The Institutionalist Approach to Public Utilities Regulation

The Institutionalist Approach to Public Utilities Regulation

EDITED BY

EDYTHE S. MILLER

AND

WARREN J. SAMUELS

Michigan State University Press
East Lansing, Michigan

♾ The paper used in this publication meets the minimum requirements of
ANSI/NISO Z39.48–1992 (R 1997) (Permanence of Paper).

Michigan State University Press
East Lansing, Michigan 48823–5202

Printed and bound in the United States of America.

08 07 06 05 04 03 02 1 2 3 4 5 6 7 8 9 10

LIBRARY OF CONGRESS CATALOGING-IN-PUBLICATION DATA

The institutionalist approach to public utilities regulation / edited by
    Edythe S. Miller, Warren J. Samuels.
        p.cm.
Includes bibliographical references.
    ISBN 0-87013-624-0
    1. Public utilities—State supervision. I. Miller, Edythe Stern. II. Samuels,
Warren J., 1933–
    HD2763 .I54 2002
    363.6—dc21

                                                            2002008419

Cover design by Heather Truelove Aiston
Book design by Nighthawk Design

Visit Michigan State University Press on the World Wide Web at:
www.msupress.msu.edu

Contents

Introduction

EDYTHE S. MILLER AND WARREN J. SAMUELS

Harry Martin Trebing has been, during the last forty or so years of the twentieth century, one of the top two or three, if not the foremost, specialists in the world in the field of public utility regulation. The domain of his reputation encompasses academics, regulators, managers of regulated utilities, lawyers, public interest advocates, and others with an interest in the field both in North America and throughout the world. Through the conferences and workshops conducted by his Public Utilities Institute at Michigan State University, often with the sponsorship of the National Association of Regulatory Utility Commissioners (NARUC); through his activities in the Transportation and Public Utilities Group (TPUG) of the American Economic Association; through invited lectures to public utility commissions and legislatures in this and other countries; and, by no means least, through his classroom teaching, Trebing has been the foremost educator in his field. To be sure, not everyone has agreed with his technical analyses and policy positions, yet, while Trebing was considered something of an "enemy" he was nonetheless respected by those whose interests he opposed.

In order to understand and appreciate Trebing's views on public utility regulation, it is necessary to see him in the tradition of Wisconsin institutional economics, particularly its treatment of the economic role of government. This tradition started with Richard T. Ely, arguably the founder of the fields of land and public utility economics, and continued with John R. Commons, Edwin E. Witte, Martin G. Glaeser (Trebing's major professor), and Harold M. Groves, as well as a group of agricultural economists in their own department in Wisconsin, such as Kenneth Parsons and Daniel Bromley. At Michigan State University, where Trebing taught for almost three decades, he was a member of a group—also consisting of Allan Schmid and Warren Samuels and complemented by several more or less like-minded others who were not from Wisconsin, such as Walter Adams, James D. Shaffer, and Robert Solo, and their students—

1

who self-consciously worked to continue and further apply the Wisconsin approach to the analysis of the economic role of government (also called law and economics, and public choice).

The Wisconsin-Michigan State approach can be outlined as follows: Markets are a function, in large part, of the institutions that help form and operate through them. These institutions are largely legal in nature. Government, or law, is both ubiquitous and important. Economic performance is to no small degree a function of the state of the law. The rights of economic significance are a function of law. Regulation, of all types, is a mode through which interests are protected or exposed to the actions of others whose interests are protected; that is, regulatory statutes and court decisions are means through which rights are formed and reformed.

The advocates of the foregoing Wisconsin approach consider it to be nonideological and non-normative, to be positive and objective. Government is important, whether one likes it or not. In their view, therefore, the idea of "noninterventionism," or laissez-faire, is either wrong or very misleading. Take regulation: When Alpha and Beta are in the same field of action, government protection of Alpha's interest as a right is the logical and substantive equivalent of denying protection to Beta's interest. So, when government regulates Beta in order to protect Alpha's interest, then governmental activism is obvious. When government, perhaps following the sentiments of "deregulation," ceases to protect Alpha's interest by regulating Beta, it looks like government is no longer activist. Yet by ceasing to protect Alpha's interest, it is now protecting Beta's interest. Regulating polluters in favor of nonpolluters is manifestly "regulation." Deregulating polluters seems like getting the government off people's backs. Yet, in no longer regulating polluters, government is, in effect, regulating, on the backs of, nonpolluters. Government is only changing the interest to which it is giving its protection.

Another aspect of the Wisconsin approach, the one that relates directly to Trebing's life work, involves competition, or rather its absence. The traditional theory of markets, from the time of Adam Smith, was that competition would assure equity and efficiency. A large enough number of sellers, for example, who were not able to collude, would be unable to victimize particular consumers because competitive markets constitute a reasonably automatic mechanism of economic control. Yet even assuming that this control mechanism prevailed effectually or even approximately at some earlier time, there is little doubt that it has been eroded. The structure of industry has been transformed by a variety of conditions, notably including technological change.

It is not surprising, therefore, that the Wisconsin institutionalists are concerned with protecting the interests of consumers, whom they see in positions exposed to monopoly or oligopoly power. The opposite of protecting consumers is not laissez-faire (whatever that may mean). It is protecting the power of those who deal with consumers, especially producers, distributors, and retailers of products whose demand is relatively inelastic.

Evolving technology and business practice has resulted, in certain sectors, in the emergence not only of economies of scale, extensively accepted as an indication of market failure or natural monopoly and therefore as requiring social intervention, but of additional barriers to entry that make competition unlikely, if not impossible. In addition to economies of scale, public utilities manifest such characteristics as high threshold levels of investment, substantial sunk costs, a high proportion of joint to total costs, substantial asset nonfungibility, significant interdependencies, control over monopoly focal points, and other limitations to both access and egress. These barriers engender important centralizing and concentrating effects that not only are inconsistent with competition but also confer upon the industries involved a market power that gives them the ability to shift costs among customer groups. Public utilities typically produce multiple services and operate in segmented markets characterized by divergent price elasticities of demand, including markets with highly inelastic demand characteristics (that is, in which there are significant elements of necessity in demand and in which reasonable substitutes are unavailable).

This combination of conditions results in a restriction of competition and the ability to exercise economic power through risk shifting, cross-subsidization, and price discrimination among classes of consumers. It is important to recognize that entry to this market is prevented by market barriers that are structural and technical rather than strictly legal or regulatory in nature, although the latter can apply as well. Thus, the removal of legal entry barriers (that is, deregulation) will not eliminate obstacles to the establishment or persistence of competition. Moreover, the existence of monopsony power in certain of the markets served, along with the relative powerlessness of a "captive customer" base, betokens the differential and discriminatory treatment of different classes of consumers. That is, firms in these industries are neither restrained by competition nor restrained, absent regulation, from manipulating price according to differing demand elasticities in the markets served. Deregulation does not bring about a condition of competition and dispersal of economic power, but of concentrated private power and of cross-subsidization and price discrimination among different consumer groups, some of whom themselves are possessed of market power. The Wisconsin approach emphasizes the importance of these situations and suggests that where social control by competitive markets does not work, social control can be effectuated by either regulation or government ownership. For the most part, economists in the Wisconsin tradition have supported regulation.

The distinctive feature of the Wisconsin approach is the administrative commission. The administrative commission is an organizational tool that, in Commons's view, for example, enabled the bringing of technical expertise to bear on complex technical issues. Neither the courts nor the legislatures, in his view, possessed the required technical expertise and concentration of specialized attention; the administrative commission did. From this standpoint, one readily intuits an affirmation of expertise and of decision making through the deployment of experts and expertise.

The ideal administrative commission would, in Commons's view, undertake its work utilizing the expertise of a variety of specialists. It would, further, involve the maximum feasible participation of interested parties (or their representatives—especially those he deemed most "enlightened" or "progressive" in each group). It would, finally, both pursue and evaluate its work on the basis of consequences, not on the basis of some a priori position or theory.

Commons understood that public policy—the product of the administrative commissions, as well as of the legislatures and the courts—was a matter of neither expertise nor consequences alone. Consequences had not only to be identified but also evaluated, for what might be a benefit from one perspective might be a cost from another. Furthermore, different experts might identify different consequences, and of course each expert might evaluate any given consequence in a different way. Public policy was, for Commons, both laden with normative content (what ought to be) and something that had to be worked out, not settled upon a priori. No single interested party and no single expert had a monopoly on normative content, or values, or on how things should be worked out.

This brings us to the major normative component of the Wisconsin approach. It is the same normative component underlying reliance on competitive markets, namely, avoiding economic and political domination by a few. The Wisconsin approach calls for pluralism in both access to, or participation in, government and the interests to which government will give its protection,.

This means, if one combines the two principal elements, that the Wisconsin approach emphasizes (1) the inevitable and ubiquitous importance of government and of governmental activism—activist even when it was ostensibly "deregulating"—and (2) the desirability of having economic and political institutions be responsive to and protective of the widest possible range of interests. That situation fundamentally accounts for the Wisconsin tradition's advocacy of effective administrative regulation of public utility companies. It also accounts for its arguments supporting the provision of adequate resources and staff in order for these independent commissions to do their work.

The great problem with regulation by administrative commission was that it became increasingly difficult over time for the commissions to be independent and effective in the performance of their function in an objective manner. Whether commissioners were elected or appointed, they were subjected, not inappropriately, not only to the winds and vagaries of politics but also to the selective perception that thinks of deregulation as "getting government off the backs of the people." Moreover, the regulated public utilities were, again not inappropriately, quite willing to influence elections and appointments to the commissions, as well as public opinion about "deregulation." Where commissioners were not, in one way or another, more or less directly beholden to the interests they were expected to control, rules and practices of commission investigations and decision making were often, if not typically, adopted which would promote, both indirectly and directly, corporate rather than customer interests. Some of these rules, practices, and policies were dictated by the legislatures and by the courts, but many were adopted by the commissions themselves. That is not to say that commissions could or should have disregarded the operating and financial health of the companies they were meant to regulate; it was in no one's interest for the companies to be weak or on the edge of failure. Yet, to numerous observers, public utility commissions generally were, in one way or another, the captives of the companies they were supposed to control, such that both the theory and the practice of the venerable concepts by which they had been set up were now passé.

Thus, in the United States from about the early 1970s, economic regulation encountered increased suspicion, if not outright hostility. There is little doubt that this was attributable at least in part to the general allegiance in the United States to a noninterventionist economic philosophy, and to the widespread distrust of the motives and performance of government in general, and even more specifically, of regulation. Yet, these sentiments had existed for a long time.

They do not explain the reasons for the antagonism toward regulation, or the extent to which it intensified during this period of time. The key to this quandary may lie in the national economic experience of the time, including that of the public utility sector, and in the mien of the economics discipline itself.

Until the early 1970s, and most particularly in the immediate post–World War II period, public utilities in the United States had experienced strong technological advances and sustained increases in demand, productivity, and growth. The real-price declines that accompanied economies of scale engendered public tranquility, if not contentment. Regulation, while not well regarded, was not an object of intense attention. From about the early 1970s, however, the economy experienced a number of simultaneous shocks that were to strike the capital- and fuel-intensive utility sector with particular force. The economy confronted, at one and the same time, both high and increasing rates of inflation and high and increasing unemployment rates (the infamous "misery index"). In the view of contemporary economic analyses, these conditions were not supposed to occur concurrently. In addition, from the early 1970s the nation endured serious economic stagnation, characterized (because of the coincident inflation) as "stagflation." Conditions of inflation and associated increases in capital costs, an oil embargo that sharply increased fuel prices, and demands for the internalization of externalities combined to negatively impact these capital- and fuel-intensive industries. Declines in technological advance and productivity further negatively affected economic performance. If this were not sufficient, congressionally mandated rate structure reform in electricity and the indexing and deregulation of gas both reflected neoclassical economic principles and intensified the sudden and severe price shock in the electric and gas markets. Sharp price increases and poor economic performance transformed public skepticism into suspicion and finally hostility.

At the same time, and to a large extent compounding public attitudes, academic criticism of regulation escalated and broadened. Prior to this time, the profession had generally accepted, if somewhat grudgingly, the existence of market failure, even while viewing its scope as in general limited to economies of scale. Market failure was not deemed an important or particularly interesting phenomenon; the appropriate subject matter of economics was taken to be the study of free markets, by far the major part of the economics curriculum. Market imperfections were dealt with as isolated phenomena, with the subject matter sequestered in classes devoted to the "social control of business," and often left to the heterodox to instruct. The majority of courses for the most part ignored the topic. Yet, even if slighted, the phenomenon of market power and its corollary, the "social control of business," was recognized by the economics profession as a legitimate, if a negligible and anomalous, field. Relentless criticism of the regulation of business as a practice, and by implication as a field, came primarily from a group of economists itself perceived as more or less outside the mainstream, or at least on its fringe, and at best as a weak rival to mainstream thought. For the most part, although there was some disagreement about the importance and extent of "market imperfections," and while economics departments devoted themselves primarily to topics centered around price formation under competitive conditions, a policy more or less of containment was maintained, with the study of "free" markets the domain of orthodoxy, and that of the control of market power ceded to heterodoxy. The economics discipline tolerated, even if it did not embrace, heterodox views. A qualified, if uneasy, consensus existed. It was not to last, however.

From about the 1970s, the neoclassical viewpoint, always the controlling view in the discipline, became more dominant and, perhaps of even greater importance, seemed determined both to carry its initial premises to logical extremes and to eliminate dissent. To a large extent, the fringe morphed into the mainstream. There occurred a hardening of the dominant laissez-faire philosophy in almost every field, but none more so than regulatory and public utility economics. Courses in the "social control of business" disappeared from curricula, reincarnated as industrial organization and presented as little more than exercises in advanced price theory.

The economics literature was suffused with a steady stream of work that minimized the existence or narrowed the extent of market imperfections and was highly critical of regulators and of regulatory policies and practices. Regulation was faulted, for example, as overly generous to the regulated industries through acceptance of such devices as rate-base padding and cost and expenditure inflation, implying that consumers were subjected to higher prices under regulation than in its absence. Regulation was also criticized as insufficiently forward-looking and inadequately attentive to appropriate resource allocation, because of a reliance on average historic, rather than marginal, costs; as overly focused on equity considerations at the expense of efficiency; and as hostile to innovation, among other charges. At the same time, the literature portrayed regulators as captives of regulated industries and inattentive to consumer needs. Moreover, academic criticism worked its way down to nonacademic tracts, ranging from government reports to the popular press, becoming the stuff of newspaper editorials and syndicated columns.

The existence of contradictions in these assessments did little to weaken their impact. There was something to appeal to all political tastes and to attract adherents from across the political spectrum: For political conservatives, for example, there was the claim that regulation elevated equity concerns over those of efficiency, and that it ignored neoclassical pricing principles; for liberals, that regulators were captives of regulated industries.

This is not to suggest that regulation did not deserve much of the censure it received. Overall, there is little doubt that many—even if not all—of the criticisms of regulation were justified. The defect in the approach was that only one solution to all regulatory deficiencies was advanced. "Regulatory reform" was posited as the solution to all regulatory ills, irrespective of their nature. Furthermore, regulatory reform was given one meaning only. It was equated with a transformation to market guidance, at best through deregulation, but at the least, through market simulation by adoption of such neoclassically approved methods as marginal cost pricing or, where that was impractical, Ramsey pricing (the inverse elasticity rule), or through the use of market-like techniques such as bidding or auction. The proposed solutions, however, did not address the underlying problem of how to control the existence of economic power or restrain its abuse. Moreover, absent from the public agenda was any discussion of other possible remedies to the persistence of market power, or to regulatory deficiencies; discussion, for example, of whether the imposition of more rigorous regulation, of extensive public planning, or of exacting structural separation would not in some cases be more appropriate correctives than simply naive deregulation.

The predicament of those who supported public utility regulation in the manner, say, of Commons was that they increasingly had to combat those who thought of regulation as interventionism in the pejorative sense and those who had willy-nilly captured regulation for their own purposes. The dominant ideology that supported the former position ironically also lent a hand to the latter, insofar as it rationalized or legitimized private ownership doing whatever it wanted, as if under effective market control. If the opponents of government regulation erred in failing to see that the alternative to regulation was not competition, as called for by the theory of markets, the supporters of regulation erred by pretending that regulation was effectively substituting for competition. The predicament of the supporters of effective regulation is obvious: it required a great deal of sophistication and objectivity to understand what regulation, in their view, was, or should be, all about.

This is the predicament in which Trebing has operated throughout his professional life as a specialist in public utility regulation. Yet, his position in this situation has at least two larger dimensions: first, he is an individual scholar, somewhat sui generis, writing on issues and in contexts relevant to his time; and second, he contributes to, fulfills, reinforces, and extends the Wisconsin tradition in analyzing the economic role of government.

Trebing was, in particular, the student at Wisconsin of Martin Glaeser. From Glaeser, Trebing either acquired or had reinforced several lessons: (1) the importance of a deep philosophical and legal comprehension of the public utility institution, one neither excluding nor limited to a comparatively narrow market structure-price discrimination analysis or a comparatively narrow structure-conduct-performance model of industrial organization; (2) the importance of technology, and therefore of empirical engineering experience and knowledge, for both general and technical issues of policy; and (3) the importance of what Robert Solo has called the planning and programming function of government, as evidenced in such infrastructure areas as Tennessee Valley Authority (TVA) and power grid.

Trebing also studied at the University of Maryland under Eli W. Clemens, under whom he wrote his master's thesis on natural gas regulation and market failure, and Allan G. Gruchy. Clemens, author of the well-known text *Economics and Public Utilities* (1950), had, himself, been a student of Glaeser. From Gruchy, Trebing learned more of the varieties of institutional economics, including his approach to economic planning. While Trebing was not convinced of the advantages of a national economic plan, Gruchy nonetheless reinforced his sense of the importance of government and of the possibilities of public utility regulation.

In his numerous publications, lectures, and presentations, Trebing scrutinized the full sweep of regulatory and public utility issues. His analyses exhibited both depth and breadth; a detailed examination of public utilities and regulation per se, and an account of how their circumstances impact and are impacted upon by the wider society. His inquiry ranged over issues of the underlying rationale and purposes of regulation; the characteristics of market structure and product demand that support or repudiate its implementation, extension, or contraction; its mechanics of operation; its strengths and shortcomings. He explored the question of where regulation could be improved, and where abandoned or relaxed. The whole range of issues consistently was explored from the standpoint of many divergent viewpoints—of supporters and critics of regulation, of regulators and the regulated, of institutionalists and neoclassicists—and from both a historical standpoint and in view of changing contemporary conditions. In the process, Trebing employed and extended the themes and techniques of the institutionalist regulatory economists who had preceded him, both those, as noted, who had been associated with the University of Wisconsin and those with other affiliations. Thus, Trebing's intellectual heritage included the work of such well-known institutional regulatory economists as John Maurice Clark, Henry Carter Adams, and James Bonbright, among others, in addition to that of Wisconsin institutional regulatory economists.

Trebing therefore built substantially upon a foundation and contributed to an edifice assembled over the years by prior generations of economists. For example, Commons, in addition to his groundbreaking pedagogy and scholarly work, had been a political ally in Wisconsin of

Robert LaFollette, with whom he worked, among other things, to establish a Wisconsin public utilities commission. They succeeded in this effort
in 1907, and Wisconsin became one of the first of two states in the nation
to initiate state commission regulation. During this time, and to build support for his practical program of reform, Commons authored reports on
public utility problems and issues. Trebing, in light of the existence of similar conditions of market power, advocated the strengthening of state and
federal regulation, through commissions staffed by independent experts,
and with warrants of continuous surveillance. He also recognized, as had
Commons, the inherent inseparability and interdependence of the theoretical and the practical, the critical fusion of theoretical analysis and the
field work necessary to validate and support it.

Trebing also shared with Commons the perception that the definition,
the very conception, of legal and economic rights, principles, and postu-
lates such as private property and the specification and differentiation of
costs is not given and fixed, but prescribed by society through law and
regulation that both influence and are influenced by popular opinion and
custom. It follows that, far from being inviolate, these definitions are subject to change (though usually not without resistance) with changing circumstance and belief. Of equal significance was Trebing's embrace of the
position, notably identified with Commons,, that collective action serves
both to restrain and to enhance individual action.

Similarly, Trebing shared with J. M. Clark an awareness of the prominent and increasing role performed by overhead, joint, and common costs
in total costs as an economy becomes increasingly industrialized. Not only
does cost composition change over time with changing technology and
industrial structure, but particularly in a multiproduct environment,
where costs of various services or products are shared, cost allocation to
particular services may be extremely arbitrary. Far from being certain and
fixed, then, cost definition, composition, and allocation is both ambiguous and capricious. It was evident to Trebing that the ability to shape cost
definition and allocation allows groups wielding that power to turn these
ambiguities to their own account. Furthermore, Trebing joined with
Clark in comprehending the existence of a social efficiency that transcends
the sum of private individual efficiencies and that must be taken into
account if we are to subsist as a viable society.

In addition to his contribution to theoretical and methodological
issues, Trebing interpreted, explained, and otherwise helped to refine the
tools of regulatory control in a manner reminiscent of Henry Carter
Adams, James Bonbright, and Martin Glaeser, who also had contributed
to both the theory and application of public utility regulation. The early

accounting systems devised by Henry Carter Adams were indispensable to the establishment of a uniform system of accounts, essential to the development of the mechanics of regulatory control. They served as essential inputs into the rate base, rate-of-return (RBROR) regulation that in subsequent years was to become an essential feature and the technical foundation of economic regulation. The principles of RBROR regulation and those of the traditional responsibilities and rights of public utilities—the obligation to serve; the quality-of-service requirement; the establishment of nondiscriminatory, nonexploitative, cost-based rates; and the opportunity (but not the right) to earn a fair rate of return—were developed and enriched by institutional regulatory economists, most notably by Bonbright and Glaeser. Trebing extended this approach in his examination of the design and potential repercussions of proposed substitutes for RBROR regulation, such as price-capping, the various forms of incentive regulation, the use of market-simulating devices such as bidding and auction, and in his emphasis on the abiding importance of cost-based rates.

Trebing also built upon the contributions of prior generations of institutional economists in his analysis of the pervasive nature and potential for abuse of industrial concentration. Market concentration has never been perceived by institutional economists as an anomaly. It is seen rather as a standard attribute of the modern economy and as a typical concomitant of industrialization and economic development. The barriers to entry and exit in the particular industries that Trebing and his predecessors enumerated were familiar characteristics of the contemporary operating environment, would not be eliminated by deregulation, and, so long as they existed, would function to preclude the development of competition. It was thus not regulation, as contended in so much of the neoclassical literature, that constituted the barrier to entry in these industries, but rather the existence of particular operating conditions; whether regulated or deregulated, industries so situated would remain concentrated and possessed of market power. When to these barriers to entry and exit is added the fact that these firms typically produce multiple products for segmented markets with varying demand elasticities and significant disparities in market power, the opportunity for cross-subsidization and exploitative, discriminatory, non-cost-based pricing is heightened. Finally, when for many the product is also a practical necessity for reasonable subsistence, the requirement for a social remedy is clear. Trebing described these conditions of modern life and industry and actively sought methods of control and remediation.

For example, Trebing encouraged the adoption of the Glaeser model, designed for application to the TVA, for allocation of joint costs in proportion to the benefits of economies of scale, scope, and joint development. The adoption of this method would permit the design of realistic cost-based rates and prevent cross-subsidization. He advocated the utilization of measures of market power and of minimum efficient scale in place of a blind confidence that potential competition would produce competitive outcomes even in the presence of market barriers and concentrated power, as contended in the dominant and currently fashionable contestability theory. He contended that the movement toward deregulation of public utilities that has occurred in recent years has resulted not in competitive markets, but rather in tight oligopoly, the temptation to target network technology to the sophisticated requirements of large-volume users and the threat of disinvestment and service deterioration in core markets.

Other proposals were specifically tailored to uniquely contemporary conditions, rather than strictly to such persistent historic problems as the existence of market barriers and the abuse of market power, for example, through cross-subsidization. For instance, in light of the expected increases in difficulty of coordination in situations of pluralistic supply, Trebing broached consideration of provision of service through development of expanded transparent common carrier networks with cost-based access, mandatory interties, and continuance of the traditional obligation to serve. The network was to be regulated, with its structurally separated unregulated marketing subsidiaries free to pursue competitive activities. Each entity would have its own board of directors and be responsible for separate debt financing. Appropriate safeguards would be required to be established to ensure integrity of affiliate transactions and structure of secondary markets.

Trebing also warned of the potential for abuse inherent in the contemporary movement toward conglomeration through merger, acquisition, joint venture, holding company formation, and diversification in public utility industries. Many of the potential risks inherent in the holding company structure had been addressed in a classic work on the holding company, written by Bonbright and Gardiner Means in 1932. These institutional economists pointed out that the holding company structure permits the employment of a variety of stratagems that are privately enriching but publicly impoverishing. They cautioned against the strategic use of the holding company as a device to move the companies that it shelters beyond regulatory control. To the extent that the holding company straddles state and national boundaries and operates across industry lines, the ability of jurisdictional regulatory bodies to oversee and control is atrophied. Where the holding company consists of regulated monopoly and unregulated nonmonopoly firms, the shifting of costs to the core customers of the regulated monopoly firm is facilitated. The capacity to monitor affiliate transactions is diluted. Insofar as the cost of borrowing for the consolidated company is based upon the blended lower-risk position of the monopoly firm and higher-risk position of the competitive subsidiary, debt costs of the regulated company will be increased, and those of the unregulated firm decreased. The higher costs will be borne by core monopoly customers. The lower cost of borrowing of the unregulated firm, in turn, will disadvantage rivals in these putatively competitive markets. Today, many of the safeguards put in place to protect against the abuses of which Bonbright and Means warned are in the process of being dismantled. Trebing is in the forefront of those cautioning against such imprudent action and its perhaps unintended consequences.

Trebing was not a blind defender of regulation. His advocacy also took the form of a critique aimed at buttressing the viability of regulation. His criticisms extended to the passivity of regulation, demonstrated by its quasi-judicial and case-by-case approach, and its failure to confront real-world developments by adopting a future-oriented planning mode. He acknowledged the authentic (even if unstable) grain of truth in capture theory. Moreover, his training sessions for regulators and regulatory staff did much in themselves to disprove the theory, for through them he instilled in decades of regulators a sense of the importance of their work and of pride in their accomplishments, while urging them toward improved and superior performance and educating them about possible hazards.

Further, while noting the shortcomings of past and present regulation, Trebing also imparted in both his written and oral work a skepticism about the alleged effectiveness and asserted efficiency of market outcomes. He questioned the acceptance of the market as the final arbiter in view of the continued existence of private market power. He demonstrated that partial deregulation has not resulted in the emergence of competition. Markets remain concentrated; high levels of profitability persist; and patterns of price discrimination, cross-subsidization, and the shifting of risk and costs continue as factors in the public utility sector. At the same time, the existence of oligopsony power on the other side of the market encourages these patterns and stimulates price leadership and other forms of conscious parallelism in monopoly markets, and rivalrous discounting in putatively competitive ones. Trebing's explanation of these and other issues was brought to life, and given fresh currency, by means of his seemingly endless store of current examples and historical anecdotes to fit almost any relevant situation.

The NARUC-sponsored and other educational programs that Trebing organized included the full reach of issues and perspectives that distinguish the field. The resulting debate eventuated in a broadening of both outlook and perceived parameters of the problems for the commissioners and staff of federal and state regulatory bodies who were the students at these sessions, and who themselves were in positions to influence policy. The airing of the many sides of disputed issues instilled a sense of balance in the participants and carried students beyond the conventional positions to which they more regularly were exposed.

In short, in keeping with the beliefs of his institutional predecessors, Trebing advanced a public interest theory of regulation. The concept of public interest regulation has a long history, reaching back at least to the seventeenth-century British common law. It was recognized even then that when a private business is "affected with a public interest," it is no longer strictly private, and a measure of social control is warranted. That is, the public interest theory of regulation comprehends the coercive ability of particular forms of private property, and looks to means of remediation, such as control of market power, prevention of monopoly abuse, and resolution of disparities among market and social values. Thus, the public interest theory of regulation recognizes the existence of a broader social efficiency, a concept of social value that includes considerations of equity, and thus surpasses the narrow concept of allocative efficiency revered in neoclassical economics. It contends that a public utility is not simply a business like any other business, with only bottom-line obligations to safeguard profits of shareholders. Public utilities operate under governmental privilege and with grants of public franchise. As such, they have public franchise obligations to return something to the community. In respect to the operation of the firm, they have the responsibility "to make it work," that is, to maintain both industrial and business viability—in the language of the early institutionalists, to maintain going plants as well as going businesses. Their obligation "to make it work" includes that of ensuring the distribution of these essential public services to all comers at reasonable, nondiscriminatory rates. "Making it work" goes beyond financial and technical considerations.

A public interest theory of regulation advances the position that public utilities, as operators of infrastructure industries and producers of required public services, have both the power and the obligation of integration. Essentially, their mandate is to facilitate and expedite the "connectedness" of individuals who otherwise might be isolated or injured by exclusion, or divided and estranged and otherwise subjugated by subordinate forms of service. In discharging this mandate, they help ensure a healthier, more viable economy. In thus advocating a public interest theory of regulation, Trebing fulfilled his heritage and kept alive the premise and promise of a regulatory economics whose purpose it is to support and improve the human condition.

As has been noted, the last half of the twentieth century was one of extensive and increasing allegiance to orthodox precepts on the part of the economics profession generally, including scholars in the subfield of regulatory economics. The price of dissent was high—often amounting to virtual professional exile or isolation. Irrespective of this cost, Trebing brought to the controversial issues involved an authoritative and often lonely voice advising of the distinct tendency in certain key industries for development on both sides of the market of dominance by a few, and of the harm these conditions could inflict on vulnerable individuals and the economy as a whole.

Trebing's framework was by choice and necessity interdisciplinary, encompassing the various fields of which regulation is comprised—economics, law, engineering, and accounting. His professional relationships also breached narrow disciplinary bounds. His teaching occurred within but also extended beyond the college campus; his students included, but were not confined to, those adhering to a typical collegiate pattern. He taught and mentored successive generations of students, whose nature and makeup ranged over the spectrum from the callow and inexperienced neophyte to the sophisticated and seasoned veteran. His conferences and workshops attracted instructors and students with diverse interests and patterns of thought—academics and practitioners; providers, consumers, and regulators; traditionalists and reformers. His teaching ranged from the "nuts and bolts" of rate base construction, to the ambiguities of joint cost allocation, and to such contentious and controversial questions as the responsibility of cost overruns and poor operating records of some of the larger, and especially the nuclear, electric plants for widespread rate hikes. His knowledge of all aspects of regulatory and public utility economics was comprehensive; his communication of these often abstruse topics exemplary. Yet for all his formal teaching and guidance, the most important lesson he imparted to his students was the importance, reasonability, and acceptability of independent thought, that is, of breaking with the orthodox and traditional and advancing to wherever the facts lead.

Harry Trebing is an academic who made a difference. Had it not been for the vitality of his teaching and writing, his comprehensive understanding of the subject matter, his ability persuasively to communicate his knowledge and perspective, the drawing power of his official NARUC programs for members of regulatory commissions, and the excellence of the many additional training programs that he organized and in which he shouldered a leading role, it is quite possible that the institutional branch of regulatory economics would by now have withered on the vine. At the least, it almost certainly would have been even more effectively silenced than it is at present. Furthermore, a distinctive voice would have been stifled, vastly impoverishing the national and global dialogue.

This volume is a reflection of the respect and admiration that various colleagues of Harry Trebing have for his technical expertise and his perspective on regulation in the context of a larger theory of the economic role of government. It is also, the truth be told, a measure of their respect and admiration for Harry Trebing the human being.

In addition to this introduction, the volume is also prefaced by a remembrance written by a long-time colleague and friend of Trebing's, David Schwartz. Part 1 includes chapters on some of the other historical origins of regulation and on the general design of utility regulation. Part 2 presents chapters on important aspects of communication, especially the Internet. Part 3 comprises chapters on costing and pricing, surely a practical matter of direct interest to consumers. Part 4 considers several aspects of so-called deregulation. Part 5 presents two different views of the social control of public utilities in historical and normative perspective.

The authors collectively dedicate this volume to Harry Trebing, and that for which he stands.

Crossing the Rubicon
with Harry Trebing

DAVID S. SCHWARTZ

Reflections on a Long and Special Friendship

My friendship with Harry Trebing, almost a half century old, has been an unqualified joy. I met Harry in the office of Dr. Martin Glaeser at the University of Wisconsin in the mid-1950s. He was then a Ph.D. candidate in public utility economics. My first impression upon seeing his "crew-cut" hair and conventional dress was that here was a future utility executive and defender of the status quo.

To admit that I was wrong is a gross understatement. Although I was correct about his reliance on traditional attire, Harry's commitment is to the general public interest, and to the persistent questioning of the conventional wisdom.

In my discussions with former students, regulatory commission personnel, utility executives, academics, and others, another facet of Harry's orientation usually mentioned is his sense of fairness and balance in all his endeavors. These qualities were the grounding for his administrative and organizational responsibilities to programs, panels, and teaching sessions as director of the Institute of Public Utilities and administrator of the NARUC education program at Michigan State University, to regional programs for regulatory commission personnel, and to numerous other projects.

As editor of the *MSU [Michigan State University] Public Utilities Papers,* Harry provided a forum for varying opinions and positions on the issues and problems of the changing patterns of public utility regulation. It is doubtful whether many of the consumer and environmental concerns raised in these papers would have been addressed in other forums.

As professor of economics at Michigan State, and as a participant in a

17

variety of forums, he has consistently provided a comprehensive assessment of the evolution of regulatory institutions in the telecommunications and energy industries. His broad background and analytical ability has enabled him to explore with singular insight the more complex issues and problems of rate equity and the reliability of services.

As behooves an adventurous spirit, Harry temporarily left academe to become a practitioner in the regulatory process. On leave from Michigan State, he served as chief economist in the Common Carrier Bureau of the Federal Communications Commission and chief economist at the Postal Rate Commission. In addition, we worked together on a National Science Foundation grant dealing with competition and regulatory reform in the energy utilities.

Reflective of his fundamental foundation in institutional economics, he served as president of the Association of Evolutionary Economics and is the recipient of the association's Veblen-Commons Award. Harry is currently professor of economics, emeritus, after retiring from Michigan State University in 1992. The majority of his time now is committed to pro bono work on behalf of consumer and public interest organizations.

Those who know Harry are aware of his reservations, to put it mildly, about flying. This has resulted in his driving thousands of miles annually to participate in numerous programs throughout the United State and Canada. An ardent Wagner fan and a member of the Wagnerian Society, Harry also will drive from Michigan to New York City for a Wagner performance at the Met. He has traveled to Bayreuth, Germany, for the Wagner Festival. Knowledgeable about auto mechanics, Harry collects antique cars and, for good measure, also collects oriental rugs.

Harry's lively, intelligent wife, Joyce, an exceptional organizer in her own right, has been a constant support through the years. Harry and Joyce are the parents of two grown sons and the grandparents of four boys.

It is no simple task to distill the qualities of such a man; nonetheless, it is not difficult to discern the basic values underpinning Harry's support for a diversity of views in controversial matters and the furtherance of basic democratic principles in general. In short, Harry is a true gentleman, possessing a brilliant mind, tremendous vitality, and unfailing good humor, always underlined by his uncompromising integrity. It is for these qualities that Harry is respected and admired, and justly so.

Intellectual Orientation: An Appreciation

Crossing the intellectual Rubicon with Harry Trebing is to know that one is well armed with a historical perspective, a comprehensive command of the relevant facts, and the analytical power to discern the evolving forces of economic power.

While Trebing's teaching and other professional activities relate to public utility regulation (or lack thereof), in fact, his writings and other endeavors reflect a broad grounding in neo-institutional economics. The structural foundation of his work is in the institutionalist tradition, and as such, part of a new generation of heterodox economists. In short, he has rejected the theoretical framework of the orthodox economists as suffering from cultural lag, a set of false assumptions, and a lack of realism.

Trebing's institutional approach serves as a guidepost to his efforts to explore the important public utility issues of the impact of tight oligopoly and the lack of effective competition. In an article examining the breakdown of meaningful coordination in public utility industries, he detailed the benefits of a high degree of coordination between a capital-intensive supply network and diverse patterns of customer usage. Trebing stressed that effective coordination enhances the possibility of network economies of scale, scope, joint production, and pooled reserves.

In the period from 1946 to 1968, coordination was achieved through public enterprises or private monopolies subject to price and earnings regulation. After 1968, a variety of external shocks resulting from the country's exposure to periods of under- or oversupply, low- to high-cost suppliers, and cumulative evidence of poor management caused a virtual collapse of the coordination function.

Trebing concluded that if regulatory intervention was limited, new entry would be restricted and oligopoly profits would be sustained. He detailed the significant negative efforts of tight oligopoly as follows:

1. Collaborative strategies through alliances, joint ventures, and mergers would increase industry concentration and reinforce oligopolistic behavior;
2. Instead of price tracking costs, the price would be a function of the strategies of the oligopolistic firms and the bargaining power of particular user groups; and
3. Profit levels would be higher than under traditional rate base/rate-of-return regulation or effective competition.

His suggestion is to implement more direct and purposeful regulatory intervention. He advocates structural separation where network economies and industry-specific barriers promote high concentration. The network will remain under regulation, but the marketing of services can be divested and deregulated. The basic services to residential and small commercial customers will remain under cost-based regulation.

Another facet of Trebing's writings relates to the turbulent changes in telecommunications. He is dismayed by the dominance of the neoclassical economists in public policy. He emphatically rejects their prescription of deregulation of private carriers and privatization of government-owned telephone systems. Further, rejecting the neoclassical arguments that efficiency gains will result from this approach, he challenges the idea of relying on new technology to overcome traditional barriers to new entrants and create new supply options, greater competitive services, and new equipment markets. His institutional overview leads to the conclusion that the oligopolistic telecommunications market is one where technology is vulnerable to manipulation by the dominant firms, which have market power and influence. He emphasizes that imperfect markets are not self-correcting, and that government intervention must assume a positive role.

Trebing's sensitivity to institutional change and the problems of protecting residential and small commercial consumers from exploitative rates in electric power supply opens up another area for study. Deregulation, vertical deintegration, unbundling, mergers, and acquisitions are the major structural and institutional changes that are transforming the electric utility industry and threatening continued universal service at reasonable rates. After the Energy Policy Act (1992) opened the electric transmission network to potential rivals, regulation could no longer serve as a source of protection for small consumers. As Trebing has pointed out, electric utility management reacted and moved aggressively to promote profit growth and secure its position in a changing industry. The following patterns emerged:

1. Electricity supply was divided into two categories—kilowatt hours as a commodity, and transmission and distribution as a service;
2. Relaxed regulation at the national level permitted the strongest utilities to establish a regional or national presence outside their traditional service areas;
3. The move toward privatization in both industrialized and developing countries created new opportunities for utilities to establish an international presence; and
4. Lax antitrust enforcement and the prospect of weakening the Public Utility Holding Company Act created incentives for mergers, acquisitions, and alliances.

In light of the vulnerability of residential and small commercial customers to exploitative rates and uncertainty of service, Trebing has examined various protective options. One is the use of a purchasing agent who can act on behalf of residential and commercial customers in the purchase of electricity and gas.

Another option is auctioning, which may take the form of auctioning the franchise to induce prospective suppliers to serve a given market, or may involve local groups inducing bidders to supply services. For the bidding/auctioning process to succeed, Trebing has emphasized the following: (1) there must be no collusion among bidders; (2) there must be adequate consumer control; (3) there must be a clearly defined price by which to judge the successful bid; (4) there must be a determination of the appropriate franchise period for the bid award; and (5) there must be a clear determination of the customer base.

A further traditional option for protecting residential and small commercial customers is municipal ownership. There are many new incentives for municipal systems to pursue buyouts of investor-owned distribution systems. The municipal system can act as a purchasing agent and can provide multiple services, such as electricity, gas, telecommunications, cable, and home security.

Another option explored by Trebing is the functional separation by line of business, and the critical need for the creation of an independent network in the electric industry. To maximize the number of buyers and sellers, it is necessary to develop a genuinely independent network or power grid. The network must have common carrier status and serve all customers, and it must be under regulatory authority. He foresees that such an arrangement would be strong incentive to expand usage of the system, minimize bottlenecks, and develop a rate structure that would promote overall efficiency.

Trebing concludes that as long as the electric industry remains highly concentrated, the prospect of effective competition protecting residential and small business customers is an illusion. He further contends that reliance on potential entry by new suppliers is a delusion.

Conclusion

A recurring theme in Trebing's discussions, lectures, and writings is the importance of market power in economic decisions. He rejects the assumptions of orthodox economic theorists that unfettered, self-correcting markets will provide optimal allocation of resources and pricing.

As a committed institutional economist, Trebing has a clear understanding of the central role of market power in the allocation of resources, the distribution of income, and the related aspects of economic efficiency.

There is no doubt that wealth buys power, and this undermines the illusory contentions of the free-market economists.

Trebing's overriding conclusion is the need for a reaffirmation of a meaningful role for government and effective social regulation.

References to Recent Writings

Articles

Trebing, Harry M. 1994. The network as infrastructure—The reestablishment of market power. *Journal of Economic Issues* 28(2): 379–89.

Trebing, Harry M. 1996. "Achieving Coordination in Public Utility Industries: A Critique of Troublesome Options" *Journal of Economic Issues* 30(2): 561–70.

Trebing, Harry M. 1998. Promoting consumer protection in a changing electric utility industry." *The Consumer Research Foundation.*

Trebing, Harry M. 1999. New challenges for the consumer movement in an era of utility deregulation. *NRII Quarterly Bulletin* 19(4):.

Book Reviews

Trebing, Harry M. 1996. Review of *The New Telecommunications: A Political Economy of Network Evolution,* by Robin Mansell, and *The Global Political Economy of Communications,* edited by Edward A. Connor. *Journal of Economic Issues* 30(1) (March 1996): 314–18.

Trebing, Harry M. 1998. Review of *Everything for Sale,* by Robert Kuttner. *Journal of Economic Issues,* 32, no. 1 (March): 237–41.

Part 1

Economic History and Theory, Market Failure, and Public Policy

Designing Utility Regulation for Twenty-First-Century Markets

W. H. MELODY

> The question for the future then becomes our estimate of the extent to which market processes will threaten economic growth and stability and of the likelihood that the redress of market failures will lie within the political capabilities of a social order whose vitality lies in the accumulation of capital.
>
> —Robert Heilbroner, *21ˢᵗ Century Capitalism*

Introduction

The role of government in regulation of private markets has varied over time in response to the particular economic and social problems of the day, and the perceived success of inherited institutional arrangements in addressing these problems. Changing circumstances, including technologies, demands, and general economic conditions, invariably have led to changing market and industry structures, which, in turn, have required a reconsideration of the appropriate public policies. New policies have been fashioned from the available knowledge of institutional relationships and the anticipated implications of specific institutional changes. As the dawn of the twenty-first century begins to reveal the dominant characteristics of a new global information economy, it is apparent that many industries and markets are changing in quite fundamental ways. A new structure of private and public institutional arrangements will be required if economic efficiency, growth, and other public policy objectives are to be achieved.

The challenge for economists and other analysts is to develop the theoretical and applied knowledge that will provide a foundation for designing effective regulation for the twenty-first century economy, its industries and markets. This chapter explores some of the major characteristics of the twenty-first-century economy and the implications for potential new forms of market regulation, building on nineteenth- and twentieth-century experience. The chapter focuses on the public utility infrastructure sector of the economy, and the telecommunication (telecom) industry in particular. Dramatic changes in technologies, demands, and public policies are transforming the former telephone industry into a new information infrastructure that will provide the foundation for a future economy based increasingly on electronic commerce.

The Historical Framework

All the major schools of economic thought have addressed particular issues of government economic policy, generally attempting to build a case for a change in the government policy of the day, or to promote a particular structure of government-market relations. Adam Smith and the classical economists sought to reduce the all-pervasive government regulation of economic activity that existed in eighteenth- and early-nineteenth-century Britain and Europe. They made a case that a greatly expanded role for private initiative, and thereby private markets, in a mixed economy would stimulate economic activity, growth, and the wealth of nations. By reference to today's classification of economic issues, the classical economists were attacking unduly restrictive overregulation by government, including the widespread granting of privileged monopolies, as barriers to economic growth. The neoclassical school of the nineteenth and early twentieth centuries extended the analysis to make a case against barriers to international trade, such as the corn laws in England, arguing that free trade (i.e., deregulation of international markets) would stimulate economic growth and national wealth—at least for Britain at that time.[1]

These developments can be seen as the beginning of a fundamental long-wave shift in the institutional structure of government-market relations in specific national and international markets that recognized the positive contribution liberalized competitive markets could make to economic growth. The theme was liberalization in all sectors of the economy where markets could function competitively. The policy changes being advocated were the dismantling of specific government regulations that were restricting economic growth and development.

The neoclassical economists attempted to establish a policy presumption in favor of liberalized markets. Government intervention should be only to facilitate the functioning of markets, to compensate for market failures, and to provide public goods and services that the market would not.

At the same time, imperfections and failures in many markets were recognized by both the classical and neoclassical economists, most notably with respect to monopoly and the provision of essential public services, including transport on roads, canals, bridges, ferries, and rail. In Britain throughout the eighteenth and nineteenth centuries, and even earlier, a variety of legislative and common law judicial constraints on the market behavior of dominant firms in these and other important markets provided early evidence for an institutional approach to directing markets more closely to the economic and social objectives of public policy.

By the mid-nineteenth century the United States had succeeded Britain as the country where markets had been given the greatest free rein in economic development, with government policy more likely to promote and subsidize private markets, through land grants and other means, than restrict or regulate them. Yet, with experience—sometimes bitter—market failures in some key industry sectors had become dramatically evident, and public policy was being developed to constrain, control, and direct market activity in the economy generally, and in a range of industries specifically. From 1870, state legislatures were beginning to experiment with ways to constrain the railroads. The Interstate Commerce Act (1887) established federal regulation of railroads. The Sherman Act (1890) established the first antitrust law. State regulation of railroads and public utilities (primarily electricity, gas, and telephones) by independent state commissions grew rapidly in the early twentieth century. The Mann Elkins Act (1910) brought interstate communication under federal regulation.

In terms of the trend of market developments in the economy of the time, the tide had turned for the new U.S. economics profession, which came of age in the late nineteenth century. The primary task for economists was no longer making a case to dismantle specific government regulations that prevented economic growth and development, but rather the more difficult task of assessing market failures and devising regulations that would overcome them. The challenge was to design structures for private and public institutional relations that would promote efficient markets and other policy objectives.

Throughout the nineteenth and twentieth centuries, the U.S. economy, more than any other, has taken the neoclassical conception of competitive markets as a cornerstone of public policy and experimented with the liberalized market wherever possible. Even when market failures have become dramatic and self-evident, the preference of government has been to attempt to fashion a system for regulating the private market rather than displacing it with government supply. Nowhere has this been more evident than in the rail and public utility industries, the sectors that provided the fundamental infrastructure for the rest of the economy during the era of great industrial expansion. Whereas nearly all other countries chose to provide these essential public infrastructure services through government monopolies, the United States fashioned a distinctive form of government regulation of private and public utility operators, attempting to make maximum use of markets even under conditions of experienced, self-evident, and generally accepted market failure.[2]

Institutional economists, most notably those working in the tradition of J. R. Commons, were instrumental in developing both the theory and methodology for this unique and distinctive institutional design of twentieth-century markets in the public utility infrastructure industries. In many respects they were following in the tradition of the classical and nineteenth-century neoclassical economists, examining the functioning and effects of different market forms and structures. They studied specific market failures and designed public policy options to help markets in different industries function more efficiently in achieving public policy objectives. Government intervention in markets was seen as a vehicle for extending the scope of efficient markets, as well as using markets as an effective vehicle for achieving other government policy objectives (Commons 1931, 1934).

The U.S. institutional economists of the early twentieth century were pioneers in developing the foundations for structuring private and public institutional relations in many sectors of the economy. Their work covered a broad range of issues relating to the functioning of markets in general, including working conditions and labor relations, product and service quality enforcement, and consumer protection, as well as the special issues associated with the infrastructure industries. Their work helped establish a tradition of studying the institutional foundations of markets, which has continued throughout the twentieth century.[3] Within this historical framework, this chapter focuses on one distinctive institutional structure, government regulation of privately owned and operated public utilities by independent government commission. U.S. institutional economists in the early twentieth century played a major role in shaping this institutional framework, and it is now being reassessed for even broader application in early-twenty-first century economies around the world. It is ironic that at a time when the U.S. economy is reaping enormous benefits as a direct result of its unique and distinctive structure of twentieth century public utility regulation, and countries around the world are adopting versions of it for the future, public utility regulation in the United States has come under the most serious criticism in its entire existence, and is currently in retreat.

The Public Utility Model of Market Regulation

Commons and the early institutionalists began to unpack the multiple dimensions of markets in a systematic manner, to assess their distinct elements and characteristics, to identify the policy and regulatory underpinnings of different industries and types of markets, to assess market deficiencies and failures, and to identify where government intervention would enhance market efficiency and other public policy objectives. For example, they documented how the provisions and enforceability of specific property and contract rights shape market opportunities and the path of market development in all industries. For transport and public utility operators, greatly expanded property rights, including use of the government's power of eminent domain, had to be granted and enforced before private markets could function effectively at all. Yet these rights had to be carefully circumscribed to protect the specific property rights of others. Clearly a balance of rights and interests had to be fashioned by the government, and this balance determined the role, shape, and effectiveness of this type of market.

The institutionalists demonstrated that government always has engaged in a wide variety of market-shaping behavior, including both promotional and constraining activities and establishing market rules. These behaviors range from patent and copyright grants to R&D to agricultural subsidies, fair labor standards, consumer information, product liability, acceptable competitive contracting terms, natural resource conservation, environmental protection and more. This is all done under the presumption that market competition will be a viable force promoting efficient resource allocation in markets with clearly defined rules. Government establishes the appropriate ground rules and modifies them periodically based on experience and changing policy objectives. Government "tunes up" these markets, promoting or regulating the deficiencies away, and steers them into open water, where they can function more efficiently, so the benefits to society will be increased and the costs decreased.

The more difficult problem has been monopoly. This is a fundamental market failure that cannot be resolved by modest shaping and steering forms of government intervention. Much more company-specific and direct intervention is required to preserve or reestablish a viably competitive market. The antitrust laws can sometimes prevent monopoly from being established by merger or acquisition. Yet once monopoly power has been obtained, the only effective way to restore competition is to break up the monopoly. Good behavior agreements with monopolists rarely work, as they are generally unenforceable, and the market remains dominated and overshadowed by monopoly power.

The problem of self-evident market failure, in the form of unstable oligopoly or natural monopoly over essential infrastructure services that must be accessible by everyone, cannot be addressed within the framework of traditional market theory. There is no natural market solution. By the late nineteenth and early twentieth centuries, the transport and public utility industries had demonstrated market failure in many respects:

1. monopolies and cartels had arisen from collusion and destructive competition;
2. there were continuing major instabilities of supply and prices;
3. extreme forms of price discrimination had developed;
4. segments of the population had been deliberately excluded from essential services;
5. virtually all classes of consumers were unhappy with the services provided and were petitioning their governments for action;
6. high fixed costs and significant economies of scale in supply had become evident;
7. even larger economies of co-ordination in these network industries had become apparent;
8. these industries required the use of significant public resources, e.g., rights of way;
9. the existence of significant positive externalities meant that private markets would not extend these services anywhere near the limits of economic efficiency, or provide universally accessible services.

In infrastructure industries that provide services on which the rest of the economy depended, demonstrable market failure and massive inefficiency could not be allowed to persist. Nearly all the rest of the world (including Britain) chose, either in advance or after observing the unfolding experience in the United States, to establish government monopolies over the essential infrastructure industries. In contrast, the dominant response in the United States was to try to preserve private markets to the extent possible. As it was obvious that the antitrust laws could not hope to solve these massive market failures, a new institutional model of direct government regulation of private markets was developed.

Much innovative research and analysis on the issue was provided by Commons and his colleagues, students, and successors at the University of Wisconsin (Commons 1924, 1934). In 1907, Wisconsin and New York were the first states to establish state Public Utility Commissions (PUC) with the legal authority to regulate these important infrastructure industries. Within a decade most states had established PUCs. During the

1930s, federal regulation was expanded by strengthening the Interstate Commerce Commission (ICC) powers over transport, and by creating new federal regulatory commissions in securities, banking, electricity and gas, communications, and airlines. The regulatory agencies were the institutions at the frontier of market development. They were often referred to as the law's substitute for competition in the public utility industries.

The public utility model of market regulation was unique in both structure and function. The regulatory agencies were established under general laws expressing government policy objectives and providing fairly wide discretion to the agencies in interpreting and implementing them. Independent regulatory commissions were seen as superior to either legislative or judicial regulation because they could acquire greater specialized expertise, monitor industry developments in detail, make more informed decisions, and make them more rapidly. Their decisions would be objective and credible because they would be independent of narrow political or corporate special interests. Their remit would be to act in the public interest.

The regulatory agencies would have special information-gathering and fact-finding powers. They would be required to follow specified administrative procedures to ensure the participation rights of all affected parties. They would be structured to be independent of backdoor political or industry influence, and required to justify their decisions both procedurally and substantively. Their decisions could be appealed to the courts. Commissioners would be appointed on the basis of qualifications for a fixed term of significant duration. Most commissions would have several commissioners with different professional backgrounds and qualifications. Commissions would be publicly accountable to the legislature for performance in meeting the specified policy objectives and to the public via annual reports. Budgetary controls for these agencies would be the same as those for other branches of government. It was hoped that this unique structure would lead to regulations, and a regulatory environment, that would stimulate a better market performance than would any other institutional structure, and would allow both economic and social policy objectives to be achieved efficiently and effectively through the market.

This model of public utility regulation left ownership and management of the utilities in the private sector, an arrangement that has some distinct advantages, from the perspective of a market economy. The firm attracts its capital, labor, equipment, and other resources from presumably competitive resource markets, where prices and conditions will be determined by private-sector market negotiations, and comparisons with competitive market results in other firms and industries can be made. Prices to consumers are more likely to reflect the economic cost of providing services, as this will be necessary if the public utility is to continue to attract the resources necessary to supply the services.

What bounds, then, must be placed on the public utility by the regulator to ensure the market failures are at least mitigated, if not eliminated? Essentially, the guidelines for regulation came straight out of the neoclassical competitive model. The focus is almost entirely on price. According to the "boilerplate" clauses of virtually all the legislation establishing regulatory agencies, prices must be "reasonable" and "not unduly discriminatory." The social policy objective of public utility regulation is equally straightforward—that is, a universal service should be established to the extent practicable. In implementing these responsibilities, regulators have broad powers to examine other aspects of utility operations, including costs and quality of service. Yet the essential criteria around which public utility regulation has revolved are the reasonableness of prices and the universality of service coverage. It is on this skeleton regulatory framework that a little meat and an enormous amount of fat has been hung during the last century.

In retrospect, it is surprising that in the legislation establishing the regulatory agencies there was no mandate to maintain existing levels of competition, to encourage competition where possible, or even to monitor whether and where competition might be possible. Regulation was seen and described as a substitute for competition. It replaced competition. It attempted to achieve the efficiency objectives of competition. Yet, regulation did not promote competition. There were primarily two reasons for this. First, regulation was being established because competition had failed. The prevailing thinking was that regulation should not be promoting a market structure whose failure was the very reason for establishing regulation. Even more important was the pervasive lobbying of the dominant utilities. They argued persuasively that if they were to be subjected to regulation because competition had failed, the trade-off was a grant of monopoly, preferably exclusive monopoly in perpetuity. Many of the early licenses and charters granted to the dominant operators were viewed as contracts, at least by the operators. The utility agreed to be regulated in return for an exclusive monopoly and the right to use the government's powers of eminent domain. Moreover, it was argued that the extension of service to unprofitable customers would be possible only under monopoly, where internal cross-subsidies could be employed.

AT&T and other dominant utilities actually saw regulation as a vehicle for taking the final steps toward creating private monopolies that would be acceptable to government. AT&T was the most vigorous, mounting an intensive lobbying program with state legislatures over the decade between 1907 and 1917 to obtain a rationalization of the telephone industry by regulation of exclusive monopoly. It was then-AT&T chairman Theodore Vail who invented the "universal service obligation," although what he meant was simply an interconnected service among exclusive monopolies operating in different geographical areas. As the dominant operator in the most populated parts of the country and in long-distance services, and as an operator that was refusing to interconnect to smaller competitors or to local telephone operators in areas that it did not own, AT&T knew that the establishment of regulation would provide a vehicle for virtually eliminating the existing competition, giving AT&T absolute dominance in the more populated geographical areas it served, leaving the less populated and rural areas to others. Thus the creation of public utility regulation as an institution changed the industry structures from unstable oligopoly to virtually closed-entry oligopoly (transport) or geographic exclusive monopoly (telephone, electricity and gas). It established a general presumption that competition was not to be encouraged, and in many states could not be encouraged because the legislative mandates specified exclusive monopoly (R. Gabel 1969).

The Performance of Public Utility Regulation

The performance of public utility regulation in the United States has been subject to heavy criticism virtually throughout its entire period of existence. Like the yawning chasm between the theory of perfect competition and the reality of massive market failure in the public utility industries, there has developed a massive gap between the theory of public utility regulation and the reality of regulatory ineffectiveness and failure. Although there have been examples of effective, and even exemplary, regulation by particular commissions from time to time, the overall weight of evidence calls into question whether public utility regulation in the United States during the twentieth century has come anywhere close to achieving its objectives. Some critics, most notably from the Chicago School, have concluded that regulation has done more harm than good (Stigler and Friedland 1962; Posner 1969). These assessments, of course, do not compare the results of highly imperfect regulation with the massive market failures that existed in these industries before regulation, and which would have continued in some form in the absence of regulation. Rather, assessments of regulation have tended to be made by consumers on the basis of service expectations, by analysts from many fields on the basis of the functioning and administrative performance of the agencies, and by economists on the basis of the implications of regulation and regulatory decisions for promoting efficient resource allocation.

The Early Years, 1907–1930s

The early period of public utility regulation, up to the time of the Great Depression in the 1930s, might be considered an experimental or learning period. Although federal regulation by the ICC played a significant role in the railroad industry, the focal point of regulation in the telephone, electricity, and gas industries was at the state level. Regulation helped provide markets in these industries with greater stability than in the past, and they grew rapidly. The percentage of the population provided with utility services grew significantly, but services generally were not extended to rural areas. These industries were major forces behind U.S. industrial expansion during this period. Yet, overall, public utility regulation was seen more as an unproductive drag on economic growth than as a facilitator of it. Consumer complaints (both residential and business) about high and discriminatory prices, poor quality of service, and failure to extend service remained at a high level. The regulated companies objected to decisions restricting their prices and appealed a high proportion of commission decisions to the courts. Potential new entrants to these markets objected to the regulatory barriers to entry.

Economists documented cases of inefficiency in these industries, many of which were linked to commission regulations or responsibilities (see Samuels and Trebing 1972). The problem of high fixed costs and significant economies of scale in the supply of joint and common outputs, which had provided a foundation for instability and market failure in the first place, could not be resolved by regulators to anyone's satisfaction. It could not be resolved by economists either, even in theory, let alone practice, but it was fairly easy to document seemingly arbitrary decisions by regulators on costing and pricing matters that could be associated with unused capacity or inefficient investments in public utility systems. For many economists, responsibility for the deficiencies and failures of markets in these industries was shifted from the inherent characteristics of the industry or the corporate managers to the regulators. Many observers concluded that the commissions simply preserved the status quo by protecting the interests of the dominant firms. Some believed many commissions had been captured by them.

Yet the most telling criticism, which tended to add credibility to all the others, was the general ineffectiveness of the administrative functioning of the regulatory process. It was not working as intended. The major culprit was the court, which seemed only too happy to play the role of super-regulator, providing microscopic reviews of regulatory decisions and imposing its (often changing) judgments on virtually all the procedural and substantive matters of regulation. Thus, a high proportion of regulatory decisions were overruled by the courts. The procedural and substantive standards of regulation were ultimately determined by the courts, without consideration of the purported expertise of the commissions or the need for expedited decision making. In this period, nearly every step in the evolution of regulatory policies and standards must be traced by following the sequence of Supreme Court decisions. This proactive role of the courts on regulatory details encouraged the utilities to attempt to manipulate the regulatory process and prompted commissions to adopt processes of lengthy hearings to try to make their decisions comply with the court's detailed requirements. Some cases on the reasonableness of utility rate proposals took more than ten years to resolve.

This, in turn, provided lucrative market opportunities for the legal profession to establish a powerful vested interest in lengthy regulatory processes and judicial appeals, and for the engineering and finance professions to build a significant market for themselves in meeting the court's requirements that reasonable rates be determined on the basis of detailed calculations of a "fair" rate of return on the "fair value" of the utility's investments in plant and facilities. The judging of fairness came to require the most detailed and elaborate studies by the professions, which when employed by contending parties reached widely varying judgments on the same matters. A new set of claimants on the consumer surplus of the public utility monopolies had been created by the manner in which the regulatory process came to be implemented.

During this period, the telephone, electricity, and gas industries expanded far beyond the scope of state jurisdiction. When regulation was established, these services were predominately intrastate in character. However, the dominant firms in these industries had grown during the period by extensive mergers and acquisitions to become large, multistate holding companies, and with an expanding national economy interstate services had become a significant portion of their output. The difficulty of trying to regulate part of a company for intrastate services in a single state when its regulatory jurisdiction ended at the state border contributed to regulatory ineffectiveness. The electricity holding companies in particular engaged in fraud and manipulation that not only rendered regulation ineffective but also contributed to the collapse of the stock market in 1929 and the following Great Depression. Therefore, as part of the overall reassessment of the institutional foundations of capitalism in the United States, the new federal regulatory agencies created in the 1930s included those for telephone and telegraph (Federal Communications Commission [FCC]), and electricity and gas (Federal Power Commission).[5]

Through these and other new federal regulatory agencies, the U.S. government decided to try to make the model of public utility regulation of private markets in the infrastructure sectors work effectively. In reality, there were few alternatives. All available evidence indicated that unregulated private markets would fail dramatically. Indeed, in the absence of regulation, both experience and economic theory suggested that in the Depression economy there would be destructive competition, instability, and disinvestment in essential infrastructure services. The only real alternative to regulation was public ownership, which was tried with new initiatives but not with established operations. Ironically, despite regulatory failure, the best alternative was more regulation; or perhaps it would be better expressed that regulation was the least bad option available. As bad as it was, it did at least appear to mitigate the worst extremes of unregulated market failure. Moreover, it was felt that federal regulation could overcome many of the weaknesses of state regulation during the earlier period.

Although economists generally had been highly critical of the ineffective performance of regulation up to the 1930s, the critics had no real alternative institutional structures or policies to suggest. For neoclassical theorists, all the options were highly inefficient in comparison to the theoretical optimum, but they had no model of regulatory reform to recommend. The dilemma for economists, and economic theorists in particular, was that their tools of analysis were not good enough to delineate and compare the relative merits of different imperfect market and institutional structures.

Economists had well-developed theories of perfect competition and monopoly. The first was efficient, the second was not. Between these two theoretical extremes, markets were imperfect, as are all real markets. The only solution economists could recommend on the basis of these theories was more competition that would move the market structure closer to the perfectly competitive model. Yet if markets are highly imperfect, as they are in the public utility industries, and the end result of competition is unstable oligopoly or monopoly, economists can only conclude from the theory that the market structure is not optimally efficient. This does not provide a basis for making any recommendations. Thus, many of the criticisms that economists directed at the industry or the regulator amounted to little more than documentation that these industries are highly imperfect and inefficient when compared with the theoretical perfectly competitive model. There was a failure of economic theory to develop the conceptual and analytical tools necessary to come to grips with the particular characteristics of markets in the public utility industries.

Nevertheless, in the face of severe limitations on the guidance from economic theory, the reform of the regulatory agencies was supported by and worked on by many institutional economists (Glaeser 1957). While some were examining different roles and functions that regulation might be able to play so as to improve the performance of these highly imperfect market structures, others were examining the characteristics of highly imperfect markets in an attempt to assess the implications of specific market imperfections and different types of imperfect market structures (Wilcox 1955). Some imperfections have greater implications and significance for economic performance than others. Clark (1940) suggested that a better standard for judging the efficiency of markets would be a more realistic theory of "workable" competition. Yet research on the characteristics of real markets was not amenable to the formulation of simple theoretical generalizations. Nevertheless, it was becoming apparent that the economic understanding of imperfect markets, and particularly oligopoly and quasi-monopoly markets, would have to improve if market theory was to contribute to the resolution of the policy issues that characterized the public utility industries.

National Regulation, 1930s–1960s

During the Depression the general decline in economic activity was associated with a decline in utility services and little new investment. Few new service extensions took place, and the penetration rate of telephone service, in particular, declined significantly, as many households were forced to give up their phones. To stimulate the rural economy, in areas that generally had little or no utility services, the federal government chose not to try to work through the regulatory commissions and the private utilities, but rather initiated massive multipurpose power projects to generate and transmit power in the unserved regions of the Tennessee Valley and the Northwest. These projects were supplemented by a rural electrification program. A new government agency, the Rural Electrification Administration (REA), provided low-interest loans, technical and management advice, and training to assist local cooperatives, private operators, and local governments in developing rural distribution systems. With the evident success of the REA program in electricity, the program was extended to telephones. Between the late 1930s and the 1950s, the great majority of rural areas acquired utility services through the creation of tens of thousands of local operators. This is how universal service in electricity and telephone was achieved.

The large private utilities (occasionally joined by the federal regulatory agencies and some state commissions) opposed the public power projects and REA programs, seeing them as competitive with the established structure of regulated private monopolies, even though these new programs would support service extension in areas that the private operators were not serving and had no plans to serve. In the face of the Great Depression and powerful populist rural political representation, however, they were unsuccessful. Yet, this united attempt by the established monopoly operators and their regulators was seen by some critics as evidence of regulatory capture, that is, the tendency for the regulators to identify with the interests of the regulated operators rather than those of the consumers they were supposed to protect (Bernstein 1955).

With the establishment of many new federal regulatory agencies in the 1930s, a two-tier system of regulation became fully developed that included federal regulation of interstate services and state regulation of intrastate services. Although intended to be cooperative, and to a degree constructively competitive, this system was often competitive in unproductive ways. Disagreements over jurisdiction led to frequent skirmishes between federal and state regulatory agencies and provided fertile ground for the utilities to appeal decisions of regulatory commissions on jurisdictional issues. Jurisdictional disputes became a significant area of activity for regulatory agencies in both the telecom and electricity and gas industries.

In addition, the jurisdictional limitations of individual regulatory agencies required that the cost and revenue data of the utility operators be allocated among jurisdictions for purposes of determining reasonable prices and profits. This forced regulators to engage in jurisdictional cost separation exercises as a major activity of great importance to all parties. As there were a variety of plausible ways for allocating costs among jurisdictions, the process invited participants to seek to gain advantage through the ongoing debates on cost separation (R. Gabel 1967). Fortunately, in 1944 the Supreme Court stepped back from its earlier role as super-regulator, adopting the "end result" doctrine in the Hope case. Regulatory decisions henceforth would be judged by the end result of those decisions, not by detailed judicial determination of the procedural and substantive details.

Nevertheless, a significant amount of new regulatory activity was generated by the requirements of the two-tier structure of regulation that had no discernible relation to promoting efficiency, protecting consumers, or extending universal service. Yet, as this regulatory structure was derived directly from the U.S. Constitution, which limits federal jurisdiction to interstate commerce, there were no other options to consider. However, it did provide a significantly expanded potential market for lawyers and consultants to ply their trade. Increasingly over this period large numbers of economists were drawn into the process by the new market opportunities for experts in the regulatory process. As a general rule, the neoclassical theorists tended to work for the utilities, arguing that proposed regulations restricting utility activities on pricing, profits, or other matters would be inefficient and would distort the market. The institutional economists tended to work for the regulatory agencies, attempting to develop and apply standards that would prevent monopoly pricing, promote improved efficiency, and extend market coverage. There were, of course, many more of the former than the latter. Nevertheless, the performance of regulation was steadily criticized by both neoclassical theorists and institutionalists, both those working directly in the regulation process and those outside it.

After World War II, a stable, growing economy stimulated utility expansion to fill out the needs for industrial expansion and urban development and to connect to the rural networks that had been established. Technological improvements in the equipment and facilities purchased by the utilities, economies of scale in expanding volumes of service, and more concentrated networks provided the basis for an era of generally declining costs and prices. Yet, economic research began to raise questions about how competitive the equipment markets were. Evidence of price fixing in electricity company purchases came to light. Concerns about AT&T's purchasing practices from its fully owned equipment-manufacturing affiliate, Western Electric,[6] prompted a federal government antitrust investigation. In addition, utility management overhead expenses were expanding disproportionately. This and other evidence was documenting the criticism that regulatory standards for judging the reasonableness of prices and profits on the basis of the operator's costs were essentially cost-plus regulation, which encouraged the artificial stimulation of costs rather than a decline in consumer prices.

Complaints about barriers to entry, either imposed or supported by regulators, continued to grow. Some firms wanted to sell equipment to the utilities, yet the utilities purchased only from affiliated or favored suppliers. In telecom, customers were prohibited from connecting equipment to the network. Firms wanted to lease capacity on the network for resale or for the provision of enhanced services. Some wanted to interconnect private networks. Still others wanted to compete for particular services. Regulations and utility tariff restrictions tended either to prevent such activities absolutely or make the entry price prohibitive in terms of cost and delay. For very large customers that had the size, resources, and economic power to supply a portion of their own telecom needs, for example, the rail, airline, and broadcast industries, drastic discriminatory rate reductions by AT&T became common practice. According to the utilities and their regulators, this was all necessary, to maximize the benefits from economies of scale, to permit the cross-subsidy of basic services in high-cost areas, and to keep prices as low as possible. Yet the mounting evidence on the failures of regulation was once again calling into question whether the institution of public utility regulation was creating more harm than good.

During this period, the federal government paid close attention to the structure and performance of the regulatory agencies, in an attempt to make them more effective. There were four special federal government commissions established to study the regulatory agencies between 1937 and 1960 and make recommendations for reform. Many recommendations were made on the powers, accountability, and administrative structure of the regulatory agencies, some of which were implemented. Yet, as the continuing saga of attempts to reform regulation suggests, there was sustained widespread frustration about the performance and effectiveness of the regulatory agencies, including dispute about not only structural and procedural issues, but also the tendency for the regulatory agencies to treat the regulated operators as clients, making the agencies vulnerable to regulatory capture. In his assessment of the history of regulation, Marver Bernstein (1972) concluded:

> [T]he greatest need in administrative regulation today is to focus attention on strategies of regulation. The primary question that we must try to answer as systematically as possible is this: For a given set of objectives, what combination of statutory provisions; regulatory powers, processes, and techniques; incentives and sanctions; political leadership; and administrative resources is likely to achieve results that approximate the goals of a regulatory program? After nearly a century of regulatory experience in an industrial economy we are unable to identify, on the basis of rigorous analysis rather than impressionistic judgments, the requisites of acceptable administrative performance—given the objectives sought, the mix of parties of interest, the state of technology, the number of firms subject to regulation, the strength of consumer interests, and the degree of danger to individuals. The talent and energy we have devoted to designing regulatory programs to protect the regulated from unfair procedures and to minimize effects adverse to regulated clienteles must now be targeted on the modest problem of designing and improving systems of regulation that have a fighting chance of achieving some useful result. (21)

Thus, after thirty years of federal regulation of public utilities, the general state of knowledge about public utility industry markets and their regulation had not advanced significantly from what had been known in the 1930s. Unregulated public utility markets would lead to unacceptable market failures. The overall performance of regulation was generally disappointing and considered to be a failure by many observers. Yet there were no realistic options. Neoclassical theorists were still reciting the competitive model, hoping that reality would eventually conform to it. Institutionalists were plugging away at the specific problems of regulation, with only modest and occasional success.

During this period the evident problem of monopoly in the economy began to command greater attention from economists. The theoretical and applied study of imperfect markets and monopoly power became a more serious subject for an increasing number of economists.[7] The common thesis through much of this work was that most markets were highly imperfect and dynamic. Markets with significant monopoly power were the general condition in most industries. There was no self-correcting mechanism that would bring markets back to the equilibrium of competition theory. An active debate developed around the conditions of "workable competition," or as Walter Adams more precisely characterized the problem in terms of neoclassical theory, "workable monopoly." There was a strong case for public policy intervention in many markets to achieve efficiency goals. Yet there was no clear guide as to what that intervention should be, especially for the special circumstances of dominant monopoly power over essential public utility services.

Activating Regulation and Competition, 1960s–1984

By the 1960s, the utility industries had reached maturity in a stable and growing economy. Universal service had been pretty much achieved. New technologies and economies of scale were providing a basis for declining unit costs. On the surface, there was considerable evidence that the institutional model of regulated public utilities was beginning to work as intended. Perhaps "workable monopoly" arrangements finally had been achieved. Yet the criticism from the economics profession expanded. The economists' critique of cost-plus regulation and the disincentive it creates for efficient resource allocation became a popular topic for academic research. The traditional empirical critiques of specific regulatory procedures and practices were supplemented by theoretical models. In particular, the Averch and Johnson (1962) model, which showed how return on investment regulation could stimulate utilities to overinvest and misallocate investment in reference to the theoretical optimum, spawned a small academic industry churning out theoretical papers on the theme for many years. It was no longer necessary for one to study a regulated industry in order to partake in the game of theorizing about the imperfections of regulation. However, no proposals for resolution of the cost-plus problem came out of this activity. Still, if there were no regulation, the investment misallocations predicted from the theory of monopoly would be many times worse than the Averch and Johnson misallocations. That was easily demonstrated by the same theoretical models.

The most constructive resolution to this problem was developed by Harry Trebing. In a 1963 article, "Toward an Incentive System of Regulation," Trebing examined the issue of incentive regulation and demonstrated that the disincentive for efficiency was not as strong in reality as claimed in theory because of inherent time lags in the regulatory process. Regulatory decisions applied only to the future, not the past. Past excess or deficient profits could not be recouped by the regulator for consumers or by the utility for shareholders. Trebing documented the various forms of incentive regulation that had been tried in the past with varying degrees of success, and showed how this type of regulation could be applied within the conventional public utility model for regulating prices and profits. By designing into the public utility model specific time lags, for example, three-year reviews, ranges of reasonableness for prices and rates of return rather than precise numbers, and shared benefits for realized profit levels that were outside the target range of reasonableness, strong incentives for efficiency could be created. These ideas for incentive regulation were not picked up immediately, but have received increasing attention over the years, playing a central role in the new "Price Cap" method of regulation initiated in Britain in the mid-1980s and now being used in a number of countries, as well as by the FCC and several state regulatory commissions in the United States.

The most significant issues of this period related to the dynamics of changing conditions in the public utility industries. Applications by potential new entrants to utility markets were increasing, and new technologies were opening potential new opportunities. The role and significance of utility services in the economy had become more important as the U.S. economy had grown. Considerable economic growth opportunities in many industries were associated with new uses and applications of utility services. These developments were most predominant in the communication industries, where radio microwave technology developments from World War II were transforming the provision of longdistance telephone transmission and making long-distance television transmission economical. International satellites had been developed, broadband coaxial cable was being developed for local distribution of television signals, and there was experimentation with something called "computer communications." In addition, the rapid growth and increasing importance of the services sector in the economy prompted many industries to examine their communication needs, costs, and opportunities more closely, and seek greater control over them.

The FCC appointed Harry Trebing as chief economist in its Common Carrier Bureau in the early 1960s. Trebing assembled a small team of economists to study the problems confronting the industry and the FCC at the time.[8] The conventional wisdom, which was almost universally accepted without question or examination, was that the telephone industry was a natural monopoly with enormous economies of scale, scope, and coordination. Its regulated uniform prices were set to cross-subsidize basic local telephone service, high-cost areas, and universal service. This delicate balance could be sustained only if the monopoly was maintained in the face of potential new entrants, whose desire to enter the market could be explained only as attempts to "cream-skim" low-cost, high-revenue segments of the market and to avoid the social cross-subsidy costs.

Clearly there was a conflict between the conventional wisdom and the claims of potential entrants, as well as the claims of some industrial user groups. In fact, Western Union claimed that AT&T's services that overlapped competitively with its telegraph and private line services were being subsidized by AT&T's monopoly telephone services. The initial task of the new economics group was simply to investigate the different claims. Yet, the mere fact of investigation raised a potential threat to the conventional wisdom. The work of the group fell into four interrelated areas: cross-subsidies, implications of new technologies, entry conditions, and adapting the traditional regulatory model to a dynamic market environment. The major reference for the group's work was the economic literature on institutions and monopoly. Ironically, the major reference for AT&T, the most pervasive monopoly in the U.S. economy, was the perfectly competitive model of neoclassical theory.

Cross-Subsidies

There were two kinds of cross-subsidies possible, (1) the social subsidy that was a central tenet of the conventional wisdom; and (2) the subsidy of potentially competitive services with profits from the monopoly services, within the framework of aggregate rate of return regulation. The first assumed perfect regulation and public service objectives driving AT&T management. The second assumed that AT&T's objectives were the same as any other private monopolist and were restrained only insofar as regulation was capable of enforcing specific constraints. AT&T's concern at this time was that major industries, such as airline, broadcast, rail, and pipeline might be licensed to provide a major portion of their own communication requirements, which could open the door to potential competition.

Theoretically, the public utility model as implemented by the FCC and state commissions provided a powerful incentive for AT&T to engage in anticompetitive cross-subsidies. The reasonableness of AT&T's prices was judged entirely by reference to the overall return on investment realized for all of AT&T's interstate and foreign services in aggregate. The reasonableness of specific prices, or the rates of return for specific services, had not been part of this process. Thus, high returns on monopoly services and low, or even negative, returns on potentially competitive services would be masked entirely by the aggregate data (Melody 1971).

Moreover, as the allowed level of actual profit was a function of the size of the investment base, preventing or restricting competition at almost any cost would maximize AT&T's investment base and its absolute level of profit, in both the short and the long run. The monopoly services would provide the necessary revenue to earn the allowed return on all of the investment, which should be as high as could be justified. The theoretical precision tuning bias for economic efficiency of slightly shifted marginal conditions in the firm's investment decisions (the Averch-Johnson effect) would be swallowed up as an insignificant part of the much larger inefficiency incentive for AT&T to engage in anticompetitive pricing. It was actually a profitable activity. Only by excluding competition totally would AT&T's allowed profit level be maximized.

There were no studies, and there was very little relevant data available on the cross-subsidy issues, and AT&T could not provide any systematic evidence on them. AT&T was asked by the FCC to undertake a cost-of service study for its seven major classifications of interstate services. AT&T selected and applied the methodology, performed the calculations, and presented the results. For the 1964 test year, the study showed that the basic monopoly public services were subsidizing the potentially competitive services, some of which were earning negative returns. This led to further studies. These showed that large business users like the airline and broadcast industries could lease lines at prices as low as 14 percent of the general tariff price, when the costs were identical. Also, special terminal devices and switches for big business were priced well below cost (Trebing and Melody 1969).

Investigation of the social cross-subsidy costs revealed a number of important results. It confirmed that AT&T did not even serve the high-cost rural areas. At the time, AT&T served less than 20 percent of the land area of the United States, but collected 85 percent of industry revenue. AT&T's highest-cost area was lower Manhattan. Its highest-cost intercity route was the northeast corridor from Boston to Washington. On the pricing side, AT&T had many different uniform tariffs for essentially the same service, and significant price variation within each tariff. One nationwide uniform tariff was applicable to any U.S. Department of Defense, another to any airline industry, another for broadcasters, and so on. At bottom, most of the claim of social cross-subsidy was really a debate over the allocation of the common costs of local exchange networks among the different services that used them, and particularly the allocation of a share of local exchange costs to long-distance services.

The conventional wisdom was that any allocation of local exchange costs to long-distance services for originating and terminating these calls was a subsidy. Yet evidence showed that local exchange networks were designed for the more sophisticated and expensive long-distance services. Local services were the inferior services. One could debate the appropriateness of the common cost allocations, but there was no evidence that there were subsidies. Moreover, these same cost allocation rules would apply to any new operator that wished to originate and terminate calls on local exchanges. There would certainly be no competitive disadvantage to AT&T (Melody 1971, 1980; D. Gabel 1991).

Neither the FCC economists nor AT&T and its economic consultants could find any evidence of a significant or systematic social cross-subsidy built into AT&T's cost or pricing structure for its interstate services that would place AT&T at a disadvantage with respect to political competition. There might have been special circumstances where social cross-subsidies might have existed and needed to be considered. These would have had to relate to the basic public long-distance services, and would have been paid through contributions to local exchange costs, which all long distance operators would have had to pay for having their services originated and terminated in local exchanges. The conventional wisdom that the existence of social cross–subsidies required that competition be prevented was not supported by an economic analysis of the evidence.

As the factual evidence relating to AT&T's anticompetitive pricing mounted ever higher, AT&T resorted to a theoretical defense. It discovered neoclassical economic theory and the beauty of the marginal cost concept to be precisely what was needed. The AT&T economists recited the theory, focusing entirely on marginal cost as the only appropriate standard for assessing the economic viability of competitive services. They argued that the standard financial test of return on investment based on actual costs was inappropriate to judge the economic viability of an individual service. This test was not optimal and required cost allocations, which were arbitrary.

What was important for AT&T management was the flexibility to apply its judgment on cost and price matters in any way it wished without being held accountable by the FCC. By adopting the terminology of marginal cost, AT&T could select whatever conception of marginal cost was appropriate, leave out of their cost studies whatever indirect and common cost categories they wished, and place any values they desired on the remaining cost elements. This, the AT&T economists claimed, was not arbitrary. It was scientific and optimal. Neither the economists nor AT&T wished to take the risk of having the economists determine a specific methodology for measuring the marginal costs of AT&T services. What was important to the economists was use of the "theoretically correct" terminology for the cost calculations. Interestingly, when an FCC hearing judge called for a one-week conference among the economists of all the parties to get agreement on cost definitions and implementation methods, the group of leading economists couldn't agree on the relevant theoretical definition of marginal cost, and never got close to implementation issues.[9] The judge was not impressed.

The FCC staff economists suggested that, theoretically, marginal cost might be an appropriate efficiency standard if it was used for the monopoly services. If prices for the monopoly services were set precisely equal to their respective marginal costs, then it would follow that AT&T could set its prices in its potentially competitive services on a level playing field with any potential competitors, as there would be no subsidies flowing between the monopoly and potentially competitive services. For AT&T management this was unthinkable and financially irresponsible, and for its marginal cost theoreticians it was suddenly impractical. They refused even to investigate this possibility.

Instead, the AT&T economists at Princeton and the Bell Labs went to work on the problem of demonstrating that AT&T's massive price discrimination and anticompetitive pricing practices were the most efficient form of pricing possible. Demonstrating significant ingenuity, they came up with what they later labeled Ramsey pricing (Baumol and Bradford 1970). With very low marginal costs, price discrimination that reflects pricing the inelastic services with very large markups over marginal cost, and the elastic services with very small markups, was not only justified but socially efficient, given a full-cost aggregate revenue requirement. Yet without credible evidence on marginal cost or demand elasticities for its different services, and with very high cross-elasticities among the different service classifications, AT&T gave up trying to demonstrate that they had been implementing Ramsey pricing before Baumol et al. had invented it.

This may have been a mistake, because Ramsey pricing quickly acquired significant popularity in the neoclassical theory literature, a popularity that has continued to this day. As Baumol (1987) oberved in his article on Ramsey pricing in the *New Palgrave,*

> That theorem states that if a monopolist who is constrained by a regulatory (or other) profit ceiling chooses to adopt the Ramsey price vector rather than some other set of prices that enable him to earn his allowed return, then under a fairly attractive set of assumptions the monopolist will be rewarded for his virtuous decision by being protected from entry by those prices. In other words, self-interest may impel a monopolist to adopt Ramsey prices because those prices are *sustainable* against entry, meaning that at those prices the monopolist will earn the profits that the constraint allows to him, but any rival firm that undertakes to enter the field will be predestined to lose money even if the incumbent undertakes no strategic (retaliatory) response. (4:51)

The AT&T economists definitely delivered the goods. Yet the FCC economists did not accept Ramsey's pricing theory as relevant or appropriate to the circumstances of regulating AT&T in a dynamic market environment. To accept static models with criteria for regulation that forced the regulator to accept the subjective judgments by AT&T management about future marginal costs that could be neither verified nor corroborated would mean handing FCC regulation over to AT&T. Its management had an overwhelming incentive to understate marginal cost in order to justify anticompetitive pricing, knowing that the actual costs for these same services would be recoverable through the aggregate revenue requirement and the monopoly service. As one would expect, Ramsey pricing has won great favor with regulated firms everywhere, and has been sold to a few regulators. It provides the foundation for the modern intellectual justification of monopoly.

After continued discussion between the AT&T and FCC economists, the theoretical precision of marginal cost gave way to the imprecision of incremental cost, and then to the further ambiguities of long-run incremental cost (LRIC). According to the AT&T economists, LRIC was an approximation of marginal cost, although Bill Vickrey maintained LRIC was simply a set of arbitrary average costs. Several rounds of fully distributed cost, return on investment, and incremental cost studies were undertaken with no sign of a resolution of the problems. Finally, in 1968 the FCC economists suggested that many aspects of the apparent price discrimination and anticompetitive cross-subsidies in AT&T's tariffs could be eliminated by simply including a provision for unlimited resale in all relevant tariffs. AT&T resisted, effectively manipulating the regulatory and judicial process to delay implementation of the resale provisions for eight years. The neoclassical theorists advising AT&T were strangely silent on the subject, in FCC meetings and proceedings, and also in the research literature.

Implications of New Technologies

Although AT&T's Bell Laboratories were the principal source of new technological developments in telecom, they were not the only source. An increasing number of new technological developments, large and small, were coming from other sources. Hughes was pioneering communication satellites, but for U.S. domestic communication would have no customers, as AT&T would decide whether satellites would be introduced into the telecom network, and if so, would have them manufactured by its manufacturing affiliate, Western Electric. Radio microwave systems, which had become the backbone of the long-distance network, were being developed by Motorola, Collins Radio, and others, but AT&T would not buy from them even when their systems were cheaper and better. Computer industry firms were experimenting with data communication, but were generally prohibited from connecting computers to telephone lines, or from controlling the parameters of communication over those lines. A number of innovative telecom customer terminal devices had been developed, but they couldn't be connected to the network. Some AT&T telephone operators were using their own money to buy lightweight headsets from a small manufacturer, in violation of AT&T policy, because Western Electric produced only heavier headsets.

The existing monopoly restrictions were denying major opportunities to a broad range of suppliers of new technological equipment, to telecom users, and even to AT&T. Indeed, as the owner and operator of the core national network, AT&T would benefit from most of these developments, as they would reduce network costs, expand network capabilities, and increase usage, all of which would increase AT&T revenue. These "potential competitors" really would be more like partners in extending the efficiency, service capabilities, and usage of the national telecom network, than direct competitors. Unless a way could be found to allow them to participate in the telecom system, the industry would suffer serious dynamic inefficiencies, with increasing negative consequences for the economy as a whole.

There were two issues arising from the review of new technological developments that were outside the debate over natural monopoly versus competition in the telecom services network and deserved special study. The first was the vertical integration between AT&T and its equipment-manufacturing affiliate, Western Electric. The case for natural monopoly generally does not extend to include monopoly over the manufacturing of equipment. If the AT&T operating telephone companies were allowed to purchase their equipment competitively, new opportunities for many independent equipment suppliers would be opened up. This issue had been examined by the Justice Department during the 1950s, but the evidence indicated the problem was becoming more serious during the 1960s, with ramifications well beyond the equipment market (Irwin 1971).

The second issue was the implications of computer communications for the future development of the telecom network. Although still in an experimental stage, and not widely recognized or understood, the FCC accepted the staff recommendation to undertake a computer inquiry (Federal Communications Commission 1971) to highlight potential future issues and gather information as a basis for future policy development. It was evident that changes from the traditional monopoly policies would be necessary if computer communication was to have a reasonable opportunity to develop (Irwin 1969). Study of these fundamental issues of long-term industry structure framed the more immediate challenges relating to specific applications for entry to telecom markets.

Entry Conditions

A study of entry conditions revealed that the FCC did not have a policy on entry. There were no provisions in the Communications Act of 1934 that required monopoly or specified entry conditions. The FCC had never specified a policy on entry conditions, except that it had always rejected new entry applications that could in any way be considered remotely competitive with AT&T. Thus, the rail, pipeline, electricity, and other specialized private networks that had been licensed for safety and security reasons could be used only to control their own specialized industry operations. Even though they had enormous amounts of unused capacity on their microwave radio networks, all their administrative traffic had to be provided by AT&T. Radio relay licenses that were granted to specialized operators to carry TV signals from the point where the AT&T network stopped to the rural hinterland areas were conditioned so that if AT&T chose to extend its network further to deliver TV signals, the radio relay licenses would be revoked. A "Hushaphone," a device that could be attached to a telephone to muffle the sound so that nearby people couldn't overhear and wouldn't be disturbed, was declared an unlawful interconnection (Federal Communications Commission 1956). The AT&T

monopoly extended even to covers on telephone directories (Trebing and Melody 1969).

When one searched for the source of an entry policy across these and other FCC decisions, it was found that the essential justification for them lay in the AT&T tariffs. All the applications violated AT&T tariff restrictions. Through its tariffs, AT&T therefore determined the FCC policy on entry conditions. By accepting the tariffs, the FCC had accepted the policy without undertaking an evaluation of its merits or implications.

An opportunity to reassess AT&T's interconnection restrictions against customer terminal attachments arose in the Carterfone case. Mr. Carter had developed an acoustical coupling device, a special cradle in which two telephones from different networks could be placed so that they could communicate directly. There was no physical connection. Carter sold it to oil and other natural resource companies to link their private systems serving the hinterland areas, where there was no telephone service, to the public telephone network. AT&T declared these unlawful interconnections, removed the Carterfones, and warned the companies about unlawful activities. Carter brought an antitrust suit against AT&T. The judge sent the case to the FCC and asked what its terminal interconnection policy was. After considerable debate within the commission, the position of the economics staff was adopted. Interconnection was to be permitted as long as there would be no technical or economic harm to the network. Technical standards would be made available to all suppliers and an independent dispute mechanism established. AT&T would have an opportunity to demonstrate that beneficial social cross-subsidies would be lost if "foreign" attachments, that is, terminals not owned by AT&T, to the network were permitted. It never attempted a demonstration.

The most important aspect of the FCC Carterfone decision (1968) is that it established an efficient entry policy for the customer terminal market that allowed other equipment manufacturers and retailers to participate in the industry's growth. It unleashed a market explosion as the standard black telephone set gave way to an enormous diversity of terminals and terminal capabilities, and the consumer electronics industry turned its attention to a potential large new market. These developments did not harm social policy. They strengthened it by helping to expand the network, improve its capabilities, diversify its potential uses, and make access easier.

The Carterfone decision demonstrated that AT&T's natural monopoly claim could not be extended to include network terminals, yet it didn't address the issue of competition in the network itself. That was being addressed in another proceeding at the FCC at about the same time. A trucking firm in Chicago wanted to lease broadband capacity from AT&T to manage its business between Chicago and St. Louis, including its communication relations with its customers. AT&T would not provide it. So the firm applied to the FCC for licenses for eleven microwave radio towers between the two cities to provide private (leased) line services. Its costs were significantly lower than AT&T's. Among other factors, it leased corners of farmers' fields for its radio towers, and Collins Radio delivered modular radio towers by helicopter for installation in a few days, compared to AT&T's policy of buying acreage and constructing virtual "bomb shelter" sites that took months to build. As the proposed applications did not challenge public network services, and AT&T's case against it was directed entirely at challenging the technical specifications and the qualifications of the applicant, the only thing at risk was the applicant's money. In its MCI decision (1969), the commission approved the MCI applications by a 4–3 vote. This demonstrated that competitive entry into supplying specialized network services was at least legally possible.

The MCI decision was followed by an avalanche of applications to the FCC for radio licenses to provide specialized network services. The staff economists urged the commission to establish a general policy on entry. Indeed, it had little choice. It was physically impossible for it to consider public hearings on all the applications. After a public policy inquiry, the FCC announced a policy permitting competition for specialized network services. Applications would be approved unless there was a significant public interest reason to investigate them (Federal Communications Commission 1971).

AT&T's response was to resist interconnection with the new entrants and introduce additional anticompetitive price reductions where needed. For many years, MCI was known as a law firm with a communication company as a by-product. It was winning in court but being delayed significantly in entering the market; FCC decisions and court rulings against AT&T could not keep up with AT&T's anticompetitive responses. MCI had its first significant revenue in 1974, five years after its first licenses had been approved. Many other applicants for specialized communication carrier licenses were defeated by the barriers to entry created by AT&T and sold out to MCI or gave up on their plans. The most innovative new application by the Data Transmission Company (DATRAN) was for a specialized national data communication network, giving credibility to the future of computer communication. Yet, in several years of trying it was never able to negotiate an interconnection agreement with AT&T for local exchange access. Just as DATRAN was about to raise its final tranche of investment financing, AT&T discovered data-under-voice, unused data transmission capacity lying beneath voice-carrying capacity on all its nationwide voice circuits. At virtually zero marginal cost, this "justified" very low prices in AT&T's new digital data service tariff filing with the FCC. After DATRAN went bankrupt, AT&T withdrew this tariff. Implementation of the FCC's competition policy was proving extremely difficult in the face of AT&T's anticompetitive responses. AT&T was making sure that the real barriers to entry, in terms of time, cost, and maximum resistance, were formidable.

Throughout the 1960s and 1970s, AT&T repeated this scenario. Anticompetitive tariffs would be established by AT&T. The FCC would hold hearings, gather evidence, and find the prices unlawful. AT&T would appeal the FCC decisions to the courts, which would eventually support the FCC and require the low prices to be withdrawn. Coincident with the withdrawal of the unlawful tariff, AT&T would file a replacement anticompetitive tariff. The FCC staff made recommendations to try to overcome this problem, including annual cost of service monitoring, the filing of more detailed information in support of new tariff filings, steps to expedite tariff proceedings, and possibilities for the selective application of longer tariff suspension periods. Some of these recommendations were implemented, yet they were insufficient to alter the trend of events. Throughout this period the FCC continued to assess the reasonableness of AT&T's overall rate of return on the basis of its aggregate financial data.

At the same time, AT&T launched a massive lobbying and public relations campaign with the FCC, the U.S. Congress, the state regulatory agencies, politicians at all levels, the press, and opinion leaders to attempt to get the FCC competition policy reversed. Its case focused on the natural monopoly and social policy benefits it claimed would be lost (deButts 1973). AT&T also turned its neoclassical economists at the Bell Labs, Princeton, and other leading universities loose on the problem to find some theoretical support for a policy reversal to monopoly protected by regulation. Once again the economists performed extremely well. They developed the theory of sustainability of natural monopoly—entry restrictions might be necessary to sustain a natural monopoly in order to realize its efficiency benefits. One could not trust the results of a market test as to whether the scale economies attributed to natural monopoly actually existed. A little bit of competition could lead to an irretrievable unraveling of the whole system, with major efficiency losses, what Melody referred to at the time as the humpty-dumpty theory of natural monopoly (see Baumol, Bailey, and Willig 1977). Yet once again the leap from the economist theory to the AT&T reality could not even be attempted by AT&T.

Throughout the 1970s there was a major struggle under way over the implementation of the FCC competition policy. The FCC Common Carrier Bureau, the new entrants, the industries that wanted to enter the telecom sector, business and residential consumer groups, and many institutional economists supported rapid implementation of the new FCC competition policy and further extension of this policy. AT&T and its vast network of economic and political powers were seeking a policy reversal. At the time, AT&T employed more than one hundred academic economists and more than two hundred small consulting firms, many run by leading academic economists. The economics departments of most leading universities were represented (Owen and Braeutigam 1978).

During the 1970s, the FCC was able to extend its competition policy to cover the introduction of domestic satellites. Later the court ruled that the MCI licenses granted by the FCC did not prevent the company from offering public network services as well as specialized services. The FCC finally was able to implement its policy allowing the resale of AT&T services, which opened opportunities for retail and enhanced services markets to develop and laid a foundation for developing data and information network services, what is known today as the Internet. Thus, a comprehensive competition policy permitting entry for the potential competitive provision of all interstate long-distance services, at both wholesale and retail levels, finally had been achieved.

Yet it was still questionable whether the FCC was capable of implementing this policy effectively, in light of AT&T's anticompetitive responses. MCI, Sprint, and other new entrants had resorted to bringing private antitrust cases against AT&T. The U.S. Justice Department had begun an antitrust investigation of AT&T's anticompetitive practices. In timely fashion, AT&T's economists once again came up with an appropriate theory to support AT&T's anticompetitive behavior. The theory of contestable markets argued that monopolies would operate at optimal efficiency as long as the possibility for entry existed. The potential for entry would force the monopoly to behave as if the market were competitive, even though it was a monopoly by all conventional economic measures. Real market competition wasn't necessary to achieve optimal results. Indeed, Baumol (1982) claimed that contestable market theory was "an uprising in the theory of industrial structure." Yet once again the link between the imaginative new theory and AT&T's actual practices was something even AT&T couldn't try to make with a straight face. The government brought its antitrust case to trial. The overwhelming evidence of nearly a quarter century of anticompetitive activity and manipulation of the regulatory process led AT&T to agree to a divestiture of its operating companies, effective 1 January 1984, rather than risk a court judgment based on the mountain of evidence.

Perhaps more dramatically than at any time in the history of utility regulation, this era of dynamic policy change driven by the FCC was one where regulation led events and opened opportunities for the development of new technologies, new services, and a restructured industry. Without this series of forward-looking and far-reaching FCC decisions in opposition to overwhelming and incessant establishment pressure from AT&T and its vast network of influence, the AT&T monopoly would have been maintained for at least another generation. The AT&T network of political influence included the Department of Defense and other federal, state, and local government agencies, many recently retired politicians, AT&T's many suppliers and favored large corporate customers, the Communication Workers Union, and recipients of AT&T's extensive program of research and charitable grants, including most major universities and a surprisingly large proportion of the leading neoclassical economists residing in them.

The forces supporting the policy changes were relatively weak in comparison—new, small firms with innovative ideas but few resources and far less political influence, industries that would benefit from the new arrangements but that shied away from direct confrontation with AT&T. Machiavelli's famous quotation described the situation well:

> There is nothing more difficult to take in hand, more perilous to conduct, or more uncertain in its success, than to take the lead in the introduction of a new order of things. Because the innovator has for enemies all those who have done well under the old conditions, and lukewarm defenders in those who may do well under the new.

In addition to the competition policy issues, the FCC Computer Inquiry was instrumental in focusing the attention of the computing industry and many other groups on the potential of teleprocessing for the future of the industry and the economy. The significance for sector development and economic growth of interconnection, resale, and enhanced services liberalization and a policy favoring competition was not well understood and was vastly underestimated, even by the future beneficiaries. These changes in telecom policy spawned a reform movement that has spread around the world and placed U.S. telecom, information infrastructure, and Internet development ahead of other countries in that transformation. This would not have happened had it not been for the forward-looking, proactive independent regulation by the FCC during this period and the refusal of the FCC economists to accept the new designer static efficiency models developed by AT&T economists as a basis for policy analysis in dynamic markets.

For economists and their theories, the twenty-year struggle to introduce competition in long-distance telecom markets exposed some puzzling ironies. Leading neoclassical theorists participated in the support of the monopoly, in an attempt to reverse the competition policy, in the defense of AT&T's anticompetitive practices, and in developing special-purpose theories to justify monopoly as competitively efficient. They never supported the liberalization of these markets before the FCC or in the economic literature, a strange silence for a school of thought based entirely on competitive markets and minimal regulation. It was institutional economists, traditionally associated with giving high priority to nonmarket and social policy objectives, who supported the introduction of a competition policy they saw as promoting both efficiency and social policy goals. The experience showed neoclassical economists distorting their theory beyond all recognition in the service of preserving monopoly power and the status quo. Alternatively, it might be concluded that the neoclassical economists simply applied their market theory to themselves and sold their services to the highest bidder. Institutional economics provided no optimal theories, but did provide an application of the economists' tools of analysis to dynamic issues and institutional change so as to develop policies and regulations for a new economic environment.

After the AT&T divestiture, the restructured telecom industry provided a more conducive environment for implementing the FCC competition policy. Yet this policy had to be implemented within a framework of public utility regulation that still required strong regulation to protect consumers of the basic monopoly public long-distance service, to maintain universal service objectives, and to ensure reasonable interconnection among competitive operators and access to customers.

Toward a Dynamic Model of Utility Regulation

Throughout this period of dynamic change in the industry and in FCC policy with respect to competition, the commission continued to regulate AT&T within the framework of the traditional cost-plus aggregate financial model. The reasonableness of AT&T's prices was judged with reference to its overall rate of return on investment for all of its interstate services. Price adjustments to maintain the rate of return at the specified level of reasonableness generally were made to the basic monopoly service. Occasionally the commission would examine returns by major service category, but it never established ongoing cost of service studies as an integral part of a new approach to regulation. There was severe resistance to any move away from the traditional regulatory approach both at the FCC and state levels, as well as from AT&T, especially when there was no compelling alternative on the table and uncertainty about what the court might say about any new regulatory model.

Yet there was a serious incompatibility between the traditional regulatory model and the new competition policy, in that the model encouraged and rewarded predatory pricing, anticompetitive cross-subsidies, and other anticompetitive practices. In fact, by continuing to use the model in regulating AT&T throughout the period in which its competition policy was being introduced, the FCC provided a positive incentive for AT&T to take the drastic steps it did to try to defeat the competition policy. Continued use of the traditional regulatory model was not compatible with a competition policy in a dynamic environment.

Harry Trebing took the lead in focusing attention on this fundamental problem and in seeking a constructive solution to it. In a 1969 article, "Common Carrier Regulation—The Silent Crisis," Trebing demonstrated the incompatibility of the traditional static regulatory model with the dynamic characteristics of the industry and the commission's competition policy.

> Regulation should not be a cloak for maintaining the status quo. Rather, successful regulation has a vested interest in maintaining flexibility and disequilibrium in the interests of encouraging innovation and change. (328)

He presented an outline of a systems approach to regulation, as follows:

> Systems planning would seek to interrelate all variables pertaining to the common carrier service, as well as general communications, in such a fashion that they can be treated sequentially and cross-sectionally. Systems analysis must interrelate (1) the over-all system integrity of common carrier communications; (2) coexistence of monopoly and competition; (3) the need to assure an inducement to superior performance and freedom of consumer choice; and (4) efficient use of public resources. (326)

That same year, in a report to the President's Task Force on Communications Policy, Trebing and Melody developed some of the key characteristics of a new model of regulation. Coherent and integrated policies on competition, interconnection, cost and pricing standards, and other factors, they said, should replace case-by-case adjudication, which needed to be minimized in the new environment. Competition needed to be seen not as a substitute for regulation but as a valuable tool of regulation that in many circumstances could be the most effective vehicle for achieving both efficiency and social policy objectives. Competition should be seen and used by regulators as a valuable asset that strengthens regulation, not as a threat or problem. Yet keeping the door for entry open and barriers to entry minimized would require vigilant monitoring and periodic regulatory intervention. Otherwise, as Boyd Nelson always emphasized in FCC staff debates, the limited competition and oligopolistic rivalry would lead directly back to a cartel or monopoly.

In a variety of publications during this period, Trebing, Melody, Irwin, R. Gabel, Bolter, and other institutional economists contributed to the development of a new approach to telecom regulation adapted to the new dynamic environment. Under conditions of mixed monopoly and competitive services, more detailed cost analysis by service category would be required to set maximum prices for monopoly services and to ensure reasonable interconnection prices for new competitors. AT&T's costs for its competitive services could be used as benchmarks to judge the reasonableness of the costs assigned to the monopoly services for the same network elements. At the same time there wase a need for much greater flexibility for AT&T in its competitive services. Use of the traditional aggregate return on investment standard needed to be abandoned to ensure that the artificial incentive for AT&T to engage in cross-subsidy was eliminated, and to permit AT&T an opportunity to earn higher returns for superior performance in its competitive services. If more detailed information was gathered and published with respect to clearly defined policies and standards, a proactive regulatory commission could perform more expeditiously and effectively in the new environment than it could in the old one.

This more open and dynamic model of utility regulation is arguably superior to the traditional model for application to any public utility under almost any circumstances. As Edythe Miller (1985) observed, "Industry structure (itself) becomes a variable." The role and significance of competition can range from very little to a lot, and it can vary over time to reflect changing industry circumstances. By keeping the entry door open and barriers to entry minimized, the regulator ensures the natural monopoly thesis is constantly put to a dynamic market test. If economies of scale and scope are extensive compared to economies of specialization when technologies, demands, and market opportunities are continuously changing, there will be relatively little competition. If not, there will be much greater competition. The task of the regulator is to ensure that this market test is based upon efficiency and responsiveness to demand, not monopoly power. Regulation is necessary to identify which markets can be contested in reality through the market test. If conditions warrant it, competitive markets ultimately could displace regulation, but the displacement will be based on the evolution of real competition, not on idealist theories or wishful thinking.

This new model need not compromise the implementation of social policy objectives, but should make it more effective. Competition and the continuing threat of competition will extend the limits of markets and convert many formerly unprofitable market segments into profitable ones, reducing subsidy requirements. Indeed, there have been many occasions in the history of utility development when the appearance of an unforeseen threat of competition suddenly transformed a monopolist's unprofitable calculations relating to extensions of utility markets into profitable ones. In addition, as most subsidies within utility networks are really judgments about the allocation of common costs, the existing allocation methods can be continued or changed in a more competitive environment. Common cost allocations can continue to be a tool for implementing social policy, although it would clarify matters if they were no longer misidentified as subsidies. Regulation must simply ensure that all competitive suppliers use the core network under the same terms. The remaining real subsidy requirements, which will be vastly reduced, can be provided directly (following the REA model), applied as a uniform indirect tax on the entire network including all suppliers, or put out to competitive bid.

Acceptance of this new model of regulation requires that regulatory agencies commit to using competition as an effective tool of regulation. For most state commissions, this has been extremely difficult in light of the fact that the AT&T divestiture still left regional Bell operating company (RBOC) monopolies supplying intrastate services, with tremendous lobbying and political power at the state level. In some states, the Bell operating companies had exclusive monopoly licenses. In others, the exclusive monopoly grant was in the legislation establishing regulation. Moreover, the other public utilities regulated at the state level, notably electric, gas, and water, were still regulated as natural monopolies under the traditional model for regulation.

In his writings, and the conferences, publications, and regulatory training programs at the Institute of Public Utilities, Michigan State University, for more than a greater century Harry Trebing has opened up the issues of dynamic regulation for research, discussion, and debate among academics, government policy makers and regulators, industry executives, and user groups. It was apparent that the dynamic developments in telecom regulation were likely to be followed by similar market-liberalizing developments in other utility industries. A new generic model of dynamic regulation had to be developed, discussed, experimented with, refined, and ultimately integrated into a new coherent structure of utility regulation (Trebing 1987). This became Trebing's focus.

The period from the 1980s forward has provided a unique opportunity for further experimentation and reform in utility regulation. Different commissions have adapted regulation to deal with competition and monopoly issues in different ways. Some have continued to regulate within the framework of the old public utility model. There has even been a case of complete deregulation. The airline industry was a regulated oligopoly, with virtually no opportunity for new entry. Both industry performance and regulation were under heavy criticism. Following the tide of the competitive movement in telecom, economic regulation of the airline industry was abolished in 1978. The industry was subject to a degree of oligopolistic rivalry. There was substantial interest in new entry, and complete economic flexibility in terms of allocating airplanes to routes. The government concluded that these highly concentrated oligopoly markets would become more competitive and perform better without the regulation that had been applied. An unregulated market would satisfy both economic and social policy objectives.

Experimenting with Deregulated Markets: 1984–2000

Following the AT&T divestiture, throughout the 1980s the indicators showed positive results for increasing competition, reduced consumer prices, and greater consumer choice in the interstate long-distance market, and the competition was beginning to extend into the international market. AT&T's market share declined to about 65 percent, and MCI, Sprint, and Worldcom grew to become significant players in the interstate long-distance market. Hundreds of retailers and enhanced service suppliers came into the market. With the regional Bell operating companies (RBOCs) no longer tied to AT&T's manufacturing arm, and network access via customers, service suppliers, and competitors all expanding, the telecom equipment markets raced ahead, drawing in firms from the computer and electronics industries and setting the stage for the future explosion in networked personal computers. Although developments in the telecom services market have received most of the attention by analysts, much greater economic growth and market diversification took place in the equipment-manufacturing sector, where much larger markets were opened up, where competition has been far more effective, and where most of the new technologies have been developed. The primary beneficial effect of the AT&T divestiture was the freeing up of consumers, large and small, to buy their telecom equipment—ranging from fancy telephones to corporate data networks and telecom operator cables, switches, and radio equipment—from any supplier.

Unfortunately, the FCC competition policy did not prompt a spread of significant competition to intrastate services, and virtually not at all to services provided on the local exchange. As all the interstate long-distance operators had to pay local access charges to have their customers' calls originated and terminated, they were paying half or more of their revenues to monopoly local exchange companies. Only a few states were promoting competition. Many were resisting it. The RBOCs were turning out to be very formidable monopolists in their regions. Fiber-optic cable rings were being built in the central business districts of large cities by competitive operators, but this was an effective competitive option only for meeting specialized needs of some large business customers.

Other countries noticed the U.S. market liberalization developments and began to move in the same direction. Canada cautiously followed some U.S. liberalization policies a decade or so later. In 1984 the United Kingdom privatized its national telecom operator (now British Telecom) and established an independent telecom regulator (OFTEL). In 1987 the European Commission issued a Green Paper announcing its intention to begin a process of telecom liberalization. New Zealand, Australia, several South American countries, and other countries around the world made policy changes in the same direction. In most countries this involved some form of privatization of the national government telecom system (Melody 1997).

During the 1980s, under the Reagan administration, the federal government's conception of both competition and regulation changed dramatically. Competition was not seen as a tool of regulation, as conceived by institutional economists and applied by the FCC. Rather, the "free market" was seen as a desirable substitute for regulation. Regulation was a barrier to market development, and the removal of regulations made markets free. Most distinctions between competitive and monopoly markets lost significance. In this newfound faith in markets, it did not really matter much how markets were structured. This led to a gradual weakening of industry regulation across the board, the most infamous example of which was deregulation of the traditional investment criteria for the savings and loan industry, which soon led to its financial collapse. Through Reagan-era appointments to commissions, utility regulation was considerably softened at both the federal and state levels. Trebing (1986) assessed the limitations of the Reagan-era deregulation program for utilities as follows:

> The combined effect of high levels of concentration, differentiated markets, retaliatory power of incumbent firms, demand/supply imbalances,

and the difficulty of setting neutral pricing guidelines indicates clearly that accelerated deregulation will not result in high levels of competition in the energy and telecommunications industries. Rather, oligopolistic market structures will emerge that are conducive to significant inefficiencies and adverse distributional effects. A more reasoned solution calls for reforming regulation to come to grips with the current problems in these industries. (627)

After the AT&T divestiture, the profit rates of all the divested Bell companies increased, and cash flow increased very rapidly because of significantly increased depreciation rates that regulatory agencies were convinced to accept. The companies used these funds to diversify their investments, not by entering one another's markets, but primarily by buying real estate and computing firms. Nearly all these ventures lost money (Rosenberg et al. 1993).

By the early 1990s, the positive trend toward increased competition in the telecom sector began to slow down and in some cases reverse itself. The major long-distance competitors convinced the FCC to declare their market to be competitive and remove dominant carrier price regulation from AT&T. Although unit costs were falling dramatically as a result of new fiber cable and network management technologies, as well as major reductions in carrier access charges paid to local exchange companies, tariff prices for long-distance calls were increasing steadily. This provided room for expanding price discrimination, where the operators could charge tariff prices to the uninformed and those without alternatives, while offering special packages to consumers who had options. This was accompanied by major increases in the rates of return realized by the major operators. Following the concentrated oligopoly model to perfection, the competition shifted from price and consumer choice to marketing and customer loyalty plans (MacAvoy 1996). Consumer fraud, particularly in the retailing sector, began to increase alarmingly. "Let the buyer beware," was becoming the theme for this competitive business. The old criticisms of regulatory capture began to return.

As the digitalization of the telecom network became pervasive and the potential for Internet services began to be recognized, the future possibilities for interindustry competition became a subject for analysis. There was considerable posturing among the major industry facilities network players. The long-distance operators (concentrated oligopoly), RBOCs (regional monopolies) and cable television companies (national firms with local monopolies) were all making threatening noises about wanting to move into one another's markets. Yet none of them were making any serious moves to do it. The RBOCs had instead chosen to invest in telephone companies in other countries, most notably newly privatized national telecom operators—usually monopolies. They were more interested in horizontal mergers to enhance their monopoly power over customer connections. AT&T primarily invested in, or engaged in joint ventures with, electronics and computing companies, such as Philips, Olivetti, and NCR, the majority of which failed, some disastrously. It seemed the potential development of competition across the major segments of the telecom industry was not going to happen. The movement to competition in the telecom sector had become stuck (Trebing 1994).

In yet another ingenious twist of neoclassical theory in defense of monopoly, Baumol developed the "efficient component pricing rule" (ECPR) as a standard for determining interconnect prices that new competitors should pay incumbent monopolists for originating and terminating services provided by the new competitors (Baumol and Sidak 1994). According to this theory, prices should not be based upon marginal cost or long-run incremental cost, but rather on the opportunity cost to the monopoly of losing business to a competitor. The ECPR would set prices equal to the incremental costs of providing the interconnection service plus the profit the incumbent would lose if the competitor took the business away. The incumbent monopoly then would be indifferent whether it, or the new competitor, got the business, as its profit would be unaffected. In implementing the Telecommunications Act of 1966, the FCC rejected the ECPR as well as cost allocations based on Ramsey pricing principles as appropriate for implementing competition policy (Federal Communications Commission 1996).

The new Telecommunications Act attempted to provide a basis for a major surge forward in competition. It liberalized all telecom markets and specified detailed conditions to promote entry opportunities at several different levels within the monopoly local exchanges. Entry to interstate and international long-distance markets by the RBOCs was prohibited until there actually had been a satisfactory level of entry at the local exchange level in their respective regions. The FCC was instructed to develop specific implementation standards, and the state commissions were to facilitate implementation of the new competition policy at the state level. The FCC adopted a standard of total element long-run incremental cost (TELRIC) for determining interconnection prices to local exchanges (Bolter 1997).

Yet the master plan of the new Telecommunications Act grossly misconceived the incentives of the dominant players. The RBOCs predictably reaffirmed their primary goal of strengthening their monopoly power over customer connections. Controlling the origination and termination of all fixed line services to customers, including interstate long-distance services, is worth much more than an opportunity to compete in the interstate long-distance market. The seven RBOCs have been reduced to four, and the CEO of SBC (which has acquired Pacific Telesis and Ameritech) has announced his goal of creating a single national company. Traditionally the horizontal merger has been one of the actions that economists and antitrust authorities have unanimously agreed is anticompetitive, creates unnecessary monopoly power, and should be prohibited. Yet the RBOC mergers have not been challenged by policy makers. Adopting a passive posture, the FCC has found them acceptable.

Picking up on the FCC and antitrust authority tolerance of mergers, MCI and Worldcom, the second and third largest players in the United States long-distance market, have merged, creating a more concentrated oligopoly. Their attempt to acquire Sprint, the fourth largest player was rejected.[10] Realizing that its access to customers will be dependent on RBOC local exchange monopolies, AT&T has purchased TCI, the largest U.S. cable TV operator, in preparation for its entry into the future broadband Internet services market. The deregulated free market is leading to significantly fewer players who can control the competition, what Trebing (1997) refers to as "tight oligopoly."

Throughout this period of merger mania in U.S. telecom, which is by no means over, the FCC has been unable to develop standards for assessing the merger proposals. By all the usual criteria of market share, or concentration measures, these mergers would have to be rejected. From a more dynamic conception of the market, the mergers do not expand or open competition in new markets; they are obvious attempts to protect markets, extend monopoly power, and create or raise barriers to entry. Because technologies are changing rapidly, and the Internet and electronic commerce are expected to change our entire conception of communications, the FCC and the Justice Department are standing idly by to see what happens. Yet the technologies driving the communications revolution are not coming from these telecom operators seeking to create and expand their monopoly power. They are coming from the equipment manufacturers in telecom, computing, and electronics, and from the computing and information services applications sector, both of which are operating in more dynamic, more innovative, and more competitive industry sectors.

The telecom operators provide the facilities network, including the connections to customers, using the technologies supplied by the equipment industry to create the capacity for the services developed by the information services applications firms. The telecom operators "stand at the gateway of commerce and collect a toll from all who pass."[11] In this environment, the FCC has virtually abandoned any serious attempt at price regulation, except to protect the interests of the industry it regulates. The long-distance carriers were even successful in getting the FCC to order them to pay lower revenue settlement payments on international traffic to developing countries, shifting monopoly profit from the developing countries to the U.S. carriers (Melody 2000). They were not required to pass through these benefits to consumers. FCC decisions, and nondecisions, identify closely with what many observers refer to as the FCC's clients, AT&T and the other major long-distance telecom operators.

Again, the neoclassical economists have been virtually silent on these developments. Perhaps it is in recognition that in these dynamic times the neoclassical model is manifestly not relevant, even in their own view. More realistically, it would seem that in the current environment of general acceptance of monopoly power, they are not needed to defend it. Institutional economists have documented the implementation failures of telecom competition policy and the failure to resist the anticompetitive accumulation of monopoly power in response. Tight oligopoly is the industry structure that the major players want. It is not what the competition policy developed earlier at the FCC and the Justice Department, or the policy stated in the new Telecommunications Act, intended. Nor is it required by the characteristics of the technologies or consumer demands.

Similar tight oligopoly market structures have developed in the liberalized electricity, gas, and airline industries. Here, too, there has been a failure to implement effective competition or regulatory policies. The dominant industry players have not been checked in their moves to enhance their monopoly power and create or expand barriers to entry. They have determined that a tight oligopoly market core, with occasional entry and exit at the margins, is what they will permit. They have taken the lead in determining the market structure policy for the industry. Trebing (1997) has observed, "unless effective regulatory mechanisms can be developed for the new environment, it will only be a matter of time before market failure requires a new wave of ad hoc regulation to address the long term adverse consequences of tight oligopoly" (39).

For the future, one might ask whether public policies will be developed to ensure these restructured utility industries operate in the public interest, and whether economists will be able to provide the evidence and analysis needed as a foundation for it.

Utility Regulation in the Information Economy

The economy is in the midst of a major transformation, from one based primarily on industrial production to one based primarily on services. New information and communication technologies and services (ICTS) are providing a foundation for the restructuring of production and distribution processes in most industries and in public services. The twenty-first-century economy is commonly described as an information, or Internet, economy that will extend the limits of markets in most major industry sectors to international and global dimensions. Commerce increasingly will be conducted electronically, that is, as e-commerce. Applications of advanced ICTS will reshape the supply and demand of the vast majority of economic, social, and even cultural activity—at least in the United States and other technologically advanced countries. These new markets based on electronic transactions are requiring the development of a new set of institutional foundations relating to security, privacy, authenticity, contracting, digital signatures, intellectual property, consumer protection, and other issues. Regulation and its enforcement on these issues in an international e-commerce virtual marketplace will determine the efficiency and the limits of e-commerce development. The information economy also raises new institutional issues relating to global financial management and banking regulation of potentially more unstable global financial markets (Melody 1999).

The foundation for the information economy and advanced ICTS will be a transformed and upgraded telecom network that will provide the information infrastructure over which the new electronic services will be supplied. Broadband telecom network connections will be needed in the workplace, home, schools, and all other centers of activity, just as the telephone is needed now. The new information infrastructure will be the most important public utility of the twenty-first-century economy. The traditional utilities will remain as important parts of the infrastructure of the new economy, but they will be transformed by their own institutional reform processes, as well as applications of the new ICTS in their sectors and the changing structure of the economy they serve. Almost all countries are in the process of developing or implementing policies relating to the establishment of new national broadband information infrastructures. These developments require a considered reassessment of public policy relating to the supply of public utility services in the new economy. What is the best institutional structure for ensuring an efficient universal provision of utility services, old and new, under conditions that are accessible by all those who desire it?

Regulatory Reform: Learning from Experience

What does twentieth-century experience teach us? A general conclusion from the preponderance of evidence is that public utility regulation in the

United States has, for the most part, failed. The occasional examples of innovative and effective regulation would appear to provide evidence for why regulation failed, not whether it has failed. Yet, whenever regulation has been reduced, weakened, or eliminated, the performance of highly imperfect utility markets has not improved in any demonstrable way. In most cases market failures have become worse, sometimes much worse. Does the mere act of establishment of the institution of regulation tend to reduce market failures, so that even with failed regulation, the result is better? Is the regulatory structure good, but the conduct and performance bad? Is regulation, like parliamentary democracy as described by Churchill, a highly inefficient and ineffective institution for trying to implement desirable public interest objectives, but still better than any alternative yet devised? An analysis of the major criticisms of regulation, and international assessments of U.S. utility regulation, suggest that this may the case.

None of the critics of regulation have suggested that the utility industries are likely to be effectively competitive markets without regulation. Nor have they questioned the importance and desirability of ensuring universal availability of utility services under reasonable conditions. The case for government intervention to address market failures and public service policy goals is widely accepted. The principal criticism is that the performance of regulation has failed badly as an effective administrative process and in promoting efficiency, although it may be able to take some credit in helping to maintain universal service coverage at reasonable prices.

There have been different approaches taken around the world with respect to the form the government intervention in public utility markets should take. The most commonly adopted model has been the direct provision of service by national or state governments. Government supply of services at the local levels has developed primarily to serve geographical areas that national or state public or private operators have chosen not to supply. A comparison of utility services development in the United States with countries that have adopted the government provision model shows U.S. utility industry development to be among the best in the world. In telecom, by many indicators (but not all), the United States has been the world leader for a long time. Although this apparent leading performance of the U.S. utility industries may be attributed in significant part to the fact that the U.S. economy is the most technologically advanced and wealthy in the world, clearly the development of the utility sectors under the U.S. model of public utility regulation has kept pace with the economy. When measured by end results, U.S. utility regulation has done no demonstrable harm to the industries, and the economic and social goals of public policy essentially have been achieved.

In fact, there is a major movement around the world for governments to privatize utilities and adopt the U.S. model of government regulation by independent authority. These governments have reached the conclusion that, at least for the future economic development of their countries, this institutional structure is likely to yield better results. Their conclusions are based on observation and assessment of the U.S. system. Most have concluded that significant amounts of private capital will be necessary to develop their utilities, and private-sector utility management is likely to provide the services more efficiently and be more responsive to consumer demands. Yet government policy direction and regulation will be necessary to ensure government policy objectives are met. The U.S. model of utility regulation provides an illustration that appears to other countries to be working rather satisfactorily.

Moreover, U.S. utility managers, government officials, and even critics of U.S. utility regulation are actively encouraging other countries to adopt the U.S. model of utility regulation. The FCC even has published a guide for developing countries that are in the process of establishing telecom regulatory agencies. One must acknowledge the powerful self-interest of the United States in promoting these changes, as many U.S. utilities are seeking investment opportunities in other countries. Nevertheless, the U.S. model of utility regulation is being held up and widely acknowledged as the "world's best practice." Within the last fifteen years, more than one hundred countries have established utility regulatory agencies. They are now identified as a key indicator of progress and successful utility reform. This will be the dominant model for the reform of utilities around the world, and for the development of the new information infrastructure of the twenty-first century. Not bad for an institution that by some standards has utterly failed for the better part of a century.

Although other countries are adopting the essential institutional structure of the utility regulatory model developed in the United States, as well as the fundamental objectives of an efficient service accessible to everyone under reasonable terms, they have learned some things from the U.S. experience and are adapting the model to their own particular circumstances. First, they are designing administrative structures to avoid an elaborate legalistic process, as has developed in the United States. They are establishing more informal processes in an attempt to provide greater flexibility and more expeditious decision making than happens under U.S. regulation. They employ, but are not dependent on, lawyers and other professional experts, at least so far. They are attempting to ensure that the regulatory process does not become a lush feeding ground for the professions.

Second, they are adopting less complex standards for decision making. The price cap model of rate regulation initially developed in the United Kingdom was developed with the specific objective of finding a standard that avoided the problems of rate of return regulation as applied in the United States. Although theoretically inferior to cost of capital based rate of return regulation, the price cap method was developed to be a simpler standard, more easily applied and more relevant to the specific concern of the U.K. regulator to stimulate large productivity improvements in a very inefficient, newly privatized national monopoly operator. Productivity adjustments are more often negotiated than determined by elaborate scientific study.

A similar approach is being taken by many countries to address carrier interconnection issues, where international benchmark comparisons and straightforward cost calculations are being used to negotiate rates, eliminating the long, adversarial, and unproductive procedures that have slowed down the development of competition in the United States for years. These different approaches to regulation are not without their problems. Yet the problems become the exception, not the norm. The important point is that many countries are experimenting with a variety of different procedures and substantive criteria within the overall framework of independent regulation of commercial utility markets dominated by a former monopoly supplier. This widespread experimentation provides fertile ground for learning and improvement.

Nearly all the new regulatory agencies are charged with a specific policy objective to promote competition as a high priority in order to move the market structure away from monopoly by the incumbent national operators as rapidly as possible. Competition has been adopted as the priority tool of regulation for implementing policy. The intention is to create as much competition as the market will permit, and to try to use competitive market forces to develop the information infrastructure as far as possible. For developing countries, the hope is that competition policy also will encourage participation in the extension of national telecom networks to unserved regions and people.

The single major criticism of U.S. utility regulatory agencies can be summarized as regulatory capture. Regulators have been primarily concerned about protecting the interests of the dominant regulated firms. The main way they have done this is by protecting the dominant firm's markets. Regulatory decisions have excluded competitors and approved anticompetitive practices by the established firms. Failure to protect consumers by allowing exorbitant and discriminatory prices has been a second-order criticism. Failure to attend to universal service goals was a major complaint during the earlier era of utility network diffusion, but is less so now that a high level of universal service coverage has been obtained.

It is difficult to pinpoint the cause of regulatory capture when it is recognized that the institutional structure of regulation has been deliberately designed to establish and preserve regulatory independence from political and industry influence. Politicians, government bureaucrats, and industry players will try to influence the regulatory agencies on the issues of the day. Yet that should be expected; indeed, that is why the independence protections have been built into the regulatory legislation. It would seem that a significant part of the problem must be traced to the culture of regulation and to the quality of the appointments of the commissioners and staff of the agencies. If commissioners are appointed on the basis of political, instead of professional, criteria, their independence may be compromised. If commission staff are primarily preparing themselves for future employment with the major regulated firms or their advisers and consultants, their independence may be compromised. If commissions are resting places for bureaucrats seeking the quiet life, it is much easier to give in to requests from, or act in the interests of, the dominant players than to do independent analysis and oppose these interests on occasion. Independent regulatory agencies require strong, independent, proactive people to make them function effectively. Throughout the history of U.S. regulation, too often they have not had them.

The commissions have been structured to be independent, but the appointments to the commissions too often have been highly dependent on political benefactors, past or future benefits from the dominant regulated firms, or personal career agendas best served by cultivating the power structure or at least not bucking the establishment. For regulation to function effectively, the commissions need people who are confident in their professional competence and who can and will resist the pressure. They must be prepared to disagree with the power structure at regular intervals. As a rule, commissions do not offer pay levels likely to attract such people as a matter of course, although they do benefit from the commitment of idealists and public interest advocates. The regulatory capture problem may be substantially reduced by incorporating a strong competition policy into the regulatory mandates, by establishing better criteria for selecting staff, and by establishing professional career structures that reward independence rather than malleability.

Experience has shown that regulatory agencies require a continuous balancing of opposing and sometimes contradictory influences. Independence from political and industry influence on decisions is vital, but engagement with politicians and industry managers is essential in order to maintain expertise and demonstrate credibility (Samarajiva 2000). An effective institutional structure is a necessary condition for effective regulation, but not a sufficient one. Success requires a proactive rather than a passive interpretation, and implementing the regulatory mandate. Passive regulation will gravitate toward making ad hoc judgments, like the courts do. Proactive regulation can lead the way in shaping regulation to achieve policy objectives in changing market conditions.

During the 1960–84 period the FCC demonstrated that regulation could lead the response to changing market conditions and fashion a path for change with enormous benefits to all parties, including the incumbent monopolist, AT&T, and its neoclassical economists who vigorously opposed it. In the key decisions that started this era of reform, FCC commissioners at the opposite ends of the political and ideological spectrum—conservative Dean Burch and liberal Nicholas Johnson—found common cause. Both had well-earned reputations for being proactive, well informed, and independent. The FCC experience demonstrates that regulation can achieve efficiency and public interest objectives in a more effective way than any other institutional structure. Yet, in order to institutionalize this kind of exceptional performance, more attention must be paid to the design of the institutional structure surrounding regulation, the culture of regulation, and the criteria and methods for making regulatory appointments.

Dynamic Regulation for Dynamic Markets

The model of twenty-first-century public utility regulation must be premised on dynamic markets and flexibility in the selection of the most appropriate procedures and substantive criteria to resolve regulatory issues. The unexamined acceptance of a static natural monopoly market structure, or indeed any market structure, must give way to an ongoing examination of market structure as a key element in regulation. Most utility markets, at least for the foreseeable future, will be characterized by tight oligopoly with fringe competition and constantly shifting market boundaries. This must be the point of reference for regulation. Competition policy can be best implemented by focusing directly on existing and potential barriers to entry and the concentration of monopoly power. No matter what the market structure happens to be at any moment in time, barriers to entry should be continuously examined and minimized, and all avenues to increased concentrations of monopoly power should be blocked except those obtained as a result of growth by superior market performance in providing services to customers. This approach to implementing competition policy will permit competition to develop wherever market conditions justify it. The industries will be in a much more flexible position to adapt to change. Moreover, an explicit policy on entry to this effect should reduce the protectionist pressure on regulators and strengthen their capability to resist what remains of it.

Other dimensions of competition policy that should be made explicit are participation and diversity. In a dynamic market, the discovery of opportunities and market potential arises from experimentation and learning. The lesson of experience in public utility development in the United States and other countries is that significant benefit has come from the participation and contributions of an enormous variety of institutional structures, including large and small private and public operators, local cooperatives, and a wide range of private and public partnerships and regulatory relations. Most of the problems and major failures have arisen because governments have attempted to apply a single model—usually private or public monopoly—and then have blocked the initiative of others. In the new environment, government policy and regulation should not only permit the participation of a variety of institutional forms of service provision, it should encourage diversity as essential for the experimentation and learning necessary for the utility industries to adapt to change most effectively.

There is an immediate need to develop and apply policies promoting participation and diversity in most utilities and countries. It is most urgent in telecom. Most developing and some developed countries do not have national networks, because the task of developing them has been reserved for national government monopolies. Other potential private or public participants have been prohibited from contributing. Privatization of the government monopolies and the licensing of competitors now is seen as a popular solution. Experience has shown that national network development will require the participation of public and private organizations at both the national and local levels. The most rapid and effective development will come when all interested participants are encouraged, instead of being restricted.

Similarly, information infrastructure development will require enormous amounts of investment over an extended period of time in all countries. In the United States it is already becoming apparent that rural communities with broadband access are attracting new businesses while those without it are losing them. The large telecom companies are bypassing most rural communities in building their information infrastructure networks. The "digital divide" between the "haves" and "have-nots" is increasing (NTIA 1999). Discussion is turning to the potential need for a program similar to the REA program, which supported rural participation in providing electricity and telephone service. Local governments and co-ops are initiating a range of activities, including building their local information infrastructures themselves, to ensure that they will be able to participate in the information economy. Electric utilities serving rural areas, such as the, Bonneville Power Administration, have discovered they can provide information infrastructure capabilities for rural communities at much reduced cost by expanding the capacity of their own communication networks, provided over their electricity rights of way. Yet these and other initiatives are being delayed by obsolete regulations, pointless debates over private versus public provision, and economic opportunism. What is needed is clear policy direction and proactive regulation directed to minimizing barriers to participation and seeking institutional diversity in the development of the information infrastructure (Parker 2000).

There will continue to be a need for maximum price regulation in markets not subject to effective competition, most notably residential and small business network connection and access charges, and interconnection options and charges for competitors to the dominant network operator. The traditional difficulties many regulators have had in regulating effectively on these issues can be reduced significantly in an environment more conducive to entry opportunities and where more comparative information is gathered, made public, and used by the regulator. In a competitive market, information is the great regulator. Regulatory authorities can use information as a much more effective tool to help achieve regulatory objectives. Benchmark comparisons and equal treatment of customers (for example, in competitive and monopoly services) and competitors is far more important to all parties than debates over the fine points of incremental cost calculations by vested interests. Similarly, regulation to achieve universal access to the information infrastructure, or any other utility service, can focus on maximum participation. The traditional regulatory debates over special utility rights and privileges should be minimized, if not eliminated.

In the new environment the regulator must play a much more participatory role in achieving public policy objectives. Regulation should be judged by improvements in the end-result objectives of universal access and opportunities to use utility services. It should carry the responsibilities for adapting its processes and procedures to achieve these objectives efficiently and effectively, for maximizing opportunities for participation, and for establishing and implementing the market rules by which the competing operators will participate. The commission must be a dynamic participant in regulating dynamic markets.

Toward an Economics of Workable Oligopoly

To regulate effectively, commissions will need to build a better knowledge base about the functioning and performance of oligopoly markets in utility network industries—ranging from lopsided duopoly through implicit cartel and tight oligopoly to more diversified oligopoly approaching monopolistic competition, as rivalry gives way to competition. This is one area where economists need to develop a much stronger body of both theoretical and applied knowledge.

The existing body of economic knowledge tells us that oligopoly yields market failure in the form of inefficiency, instability, and indeterminacy. Too little output is produced and too much capacity is established for that output so that excess capacity will serve as an artificial barrier to entry. The rivalry tends to focus on non-price factors, often heavy marketing, which provides an additional artificial barrier to entry. Prices are generally set well above costs, and significant price discrimination is typical, except when external factors or a rise in uncertainty stimulates a price war. Concentrated oligopolies often engage in explicit or implicit self-regulation. Some oligopolies engage in significant R&D and technological development, which can lead to crashing the barriers to entry of another industry, interindustry rivalry, and "waves of creative destruction." Yet the transition to the new paradigm may be highly inefficient and path dependent, leading to new industry arrangements which are far from efficient, and very often simply restructured oligopoly.

The traditional analysis is helpful to a degree, and utility regulation attempts to address some of the inefficiency characteristics of concentrated oligopoly. However, economic analysis of market failures and imperfect markets in recent years has developed additional insights into some of the distinct characteristics of utility markets. Developments in the economics of networks have clarified the characteristics of both production and consumption network externalities (Economides and Encaoua 1996; Shapiro and Varian 1999). This becomes extremely significant in the utility industries as capacity networks are unbundled from service networks and an increasing number of players participate interdependently in competitive and cooperative relations to develop capacity and supply services. Opportunities for strategic opportunistic behavior, such as imposing network costs on others while realizing revenue from the contributions of others, will tend to promote inefficiency and instability. There are significant economies of scale and scope in networks, but we have learned that most of these can be achieved without being internalized to the firm. For many information services on the information infrastructure, there are increasing returns in market expansion. Markets with these distinctive characteristics need rules if operator initiative is to be directed toward efficiency and universal service development. Regulation can influence where the oligopoly market rivalry is focused.

Utility networks provide multiple service outputs using common capacity. The problem of common cost, addressed brilliantly by J. M. Clarke (1923) long ago in reference to railroads, and by others since then, remains an important issue for regulation. Moreover, the common cost characteristics of utility networks provide an important avenue where regulation can develop methods of common cost assignment that will capture externalities, encourage network extension, reduce barriers to entry, and provide a level playing field for more effective competition.

Other areas of more recent economic analysis that can contribute to strengthening the intellectual foundation of utility regulation include information economics, and particularly models examining the implications of asymmetric information. The analytical work on the theory of contestability can be reworked to an objective of promoting competition rather than defending monopoly, and refined to identify levels of contestability linked to barriers to entry. Dynamic modeling examining the implications of utility legacy networks and path dependency can shed light on technological trajectories, network tipping, and technology lock-in issues (David 1975; Shapiro and Varian 1999). The economics of standards development, protocols, and interfaces in open and closed networks can provide a basis for a better understanding of network evolution. The challenge for economists is to begin to integrate these and other contributions to the study of imperfect and dynamic markets into a more coherent body of theoretical knowledge about the utility industries, and to the development of applied guidelines for utility regulators. This work can provide an economics of workable oligopoly with applications that will be relevant not only to the utilities industries but also to other industries with "tight oligopoly" structures.

Conclusion

In the twenty-first century, public utility regulation will play an expanded but very different role than it did during the twentieth century. For the next decade, as different countries and regions experiment with different interpretations and applications of the basic model of utility regulation, regulatory institutions will be in the process of design and redesign, after which the more effective approaches and methods will begin to become widespread. These developments will provide interesting and challenging opportunities for all economists who study real, as opposed to idealist, markets, and for institutional economists in particular.

If the open, dynamic model of utility regulation suggested here is applied, the probability of achieving better results than were achieved during the twentieth century should be greatly increased. Moreover, even in the event of regulatory failures—and we must expect some—there is far less risk of regulation contributing directly to the preservation of monopoly power and related market failures. The probability of regulatory capture should be significantly reduced. When regulatory failure does occur, it is likely to lead to an unregulated tight oligopoly or implicit cartel, the market failure that would exist if there were no regulation. Regulatory failure should not create additional barriers to entry, as it typically did during the twentieth century

With utility regulation being applied in many countries, there will be increased opportunities for international comparisons and the development of international benchmarks and best practice standards. Some regulatory issues already are growing beyond the nation state and require either cooperative regulation across regions (e.g., NAFTA, European Union) or a new tier of regulation. Others are requiring increased governance at the global level through organizations such as the World Trade Organization and the International Telecommunication Union.

During the twentieth century the linkage between mainstream neoclassical economic theory and the study of regulatory institutions for highly imperfect markets was weak and often in opposition. Institutional economists provided the economic support and ongoing critical analysis necessary to improve those regulatory institutions, in the face of continuing opposition from the regulated industries and most neoclassical economists. There are signs that all groups have learned from the twentieth-century experience. More traditional economists are shifting their attention away from the neoclassical model, which has been experiencing diminishing returns of late, to the study of imperfect markets. Institutional economists have integrated competition more effectively into their models of regulation. For the future, imperfect markets and market failure will be the area on which mainstream theorists and institutionalists can find common cause. Institutional arrangements for making oligopoly markets workable in achieving public policy goals will be a central issue in economic and policy studies. Regulatory agencies can become institutions at the frontier of shaping and directing markets in the twenty-first-century information economy. They can be instrumental in developing and applying the governance necessary to prevent or redress market failures and keep them from threatening economic growth and stability.

Notes

Thanks to Walter Bolter and Jerry Duval for discussions on several issues covered in this paper during its preparation.

1. Perhaps reflecting its proximity to the United States, as well as its vast land area and limited population, Canada made extensive use of both private markets and government supply in developing its transport and public utility infrastructures. For example, two national rail networks were developed, one private, one government-owned. Canada also adopted the general model of public utility regulation of private monopoly suppliers, after observing developments in the United States.

3. Surprisingly, the school of economics that has carried forward the "neoclassical" name throughout the twentieth century has steadily retreated from the study of real industries and markets, generally confining itself to designing ever more "elegant" theoretical restatements of the perfectly competitive model. For these myopic neoclassicals, the theory—like HAL in the film 2001—has been transformed from a useful tool of analysis to their master. Thus their primary role has been reduced to reciting economic ideology. Nevertheless, in the later half of the twentieth century they have dominated the economics faculties at U.S. universities, and supported dominant institutions and the status quo.

5. The problem of failure of the general economy required attention to private and public institutional relations of a new form. Keynes focused on the problem of deficient demand and unemployed resources, making the case for an expanded role of government in the management of national economies to achieve full employment of capital and human resources, but at the macro level. Although this subject is not within the bounds of this chapter, it added another dimension of economic regulation that is now a part of the institutional foundations that are essential for private markets to function efficiently.

6. Since spun off as Lucent.

7. Major contributions came from Berle (1932, 1959), Chamberlin (1932), Robinson (1933), Lerner (1933–34), Clark (1939, 1961), Bain (1941, 1959), Schumpeter (1942), Fellner (1949), Galbraith (1952), Machlup (1952), Adams (1954), Mason (1959), and others.

8. At the beginning the core group was made up of Boyd Nelson, William Melody, Manley Irwin, and Edwin Winslow. This group was often assisted by Richard Gabel, industry economist with the U.S. Department of Commerce, and by Norman Schwartz, FCC attorney, who overcame the ever-present claims that the economists' proposals for change were unlawful. Soon after, Trebing became

founding director of the Institute of Public Utilities at Michigan State University, although he maintained an ongoing working relationship with the group.

9. The group included William Vickrey (1996 Nobel Prize winner), W. Baumol, J. C. Bonbright, P. Davidson, A. Kahn, H. Wein, and others.

10. As AT&T's market share in the interstate long-distance market has fallen below 50 percent, the share for the new merged MCI Worldcom approaches 40 percent (Rosenberg and Clements 2000).

11. Munn v. Illinois (1877) 94 US 113.

References

Adams, W. 1954. The rule of reason: Workable competition or workable monopoly? *Yale Law Journal* 63.

———. 1958. The role of competition in the regulated industries. *American Economic Review*. (May): 527–43.

Averch, H., and L. Johnson. 1962. The firm under regulatory constraint. *American Economic Review* 52.

Bain, J. S. 1956. *Barriers against new competition.* Cambridge, Mass.: Harvard University Press.

———. 1959. *Barriers to new competition: Their character and consequences in manufacturing industries.* Cambridge, Mass.: Harvard University Press.

Baumol, W. J. 1987. Ramsey pricing. In *The new palgrave: A dictionary of economics*, 4:51. London: Macmillan.

Baumol, W. J., E. E. Bailey, and R. D. Willig. 1977. Weak invisible hand theorems on the sustainability of prices in a multiproduct monopoly. *American Economic Review* 67 (June): 350–65.

Baumol, W. J., and D. F. Bradford. 1970. Optimal departures from marginal cost pricing. *American Economic Review* 60 (June): 265–83.

Baumol, W. J., J. C. Panzar, and D. G. Willig. 1982. *Contestable markets and the theory of industrial structure.* New York: Harcourt Brace Jovanovich.

Baumol, W. J., and J. G. Sidak. 1994. *Toward competition in local telephony.* Washington, D.C.: MIT Press and American Enterprise Institute.

Berle, A.A., and G. C. Means. 1932. *The modern corporation and private property.* New York: Harcourt, Brace and World.

Bernstein, M. H. 1955. *Regulating business by independent commission.* Princeton, N.J.: Princeton University Press.

———. 1961. The regulatory process: A framework for analysis. *Law and Contemporary Problems* 26.

———. 1972. Independent regulatory agencies: A perspective on their reform." In *A critique of administrative regulation of public utilities,* ed. W. J. Samuels and H. M. Trebing. East Lansing, Mich.: MSU Public Utilities Papers.

Bolter, W. G. 1997. Moving to full liberalisation under the U.S. Telecommunications Act of 1996: Interconnection, costing, and other entry issues. In.

Telecom reform: Principles, policies and regulatory practices, ed. W. H. Melody. Lyngby: Technical University of Denmark, Den Private Ingeniørfond.

Bonbright, J. C. 1961. *Principles of public utility rates.* New York: Columbia University Press.

Brock, G. 1994. *Telecommunication policy for the information age.* Cambridge, Mass.: Harvard University Press.

Chamberlin, E. H. 1932. *The theory of monopolistic competition.* Cambridge, Mass.: Harvard University Press.

Chessler, D. 1996. *Determining when competition is "workable": A handbook for state commissions making assessments required by the Telecommunications Act of 1996.* Colombus Ohio.: National Regulatory Research Institute.

Clark, J. M. 1923. *Studies in the economics overhead costs.* Chicago: University of Chicago Press.

———. 1939. *Social control of business.* New York: McGraw-Hill.

———. 1940. Toward a concept of workable competition. *American Economic Review* 30.

———. 1961. *Competition as a dynamic process.* Washington, D.C.: Brookings Institution Press.

Commons, J. R. 1924. *The legal foundations of capitalism.* Madison: University of Wisconsin Press.

———. 1931. Institutional economics. *American Economic Review* 21.

———. 1934. *Institutional economics: Its place in political economy.* Madison: University of Wisconsin Press.

David, P. 1975. *Technical choice, innovation and economic growth.* Cambridge: Cambridge University Press.

deButts, J. D. 1973. An unusual obligation. Speech before the annual convention of the National Association of Regulatory Utility Commissioners, Seattle, Washington.

Demsetz, H. 1968. Why tegulate utilities? *Journal of Law and Economics* 11.

Economides, N., and D. Encaoua. 1996. Special issue on network economics: Business conduct and market structure. *International Journal of Industrial Organization* 14.

Federal Communications Commission (FCC). 1966. Regulatory and policy problems presented by the interdependence of computer and communication services and facilities, Notice of Inquiry, Docket No. 16979, FCC 66–1004, 9 November. Supplemental Notice of Inquiry, FCC 67–239, 2 March 1967. Report and Further Notice of Inquiry, FCC 69–468, 1 May 1969.

———. 1968. Use of the Carterfone device, 13 FCC 2d 420 (1968).

———. 1969. Microwave Communications, Inc., 18 FCC 2d 953 (1969).

———. 1971. Computer I. CC Docket No. 16979, 29 FCC 2d 879, 906. Washington.

———. 1976. Regulatory policies concerning resale and shared use of common carrier services and facilities. Docket No. 20097, Report and Order. Washington.

———. 1996. First report and order re implementation of the local competition provisions in the Telecommunications Act of 1996, and interconnection between local exchange carriers and commercial mobile radio services providers. 8 August. Washington.

Fellner, W. 1949. *Competition among the few.* New York: Knopf.

Gabel, D. 1967. *Development of separations principles in the telephone industry.* East Lansing: Michigan State University.

———. 1991. An application of stand-alone costs to the telecommunications industry. *Telecommunications Policy* (February): 75–84.

Gabel, R. 1969. The early competitive era in telephone communication, 1893–1920. *Law and Contemporary Problems.* Durham, N.C.: Duke University School of Law.

Galbraith, J. K. 1952. *American capitalism.* Boston: Houghton Mifflin.

Glaeser, M.G. 1927. *Outlines of public utility economics.* New York: Macmillan.

———. 1957. *Public utilities in American capitalism.* New York: Macmillan.

Gray, H. M. 1940. The passing of the public utility concept. *Land Economics* 16:8–20.

Hope Natural Gas v. FPC (1944). 320 U.S. 591.

Irwin, M. R. 1969. Computers and communications: The economics of independence. In *Law and Contemporary Problems.* Durham: Duke University School of Law.

———. 1971. *The telecommunications industry: Integration vs. competition.* New York: Praeger.

Lerner, A. P. 1933–34. The concept of monopoly and the measurement of monopoly power. *Review of Economic Studies* 1:157–75.

Machlup, F. 1952. *The economics of seller's competition.* Baltimore: Johns Hopkins University Press.

MacAvoy, P. W. 1996. *The failure of antitrust and regulation to establish competition in long distance telephone services.* Cambridge, Mass.: MIT Press and Washington, D.C.: AEI Press.

Mason, E. S. 1959. *Economic concentration and the monopoly problem.* Cambridge, Mass.: Harvard University Press.

Melody, W. H. 1971. Interservice subsidy: Regulatory standards and applied economics. In *Essays on public utility pricing and regulation,* ed. H. M. Trebing. East Lansing: Mich.: MSU Public Utilities Studies.

———. 1980. Competition and subsidies as instruments of social policy in telecommunications. In *Energy and communications in transition,* ed. H. M. Trebing. East Lansing: Michigan State University Press.

———. 1986. *Telecommunication: Policy directions for the technology and information services. Oxford surveys in information technology.* Vol.3. Oxford: Oxford University Press.

———. 1989. Efficiency and social policy in telecommunication: Lessons from the U.S. experience. *Journal of Economic Issues* 23 (September): 657–88.

————. 1997. *Telecom reform: Principles, policies and regulatory practices.* Lyngby: Technical University of Denmark, Den Private Ingeniørfond.

————. 1999. Telecom reform: Progress and prospects. *Telecommunications Policy* 23:1.

————. 2000. Telecom myths: The international revenue settlements subsidy. *Telecommunications Policy* 24:1.

Miller, E. S. 1985. Controlling power in the social economy: The regulatory approach." *Review of Social Economy,* 43.

————. 1995. Is the public utility concept obsolete? *Land Economics* (August).

NTIA. 1999. *Falling through the net.* Washington D.C.: U.S. Department of Commerce, July.

Owen, B., and R. Braeutigam. 1978. *The regulation game.* Cambridge, Mass.: Ballinger.

Panzer, J. C., and R. D. Willig. 1977. Free entry and the sustainability of natural monopoly. *Bell Journal of Economics* 8.

Parker, E. B. 2000. Closing the digital divide in rural America. *Telecommunications Policy* 24 (4).

Posner, R. A. 1969. Natural monopoly and its regulation. *Stanford Law Review* 21.

Rosenberg, Borrows, Hunt, Samarajiva, and Pollard. 1993. Regional telephone holding companies: Structures, affiliate transactions and regulatory options. In NRRI 93–05, Columbus, Ohio.

Rosenberg, E. A., and M. Clements. 2000. Evolving market structure, conduct, and policy in local telecommunications. In NRRI 2000–02, Columbus, Ohio.

Samarajiva, R. 2000. Establishing the legitimacy of new regulatory agencies. *Telecommunications Policy* 24 (3).

Samuels, W. J. 1971. Externalities, rate structure, and the theory of public utility regulation. In *Essays on Public Utility Pricing and Regulation,* ed. H. M. Trebing. East Lansing, Mich.: MSU Public Utilities Studies.

Samuels, W. J., and H. M. Trebing, eds. 1972. *A critique of administrative regulation of public utilities.* East Lansing, Mich.: MSU Public Utilities Papers.

Schumpeter, J. 1942. *Capitalism, socialism and democracy.* New York: Harper.

Shapiro, C., and H. R. Varian. 1999. *Information rules: A strategic guide to the network economy.* Boston: Harvard Business School Press.

Shepherd, W. G. 1975. *The treatment of market power.* New York: Columbia University Press.

Steiner, P. O. 1975. *Mergers: Motives, effects, and policies.* Ann Arbor: University of Michigan Press.

Stigler, G. J. 1971. The theory of economic regulation. *Bell Journal of Economics and Management Science* 2.

Stigler, G. J., and C. Friedland. 1962. What can regulation regulate? The case of electricity. *Journal of Law and Economics* 5.

Trebing H. M. 1963. Toward an incentive system of regulation. 72 *Public Utilities Fortnightly,* July 18.

Trebing, H. M. 1969. Common carrier regulation—The silent crisis. In *Law and Contemporary Problems*. Durham, N.C.: Duke University School of Law.

———. 1984. Public utility regulation: A case study in the debate over effectiveness of economic regulation. *Journal of Economic Issues* 18.

———. 1986. Apologetics of deregulation in energy and telecommunications. *Journal of Economic Issues* 20.

———. 1994a. Institutionalist contribution to public utility regulation. In *The Elgar companion to institutional and evolutionary economics*, ed. G. M. Hodgson, W. J. Samuels, and M. R. Tool. Northampton, Mass.: Edward Elgar.

———. 1994b. The networks as infrastructure—The reestablishment of market power. *Journal of Economic Issues* 28 (2).

———. 1997. Emerging market structures and options for regulatory reform in public utility industries. In *Telecom reform: Principles, policies and regulatory practices*, ed. W. H. Melody. Lyngby: Technical University of Denmark, Den Private Ingeniørfond.

———, ed. 1971. *Essays on public utility pricing and regulation*. East Lansing, Mich.: MSU Public Utilities Studies.

Trebing, H. M., and W. H. Melody. 1969. An evaluation of pricing practices and policies in domestic communications. Staff Papers, President's Task Force on Communications Policy, Clearinghouse for Federal Scientific and Technical Information, Springfield, Virginia, June.

Wilcox, C. 1955. *Public policies toward business*. Chicago: Irwin.

Public Utilities in the Perspective of the Gemeinwirtschaftslehre

JOHANNES M. BAUER

Introduction

This chapter reviews the theoretical and practical positions of the theory of the social economy (*Gemeinwirtschaftslehre*), a school of thought whose influence is largely limited to the German-speaking European nations of Austria, Germany, and Switzerland. Drawing on multiple intellectual roots in the eighteenth and nineteenth centuries, such as romanticism and socialism, the movement developed several interesting views of the role of the social economy (*Gemeinwirtschaft*) in a market economy. The social economy was delineated from the private capitalist economy by its pursuit of goals other than profit maximization. Most authors include state- and municipally-owned enterprises, cooperatives, and trade unions' and other associations' enterprises (*freigemeinwirtschaftliche Unternehmen*) into this segment of the economy. A few authors would also include regulated private firms (*öffentlich gebundene Unternehmen*) into the social economy.

During the evolution of the theory of the social economy, contributions originated from different methodological perspectives. Since the mid-nineteenth century, different theoretical positions had coexisted, and their influence on practical policy varied greatly. More radical early proponents viewed the social economy as a medium of transformation from a capitalist to a socialist society. The members of the classical school (approximately 1860–90) saw it as a stopgap (*Lückenbüßer*) in situations where the private market economy failed to achieve certain socially desirable goals. The most widely accepted modern school views the social economy as an instrument of public policy. This position—commonly referred to as instrumental thesis (*Instrumentalthese*)—emphasizes that the social economy is but one of several instruments available to the government to attain public interest goals. Unlike neoclassical economics, which focuses on market failure as the main rationale for government intervention in the economy, the instrumental thesis recognizes that there is no generic set of circumstances meriting government intervention. Rather, the substance of public interest objectives needs to be defined in a political process. Whether or not the social economy is an effective instrument for pursuing a specific objective needs to be establishedon a case-by-case basis.

This chapter is organized as follows: the next section briefly reviews the early historical origins of the theory of the social economy. Section three discusses the classical period, and the subsequent section the degeneration of the school during World War I. The following section outlines the main positions of the instrumental thesis and its translation into specific policies for public utilities and infrastructure industries. The final section provides an assessment of the intellectual contribution of the theory of the social economy and its influence on practical policy decisions and offers some conclusions.

Many of the basic notions of the school have been introduced into the current debate on privatization and deregulation, but its influence has been weakened by the resurgence of laissez-faire politics. Despite its relative decline, the theory of the social economy can be seen as an alternative concept providing a normative foundation for the delineation of the respective roles of the public and the private sectors of the economy, which is of continuing interest.

Roots

The theory of the social economy has its early roots in the work of German thinkers of the eighteenth and nineteenth centuries; it also has certain similarities to the cooperative movement and the Fabian socialism of nineteenth-century England (Snow 1988, 2). The more recent intellectual development of the theory can be divided into a classical period, a reformulation (and, arguably, degeneration) of the approach during and after World War I, and a modern period, which will be covered in the next sections.

The earliest influences can be found in mercantilism, a period during which the state was actively involved in strengthening the economic base of its dominion, for example, by founding manufactures and issuing privileges to the private sector to operate certain businesses. German cameralism subsequently outlined a dualistic role for the state, which was adopted later by the theory of the social economy. On the one hand, the state should contribute to a laissez-faire economy by eliminating obstacles to the working of free market forces, such as price controls or trade associations. On the other hand, the state should remain prepared to intervene if private enterprise failed to achieve its tasks (Justi 1758; Sonnenfels 1804). However, as later also became characteristic of the theory of the social economy, no clear definition of the instances requiring such state intervention was provided.

Other roots can be found in German romanticism, the cooperative movement, and the early writings of the German Historical School. According to Snow (1988, 3), who briefly synthesizes the positions of major romanticists, Baader (1835) "saw corporations and associations as means of integrating the poorer classes into society and reducing the maldistribution of wealth." Müller (1810) opposed individualism, laissez-faire, and a "rational" social order, stressing instead historical conditions that he characterized as "organic." The notions of a complementary relationship between the private sector and the state and the view of the latter as a tool for achieving social policy goals became later cornerstones of the theory of the social economy.

Representatives of cooperatism envisioned a fundamental social transformation of the private capitalist system. All consumers were to participate in the economic decisions of a society through consumer cooperatives. These cooperatives, in turn, were to be organized at higher levels to govern the distribution of goods and services and eventually also their production. Later, more pragmatic versions of the cooperative movement realized the utopian nature of these early approaches. However, consumer cooperatives continued to be seen as an important factor in overcoming the structural defects of the private capitalist system. As well, they were seen as an instrument to facilitate the regional and national planning of economic activities through economic councils and chambers. In Germany and to a lesser degree in Austria and Switzerland, cooperatives developed into an important economic force in certain sectors, such as banking, insurance, and retail trade.

A clear view of the state as an economic actor also emerged from the writings of the German Historical School. In particular, List (1841) argued in favor of an active role for the state in supporting the growth of new industries. Contrasting the work of Adam Smith on free trade, List was in favor of (moderate) protective tariffs to help national industries become competitive at an international level. List also suggested that the state take a leading role in developing infrastructures, most importantly, a system of railroads. The role of the social economy in promoting economic goals and in particular the contribution of infrastructure industries was an important theme in the later practical and theoretical discussions.

The socialist movement had a strong influence on the development of the theory of the social economy. Early socialists differed widely in their analysis of the role of the state and of state-owned enterprises. Since the late seventeenth century, several German writers had promoted a view of the state as an engine of social transformation. Fichte (1800), one of the proponents of state socialism (*Staatssozialismus*), saw a moral obligation for the state to provide employment for everyone and regulate trade, production, and distribution. Marx and Engels, on the other hand, saw the state as an institution necessary to stabilize capitalism. In its role as an ideal capitalist (*idealer Gesamtkapitalist*) it secured the legal foundations of the capitalist system. As a real capitalist (*wirklicher Gesamtkapitalist*) it secured the material basis of capitalism through state ownership of means of production (Marx and Engels 1972). Thus, in their view, nationalization of enterprises would not overcome the fundamental contradictions of capitalism but rather aggravate them (Ambrosius 1984, 17).

A similar division affected practical policy. Most members of the reformist social democratic movement viewed state ownership as a stepping-stone toward a socialist society. At the same time it was cautioned that the state continued to represent the interests of the ruling class. Nationalization was thus no panacea but should be evaluated in each individual case based on its impacts on the working population. Based on this framework, social democrats asserted that monopolies like the railways should be publicly owned, in order to avoid an abuse of market power. Orthodox socialists, on the other hand, continued to assert that the state was an integral component of the capitalist economy. Many saw a great danger in the combination of political and economic power and insisted that public ownership of enterprises was the worst form of capitalism.

Socialists more readily endorsed public ownership at the municipal level. Likely, this was due to the observation that municipal enterprises were indeed operating in the public interest of the communities. During the second half of the eighteenth century, many municipalities and cities began to provide public utility and transportation services, community housing, and financial services, among others. Cities like Vienna embarked on broad-based investment programs intended to transform society into a more egalitarian community. The experience with communal enterprise provided practical models for the further development of the theory of the social economy.

The Classical Period

Although they came from very different intellectual traditions than the socialists, the classical representatives of the theory of the social economy were strongly influenced by these debates. Increased state intervention in the economy as well as the nationalization of many private activities in the late nineteenth century forced conservatives and liberals to address questions related to the functions of the social economy. The three main writers shaping the conceptual outlook during this period were Albert Schäffle (1831–1903), Emil Sax (1845–1927), and Adolph Wagner (1835–1917). All three authors had close ties to Vienna and witnessed some of the early experiments in municipalization. Schäffle held academic positions in Germany and Vienna and briefly served as secretary of commerce under Count Hohenwart in Austria. His writings were apparently widely misinterpreted, and Schäffle mistakenly acquired the reputation of a fierce and dangerous socialist. Wagner held teaching positions in Vienna before leaving for Prague and later Berlin. Sax acquired his habilitation at the Technical University of Vienna and held a university position in Prague.

Intellectually, Schäffle and Wagner belonged to the historical school and stood thus outside of the emerging marginal utility school of economics. Sax wrote in the tradition of neoclassical economics. Although he was a social-conservative thinker, Wagner claimed the term "state socialism" for his conceptual approach. He became known as a rostrum socialist (*Kathedersozialist*) for his strong engagement with social reforms. All three scholars accepted the private capitalist market system and aimed their proposals at mitigating negative impacts of industrialization. This basic approach clearly distinguished them from the socialist goal of system transformation, on the one hand, and from the dominant position of liberalism, on the other.

Schäffle (1873) first formulated an integrated approach that was later dubbed the "dual conception" of the social economy (Ritschl 1955). An admirer of the merits of the private capitalist economy, he saw the social economy as subsidiary but necessary in order to correct the failures of the market system. The (central) state, he felt, should not take on functions that could be more effectively carried out by lower level government institutions or the private sector. Unlike Wagner, Schäffle did not claim any moral superiority of the social over the private economy. He also believed that the social economy would shrink over time, as the private sector would be able to take on some of its tasks.

Wagner (1887) deviated in several important respects from Schäffle. He argued that the expansion of the private market system would place increasing demands on the public sector, for example, to provide infrastructure services, ultimately leading to the relative expansion of the social economy. Wagner saw this as a fundamental tendency within the mixed economic system and formalized it in his famous "law of increasing state activity." Although he did not question private ownership of the means of production, and repeatedly pointed out the indispensable function of the private economy for rational production, he emphasized the a priori moral and ethical superiority of the social economy. Wagner's use of the term "state socialism" was met with considerable reservation, although his position was clearly one of social conservatism with a strong belief in social reform driven by a societal elite.

It is interesting to compare and contrast the positions advocated by Sax (1887) with those of Schäffle and Wagner. Sax engaged in a famous debate with Wagner on the most appropriate policy toward the railroads. This railroad controversy (*Eisenbahnenstreit*) reviewed the pros and cons of different institutional approaches. Wagner strongly endorsed nationalization as a precondition to meet the public interest obligations of the railways. In contrast, Sax emphasized the advantages of public regulation of private enterprises. Such "delegated enterprises" would combine the advantages of efficient private management with service in the public interest. Like Schäffle and Wagner, in Sax's conception the social economy (essentially a theory of regulated enterprises) was auxiliary to the private economy. All three authors agreed that the boundary line between the private economy and the social economy was flexible and dependent on technological and political developments. Likewise, the meaning of the term "public interest," they agreed, could not be determined once and for all but required continuous reinterpretation.

War Economy and Interwar Period

The idealization of the state before and shortly after World War I heavily burdened the further conceptual development of a theory of the social economy. Writers such as Edgar Jaffé or Wichard von Moellendorf glorified the war economy—characterized by central planning of resource allocation and prices—as a model for the emerging peacetime economy. In their view, the war had established an exemplary order for the economy. A continuing "militarization of the economy" was called for with the purpose of strengthening the state. The omniscient state, pursuing the national interest, was seen as superior to individual enterprises. Economic efficiency and achievement were first and foremost a national task that would indirectly also benefit individuals.

Later proponents of the theory of the social economy distanced themselves clearly from these positions, which were considered politically dangerous (Thiemeyer 1973, 13). In the late nineteenth century, the attitudes of the socialist and the liberal political forces differed, although some overlaps developed. The establishment of a parliamentary democratic political system had created conditions in which the reformist social democratic movement could expand its influence. After it became evident that no revolutionary socialist transition would happen, public enterprises were again increasingly looked at as a vehicle for the expansion of economic democracy. State-owned enterprises were seen as noncapitalist enclaves within the market economy. According to Ambrosius (1984, 59), three features were deemed characteristic for public enterprises. First, while they were to produce for the market, their management could be directly instructed to serve public interest goals. Private, profit-oriented firms would not be willing to pursue such goals unless specifically compensated. Second, while the basic relationship between labor and capital continued, private capitalists were replaced with public officials. Third, decisions as to the use of economic surplus were to be made by a democratically elected institution rather than by private capitalists.

During the interwar period, no clear operational concept of the meaning of social economic behavior was developed. However, the foundations for refinements after World War II were laid. Within the capitalist order, it was felt that public enterprises should realize certain social economic goals. Four aspects of this role deserve mentioning, as they influenced the later discussion. Public enterprises should, first, it was thought, strive to serve demand for their services rather than maximize profits. Second, such enterprises should become an integral part of overall economic policy making and planning rather than strictly pursue narrow managerial and shareholder goals. Third, their decision-making processes should be structured in a democratic rather than a hierarchical way. Fourth, they should replace private capitalist exploitation with progressive wage policies and improvements in working conditions (Ambrosius 1984, 60).

During this period, the liberal political movement was essentially divided into three streams. Some liberals saw the public economy as incompatible with the market economy. State ownership could only temporarily be justified where, due to insufficient profitability, the private sector had failed to provide necessary goods and services (von Mises 1922). Representatives of the Austrian and ordo-liberal schools of economics also criticized the lack of a theoretical basis for much of social economic thinking. Other strands of liberalism accorded a more permanent role to the public economy but essentially limited it to naturally monopolistic industries. Lastly, moderate liberals saw the social economy as an integral part of the private capitalist system.

This latter strand came closest to the position of the classical school of the theory of the social economy. Its attempts to develop a more specific set of objectives for the public economy have influenced the discussion since. Main tasks for the social economy were seen to be urban planning and infrastructure development. In contrast to past practice, it was now recommended that state enterprises should contribute to macroeconomic stabilization policies through anticyclical investment and employment policies. Prices should be set to support distributional goals, for example, by providing affordable service to low-income families. Moreover, the social economy was to contribute to fiscal policy and competition-policy goals.

The *Instrumentalthese*

The contemporary theory of the social economy builds on these approaches. Writers in this tradition largely agree that the social economy is a complement to the private enterprise system. Its main distinctive feature is the adoption of public interest goals that would not be pursued by private, profit-oriented enterprises. As in the classical school, there is a consensus that there is no rigid boundary between the realms of the social and the private economy. Rather, this boundary is dependent on political and economic conditions. However, there is a broad debate as to the nature of social economic behavior and the specific set of objectives that should govern social economic enterprises.

In a narrow perspective, social economic behavior is equated with the renunciation of profits. Thiemeyer (1973, 24) has pointed out the logical limitations of this delineation. For example, according to this proposed definition, independent of its goals and functions for the community, an urban energy company earning profits would not be considered part of the social economy. However, if it were integrated into a municipal holding company and used its profits to alleviate the deficit of other services, such as urban transportation, it would be considered part of the social economy. To avoid such inconsistencies, most authors prefer to delineate the social economy based on the purpose or intent of the enterprise and not its ownership, organization, or actual conduct.

This is most distinctly expressed in the instrumental thesis (*Instrumentalthese*) of social economic enterprise. In this view, social economic enterprises are instruments of public policy. According to Thiemeyer

(1973, 26) the theory of the social economy does not have to address the question as to whether the social economy is superior to the private economy. This is a political question and can be dealt with outside of the scholarly community. Neither can such a theory define once and for all what the appropriate goals of social economic enterprise should be. Rather, these need to be developed in a political debate, based on explicit and transparent political views and attitudes. Therefore, the specific substance of socioeconomic behavior cannot claim general validity, like scientific statements do. The role of the theoretician is thus confined to deciding whether or not the social economy is the most appropriate method to achieve the proposed goals (Thiemeyer 1975).

In order to allow such a political dialogue, social economic goals need to be expressed specifically in a catalog of duties. The list of possible objectives for the social economic enterprises, often called their performance conception (*Leistungskonzeption*), encompasses:

- Resource allocation goals, such as the provision of an optimal quantity of naturally monopolistic services and of public or merit goods.
- Stabilization goals, such as the pursuit of an anticyclical investment policy in support of overall macroeconomic goals.
- Employment policy goals, such as the maintenance of high employment levels during times of recession (Nowotny 1982).
- Industrial policy goals, such as the stimulation of national innovative activity.
- Regional policy goals, such as fostering the development of remote regions through the pricing of services and the channeling of investment funds.
- Distributional goals, such as the reduction of income inequalities.
- Social political goals, such as the provision of services at subsidized rates to assist businesses and, indirectly, the population of rural areas.
- Urban planning goals, such as the optimization of land use.
- Competition policy goals, such as the mitigation of market power.

It is widely accepted among the proponents of the theory of the social economy that one of the most important instruments in pursuit of these goals is the ability of management to implement a multifaceted price policy. In this respect the modern theory of the social economy diverges significantly from the American regulatory debate and in particular the neoclassical position on the optimal pricing of utility services. In the United States, regulation was historically seen as a substitute for market forces. Institutionally oriented writers—and until recently U.S. regulatory practice—have emphasized that the prices charged by a utility should reflect its embedded, fully allocated costs. Neoclassical economists have, within the particular assumptions of their paradigm, highlighted the desirable efficiency implications of marginal or incremental cost pricing. Both standards are ultimately inspired by the outcomes of a competitive market, where there is a strong tendency for prices to converge to the costs of service provision. (Despite the fundamental differences in their methodological approaches, the prescriptions of the two schools of thought are identical in market equilibrium.)

For several reasons, these positions are regarded as fundamentally flawed by the proponents of the modern theory of the social economy. In the words of Thiemeyer (1983, 407),

> There is the erroneous belief that competition might be simulated by imposing restrictions on profits and particularly by orienting prices (tariffs) to "real" cost. The linking of prices to costs is incorrect, not merely because the "correct" cost cannot be determined. It is wrong not merely because, in the eagerness to determine these "correct" costs, an avalanche of ever more precise governmental regulations as to the way in which costs are to be calculated is set in motion (which as a rule stick to outmoded full cost principles). The linking of prices is wrong above all because it robs the enterprise of the most important instrument it possesses, to fulfill its (public) tasks: a multifaceted price policy, which is adequate for this purpose.

It follows from this endorsement of a flexible pricing policy that the theory of the social economy is not principally against internal cross-subsidization. Such pricing may be justified under certain conditions and if it is instrumental to reach social economic goals. Unlike the older social economic approaches, the newer writers do not endorse uniform spatial pricing as a cornerstone of social economic behavior. Likewise, they do not generally condemn cream skimming by enterprises from outside the social economy. Rather, a case-specific evaluation of such pricing policies is called for to distinguish situations in which selective competition may actually improve the efficiency of the social economy from others in which efficiency is diminished.

For individual enterprises, the social economic goals need to be determined by their owner or governing body. The specificity of objectives is an important precondition for a rational debate over the meaningfulness of these goals. Thiemeyer (1973, 1975) emphasizes that the substance of social economic behavior cannot be determined in the abstract. Conflicts of interest and different views as to the appropriate goals of social economic enterprises must be expected. Unlike proponents of the modern political economy of regulation, which warn that policy makers may be captured by special interest groups, supporters of the theory of the social economy believe that a political dialogue will eventually lead to agreement on a catalog of duties.

This optimistic view also minimizes potential problems emanating from the interaction between the political system and the social economy. Aharoni (1986) has drawn attention to the widespread problem of state-owned enterprises as "agents without a principal." This observation results from the fact that the political system typically is structured in multiple centers of decision making that attempt to influence the specific goals and conduct of the social economy. Moreover, the political principals (e.g., secretaries of energy or commerce) may change quite often and in response to developments that are unrelated to the performance of the social economy. This may cause disturbances for the managers of social economic enterprises that reduce their efficiency. The current dissatisfaction with the performance of social economic enterprises seems to be partially related to these dilemmas of governance. Rather than establishing effective governance structures, many governments have opted to privatize large segments of the former social economy.

Practical Influence

Overall, it seems that the theory of the social economy has had a stronger influence on practical policy making than on the academic discourse on the organization of economic activity. Many representatives of the various conceptual approaches also held temporary government functions or served in advisory roles to policy makers. Moreover, social economic thinking was often adopted by the stakeholders in political debates without explicit reference to the conceptual underpinnings. Trade unions, chambers representing worker interests, and industry associations all at one point or another promoted the cause of the social economy. In Germany, Austria, and Switzerland, the social economy had expanded in several major waves toward the end of the nineteenth century and after the two World Wars. By the early 1980s, the public sector played a major role in certain areas of manufacturing, the banking sector, transportation, communications, and many local services.

Beginning in the early 1980s, the generally sympathetic attitude toward public enterprises and the social economy was gradually displaced by a more skeptical outlook. Factors contributing to this shift include the increasing fiscal difficulties of the public sector and the often-poor performance of social economic enterprises. Moreover, a widespread perception emerged that many social economic enterprises had established rather generous working conditions and compensation packages at the expense of the general public. Lastly, after an extended period of slow growth and high unemployment, a generally negative view as to the problem-solving capacity of the public sector took hold of public opinion. As a result, national governments gradually began to reduce the scope of the social economy through measures of privatization and liberalization.

At the forefront of this movement in Europe stood the United Kingdom under Margaret Thatcher, who made privatization a major part of her election campaign in the late 1970s. The other European nations endorsed privatization as a solution to revitalize their lackluster economies only with a significant delay. It is interesting that the European Union (EU) has not formally issued a policy recommendation in favor of privatization but rather focuses on the issue of liberalization and the abandoning of exclusive monopoly privileges. The three nations more strongly influenced by social economic thinking have recently sold major segments of public enterprises. Telecommunications assets usually command the largest revenues.

In the EU, the privatization volume increased from $98.5 billion between 1990 and 1994 to $265 billion for the period from 1995 through 1999 (Organisation for Economic Co-operation and Development 2000). The increase is much sharper in Germany and in Austria, where the privatization volume during the same periods increased by a factor of twenty-one and eight, respectively. As a result of privatization measures, the publicly owned segment of the economy has shrunk considerably. Moreover, many enterprises that remain formally in public ownership were reorganized as corporations according to private company law and instructed to act like private, profit-oriented firms.

The deregulation debate is not necessarily seen as damaging to the cause of the theory of the social economy. Influential scholars regard it as a welcome opportunity to critically review the present role and performance of social economic enterprises and redefine their tasks in the light of changed economic circumstances. At the same time, the school distances itself from the neoclassical belief in self-regulating markets and incremental cost pricing (Thiemeyer 1983).

This reduced practical influence is mirrored in the theoretical status of the theory of the social economy. Several academic journals were founded to disseminate social economic thinking, including the *Annals of Public and Co-operative Economy* and the *Zeitschrift für öffentliche und gemein-wirtschaftliche Unternehmen*. Whereas these journals historically were open to contributions from various paradigms, the number of articles originating in the neoclassical approach is increasing recently. The orthodox neoclassical regulatory paradigm also dominates the European debates on appropriate policies toward sectors with a significant degree of structural market power.

There are multiple channels through which neoclassical thinking has become the leading paradigm for regulatory reform. During the past years, several programs dealing with regulatory issues were founded in traditional economics departments and business schools. In a growing market for knowledge and expertise, consulting firms strategically advise policy makers and firms. Staff and lead consultants typically are recruited from orthodox economics departments, solidifying the influence of the traditional neoclassical paradigm. In all, while the theory of the social economy could provide the intellectual platform for a rejuvenation of forces in favor of a mixed economy, currently its influence is waning.

Summary

The theory of the social economy evolved from various roots in the eighteenth and nineteenth centuries. Despite attempts to develop a positive theory of social economic enterprise, it is essentially a normative framework. Several strands of social economic thinking that range from more radical socialist proposals to more reformist approaches can be distinguished. The more recent versions of the theory, building on foundations developed during the "classical period" of the school, have in common that the social economy is seen to be complementary to the private capitalist economy. In a narrower sense it can be seen as a stopgap in situations where the private market economy fails.

The broader formulation of the instrumental thesis conceptualizes the social economy as one of the instruments of public policy. Operational public interest goals ought to be developed on a case-by-case basis by the political system. Unfortunately, the theory never developed its notions in a more formal way and was discredited by mainstream economists. Perhaps the somewhat idealistic notion that the public interest could be defined and executed in a sufficiently precise way has been disappointed by the poor performance of many social economic enterprises. As a result, the theory of the social economy has recently been weakened in its practical importance. Nevertheless, it constitutes an interesting alternative to the faith in unfettered market forces that currently dominates public policy in the public utilities industries.

References

Aharoni, Yair. 1986. *The evolution and management of state-owned enterprises.* Cambridge, Mass.: Ballinger.

Ambrosius, Gerold. 1984. *Der Staat als Unternehmer.* Göttingen: Vandenhoeck & Ruprecht.

Baader, Franz Xaver von. 1835. *Über das dermalige Missverhältnis der Vermögenslosen oder Proletairs zu den Vermögen besitzenden Classen der Societät.* Munich: Georg Franz.

Eynern, Gert von. 1958. Das öffentlich gebundene Unternehmen, *Archiv für öffentliche and freigemeinwirtschaftliche Unternehmen* 4:1–59.

Fichte, Johann Gottlieb. 1800. *Der geschlossene Handelsstaat.* Tübingen: Cotta.

Justi, Heinrich Gottlieb von. 1758. *Staatswirtschaft.* Leipzig: Breitkopf.

List, Friedrich. 1841. *Das nationale System der politischen Ökonomie.* Stuttgart and Tübingen: Cotta.

Loesch, Achim von. 1977. *Die gemeinwirtschaftliche Unternehmung.* Cologne: Bund Verlag.

Marx, Karl, and Friedrich Engels. 1972. *Works.* Berlin: Dietz.

Mises, Ludwig von. 1922. *Die Gemeinwirtschaft: Untersuchungen über den Sozialismus.* Jena: Fischer.

Müller, Adam Heinrich. 1810. *Die Elemente der Staatskunst.* Berlin: Sandler.

Nowotny, Ewald. 1982. Nationalized industries as instrument of stabilization policy: The case of Austria, *Annals of Public and Cooperative Economy* 53 (1): 41–57.

Organisation for Economic Co-operation and Development (OECD). 2000. *Financial market trends 2000.* Paris: OECD.

Ritschl, Hans. 1955. Die öffentlichen Unternehen in der Marktwirtschaft, *Die öffentliche Wirtschaft* 5:2.

Sax, Emil. 1887. *Grundlegung der theoretischen Staatswirtschaft.* Vienna: Holder.

Schäffle, Albert. 1873. *Das gesellschaftliche System der menschlichen Wirtschaft.* 2d ed. Tübingen: Laupp'sche Buchhandlung.

Snow, Marcellus S. 1988. The state as a stopgap: Social economy and sustainability of monopoly in the telecommunications sector, *Review of Social Economy* 46 (1): 1–23.

Sonnenfels, Joseph Reichsfreiherr von. 1804. *Grundsätze der Polizei, Handlung und Finanzen.* Vienna: Kurzböck.

Thiemeyer, Theo. 1975. *Wirtschaftslehre öffentlicher Betriebe.* Reinbek bei Hamburg: Rowohlt.

———. 1973. *Grundsätze einer Theorie der Gemeinwirtschaft.* Frankfurt am Main: Europäische Verlagsanstalt.

———. 1983. Deregulation in the perspective of the German Gemeinwirtschaftslehre, *Journal of Institutional and Theoretical Economics* 139 (3): 405–18.

Wagner, Adolph. 1887. Finanzwissenschaft und Staatssozialismus, *Zeitschrift für die gesamte Staatswissenschaft* 43:37–122, 675–746.

Part 2

New Technology, the Network, and the Political Economy of Information

The Political Economy of Information and Communication

ROBERT E. BABE

> The very concept of a knowledge industry contains enough dynamite
> to blast traditional economics into orbit.
>
> —Kenneth Boulding

Information and Neoclassical Economics

Importance of Information in Neoclassicism

In 1937 Ronald Coase published a now-classic article proposing an information/communication-based theory of the firm.[1] In 1945 an equally influential piece by Friedrich von Hayek described the automatic information-generating properties of markets: "The marvel is," Hayek there rhapsodized, that "without an order being issued, without more than perhaps a handful of people knowing the cause, [price changes cause] tens of thousands of people whose identity could not be ascertained by months of investigation . . . [to] move in the right direction."[2] Prices, for Hayek, then, are informational. Note also Kenneth Arrow's more recent formulation of the same proposition:

> The competitive system can be viewed as an information and decision structure. Initially, each agent in the economy has a very limited perspective. The household knows only its initial holdings of goods (including labor power) and the satisfactions it could derive from different combinations of goods acquired and consumed. The firm knows only the technological alternatives for transforming inputs into outputs. The "communication" takes the form of prices. If the correct (equilibrium) prices are announced, then the individual agents can determine their purchases and sales so as to maximize profits or satisfactions. The prices are then, according to the pure theory, the only communication that needs to be made in addition to the information held initially by the agents. This makes the

market system appear to be very efficient indeed; not only does it achieve as good an allocation as an omniscient planner could, but it clearly minimizes the amount of communication needed.[3]

Coase and Hayek, as well as Arrow, were awarded Nobel Prizes, largely in recognition of their work on information in economic theory. Over the years other eminent economists of neoclassical persuasion, notably George Stigler and Gary Becker, have been recipients of Nobel Prizes— again, largely for work on information and communication in economics.[4] It is abundantly clear, then, that prices as information and communication are of utmost importance to economic theory.

As it turns out, however, information and communication are highly problematic for neoclassical theory—to such an extent, it is argued here, that neoclassicism's very foundations are undermined. In this section we discuss four issues posed by information and communication that undermine the neoclassical theoretical edifice. These issues are uncertainty, public goods, externalities, and power.

Uncertainty

By the time Stigler began addressing the "economics of information" in the early 1960s, information and communication had already become highly problematic for neoclassical theory. Whereas price theorists recognized that for markets to function "perfectly" there needed to be "perfect knowledge," forty years prior to Stigler's seminal piece Frank Knight had proposed that *profit* is a measure of market *imperfection*.[5] He attributed profit to *uncertainty,* uncertainty being defined as a deficiency in knowledge or information.[6] Stigler's aim in 1961 had been to diminish the importance for economic theory of uncertainty—that is, to restore "faith" in the perfectibility of markets—by proposing that markets for price information will arise spontaneously in the face of uncertainty over prices, and further that these markets will generate price information sufficient to alleviate, if not indeed eliminate, uncertainty.[7] Stigler looked, in other words, to the commodification of information for the solution to the problem of uncertainty.

Since the 1960s there has been, in practice, a heightening in the commodification of information: New information markets have arisen (copyright and patents have been extended, for instance, to cover even biogenetic information); encryption technologies have been developed to prevent nonpayers from accessing electronically encoded information; and there has been a diminution in the size of the public sphere (public broadcasting and public libraries, for example) relative to user-pay sectors. All these developments point to increased commodification on a broad scale of information, indicating perhaps that Stigler's "solution" to the problem of uncertainty is being pursued enthusiastically.

There are other strategies, too, that may serve, inter alia, to reduce uncertainty: mergers (both horizontal and vertical) and heightened advertising, for example, can reduce the vagaries of competition by increasing market control, firming up supplies, and managing consumer demand.[8] These strategies, however, it can be argued, sacrifice other requisites of market "perfection," and therefore may be undesirable in and of themselves. In that light we ought to give full scrutiny to Stigler's "solution" of commodifying information as a means of relieving uncertainty. Consideration of problems inherent to the commodification of information, however, will cause us in the end to reject *in principle* the commodification of information, and indeed to reject market prices as effective indicators of what economic activity should be.

Public Goods

Over the past forty years or so there has arisen the still burgeoning subfield of "information economics," a largely theoretical endeavor devoted to considering problems raised by information for neoclassicism. One conceptual difficulty concerns information's status as a "public good," meaning that one person's use of information does not diminish use by others. Kenneth Boulding summarized well information's attributes in this regard:

> When a teacher instructs a class, at the end of the hour presumably the students know more and the teacher does not know any less. In this sense the teaching process is utterly unlike the process of exchange. . . . In exchange, what one gives up another acquires; what one gains another loses. In teaching this is not so. What the student gains the teacher does not lose. Indeed, in the teaching process, as every teacher knows, the teacher gains as well as the student. In this phenomenon we find the key to the mystery of life.[9]

Since information is a public good, as Boulding so eloquently explained, it follows that information *should not* be commodified. Private property rights to information should neither be legislated nor enforced. Private property, after all, excludes nonowners from use, even though their use would not detract from others using the same information. Free access to information, in other words, satisfies neoclassical economics' "Pareto-efficiency" requirement whereby one (indeed many people) can be made better off without anyone being made worse of.

The principle that information is a public good has received wide recognition historically, and forms the basis upon which public libraries, public education, public television, access to information legislation, public funding of research and development, and so forth have been founded.

An absence of private property rights, however, as warranted by information's status as a public good, would mean, of course, that markets for information will not develop; markets, after all, concern exchanges of *private* property. Moreover, attempts to impose private property rights upon information (e.g., through copyright legislation) will never be fully successful (e.g., the undetected "pirating" of information through illegal reprography) due to information's inherently public good character, meaning that markets will not develop to the extent they otherwise would. In brief, exclusive reliance on markets to generate and distribute information will result, according to neoclassical criteria, in suboptimal levels of information production.[10]

Stigler's "solution," in other words, is highly problematic—both in theory and in practice. His "solution," in fact, highlights problems within neoclassicism that go well beyond that of deficient price information. By neoclassical economics' own efficiency and welfare-maximizing criteria, any and all commodifications of information are inefficient: copyright, patents, signal scrambling, pay-as-you-use, tuition fees, international accords dealing with commodity trade in knowledge and information—indeed, *user fees of all types*—contradict neoclassicism's own Pareto efficiency criterion, since one person's use does not detract from use by others.

Firms specializing in the production and distribution of information understand well information's inherent public good nature. That is why they put such effort into lobbying to have copyright laws enhanced, to have enforcement of copyright strengthened, and to have penalties for violation of copyright increased. It is also why new means of encryption that defend against unauthorized (i.e., nonpaying) users are continually developed. Huge sums are spent each year in terms of technological development, lobbying, surveillance, and legal enforcement to inhibit people from copying or accessing information for which they have not paid—a misallocation of resources on a monumental scale!

Many have speculated that developed countries have entered a new era, a veritable Information Age. They have contended that ours has become an Information Economy. Information workers, according to Fritz Machlup and Marc Porat, now account for upward of 50 percent of the U.S. labor force.[11] In these circumstances, to recognize that neoclassical economics (which focuses on markets, that is, on private commodity exchanges) is ill-equipped to handle dilemmas posed by uncertainty and by the public good nature of information is akin to concluding, one might judge, that neoclassicism is irrelevant in our day.

Externalities

As if information's status as a public good were not serious enough for neoclassical price theory, a further difficulty has become evident also— that of "externalities," or third-party effects. Externalities initially were explored most rigorously by A. C. Pigou, a disciple of Alfred Marshall, in *The Economics of Welfare*.[12] There Pigou focused on discrepancies between individual economic interests and those of the community. He explained that even in the purely competitive economies proposed by economic theory, private and social interests diverge when third parties are affected by private transactions. Seen from the standpoint of information and communication, the existence of externalities means that prices give improper signals on what to produce, how much to produce, and for whom.

In response to this challenge there has arisen yet another vast subfield— "environmental economics"—which, like "information economics," attempts to salvage neoclassicism in the face of acknowledged breakdowns attributable to faulty information/communication. Again, one of the principal theoreticians has been Ronald Coase. In his second classic article Coase proposed that if rights to pollute or rights not to be damaged by pollution are traded in the marketplace, problems posed by externalities are in principle resolvable through market-based activity.[13]

For "environmental economists" ever since the appearance of Coase's article, problems posed by externalities, and particularly problems of environmental degradation, have been viewed as being "informational" in the sense that unadjusted market prices are understood as not incorporating all relevant costs and benefits. One "solution" proffered, therefore, has been to "auction off" rights to pollute. Neoclassicists believe that the costs of acquiring pollution rights will be reflected in the prices charged for the final goods or services, making those processes better reflective of social costs and benefits. Moreover, neoclassicists believe that the highest bidders for these rights will be those producers best able to meet society's needs, since they by definition will be the ones with the incentive to pay the most, as it is they who will be able to recover the additional costs through higher prices, even in competitive markets. Alternatively, neoclassicists propose that market prices be "adjusted" through taxes or otherwise—again with a view to more closely aligning prices to social cost. The intent in both cases, in other words, is to "internalize the externalities"—that is, to extend the bounds of commodity exchange by incorporating more fully monetary representations of *all* (third-party) consequences.

The commodification of the right to pollute is welcomed by business, of course, as this presents yet further opportunities to engage in commodity trade, and in particular to pursue new avenues for profit making by buying and selling pollution rights. Business may be less favorably disposed to pollution taxes, of course, although even here, to the extent that firms face higher costs if they pollute, new profit opportunities emerge for companies that develop emission-reduction technologies. Once again, to proponents of these policies, markets are seen not only as being consistent with, but as actually contributing to environmental well-being.

However, as was the case with the commodification of price information, so too with "internalizing the externalities": serious problems for economic theory and economic practice arise. First, as noted by Herman Daly and John Cobb, even *adjusted* market prices can reflect only *relative* valuations of commodities and resources; prices in principle provide no guidance whatever as to the appropriate *scale* of the economy relative to the biosphere. Since the economy is but a subsystem of the finite ecosystem, this limitation is of prodigious importance. Daly and Cobb express their concern this way:

> Obviously the world is not static. But equally obviously the diameter of the earth is not expanding. The solar flux and the turnover rates of biochemical cycles stay roughly constant, regardless of the interest rate or the growth of GNP. Consequently the economy (subsystem) becomes larger relative to the ecosystem and stresses the parent system to an ever greater degree.[14]

There are abundant indicators that global economy is already too large relative to the ecosystem: ozone depletion, species extinction and loss of genetic diversity (each year, twenty thousand species disappear forever), the greenhouse effect and global warming, toxification of air and ground water, desertification of arable land (each year six million hectares are degraded to desertlike conditions), growing disparities between rich and poor partly on account of undue exploitation of the earth's resources, and so forth.[15]

Worse still, according to current systems of accounting, the greater the environmental degradation, the greater our "well-being," at least as currently measured by the price system: cleanups of toxic spills, sun creams to compensate for ozone depletion, medical expenses incurred as a result of radioactive contamination, price increases due to the depletion of resources—all these raise GNP and per capita income!

Furthermore, prices reflect only *human valuations.* Yet human preferences, in addition to being often ephemeral and easily manipulated by advertisers and other professional persuaders, discount heavily future outcomes. Assuming a 10 percent discount rate, for example, one thousand dollars thirty years hence is worth only $57.31 today! (A lower discount rate would raise the present value of the $1,000 somewhat, but the point still remains: the price system inherently trivializes outcomes occurring in only a few decades). Built into our entire system of monetary representations of value is a trivialization of the future. In this light one must question whether decisions with irreversible, virtually eternal consequences—concerning activities that could lead to the extinction of species, the depletion of resources, the buildup of nuclear stockpiles with half-lives of thousands of years, and so on—should be made on the basis of the momentary preferences of today's "consumers," even if and when reflected in "adjusted" market prices. The price system, again, even when operating "smoothly," is an abysmally poor guide for making decisions concerning long-term survival.

Power

As if the foregoing problems with neoclassical treatments of information and communication were not serious enough, there is also the issue of power. Neoclassicism congenitally proposes the existence of, if not "pure," then at least "workable" competition, "contestable markets," and so forth, thereby supporting the proposition that decentralized markets *spontaneously* or *nondeliberatively* generate and diffuse price information in the appropriate quantity and of sufficient quality. Yet looking at the real world, few (apart from neoclassical diehards) can help but espy great and increasing concentrations of economic power. In other words, for important sectors of the economy, price information does not *arise;* it is *set,* and set in such a way that the parties doing the setting gain inordinately.

Pursuing the logic of neoclassicism, the problem of concentrated economic power in fact is simply a matter of prices, viz. undue control over the production of price information. Just as "environmental economics" proposes that adjusted market prices can rescue neoclassicism and markets from the problems of environmental degradation, and just as "information economics" purports to save neoclassicism from the ravages of uncertainty, so too with regard to monopolistic price setting does "public utility economics" purport to salvage neoclassicism from problems posed by the power to set prices.

Public utility economics historically has recognized or proposed that certain key industries or sectors are "naturally monopolized": telephones, telegraphs, and pipelines, for instance. The recommendation has been, therefore, that a regulatory commission oversee the operations of the "public utility," and that the commission set prices that will simulate competitive markets. Once again, prices are regarded as being not only informational but in principle perfectible, and the problem of monopoly is thereby reduced to one of pricing.

Debates have raged over the years as to exactly what formula or formulae for a public utility best simulates competitive results—cost of service versus value of service pricing, for instance, and with regard to the former, marginal cost pricing versus fully allocated cost pricing.[16] It has been shown convincingly, however, that there is a fundamental contradiction in setting prices for public utilities: if marginal cost pricing is used, an unsubsidized public utility normally will lose money on account of uncompensated overhead costs and declining average costs—and hence go out of business; if fully allocated cost pricing or value of service pricing is used, however, the utility confronts incentives to become unduly capital-intensive (rate base padding) and thereby not only become inefficient but also engage in predatory pricing in otherwise competitive markets.[17] There is also a substantial literature pointing to the "capture" of regulatory commissions by the firms and industries they purport to "regulate"—an aspect of power well transcending mere price-setting.

Public utility economics aside, however, concentrated power raises further profound informational and communicatory concerns—none of which are much acknowledged in the vast literature that is neoclassical economics. One of the gravest is the capacity of concentrated media owners and advertisers to affect tastes and preferences, quite undermining the goal of "consumer sovereignty" which purportedly underlies neoclassicism. The origin and dynamics of tastes and preferences are conveniently shunted aside by neoclassicism through the self-imposed doctrine of "de Gustibus non est disputandum" (one does not discuss tastes).[18] If and when concentrations of media power *are* acknowledged, however, questions regarding the origin and manipulation of tastes and preferences *must* arise.[19]

Inferences and Possibilities

Neoclassicism's problems, in all the cases addressed here, stem from an inordinate faith in the capacity of the price system to serve as an efficacious and beneficent medium of information and communication, and from neoclassicism's incapacity or unwillingness to envisage constructively modes of human interaction other than that of commodity exchange.

Inconsistencies and other inadequacies in neoclassical treatment of information and communication, one might well conclude, should long ago have relegated neoclassicism to the status of a footnote in the history of economic thought. Of course, this has not yet happened; neoclassicism's longevity and persistence therefore merit extended research and speculation.

One explanation might be a perceived absence of alternatives: if, despite gross deficiencies, neoclassicism is all there is, one might argue, it is better to stick with that until something better comes along. This chapter therefore now turns to the origins of alternatives to neoclassicism's treatment of information and communication, to show that superior modes of analysis do indeed exist. Collectively these theories can be termed *the political economy of information and communication.*

Origins of the Political Economy of Information and Communication

This section summarizes the communication thought of three seminal economists—Harold Innis, Dallas Smythe, and Kenneth Boulding. Each made substantial contributions toward resolving, or rather transcending, the informational and communicative dilemmas inherent to neoclassicism. Individually and in combination these writers provide analyses that are more logically consistent than those of "information economists," "environmental economists," and "public utility economists." Furthermore, each theorist points us toward more holistic modes of understanding, whereby the economy is viewed as but a subset of larger political, social, cultural, and indeed ecological systems. For that reason, although working independently of one another, all three can properly be spoken of as being institutional economists; each certainly displays a certain indebtedness to Thorstein Veblen, again making such an appellation apropos.

All three, moreover, recognize the dynamic, *penetrative properties* of the price system; prices and markets penetrate and transform hitherto uncommodified human relations and practices, weakening or wiping out considerations of kinship, love, tradition, religion, national sovereignty, community, and so on. In addition, the price system is understood by these writers as being but one among many modes of human communication, even though in the modern world it continues to increase in relative as well in as absolute importance. Furthermore, asymmetries in the distribution of power based on unequal capacities to create, disseminate, and receive information (including price information) are recognized to be of special importance.

It is remarkable how consistent the treatments of information and communication are in the writings of these three formidable theorists, and this notwithstanding their ostensibly different starting points, scope, and modes of analysis. Harold Innis was an economic historian who conceived a media theory that proposes that the mode of communication is a central variable explaining the evolution of cultures and relations of dominance and dependence among economies. Innis's analysis encompassed the rise and fall of civilizations within the course of human history. The scope of Dallas Smythe's analysis, by contrast, is much narrower, confined largely to late-nineteenth- and twentieth-century media industries within capitalism. However, like Innis, Smythe viewed control over the means of communication as the single most important source of power, and on that presumption proceeded to analyze media as instruments of class power and as loci of struggle. In 1948 Smythe joined the faculty of the newly established Institute of Communications Research, University of Illinois, where he began teaching the first course anywhere on the political economy of communication.[20] In his course, Smythe focused primarily on electronic media—telegraph, telephone, radio broadcasting, and television—and on radio spectrum allocation. He was concerned particularly with how these fields were organized, how they interrelated as industries, and with the development of public policy, especially at the domestic (American) level but internationally as well.[21] Finally, Kenneth Boulding—a founder of general systems theory and steeped in ecological understanding—recognized communication as the universal means whereby systems interact with one another. Boulding extended the analysis of information, communication, and production well beyond the limits adopted by Innis and Smythe, to encompass all biological processes. Yet his media theory also echoes those of Smythe and Innis, insofar as he, too, saw people and cultures as being manufactured through communicatory processes. Furthermore, Boulding recognized that different media and different usages of media result in profound cultural differences.

The three analysts, it is argued here, cohere to, supplement, and complement one another, and together point to a political economy of information and communication far superior to neoclassicism.

Harold Adams Innis[22]

Even as Knight, Coase, Hayek, and others were speculating on the generation and sufficiency of price information in the market economy, and on its importance within economic theory, a brilliant albeit maverick economic historian at the University of Toronto, Harold Adams Innis (1894–1952), was quietly addressing the roles of information and media in *defining* economic activity and in apportioning economic power. Innis believed that economic models developed in older, industrialized economies should not with impunity be applied to emergent, peripheral ones. Rather, economic history and economic theory should be closely integrated: history should, in fact, constitute the main test of economic theory. Innis's intent, therefore, was to develop a "philosophy of economic history or an economic theory suited to Canadian needs."[23]

In undertaking that task he identified three factors as paramount—Canada's trading dependence on other countries; her geography, particularly the inland water systems and the pre-Cambrian shield; and the unique character of her natural resources or "staples." Building on Thorstein Veblen's work, which he studied intently while doing doctoral work at the University of Chicago, Innis saw technological developments, particularly in the fields of transportation and communication, as interacting with geography and staples to disrupt established patterns. Tensions result, Innis advised, when groups controlling technologies associated with staples' extraction trade with traditional (or "time-bound") cultures. Trade in staples, Innis insisted, "biases" development in peripheral countries, giving rise to political, economic, and cultural dependence. (Parenthetically, we note that the contrast between Innis's staples theory and neoclassicism's static "theory of comparative advantage" is pronounced: comparative advantage proposes fixity to factor endowments, including the capital infrastructure and the educational attainment of the labor force, and from that premise argues that countries inevitably gain by specializing in the production of commodities for the purpose of international trade).[24]

Retrospectively we see germinating in Innis's discourse on staples a rich theory of communication. The production or extraction of natural resources constituted "communication" for him, since staples, combined with technology and geography, create singular environments or ecosystems which *mediate* and hence direct or "bias" human relations.[25] Furthermore, staples are the agency bringing into contact peoples or civilizations previously isolated, setting up thereby reciprocal relations of dominance and dependence.

With regard to the fur staple, for example, Innis noted a drastic impact on North America's indigenous peoples, who exchanged furs for "iron goods" such as hatchets, knives, scissors, needles, and, most significantly, muskets, quite disrupting their way of life. As Innis commented,

> The history of the fur trade is the history of contact between two civilizations, the European and the North American. . . . Unfortunately the rapid destruction of the food supply and the revolution in the methods of living

accompanied by the increasing attention to the fur trade by which these products were secured, disturbed the balance which had grown up previous to the coming of the European. The new technology with its radical innovations brought about such a rapid shift in the prevailing Indian culture as to lead to wholesale destruction of the peoples concerned by warfare and disease.[26]

Likewise, the forestry staple changed completely a way of life. According to Innis's historiography, timber supplanted fur as a key staple for export, and like fur, "was adapted . . . to the cheap water transportation of the St. Lawrence." It contrasted with fur, however, in terms of weight, bulk, and value.[27] Whereas the manufacture of fur products, such as hats, was undertaken largely in Europe, timber's bulk and weight meant that manufacture "took place close to its source."[28] Canada consequently exported square lumber instead of raw timber to the United States.

In Eastern Canada a large number of lumber companies also shifted to the production of pulp and paper.[29] Paper is, of course, a medium for written communication, and accordingly is part and parcel of modernity. Exports of paper to the United States had dramatic consequences for the American newspaper industry, and hence for the whole of North America. Innis noted, for instance, that in St. Louis between 1875 and 1925 there was a decline in the space allocated to news from 55.3 percent to 26.7 percent, and a concomitant increase in the space devoted to advertising. Given this development, the newspaper industry, perforce, accommodated itself more thoroughly to the demands of advertisers. Consequently, relations between the newspaper and the commercial world "narrowed": on the one hand, large business organizations began to build "goodwill" through newspaper advertising; on the other, newspapers themselves became large, oligopolistic enterprises reluctant to rile advertisers.[30] A new view of the world was being socially constructed at the behest of advertisers by the emerging mass media.

Finally, it is evident that in his staples writings Innis understood money to be a potent medium of communication. He chafed, however, at neoclassical treatments, whereby money is viewed as a neutral (or "unbiased") medium of exchange.[31] In his view, money and prices "penetrate" indigenous cultures, annexing them to increasingly larger trading, financial, cultural, and political systems. In the process, local relations based on hierarchy, kinship, tradition, love, empathy, culture, religious sensibilities, and intrinsic value (in Adam Smith's phrase, "moral sentiments") are split apart, wiped out, and replaced by the impersonality of money value and commodity exchange.

In his last few years Innis turned from staples to communication media per se. Briefly, he proposed a dialectic of "time-binding" versus "space-binding" media, the former inducing or supporting local community and continuity, the latter individualism, impersonal relations, geographic empire, and incessant change. In setting forth his communication thesis, Innis turned from Canadian history to the veritable rise and fall of civilizations.[32] He asked: What is the role of communication media in defining society, in maintaining social stability, in inducing social change, and in fostering empire and control? According to James W. Carey, in responding to such questions Innis "founded the modern studies that now exist under the banner of media imperialism."[33]

Implicitly at least, Innis regarded media as being in some ways similar to staples; just as harvesting new staples helps bring about fundamental political, economic, and cultural struggle and change, so, too, do "inventions in communication compel realignments in the monopoly or oligopoly of knowledge."[34] Regarding clay tablets and cuneiform script, for instance, he wrote:

> Dependence on clay in the valleys of the Euphrates and Tigris involved a special technique in writing and a special type of instrument, the reed stylus. Cuneiform writing on clay involved an elaborate skill, intensive training, and concentration of durable records. The temples with their priesthoods became the centres of cities. A culture based on intensive training in writing rendered centralized control unstable and gave organized religion an enormous influence.[35]

The point is made again with regard to paper and Chinese pictographs. Although the Chinese developed paper, a most flexible medium for encoding messages, their symbol system, consisting of well over 1,500 characters, being highly complex, necessitated the emergence of "a learned class." This served to foster the rise of "expert" opinion, which denigrated traditional knowledge. Complexity of the written language for Innis, in other words, explained the persistence of hierarchical political and religious institutions in the face of a light and flexible writing material. In Europe by contrast, albeit several centuries later, the much simpler phonetic alphabet combined with paper to hasten "the growth of commerce."[36] Innis, then, saw the physical materials upon which messages are inscribed as combining with the means of inscription to constitute distinct "amalgams"—paper-plus-phonetic alphabet being distinctly different from paper-plus-Chinese-characters, for example.

Innis regarded the quest for power as underlying all technological change, and hence also as being a key explanation for cultural transformation. He believed that each medium of communication is normally controlled by a particular elite—a priesthood, perhaps, in the case of certain time-binding media, and press barons and advertisers in the case of today's newspapers. At every stage of development, however, he maintained, some groups try to bypass entrenched "monopolies of knowledge" by innovating new media of communication.

Innis further insisted that balance is needed between institutions, practices, and media exerting control through time and those managing control over space.[37] Undue emphasis on one mode of control or organization relative to the other inevitably leads to dis-organization.[38] For our present space-biased era Innis made an impassioned "plea for time." He wrote: "The modern obsession with present-mindedness . . . suggests that the balance between time and space has been seriously disturbed with disastrous consequences to Western civilization."[39]

Dallas W. Smythe

A second seminal figure in the political economy of information and communication was Dallas W. Smythe (1907–92). Political economy for Smythe meant not only studying communication industries from an economic point of view, but, even more importantly, *integrating* communication studies and economics into a new approach. Standard economics, he averred, is woefully deficient because it does not recognize the dynamic power implications of communication. Likewise, however, mainstream communication studies is lacking because it seldom acknowledges the economic base of much communicatory activity. Hence, *the political economy of communication,* as Smythe formulated it, draws out the economic base of communicatory activity while at the same time showing the power repercussions of communicatory control for the economy and for economic organization.

Always a dissenter, Smythe's radicalism intensified with age. He began in the early 1950s writing tightly focused content analyses of television programming in selected communities, but by the 1970s was linking electronic communication to power aspects of the entire capitalist order.[40] In Smythe's view, monopoly capitalism could not have arisen without the mass media. Indeed, he attested, beginning with mass circulation daily newspapers in the 1890s, monopoly capitalism in its formative stage *invented* the mass media.

Monopoly capitalism, a term Smythe borrowed from Marxist economists Paul Baron and Paul Sweezy, refers to the increasingly global private enterprise system now dominated by but a few hundred gigantic corporations.[41] For Smythe, in this context, mass media were to be understood primarily not as producers of mass media messages, but rather as producers of *people*—that is, as causing people to display "appropriate" behavior and to ascribe to a "correct" set of beliefs.[42] "Correct" beliefs, for Smythe, included such (to him erroneous) notions as the following:

- that personal possessiveness is essential to human beings;
- that the main goal of life is to consume commodities and services;
- that freedom and conflict are individual, not collective matters;
- that commodities and services do not educate or form values; they merely contribute to people's comfort and pleasure;
- that a conflict of ideas need not be resolved; every person to his or her own taste and belief;
- that it is possible and desirable to be neutral or objective while working in the mass media, educational institutions, government and business; it is not, as Mark Twain put it, a question of "Who are you neutral against?"
- and most importantly, that "you can't change human nature"; the status quo is timeless.[43]

In addition to inculcating *beliefs* such as these, Smythe advised, media under monopoly capitalism also "screen in" *values*, like the following:

- *that private is better than public;* private business is deemed to be clean and efficient whereas public and governmental affairs are dirty and inefficient;
- *that prices charged by private businesses are good;* taxes, however, since they fund public goods, which do not meet "the market test" of profitability, are by definition bad;
- *that private property is virtually sacred;* hence public planning and the public regulation of business are inherently bad;
- *that technology and winning are of utmost importance;* "We learn from professional sports"—for instance, Smythe explained that "nice guys finish last."[44]

According to Smythe it was not merely mass media, however, that inculcate capitalist values and beliefs. Fronting the relatively few giant corporations was a "cluster of institutions" that he referred to as the *Consciousness Industry* (CI). He wrote: "[CI is] most directly concerned with the design of consumer goods and services, their packaging, audience production, advertising, and marketing,"[45] CI consists of

the advertising/market research agencies plus the mass media. Backing them are the educational system, photography and commercial art. In the next rank are professional and pre-professional sports, comic books, parlor games (such as Monopoly), recorded music, tourism, restaurants, hotels and transportation. In the next rank are other consumers goods industries—the Homogeneous Package Goods (soaps, soft drinks, etc.) and the consumer durables (such as household appliances, motorcycles and automobiles). As backdrop for CI are the industries which bind together the whole Monopoly Capitalist system: the Military-Industrial Complex, telecommunications, banks, insurance, finance, real estate, the gambling industry, and crime, both organized and unorganized.[46]

CI, in brief, is wide-ranging and, according to Smythe, is the "indispensable foundation of the capitalist politico-economic system."[47] Smythe undoubtedly would agree that neoclassical economic theory is a part of the persuasive communication put out by the oppressive Consciousness Industry. Smythe further opined that CI had largely superseded military power as the primary means of imperial control.[48]

Kenneth E. Boulding[49]

Finally, we turn to Kenneth E. Boulding (1910–93). For Boulding *all* economic activity is informational and communicatory. *Production,* for example, "whether of a chicken from an egg or of a house from a blueprint," according to Boulding, is a process whereby "some kind of information or knowledge structure is able to direct *energy* toward the transportation, transformation, or rearrangement of materials into less probable structures than those existing at the start of the process."[50] When a seed germinates in the ground, for example, its informational or knowledge structure (DNA) utilizes stored energy to draw selectively upon nutrients or "building materials" in the soil to produce its *phenotype* (i.e., the plant). Similarly, a housing contractor, after studying a blueprint, utilizes energy to assemble and rearrange construction materials, which thereupon take a form more complex or improbable than had existed previously.

So universal, indeed, is this process of production/communication that Boulding recommended replacing economics' prototypical triad of land-labor-capital as the factors of production with a new triad comprised of energy-materials-information.[51] A major advantage of Boulding's proposal is an implicit recognition that most "production" occurs *outside of markets,* notwithstanding the neoclassical economists' contention that externalities are exceptional; under Boulding's formulation, it is readily apparent that not all factors of production are intrinsically commodified, in stark contrast to the land-labor-capital triad.[52] A further implication of the revised triad is that human economic activity occurs only within the context of a larger ecosystem, an insight often disregarded by mainstream economists but one that, if continually borne in mind, should foster increased awareness of and heightened respect for the environment.

All production, both organic and inorganic, Boulding advised, entails *selections*. Through sequences of behavior, knowledge structures "recognize" and correct divergences between actual and ideal states.[53] Such homeostatic sequences are known also as cybernetic mechanisms. Embryology is the study of cybernetic mechanisms in developing organisms, but analogously human decision makers bring mental contexts or "images" to production processes with the intent always of reducing differences between actual and desired states.[54]

Boulding distinguished among three main types of human artifacts or *social species*, namely: *material artifacts*, that is, material structures and objects such as buildings, machines, and automobiles; *organizational structures*, that is, human institutions, ranging from extended families and hunting bands to transnational corporations, governments, and churches; and *biological artifacts*, under which heading he included not only plants and animals altered by domestication, selective breeding, and genetic engineering, but also human beings. Humans, he advised, are to a considerable extent artifactual. Whereas every person is, of course, produced *biologically* in accordance with information inherent to the genetic makeup of the original fertilized egg, people are also "produced" *culturally* in the sense of acquiring learned images, knowledge, languages, and skills.[55] (Boulding often jokingly compared his notion of the artifactual nature of human beings to what he termed neoclassical economics' thesis of the "immaculate conception of the indifference curve.")

Organic species and social species alike constitute components of *ecosystems*, defined by Boulding as "interacting populations of different species in which the birth and death rates of each population are a function of its own size and the size of the other populations."[56] Species, whether organic or social, occupy *niches*, that is, equilibrium populations of phenotypes in their ecosystems.[57] Social species are similar to organic species in the sense that both are "selected" for occupancy of niches. Commodities, for instance, at any moment have a population or stock that increases through production and decreases through consumption, and, like biological species, they interact continuously, influencing each other's birth, growth, and death rates.

Modes of species' interaction are various. Petroleum and automobiles, for Boulding, are in continuous symbiotic interaction, whereas intercity trains and buses tend to interact competitively. Social artifacts may also be competitive with organic species (for example, automobiles with horses), or cooperative with them (for instance, chemical fertilizers with domesticated crops). Boulding also analyzed predator-prey relations and host-parasite relations.[58] He wrote: "The fundamental principle of ecological evolution [is that] everything depends on everything else."[59]

Furthermore, Boulding compared two types of production. In *biogenetic production,* "genetic information (or 'know-how') is transmitted by genes from one generation to the next." In *noogenetic production,* "learned structures in central nervous systems or their equivalents . . . [are transmitted] by a learning process."[60]

In transmission, however, information can be subject to alteration ("mutation"), a change often referred to as *evolution.* Boulding defined evolution as "a process of cumulative change of know-how."[61] *Noogenetic evolution* occurs when knowledge transmitted from one generation to another undergoes change and becomes subject to cognitive social selection.[62]

Modes of communication (i.e., media) carry signs and symbols to their destination. Physical systems, then, are "agents of communication." In biogenetic systems the agent or carrier is DNA, genetic information being encoded in a double helix of carbon atoms with attached atoms of oxygen, hydrogen, nitrogen, and carbon. In human social systems, by contrast, modes of communication (media) change through time, and these changes for Boulding (as for others such as Harold Innis) are at the very heart of societal evolution. In nonliterate societies, "noogenetic" communication is limited to verbal rituals, poems, legends, ceremonies, and so forth. Writing, however, inaugurated what Boulding called the "disassociated transcript,"[63] expanding enormously the temporal and spatial dimensions of communication and learning.[64] Without records, complex organizational continuity from generation to generation would have been impossible. Nor could decision makers have transmitted instructions as effectively over space to distant peripheries. With writing, however, the "total body of human knowledge potentially accessible to an individual grew constantly, as each generation left its deposit. . . . It was no accident," Boulding added, "that [Western or modern] science comes along with printing."[65]

Innovations in media for Boulding, then, are at the heart of the "organizational revolution," by which he meant the "great rise in the number, size, and power of organizations of many diverse kinds, and especially of economic organizations."[66] He maintained that evolving media enable organizational growth in two principal ways. First, media help overcome external constraints. Revolutions in transportation (for example, railroads, steamships, automobiles, airplanes) and in communication (telegraph, telephone, radio), "pushed back the limitations of the environment [enabling organizations] to expand farther into [their] environment."[67] Second, media like typewriters, duplicators, calculators, and computers facilitate internal communication. Without changes in media technology, internal communication for growing organizations would have become increasingly difficult.

Indeed, communication media help alter fundamentally geo-social/cultural structures. Over the past couple of hundred years, Boulding observed, "the world has changed from being a set of a considerable number of fairly isolated social systems . . . into something approaching a single social system."[68] Initially ocean transport enabled transoceanic migrations and world trade; subsequently the telegraph, telephone, transoceanic cables, radio, television, communication satellites, and optical fibers have played "an overwhelmingly important role in this transformation into a single world system,"[69] eroding local cultures and substituting in their place "superculture."[70]

Conclusion

Let us turn now to how the political economy of information and communication, as inaugurated by these three seminal thinkers, transcends the problems inherent to the neoclassical approach.

Uncertainty. Contrary to neoclassicism, in the political economy of information and communication there is no notion of prices being a "perfect" means of communication, nor of price being the definitive representation of value. Furthermore, in political economy virtually all social interaction, whether narrowly "economic" or not, is understood as being evolutionary, dynamic, undetermined, and hence in some respects unpredictable. Information in the political economy model, in fact, is seen as often *increasing* uncertainty, in the sense of provoking change, hardly reducing it, as is the view within neoclassicism. A nondeterministic model, then, is substituted for neoclassicism's deterministic one, and instead of "uncertainty" being viewed as an anomaly to be overcome, it is understood as being intrinsic to existence. For political economy, therefore, a main problematic is adapting to continually changing circumstances.

For political economists, moreover, information transcends mere price information, although price information certainly is understood to be important, since it often displaces other modes of information and communication, albeit often to the detriment of democracy, community, and the environment. In political economy, then, information and communication are understood less in terms of causing or enabling optimality and equilibria, and much more as inducing evolutionary transformation. Favorite neoclassical concepts such as maximization and equilibrium are rendered meaningless in the context of evolutionary political economy.

Externalities and Public Goods.   In the political economy of information and communication, people, and all else, are understood as being radically interdependent. Economic processes are understood, for example, as being interrelated bidirectionally with social, political, cultural, communicatory, and indeed ecological processes. Likewise, individuals (whether "producers" or "consumers") are understood as themselves being products of social interaction.

According to political economy, moreover, human interaction (i.e., communication) is not conceived as consisting solely of commodity exchanges, and even those interactions that in the first instance typify commodity exchanges are recognized as having unavoidably broader consequences. Since "externalities" in the neoclassicists' sense of the term both abound and are deemed to be omnipresent and unavoidable, the very concept of an "externality" loses its significance.

According to political economy, furthermore, societies and cultures are recognized as being informational. People are born into ongoing systems of symbolic interaction, they make their mark there, and die, even as the culture continues to evolve. Our actions are public actions that contribute to societal evolution, and in that sense all human artifacts are communicatory and thereby fit the neoclassicist's definition of a "public good." While this poses no particular problem for the political economy of information and communication, it does render problematic key neoclassical concepts like "consumer sovereignty," private property, individual demand, utility functions, and so forth.

Power.   Nor does the political economy of information and communication abstract from asymmetries in the distribution of power. To the contrary, the capacity to communicate is recognized as being a principle site of power, as is the capacity to attain information. For those interested in achieving social change, access to the means of communication is understood as being vital.

Much more, of course, could be said. Perhaps in closing, however, it is sufficient to speculate on why the political economy of information and communication, as formulated particularly by these three remarkable thinkers, has not received wider acclaim. One explanation is psychological: political economy casts aside the "psychic balm"[72] of a deterministic, mechanistic economic model in favor of radical indeterminacy. A second explanation concerns knowledge systems as instruments of power: the political economy of information and communication, after all, raises issues relating to the distribution and use of communicatory power that those in control of the means of communication might possibly wish not to be raised publicly. Other explanations can be conceived as well.

To the extent, however, that the political economy of information and communication resolves or transcends problems of information and communication inherent to neoclassicism, political economy certainly deserves wider exposure.

Notes

Many thanks to Edward Comor, Paul Anglin, Warren J. Samuels, and Edythe Miller for insightful comments on a previous draft. The author is Jean Monty/BCE Chair of Media Studies, Faculty of Information and Media Studies, University of Western Ontario, London, Canada.

1. Ronald Coase, "The Nature of the Firm," in *Readings in Price Theory*, ed. George Stigler and Kenneth Boulding, (Homewood, Ill.: Irwin, 1952), 331–51.

2. F. A. Hayek, "The Use of Knowledge in Society," *American Economic Review* 35 (1945): 526–27 (emphasis added).

3. Kenneth Arrow, "The Economics of Information," in *The Computer-Age: A Twenty-Year View*, ed. Michael Dertouzos and Joel Moses (Cambridge, Mass.: MIT Press, 1979), 306–17.

4. For this article neoclassicism is defined as the mainstream of modern economics, arising from the work of Alfred Marshall and the Austrian economists (Menger, Böhm-Bawerk, and von Wieser) in the early decades of the twentieth century. Neoclassicism focuses on the market and the system of prices arising from market activity without inquiring very much into factors giving rise to and sustaining particular market relations in the first place. Furthermore, in neoclassicism there is a basic tenet that markets and the price system are efficacious means of generating information and making decisions as to what to produce, how much, and for whom. The overriding criterion for judging is "Pareto Optimality," whereby an event can be declared to be an improvement only if one person's situation is improved without others becoming less well off.

5. This is "profit" in the economic, as opposed to the accounting, sense. "Economic profit" is the return to capital over and above the cost of capital.

6. Frank Knight, *Risk, Uncertainty and Profit* (1921; reprint, Boston: Houghton Mifflin, 1946).

7. George Stigler, "The Economics of Information," in *The Organization of Industry* (Homewood, Ill.: Irwin, 1968), 171–90. See also Stigler, "Information in the Labor Market," in *The Organization of Industry* (Homewood, Ill.: Irwin, 1968), 191–207.

8. See, for example, John Kenneth Galbraith, *The New Industrial State* (Boston: Houghton Mifflin, 1967).

9. Kenneth E. Boulding, *The Image: Knowledge and Life in Society* (Ann Arbor: University of Michigan Press, 1956), 35.

10. There is a huge distribution of income question here too. Insofar as information/knowledge remains with the seller even after trade, parties specializing in the production of information/knowledge will become increasingly wealthy compared to those specializing in producing non-public goods. The implications for international trade and first world—third world relations are immense indeed.

11. See particularly Fritz Machlup, *Knowledge: Its Creation, Distribution and Economic Significance. Volume 1: Knowledge and Knowledge Production* (Princeton, N.J.: Princeton University Press, 1980); and Marc Porat, *The Information Economy: Definition and Measurement, Special Publication 77–12 (1)* (Washington, D.C.: Office of Telecommunication, U.S. Department of Commerce, 1977).

12. A. C. Pigou, *The Economics of Welfare*, 4th ed. (London: Macmillan, 1932).

13. Ronald Coase, "The Problem of Social Cost," *Journal of Law and Economics* 3 (1960): 1–44.

14. Herman Daly and John Cobb Jr., *For the Common Good: Redirecting the Economy Toward Community, the Environment and a Sustainable Future* (Boston: Beacon Press, 1989), 143.

15. See, for example, David Suzuki, *Time to Change* (Toronto: Stoddart, 1994); and World Commission on Environment and Development, *Our Common Future* (Geneva: Oxford University Press, 1987).

16. See, for example, James Bonbright, *Principles of Public Utility Rates* (New York: Columbia University Press, 1961).

17. Harvey Averch and Leland Johnson, "Behavior of the Firm Under Regulatory Constraint." *American Economic Review* (1961): 1052–69.

18. George Stigler and Gary Becker, "De Gustibus Non est Disputandum," *American Economic Review* 67 (1977): 75–90.

19. See, for example, John Kenneth Galbraith, *The New Industrial State* (Boston: Houghton Mifflin, 1967); also, Tibor Scitovsky, *The Joyless Economy: An Inquiry into Human Satisfaction and Consumer Dissatisfaction* (New York: Oxford University Press, 1976).

20. John Lent, "Interview with Dallas W. Smythe," in *A Different Road Taken: Profiles in Critical Communication,* ed. John A. Lent (Boulder, Colo.: Westview Press, 1994), 43.

21. See particularly Dallas W. Smythe, *The Structure and Policy of Electronic Communication* (Urbana: University of Illinois, 1957).

22. The sections on Innis and Smythe are derived from my book, *Canadian Communication Thought: Ten Foundational Writers* (Toronto: University of Toronto Press, 2000).

23. Harold A. Innis, "The Teaching of Economic History in Canada," in Harold A. Innis, *Essays in Canadian Economic History,* ed. Mary Q. Innis (Toronto: University of Toronto Press, 1956), 3.

24. See particularly Daly and Cobb, *For the Common Good*, 209–35.

25. See Barrington Nevitt, *The Communication Ecology: Re-presentation versus Replica* (Toronto: Butterworths, 1982), 100–104.

26. Harold A. Innis, *The Fur Trade in Canada: An Introduction to Canadian Economic History* (Toronto: University of Toronto Press, 1930), 388.

27. Harold A. Innis, "The Lumber Trade in Canada," in H. A. Innis, *Essays in Canadian Economic History* (Toronto: University of Toronto Press, 1956), 242.

28. Ibid., 243.

29. Ibid., 246.

30. Harold A. Innis, "The Newspaper in Economic Development," in *Political Economy in the Modern State* (Toronto: Ryerson Press, 1946), 27.

31. Harold Innis, "The Penetrative Powers of the Price System," in H. A. Innis, *Essays in Canadian Economic History*, ed. Mary Q. Innis (Toronto: University of Toronto Press, 1956), 252–72.

32. According to Robin Neill, Innis inaugurated his writing on communication when U.S. hegemony was coming to the fore, and his "intense nationalism was aroused" as a result. If Gibbon wrote *The Decline and Fall of the Roman Empire* about Britain and not about Rome, as Innis said he had, then, Neill declared, Innis in the same sense wrote his history of communications "about Canada and not about Egypt, Greece, and Europe." Robin Neill, *A New Theory of Value: The Canadian Economics of H. A. Innis* (Toronto: University of Toronto Press, 1972), 17.

33. James W. Carey, "Culture, Geography and Communications: The Work of Harold Innis in an American Context," in *Culture, Communications, and Dependency*, ed. William H Melody, Liora Salter, and Paul Heyer (Norwood, N.J.: Ablex Publishing, 1981), 80.

34. Harold A. Innis "Minerva's Owl," in *The Bias of Communication* (1947; reprint, Toronto: University of Toronto Press, 1951), 4; emphasis added.

35. Ibid., 6.

36. Ibid., 20.

37. Harold A. Innis, "The Problem of Space," in *The Bias of Communication* (Toronto: University of Toronto Press, 1951), 111.

38. Harold A. Innis, "A Plea for Time," in *The Bias of Communication* (Toronto: University of Toronto Press, 1951), 64.

39. Ibid., 76.

40. Dallas W. Smythe, "Reality as Presented by Television," in *Counterclockwise, Perspectives on Communication*, ed. Thomas Guback (Boulder, Colo.: Westview Press, 1994): 61–74.

41. Smythe defined capitalism as "a system based on private property in the means of production and consumption and on the appropriation of the surplus product of labor by the owners of capital; it is a worldwide system of interrelated markets for commodities." (Dallas W. Smythe, *Dependency Road* [Norwood, N.J.: Ablex Publishing, 1981], 2).

42. Ibid., 13.

43. Dallas W. Smythe, "Culture, Communication 'Technology' and Canadian Policy," the 1986 Southam Lecture, *Canadian Journal of Communication* 12 (1986): 2.

44. Ibid., 17.

45. Dallas W. Smythe, "Communications: Blindspot of Economics," in *Culture, Communication, and Dependency: The Tradition of H. A. Innis,* ed. William H. Melody et al. (Norwood, N.J.: Ablex Publishing, 1981), 112.

46. Smythe, "Culture, Communication, 'Technology' and Canadian Policy," 8.

47. Smythe, *Dependency Road,* xiii.

48. This declaration, incidentally, is endorsed by representatives of America's military-industrial establishment. See Joseph S. Nye Jr. and William A. Owens, "America's Information Edge," *Foreign Affairs* (March/April 1996): 29.

49. This section is based on my chapter on the communication thought of Kenneth Boulding in *Communication and the Transformation of Economics* (Boulder, Colo.: Westview Press, 1995).

50. Kenneth E. Boulding, *Ecodymamics: A New Theory of Societal Evolution* (Beverly Hills, Calif.: Sage Publications, 1978), 12, 34.

51. This is not the "information" of Shannon and Weaver's "mathematical theory of communication," however. For Boulding, information "involves not only improbability of structure, but the structure's ability to 'instruct'; that is, to be a code of selection according to a program" (ibid., 13).

52. See, in particular, Karl Polanyi, *The Great Transformation: The Politics and Economic Origins of Our Time* (1944; reprint, Boston: Beacon Press, 1957).

53. Boulding, *Ecodynamics,* 108.

54. Kenneth E. Boulding, *The Skills of the Economist* (Toronto: Clarke, Irwin and Co., 1958). According to Boulding, when messages confirm that a discrepancy exists between actual and ideal states, ensuing action can be of three types: First, action can modify the ideal image internally, bringing it more in line with the existing state of affairs (one becomes more "realistic"). Second, energy may be expended on the external environment with the intent of bringing that more in line with the ideal. As a third, and probably most common possibility, action can modify both the ideal and the real. In any event, decisions or actions stem not merely from the flow of sensory stimuli, as would be the case with purely mechanical systems of cause and effect, but from "the change in context which that information provides" (ibid., 90).

55. Kenneth E. Boulding, *Evolutionary Economics* (Beverly Hills, Calif.: Sage Publications, 1981), 24.

56. Kenneth E. Boulding, *The World as a Total System* (Newbury Park, Calif.: Sage, 1985), 23–24

57. Kenneth E. Boulding, "The Limits to Societal Growth," in Elise Boulding and Kenneth E. Boulding, *The Future: Images and Processes* (Thousand Oaks, Calif.: Sage Publications, 1995), 27.

58. Kenneth E. Boulding, *Conflict and Defense: A General Theory* (New York: Harper and Row, 1962).

59. Boulding, *Ecodynamics*, 224, 31.

60. Boulding, "The Limits to Societal Growth," 27.

61. Kenneth E. Boulding, "World Society: The Range of Possible Futures," in *How Humans Adapt: A Bicultural Odyssey*, ed. Donald J. Ortner (Washington, D.C.: Smithsonian Press, 1983); reprinted in Kenneth E. Boulding and Elise Boulding, *The Future: Images and Processes* (Thousand Oaks, Calif.: Sage Publications, 1995), 47.

62. Boulding, "The Limits to Societal Growth," 27.

63. Boulding, *The Image*, 65.

64. Boulding, *Evolutionary Economics*, 122.

65. Ibid., 128.

66. Kenneth E. Boulding, *The Organizational Revolution: A Study in the Ethics of Economic Organization* (1953; reprint, Chicago: Quadrangle Books, 1968), xiii.

67. Ibid., 25.

68. Boulding, *The World as a Total System*, 148

69. Ibid., 148.

70. Ibid., 151.

71. Warren J. Samuels, introduction to *Economics as Discourse: An Analysis of the Language of Economists* (Boston: Kluwer Academic Publishers, 1990).

References

Arrow, Kenneth. "The Economics of Information." In *The Computer-Age: A Twenty-Year View*, edited by Michael Dertouzos and Joel Moses, 306–17. Cambridge, Mass.: MIT Press, 1979.

Averch, Harvey, and Leland Johnson. "Behavior of the Firm under Regulatory Constraint." *American Economic Review* (1961): 1052–69.

Babe, Robert E. "The Place of Information in Economics." In *Information and Communication in Economics,* edited by R. E. Babe, 41–67. Boston: Kluwer Academic Publishers, 1994.

———. *Communication and the Transformation of Economics.* Boulder, Colo.: Westview Press, 1995.

———. *Canadian Communication Thought: Ten Foundational Writers.* Toronto: University of Toronto Press, 2000.

Bonbright, James. *Principles of Public Utility Rates.* New York: Columbia University Press, 1961.

Boulding, Kenneth. *The Organizational Revolution: A Study in the Ethics of Economic Organization.* 1953. Reprint, Chicago: Quadrangle Books, 1968.

———. *The Image: Knowledge and Life in Society.* 1956. Reprint, Ann Arbor: University of Michigan Press, 1961.

———. *The Skills of the Economist.* Toronto: Clarke, Irwin and Company, 1958.

———. *Conflict and Defense: A General Theory.* New York: Harper and Row, 1962.

———. "The Knowledge Industry." *Challenge* (May 1963): 36–38.

———. *Ecodynamics: A New Theory of Societal Evolution.* Beverly Hills, Calif.: Sage Publications, 1978.

———. *Evolutionary Economics.* Beverly Hills, Calif.: Sage Publications, 1981.

———. "World Society: The Range of Possible Futures." In *How Humans Adapt: A Biocultural Odyssey,* edited by Donald J. Ortner. Washington, D.C.: Smithsonian Press, 1983. Reprinted in Kenneth E. Boulding and Elise Boulding, *The Future: Images and Processes.* Thousand Oaks, California: Sage Publications, 1995.

———. *The World as a Total System.* Newbury Park, Calif.: Sage, 1985.

———. "From Chemistry to Economics and Beyond." In *Eminent Economist,* edited by Michael Szenberg. Cambridge: Cambridge University Press, 1992.

———. "The Limits to Societal Growth." In Elise Boulding and Kenneth E. Boulding, *The Future: Images and Processes,* 26–38. Thousand Oaks, Calif.: Sage Publications, 1995. First published in *Social Growth: Processes and Implications,* ed. Amos H. Hawley (New York: Free Press, 1979).

Carey, James W. "Culture, Geography and Communications: The Work of Harold Innis in an American Context." In *Culture, Communications, and Dependency,* edited by William H Melody, Liora Salter, and Paul Heyer, 73–91. Norwood, N.J.: Ablex Publishing, 1981.

Coase, Ronald. "The Nature of the Firm." In *Readings in Price Theory,* edited by George Stigler and Kenneth Boulding, 331–51. Homewood, Ill.: Irwin, 1952. First published in *Economica* 4(1937): 386–405.

———. "The Problem of Social Cost," *Journal of Law and Economics* 3 (1960):1–44.

Daly, Herman, and John Cobb Jr. *For the Common Good: Redirecting the Economy Toward Community, the Environment and a Sustainable Future.* Boston, Mass.: Beacon Press, 1989.

Galbraith, John Kenneth. *The New Industrial State.* Boston: Houghton Mifflin, 1967.

Hayek, F. A. "The Use of Knowledge in Society." *American Economic Review* 35 (1945): 526–27.

Innis, Harold A. *The Fur Trade in Canada: An Introduction to Canadian Economic History.* 1930. Reprint, Toronto: University of Toronto Press, 1962.

———. "The Newspaper in Economic Development." In *Political Economy in the Modern State,* 1–34. Toronto: Ryerson Press, 1946.

———. "Minerva's Owl." Presidential Address to the Royal Society of Canada, 1947. In H. A. Innis, *The Bias of Communication,* 3–32. Toronto: University of Toronto Press, 1951.

———. "A Plea for Time." In *The Bias of Communication,* 61–91. Toronto: University of Toronto Press, 1951.

———. "The Problem of Space." In *The Bias of Communication,* 92–131. Toronto: University of Toronto Press, 1951.

———. "The Lumber Trade in Canada." In H. A. Innis, *Essays in Canadian Economic History*, edited by Mary Q. Innis, 242–51. Toronto: University of Toronto Press, 1956. First published in *The North American Assault on the Canadian Forest*, edited by A. R. M. Lower et al. (Toronto: Ryperson Press, 1938), vii–xvii.

———. "The Penetrative Powers of the Price System," in H. A. Innis. *Essays in Canadian Economic History*, edited by Mary Q. Innis, 252–72. Toronto: University of Toronto Press, 1956. First published in *Canadian Journal of Economics and Political Science* 4 (1938):299–319.

———. "The Teaching of Economic History in Canada." In Harold A. Innis. *Essays in Canadian Economic History*, edited by Mary Q. Innis, 3–16. Toronto: University of Toronto Press, 1956. First published in *Contributions to Canadian Economics* 2 (1929).

———. "The Passing of Political Economy." In *Staples, Markets, and Cultural Change*, edited by Daniel Drache, 438–42. Montreal and Kingston: McGill-Queen's University Press, 1985. First published in *Commerce Journal* (1938).

Knight, Frank. 1946. *Risk, Uncertainty and Profit*. Boston: Houghton Mifflin, 1946.

Lent, John A., ed. "Interview with Dallas W. Smythe." In *A Different Road Taken: Profiles in Critical Communication*. (Boulder, Colo.: Westview Press, 1994).

Machlup, Fritz. *Knowledge: Its Creation, Distribution and Economic Significance. Volume 1: Knowledge and Knowledge Production*. Princeton, N.J.: Princeton University Press, 1980.

McLuhan, Marshall. Introduction to *The Bias of Communication*, by Harold A. Innis. Toronto: University of Toronto Press, 1971.

Neill, Robin. *A New Theory of Value: The Canadian Economics of H. A. Innis*. Toronto: University of Toronto Press, 1972.

Nevitt, Barrington. *The Communication Ecology: Re-presentation versus Replica*. Toronto: Butterworths, 1982.

Nye, Joseph S., Jr., and William A. Owens. "America's Information Edge." *Foreign Affairs* (March/April 1996).

Pigou, A. C. *The Economics of Welfare*. 4th ed. 1920. Reprint, London: Macmillan, 1932.

Polanyi, Karl. *The Great Transformation: The Politics and Economic Origins of Our Time*. 1944, Reprint, Boston: Beacon Press, 1957.

Porat, Marc. *The Information Economy: Definition and Measurement, Special Publication* 77–12 (1), Washington, D.C.: Office of Telecommunication, U.S. Department of Commerce, 1977.

Samuels, Warren J., ed. *Economics as Discourse: An Analysis of the Language of Economists*. Boston: Kluwer Academic Publishers, 1990.

Scitovsky, Tibor. *The Joyless Economy: An Inquiry into Human Satisfaction and Consumer Dissatisfaction*. New York: Oxford University Press, 1976.

Smythe, Dallas W. *The Structure and Policy of Electronic Communication*. Urbana: University of Illinois, 1957.

———. *Dependency Road*. Norwood, N.J.: Ablex Publishing, 1981.

———. "Communications: Blindspot of Economics." In *Culture, Communication, and Dependency: The Tradition of H. A. Innis*, edited by William H. Melody et al., 111–25. Norwood, N.J.: Ablex Publishing, 1981.

———. "Culture, Communication 'Technology' and Canadian Policy." The 1986 Southam Lecture, *Canadian Journal of Communication* 12 (1986):1–20.

———. "Reality as Presented by Television." In *Counterclockwise, Perspectives on Communication*, edited by Thomas Guback, 61–74. Boulder, Colo.: Westview Press, 1994. First published in *Public Opinion Quarterly* 18 (summer 1954): 143–56.

Stigler, George. "The Economics of Information." In *The Organization of Industry*. Homewood, Ill.: Irwin, 1968, 171–90. First published in *Journal of Political Economy* 69 (1961).

———. "Information in the Labor Market." In *The Organization of Industry*.. Homewood, Ill.: Irwin, 1968, 191–207. First published in *Journal of Political Economy* 70 (1962).

Stigler, George, and Gary Becker. "De Gustibus Non est Disputandum," *American Economic Review* 67 (1977): 75–90.

Stiglitz, Joseph. "Information and Economic Analysis: A Perspective." *Economic Journal* 95 (1985): 21–41.

Suzuki, David. *Time to Change*. Toronto: Stoddart, 1994.

Williams, Raymond. "Advertising: The Magic System." In *Problems in Materialism and Culture*, 170–95. London: Verso, 1980.

World Commission on Environment and Development. *Our Common Future*. Geneva: Oxford University Press, 1987.

Policy Challenges
in the Age of the Internet

MAURICE ESTABROOKS

Introduction

About a half-century ago, during the Second World War, scientists and engineers around the world became engaged in a race to build the world's first automatic computing machine. Their efforts initiated a self-sustaining process of innovation, development and commercialisation that has changed the course of social and economic evolution. Their search led to the development of the world's first transistor, the first stored program digital computer, the first general purpose mainframe computer, the first microprocessor, and the world's first personal computer. All of these developments initiated the information revolution of the sixties, seventies, and eighties. Complementing these were equally significant developments in digital switching and transmission systems including communications satellites and optical fibres, which initiated the telecommunications revolutions of the seventies, eighties, and nineties.

This process of technological innovation and commercialization and rapid social and economic change is still going on today. The personal computer has evolved into a multimedia, communicating machine. Wireless, hand-held, multimedia devices with text, voice, sound and image communications capabilities are coming onto the market today. It is developments in broadband optical and wireless communications systems and the Internet that constitute the leading edge of this ongoing technological revolution today.

In the short time span of a decade, the Internet has evolved from relative obscurity to one of the most influential information and communications mediums in history. It has grown to penetrate homes more rapidly than did telephone, radio, television or cable television. It has resulted in the creation of new industries. Three of the most significant are the

Internet services provider industry, the multimedia publishing industry and the electronic commerce industry. The Internet, however, has also begun to drive developments almost every sector of the economy. These include the telephone, cable television, information, and entertainment industries as well as banking and financial services, and travel, retail, and wholesale services. An Internet-based marketplace has already become an economically efficient and practical reality for the sale and purchase of everything from computers, clothing, and groceries to automobiles and even homes. Most of the leading banks now provide an entire range of online financial services, including savings, loans, and bill payment services over the Internet. Computerized trading has taken over most of the stock exchanges worldwide of the world, transforming them from physical floors to network-based trading systems. The Internet now provides individuals at home and the office with online access to the trading systems of most of the leading stock exchanges so they can buy and sell stocks and options instantaneously. All of the leading publishers, record producers, broadcasters, and software producers have embraced the Internet as a means of marketing and distributing their products and serving their clients.

The purpose of this paper is to examine the technological and economic forces that are propelling this evolution of the Internet and this transformation of economic society. Another objective is to assess the social, economic, and policy significance of these developments for the future.

The first section identifies some of the unique technological and economic processes that are driving this technological transformation of society. The next part describes some of the unique features, functionalities, and applications of the Internet and argues that the Internet has the potential to evolve into a universal information processing, communications, and trading and transactions infrastructure that will continue to transform economic activity for decades to come. The third part examines the significance of the evolution of electronic markets and of the network economy. This trend toward an electronic marketplace will continue to change the structure of entire sectors, markets, and the economy as a whole. The final section examines some of the social and economic implications of the rise of the Internet economy and the challenges it poses for public policy.

An Examination of the Driving Forces

No one foresaw and no one could foresee the spectacular growth of the general-purpose mainframe computer when it was introduced in 1964. No one foresaw the even more rapid growth of the IBM personal computer when it was introduced in 1981. Furthermore, no one foresaw the even more spectacular growth of the Internet when it evolved into a public information and communications infrastructure in the early nineties. The reason no one could foresee their impacts is that no one was aware of all of the powerful technological and economic forces driving them. We are fortunate today because we have a much better understanding of these forces and we can use this understanding to make some reasonably reliable forecasts and predictions of the future of the Internet and its social and economic implications.

There are five or more key technological and economic forces driving the computer, microchip, and communications revolutions and the evolution of the Internet. The best known is Moore's Law. It states that the density and the processing speed of integrated circuits (i.e., the microprocessors that power all computer and communications machines) are doubling every eighteen months. Over the past thirty years, this has translated into an increase in performance of over 100 million percent—truly a phenomenal growth rate. The current view (as of 2001) is that Moore's Law can be extended for another fifteen to twenty years or more. This implies a continuing increase in processor speed by a factor of as much as 16,386 in the next two decades. This means that by 2020, personal computers will be capable of operating at speeds as high as 10,000 GHz to 100,000 GHz. (IBM announced in early 2002 that it would begin shipping a new generation of microchips operating at a speed of 110 GHz.) Furthermore, the power consumption of a semiconductor chip is declining by as much as 30 to 40 percent with each new generation. The implications of these developments stagger the imagination. How will this enormous processing power be used? What are the implications for the economy and for society?

However, there appears to be a Moore's Law equivalent driving every component element of the Internet, from digital storage, switching, and transmission speeds, bandwidth and throughput capacity. Since network servers and switches are powered by microprocessors, their processing speeds are also increasing at the same rate as Moore's Law. However, the capacity of digital storage devices is increasing at a rate that is even greater than that of Moore's Law. According to IBM, technological advances are making it possible to continue to double the capacity of digital storage devices each year. (IBM expects that by 2011, the average PC will have 20 terabytes of storage, that is, 1,000 times the capacity of the average PC in 2001.) Massive storage area networks are currently under development that will constitute an infrastructure for selling inexpensive online storage as a business to anyone who wants it. In addition to the capacities of individual network elements, the throughput capacity of the Internet has been doubling each year as a result of the duplication and replication of network linkages, switches, and servers.

A Moore's Law equivalent also applies to the transmission capacities of optical networks. Here too, dramatic advances have already been made and more are expected in the future. Between 1996 and 2000, the capacity of a single strand of a commercially deployable optical fiber transmission system grew from 40 Gbits/sec to 960 Gbits/sec, a factor of 24 in just four years. (The technology is referred to as Dense Wave Division Multiplexing or DWDM.) This growth constitutes more than a doubling of capacity each year and the capacity limits of optical fiber systems have not yet been reached. Nortel Networks announced the first shipments of its terabit optical fiber systems in 2000. Much greater speeds are expected in the future. Engineers in Japan announced in March 2001 that they had succeeded in achieving a speed of 10 trillion bits per second over a single optical fiber.

The holy grail of the communications industry is the all-optical network. The objective is to completely eliminate all electronic components and systems in the networks of tomorrow. This will abolish the need for thousands upon thousands of expensive amplifiers and other equipment to convert optical signals to electronic signals, amplify and switch them and convert them back again. The technology will also make it possible to transmit optical signals over far greater distances, i.e., over thousands instead of hundreds of miles, without amplification or regeneration. These and other enhancements will make it possible to provision very efficient, high speed networks at very low cost.

The elimination of storage bottlenecks and processing, switching, and bandwidth constraints in the networks of tomorrow combined with continued declines in cost point to several seemingly inevitable consequences for the evolution of the Internet. First, it means that the functionality of the Internet will increase to provide the complete range of sound, voice, video, and entertainment, education, and business services that visionaries have long promised. Secondly, it means that the incremental costs of network processing, switching, and transmission, and therefore of transactions processing and content distribution will continue to plummet to the point that these costs will become virtually zero. Thirdly, it means that the Internet will inevitably become a much more economically attractive means to deliver a wide variety of business, entertainment, educational, and personal productivity services, from business services involving e-commerce and workgroup applications to interactive entertainment and educational services.

There are several provisos to this forecast. The first is that the Internet can be made a safe, secure, and reliable means of delivering this multitude of services. The second proviso is that markets will develop for these applications and revenues can be generated to pay of their development, production, and delivery. The limiting factor in other words is not technology. It is demand and industry and market conditions. If Say's Law continues to hold as it has the past, businesses will take advantage of the enormous potential that the technology provides and create markets for these services.

As the cost of doing business in the so-called "virtual space" of the Internet continues to plummet and the social and economic cost of the doing business in the real economy continues to increase, it will become increasingly attractive to deliver all information, entertainment, and education services and to conduct business generally over the Internet. The implication is that there are major changes and challenges ahead for industries ranging from telecommunications, broadcasting, entertainment, and banking and financial services to business and work itself.

There appears to be at least three other distinctive but complementary economic and technological forces at work that propelling the information and communications revolutions. The first can be called the "dematerialization effect." The dematerialization effect manifests itself in the massive reduction of physical materials (i.e., hardware) in information processing equipment, machinery, and infrastructures as more and more physical components, devices, equipment, and entire systems are condensed and integrated into a single microprocessor chip. Microprocessor-controlled machines and systems are lighter in weight, smarter in their operation, use far fewer physical components, and far less materials and energy than their mechanical, electrical or electromechanical counterparts. They are therefore far more efficient to operate and maintain. This dematerialization effect is resulting in the creation of increasingly powerful digital processing and communications machinery and network infrastructures that have (artificial) intelligence in their own right. It is also reducing the use of physical materials and energy in all physical design, development, and production processes.

Complementing this dematerialization process is the equally powerful process that can be called a "knowledge creation" or "digital content creation" or "software-creation" process. This process or force manifests itself in the growth and proliferation of digital commodities that can be designed, created or captured, and stored, marketed, sold, and delivered and even consumed online in their digital form. (Digital commodities are to be distinguished from their physical or "atom-based" commodities, which occupy physical space and are subject to conservation laws of physics.) Software and information (stored digitally), in their broadest manifestations, are the best examples of digital commodities. This new class of commodities includes all content comprising any combination and all combinations of text, numbers, statistics, graphics, images, voice, and sounds. It includes music, video, film, radio and television productions, and indeed any kind of information that can be represented digitally. Digital commodities span the full range of information and communications applications from business and medicine to entertainment and education. The process of digital commodity creation has almost infinite possibilities in terms of the variety and sophistication of digital content that can be designed, created and used.

The digital commodity creation and dematerialization processes also complement one another. Scientists, engineers, and architects use computer-aided design and simulation software to model, simulate, and study complex designs, systems, and processes without the use of physical media or materials. Engineers use the same technology to optimize component and systems designs and translate these designs into instructions for computer-aided manufacturing systems. Artists and animators use the technology to create photo-realistic, animated videos, and full-length movies. (The computer game industry has used the same digital animation technology to single-handedly create the video game industry, by far the biggest segment of the entertainment industry.) All of these processes represent enormous savings in physical materials.

Another example of the complementary nature of the digital commodity creation and dematerialization processes is the substitution of information storage and communications media based on recording materials such as paper, including paper cash, and celluloid film, for example, by electronic and optical communications media in the form of digital electronic and optical storage and display devices. In the film industry, for example, it has been estimated that the use of digital cameras, digital editing systems, digital storage and distribution systems, and digital displays and projection systems has reduced the costs over celluloid productions by as much as 90 percent. Furthermore, the quality of digital pictures and movies is far superior. Superior quality, and time and cost savings are three of the drivers of high-definition television.

There is yet another attribute—an economic one—that will continue to drive the creation of a digital and an Internet-centered world in the future. It is derived from the fact that digital goods and services are not subject to the same exclusion principle as are material or atom-based goods and services. This means that the use or consumption of digital goods and services by one does not limit its use or consumption by others. It means that as the marginal cost of processing, storage, and distribution—and of transactions generally—declines toward zero, the technology revolution is creating a situation where more and more digital information products and services can be supplied at a very low cost or even given way at no charge.

Giving things away is another term for sharing and sharing has been one of the principal driving forces behind the rapid acceptance, growth, and use of the Internet. The implication is that the Internet will evolve to become an increasingly powerful medium for the sharing of resources, including information, software (broadly defined), and of ideas, knowledge, and experience among all of those who have access to it. This potential for sharing the information and intellectual resources of the world has never been as great as it is today. The promise of technology in the new millennium is that people throughout the world will have the opportunity to share their ideas, their knowledge, and their dreams on a scale never before realizable. This could produce social, and economic value on an unimaginable scale. This is why Internet access could become so important to public policy in the coming decades.

Universal Functionality and Enabling Capabilities of the Internet

One of the reasons that the Internet (and the computerized network or networks it has come to constitute) is so important is that there is seemingly no limit to its functionality and the scope of the applications and services that can be provided over it. The following is a brief description of some of the key functional capabilities and applications of the Internet that make its potential so great.

The Internet as a Multimedia Communications System

The most popular application of the Internet by individuals at home and in business by far is electronic mail. E-mail is a very simple and inexpensive way for people to exchange information, distribute documents, and coordinate their activities. This capability is universally accessible to anyone with a telephone, a computer, and an account with an Internet services provider, and it operates round the clock, seven days a week. E-mail also constitutes a very cost-effective means for business to conduct invoicing and billing activities. Even though the bandwidth of the Internet for most home users is still very limited, people can still distribute images, photographs, and content involving sounds and music as attachments. Broadband access will resolve the bandwidth limitations in the local network and open up new kinds of applications. Residential homes with digital cable modems (or Digital Subscriber Line modems) can already receive high-quality audio content, including music, as well as video content. Voice mail could become one of the next "killer" applications of the Internet.

A Publishing Medium

The second most popular application of the Internet is as an information distribution and publishing medium. Literally anything and everything that can be printed today can be, and is being, published on the Internet and much more. There are hundreds of media portals specializing in every aspect of publishing. They include portals for newspapers, periodicals, academic journals, e-zines (i.e., electronic magazines) book reviews, movie, and film reviews. Some portals publish entire books on the web. What makes the Internet unique is its capability to make any person, any group or any organization a self-publisher as long as they have a computer, a telephone line, and an account with a service provider. Internet publishing continues to be one of the forces driving Internet developments. A few publishers have decided to abandon their old publishing model and completely embrace the Internet as a publishing and distribution medium. Thompson Corporation for example has sold off its entire newspaper chain to concentrate on its online publishing business.

The Internet as a Virtual Library Medium

Another significant feature of the Internet is its virtual library capabilities. The Internet already constitutes by far the largest and most up-to-date library in the world. Indeed, the national libraries of most industrialized nations are already accessible via the web and governments are adding more libraries and a greater variety of content each year. The subject matter of web libraries ranges from entertainment, cinema, gourmet food, news, weather, and sports to market research reports, stock market quotations, science, technology, engineering, medicine, health care, and education. It is also universally accessible and inexpensive to use. These attributes make it a valuable research tool for scholars, scientists, technologists, and the masses. In the future, the Internet could become an enormous virtual audio and video education and entertainment library.

A Collaboration Medium

One other powerful feature of the Internet is its capability to bring people together wherever they are located into a social, workgroup or business environment so they can communicate and collaborate as if they were in the same office or building. Indeed, no other information or communications medium can match the attractiveness of the Internet as a many-to-many, interactive, multimedia collaboration medium. The purpose of collaboration can be to create and share ideas, information, and knowledge, or engineering and architectural designs. It can be for the purpose of learning or education in a group environment or participation in a conference. Organizations are taking advantage of the potential to conduct business—both internally and with other organizations—electronically over any distance, inexpensively, and productively, through video conferencing, for example. Electronic collaboration in this way is giving rise to new kinds of work environments, such as virtual work groups, tele-working, and small home-office businesses.

A Low-Cost Medium for Accessing and Distributing Digital Commodities

Perhaps the greatest and most significant long term potential of the Internet is to enable access to, and distribution of, digital commodities. As explained above, these include reports, images, photographs, as well as cultural, education, and entertainment content, including music, videos, films, and other such products. No other medium can currently match the Internet in terms of its speed, timeliness, accessibility, convenience, and low-cost for delivering a wide variety of news, reports, statistical publications, and other kinds of content on demand. Most businesses already have broadband access. As local telephone and cable television companies expand their broadband access service offerings, more and more households will be able to receive real-time audio, video, and multimedia educational and entertainment programs on demand.

The Internet as a Commerce Medium

Electronic commerce is widely viewed as the greatest "killer application" of the Internet and, indeed, statistics appear to support this premise. The Internet is far superior to telephone, fax, and other electronic means of communications because it is capable of facilitating most, if not all, of the activities necessary to conduct business. Its greatest potential by far is as a buying, selling, and trading and exchange medium. You can buy, sell, and pay for just about anything over the Internet that you can in the real market, and much more because the market and the sources are worldwide. A rough estimate is that the cost of an online transaction over the Internet is less than one-tenth the cost of a face-to-face transaction. Market researchers estimate that the electronic commerce marketplace will explode to reach between three and five trillion dollars by 2005. About 80 percent of the market is expected to be in the business-to-business segment, with the remaining 20 percent coming from in the business-to-consumer segment.

The missing prerequisite to the widespread acceptance of e-commerce is the existence of a reliable and secure online payment system. A number of companies are vying to become the Microsoft of the online payments system of the future. One of these is PayPal. eBay has a service called Bill-Point and Citigroup has a person-to-person system called c2it. The leading banks and credit card companies are also developing their own online payments system.

A Monetary and Banking Medium

Money and banking are also natural applications of the transactions and e-commerce capabilities of the Internet. Indeed, all of the activities associated with money, including deposit, withdrawal, and payment, are purely information and transactions processing in nature and are therefore natural applications of Internet mediation. Most of the big banks now provide Internet banking as a basic service, and some are encouraging their customers to do all of their banking, bill payment, and other transactions on the Web. One of the reasons for this is the low cost of the service. Another reason is that banks see the Internet as a means of providing many new kinds of services and generating new sources of revenue. Banks have had to move quickly because of the entry of new competitors called "virtual banks" into their business. Virtual banks are distinguished from traditional banks by the absence of local physical or "brick-and-mortar" outlets or a physical retail distribution system. Pure, "stand-alone" virtual banks, however, have had difficulty surviving in the tough competitive environment. So the trend recently has been to marry virtual banking and brick-and-mortar banking. This favours the big institutions. The big banks and brokerage companies are encouraging their clients to do business online because it will enable them to cut their costs and provide new services.

The Internet as a Securities Brokerage and Trading Medium

It is through developments in the securities brokerage and investment business where the Internet has gained so much popularity in the past five years. Every brokerage company today must have an online service to survive and grow. Many of the leading online brokerage companies have collaborated to form communications trading networks and are now vying to become an exchange in their own right. They want to challenge the NASDAQ and New York Stock Exchange. As with banking, the Internet has certain advantages when it comes to providing brokerage and investment services. These include instant, online access to market data and the trading networks, low-cost, and potentially universal accessibility and round-the-clock services. Every player in the financial services sector, not only banks and brokerage companies, but the securities and commodities exchanges have also moved or are in the process of moving to supply their services over the Internet.

The Internet as a Travel Reservations, Ticketing and Registration Medium

One of the oldest and most successful online computer applications is in the travel, accommodations, and tourism industry. The American Airlines' Sabre System came to enjoy a virtual monopoly on airline reservations in the United States until antitrust authorities had to curb its power. The Sabre System, however, was designed for travel agents. The Internet has been designed for individuals end users, thus making it possible for travellers to by-pass travel agents altogether. On line reservations services like Microsoft's Expedia and American Airlines' Travelocity enable individuals to check flight schedules, make reservations, and purchase tickets online. This new way of travel planning appears to have caught on. More than fifty percent of the customers of Southwestern Airlines now book their reservations and buy their tickets online. Five of the leading airlines in the United States launched their own online booking and ticketing system, called Orbiz, in June 2001. These systems enable individuals to search for the cheapest fare, book reservations, pay for their tickets online, and receive an e-ticket. They can also reserve a hotel room, rent a car, purchase tickets for the theatre, and reserve seats at a restaurant. All of the leading hotel and motel chains, car rental agencies, and theatres are now well represented on the Internet. The reason for this is convenience, accessibility, and low-cost.

Auction Markets on the Internet

Web auctions have become one of the most popular and lucrative applications on the Internet. There are a number of reasons for this. Like all online markets, there are no limits to the number of buyers and sellers who can participate in a Web auction. Web auctions also operate independently of geography, like all online markets, so buyers and sellers can be located in any part of the world. They also operate around the clock on a seven-days-a-week, twenty-four-hour-a-day basis, and there is effectively no limit to the kind of products that can be posted for sale. Buyers and sellers can also communicate with one another through e-mail.

Companies like e-Bay, by far the dominant Web auction company in the world, have been able to take advantage of these and other network effects that the Internet has made possible to gain a strategic advantage over their rivals. Once a company like e-Bay achieves a certain critical customer base, it is able to take advantage of these network effects that enable it to grow in a self-sustaining way until it becomes the dominant supplier in the industry. (The network effect works in an analogous manner to that of the telephone industry. AT&T was able to monopolize the business in the part of the twentieth century.)

A Mass Merchandising Medium

Merchandising has been perceived as another "killer application" from the time the Internet was in its infancy. However, the Internet has not turned out to be the superior mass merchandizing medium many expected—at least to date. There certainly are advantages to Internet-based merchandising. They include ready access to catalogues and brochures on demand. Customers can shop and buy at any time of the day independent of where they live and, they have considerable choice in where they buy. There are, however, disadvantages to online merchandising. Goods have to be shipped from the warehouse but this can increase the cost and the price of the merchandise. It also takes time to ship the goods. This may explain why Internet-based mass merchandisers have been unable to effectively compete with the big discount chains, especially on price. Nevertheless, the big retail chains are showing increasing interest in the Internet as a means of complementing their physical distribution system. In fact, Wal-Mart, Sears, J. C. Penney, The Gap, and most of the other big retail chains have launched Web-based businesses.

Infrastructure for Delivering Music and Entertainment Programs On-Demand

One of the greatest potentials of the Internet is as a broadcasting and entertainment medium for delivering radio, television, and multimedia programs to users on demand. Napster, a dot-com company that began operation in 1999, demonstrated that online sharing and distribution of music can be wildly popular with the masses. (Napster was closed down in 2001 by the major record companies for infringing on copyright laws.) Realizing the inevitability of online music distribution, the leading record companies have started their own fee-based service. AOL Time Warner, Bertelsmann, EMI Group, and RealNetworks have teamed up to launch their service called MusicNet. Sony Music Entertainment, Vivendi Universal, and MSN have launched a competing service called Pressplay. Five of the world's biggest movie studios, including Sony Pictures, Paramount Pictures, and Metro Goldwyn Mayer Inc., also announced in August 2001 a joint movie service that offers a broad selection of films to broadband users in the United States on demand. Music and movie distribution services could become highly lucrative with the spread of broadband Internet access.

An Educational Programming, Learning and Distribution System

Most of the same technologies that are being developed for delivering entertainment content can be and are also being used for delivering educational content. An additional feature of online education is interactivity, something which no other online medium provides. A growing number of universities are moving to provide distance learning over the Internet. Business schools have been among the leaders in this trend to providing online education. The Harvard Business School announced in July 2000 that it would put several of its basic courses online. In what was widely viewed as the strongest vote yet for online education, the Massachusetts Institute of Technology announced plans in April 2001 to make the materials for nearly all its courses freely available over the Internet in the next ten years.

These are just a few of some of the most promising applications and services that can be delivered over the Internet. The number and variety of applications is seemingly unlimited. This is why one can conclude that the Internet has potentially universal applications to all social, economic, and business activities.

The Internet and the Evolution of E-Markets

Some of our oldest and most sacred institutions could be sacrificed in the name of technology and economic efficiency as the transition to the Internet-based economy speeds ahead to its ultimate conclusion. One of these is the institution of the market. Economic textbooks define a market as a place where buyers and sellers meet to transact business. Throughout history, buyers and sellers have met in physical locations—in towns, villages, and cities—to transact business in a face-to-face manner. However, it is becoming increasingly common for people to transact their business over the Internet, without ever meeting face-to-face. It is already possible to perform most of the activities normally conducted in the marketplace in an electronic fashion from a single computer terminal in an office or a home located almost anywhere in the world. These include the usual information-related and communications-related activities, as well as payment, accounting, and settlement activities. In those cases where the deliverable is a digital commodity or a service, the Internet is capable of serving as the delivery or distribution system. In other cases, where the deliverable is a physical commodity, such as clothing or a computer, the Internet is capable of facilitating its delivery, by courier, for example.

Fully electronic markets already exist and are growing in number as more and more companies move to do business online, both with one another and with customers. Companies like Amazon.com sell just about everything over the Internet. Dell Computers has become the number-one seller of computers by selling all of its products over the Internet. General Electric buys from its suppliers electronically, through a competitive bidding process. Intel, IBM, and Microsoft are committed to selling as many of their products as possible over the Internet. All of the major brokerage companies have given their customers the option of buying and selling stock, bonds, and options over the Internet. By far the greatest potential (and most of the action to date) is in the business-to-business segment. Companies in every sector of the economy, from manufacturing, and oil and gas exploration, to the airlines and trucking industries have been forming consortia to create virtual markets where they can do much of their business electronically. The reasons are economic, that is, cost savings, and convenience.

Based on developments that are currently taking place and those that are expected to take place in the coming decade and beyond, it is realistic to conclude that one of the greatest legacies of the Internet will be the transformation of the market economy and the evolution of a fully electronic market economy. These electronic markets have come to be known by various names. Some have called them *cybermarkets*. Others have termed them *e-markets*. Still others refer to them as *virtual markets*. These terms are used interchangeably in this chapter. An e-market is defined as a market that is mediated by electronic computers and communications networks and the Internet in virtual space or cyberspace.

E-markets are online markets where buyers and sellers meet to do business and communicate, yet never actually see one another in person. They are markets where buyers and sellers transact business through screen-based activities, where money changes hands in its electronic equivalent between computers, from a screen and a keyboard. They are markets where digital commodities and digital services are sold as naturally as groceries are at the local supermarket. The following are some of the other outstanding characteristics of e-markets:

Very Low (Near-Zero) Transaction Costs

E-markets are distinguished by their extremely low (near-zero) transaction costs. Transaction costs include the costs of information search, retrieval, decision-making, and buying, selling, and payment. Very low transaction costs, in turn, translate into increased economic efficiency and an expansion in the variety of products that can be traded and exchanged. The greatest payoff by far is in the business-to-business segment and this is indeed where most of the investment is taking place.

Low (Near-Zero) Distribution Costs of Digital Goods and Services

E-markets are also characterized by very low, near-zero costs for distributing digital products and digital services. These include information, news, reports, multimedia entertainment, and educational content, as well as software products. The services include personal communications services, including multimedia E-mail, group conferencing services, and transactions services.

Information-Intensive Markets

E-markets are distinguished by their high information intensity. Information technology makes it possible to collect, produce, store, retrieve, and distribute massive volumes of information, accurately, instantaneously, and at low cost, and to make it accessible more conveniently and in a greater variety of forms to the individuals, organizations, and institutions that participate in these markets. More accessible, less expensive, and more accurate information, in turn, contributes to improve decision-making, reduced risk, a more efficient marketplace, and a more productive, fast-growing economy.

Potential Universal Accessibility

Another attribute of e-markets is that any person can access them wherever they are located as long as they have a computer, a modem, and access to a telephone line, a satellite or cable television, as well as an online account with an Internet service provider. Carriers are investing heavily in the new generation of wireless technology to enable customers to access e-markets from anywhere at anytime.

Interaction of Anonymous Market Actors Through Screen-Based Activity

Another characteristic of e-markets is that buyers and sellers are completely anonymous. They interact at a distance through screen-based trading systems. Buyers and sellers simply enter their bid and asking price respectively, and computer-based trading systems do the order matching and trading functions automatically.

Operating Independently of Location, Geography and Time Zones

E-markets operate increasingly independently of location and economic and political boundaries. They are 24–7 markets, that is, they operate around the clock, seven-days-a-week, twenty-four hours a day. E-markets are also global markets.

Potentially Unlimited Numbers of Buyers and Sellers

Unlike traditional markets, there are no limits to the number of buyers and sellers that can participate in an electronic or virtual marketplace. Electronic markets can accommodate an almost unlimited number of participants.

E-Markets Are Near-Perfect Markets

E-markets are possibly the nearest we can come to the textbook definition of perfect markets. Near-prefect markets are characterized by near-perfect information, near-zero transactions costs, and the absence of barriers to entry. Under the near-perfect market model, there are many sellers, supplying a complete range of differentiated products and various prices, and many buyers vying for these products.

In the coming decades, the Internet will enable us to see how close we can come to this textbook definition of perfect markets, and, in doing so, will allow us to determine what the consequences will be. If the experience of the online brokerage industry is any indication, e-markets will sometime become explosively turbulent.

Evolution of a Network-Centric Economy

All of this evidence suggests that the Internet will continue to spread throughout all private- and public-sector organizations in the coming decade and will connect them into an interactive and interacting entity. It will evolve into an all-encompassing, all-powerful, interactive information and communications medium, and a transactions and trading medium that will come to dominate commerce, trade, politics, and culture in the decades ahead. All businesses and public-sector organizations, and all households, all individuals, and all markets will come to depend on this infrastructure for conducting their day-to-day activities.

This dependency of all organizations on networks and the Internet in particular represents a new milestone in the evolution of economic society. It is giving birth to a new organizational paradigm, that is coming to be known as the *network-centric organization* and which will grow to dominate society over the course of the coming millennium. Network-centric organizations are those that depend on the Internet infrastructure for their efficient operation and their growth and profitability. They include not only individual businesses, but supply chains, markets, and entire economic systems and organizational entities that will come into being in the future. Network-centric organizations are unique in the sense that their social and economic value is derived from the functionality (and low-cost) of their network infrastructures, the activities that can be conducted over them, the resources that can be accessed through these infrastructures, and the services that can be supplied over them. These resources include information, knowledge, software, money, capital, and specialized services, as well as people and other organizations connected to them and accessible through them. There may be no limit to the kinds of activities that can be conducted over these network infrastructures, the kinds of services that will be provided over them, or the kinds of business that will be transacted in this evolving network-centric marketplace.

New Frontiers of Convergence

The Internet has given new meaning and new significance to the concept of convergence. From a technological perspective, convergence refers to the capabilities of the new network infrastructures to provide an almost unlimited variety of services. These capabilities include the carriage of various kinds of information and communications services, the storage and distribution of various kinds of content, the processing of various kinds of financial transactions, and the trading and exchange of goods and services. From a business and economic perspective, convergence refers to the capabilities of companies to provide a much wider variety of services that were formerly supplied separately, by different companies in various industries or sectors. The industries involved in this phenomenon of Internet convergence include telecommunications, cable television, radio and television broadcasting, entertainment, publishing, and information and banking and financial services. The Internet is being engineered to deliver all of these services and many more. One of the consequences is the erosion and possibly the complete elimination of the boundaries—functional, geographical, and other kinds of boundaries—that separated non-competing industries and sectors of the economy. This process of convergence is expected to dominate market developments, corporate strategies, public policies, and the evolution of economic systems in the coming decade and beyond.

The Significance of Convergence and the Full-Service Supply Strategy

Convergence is significant in the context of corporate strategy and public policy because it can bestow strategic competitive advantages on companies that supply a complete range of services tailored to meet the needs of individual customers. The strategy of developing a full complement of services to meet the needs of all customer classes has come to be known as the full-service supplier strategy (alternatively, the one-stop-shopping or supermarket strategy). The following are some of the key elements of the full-service supply strategy:

Full Service Supply Capability

The strategy calls for the supply company to provide a complete range of services to meet the customized needs of each class of customer. The customer base can include low-, medium- or high-income households, small, medium, and large companies, and entire sectors. The range of services provided can include distribution and communications services, information and entertainment, and banking and financial services.

Branding

One of the prerequisites to success in the economy of converging industries is a nationally and internationally recognized brand name.

Branding has always been one of the most important elements to business strategy especially to gaining market share and dominating markets but it is very costly. Corporate size is therefore very important. Advertising is one of the biggest items in the budgets of the leading telecom, broadcasting, and media companies as it is for manufacturing and banking companies. However, there are important linkages between branding and economies of scale and scope. The greater the scope of services supplied the more effective advertising and branding strategies can be. The Internet itself has become a critical element in the branding strategies of most companies, but especially those involved in the convergence game. This is one additional reason why telecommunications, broadcasting, publishing, entertainment, and banking companies have had to embrace the Internet.

Economies of Scale and Scope

The convergence strategy leverages on the capability of the supply company to take advantage of economies of scale and scope in its internal networks (as well as in public infrastructures) and its internal operations to deliver all of the relevant services at a cost that is lower than that of its competitors.

Bundled Services

The full-service strategy also leverages on the ability of the supply company to exploit the low-cost processing and service delivery capabilities of its distribution systems to bundle all of the services into a single package and to price these below the prices that competitors can offer individually. This enables the supply company to develop a system of pricing incentives that targets all classes of customers and encourages them to purchase entire packages of services.

Mergers and Acquisitions

The principal means of pursuing the full-service or one-stop-shopping strategy is through mergers and acquisition of companies in both competing and non-competing industries. The purpose of mergers and acquisitions is to achieve economies of scale and scope in their network operations and distribution systems. The alternative—that is, to expand by developing new services from within—is considered to be too costly and too time consuming to be effective. Mergers and acquisitions do have certain advantages, despite their record of failures. They can maximize time to market, which many companies consider essential to achieving the objectives of the convergence strategy.

Four Axes of Convergence

There are at least four identifiable axes of convergence. The first focuses on network infrastructure and services. The second focuses on content and carriage. The focal point of the third is electronic commerce. The focal point of the fourth is banking and financial services. The following is a brief description of each:

Network Infrastructure and Services

Infrastructure constitutes the first dimension of convergence. The objective of strategy here is control over the communications and distribution infrastructure and the services that can be delivered over it. Control in this case is exercised through the ownership of high-capacity, broadband, wire-line, and wireless network infrastructures, including high-speed Internet access. The objective here is to provide a complete package of communications and related services to residential and business customers. The purpose of AT&T's takeover of TCI, for example, was to provide AT&T with broadband access to the residential marketplace for the purpose of providing local telephone, television, and high-speed Internet services. The purpose of MCIWorldCom's proposed takeover of Sprint was to gain control of Sprint's wireless delivery system. Broadband Internet access via telephony, cable, and satellite along with broadband wireless services are currently on the leading edge of this convergence of infrastructure.

Content, Packaging and Distribution

The second focus of convergence is on content and carriage or distribution. Control in this case is exercised through the ownership of the capabilities to gather or produce news, information, and audio, video, entertainment, and education content to feed the various growing bandwidth and distribution channels. One of the prerequisites to success is the ownership of Internet portals and the capability to deliver audio, video, and multimedia content over interactive, broadband networks. There is a view in the industry that companies with strong Internet holdings are a natural match for traditional companies whose strength is in content and carriage. As discussed in the following, the purpose of AOL's takeover of Time Warner was to combine AOL's Internet holdings with Time Warner's content and distribution holdings.

Electronic Commerce

The third focus of convergence is e-commerce, that is, the provision of the entire range of related services over the Internet. This includes the buying and selling of goods and an entire suite of business services to businesses and households. This biggest segment by far is the business-to-business segment but the business-to-consumer segment is also very important to all of the suppliers. Here again, control is exercised through the ownership of leading Web commerce portals and the marketing, advertising, sales, and distribution of goods and services over it. The services marketed include information, online shopping, and personal productivity and decision-making applications, as well as billing and payment services, auctions, travel reservation services, and so on. Telecom companies, banks, and postal services organizations view e-commerce as a natural extension of their services. However, so do companies in other industries and sectors. One of the objectives of the AOL Time Warner deal was to sell Time Warner's content over the Internet.

Banking and Financial Services

The fourth focal point of convergence is the provision of a complete suite of financial services to both businesses and consumers. Again, control is exercised through the ownership of Internet portals, electronic banking networks, and systems to provide a complete range of online banking, investment, insurance, and brokerage services. This sector of economic activity is in the early stage of convergence. Most of the big banks have moved aggressively into virtual banking. Both Bank of America and Citigroup have developed their own virtual banking subsidiaries to complement their physical distribution systems. Most of the leading brokerage and investment companies have either developed or are in the process of developing their own online brokerage, investment, and banking subsidiaries (primarily through mergers and acquisitions). Another target of their strategies is business-to-business commerce.

Leading companies in all of these sectors are pursuing strategies to enable them to become the dominant player in their own sector. Some have begun to cross international, industrial and sectoral boundaries in search of growth, profit, and market domination.

Convergence Strategies

Convergence has been behind most of the merger boom in the telecommunications, broadcasting, and entertainment industries in recent years.

This boom is expected to accelerate in the coming decade as it spreads to other sectors, notably the banking and financial services sector. Convergence is also rapidly becoming a worldwide phenomenon. It is expected to dramatically change the structure of the entire marketplace and the economy in the coming decade.

The following is a brief description of the convergence strategies of a few of the leading companies in each of four areas:

AT&T's All-in-One Convergence Strategy

AT&T knows the convergence game better than any other company. The company has been pursuing a convergence strategy since the early days of the computer and communications revolution back in the sixties and seventies. AT&T is still the biggest supplier of local, long-distance, and international telecommunications services in the United States. It is a major player in wireless communications services. (AT&T acquired McCaw Cellular in 1993.) AT&T's WorldNet Service subsidary is one of the leading Internet service providers in the United States, serving more than 1.5 million customers. AT&T's most ambitious play to date, however, has been in the cable television and media sector.

In 1998, AT&T announced the $55 billion acquisition of TCI in the cable television industry, giving the company access to 14.5 million subscribers nationwide. In 1999, it announced the $62 billion acquisition of MediaOne Group Inc. These two acquisitions made AT&T the biggest cable television company in the United States, with more than 25 percent of the total customers. AT&T is also a majority owner of Excite@Home in broadband access. MediaOne Group owns 25 percent of Time Warner Entertainment. Another AT&T subsidiary, Liberty Media, owns broadcasting businesses in the United States, Europe, and Asia and is intent on expand there. These acquisitions make AT&T one of the leaders in the convergence of voice services, broadband distribution, and high-speed Internet services, as well as television broadcasting and content production. Other telecom companies are expected to follow AT&T's lead.

AOL Time Warner's Convergence Strategy

America Online and Time Warner have created what many believe could become a model of how the Internet will redefine the corporate and economic landscape in the new millennium. The $183 billion takeover, announced on 10 January 2000 by America Online, was billed as the biggest corporate takeover in history. The media called it a merger of a stodgy, old-world company and a new, fast moving, high-growth New Economy company, making it a model for the twenty-first century. The purpose of the deal was to take advantage of the synergies between the content and the distribution capabilities that were being created by the high-speed, interactive, multimedia capabilities of the Internet.

Time Warner's traditional strengths have been in content production, cable television, and television broadcasting. Its subsidiary, Time Warner Entertainment, owns Home Box Office, Warner Brothers Studios, and television channels TBS, TNT and CNN. Time Warner Cable is the second-biggest cable television company in the United States, with 20 percent of subscribers. (The company was the number one supplier before AT&T's takeover of TCI.) AOL's strengths are in Internet access and portal services. It is by far the biggest Internet services company in the world. On 24 February 2000, Time Warner followed up with an announcement that it was acquiring EMI, one of the top music publishers in the world, for $20 billion. This acquisition makes EMI-Time Warner the biggest supplier of music content in the world.

Executives at AOL and Time Warner explained at the time of their merger that the rationale behind the strategy is to unlock multi-billion dollar synergies that will translate into cost savings and revenue generation for years to come. They explained that the two companies together would reach over one hundred million households. Each was able to cross-sell the other's products and advertise on the other's distribution system. AOL, for example, is able to sell music from EMI and Time Warner on its Web portal. Time Warner is also strong in magazine publishing. It publishes *Sports Illustrated, Time,* and *People* magazines. This, too, opens up new opportunities for cross-selling and advertising for both companies. Both companies are also able to provide telephone services over their distribution systems. They are also able to provide online shopping, bill payment, and e-commerce services through AOL's portal. The two companies have are developing a television set-top box with Internet capabilities.

Bell Canada Enterprises

The AOL Time Warner deal has established a model that other companies are expected to emulate. One of the first to do so has been Bell Canada Enterprises (BCE). Bell Canada, BCE's telephone subsidiary, is the dominant supplier of local, long-distance, and international telephone services in Canada. BCE is also strong in cellular telephone services throughout Canada. It is also majority owner of Telesat Canada, Canada's national satellite services company, which provides services to businesses and cable and television broadcasting companies. In addition, BCE owns Sympatico, Canada's leading Internet services portal company and access provider and its subsidary, BCE Emergis, is one of Canada's leading e-commerce companies. In February and March 2000, BCE made two big moves to model itself on AOL Time Warner. It agreed to purchase Teleglobe Inc., which owns a cable network spanning both the Atlantic and the Pacific Oceans. Teleglobe also offers services in the United States. Weeks later, BCE announced the takeover of CTV, Canada's largest private broadcaster.

In September 2000, the company announced an agreement to purchase most of the online assets in Canada of Thompson Corporation, which owns the Toronto *Globe and Mail,* Canada's leading business newspaper. (Thompson Corporation owns one of the largest newspaper chains in the world.) The *Globe and Mail* also operates a number of successful electronic businesses. BCE has merged these operations with CTV. BCE's chief competitor, Rogers Communications, is Canada's biggest cable television company. It, too, is pursuing a convergence strategy similar to BCE's.

Citigroup's All-in-One Convergence Strategy

Convergence is also taking place throughout the banking and financial services sector. One of the leaders is Citigroup, which provides a complete range of financial products and services to over one hundred million consumers, corporations, governments, and institutions in one hundred countries. Citigroup was formed in 1998 with the merger of Citicorp and Travelers Group. Through its various subsidiaries that include Citibank, Salomon Smith Barney, CitiFinancial, and Primerica, Citigroup provides consumer banking and credit services, corporate and investment banking services as well as insurance, securities brokerage, and asset management services. The company has set its sights on the Internet as a new frontier to conquer.

In March 2000, Citigroup announced the formation of a full-services virtual bank called CCiti f/i. The new subsidiary enables customers to perform daily banking and investing activities over the Internet. Clients can transfer funds, pay bills, place stock orders, and customize financial reports. Other services include certificates of deposits, insured money market accounts, free online bill payment, and ATM services. Citigroup has moved into the business-to-business commerce market. The company's e-commerce subsidiary, e-Citi., is building an online marketplace for corporate buyers in collaborating with Commerce One. The company's procurement portal hosts vendor catalogues and provides such services as online currency exchange rates, financing, digital certificates and electronic bill payment. Citigroup also offers an online person-to-person payments system called c2it, which could become as valuable as the company's vast credit card operations.

Other Company Strategies in Cyberspace

The following are several other examples of the potential of the Internet to drive corporate strategy and industrial and economic change in the coming decade:

In February 2000, Reuters PLC, one of the world's leading news and information service organizations, announced a bold strategy to transform itself into an Internet-centric services company. It announced plans to bypass many of its big retail customers that resell its information products and begin selling directly to end-users over the Internet. In the same month, Thompson Corporation announced that it was selling off all of its newspapers (with the exception of the Toronto's *Globe and Mail*) to concentrate on its electronic information services business.

On 25 February 2000, General Motors Corp., Ford Motor Corp., and DaimlerChrysler AG announced a joint venture to create an electronic commerce services company that will combine the annual $240 billion purchasing operations of the three companies. The plan is to create an Internet-centric platform that will link tens of thousands of suppliers, partners, and customers worldwide into a single marketplace. The advantages they cited included convenience, cost savings, improved services, and heightened customer satisfaction. GM and Ford are also working on their own to reinvent themselves into built-to-order car makers by enabling consumers to go online, design their own cars and have them delivered to their homes in days.

Observations on the Future

If the technological and economic trends identified above continue as expected, all organizations and the entire economic system will become densely interconnected by a variety of networks to create an online and interactive system of organizations. This interconnected economy will be one in which businesses, governments, households, and individuals inter-act online with one another and with fully automated server and trading and transactions systems, in real-time, to communicate, inform, make decisions, and do business. Real-time economic interaction among busi-ness and eventually with consumers will become the modus operandi of the millennium economy.

The dramatic decline in transactions costs will continue to lower the cost differentials between market-based and non-market-based activities. This will make it possible to produce, market, and deliver an ever widen-ing variety of products and services that were previously impossible or too costly to produce or supply. In such cases, the effect will be to enhance market-based activities. In other cases, the opposite will occur. That is, it will become cost-effective for businesses to internalize and integrate for-mer market-based activities and provide these within and to customers.

One of the consequences will be the emergence of fully integrated sup-ply chains that will come to dominate the network economy of the future. These supply chains will interconnect retailers, producers, suppliers, and primary producers into a single, interactive production supra-organiza-tion. Integrated supply chains will become the dominant feature in indus-tries extending from automobile, aircraft and electronic equipment manufacturing to clothing, pharmaceutical and chemical production. These supply chains will grow to become global entities in their own right and they will transform the structure of entire sectors worldwide. There is a distinct possibility that two or three of these global supply chains could emerge to dominate entire industries and national and global markets.

The networked economy will also redefine the nature and scope of com-petition in many industries. It will erode previous sources of strength and force companies to seek out new sources of strategic competitive advan-tage. This will require greater emphasis on managing strategic relationships and partnerships among suppliers, distributors as well as direct competi-tors. Corporations will also be forced to seek out and gain new sources of economies of scale and scope in their operations through such partnerships and through specialization and the bundling of products and services.

Competition in the network economy will force companies to increas-ingly focus on their core competencies but it will also force them to out-source more non-core activities to remain competitive. Outsourcing will become more common in many industries as companies find it economi-cally attractive to contract out entire segments of non-core activities to other companies that specialize in these new kinds of activities and can provide them more efficiently.

The rise of the Internet economy will continue to erode barriers to entry in industries ranging from publishing and information and communications services to advertising, travel, entertainment, and banking and financial services. As incumbent businesses embrace the new infrastructure and integrate it operationally and strategically into their business model, however, the effect could be to erect new kinds of barriers to entry.

One of the inevitable consequences of the evolution of the Internet economy is "disintermediation," that is, the bypass (or complete elimination) of traditional intermediaries in the production and distribution chain. Some of the groups already affected include travel agents, sales agents, bank clerks, and brokers. At the same time, the Internet is creating new kinds of intermediaries. In fact, the Internet revolution is all about re-intermediation of business activity but in different ways and by new kinds of intermediaries. Almost every online company constitutes an intermediary of one kind or another.

By its very nature, the electronic mediation of business, government, and household activities favours horizontal relationships over hierarchies. That is, it favours the interaction among equals, among peer groups, among producers and suppliers and suppliers and their customers. One of the long-term consequences will likely be a relative decline in vertically integrated structures and the growth of horizontal, "peer-to-peer" or "market-type" relationships.

The evolution of the online, real-time, interactive economy will continue to enhance productivity and the efficiency of businesses in all sectors of the economy. It will enhance consumer choice by bestowing greater information and communications power on individuals. To this extent, it will empower consumers and enhance consumer sovereignty. To the extent that information power will also serve to curb the ability of companies to control prices, the effect will be to reduce inflationary pressures.

At the same time, the evidence presented above, in the communications, media, and banking and financial services sectors, for example, appears to corroborate the view the Internet also favours corporate size and corporate concentration. It appears to be bestowing enormous economic power on a few large corporations at the expense of smaller and medium-size corporations. In fact, information technology and the Internet could eventually make it possible for a handful of corporations in each industry to dominate world markets.

The "dematerialization process" will continue to reduce the material composition of economic activity. This will be accompanied by the continued growth in knowledge-based, information and communications-based, and services-based activities. The implication is that a growing proportion of economic and productivity growth (along with the growth of wealth, value, welfare, and employment) in the coming decades will become derived from the growth of production and distribution of information, knowledge, software, and digital commodities and network-based services.

The information and communications revolutions (and the complex of forces described in the beginning of this chapter) will continue to stimulate invention and accelerate the production and distribution of knowledge as it has in the past. Computer modelling and simulation tools will magnify the ability of scientists to study, analyse, and better understand some of the most complex systems and processes in nature. Information and communications networks will enhance the enable of scientists and engineers to collaborate and share information and knowledge resources with colleagues throughout the world. In this sense, the technology revolution will continue to accelerate the process of discovery and enabled mankind to push back the frontiers in every field of science. The Human Genome Project is a good example of how information and communications technologies have accelerated scientific developments in recent decades. The purpose of the project (initiated in 1990) is to identify and study the 30,000 or more genes that make up the human DNA. Among its many other objectives is the development of tools that will enable scientist to create designer drugs and designer genes to fight some of the most deadly human diseases. Without the advanced information technology and communications tools, the project would have taken decades instead of the thirteen years to complete. In this sense, the information revolution has made a vital contribution to launching the biotech revolution and advancing the genetic engineering age.

Some Policy Implications

The technology revolution and the Internet will continue to change society in the coming decades. It will present both threats and opportunities for businesses, governments, and individuals. The challenge will therefore be to embrace change because change is inevitable. For governments, the challenge is to develop policies and regulations that facilitate rather than impede change and enable all members of society to share the benefits. Below are some areas where policy research and policy action are required.

Infrastructure Policies

One of the most important responsibilities of national governments in the networking age continues to be the timely development of a modern, efficient broadband infrastructure that meets the needs of businesses, governments, public institutions, households, and individuals. This infrastructure must incorporate open systems standards for switching, transmission, and interconnection. A viable infrastructure policy should also foster equitable access by disadvantaged groups in society and by those living in underserved rural or remote areas of the country. This will help to stem any threat arising from the possible creation of a digital divide.

Content Policies and Regulations

Content will drive the evolution of networks in the future. This will require government action on at least two fronts. First, policies and programs are necessary to ensure that certain kinds of content are made available online to the public in a timely manner. Governments must seize the opportunities at hand to use the information infrastructures to improve the full range of services they provide to the public. This includes its traditional regulatory and licensing activities. Many governments around the world have developed national programs designed to foster the digitization of library and heritage collections and making these accessible online. The second area where government action is required is the development of effective policies and regulations that ensure that the online content serves the public interest. This will require extending existing laws and developing new laws that prohibit the use of the network for the purposes of engaging in criminal activities including fraud as well as slander and discrimination.

Copyright Policy

Copyright laws must continue to be updated and strengthened to protect the rights of the creators of intellectual property in the networking age. Composers, authors, writers, artists, and designers worldwide must be adequately compensated for their work and their contributions to society. This is even more important in the networking age because digital content can be easily accessed online and copied and distributed anywhere in the world.

E-Commerce Policies and Regulations

Electronic commerce is also expected to drive the evolution of the Internet and the network economy in the millennium. This too will require policies that clarify the rights and obligations of buyers and sellers of online goods and services. An obvious prerequisite to the evolution of an online marketplace is a low-cost, secure, and easy-to-use online payments system. Governments must take the lead in developing such a payment system and ensuring that it is efficient, reliable, secure, and accessible to everyone. Governments must also ensure that taxation policies, laws, and regulations are updated for the networking age. This will require harmonization of existing laws and regulation and ensuring the efficient and non-discriminatory treatment of online transactions.

Network Security and Personal Privacy

As society becomes increasingly dependent on networks and network infrastructures, so too will it become increasingly vulnerable to those elements in societies around the world who seek to use the network for malicious and criminal purposes. This includes the unauthorized and illegal access to corporate databases and personal files of information. National policies are therefore required to protect the security and integrity of the national and global information and communications infrastructure. Laws and regulations must also ensure the privacy and security of files of personal information and serve and protect national security.

Administration of Boundary Problems

One of the great challenges of governments will be the effective regulatory administration of boundary problems. Technology is eroding or eliminating many of the industrial and geographical boundaries that served to define markets in the past. It is also eroding many of the regulatory boundaries that were designed to curb corporate power and protect the public interest. The challenge for governments is to update and strengthen these policies and regulations and create new ones that serve the public interest in the networking age. Among the greatest challenges will be resolving the regulatory and boundary problems in the banking and financial services and information and communications sectors.

Transborder Policies

One of the consequences of the evolution of the network economy will be the continued rapid growth of information, communications, and trade and financial transactions across international borders. Governments must ensure that ensure that these digital flows conform to domestic and international policies, laws, and regulations. This will require some means of monitoring these flows of information, communications, and commerce. It will also require agreements among nations to harmonize national laws and regulations.

Antitrust Policy

Mergers and acquisitions are expected to continue to drive national and global economic and industrial developments in the coming decades as entire sectors embrace the Internet as a vital way of doing certain kinds of business. Left to the unfettered forces, the result could be that key sectors of the world economy, including information, communications, and banking and financial services, will become dominated by perhaps two or three global supra-corporations. It is unlikely that such an outcome will be in the public interest. This suggests we may need a new kind of global institution, possibly on the model of the World Trade Organization to exercise regulatory oversight at the global level to ensure that mergers and acquisitions are in the public interest.

Control and Stability in Global Electronic Markets

Convergence and the globalisation of the financial services sector also pose significant challenges for governments. The Internet has reduced the transactions costs of communicating and doing business by at least an order of magnitude and it has made it possible for millions of people to access financial markets directly. Trading volumes on the securities and futures exchanges have soared as a result. This trend is expected to continue as the networks grow and expand to interconnect more businesses and people in more nations. At the same time, these same electronic networks have integrated world financial markets to the point that they have effectively become one. However, this "democratization" of the world financial markets has turned them into veritable casinos ruled by day traders, hedge players, and gambling addicts. The result has been unprecedented speculation and volatility that have at times threatened the stability of the global financial system. A serious problem in one part of the world automatically becomes a world problem. The entire national and global banking systems are evolving into a single system.

The world clearly needs new kinds of controls to stabilize world financial markets. It may be that voluntary limits (or self-regulation) of some kind will be sufficient to curb excessive speculation and volatility in global markets. It may become necessary to increase the cost of currency and futures trading by artificial means as some have argued to reduce speculation and dampen shock waves to the system. It may be that we will eventually come to realize that we need to exercise greater regulatory oversight to control and stabilize world financial markets. This many require a new kind of global financial institution. Maybe the world is not yet ready to cope with free-wheeling, frictionless, global markets.

Balancing Democracy and the Rights and Freedoms of Individuals

The evolution of the broadband, multimedia network age will continue to strengthen democracies around the world as the various information and communications revolutions have in the past. The evolving multi-media infrastructure is giving both legitimate and illegitimate groups in society the means to organize themselves on a global scale that was never before possible. On the one hand, it is giving legitimate working groups in business, professional, and quasi-governmental organizations on various continents the means to collaborate for the legitimate purposes. On another hand, this same infrastructure is providing illegitimate groups engaged in a variety of criminal activities extending from fraud, drug smuggling, and promoting anarchy to trafficking in drugs and child pornography the means to collaborate and organize themselves to carry out their activities on a global scale. This suggests the need for certain kinds of network surveillance activities to guard against the use of our global information highways for illegal and illegitimate purposes. Maybe we will have to give up certain rights and freedoms in return for public safety and security.

Standards for Measuring Value, Wealth, Performance and Economic Growth

One of the arguments of this chapter is that the ongoing information and communications revolutions are precipitating a profound social and economic transformation. At the core of this process is a transformation from a materials-intensive and energy-intensive economy to an information-intensive, communications-intensive, software-intensive network-based, and knowledge-based services economy. One of the consequences is that many of our basic business and economic concepts are becoming obsolete. Most of the metrics we use today to measure corporate, industrial, and economic performance have been developed over the centuries for an industrial economy based on the intensive use of raw materials, manpower, and energy and the production of equipment, machines, and physical products. The old measures of economic activity and economic performance are becoming less relevant in the new age in which a growing proportion of commerce and of social and economic activity is mediated by intelligent machines and multimedia networks.

The millennium economy will require the development of new concepts and new metrics for measuring social and economic progress and corporate and economic performance. It will require the synthesis of new concepts for measuring value, wealth, and output and of productivity and performance. This will require fundamental changes in accounting standards including the system of national accounts. The new accounting standards must be capable of measuring what are referred to as intangibles. They include the stocks of knowledge and of human and knowledge capital. They also include stocks of intelligent machines and infrastructures. However, they must also include the information content, digital commodities, and communications and transactions that flow through the global network infrastructures. Governments must take the lead in the process of redesigning and reinventing (and enforcing) these and many other kinds of measurement and accounting standards.

Concluding Remarks

One of the unique features of capitalism in the millennium will be the emergence of network-based organizations and the network-based services economy. The information highways being build today will grow and evolve in the coming decades to connect businesses, homes, governments, and individuals into a dense mesh of communications linkages. This system of networks will become a defining feature of economic organization as all economic actors become interconnect into a single, online global system, operating in real-time. The network age will stimulate economic growth and productivity and create new sources of wealth. It will also pose new challenges for businesses, governments, and individuals. For governments, the challenge will be to develop the appropriate policies and regulations that will foster the development of this new social and economic age and ensure that it benefits all classes of society nationally and worldwide. This will require a revolution in institution building. It will require governments to design and create new kinds of institutions at both the national and global levels to serve this purpose. This is one of the great challenges that governments will face in the millennium.

Postscript

The process of economic evolution and transformation is seldom a smooth one. No change in recent decades has been more dramatic than the technology boom that began in the early nineties and the bust that followed it in 2000 and beyond. The stock market bubble along with subsequent developments have exposed serious flaws in our policy-making and regulatory institutions that need to be corrected as we move forward.

The bubble in technology stocks was caused by many factors that reinforced one another. The Y2K problem: The explosive growth of the Internet: The race to buy virtual real estate and build dot-com companies on the Internet: All of these called for massive investments in technology and communications infrastructures. But the bubble was also caused by massive speculation and "irrational exuberance." The rise of a new breed of online investor and of the day-trader exacerbated the frenzy. All of these factors resulted in a massive over-investment and excessive capacity in every segment of the high technology sector, from microchips and computer and telecom equipment to telecom and Internet infrastructures. The result has been a massive economic downturn that has affected the growth and profitability of every company in the technology and telecom sectors. This downturn has made many of the leading companies in these sectors vulnerable to the very high debt loads they have been carrying.

The technology bust has left many small, new innovative entrants in many of the most promising segments of the high technology sector without sufficient revenues to finance their operations. It has even jeopardized some of the biggest blue-chip companies, especially in the telecom sector, whose fortunes have never been questioned. Global Crossing filed for protection in early 2002 and the future of Level 3 Communications, Williams Communications, and 360 Networks is in question. Several of the long distance carriers in the United States are carrying so much debt that their credit ratings are being downgraded to near-junk status. AT&T is being forced to unravel its cable strategy. The stock prices of Lucent Technologies and Nortel Networks have plummeted to a fraction of their highs in 2000.

The collapse of the technology boom has triggered a massive merger and consolidation extending across entire sectors as big companies buy out small competitors and as incumbents acquire new entrants at fire sale prices. The real threat is that if the telecom bust persists, it could jeopardize the success of the Telecommunications Act of 1996. The Act was intended to create a thriving competitive industry by boosting the fortunes of new, innovative entrants into the market. Unless the fortune of these smaller companies is reversed, the telecom sector (along with the Internet) could once again become dominated by regional monopolies.

The bubble in technology stocks and subsequent meltdown has also exposed serious flaws in our systems of regulation and policy-making. It has exposed the ability of senior corporate executives to manipulate the system through insider trading for their own personal advantage at the expense of employees and small investors. It has also exposed the faulty accounting practices of many of the most respected technology and non-technology companies. It has exposed the ability of accountants and auditors to manipulate information to their own advantage and of their clients. Finally, it has exposed conflict of interest and biased reporting among investment analysts and the brokerage, accounting, auditing, and consulting arms of many leading firms.

Resolving these and other problems identified in this chapter represents just some of the challenges policy-making and regulatory institutions are facing as we enter the millennium.

Emerging Internet Oligopolies: A Political Economy Analysis

MICHELE JAVARY AND ROBIN MANSELL

Introduction

Public utility regulation has been charged historically with protecting the public's interest. The behavior of monopoly or dominant incumbent suppliers in the telecommunication industry that may be consistent with the public interest has long been subject to controversy, as has the issue of whether public intervention is needed to protect that interest. Viewpoints have varied between two poles. On the one hand, a "light touch" regulatory apparatus has been championed to promote the free play of market forces. On the other, regulatory intervention has been deemed essential to provide the discipline of the market and to protect the public interest in the development of infrastructure and services (Horowitz 1989). Debates about the need for regulatory oversight and the impact of regulatory intervention in the United States have been continuous and often acrimonious.[1] With the establishment of a formal regulatory apparatus in the United Kingdom in 1984 there have been varying degrees of controversy over how best to ensure that the behavior of incumbent firms and new entrants in the telecommunication industry is consistent with the public interest.[2]

The issues of whether, and in what form, regulation should be applied to the rapidly changing telecommunication infrastructure and related information and communication service markets are now considerably more complicated than they were in the monopoly era of telecommunication. From the mid-1990s in the United States and Europe the spread of the Internet as a platform for service applications for citizens and for the commercial sector has been challenging the incumbency of traditional telecommunication operators. Internet developments have provoked questions about whether new forms of regulation are needed to ensure that the evolutionary forces in the market for Internet access and related

162

services produce outcomes that are in line with the public's interest in high-quality, low-cost services. Is there a case for regulatory intervention to protect the public's interest in the deployment of services that use the Internet as a platform?

For some analysts, such as Jason Oxman of the Federal Communications Commission (FCC) Office of Plans and Policy, the answer to this question is negative.[3]

> Fundamental lessons learned from the Commission's thirty year deregulatory approach towards data networks include: do not automatically impose legacy regulations on new technologies; when Internet-based services replace traditional legacy services begin to deregulate the old instead of regulate the new; and maintain a watchful eye to ensure that anticompetitive behavior does not develop, do not regulate based on the perception of potential future bottlenecks, and be careful that any regulatory responses are the minimum necessary and outweigh the costs of regulation. (Oxman 1999, 3)

Given the nascent development of electronic commerce and the relatively immature Internet service provider (ISP) market, Oxman argues that there is no basis for regulatory intervention at present because of the large number of entrants into this market. In contrast, François Bar et al. (1999, 3) argue that the FCC's support for "unregulation" of Internet developments "constitutes a fundamental policy reversal." They suggest that sustained policy intervention is needed to encourage the continuing evolution of an open network infrastructure and services.

As an observer of successive generations of technological innovation and their deployment in the telecommunication industry, Harry M. Trebing has brought substantial evidence to bear on the implications of changes in the structure of the industry, and the performance and conduct of both incumbents and new entrants. He has detected flaws in the "de" or "un" regulationists' reliance upon market forces by demonstrating empirically that market developments, in many instances, have been inconsistent with an adequate standard of protection of the public interest. With William G. Shepherd (1995), he has argued that market entry is rarely free and without limit and he has demonstrated that new entrants are often unable to establish themselves without fear of retaliatory moves on the part of incumbents (Trebing 1995, 404). He has suggested that, "the network is a form of commons and the societal goal should be to permit the greater participation of everyone in this facility . . . The danger is that the discretion inherent in tight oligopoly will make the design and planning of the network more responsive to the monopsony power of the large user, or to the strategy of the incumbent firm as it seeks to enter new markets" (Trebing 1995, 409). A principal consideration in determining the need for regulation and other forms of policy intervention is whether the benefits and opportunities associated with technological innovation are likely to "be distributed on the basis of carrier discretion" (Trebing and Estabrooks 1995, 543). Insofar as this is so, then the outcome "undoubtedly will be influenced more strongly by relative demand elasticities than by social values" (Trebing and Estabrooks 1995, 543).

In the face of a new generation of technological innovations embodied within the Internet, as well as its rapid diffusion, there is a growing need for independent assessment of the "proper role for government surveillance and intervention" (Trebing and Wilsey 1993, 274). We begin our assessment with the observation that competition is best understood as an evolving process, rather than as an end-state.[4] Thus, firms should not be regarded as "powerless economic agents adjusting passively to parametrically given techniques, prices and quantities but as agents actively seeking the reorganization of production and market activities in the context of rivals' possible reactions" (Corsi 1991, 124). The competitive process that is engaging the firms in the ISP market may give rise to positive economic and social outcomes. Alternatively, it may contribute to the persistence of "monopoly focal points" and the emergence of an intensely oligopolistic industry structure (Trebing 1998, 62). This is the central issue that is addressed in this chapter.

The phenomenal growth of companies providing access to the Internet in the United States and in the United Kingdom has suggested to some observers that rapid technological change and innovation are producing Schumpeterian (1961) "creative gales of destruction" that have sufficient strength to eliminate monopoly focal points, thereby removing any grounds for regulatory intervention to protect the public interest. Trebing has treated such conclusions with considerable suspicion. In fact, the dynamics of technological change may even strengthen the market power for key players in the industry (Trebing 1998, 61). Our analysis of the dynamics of the Internet industry focuses on the implications of the interplay between technological change and the control and coordination of the emerging knowledge base and capital flows within the industry. We conclude that there are strong signals that the processes of "creative destruction" are leading not to the erosion of market power but to its reconstitution.

The outcome of the reconstitution of an oligopolistic industry is inconsistent with the public's interest in the evolution of a network "commons." We also suggest that it will be extremely difficult to address these developments within the confines of traditional industry-specific regulation. We acknowledge that digitalization and major changes in the cost/performance characteristics and architectures of the technological infrastructure for information and communication services are central features of the turmoil in the ISP industry and that there is considerable scope for new entry. Our examination of the investment strategies of key players in the ISP market in the United Kingdom illustrates, however, that strategies are being implemented to monopolize the coordination and control of the complex knowledge base that is necessary for the supply of new services. The creation of new "monopoly focal points" is achieving more than a redefinition of control over the scale of market power on a spatial basis (that is, the extension of control from national to global markets). It is also achieving a reconfiguration of the *scope* for market power (that is, its extension into the control of new combinations of technological, knowledge, and financial lock-ins as a means of securing the generation and appropriation of economic rents).

This argument is developed through an analysis of the financial linkages that underpin the evolution of the ISP market in the United Kingdom. A survey of consolidations, alliances, and merger activity during 1999 provides the basis for an analysis of the various forms of lock-ins that are occurring within the emergent ISP industry. In the second section, insights arising from research on the relationships between the innovative technological architecture of the Internet and its market dynamics are highlighted. In the third section a description of the networks of investors in the ISP market in the United Kingdom is provided as a basis for an examination of the evolutionary pathways for the further development of the ISP market, which is presented in the fourth section. In the concluding section we reflect upon the implications of recent market developments for policy and regulation aimed at the protection of the public interest in the evolution of Internet-related services.

Researching Internet Market Dynamics

The focus of our analysis is on the evolving structure of markets for the supply of Internet access and the provision of Internet-related services by ISPs. The Internet has been defined as "an international network of interconnected computers enabling millions of people to communicate with one another and to access vast amounts of information from around the world" [footnote omitted] (Federal Communications Commission 1999, 3). An ISP "is an entity that provides its customers the ability to obtain on-line information through the Internet" (Federal Communications Commission 1999, 3). Multiple ISPs may be involved in the transmission of Internet traffic from its origin to its destination, as shown in figure 1.[5]

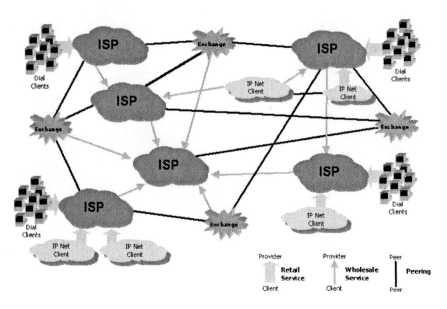

Figure 1   Schematic View of ISP Configurations
Source: Huston 1999.

The Internet emerged as a network to support defense-related scientific research. As Leiner suggests, however, economic issues have become increasingly salient as the network has become accessible to users outside the scientific community (Leiner et al. 1998). The Internet differs from earlier networks because the choice of any individual technology is not dictated by a particular network architecture. Instead, technologies can be selected by a provider and made to "interwork" with other networks through a meta-level "Interworking Architecture." The open architecture of the Internet means that networks can be "separately designed and developed, and each may have its own unique interface, which it may offer to users and/or other providers, including other Internet providers. Each network can be designed in accordance with the specific environment and user requirements of that network" (Leiner et al. 1998, 4).

The distinctive characteristics of the Interworking Architecture have been offered in support of the view that the evolutionary pathway is such that suppliers do not face barriers to market entry or exit. With the growth of the Internet to an estimated fifty-six million hosts by July 1999 and some seven million World Wide Web sites by August 1999 (Zakon 1999), commercial exploitation has been accompanied by fierce price competition in some segments of the markets served by ISPs. Geoff Huston (1999, 1) argues, however, that, underneath the veneer of a highly competitive Internet service market is a somewhat different environment, in which every Internet Service Provider (ISP) network must interoperate with neighboring Internet networks in order to produce a delivered service outcome of comprehensive connectivity and end-to-end services, and therefore, every ISP must not only coexist with other ISPs but also must operate in cooperation with other ISPs.

Internet carriage service, that is, traffic distribution, has become a commodity service that provides little opportunity for product differentiation. In the traffic wholesale business, a relatively low rate of financial return is the norm. Most ISPs, therefore, are seeking to participate in service retail markets, where there is potential for differentiating products and for increasing profit margins.

The interdependencies between ISPs mean that there is a hierarchy within the Internet structure. For example, there are a small number of global ISP transit operators, a second tier of national ISP operators, and a third tier of local ISPs. At each tier, the ISPs are clients of the tier above, as shown in figure 2. However, because there is a strong incentive to reduce costs and maximize revenues, ISPs often seek to establish direct interconnections that bypass this hierarchical relationship. The aggregation of ISPs provides a basis for exploiting economies of scale and scope and for strengthening market position.

Huston (1999, 2) envisages two different trajectories for the evolution of the ISP market. On the one hand, a trajectory may emerge where quality of service differentiation and end-to-end tariffs are introduced in the

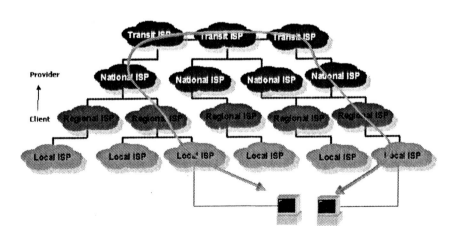

Figure 2   Layering of ISP and Potential for Consolidation.
Source: Huston 1999.

Internet together with financial settlement arrangements between ISPs resembling those for telephony interconnections. On the other, the current Internet "uniform best effort environment," which offers no basis for a uniform approach to revenue distribution, may prevail. In this case, incentives for the continuing consolidation of ISPs are likely to remain strong. Huston (1999, 23) suggests that, "the Internet market is not a sustainable open competitive market. Under such circumstances there is no natural market outcome other than aggregation of providers, leading to the establishment of monopoly positions in the Internet provider space." This evolutionary trajectory suggests that the competitive process will lead to variety reduction through increasing concentration in the industry and to the emergence of new "monopoly focal points."

In the United States, the FCC appears to support the first trajectory as the more likely evolutionary pathway. On this basis, it was decided that there is no need for regulatory intervention, at least at present (Federal Communications Commission 1999). The FCC based its decision on data indicating that the competitive process has enabled many small ISPs to populate the market, often serving the same geographical or "local" customer base. In 1998, for example, more than 92 percent of the population in the United States had access to a competitive local ISP market (Downes and Greenstein 1998). However, Thomas A. Downes and Shane M. Greenstein caution against drawing conclusions on the basis of this evidence about the presence or absence of barriers to market entry. They point to the relatively high start-up and running costs associated with developing viable ISP businesses and they allude to the knowledge base that is increasingly essential for the provision of added value and differentiated services.

> As an economic matter, starting and operating a node for a dial-up ISP involves many strategic considerations [references omitted]. Higher quality components cost money and may not be necessary for some customers. High-speed connections to the backbone are expensive, as are fast modems. Facilities need to be monitored, either remotely or in person. Additional services, such as web-hosting and network maintenance for businesses are also quite costly, as they must be properly assembled, maintained, and marketed. Providing added value may, however, be essential for retaining or attracting a customer base. (Downes and Greenstein 1998, 6)

From a public interest point of view, Downes and Greenstein (1998, 21) suggest that "Many issues will remain unresolved [for universal access] until future research on access analyzes the *precise determinants of firm entry and expansion strategies*" [emphasis added].

Further evidence in support of the second evolutionary trajectory for the ISP market is offered by Padmanabhan Srinagesh (1997, 152), who suggests that the ISP market is one in which, "prices have not lined up neatly with costs. . . . Competition among firms with sunk costs can be problematic, especially when there is excess capacity. . . . Owners of physical networks may decide to avoid potentially ruinous price competition by *integrating vertically and differentiating their services*" [emphasis added]. Srinagesh also highlights the importance of the knowledge base that is an essential component of ISP services such as customer support, information content, and methods of improving the reliability and quality of services. Both Srinagesh and William H. Lehr and Martin B.H. Weiss (1996) argue that these knowledge-related activities provide the basis for product differentiation and for adding value to Internet businesses. If substantial economic returns are to be generated, it is likely that ISPs will need to establish new "monopoly focal points," not necessarily over access to the Internet, but over the information and content and the knowledge base that are essential for product differentiation.

The economic viability of alternative business models for Internet-based content provision also has been a subject for investigation. For example, Jeffrey K. MacKie-Mason et al. (1996) suggest that the structure of the Internet architecture affects content provision in different ways depending upon whether the network is designed to be "application-aware" or "content-aware." In the former case, ISPs can identify the general type of applications that are being invoked by users, for example, e-mail, audio playback, or interactive video. In the latter case, the network can also be used to monitor and control the content that is transported. They argue that "network architecture can have important implications for the nature of information goods" (MacKie-Mason 1996, 205) and that ISPs can play an editorial role in selecting the content made available to consumers. These features mean that ISPs are likely to have strong incentives to consolidate their control over the knowledge base that permits this "editorial role" to be performed.

ISPs are focusing on retailing a host of information products and services under a variety of business models, and they have the potential to become significant intermediaries between citizens or customers and information creators (Eliasson 1999). Their potential for growth depends upon whether they can "lock in" their customers in a way that establishes a foundation for growth. This requires more than the achievement of traditional forms of "lock-in" that have characterized the carriage business in the telecommunication industry or the content business in the broadcasting and cable industries. It also requires the sealing of supplier-client relationships with respect to information and content, and it requires money. As Gunnar Eliasson (1999, 6) suggests, the ISPs link communication transport infrastructures with the "syndication of electronic content." Consolidation of this linkage requires a combination of capabilities for knowledge generation that are required for innovation and the creation of new value-added products and services. This is similar to developments in other high-technology industries where business success depends upon a match "between the development and deployment of bodies of technological knowledge, on the one hand, and commercially successful (or useful) working artifacts, on the other" (Pavitt 1997, 11). The innovative performance of ISPs is likely to depend upon cognitive mechanisms that affect the boundaries of the knowledge base that firms are capable of exploiting; upon the specific types of coordination mechanisms that are used to support learning and innovation; and upon the control mechanisms that are in place for allocating resources between the divisions and business units of a firm.

In order to assess which of the two alternative trajectories for ISP market development is likely to prevail, it is essential to consider several dimensions of the competitive process in addition to those that are highlighted in this section. It is necessary to examine the transformations in financial markets that are influencing the capacity of ISPs to exploit new technological opportunities. To achieve a sustainable linkage between the carriage of "bits" and the provision of information services, new sets of financial flows must be organized and controlled and the institutional conditions must be put in place to secure good economic returns. In the next section, we focus on developments in the ISP market in the United Kingdom. We hypothesize that the mergers and acquisitions in the ISP market will display a pattern whereby economic rents are being extracted by financial institutions in ways that (1) bypass barriers to entry in existing markets; (2) reconfigure the market so as to reduce the high costs of learning associated with knowledge creation and the time needed to achieve customer lock-in; and (3) protect and control financial returns for investors.

The predominant viewpoint among policy makers in both the United States and the United Kingdom is that it is too early to employ regulation in the ISP market because this would threaten its growth potential. Another viewpoint is that "the broader consequences of oligopoly will be to adversely affect the infrastructure as a platform for supporting productivity growth throughout the economy" (Trebing 1998, 65). The industrial dynamics of the ISP market are important because its prospects are intertwined with major shifts in economic activity within industrialized economies and with the distribution of employment opportunities and income.[6] Insofar as the trajectory for Internet evolution implies new bifurcations in the market and the potential for lock-in, there may be a strong case for regulation to protect the social or public interest in Internet developments.

The Evolving Internet Service Provider Market in the United Kingdom[7]

The ISP market in the United Kingdom is rapidly developing and, because of its smaller scale, compared to the United States, it provides an interesting basis for analysis of the features of investment and their implications. The ISPs in Britain fall into three categories: (1) national Internet access providers serving mainly British companies, using reciprocal or peering arrangements with overseas firms to provide international service; (2) international Internet access providers including companies that own, or are building, worldwide networks; and (3) private network providers, including the majority of national and international data networking service firms that use private network infrastructures and management, such as the large telecommunication companies, computing service companies, and a number of small private network operators (Durlacher 1997). In the first quarter of 1997, nearly all the ISP activity in the United Kingdom was in the first category. The market showed signs of becoming bifurcated between the dial-up access market and the access and related services market for corporate users, where efforts were under way to achieve product differentiation and there were expectations of market consolidation (Durlacher 1997).

By July 1999, there were about 5.8 million dial-up users of ISP services (including subscription-free services) in the United Kingdom and the first non-metered usage ISP services were expected in the fourth quarter of the year (Durlacher 1999a). The number of ISPs providing high-speed leased line access services was growing rapidly. It was estimated that close to 99 percent of large organizations were connected to the Internet and that as many as 95.6 percent of British-owned companies were outsourcing some services, including web hosting, remote access, web design, and consulting (Durlacher 1999b). By 1999, in the dial-up market efforts were under way to secure a basis for further growth. Our analysis focuses on this market because the target customers are mainly citizens, consumers, and smaller firms. Tables 1 and 2 show the estimated market shares held by the subscription-free and subscription-based segments of this market as of July 1999.

Table 1   Estimated Market Shares Held by Five of the Top Suscription-Free ISPs in July 1999

Subscription-Free Dial-Up ISP	No. of Subscribers (in '000s)	Market Share (%)
Freeserve	1,250	32
X-Steam	270	7
Curran Bun	250	6
breathenet	225	5
Line One	200	5
Other	1,745	44
Total	3,940	99

Source: Durlacher, 1999b

The ISP market in the United Kingdom differs considerably from that in the United States in a major respect in addition to its relatively smaller size. In Britain, end users pay charges for local dial-up connections to the ISP, in contrast to the flat-rate pricing of local service in most places in the United States. In the United Kingdom, ISPs may offer a flat rate for monthly service, and by the middle of 1999 they had started to offer "free" services. In addition, leased lines required by ISPs in the United Kingdom are more costly than in the United States. Our analysis is based on investor and supplier activity at the end of August 1999. We map the patterns of ownership and control that link investors and the large ISPs in this market in the following section to provide a basis for examining two closely related

Table 2   Estimated Market Shares Held by Five of the Top Fee-Paying ISPs in July 1999

Fee-Paying Dial-Up ISP	No. of Subscribers (in '000s)	Market Share (%)
AOL	600	29
CompuServe	400	20
Demon	175	96
BT Internet	115	6
Global Internet[a]	100	5
Other	644	31
Total	2,034	100

[a]Global Internet is the wholly-owned subsidiary of Internet Technology Group (ITG)
Source: Durlacher, 1999b

processes of consolidation. The first involves the large firms that emerged following the wave of market liberalization that affected the former public utility operators. The second involves a new tidal wave of American investors in the United Kingdom and continental European markets.[8]

The Giants' Trail: Growth and Transformation

Rapid growth in the numbers of British companies offering Internet access and services occurred in the first half of the 1990s. This early phase in ISP development was marked by the growth of new entrants, some of which achieved a relatively strong leadership position. In July 1999, for example, Demon Internet was ranked second to America OnLine/CompuServe in terms of market share in the subscription dial-up market, and Global Internet (a subsidiary of ITG—Internet Technology Group) was ranked fourth (Durlacher 1999a). Other fast-growing new entrants have maintained a high profile during the consolidation of the ISP industry. For example, Internet Network Services was ranked fifth in terms of market share in the subscription dial-up market in March 1997 (Durlacher 1997). These estimates of market position serve as benchmarks of the significance of the new entrants' remarkable growth and of their efforts to sustain their positions in a rapidly changing market.

It is not only the fast-growing entrepreneurial ventures that have been securing their positions in the ISP market in the United Kingdom. The incumbents that emerged from the privatization of the public utilities, including electricity and telecommunication as well as the broadcasting authorities, have also been assessing the scale and scope of these markets. Since the mid-1990s, the incumbents have been intensifying their strategies for entry into the ISP market and strengthening their positions in the market segments related to services for consumers and small businesses as well as those aimed at the large corporate users. By the end of the 1990s, following a wave of mergers and acquisitions, the incumbents had acquired many of the most successful early entrants. They also had forged global partnerships or merged their operations with American-owned companies. In the following, we depict some of these developments for the largest ISPs and we map some of the alterations in their ownership and control structures. Figure 3 provides an outline of the landscape of the consolidation of the ISP market in the United Kingdom.

We begin with the trail established by entrepreneur Cliff Stanford, who launched Demon Internet in 1992 with a personal investment of £20,000. The history of the phenomenal growth of Demon Internet as an ISP focused mainly on corporate clients is instructive. Demon reached a turn-

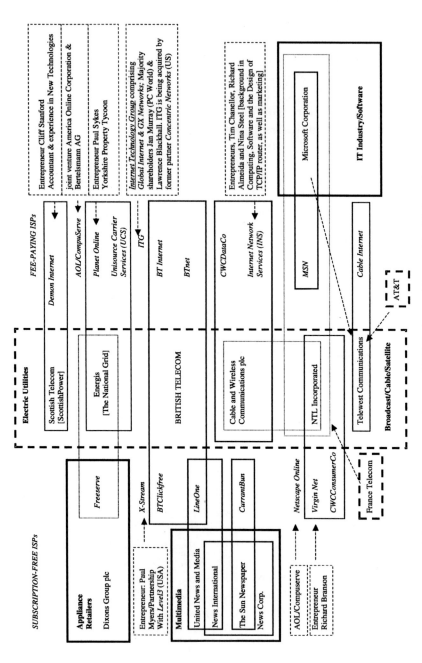

Figure 3 Consolidation of Major Incumbents of UK Industry (Ownership Linkages).
Source: compiled by authors.

ing point in May 1998 when, after six years of development of a customer base from zero to 180,000, the company was acquired by Scottish Telecom. Stanford made a personal fortune of £66 million and went on to create a new venture, Redbus, a consultancy company for innovators, entrepreneurs, and business start-ups. Demon became a wholly owned subsidiary of Scottish Telecom. The trail does not end here, however. Scottish Power plc, Scottish Telecom's parent, was formed following the privatization of the electricity supply industry in 1990 and the breakup and flotation of the Central Electricity Generating Board (CEGB). It has followed a global strategy for growth like most of the privatized offspring of the former publicly owned utilities.

In December 1998, the same year as the acquisition of Demon, Scottish Power announced a merger with PacifiCorp, an electric utility in the United States. As a result of this merger, PacifiCorp became a wholly owned subsidiary of ScottishPower, the agreed name for the newly integrated company, and ScottishPower expected to enhance the potential for global expansion. Similarly, Energis, the telecommunication network operator and spin-off from the National Grid, the transmission branch of the former CEGB, has consolidated its competitive position in the market vis-à-vis the largest incumbent, British Telecommunications plc., or BT. BT, the former monopoly telecommunication operator, continues to control some 80 percent of the revenues generated by domestic telephone services in the United Kingdom. One aspect of the competitive response by Energis and Scottish Telecom has been to establish a network capacity sharing agreement.

Like Scottish Telecom, Energis has sought to strengthen its position in the information services market by acquiring Planet Online in August 1998. Planet Online is a new entrant in the Internet access and service provider market. Formed in July 1995 in Leeds with the financial backing of Yorkshire property tycoon Paul Sykes, Planet Online was launched in September of the same year. Focusing on providing high-performance Internet and intranet solutions for the corporate business market, the company enjoyed substantial growth and achieved a turnover of £24.7 million in March 1998. Paul Sykes realized a £41 million capital gain from the sale of Planet. Energis, having consolidated its position in the corporate market, was instrumental in the launch of Freeserve.[9] This is the largest subscription-free ISP in the consumer segment of the market, and the company was a wholly owned subsidiary of Dixons Group plc.

Freeserve's launch followed in the innovative footsteps of a small new entrant, X-Stream. This company had started a subscription-free ISP service funded by advertising revenues early in 1998. Dixons Group plc,

Freeserve's parent, in contrast to X-Stream, had substantial assets and a strong position in the consumer retail market. This has provided the venture with considerable "launching" as well as "staying power." With nearly 33 percent of its shares held by four of the most prominent financial institutions in the City of London,[10] Dixons Group, which is the largest retail outlet for electrical appliances in Britain, provided Freeserve with a secure financial base and a large potential customer base. This backing helped to take Freeserve to a leadership position in the consumer market in the record time of four months. Through a partnership with Energis, Freeserve obtained access to the necessary infrastructure and used the Dixons Group's extensive distribution network of 350 stores to offer Microsoft's free Internet Explorer software.[11] BT's quasi-monopoly position in the domestic market means that the majority of dial-up calls destined for Freeserve, and which are carried over the Energis network, originate on BT's facilities. Nevertheless, Freeserve and Energis have reaped the benefit of their partnership. Freeserve has been able to generate revenues by taking a share of the revenues from the telecommunication usage tariffs charged by BT to end users for carrying traffic over its network, a percentage of which are rebated to Freeserve's carrier, Energis.

The subscription-free dial-up ISPs appear to be developing a thriving market. However, there is one important reservation. Since January 1999, there has been an increase of 50 percent in the average number of failed dial-up calls (Murphy 1999). The growth of the new entrants in the subscription-free dial-up market is being accompanied by the rapidly increasing presence of large media companies. News Corporation and Rupert Murdoch's *Sun* newspaper, for example, launched a successful ISP named CurrantBun in 1998.[12] By harnessing the advertising power of its owners, CurrantBun was able to achieve third position in this segment of the market by July 1999. LineOne, a joint venture between BT, News International (a News Corporation subsidiary), and United News and Media, was in fifth position in 1999 (Durlacher 1999a).[13] To meet the competition, BT also launched a subscription-free dial-up ISP named BTClickfree. Freeserve continued to dominate the subscription-free segment of the market, with an estimated 32 percent market share in July 1999 and some 1.32 million active registered accounts as of June 1999. To consolidate their partnership, Energis acquired 5 percent of Freeserve's ordinary shares in June 1999 (Computerwire Inc. 1999) and, as a result of Freeserve's initial success, Dixons' share price has doubled (Murphy 1999).

The growth of the subscription-free dial-up market has led to numerous disputes and protests between the competitors. For example, America Online (AOL) UK has claimed that ISPs that are linked to telecommunication network operators are putting the ISPs that are independent at an unfair disadvantage (Computergram International 1999). Although there are concerns about the viability of the small "free" ISPs that provide services for charitable or educational organizations, this issue is not likely to be the concern of AOL UK. In the consumer market targeted by ISPs, attention is focusing on the potential for loss of revenues further along the value-added chain. It is also focusing on the use of subscription-free dial-up ISPs as a potentially loss-making marketing tool to achieve customer lock-in to virtual mazes of carefully designed electronic commerce galleries. Advertising provides an uncertain foundation for future revenue growth and it will be necessary for these ISPs to devise ways of creating new opportunities for sustained growth. As we discuss in the following, America Online Corporation, based in the United States, entered the British subscription-free dial-up ISP market with the launch of Netscape Online in the autumn of 1999.

National Grid plc,[14] the parent company of Energis, like its counterpart ScottishPower, has been forging partnerships and consolidating its market overseas.[15] National Grid plc is to acquire the New England Electric System (NEES) and, subsequently, Eastern Utilities Associates (EUA) after approval of the merger by the state authorities.[16] Changes in the National Grid's corporate structure have been agreed upon by its shareholders. By the autumn of 1999, approximately 15 percent of the company's stock was held by two prominent financial institutions, HSBC Investment Bank and a subsidiary of the Prudential Corporation plc. The Prudential Corporation also holds a significant 6.03 percent share of Scottish Power plc. Scottish Power's strong growth rate is underlined by its substantial increase in dividend payments, averaging 12.7 percent per annum (Scottish Power plc 1999).

The merger of Scottish Power with the American electricity supply company PacifiCorp was strongly recommended to PacifiCorp's shareholders, with a full guarantee of the value of their shares. Under this agreement, the premium for PacifiCorp's shareholders was guaranteed at 26 percent above the market price of the company's common stock. The conversion of PacifiCorp shares into American Depository Shares or ScottishPower ordinary shares was guaranteed on a tax-free basis, and fractional shares were to be paid in cash. For its part, the National Grid announced exceptional dividend payments of 44.7 pence per share in 1998. This means of improving capital efficiency was achieved by returning "*excess* capital" to shareholders. BT's failed attempt at a merger with MCI was replaced by partnership agreements with AT&T, while, at the time of writing, MCI-WorldCom was planning a merger with SPRINT, another of the large telecommunication network operators in the United States.

Developments in the ISP market in the United Kingdom have been characterized by the convergence of the ISPs with the telecommunication network operators. This has taken place against a backdrop of the changes since privatization in both the telecommunication and electricity sectors in the 1980s and 1990s. In the former case, these changes have been characterized by the slow erosion of BT's monopoly position. In the latter, they have been characterized by the entry of the incumbents into related technological fields. For example, some of the electricity companies have diversified from transmission into the telecommunication sector. However, these ventures are proving to be very unstable.

Other developments in the ISP and the telecommunication market in the United Kingdom have provided the foundation for a different process of convergence in the knowledge base that supports the emerging industry. They have also contributed to a process of redefinition and consolidation of the economic and corporate governance of associated markets. These developments are related to transformations in the cable television industry, which follow, in part, from the privatization of the Independent Broadcasting Authority. This process of transformation is illustrated by the experience of National Transcommunications Limited Inc. (NTL Inc.) and the corporate restructuring of Cable & Wireless Communications plc (CWC), a subsidiary of Cable & Wireless plc. This restructuring involved the division and reintegration of CWC, and its acquisition of the ISP Internet Network Services (INS), a new entrant in the British market.

NTL Inc. was established in 1997 as a result of the acquisition of the privatized transmission network of the former Independent Broadcasting Authority (IBA), National Transcommunications Ltd. The former engineering arm and network backbone of the IBA was acquired by a small entrepreneurial cellular telephone company that had entered the cable and telecommunication industry under the name of International CableTel (NTL Inc. 1998). The new company, NTL, resulted in the merging of state-of-the-art engineering capabilities for the development and management of terrestrial and satellite networks and fiber-optic technologies. NTL's consolidation of its technological assets and capabilities and its positioning in related segments of the market have produced a blazing trail of acquisitions. For example, in the year following its formation, NTL signed contracts with the telecommunication carrier Energis and the (indirectly) wholly owned subsidiary of the FMR Corporation (the Fidelity Management and Research Company/Fidelity Group), Colt Telecom, which had been operating in the United Kingdom market. [17] By 1999, NTL had acquired ComTel (including Telecential Communications), all the cable television and telecommunication outstanding stock of ComCast UK Cable Partners Ltd. via its subsidiary NTL Bermuda Ltd., as well as Diamond Cable. To consolidate its regional networks, NTL had also acquired Eastern Group Telecoms (in the United Kingdom) and, respectively, 40 and 30 percent of the outstanding stock of CableTel Newport with cable television and telecommunication franchises in South Wales. It also acquired Cable Enterprise Inc., the owner of cable television and telecommunication franchises in the northern suburbs of London. These consolidations were compounded by the purchase of the largest Irish cable television provider, Cablelink Ltd. All these companies became wholly owned subsidiaries of NTL.

Parallel to these acquisitions, NTL had developed a base of two hundred thousand customers in the Internet market. With a strong partnership as backbone provider and as part owner of the subscription-free dial up ISP Virgin Net, NTL added entrepreneur Richard Branson's brand name to its market assets.[18] In 1999, NTL Inc. declared that it had become "the largest broadband telecommunications provider in the UK and Ireland as measured by number of customers" (NTL Inc. 1999). The competitive challenge mounted by NTL appears to have heightened the pressure on the incumbent telecommunication operators in the local services market. BT felt the pressure when NTL acquired BT Cable Services in July 1999, but the main competitive threat has been to Cable & Wireless Communications plc. Trends toward the further consolidation of the ISP market are suggested by the developments that led to the restructuring of Cable & Wireless Communications plc (CWC) and that produced a turning point in the expansion of NTL Inc. The restructuring of CWC took place against the background of a transaction between Cable & Wireless Communications and NTL that occurred at about the same time as the acquisition by NTL of BT Cable Services. The details of this transaction provide a glimpse into the process of redefining the market scale and scope for NTL and Cable & Wireless. The transaction also affected Telewest Communications, another competitor in the British cable market.[19]

The transaction between NTL and CWC established a framework for the reorganization of the two companies' core market, extended their geographical coverage, and defined new boundaries for their operational domains of expertise as well as their future development. These developments provide a foundation for future "lock-in" of the customer base that is likely to influence the coordination and control of capital flows. Cable & Wireless Communications (CWC) plc, a 53-percent-owned subsidiary of Cable & Wireless plc, was created as the result of a merger between NYNEX Cablecomms, Bell Cablemedia, Videotron, and Mercury Communications in April 1997 (Cable & Wireless Communications plc 1999).

With this merger, CWC took the lead in the consolidation of the cable industry and became the first British cable operator to offer digital television. As a result, in 1998 CWC was the largest provider of integrated telecommunication and television services, measured by revenue. It had a broad range of facilities and provided local, national, and international voice, data, and Internet services. It was among the largest British carriers of wholesale telecommunication traffic, and the ninth-largest carrier of international telecommunication traffic. In July 1999, Cable & Wireless plc, Cable & Wireless Communications plc (CWC) and NTL Inc. made a joint announcement regarding the restructuring of CWC and the subsequent separation of the company's business into two branches: CWC DataCo, with its corporate, business, international, and wholesale operations, and CWC Consumer Co, comprising the consumer cable, telephone, Internet, and television operations. While Cable & Wireless plc acquired complete control over CWC DataCo, the ownership of CWC Consumer Co was transferred to NTL Inc. The acquisition of CWC Consumer Co made NTL the largest cable television company in the United Kingdom, ahead of Telewest Communications. NTL's consolidated cable network covers over half of the British households passed by cable. With full control over DataCo, Cable & Wireless plc set out to integrate its corporate and business activities in the global market and shifted its focus toward rapid growth of the corporate data and Internet markets. The restructuring was designed to enable the company to consolidate and rationalize its operations to compete more effectively in the international end-to-end business services market.

The transformation of the NTL and Cable & Wireless businesses was accompanied by settlements that resulted in the reorganization of capital flows. The acquisition of CWC Consumer Co. and BT Cable Services by NTL was backed by financing from France Telecom. An agreement with France Telecom enabled NTL to recover the cash paid to CWC shareholders and gave France Telecom a 25-percent stake in NTL. The transaction between CWC and NTL also resulted in CWC receiving approximately 10 percent of NTL's common shares.[20] Microsoft Corporation contributed to NTL's refinancing by investing US$ 500 million in NTL convertible preferential shares as part of an agreement to support the deployment of high-speed voice, video, and data services. This was intended to boost NTL's capacity to develop innovative services and to implement new technologies (NTL Inc. 1999). As a result, Microsoft holds about 5.25 percent of NTL stock. The consolidation of CWC and the acquisition of the remaining shares in CWC DataCo involved a redistribution of shares from the new company.[21] At the Cable & Wireless plc annual general meeting in July 1999, the chairman, Sir Ralph Robins, presented the company's plan for a worldwide strategic repositioning with a concentration on the development of the data and Internet businesses. The earlier acquisition of MCI's Internet business in the United States in September 1998 was consistent with this announcement, as was the acquisition of Internet Network Services (INS) in the United Kingdom.

Internet Network Services (INS) (Holdings) Ltd. was created in 1995 by three entrepreneurs. Tim Chanellor, founder and managing director, had considerable experience in the computer industry. His entrepreneurial record had been established following the launch of a business that manufactured and distributed IBM PC-compatible machines in Taiwan. After selling this business to investors, he worked as an independent consultant. He entered the Internet business in 1990 by designing, building, and selling dial-up systems to corporate customers and education establishments. Nina Steel was experienced in marketing and Richard Almeida was responsible for the design, construction, and operation of TCP/IP routers that were used to support the backbone of the early university networks in the United Kingdom.

INS was supported by two key investors: Baring Communications Equity and Spectrum Equity Investors LP. By 1997, INS was ranked fifth among the Internet access and service providers in the United Kingdom (Durlacher 1997, 2). INS achieved a 150 percent growth rate between 1996 and 1997 and a phenomenal 550 percent growth rate in 1997–98, prior to its acquisition by Cable & Wireless. In 1998, before it was acquired by Cable & Wireless plc, INS purchased Wisper Bandwidth plc, a company founded in 1996 with the ambition of becoming a global Internet backbone provider. The acquisition of Wisper gave INS an increased European presence and direct connectivity with several major European business centers. INS was highly regarded for the quality of the service it provided to corporate users by offering customized solutions, such as filtered Internet connectivity, web hosting, managed colocation services, Virtual Private Networks, and extranets and intranets. INS fits well with the profile needed to accomplish the Cable & Wireless strategic repositioning (Cable & Wireless Communications plc 1999).

Telewest Communications plc, a major competitor of NTL and a strong potential competitor of Cable & Wireless in the global data and Internet services market, consolidated its position in 1998. Telewest Communications' major shareholders are Microsoft Corporation and Libert Media, a subsidiary of AT&T, with 29.9 and 21.6 percent of its stock, respectively. Telewest set out to expand its activities in the corporate segment of the ISP market in the United Kingdom with the development of

Cable Internet, a data and Internet service provider launched in 1995. Following NTL's acquisition of CWC Consumer Co, Telewest's prospects for market expansion in the United Kingdom were constrained, and it now ranks as the second-largest cable operator in the market.

Developments in the market in Britain also have been affected by a transaction between giants MCI-WorldCom and America OnLine Corporation (AOL). In the last quarter of 1997 and in early 1998, MCI-WorldCom and AOL in the United States agreed to a bilateral sale and purchase of assets involving ANS Communications Inc. and CompuServe, the respectively wholly owned subsidiaries of AOL and MCI-WorldCom. CompuServe provides Internet access connections and innovative customized applications. It has a large worldwide subscriber base. ANS Communications Inc. is a managed network service company that provides Internet connections, remote dial-up access, and security solutions. The company claims to manage one of the largest and fastest Internet services in the world, and it is expanding.

As a result of the agreement between AOL and MCI-WorldCom, MCI-WorldCom transferred the CompuServe business to AOL together with a cash transaction of US$ 147 million, and ANS Communications Inc. was transferred to MCI-WorldCom. The transactions were complemented by a settlement of US$ 75 million from the German publishing company, Bertelsmann AG, resulting in a 50 percent interest in the newly created joint venture involving CompuServe Corporation. AOL generated US$ 207 million as a result of these transactions and consolidated the "material conditions" for a strategic agreement with MCI-WorldCom.

This agreement sealed an important collaborative relationship aimed at the development of high-capacity networks within and outside the United States. However, the foundation of the settlement and the relationship between AOL and MCI-WorldCom are multifaceted and run much more deeply than this. AOL's entry into the ISP market in the United Kingdom highlights several other aspects of the momentum achieved as a result of the consolidation of corporate, financial, and knowledge networks and the contribution of the latter to the design and implementation of corporate strategies. These developments have contributed to the leading position that AOL has achieved in the United Kingdom market in approximately three years. Figure 4 shows the corporate network surrounding AOL, MCI-WorldCom, and Verio Inc. This figure highlights developments that have shaped the ISP market in the United Kingdom.

Three elements are particularly important in this set of network relationships. The first relates to the coordination and control of financial flows and the recurring presence of at least one common investor with a

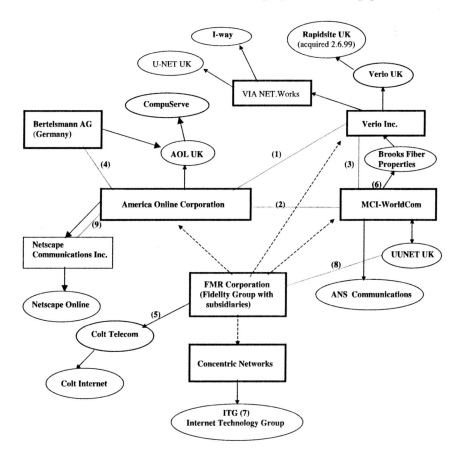

Figure 4   Corporate, Financial and Information Networks.

1. America Online Corporation has a partnership agreement with Verio Inc.
2. AOL's chairman and chief executive, Stephen Case, sits on the board of MCI-WorldCom. Stephen Case is member of the board of directors of the New York Stock Exchange.
3. MCI-World-Com's director, James C. Allen, sits on the board of Verio Inc.
4. CompuServe is a joint venture between AOL and Bertelsmann AG.
5. Colt Telecom is the indirect wholly owned subsidiary of FMR Corporation; FMR Corporation is owned/controlled by Edward C. Johnson III and Abigail P. Johnson and is known as "Fidelity."
6. Brooks Fiber Properties Inc. is a wholly owned subsidiary of MCI-WorldCom.
7. ITG (Internet Technology Group) is being acquired by its partner, Concentric Networks.
8. See History of UUNET on its web site accessed on 8 October 1999. In UUNET Technologies Inc. SEC Filings, FMR Corp. was recorded as a significant shareholder with a 6.55 percent holding in 1996 prior to its merger/acquisition by MCI-WorldCom.
9. America Online acquired Netscape Communications Inc. in 1998. As a result of the merger Netscape's cofounder, Marc Andreessen, was appointed chief technology officer of AOL in the United States.

Source: Compiled by authors.

significant financial stake in three of the major players in the network. In this instance, FMR Corporation, also known as the Fidelity Group, has significant holdings in AOL, Verio Inc., and MCI-WorldCom. Its significant position in the network is compounded by the fact that it is related to two other players in the United Kingdom telecommunication and ISP market. One of these is Colt Telecom, an indirect wholly owned subsidiary of FMR Corporation. Colt Telecom is also a partner of NTL, alongside Energis, as we saw in the earlier discussion, and the parent of Colt Internet, which was launched in 1993 in the United Kingdom. The other is Concentric Networks of the United States, which was in the process of acquiring a partner, Internet Technology Group (ITG), in the summer of 1999. ITG is the parent of Global Internet, which was ranked fifth in the subscription-based dial-up market behind AOL, CompuServe, Demon Internet, and BT Internet in July 1999 (Durlacher 1999a).

The second element that comes to light from this analysis of these networks of relationships is that another significant investor in Verio Inc. is Brooks Fiber Properties, a wholly owned subsidiary of MCI-WorldCom since January 1998.[22] This means that 28 percent of Verio Inc. stock is held in the hands of two of the prominent players in the network that we are considering here. The third element relates to the coordination and control of knowledge flows within this network of organizations. This aspect can be illustrated by examining the shared directorships between AOL and MCI-WorldCom and between MCI-WorldCom and Verio Inc., as well as the partnership between AOL and Verio Inc.

AOL's chairman and chief executive, Stephen Case, is a member of the board of MCI-WorldCom. He is also a member of the board of directors of the New York Stock Exchange. MCI-WorldCom's director, James C. Allen, is a member of the board of Verio Inc. MCI-WorldCom gained a presence in the United Kingdom ISP market through a merger with UUNET in 1998, a leader in the market with an estimated 33-percent share in 1997 (Durlacher 1997). AOL's partnership with Verio Inc. was forged in the United States and was an essential element in the strategic development of AOL/CompuServe's leadership position in the United Kingdom after the company's launch in January 1996. AOL has an exclusive agreement with Verio Inc., a large Web-hosting company and business-oriented ISP in the British market, which has targeted small- and medium-sized businesses. A survey of 1,100 companies in July 1999 estimated that Internet penetration among small- and medium-sized enterprises in the United Kingdom had increased by 37 percent over the preceding twelve months, to reach 77 percent. However, this growth was accounted for mainly by the uptake of subscription-free services, and it was estimated that only 1 percent of these companies was making full use of the Internet's potential (Durlacher 1999a). Verio Inc. launched Verio UK in 1997. Verio UK consolidated its position in June 1999 by acquiring a domain name registration company called Rapidsite UK, which had been launched in 1997. The parent company, Verio Inc., is also a substantial investor in VIA NET.Works, which owns two British entrants in the ISP market, I-way and U-NET UK, launched, respectively, in 1995 and 1994.

On the strength of these financial and strategic partnerships, AOL started an aggressive campaign to build market share in the British market in both the consumer and business segments, which are the core competence domains of CompuServe. By the summer of 1999 AOL, together with CompuServe, had achieved a one-million-strong subscriber base in the British market. AOL's acquisition of Netscape Communications Corporation, which was consolidated by a stock-for-stock transaction valued at US$ 4.2 billion, gave AOL control of the most popular web portal in the British market, thereby reinforcing the potential of electronic commerce for both companies. This strategic merger was further consolidated with the appointment of Netscape cofounder Marc Andreessen as chief technology officer of AOL in the United States (America OnLine 1999b). Building on the strength of the acquisition of this portal, AOL launched a new venture, Netscape Online, in the subscription-free ISP market in the United Kingdom through a retail distribution agreement with Kingfisher plc in September 1999. Earlier in the same month, Netscape Online software was co-branded with Woolworths for distribution in the United Kingdom (America OnLine 1999a).

In 1998, AOL had begun consolidating its core businesses in the United States by acquiring companies that were active in various segments of the interactive Internet service markets.[23] These acquisitions equipped AOL with the necessary tools for the provision of highly customized services. The business strategy is aimed at encouraging users of the services to invest their time in tailoring services to match their preferences. Once they have invested their time, it is expected that users will perceive the "switching" costs of exiting AOL services as being relatively more significant, thus strengthening the company's capacity to lock in customers and build market share. This strategy is illustrated in the following quotation.

> Personalization and Control Features—Members can personalize their [the member's] experience on the AOL service through a number of features and tools, including a reminder service that sends e-mail in advance of important events, stock portfolios that automatically update market prices, Mail Controls, which allow members to limit who may send them e-mail and to block certain types of e-mail, Favorite Places, which allows members

to mark a particular Web site or AOL areas, and Portfolio direct and News Profiles, which send stories of particular interest to members. The AOL service offers Parental Control to help parents form their children's online experience, including tools that limit access to particular AOL areas or Web sites or to certain features (for example, the AOL Instant Messenger service or receiving files attached to e-mail or embedded pictures in e-mail, or access to premium services). The Marketing Preferences feature enables members to elect not to receive certain marketing offers. (America OnLine 1999c, 4)

Within the United States, AOL has been reorganized into three components: the Interactive Service Group, the Interactive Properties Group, and the AOL International Group, which oversees AOL and CompuServe services outside the United States. This restructuring appears to have created the conditions for achieving technological and information "lock-in" in a variety of areas that may help to secure the company's development with respect to both market scale and scope.

Summary

The changes in the ISP market in the United Kingdom are reminiscent of the reconfiguration and emergence of "monopoly focal points" in earlier phases of the evolution of network-related industries. Our analysis of the technological, financial, and knowledge networks that support the growth of the Internet-based information and communication services market in the United Kingdom illustrates the way in which the emerging focal points are shaping the new segment of the industry. Recent transformations have begun to produce service differentiation through various forms of market control. This process is marked by a bifurcation between the subscription-free dial-up ISP market, which mainly targets consumers and small firms, and the subscription-based dial-up ISP market, which increasingly is targeting corporate customers. In the British market, emerging corporate linkages are characterized by the convergence of the ISPs with telecommunication network operators. These developments are taking place against the backdrop of the erosion of BT's monopoly position in the domestic market and the entry of large incumbents from the electricity industry and the former public broadcast distribution sector. These changes have been accompanied by joint ventures and partnerships between the ISPs and the media, information technology and software firms.

The large British-owned incumbent firms have been establishing a strong presence in global markets, but they have met fierce competition in their domestic market from American-owned firms. The British-owned incumbents have been seeking to strengthen their positions through acquisitions or mergers with American-owned companies, while the American-owned companies have been consolidating their positions in their own domestic market, as in the case of AOL. On the strength of their alliances in the American domestic market, American-owned firms such as AOL/CompuServe have enjoyed a swift and initially successful launch in the British domestic market, and they have been expanding into the continental European market. Continental European telecommunication network operators, such as France Telecom, have also increased their presence in the British market.

The Race for the Self-Fulfilling Prophecy

We suggested at the beginning of this article that the emergence of new "monopoly focal points" in the ISP market involves more than a redefinition of the scale of the market power accruing to companies that are participating in markets associated with the development of the Internet. The analysis in the preceding section suggests that the emergence of the new focal points involves a reconfiguration of control over key components of the knowledge base. This process appears to be the result of the innovative combination of technological, financial, and knowledge networks in ways that achieve effective customer lock-in. Insofar as this strategy is successful within the domestic market, there is a case for national governments to intervene to ensure that the market evolves in a way that is consistent with the interests of citizens, consumers, and small firms.

One conception of the Internet that has found widespread acceptance is that its open architecture supports an information and communication "commons," where social, cultural, and economic aspirations of all kinds are valued. An alternative conception envisages the emergence of a bifurcated networking environment. In this view, and in the particular case of the United Kingdom market, the provision of sophisticated intranet and extranet services for large business users is consistent with the circulation and accumulation of financial capital in the interest of very large (mainly foreign) firms. This development will have profound public interest implications if it occurs in parallel with long-term underinvestment in the Internet infrastructure and in the information and content of services that are accessible and affordable for citizens, consumers, and small firms. Indeed, it is this development trajectory that appears to be emerging in the market in the United Kingdom.

Interpreting the Trail: Consolidating Financial and Technological Control

Building a new industry in an uncertain technological and commercial environment requires massive investment. The process of building the ISP market can be expected to give rise to new predominant forms of corporate relationships, and these must be expected to influence the market dynamics and trajectories within both the new industrial segment and related existing market segments. The implications of linkages between sources of finance and control over the strategic behavior of enterprises are a central theme in the literature on the determinants of corporate organization and industrial structure. The problems of financing large-scale operations are described in this literature as being central to the implications of a separation of corporate ownership and control.

For example, when the concentration of economic activities forced the breakdown of family "tenure" and the increasing importance of capital raised on the stock exchange, liberal management theorists argued that decision-making power over the coordination and control of corporate assets would be entrusted to corporate managers (Berle and Means [1932] 1968). Marxist analysts, in contrast, tended to highlight the greater significance of the development of finance capital for the emerging joint-stock corporation. Stanislav M. Menshikov (1969), for instance, regarded the joint-stock company as an indicator of the growing power of financiers over corporate affairs. While the former expected the development of the joint-stock company to give rise to managerial autonomy, the latter suggested that "property" would remain a central determinant of the power structure influencing the behavior and performance of corporations.

In the 1980s, research by John Scott (1985, 1986) and Beth Mintz and Michael Schwartz (1985) revisited debates about the role of finance and corporate control. Drawing on Mintz and Schwartz's work, Scott (1993) argues that while decision making may be insulated from direct intervention by shareholders, the shareholders' control derives from property relationships and the legal rights conferred by share ownership. Share owners have rights over the disposition of income, and they have voting powers with respect to corporate affairs. In questioning the polarized views of the liberal management and Marxist theorists, Scott (1993, 295) argues that control should not be considered in terms of a *simple* relationship between ownership and managerial powers of decision making. Instead, issues of control should be considered within the context of the "institutional constraint" that is exercised by shareholders over decision-making processes. This constraint is embedded in the dynamics of a given share ownership structure. Thus, he argues that "it is now the strategic actions of the financial intermediaries in Britain and in the United States which are most influential in determining the constraints under which enterprises act" (Scott 1993, 295). Scott's view of the implications of linkages between sources of corporate finance and control over the strategic behavior of enterprises transcends the positions of the liberal managerial and Marxist theorists. For Scott, issues of ownership and control must be considered in the light of relations of power and the constraint created through networks of intercorporate relationships (Scott 1993, 294).

The development of the British ISP market illustrates how networks of intercorporate relations have been sealed through shareholder arrangements that bind sets of (multinational) financial organizations and firms. In some instances, these relationships are reinforced by interlocking directorships. We have underlined the significant presence of a small number of large financial institutions as shareholders that are at the heart of the emerging ISP corporate networks in the United Kingdom. These institutions include the Prudential Corporation, HSBC Investment Bank, Mercury Assets Management, Merryll Lynch & Co. in the United Kingdom, and the FMR Corporation in the United States. We have also highlighted the intercorporate direct and indirect shareholdings between companies, such as Microsoft and AT&T's investments in Telewest Communications, and MCI-WorldCom's indirect holding in Verio Inc. via its subsidiary Brooks Fiber Properties. Our map of developments in the ISP market in the United Kingdom appears to corroborate Scott's assessment of the significance of institutional shareholders within networks of corporations.

However, the institutional constraint highlighted in Scott's work is also expressed through the conditions created by ownership relations for the coordination and control of capital flows (Mintz and Schwartz 1985). These, in turn, influence the conditions for the production of goods and services. John M. Keynes ([1936] 1973) identified the significance of these "new" property relations for the dynamics of industrial growth that emerged alongside the development of joint-stock companies. He argued that these dynamics would constrain capital flows and that they would overcome the "pragmatically" grounded expectations of entrepreneurs. For example,

> With the separation between management and ownership which prevails today and with the development of organised investment markets, a new factor of great importance has entered in, which sometimes facilitates investments but sometimes adds greatly to the instability of the system. . . . But the stock exchange revalues many investments every day and the revaluations give a frequent opportunity to the individual . . . to revise his commitments. It is as

though a farmer, having tapped his barometer after breakfast, could decide to remove his capital from the farming business between 10 and 11 in the morning and reconsider whether he should return to it later in the week. . . . Thus certain classes of investments are governed by the average expectation of those who deal on the Stock Exchange as revealed in the price of shares, rather than by the genuine expectations of the professional entrepreneur [footnote omitted]. (Keynes [1936] 1973, 150–51)

The ISP "constellation" in the United Kingdom appears to be subject to the increasing pressure of large institutional shareholder expectations and the accompanying set of institutional norms that constrain the coordination and control of capital flows in the emerging market. The predominant expectations are for an increasingly rapid turnover time of capital and rapid growth in profits. These expectations are punctuating strategic decision making within the ISP firms. While this is significant for the potential for financial lock-in, the evidence of the "trail" of investment suggests further implications for the evolution of this market. To highlight these, it is necessary to consider the processes of technical change and innovation in this industry and their implications for service production.

The dynamics of technical change and innovation are largely unexplored in the literature we refer to previously. Yet, speculation as to the significant growth potential of the ISP market is substantially dependent on the exploitation of new information and communication technologies and the deployment of new products and services. New technological opportunities often give rise to a period of transition during which the new technologies and services are diffused and implemented. This requires not only *sustained* large-scale capital investment but also substantial learning time, especially in the case of complex technological systems like the Internet. The deployment of high-bandwidth infrastructures is creating the conditions for the delivery of a large (capacity) throughput for new information and communication services, and there is growing excess capacity in some parts of the infrastructure. However, the capital invested in the infrastructure has an engineering life cycle spanning several decades, and this is creating intense pressures for the realization of short-term expectations for a return on capital. In the highly competitive ISP market, the risk for investors is substantial. As a result, there is increased tension between the financial expectations of investors and the constraints created by the technological system in terms of both time and learning opportunities. This tension is being resolved under present market conditions through strategies that promote a rapid scaling up of the use of available infrastructure capacity. In the ISP market, the predominant strategies appear to be aimed at creating opportunities to exploit scale economies in infrastructure provision through consolidation between ISPs and network facility providers, and achieving economies of time through intensification of the development and marketing of increasingly higher-value added services.

The ISPs' strategies for achieving rapid returns on their financial backers' investments differ from those that characterized the formerly separate telecommunication carriage and content industries. The major players in the ISP market appear to be devising strategies aimed at achieving quasi-monopoly positions in newly differentiated segments of the market. Their redefinition of the *scope* of the ISP market seems to be aimed at increasing their capacity to integrate and systematize learning to support production and distribution in new market areas.[24] To the extent that this is achieved, it creates the conditions for optimizing their use of network capacity and securing a return on capital at a pace that may meet the expectations of financial institutions and other firms in their networks that are providing financial resources.

Recent developments in the ISP market in the United Kingdom have been marked by a wave of acquisitions of small new entrants by large British-owned incumbents and by American-owned firms. These acquisitions may be playing an important role by reducing the time needed to learn and experiment in the new market and the time needed to build market presence. By acquiring the new entrants, the acquiring firms draw in the capabilities needed to develop new value chains that have scope for future development. At the same time, these acquisitions and mergers offer opportunities to increase control over the revenues generated by the expansion of network capacity use and the sale of higher-value added goods and services.

The lesson from the restructuring of Cable & Wireless Communications and the development of NTL is that the realization of technological, financial, and knowledge lock-ins is dependent upon strategic repositioning aimed at streamlining the scale *and* scope of the large ISPs' markets. The present round of repositioning is occurring alongside substantial capitalization. As the cases of NTL and Cable & Wireless Communications, and AOL and MCI-WorldCom, indicate, asset "swaps" are not uncommon. These asset exchanges are generating substantial revenues for large shareholders and creating positive feedback that, in turn, gives rise to higher expectations and further speculation.

For the entrepreneurs who invest in the ISP business, exit represents an opportunity to capitalize on intangible assets embodied in learning and technological innovation. Acquisition of the small start-ups offers a way for these companies to access bandwidth and generates funds for business expansion. Some new-entrant ISPs have managed to sustain their growth through partnership agreements. For example, the subscription-free dial-up ISP, X-Stream, has a partnership agreement with Level 3 Communications of the United States (X-Stream 1999). This strategy also was initially chosen by the Internet Technology Group (ITG), one of the new entrants in the subscription segment of the ISP market. However, in this case, ITG is being acquired by its partner, Concentric Networks.

Our analysis of the linkages between the players in the top layer of the ISP market for dial-up access in the United Kingdom illustrates that, despite the nascent characteristics of this market and the appearance of multiple new entrants, there is a trail of financial capital suggesting that the evolution of the ISP market will not necessarily be consistent with a broad interpretation of the public interest of citizens, consumers, and small firms. The processes of creative destruction and the flurry of new entry in the ISP market do not appear to be delivering a very high quality of service for these users. The subscription-free dial-up ISPs are engaged in a frenzy of competition that is accompanied by their failure to sustain high-quality services for the end user. For example, the rate of dial-up failure in 1999 increased by 50 percent over the previous year, and some companies are offering technical support for their customers at premium telephone tariffs ranging from fifty pence to one pound per minute. Waiting times on technical support lines managed by automatic answering services can be up to ten minutes.[25]

The competitive process in the nascent ISP market in the United Kingdom is generating opportunities for British-owned small new entrants that are championed by entrepreneurs. Some have realized large capital gains through timely exit strategies. For the firms that have acquired the early start-ups or extended their services from the United States into the United Kingdom, there is evidence of consolidation and of the formation of tightly woven webs or networks of control. However, the stability of these firms is uncertain. Their high levels of capitalization are associated with the valuation of intangible assets, that is, of their technological capabilities and competencies. The wave of investment in the United Kingdom is the result of a "propensity to speculate" on technological and market potential rather than on the potential of tangible assets.

Speculative trends are not simply directed to existing tangible assets but to the potential benefits that might be lost if the assets supporting innovation are not controlled or acquired (Langlois and Robertson 1995, 133–34). As such, speculative activity on tangible assets becomes the manifestation of the future expectations of financial (and corporate) investors. It does not rely upon the *present* value of productive assets—that is, these assets are depreciating and are being "consumed." In the face of uncertainty and a highly competitive environment, investors anticipate productive and innovative capacity. The resulting financial value assigned to assets is a reflection of the potential benefits of intangible assets such as expected developments in technology, learning, and innovative products and services. It reflects the competencies available for future production and, therefore, the realization of future income.[26]

For these firms a critical issue is time. Stock market investors could curtail the ISP boom if the speculative future fails to materialize. In order to sustain a high level of capitalization, the major players in the dial-up ISP market must learn how to transform prophecy into reality. They must overcome the hurdles of uncertain trends in technological development, the uneven deployment of infrastructure capacity, and skill deficits for service production and within potential user communities. They also face the challenge of integrating new sets of capabilities for both carriage and content creation and for marketing within their organizations and building strong relationships with their customers.

Conclusion

On the basis of the empirical evidence we have presented in this chapter, it appears likely that the predominant interest of investors who own the most significant ISPs in the United Kingdom market is in promoting attractive conditions for short-term revenue growth and the maintenance of high levels of capitalization. The development of the British ISP market suggests a trend toward the emergence of an oligopolistic industry that is inconsistent with the evolution of a network "commons" that would be responsive to social values. Our analysis exposes the networks of control that are emerging through a reconstitution of market power in the ISP market. It illustrates trends that seem to favor: (1) the consolidation of the market in the hands of financial investors whose primary interests are in the rapid turnover time of capital rather than in the long-term development of services targeted at citizens, consumers, and smaller firms; (2) a race between a small number of large players to consolidate the knowledge base (competencies and capabilities) needed to succeed in the new markets; and (3) increasing barriers to entry for small players that confront constraints on their capacity to expand and to offer financially viable services as alternatives to those provided by the large players. The combination of these trends is likely to produce pressure for the reduction of variety, an outcome that runs counter to the view that the Internet's open architecture encourages diversity in the supply of content and information services.

In the light of these observations, it seems likely that American-style "unregulation" will be inappropriate for the governance of Internet-related markets in the United Kingdom. In the absence of market intervention, the market terrain seems likely to be left to multinational players. This will marginalize small regional players within niche markets with limited scope for growth. The large ISPs have strong incentives to lock in users in order to secure future revenues and to maintain high rates of capitalization. The strategies for achieving lock-in have expanded beyond those that were characteristic of the formerly segmented carriage and content industries. Liberalization has opened up new opportunities for competitive entry, but the privatization of the incumbents within the domestic market has altered the dynamics of the new markets. As Mintz and Schwartz (1985, 252) have argued with respect to transformations within the U.S. economy, "collective decision making within the business world directs capital flows that commit the resources of the country as a whole to the projects selected by the financial institutions." In the case of the ISP market in the United Kingdom, the networks of intercorporate relations, which are forming around a few core financial institutions and the top ISPs, appear to be "committing" the United Kingdom to trajectories for the evolution of Internet services that favor the large business users.

In the light of these developments, it will be important to investigate the emergence and exercise of "market power" in the ISP market in a way that exposes the interdependencies between technological change, innovation, and the role of finance in the process of competition. The current trajectory for ISP development is consistent with the interests of large corporations and expectations for strong revenue growth and rapid capitalization. In the light of the bifurcation of the ISP market and these incentives, opportunities for safeguarding the public interest are likely to come to light only through a more systematic analysis of the interplay between these factors and the sociopolitical conditions in which they are embedded.

The two poles that we highlighted in the introduction to this chapter treated regulation as a means of promoting the free play of market forces, on the one hand, and, on the other, as a necessary means of restoring the discipline of the market where monopoly or substantial market power are present. Both these poles of the regulatory spectrum are predicated upon the assumption that market forces can deliver economically and socially desirable outcomes. We acknowledge that regulation of some aspects of the carriage and content industries will continue to be needed to address the problems created by conventional "monopoly focal points." However, our analysis suggests that traditional forms of industry-specific regulation will not provide a satisfactory means of protecting the public interest in the emergent market. The newly articulated "focal points" of power in the ISP market will need to be tackled through new forms of regulation and governance. These will need to be formulated in the light of a better understanding of the evolutionary sources of market power and their implications for social, economic, and technological outcomes.

Notes

1. This has been so since the establishment of the Interstate Commerce Commission (ICC) in 1887. The ICC was created to stem turmoil in the railway industry. It was abolished in 1995 with the creation of the Surface Transportation Board. The Federal Communications Commission (FCC) was established by the Communications Act of 1934 and is charged with regulating interstate and international communications by radio, television, wire, satellite, and cable.

2. British Telecom became a public limited company on 1 August 1984 and 51 percent of the company's shares were sold to the public in November of the same year. The company faced competition from Mercury when it launched services initially in the City of London in 1993 and from cellular radio network service licensees granted to Cellnet and Vodafone. A director general of telecommunications was appointed and the Office of Telecommunications was established in 1984.

3. Oxman cites evidence of the low barriers to entry for Internet service suppliers in support of his argument in favor of "unregulation"; "Over 6,000 Internet Service Providers (ISPs) today offer dial-up service to the Internet, and over 95% of Americans have access to at least four local ISPs [footnote omitted]. Although America OnLine, with over 18 million world-wide members, dominates the ISP field, millions of Americans rely on small one POP [Point of Presence] [footnote omitted] or medium-sized ISPs for their service, ISPs that may serve several hundred or fewer customers" (Oxman 1999, 17).

4. This view is closely aligned with the depiction of competition given by Clark (1961) and is deeply embedded in Melody's (1986) analysis of developments in telecommunication markets. More generally, we take a classical approach, which analyzes competition "not as a state of affairs, but as a dynamic process linking technical change with market behaviour" (Corsi 1991, 113) and which links processes of division of labor through technical change with the evolution of market structure.

5. The technical definition of the Internet was determined by the Federal Networking Council (FNC) in October 1995 (Leiner et al. 1998; see also Zakon 1999). The National Science Foundation lifted restrictions on the commercial use of the Internet in the United States in 1991, and by 1995 the Inter-

net backbone network was entirely operated by private network operators. In the United Kingdom, the start of the JANET service using the TCP/IP began in 1991.

6. See Department of Commerce (1999); Department of Trade and Industry (1998); and European Commission High Level Group of Experts (1997).

7. This section draws extensively on evidence from company annual reports and accounts, information obtained from company web sites and press releases, newspaper articles, and so on, the details of which are available from the authors. Substantial information was obtained from U.S. Securities and Exchange Commission (SEC) Filings, particularly schedules 13D and 13G. The "Guide to Corporate Filings" can be accessed at http://*www.sec.gov*. Detailed references to all documentation can be obtained by contacting the authors.

8. A first wave of inward foreign investment occurred in the early phase of liberalization in the cable and telecommunication industry in the mid-1980s. There was a substantial inflow of investment into the cable television industry by American-owned firms. This was followed by a period of disappointing cable (and later telephony) market development and consolidation of ownership. There has been a recent flurry of investment as cable companies position themselves in the Internet access market (Collins and Murroni 1996).

9. Energis also acquired Unisource Carrier Services (UCS) from Unisource NV, a well-established telecommunication network provider, offering Internet access and services.

10. The major shareholders in Dixons Group plc are Merrill Lynch & Co. Inc., with 11.95 percent of common stock, Mercury Asset Management Ltd, with 10.94 percent, Capital Group Companies Inc., with 7.03 percent, and the Prudential Corporation Group of companies, with 4.02 percent.

11. The Labour Party in Britain distributed Freeserve's software as part of an advertising campaign with *Labour Inside,* vol. 1, in October 1999.

12. In October 1999, CurrantBun was expected to be relaunched with a new name at a marketing cost of £4 million.

13. LineOne was a subscription-free ISP. The company moved into the subscription-free segment of the ISP market as a result of the growing strength of competitors in the consumer segment of the market.

14. The National Grid plc was formed in March 1990 as part of the privatization of the electricity supply industry in England and Wales. It was owned jointly by twelve regional electricity companies until it was floated on 11 December 1995 on the London Stock Exchange. Energis was formed in 1993 as a telecommunication spin-off of the National Grid's electricity transmission activities.

15. The National Grid formed a consortium with SPRINT and France Telecom and won the license to operate national and international telecommunication services in Brazil.

16. The Massachusetts Department of Telecommunication and Energy must approve the merger. The National Grid plc made financial provisions for the acquisition of EUA in its agreement for the acquisition of NEES.

17. Colt Telecom launched an ISP in the United Kingdom, Colt Internet, in 1993. Colt Telecom selected NTL to terminate its switched traffic outside London and to provide leased digital private circuits between London and major cities in the United Kingdom.

18. NTL Inc. owns just under 50 percent of Virgin Net's common stock.

19. It is important to note that Telewest is a subsidiary of Microsoft and Libert Media, and Libert Media is a subsidiary of AT&T. Microsoft and Libert Media hold, respectively, 29.9 percent and 21.6 percent of Tele-west's stock. NTL, Cable & Wireless, and Telewest compete in the United Kingdom.

20. As a result of the transaction, "Existing CWC Shareholders will receive 3.6301 shares of new NTL Common Stock and 190.18 pounds in cash for every 100 CWC Shares held (and so on in proportion to their holdings, assuming no adjustment is made). CWC Shareholders' entitlements to fractions of new NTL Common Stock will be aggregated and sold in the market and the net proceeds paid to the relevant CWC Shareholders" (Cable & Wireless plc 1999).

21. At an exchange rate of 46.250 for 100 (former) CWC shares.

22. "Effective at 11.58pm on 29 January 1998, WorldCom Inc. ("WorldCom") acquired the company pursuant to the merger (the "Merger") of BV Acquisition, Inc., a wholly-owned subsidiary of WorldCom, with and into Brooks. Upon consummation of the merger, the company became a wholly-owned subsidiary of WorldCom" (Brooks Fiber Properties Inc. 1998, 3).

23. These acquisitions included MovieFone Inc., a major movie guide and ticketing interactive service; Spinner Networks Inc., which provides music over the Internet; When Inc., offering a personalized event directory and calendar services; At Wet Inc.; and Personal Logic Inc.

24. The benefits of the division of labor and specialization have long been the subject of the analysis of changing industrial structure. Adam Smith argued that the division of labor, technical change, and specialization are essential to the saving of production and circulation time and to the ability to increase capacity throughput (Smith [1776] 1997, 7).

25. Calls were made by the first author to premium-rate technical support lines. X-Stream responded in just under ten minutes, and the call was charged at a rate of fifty pence per minute. These costs in time and money must be added to those paid by the customer for use of online services.

26. "Money, in its significant attribute is, above all, a subtle device for linking the present to the future" (Keynes [1936] 1973, 293–94).

References

America OnLine. 1999a. Press release. America OnLine, at http://www.aol.co.uk/press/releases/1999/pr990824b.htm. Accessed on 27 September 1999.

———. 1999b. Press release. America OnLine, at http://www.aol.co.uk/press/releases/1999/, dated 17 February.

———. 1999c. Securities Exchange Commission (SEC) filings, form 10-K. Securities Exchange Commission (SEC), 30 June, Washington, D.C.

Bar, F., S. Cohen, P. Cowhey, B. DeLong, M. Kleeman, and J. Zysman. 1999. Defending the Internet revolution in the broadband era: When doing nothing is doing harm. Berkeley Roundtable on the International Economy (BRIE), University of California at Berkeley, E-conomy Working Paper no. 12, August, Berkeley, Calif.

Berle, A. A., and G. C. Means. [1932] 1968. *The modern corporation and private property*. Rev. ed. New York: Harcourt Brace.

Brooks Fiber Properties Inc. 1998. Securities and Exchange Commission (SEC) filings, submission 10K-405. Securities and Exchange Commission, 29 January, Washington, D.C.

Cable & Wireless Communications plc. 1999. CWC annual report 1999. Cable & Wireless Communications plc, London, at http://www.cwcom.co.uk/investorsmainpages/annua199/. Accessed 29 October 1999.

Cable & Wireless plc. 1999. Press releases. Cable & Wireless plc, at //206.142.4.70/press/1999, London.

Clark, J. M. 1961. *Competition as a dynamic process*. New York: Brookings Institution Press.

Collins, R., and C. Murroni. 1996. *New media, new policies: Media and communications strategies for the future*. Cambridge: Polity Press.

Computergram International. 1999. Oftel recommends price competition in free ISP Market. *Computerwire Inc*, 11 March.

Computerwire, Inc. 1999. Energis to buy into Freeserve, network briefing. *Computerwire Inc*, 25 June.

Corsi, M. 1991. *Division of labour, technical change and economic growth*. Aldershot: Avebury.

Department of Commerce. 1999. The emerging digital economy II. U.S. Department of Commerce, Washington, D.C., June.

Department of Trade and Industry. 1998. Our competitive future: Building the knowledge driven economy, the 1998 competitiveness white paper. Department of Trade and Industry, London, December.

Downes, T. A., and S. M. Greenstein. 1999. Do commercial ISPs provide universal access?" Tufts University and Northwestern University, paper prepared for the Telecommunication Policy Research 1998 Conference, 2 December 1998, Medford, Mass., and Evanston, Ill., http://skew2.kellogg.nwu.edu/~greenste/research/. Accessed 27 August 1999.

Durlacher. 1997. The Durlacher quarterly Internet report. Durlacher, corporate edition, London, Q1 1997 at http://195.224.46.246/internet_report/article2.htm. Accessed 29 September 1999.

———. 1999a. Free access providers bring subscription dial-up market to a standstill. Durlacher, news release, London, 26 July, http://www.durlacher.com/news/newsdetail.cfm?ID=8. Accessed 29 September 1999.

———. 1999b. High speed Internet access market represents ú320 m opportunity for disenchanged UK ISPs. Durlacher, news release, London, 18 May, http://www.durlacher.com/news/newsdetail.cfm?ID=3. Accessed 29 September 1999.

Eliasson, G. 1999. The Internet, electroinc business and the EURO—On information products, market transparency and Internet economics. Royal Institute of Technology, Stockholm, mimeo, 2 February.

European Commission High Level Group of Experts. 1997. Building the European information society for us all: Final policy report of the high-level expert group, Directorate General for Employment, Industrial Relations and Social Affairs. Office for Official Publications of the European Communities, Luxembourg.

Federal Communications Commission. 1999. In the matter of implementation of local competition provisions in the Telecommunications Act of 1996, intercarrier compensation for ISPP-bound traffic, declaratory ruling in CC docket no. 96–98 and notice of proposed rulemaking in CC docket no. 99–68. Washington, D.C., 25 February.

Horowitz, R. 1989. *The irony of regulatory reform: The deregulation of American telecommunications.* Oxford: Oxford University Press.

Huston, G. 1999. Interconnection, peering and settlements. Based in part on G Huston, *ISP Survival Guide* (New York: John Wiley & Sons, 1998), http://www.telstra.net/gih/peerdocs/peer.html. Accessed 25 September 1999.

Keynes, J. M. [1936] 1973. *The general theory of employment, interest and money.* London and Basingstoke: Macmillan Cambridge University Press for the Royal Economic Society.

Langlois, R. N., and P. L. Robertson. 1995. *Firms, markets and economic change.* London and New York: Routledge.

Lehr, W. H., and M. B. H. Weiss. 1996. The political economy of congestion charges and settlements in packet networks. *Telecommunications Policy* 20(3): 219–31.

Leiner, B. M., V. G. Cerf, D. D. Clark, R. E. Kahn, L. Kleinrock, D. Lynch, J. Postel, L. G. Roberts, and S. Wolff. 1998. *A brief history of the Internet.* http://www.iso.org/internet-history: 20 February. Accessed 16 August 1999.

MacKie-Mason, J., S. Shenker, and H. R. Varian. 1996. Service architecture and content provision: The network provider as editor. *Telecommunications Policy* 20(3): 203–18.

Melody, W. H. 1986. Telecommunication—Policy directions for the technology and information services. *Oxford Surveys in Information Technology* 3: 77–106.

Menshikov, S. M. 1969. *Millionaires and managers.* Moscow: Progress Publishers.

Mintz, B., and M. Schwartz. 1985. *The power structure of American business.* Chicago and London: University of Chicago Press.

Murphy, K. 1999. UK-Internet—How free can an ISP be? network briefing. *Computerwire Inc.,* 3 May.

NTL, Inc. 1998. NTL annual report and accounts. NTL Inc., London, at http://www.ntl.com/investors/. Accessed 22 October 1999.

———. 1999. NTL first quarter 1999 financial results. NTL Inc., London, at http://www.ntl.com/investors/quarterly/1st-1999. Accessed 11 August 1999.

Oxman, J. 1999. The FCC and the unregulation of the Internet. Federal Communications Commission, Office of Plans and Policy working paper no. 31, July, Washington, D.C.

Pavitt, K. 1997. Technologies, products and organisation in the innovating firm: What Adam Smith tells us and Joseph Schumpeter doesn't. SPRU University of Sussex, CoPS working paper no. 40, September, Brighton.

Schumpeter, J. A. 1961. *The theory of economic development: An inquiry into profits, capital, credit, interest and the business cycle.* Oxford: Oxford University Press.

Scott, J. 1985. *Corporations, classes and capitalism.* 2d rev. ed. London: Hutchinson.

———. 1986. *Capitalist property and financial power: A comparative study of Britain, the United States and Japan.* Brighton: Wheatsheaf Books.

———. 1993. Corporate groups and network structure," in *Corporate control and accountability: Changing structures and the dynamics of regulation,* edited by J. McCahery, S. Picciotto, and C. Scott, 291–304. Oxford: Clarendon Press.

Scottish Power plc. 1999. Annual report 1998–99. Scottish Power plc, http://www.scottishpower.plc.uk/ara99/.

Shepherd, W. G. 1995. Contestability vs. competition—Once more. *Land Economics* 71(August): 299–309.

Smith, A. [1776] 1997. *The wealth of nations, books I, II, III.* London: Penguin Books.

Srinagesh, P. 1997. Internet cost structures and interconnection agreements, in *Internet economics,* edited by L. McKnight and J. Baileym, 121–54. Cambridge, Mass.: MIT Press.

Trebing, H. M. 1995. Structural change and the future of regulation. *Land Economics* 71(3): 401–14.

———. 1998. Market concentration and the sustainability of market power in public utility industries. *National Regulatory Research Institute Quarterly Bulletin* 19(1): 61–67.

Trebing, H. M., and M. Estabrooks. 1995. The globalization of telecommunications: A study in the struggle to control markets and technology. *Journal of Economic Issues* 29(2): 535–44.

Trebing, H. M., and M. F. Wilsey. 1993. The limitations of deregulation—An overview. *Utilities Policy* 3(4): 274.

X-Stream. 1999. Press releases. X-Stream, at http://*www.x-stream.com*/uk/ flash/1024res.html, 18 October. Accessed on 19 November 1999, London.

Zakon, R. H. 1999. Hobbes' Internet timeline v4.2. August, Internet Society, http://infor.isoc.org/guest/zakon/Internet/History/HIT.html. Accessed 19 September 1999.

Part 3

Costing and Pricing
and the Public Interest

Regulation of Retail Telecommunications Rates

DAVID GABEL

Introduction

The regulation of the telecommunications market has changed radically in the past forty years. While various regulatory and judicial decisions opened up limited sectors of the telecommunications market during the post–World War II era, the passage of the 1996 Telecommunications Act created radical new opportunities for rivalry.[1] The law established ground rules that afforded entrants the opportunity to compete by using their own network facilities, relying in part or in whole upon the incumbents' network facilities, or by reselling existing retail services.

The purpose of this chapter is to examine the degree to which utility commissions can exercise forbearance in the economic regulation of retail services in light of recent, or prospective, market developments resulting from the Act.[2]

The Evolution of Retail Services Regulation, from Rate Base to Price Cap Regulation

Traditionally, regulation established rates that were designed to afford a regulated telecommunications firm the opportunity to earn a fair return on investment. Regulators referred to the amount of investment that was included in the rate calculation as the rate base.[3] With rate base regulation, a firm's potential profits increased as its level of investment expanded. In a well-known article economists Averch and Johnson hypothesized that this direct link between investment and profits biases firms' investment decisions in favor of excess capital, relative to other inputs. This investment bias, they go on to argue, is not likely to lead to cost-minimizing outcomes in the provision of service.[4]

Rate base regulation was also faulted for not providing incentives for firms to minimize production costs. Critics pointed out that basing rates on booked expenses, especially in markets where rivalry was lacking, provided no incentive to minimize these costs.[5]

Partially as a response to these concerns the United Kingdom began, in 1984, to experiment with a new form of economic regulation of retail telecommunications services. This was price cap regulation. Price caps were introduced as a means of improving the efficiency of telecommunications prices. Price cap regulation is designed, in principle, to reward overall productivity rather than just capital investment. Since all that is being regulated is the price of the services provided, in theory, it will create incentives for firms to allocate resources optimally between capital, labor, and materials.[6] Rather than relying on regulators to undertake a periodic review of the existing rates, price cap regulation provided a systematic method for adjusting rates to reflect productivity gains. Under price caps, retail rates are adjusted on an annual basis to reflect the higher rate of productivity growth achieved in the telecommunications industry relative to the rest of the economy. The regulatory price adjustment mechanism is designed to emulate the behavior of competitive markets, where changes in a sector's total factor productivity growth is typically reflected in the final price of that sector's retail products.

Subsequent to its introduction in the United Kingdom, price cap regulation had been widely adopted by regulatory agencies around the world.[7] In the United States price cap regulation has replaced rate-of-return regulation in 70 percent of the states in the country, plus the District of Columbia.[8] This widespread adoption is attributable to the perceived shortcomings in rate base regulation and a belief that the administrative costs of price cap regulation would be lower than those of traditional rate base regulation.

Price caps provided an orderly method for making marginal adjustments to retail rates. Annual price adjustments ranged from price reductions of approximately 3 percent, to none at all. While arguably an improvement of the price record under rate base regulation, the pro-competition measures of the recently enacted Telecommunications Act of 1996 might bring better improvements still.

The Telecommunications Act of 1996

On 8 February 1996 the Telecommunications Act of 1996 (the "Act") was signed into law. The 1996 Act is a comprehensive overhaul of the

Communications Act of 1934, making significant changes in the law affecting the regulation of broadcasting, cable, and telephony with less extensive changes in satellite and spectrum regulation and in the FCC's own internal processes.[9]

Broadly speaking, the intent and purpose of the act was "to provide for a pro-competitive, de-regulatory national policy framework designed to rapidly accelerate private sector deployment of advanced telecommunications and information technologies and services to all Americans by opening all telecommunications markets to competition, . . ."[10] thereby securing "lower prices and higher quality services for American telecommunications consumers. . . ."[11]

One of the principle goals of the act regarding the provision of telephone service was to open the local exchange and exchange access markets to competitive entry.[12] In advancing this goal the interconnection section of the act, section 251, imposes several obligations on the Incumbent Local Exchange Carriers. Three important obligations are:

1. *Interconnection*. Incumbent Local Exchange Carriers (ILECs) have the duty to enable competitors to interconnect with the ILECs' network, for the transmission and routing of exchange service and exchange access, at any technically feasible point within the network. These services must be offered at rates, terms, and conditions that are just, reasonable, and nondiscriminatory.
2. *Unbundled access*. ILECs must provide unbundled network elements (UNEs) to competitors at any technically feasible point within the network. UNEs must be provided in a manner enabling them to be combined to provide telecommunications service at rates, terms, and conditions that are just, reasonable, and nondiscriminatory.
3. *Resale*. ILECs must offer all their retail services for resale by competitors at wholesale rates.[13]

Among the rules devised by the FCC for the implementation of the interconnection section of the act are the rules establishing the methodology to be used in determining the rates at which unbundled network elements (UNEs) and interconnection will be made available by the ILECs to their competitors. The methodology the FCC has chosen to adopt for this purpose is the Total Element Long Run Incremental Cost (TELRIC) Plus methodology.[14] According to the FCC, this methodology is a forward-looking pricing methodology that replicates how competitive markets actually operate, and best approximates what it would actually cost an efficient, competitive firm to produce UNEs and to provide interconnection.[15] The commission and its supporters believe that the TELRIC Plus pricing of UNEs and interconnection will adequately compensate the ILECs for all forward-looking costs of providing UNEs and interconnection, including the costs of capital, and will provide for a reasonable allocation of joint and common costs.[16] Proponents of TELRIC aver that, since prices are driven to forward-looking costs in competitive markets, and because the TELRIC Plus methodology replicates how competitive markets operate, TELRIC Plus provides ILECs with a constitutionally sufficient approximation of the fair market value of their property in a competitive market.[17]

By making UNEs and interconnection available to ILEC competitors at TELRIC Plus based rates the FCC was intending to "facilitate competition on a reasonable and efficient basis by all firms in the industry by establishing prices for interconnection and unbundled elements based on costs similar to those incurred by the incumbents. . . ."[18] Allowing competitors access to the ILEC network in this manner would, the FCC hoped, enable them to provide telecommunications services to consumers in an efficient and competitive manner, which would drive retail prices down to their competitive levels.[19]

While the FCC has adopted the TELRIC Plus methodology for the setting of interconnection and UNE rates, and has adopted other rules regarding the interconnection, UNE, and resale obligations of the ILECs, it is up to the various state commissions to actually establish the rates and to enforce the obligations in a manner consistent with the intent of the act.

As I argue in the following, I believe that this opens up the possibility for state commissions to experiment with a more light-handed regulatory approach for retail rates than has heretofore been possible under either rate-of-return or price cap regulation, given the conditions outlined later in the chapter.

Is It Possible to Forgo the Regulation of Retail Rates?

The passage of the 1996 Telecommunications Act created a regulatory structure that was designed to encourage rivalry through the offering of competitive telecommunications services. To date, what competition has emerged has been concentrated in the urban markets. In these markets, entrants have targeted both residential and business customers.[20] For example, a new supplier of telecommunications services, RCN, offers customers an attractive bundle of telecommunications and entertainment services that results in substantial savings. As shown in the table below, the level of savings experienced by a user in Newton, Massachusetts, greatly

	Rates Prior to Entry	RCN
Two telephone lines	$100	
Cable television	$38	
Cable modem	$40	
Internet service	$20	
Thirty Commercial-free radio channels	Not applicable	
Total	$198	$139

Figure 1   Price Savings Due to Facility Based Competition: An Example.

exceeds the level of price reductions that were being achieved under price cap regulation. The advent of competition lowered the user's rates by 42 percent, a value that greatly exceeds the reductions realized under the current price-cap regulations.[21]

Other cable companies also offer bundles to residential customers that provide significant savings. For example, NTL, a large cable operator in the United Kingdom, offers a bundled package of telephone service and seven free additional television channels, at the *same* monthly charge that British Telecommunications (BT) assesses for telephone service alone.[22]

The fact that substantial price savings are offered by RCN and other facility-based providers is not surprising. The construction of a telecommunications or entertainment network requires large fixed and sunk costs. Once the network is constructed, the firm must obtain a substantial share of the market in order to avoid operating at a sizeable cost disadvantage.[23] Consequently, the cost structure of the industry dictates that the facility-based entrant price services aggressively.

An entrant that relies on resale or the leasing of unbundled network elements (UNEs) faces less of an imperative to aggressively price services. Whereas this type of entrant has not incurred fixed costs of similar magnitude, it can rely to a greater extent on the umbrella pricing of the incumbent. This type of entrant can slowly build up its market share without engaging in price warfare with the incumbent.

However, even an entrant engaged solely in resale will incur substantial fixed costs in establishing a visible presence in the market and in training its workforce.[24] An entrant choosing to break into the market through the leasing of unbundled network elements will incur these costs in addition to those of collocating the equipment necessary for the leasing of

UNEs. As is the case with facilities-based providers, the presence of these nontrivial fixed costs would spur these entrants to aggressively pursue signing up customers for their services in order to recover their fixed costs from a large customer base.

According to the FCC, the act allows an entrant to lease UNEs from incumbent carriers at TELRIC Plus rates, which are equivalent to the economic cost of production of the network elements involved.[25] Since the economic cost of production is typically below the embedded cost-of-service, this provides entrants with the opportunity to offer service at a price that is lower than the incumbent's existing retail price levels.[26] This gives would-be market entrants a strong incentive to pursue this method of entering the market and has even greater potential than resale to bring competition to the local market. In fact, recent FCC data indicates that competing carriers have a collocation presence in central offices serving almost 50 percent of the nation's local telephone lines.[27] The extent of this presence has the potential to place a viable constraint on the pricing of retail telecommunications services, even in markets lacking numerous facility-based suppliers of those services.[28]

In addition to the resale and UNE leasing opportunities afforded by the act, there is a third option made possible by the fact that the act allows competing carriers to purchase combinations of network elements, also at TELRIC Plus rates.[29] This gives competing carriers the option of "leasing an incumbent's entire set of UNEs—a method that has come to be called the UNE-Platform."[30] This option may be even more cost-effective than the leasing of individual UNEs, as the leasing of the entire platform does not necessarily require a competing carrier to incur collocation costs. Preliminary evidence from New York, where the FCC recently concluded that Bell Atlantic had opened its local market to competitors and granted it the ability to provide inter- and intrastate long-distance service, indicates that the leasing of the UNE-Platform is an option that a large number of competing carriers will be likely to pursue.[31] This view is further enforced by a General Accounting Office report that noted: "In one of the five states we visited, the Bell Company was being explicitly required to offer the platform, and a competing carrier reported that, as a result, the company had acquired upwards of 60,000 new local residential customers in that state during the first 5 months of 1999."[32]

Given these recent developments, I believe that it may be worthwhile experimenting with a more light-handed approach to the regulation of retail services, one that would utilize the resale and UNE leasing opportunities made possible by the Telecommunications Act of 1996 to encourage new providers to enter the market, thereby putting a competitive restraint on the pricing of retail services.

I offer this proposal based on my assessment of the strength of the two alternatives, rate base regulation and price caps. Returning to rate base regulation is a nonissue, as there seems to be little or no interest in doing so. Effective rate base regulation requires significant labor resources and it's therefore expensive to implement. In light of the resources that commission are expending on estimating the cost of unbundled network elements and interconnection, I believe it is advisable for the agencies to concentrate their resources on issues surrounding the 1996 Telecommunications Act rather than reviewing embedded cost data. Furthermore, with the convergence of telecommunications, data, and entertainment services through a common platform, rate base regulation is increasingly difficult to implement, because it is hard to separate the regulated from the nonregulated services.

As regards the present dominant system of regulation, price caps, there are shortcomings with this regulatory methodology as well. Arguably the greatest shortcoming of price caps is the tepid price mechanisms adopted by regulatory commissions in the United States. When the federal and state regulatory commissions adopted price caps in the early 1990s, they had little or no experience in measuring total factor productivity. Lacking familiarity with this issue, the commissions relied on the advice of the local exchange companies, which told them that the rate of total factor productivity growth was only slightly different than the rate for the entire economy. Consequently, despite the acceleration in demand for telecommunications services and the decline in the cost of many important inputs, the rate of price change did not reflect the underlying cost structure of the industry. As illustrated in table 1, following, this resulted in firms earning rates-of-return that greatly exceeded their authorized rate-of-return.[33] Under price caps, firms are generally entitled to retain these higher earnings.

The inability of price cap regulation to effectively deal with the market effects of the unanticipated explosion in demand for telecommunications services, and the concomitant decline in the cost of providing those services, highlights an advantage of rate base regulation relative to price cap regulation. Under rate base regulation, when something unanticipated like this happens, regulators are in a better position to speedily step in and make an adjustment to reflect the new conditions. Under a price caps regime, on the other hand, regulators typically establish a term of three to five years duration, during which time a firm's retail price is allowed to rise by a prearranged formula. During this time period the firm is not subjected to any

Table 1 Return on Regulated Net Investment f or Selected Price Cap Companies.

Company	State	Company Return on Regulated Net Investment 1996[a]	Company Return on Regulated Net Investment 1997	Company Return on Regulated Net Investment 1998
Ameritech	Illinois	25.98%	28.82%	28.50%
Ameritech	Michigan	33.54%	37.59%	38.29%
Ameritech	Ohio	23.60%	24.41%	26.14%
Ameritech	Wisconsin	29.16%	29.35%	46.80%
Bell Atlantic	Delaware	10.04%	11.86%	13.09%
Bell Atlantic	Maryland	13.59%	13.48%	14.61%
Bell Atlantic	New Jersey	10.24%	8.57%	13.48%
Bell Atlantic	Pennsylvania	9.53%	9.03%	10.56%
Bell Atlantic	Virginia	7.35%	12.00%	19.05%
Bell Atlantic	West Virginia	12.05%	15.54%	15.50%
Bell Atlantic	Maine	16.29%	16.25%	15.36%
Bell Atlantic	Massachusetts	16.84%	14.04%	15.80%
Bell Atlantic	New York	11.79%	7.80%	3.66%
Bell Atlantic	Rhode Island	18.34%	18.86%	18.37%
SBC	Kansas	9.72%	9.29%	10.54%
SBC	Missouri	10.28%	12.03%	8.89%
U S West	Colorado	8.79%	11.15%	8.88%
Return on Regulated Investment for the 150 largest telephone companies[*]\		14.19%	13.24%	14.13%

[a]The rate-of-return was derived using data from the Federal Communications Commissions Automated Report Management Information System (ARMIS) Report 43–01. The return is for the combined federal and state regulated operations.

Within ARMIS the federal rate-of-return is calculated by dividing the net return by the net investment. Net return is derived by adding together the total operating revenues and other operating income and subtracting from that sum the operating expenses, federal and other taxes, non-operating items. Subtracting the reserves from the sum of plant in-service and other investments derives the net investment. We have applied the same methodology to the combined state and federal data.

[b]These figures were calculated by taking the sum of ARMIS row 1910, Average Net Investment, for the 150 large independent phone companies in the ARMIS database and dividing this by the sum of ARMIS row 1915, Net Return, for the same 150 companies. These figures include data from companies operating under both Price Cap and Rate-of-Return regulation.

regulatory adjustment, regardless of any changes that might be taking place in the market.

What this has meant is that, during this period of tremendous decline in the cost of providing telecommunications services, the price cap regime has not provided the low rates to customers that would be achieved under competition or perhaps under rate base regulation.[34]

In light of the general lack of interest in returning to rate base regulation, as well as the failure of price caps to reflect the underlying productivity being achieved in the telecommunications industry, I feel that regulatory commissions need to try experimenting with another way of reining in retail prices. Given the competitive opportunities created by the act and the proliferation of resellers of telecommunications services in the market, I suggest that the time has come to experiment with rivalry to restrain the prices of the incumbents, but only if the following conditions are satisfied:

1. The imposition of a price ceiling for local telephone service;
2. Parity pricing between rural and urban areas;
3. Imposition of quality-of-service standards and penalties;
4. Full access to operational support systems;
5. Agreement to adhere to TELRIC pricing principles; and
6. Imposition of a built-in mandatory review process.

In the following section I develop the basis for these conditions and describe more fully how I envision them being implemented.

Price Ceiling for Local Telephone Service

The price of exchange service merits continued price protection until we reach a stage of competitive development where the incumbent provider does not have market power and we do not observe suppliers practicing price collusion.[35] In order to protect those customers with the fewest competitive options for this service, the current recurring and nonrecurring prices of exchange service should become the rate ceiling until there is more competitive entry into the market.[36] Of course, a reliance on rivalry, such as I propose, would mean that regulators would not impose any price controls on other retail services (e.g., long-distance or vertical services).[37]

The imposition of this price ceiling should not be construed to preclude incumbent local exchange carriers (ILECs) from creating and packaging for sale new service options that might involve increased prices for exchange service. For example, an ILEC might want to compete by offering unlimited calling for a 50 percent premium. What I am suggesting with the constraint proposed here is that, at a minimum, all customers be allowed to purchase exchange services at a price capped at the current price at which that service is being offered and that new service offerings on the part of the ILECs could not be used to replace this basic package. In other words, consumers would have to be given the option between the existing exchange rates and any other exchange service plan that an ILEC might come up with.

Parity Pricing between Rural and Urban Areas

As described previously, rivalry has been concentrated in urban areas. In this section I argue that because of the 1996 Telecom Act's pricing rules, it is not necessary to limit regulatory forbearance to urban areas. Pricing parity between rural and urban areas is something that is clearly called for under section 254(b)(3) of the Telecommunications Act of 1996, which states that:

> Consumers in all regions of the Nation, including low-income consumers and those in rural, insular, and high cost areas, should have access to telecommunications and information services, including interexchange services and advanced telecommunications and information services, that are reasonably comparable to those services provided in urban areas and that are available at rates that are reasonably comparable to rates charged for similar services in urban areas.

Consequently, even if no resellers offer service in rural areas, subscribers in these territories must be offered the same price packages and options that are provided to customers in more competitive markets. Determining what this means as far as local exchange rates are concerned presents some problems. For example, are exchange rates supposed to be comparable in terms of rates or in terms of the number of customers that can be reached per dollar spent? However, under the scheme I am proposing here, this issue is of reduced importance due to the rate ceiling I propose imposing on exchange service. This constraint will prevent the ILECs from raising the price of exchange service in rural areas.

Because of the potential problem of lack of information concerning the availability of promotional pricing packages when rivalry is lacking, and to eliminate any possibility of promotional red-lining, I would suggest that regulatory commissions require companies to use standardized promotional offering bill inserts which would be sent to all customers, regardless of location. Commissions should also consider requiring companies to offer, through their telephone representatives, nondiscriminatory access to information concerning promotional packages, also regardless of a customer's location. To ensure that this requirement is being followed, commissions can periodically test to make sure that nondiscriminatory access is being provided to these packages. For example, someone from the commission could call and say he or she is moving to a rural area and inquire about phone service availability and pricing options and then call back later and state that he or she is moving to an urban area and make the same inquiry. The caller should be offered the same options for both locations.

Quality-of-Service Standards and Penalties

Where incumbents do not face facility-based competitors, they may lower their quality of service in order to raise their short-run profits. If such degradation in service quality were to occur, this would be harmful to society. In order to insure the provision of adequate telephone service, regulatory commissions need to establish quality-of-service standards at the wire center level. Telephone companies should be penalized if their service at any wire center falls below the standards established by a commission.[38] The penalties should be explicitly designed so that the magnitude of the penalty is greater than the cost savings achieved through the provision of inadequate service. If large penalties are not established, companies may elect to provide poor service. This would be a suboptimal outcome because the private decision of the firm would not reflect the externalities imposed on users of the telecommunications services. When poor service is provided, a cost is imposed on the utility's customers. This cost should be reflected in the establishment of the penalty. Doing this would insure that the penalty is effective in providing firms with the incentive to maintain service quality at desirable levels.

Access to Operational Support Systems

Entry by resellers is greatly aided if they have nondiscriminatory access to an incumbent telephone company's operational support systems.[39] The federal act requires incumbent local exchange carriers to take the necessary steps to create electronic interfaces that will provide entrants with ordering processes that are equal to the ordering processes available to themselves.[40] Prior to obtaining the retail pricing freedom described previously, a state regulatory commission must make a finding that the incumbent local exchange company's operational support system is "commercially available and sufficient to handle reasonable, anticipated commercial volumes."[41]

Agreement to Adhere to TELRIC Pricing Principles

As was mentioned earlier, at note 17, the FCC's pricing methodology has given rise to numerous constitutional challenges and, in fact, has recently been vacated by the U.S. Court of Appeals for the Eighth Circuit in a decision which will likely be appealed to the Supreme Court, where there is the possibility that the decision will be over ruled.[42] For this reason, commissions seeking to implement the market-based proposal I am putting forth here will have to obtain agreement from telecommunications providers to adopt, and adhere to, TELRIC pricing principles regardless of how the Supreme Court eventually rules on this issue. Firms will agree to do this, I believe, because under the approach I am proposing here a much wider variety of products and services will be free from regulatory oversight as to pricing than would have been permitted under either rate of return or price cap regulation. Thus, under the light-handed approach I am advocating, firms will be able to keep more of their profits, while a failure to abide by TELRIC would result in their being submitted to continuing rate of return or price cap regulation.

Built-In Mandatory Review Period

Competition in the market for local exchange service has yet to move significantly beyond the urban markets. Thus, there is not enough data upon which to build a credible forecast as to how retail prices and markets might evolve under the scheme I have proposed here. For this reason there should be a review, say in three to five years' time, of how the plan is operating. This review would examine, to mention only a few items, how much competition had developed in the market in the interviewing years; the current prices of retail services relative to what those services were priced at prior to the beginning of the review period; and the variety of services being offered at the end of the review period relative to what was being offered at the beginning of the period. If this review indicates problems with the light-handed approach advocated here, then commissions may have to go back to the drawing board, or move back to some version of rate based or price cap regulation.

Such a move would not be without precedent. The government of New Zealand, a country that has not only been the most avid advocate of light-handed regulation, but that actually originated the term, has recently decided that its regulatory approach needs to be reviewed in light of the recent changes in the telecommunications markets.[43] This move on the part of New Zealand's government illustrates the point that, in a market dominated by a single provider, relying solely on potential competition to obtain reasonable rates and to spur innovative technological developments, might be ineffective.

Is This Approach Suitable in All Cases?

In the preceding paragraphs I have argued the case for a more light-handed regulatory approach and outlined the conditions I believe necessary for this approach to be successful in introducing meaningful competition into the local telecommunications services market. However, due to the diversity of local institutional factors governing the responsiveness of state commissions to the exercise of economic and political power, this approach is not without its potential pitfalls.

Regulatory institutions tend to promote political coalitions and constituencies in order to survive and prosper.[44] These institutional conditions will, necessarily, vary from state to state and have a significant impact on the type of market transition that will occur. As Trebing has observed, the success of the type of light-handed regulatory approach I am suggesting, "depends almost entirely on the level of competition that can be expected to emerge. If one assumes a reasonably smooth transition to workable competition, then the chances are good. If one assumes a transition to tight oligopoly, then the resulting markets will be flawed and a new form of regulatory oversight will be required."[45]

Given the high level of concentration prevailing in most state telecommunications markets, workable competition will develop only in states whose commissions do not ignore "the impact of dominant players for whom the network becomes a vehicle for enhancing market power."[46] In some states, prevailing institutional conditions may cause a commission to do just that. The Department of Public Utility Control (DPUC) in Connecticut provides an example of an institution acting in just this manner.

Connecticut is a rich, densely populated state; just the type of market where one would expect to find competitive entry in the provision of telecommunications services and products. However, Southern New England Telephone (SNET), now owned by SBC, has for years dominated the market in Connecticut. Over the course of this long period of monopoly control, SNET and the Connecticut DPUC have developed an institutional relationship that is strongly supportive of SNET's interests and that militates against the opening up of the Connecticut market to competition. In case after case the DPUC has taken the stance that what SNET claims to be their costs, are their costs. The commission does not believe that SNET has an incentive to overstate its costs or the costs of an efficient operator. For example, in a recent decision the DPUC declared that SNET has the incentive, despite the lack of any serious competitive pressures to do so, to propose UNE costs and prices that reflect the operation of an efficient firm.[47] The DPUC justified this decision on the grounds that if SNET overstates its costs and offers expensive UNEs, "it may lose customers to more efficient providers."[48] This statement completely ignores the importance of the economies of scale in this industry, which enables a dominant firm, such as SNET, to overstate its costs without that necessarily leading to large competitive losses.

Given an attitude such as this on the part of a state commission, it would not be possible for TELRIC to provide the same type of binding constraint on an ILEC that UNEs would in a state whose UNEs reflect reasonable estimates of prospective costs.

For states such as Connecticut, where the institutional history of the regulatory commission is such that the light-handed approach broached here would not work, the only solution would be to remain under a price cap or rate of return type of regulatory control. These traditional forms of regulation provide some consumer protection, and the controls must be sustained absent the development of effective competition.

Conclusion

The proposal I have outlined here should not be construed as a call for the elimination of economic regulation. After all, the proposal does contain some rate protection for arguably the two most important retail telecommunications services, local and toll. For local service, as outlined previously, I propose a price ceiling. Regarding toll service, as I mention in note 2, I believe that access rates should remain regulated.

Nor should this proposal be viewed as a one-size-fits-all regulatory framework that is applicable to all states. The light-handed approach broached here is predicated on the assumptions that state commissions have a strong commitment to implementing the competitive provisions of the act, understand the impact that dominant network providers have on the structure of the local telecommunications market, and are willing to use that commitment and understanding to vigorously neutralize network monopoly focal points by focusing on getting the prices for UNEs and interconnection right. As the example of Connecticut illustrates, these assumptions do not necessarily apply to all state commissions. This means that the act's intended transition to competitive markets for the provision of telecommunications service will undoubtedly be an uneven one, transitioning to workable competition in some states and to tight oligopoly in others.

Notes

I gratefully acknowledge the research assistance, comments, and suggestions provided by Scott K. Kennedy.

1. *Telecommunications Act of 1996*, Pub. L. No. 104–104, 110 Stat. 56 codified at 47 U.S.C.A. 151 (West Supp. 1996).

2. I do not discuss termination of regulation of wholesale rates because the 1996 Telecommunications Act requires the government to be an arbitrator of disputes over interconnection, resale, and unbundled network element prices. Furthermore, because a subscribers' local exchange carrier effectively controls a bottleneck facility, regulators will need to continue to control the price of access.

Since the passage of the 1996 Telecommunications Act, states have focused their resources on the pricing of wholesale, rather than retail, services. U.S. General Accounting Office, *Development of Competition in Local Telephone Markets*, January 2000, 30–31.

3. See, for example, Connecticut Department of Public Utilities, Re: Application of the Southern New England Telephone Company for Financial Review and Proposed Framework for Alternative Regulation, Docket No. 95–03-01, 13 March 1996. "A rate base consists of a company's net plant and other major assets that require company investments in order to provide ratepayers with quality service."

4. The essence of the case against rate base regulation is contained in the famous H. Averch and L. L. Johnson article, "Behavior of the Firm under Regulatory Constraint," *American Economic Review* 52 (1962): 1052–69. Since this article appeared, other economists have tested Averch and Johnson's hypothesis that rate base regulation distorted the inputs that were used to provide service. A summary of these studies can found in Sanford V. Berg and John Tschirhart, *Natural Monopoly Regulation: Principles and Practice* (Cambridge: Cambridge University Press, 1988), 332–81.

5. See, for example, ibid., 497–520.

6. See, for example, Maine Public Utility Commission, Re: Investigation Into Regulatory Alternatives for the New England Telephone and Telegraph Company d/b/a NYNEX, Docket No. 94–123, 15 May 1995.

7. Organization for Economic Co-Operation and Development, *Price Cap Regulations for Telecommunications: A Review of Policies and Experiences*, DSTI/ICCP/TISP (94) 3, 24 May 1994; and Ray Lawton, NRRI report to Idaho Commission, *Alternative Forms of Regulation: A Status Report*, 23 May 1994.

8. Bob Rowe, "Strategies to Promote Advanced Telecommunications Capabilities," *Federal Communications Law Journal*. 52, no. 2 (2000): 394n. 51.

9. Thomas G. Krattenmaker, "The Telecommunications Act of 1996," *Federal Communications Law Journal*, November 1996, 49 Fed. Com. L.J. at 1

10. *Conference Report On S. 652, Telecommunications Act Of 1996*, Congressional Record: 1 February 1996 (House), p. H1145

11. From the opening paragraph of the *Telecommunications Act of 1996*, Pub. L. No. 104–104, 110 Stat. 56 (codified at 47 U.S.C.A. 151 [West Supp. 1996]).

12. *Implementation of the Local Competition Provisions in the Telecommunications Act of 1996*, First Report and Order, FCC 96–325, released 8 August 1996, at ¶3.

13. *Telecommunications Act of 1996,* 251.

14. In its decision filed 18 July 2000 in *Iowa Utilities Board,* No. 96–3321, the 8th Circuit Court has vacated the FCC's TELRC pricing rules. This ruling will, in all likelihood, go on to the Supreme Court.

15. Implementation of the Local Competition Provisions in the Telecommunications Act of 1996, First Report and Order, FCC 96–325, released 8 August 1996, at ¶679.

16. See ibid., at ¶679, ¶700, and ¶¶697–98.

17. E. Sanderson Hoe and Stephen Ruscus, "Taking Aim at the Takings Argument: Using Forward-Looking Pricing Methodologies to Price Unbundled Network Elements," *Commlaw Conspectus* (summer 1997), 236. It should be noted that the FCC's pricing rules have proven to be extremely contentious. One of the principle ILEC objections to the TELRIC method is that, because it is a forward-looking costing methodology, it fails to permit the recovery of "historical" and "embedded" costs, or, in the language of the regulatory battles of an earlier era, fails to permit the recovery of an ILEC's "prudent investment" in its physical plant and infrastructure and so constitutes a taking of ILEC property. See, for example, First Report and Order at ¶670, also Joint Motion of GTE Corporation and the Southern New England Telephone Company for Stay Pending Judicial Review in CC Dkt. No. 96–98 (28 August 1996), 12–13, and Hoe, *Commlaw Conspectus,* 239.

18. Implementation of the Local Competition Provisions in the Telecommunications Act of 1996, First Report and Order, FCC 96–325, released 8 August 1996, at ¶679.

19. Ibid.

20. U.S. General Accounting Office, *Development of Competition in Local Telephone Markets,* January 2000; and In the Matter of Implementation of the Local Competition Provisions of the Telecommunications Act of 1996, CC Docket No. 96–98, Third Report and Order and Fourth Further Notice of Proposed Rulemaking, 5 November 1999, pars. 10–11.

21. The table understates the savings achieved with facility-based competition because I have not controlled for the larger number of telephone features and television stations provided in the bundled RCN rate of $139 per month.

22. Morgan Stanley Dean Witter, "NTL Inc. (NTLI.O): Leaders in Innovation," 9 April 1999, European Investment Research. For example, a promotion downloaded from www.askntl.com, the NTL website, on 13 December 1999 contains the following offer: For £9.25 per month, discounted to £4.62 per month till March 2000 if a customer signs up before the end of the year, a customer who signs up on to the NTL cable network will get phone service; BBC1, BBC2, ITV, Channel 4 and Channel 5, plus 7 cable channels including QVC, British Eurosport, BBC News 24, Guest channel, Local channel, TV Travel Shop, and BBC Parliament on the TV; and free internet access, hooked up to TV or PC and metered at only 1p per minute. BT currently charges £9.25 per month for basic phone service only.

A recent report by Ovum notes that this practice has also been followed by cable telephony operators in Japan, who have been paralleling Nippon Telephone and Telegraph's (NTT) tariff structures and offering more for less. Source: Peter Falshaw, Jim Holmes, and Daniel Baker, *Local Service Competition: Breaking the Bottle Neck*, a report by Ovum Consulting, Ltd., October 1998, section D1.4, *Segmentation Strategies*, 28.

23. In the Matter of Implementation of the Local Competition Provisions of the Telecommunications Act of 1996, CC Docket No. 96–98, Third Report and Order and Fourth Further Notice of Proposed Rulemaking, 5 November 1999, par. 13.

24. Even these pure resellers are likely to invest in facilities at some point, as indicated by the following comment: "the resellers we interviewed almost universally told us that resale is not a profitable means of providing local telephone service. They noted that resale can be a good way to enter the market quickly and build a customer base before investing in facilities." *Development of Competition in Local Telephone Markets*, U.S. General Accounting Office, GAO/RCED—00–38, January 2000, 18.

One important lesson learned from the airline industry is that fixed and sunk capital costs are not limited to capital investments. See, for example, Michael Levine, "Airline Competition in Deregulated Markets: Theory, Firm Strategy, and Public Policy," *Yale Journal on Regulation* 4 (1987): 393–494.

25. These UNE rates are significantly lower than the wholesale rates incumbents are required to provide to resellers. As has been observed, "there is not a great enough difference between the wholesale rates resellers pay incumbent carriers for service—rates set by state commissions in accordance with specifications in the 1996 act—and the retail prices resellers can charge their own customers." U.S. General Accounting Office, *Development of Competition in Local Telephone Markets*, 19.

26. David Gabel and David Rosenbaum, "Who's Taking Whom: Some Comments and Evidence on the Constitutionality of TELRIC," *Federal Communications Law Journal* (March 2000): 270–71.

It should be noted that an entrant incurs other costs in addition to the leasing of UNEs. The setting of UNE prices at a rate that is less than the embedded cost-of-service is not, in itself, sufficient for insuring that market entry via the leasing of UNEs will be profitable.

27. U.S. General Accounting Office, *Development of Competition in Local Telephone Markets*, 19.

28. There is a potential sticking point here: how does one ensure that the TELRIC-based prices resellers are obtaining from incumbents will be passed along to consumers in the form of rate reductions? The fact that the rate reductions obtained by the long-distance carriers have not been passed along to consumers makes this a legitimate concern. The only way to absolutely ensure that this does not happen in the reseller's market would be to regulate resellers' retail rates, which I don't believe is an attractive option. I believe that counting on the

development of competitive resellers markets to produce consumer price savings over the long term is a risk worth taking.

29. In the Matter of Implementation of the Local Competition Provisions of the Telecommunications Act of 1996, CC Docket No. 96–98, Third Report and Order and Fourth Further Notice of Proposed Rulemaking, 5 November 1999. The platform of unbundled network elements provides a competitor with the incentive and ability to package and market services in ways that differ from the incumbent's existing service offerings.

30. U.S. General Accounting Office, *Development of Competition in Local Telephone Markets*, 20.

31. "Mr. Denney noted that in New York, AT&T is serving a large number of customers using the UNE platform." In *Twenty-Fourth Supplemental Order Rejecting Tariffs; Authorizing Refiling;* Before the Washington Utilities and Transportation Commission, In the Matter of the Pricing Proceeding for Interconnection, Unbundled Element, Transport and Termination, and Resale, Docket No.UT-960369; and In the Matter of the Pricing Proceeding for Interconnection, Unbundled Elements, Transport and Termination, and Resale for US WEST, Docket No.UT-960370; and In the Matter of the Pricing Proceeding for Interconnection, Unbundled Elements, Transport and Termination, and Resale for GTE Northwest, Incorporated, Docket No.UT-960371, at ¶18.

32. U.S. General Accounting Office, *Development of Competition in Local Telephone Markets*, 20.

33. The federal authorized rate-of-return is 11.25 percent. The rate authorized by the state commissions varies but has generally been in the range of 10 percent. See, for example, New Mexico State Corporation Commission, Interconnection Contract Between AT&T Comm. of the Mountain States, Inc. and GTE Southwest, Inc. Pursuant to 47 U.S.C. 252, No. 97–35-RC, at Para. 90 (1997).

34. The steep declines in the unit cost of providing telecommunications services that I am referring to have been primarily the result of: (1) Technological innovation, which has led to long-term increases in efficiency; and (2) The explosive increase in network demand and usage telecommunications service providers have experienced in the past decade. It is the long-term cost savings attributable to these two factors that the price cap regime has failed to pass on to consumers. For example, ten years ago computers were much more expensive and less efficient (and less efficiently produced) then they are currently. The demand for computers was also considerably less then it is currently. Technological innovation leading to more efficient computers and production standards, combined with the huge surge in demand for computers, has resulted in a steep decline in costs, which, in turn, has been passed on to consumers in the form of lower prices overall. That is, a high-end computer today is not only more powerful then a high-end computer of ten years ago, it is also less expensive. Nothing similar has happened in the telecommunications industry. That is, despite steep declines in the costs of telecommunications equipment and surging demand for second lines and vertical features, overall consumer prices have not declined significantly.

35. Because the fixed customer access line charges associated with access to the toll network are included in the price of exchange service, these charges would necessarily fall under the rate ceiling scheme I am proposing here. Whereas a goal of regulation is to emulate competitive market behavior, a price ceiling for exchange service makes sense in the interim because under conditions of rivalry the price of network access should not increase.

36. The price ceiling should be constructed to preclude the addition of special surcharges to the fixed monthly charge due to regulatory decisions. Under price caps there is a procedure whereby commissions may authorize adjustments to rates to reflect changes in regulatory rules. These changes could lead to an increase or decrease in a firm's costs. Whereas I am proposing that incumbent local exchange carriers be permitted to retain the earnings associated with factors that lead to a reduction in production costs, the process should be symmetrical. If the regulatory rules lead to an increase in production costs, the firm should not be permitted to pass on this increase in the form of a higher fixed monthly charge. As the carrier is free to select its rates for other services, the constraint on the fixed monthly charge would not preclude the supplier from raising other rates if regulation increases its production costs.

37. As pointed out above, there will remain a need to regulate the access price charged for originating and terminating toll calls. Furthermore, rate protection for retail toll service is necessary for markets where customers cannot obtain equal access to interexchange carriers.

Arguably, in an era when telephone lines are increasingly tied up with calls to Internet service providers, certain vertical features, such as call-waiting or caller-number identification, are necessities that also merit price protection. On the balance of things, I favor not providing price protection for these services. Some price protection will be provided through the threat of entry.

38. A telephone company has the greatest incentive to provide good service in competitive markets. By establishing penalties based on the performance at the wire center, companies will be deterred from relying on the average performance of the firm to hide inadequate service provisioning at monopoly markets. Ideally a cost/benefit analysis would be undertaken as to the quality-of-service decisions made by the firm, possibly with customers having some input as to preferred quality-of-service levels, before any penalties are imposed.

39. The operational and support systems are the computer systems and personnel that entrants use to place orders and provision local telephone service.

40. *In the Matter of the Interconnection Contract Negotiations Between AT&T Communications of the Mountain States, Inc. and U S WEST Communications, Inc., Pursuant to 47 U.S.C. Section 252,* New Mexico State Corporation Commission, Docket No. 96–411-TC, at 386; and *Matter of the Application of Ameritech Michigan Pursuant to Section 271 of the Communications Act of 1934 as Amended, To Provide In-Region, InterLATA Services In Michigan,* CC Docket No. 97–137 Memorandum and Order (released 19 August 1997), ¶139.

41. *In the Matter of Application by Bell Atlantic New York for Authorization*

Under Section 271 of the Communications Act to Provide In-Region, InterLATA Service in the State of New York, CC Docket No. 99–295, Memorandum Opinion and Order, 22 December 1999, Par. 10.

42. U.S. Court of Appeals for the Eighth Circuit in *Iowa Utilities Board,* No. 96–3321, decision filed 18 July 2000, 36.

43. *Ministerial Inquiry into Telecommunications: Issues Paper,* April 2000, 1, available from www.teleinquiry.govt.nz.

44. Harry M. Trebing, "Structural Change and Regulatory Reform in the Utilities Industries," *American Economic Review* 70, no. 2 (1980): 388.

45. Harry M. Trebing, "Structural Change and the Future of Regulation," *Land Economics* 71, no. 3 (1995): 404.

46. Ibid., 411

47. See, for example, Connecticut Department of Public Utility Control, Decision in Docket No. 00–01–02, *Application of the Southern New England Telephone Company For Approval Of Cost Studies For Unbundled Network Elements,* 29 June 2000.

48. Ibid., 19.

Public Interest Regulation, Common Costs, and Universal Service

ROBERT LOUBE

Introduction

The landscape of the telecommunication industry has been dramatically altered in recent years. Changes have occurred in the industry's legal foundation, market structure, and technological delivery systems. First, the Telecommunications Act of 1996 (hereafter referred to as the 1996 act) rewrites the relationship between government and the carriers. The 1996 act relies on the competitive marketplace rather than regulation to police the industry. To foster competition, incumbent local exchange carriers are required to interconnect with entrants, rent their networks to entrants, and allow entrants to resell the incumbents' services. After meeting certain conditions, the Bell companies will be allowed to offer long-distance services in competition with AT&T, MCI-Worldcom, and the other interexchange carriers. The 1996 act recognizes, however, that competition will erode the current support for universal service. It requires the FCC and the state commissions to devise alternative mechanisms to support universal service.

Second, the telecommunications industry's market structure is being transformed by a series of mergers, re-arrangements and bankruptcies. The seven Regional Bell Holding Companies are now four as a result of SBC's merger with Pacific Telesis and Ameritech, and Bell Atlantic's merger with NYNEX. Bell Atlantic merged with the largest independent company, GTE, to form Verizon. ATT has been a spinning top that appears to have spun off the table. First, it became a cellular company through its merger with McGraw and a cable company through its merger with TCI. Now, ATT is dissolving into three functionally separate companies. The second largest long-distance company, Worldcom, is the product of a series of mergers. Competitive entrants such as Global Crossing, Winstar, Rhythms, and Northpoint are bankrupt. The reasons behind the mergers include the companies' desire to reduce costs by enhancing buying power and spreading overhead costs over more markets, and their wish to provide customers with a complete array of services (local, long-distance, data, wireless, and video). The bankruptcies flow from the inability of entrants to overcome the entrenched market and political power of the incumbents.

Third, the industry's technology delivery systems are being redesigned to meet the explosive demand for data services. The growth in data services fueled by the exponential growth in Internet services has reached the point where some analysts believe that half the traffic carried over communications networks is data rather than voice.[1] The design change affects not only the last mile of plant but also the central office and transmission function.

The last mile of plant can be either a twisted copper pair, coaxial cable, or wireless. Each type of plant was designed for one purpose, and transforming the plant into a multipurpose medium requires costly upgrades. Thus, it is not clear which plant type will dominate the communications network of the future, or whether there will be multiple networks, each providing a specialized service. For example, the telephone industry's twisted copper pair was designed to provide voice-grade service. The twisted copper pair provides a dedicated voice-grade path to every end user. It can be upgraded to provide data services such as asymmetric digital subscriber line (ADSL) by adding multiplexing equipment at either end of the loop. That equipment combines the voice and data traffic at the originating end, and separates the traffic when it terminates at the central office. To use the electronic equipment, it is necessary to reduce the length of the loops and remove the loading coils and bridge taps. The coaxial cable on which the cable industry relies contains sufficient bandwidth to provide data services. It, however, does not provide dedicated service; therefore, the cable network can become congested when a significant number of customers use the system simultaneously. Moreover, many cable systems contain numerous one-way amplifiers that have to be replaced by two amplifiers and fiber systems. Finally, while wireless systems offer greater customer convenience, these systems must overcome quality and bandwidth problems if they are to compete for data services.

The alternative configurations for central office and transmission facilities are circuit-switched systems with dedicated transmission trunk channels or packet switches with shared transmissions facilities. The circuit-switched network provides a dedicated path for voice traffic. The dedicated path creates a high-quality voice-grade service, but limits the ability of the network to transmit data services. These switches also have built-in advanced features and established billing procedures. Alternatively, packet-switching networks using shared transmission protocols allow bandwidth to be dynamically allocated among users. These protocols match the bursty nature of data traffic. Traffic from numerous users can be packetized in sequence to fill the gaps between the data bursts arriving from any one of the users. It is very difficult, however, for a packet system to guarantee the arrival times required for voice service. To make such a guarantee, packet systems would either have to reduce the quality of service to nonvoice users or build excess capacity. Currently it is not clear which technology will dominate future networks. The question is whether the established carriers can migrate their embedded base of switches into the data world or whether the new entrants will be able to transform the internet protocols so that high-quality voice and video services can be merged with data services and a billing system can be devised for these services.[2] At least one manufacturer has released an upgrade of the circuit switch that adds packet services to its basic circuit switch.[3] On the other hand, entrants are providing data services using only packet switches. Upgrading these packet switches and transmission networks so that they will be able to provide quality voice service is technically possible. However, the industry has not yet developed the requisite coordination schemes and billing systems required for the commercial success of Internet telephony.[4]

How well the industry performs in this new environment, and who will benefit from that performance, depends in part on how regulators define and accomplish their tasks. Economists have provided regulators with a variety of principles that can be used to define the scope and practice of regulation. The purpose of this chapter is to examine how public interest regulation defines the regulators' task and whether public interest—oriented economists have provided regulators with the tools required to meet the challenges of the new communications environment. Public interest regulation reflects the need for regulation to consider more than market outcomes. It is identified with achieving higher levels of efficiency, protecting customers who do not have economic power, providing universal service, and setting minimum prices consistent with internalizing social costs.[5] First, this chapter examines public interest regulation as defined by Harry Trebing. Second, it discusses the relevance of determining a reasonable allocation of common costs in the current regulatory environment. Third, it examines the neoclassical alternatives for allocating common costs. Fourth, it shows the viability of the alternative justifiable expenditure model for allocating common costs in the current environment. Fifth, it reviews the evolving history of universal service. Finally, it discusses the efficiency of universal service.

Harry Trebing and Public-Interest Regulation

Public interest regulation has not had many supporters in recent years. Neoclassical economists reduce regulation to a set of efficient pricing rules.[6] Like "lonesome George," the last remaining Pinta tortoise on the Galapagos Islands, Harry Trebing continues on as one of the few remaining proponents of public interest regulation.[7] Trebing's definition of public interest regulation includes the need to develop institutions that lead to a higher level of efficiency within the economy, to maintain and extend universal service, and to establish the lowest prices that are consistent with internalization of social costs. He emphasizes that regulation, like all other institutions in the economy, must evolve. What worked in one era will not work in another, because the problems that firms and individuals face constantly change.[8] He specifies that regulation deals not only with monopoly situations but also with oligopolies. He agrees that regulation should use competitive forces when possible, but cautions that the existence of a few entrants in part of a market is not the same as ubiquitous competition in all segments of the market.[9] To integrate these concerns, Trebing believes that regulatory planning must be conducted on an industry-wide basis, and must identify areas of inadequate service, develop least-cost planning options, determine when and where to use competition, and understand how firms use economic power to thwart public interest benefits and to transform regulation into a vehicle of private gain.[10]

Higher efficiency measures the extent to which an economy reflects emerging social values. It deals not only with how well the economy produces material goods but also with whether the economy reflects social choices regarding freedom, equity, and compassion. It attempts to measure well being not only through market choice, which is limited because all market choices reify the current income distribution, but also political and social choices.[11]

In telecommunications, the emerging social values include relying more on competitive forces to determine prices rather than allowing regulatory commissions to review the legitimacy of the prices of franchised monopolies. This reliance is tempered with the requirement to maintain and promote universal service, and to prohibit noncompetitive services from subsidizing competitive services. Neoclassical economists, stressing the administrative nightmare of regulation and the objective beauty of the market, assert that now is the time for all regulators to retire.[12] Trebing, however, stresses the need to identify residual monopoly markets, establish and supervise an interconnection policy for carriers, tie incentive systems to performance, and constrain cross-subsidization and price discrimination by developing cost-based caps on rates.

First, to identify residual monopoly markets, Trebing not only analyzes demand and supply characteristics but also firm interdependence. On the supply side, a competitive market is characterized by the existence of five or six viable rivals, with no single dominant firm and low barriers to entry. On the demand side, all markets should be elastic and firms should not be able to segment the market for the purposes of price discrimination. The Landes-Posner index, which incorporates market share, demand, and supply elasticity, is a good tool for measuring the level of competition. Trebing holds that Landes-Posner index value of .5 or less indicates the existence of competitive markets. Firm interdependence is indicated by conscious parallelism in pricing and corporate expansion policies.[13] For example, long-distance companies have mimicked each other with regard to the size of price reductions, the timing of the reductions, and the drift from distance-based rates to postal rates. With regard to corporate expansion, Sprint matched AT&T's move into the wireless industry, and MCI-Worldcom's desire to purchase Sprint is driven by MCI-Worldcom's lack of a wireless offering.

Second, long before the current system of unbundled network elements became law, Trebing proposed that the telephone carriers be required to interconnect their systems and rent capacity to entrants. The purpose of this proposal was to mitigate the need of rivals to replicate the network of incumbent carriers.[14] Gross investment in the existing local network is $317.8 billion.[15] A forward-looking estimate of the plant used just for local exchange carriers is $179.2 billion.[16] Clearly, replicating this plant five or six times to establish viable rivals is not practical. Price and service quality conditions for renting the network must be supervised by the regulator because the incumbent has the obvious incentive to price these services high and provide poor quality of service in order to increase entrant's cost and reduce the quality of service an entrant could provide.

Third, price cap regulation, the current method used to regulate most large telephone carriers, has not lived up to its potential. Price caps allow prices to change based on a formula that is independent of the carrier's own cost. This separation is intended to eliminate the carrier's incentive to expand its rate base to increase profits, cross-subsidize one market with profits from another through strategic cost shifting, and pad expenses that are simply passed through to their customers. These projected benefits have not been realized. Instead, price caps have allowed carriers to retain above-normal profits and subsidize competitive markets.[17] These results are attributed to the failure to periodically true-up the price cap mechanism to actual costs and the difficulty in defining the productivity offset.[18] Moreover, the incentive to reduce cost contains the perverse incentive to reduce quality rather than forcing the carrier to become more efficient. To remove this incentive, profits must be tied to quality-of-service standards. Such a tie can be incorporated into price cap regulation. When performance meets a reasonable standard, then the carrier is allowed to use an unadjusted productivity offset based on the industry's overall performance. Poor performance will be penalized with a high productivity offset, and superior levels of performance will be rewarded with a low productivity offset.

Fourth, Trebing proposes to use the alternative justifiable expenditure method to allocate common costs and establish cost-based rate caps. This method was developed by Martin Glaeser to allocate the cost of TVA dams among electric power development, navigation, and flood control. The method starts by defining common cost as the difference between the total cost of the multipurpose system and the sum of the service-specific directly assignable costs. Next, the benefits of the multipurpose network to each service are estimated as the difference between the service stand-alone cost and the service-specific directly assignable costs. The common costs assigned to each service equal the ratio of the benefit to each service divided by the sum of the benefits to all services times the common cost associated with the multipurpose system. The total cost assigned to each service is the sum of its common cost assignment and its service-specific directly assignable costs.[19]

The Glaesser method provides a reasonable solution to the common cost allocation problem because, first, it assigns the benefits of joint production in direct proportion to the benefits received by each service. Second, because it recognizes that cost causation is related to all services that benefit from joint production, it provides a reasonable method for fulfilling the regulatory mandate that common cost should be allocated among all services. Finally, it establishes a reasonable price ceiling for monopoly services, preventing a carrier from shifting all of the benefits from joint production to competitive markets.[20]

Common Costs and Unbundled Network Elements

Common costs are costs incurred in the production of several services, which remain unchanged as the relative proportion of those services varies. Common costs dominate the cost of production of telephone services. For example, a local loop, the wire, trenches, and poles that connect each customer to a central office provides local exchange, private line, data, state toll, and interstate toll services. Once the local loop has been installed, changes in the relative proportion of these services will not affect the cost of the loop. While there is no unique way to assign the common costs to the services, firms clearly have an incentive to recover common costs disproportionately in markets where they do not have competition, and recover little if any common costs where competition is intense. In many industry cost studies, this incentive translates into the assignment of loop costs to monopoly services.[21]

The 1996 act requires incumbent carriers to offer a new service, unbundled network elements (UNEs), to entrants. The 1996 act defines an UNE as a facility or equipment used in the provision of a telecommunications service including features, functions, and capabilities that are provided by such facility or equipment.[22] The purpose of UNEs is to jump-start competition. A competitor does not have to duplicate the entire network of the incumbent carrier in order to provide reasonable service throughout a given geographic territory. Instead, the competitor can build a part of a network and purchase the rest of the network from the incumbent. For example, a competitor can place a switch and a fiber ring in the business district of a city and then reach outlying businesses and residential customers through the purchase of unbundled loops.

The 1996 act specifies that regulating UNE prices is the joint responsibility of state and federal regulators. While there has been a tension regarding where state regulators' authority ends and that of federal regulators begins, there has been general agreement regarding the use of the total element long-run incremental cost methodology (TELRIC) to determine UNE prices.[23]

To understand how total element long-run incremental cost (TELRIC) methodology mitigates the common cost allocation problem, it is informative to review how the FCC anticipated that it would be used. Incremental cost can refer to any change in output. To determine cost, regulators must specify the size of the change, the time period when the change occurs, and whether the change affects peak or off-peak demand. Many incremental cost studies adopt a time period equal to a planning horizon to measure the increment. The FCC uses the term "total" to define the increment as the difference between zero output and the current output.[24]

"Long-run" refers to an economic planning period. While it is sometimes referred to as a period long enough so that all of a firm's costs become variable, such a situation rarely occurs in practice. Normally a firm's cost structure contains a mixture of fixed and variable costs. Thus, the term "long-run" refers to an ahistorical planning moment at which time all of a firm's costs are variable.[25]

Incremental cost is also defined as the economic cost of providing a service. Economic cost requires that cost be measured using only current input prices, the most efficient network configuration, and the technology currently available to determine investment levels and expenses.[26] Economic cost will be less than the costs derived from a company's books whenever the impact of technological change is greater than the impact of inflation, or if input prices are decreasing. In the case of telephone switching and interoffice transmission, it is generally accepted that not only has there been technological advance, but also input prices have decreased. Thus, economic cost will be below book cost. In the case of outside plant, because it is possible that inflation in construction costs outweighs technical advances, it is not clear whether economic loop costs will be less than book loop costs. Adopting the most efficient network requires the TELRIC cost model to redesign the network and build the entire network in a static ahistorical moment.

The term "element" is unique to the UNE costing methodology. A network element corresponds to an entire facility such as a local loop or the switch. Costing an entire network element significantly reduces the amount of common costs that must be allocated to various services. The cost of the local loop is no longer divided among local exchange, private line, state toll, interstate toll, and data services that use the loop. The remaining common costs, such as corporate overhead expenses, must still be allocated, but that allocation is across a very large revenue base. It is believed that a reasonable amount of these costs could be allocated among all services without burdening any particular service or harming the competitive process. As a result, TELRIC pricing of network elements would be free of the battles over common cost allocation that have plagued all communications costing exercises in the past.[27]

The consensus regarding the measure of a UNE as the entire facility has been short-lived. Entrants who purchase UNEs contend that the requirement to purchase the entire facility increases their costs and puts them at a fundamental disadvantage when competing with incumbent local exchange carriers. Entrants interested in using UNEs to provide voice-grade service maintain that purchasing a UNE built to provide both voice and data service is not reasonable. Instead, they want to pay for a voice-grade loop.[28] Entrants interested in providing data services believe that they should not pay for the voice-grade part of the loop.[29]

Recently, the FCC ordered the incumbent carriers to divide the loop between its voice and data capabilities and allow entrants to purchase data capabilities as a separate UNE. The FCC did not specify how the prices of the two pieces of the loop should be determined. Rather, the order established general guidelines, leaving to the states the responsibility for determining prices of the network elements.[30] As the states investigate this issue, they will discover that they must establish a reasonable mechanism for allocating common costs. As they attempt to do this the common cost allocation problem will emerge to confront regulators once again.

Common Cost Recovery and Neoclassical Economics

Neoclassical economists employ two methods to allocate common costs: Ramsey pricing, which attempts to minimize efficiency losses, or the max/min rule, which prohibits cross-subsidies.

Ramsey pricing starts from the proposition that if prices for all services cannot be set equal to incremental cost due to a regulatory constraint or the existence of common costs, then the next best thing to do is to minimize the deviation away from the optimal solution. Ramsey pricing is the solution to a constrained maximization problem, where social welfare in the form of consumer surplus is maximized and the constraint requires that firms break even.[31] This proposition is simplified to the inverse elasticity rule. This rule asserts that price changes should be inversely proportional to elasticity. Price changes will be large in inelastic markets and small in very elastic markets. In other words, if there is a need to raise additional revenue, the firm should capture that revenue in markets where the customers have no choices and the firm has a lot of economic power. Because regulators recognize this outcome, they have been reluctant to adopt Ramsey pricing. For example, the FCC concluded "that an allocation methodology that relies exclusively on allocating common costs in inverse proportion to the sensitivity of demand for various network elements and services may not be used. We conclude that such an allocation could unreasonably limit the extent of entry into local exchange markets by allocating more costs to, and thus raising the prices of, the most critical inputs, the demand for which tends to be relatively inelastic. Such an allocation of these costs would undermine the pro-competitive objectives of the 1996 Act."[32]

Companies, however, continue to sponsor pricing schemes based on Ramsey pricing. The most recent version of these is a plan sponsored by the Coalition for Affordable Local and Long-distance Service, or CALLS, a coalition consisting of AT&T, Bell Atlantic, Bell South, GTE, SBC, and Sprint. The CALLS proposal is built around three main principles. First, the subscriber line charge (SLC) caps for residential and single business customers will be allowed to increase from $3.50 to $7.00. While rates do not have to increase to the cap, there is good reason to believe that in many instances they will because revenue now collected from other charges, both loop-related and non-loop-related, are proposed to be collected through the SLC. For example, while the multiline business SLC cap remains at $9.20, the presubscribed interexchange carrier charge (PICC) and the common carrier line charge (CCLC) will disappear into the SLC. The residual interconnection charge (RIC) and 25 percent of switching costs will be transferred to the common line basket. The results of these transfers move revenue recovery from the traffic-sensitive markets to the common line basket, and then within the common line basket move revenue recovery from multiline business customers to residential and single-line business customers. The second principle is to reduce the traffic-sensitive access rates not only by shifting revenue to the common line basket but also by assigning all of the benefits derived from the productivity offset to traffic-sensitive rates. These reductions will decrease the traffic-sensitive rates from an average of eighty-six cents per minute to fifty-five cents per minute. The CALLS proponents contend that these access reductions will translate into lower long-distance rates. The third principle is to provide a $650 million universal service fund increase to the large incumbent carriers to offset alleged implicit subsidies that are contained in access charges.[33]

The first problem with the proposal is that the simplifying assumption, required to change the Ramsey rule into the inverse elasticity rule, does not hold in the case of telecommunications services. That assumption requires the demand for basic service to be independent of the demand for other services. Clearly these services are complements. When services are complements, Ramsey pricing suggests that it is efficient to price the inelastic basic service below incremental cost.[34] Thus, the efficiency claims of the CALLS proposal are illusory. The second problem with the proposal is that it increases those access prices that competition for customers will drive down. In a competitive market, firms seeking market share will not be able to charge customers for the simple right to be connected to the network by a particular firm. Rather, the firm will recover its access costs through the sale of usage services. Thus, the CALLS proposal will not mimic a competitive market outcome. The CALLS proposal will, however, reduce the risks faced by incumbent firms by shifting revenue recovery to the customers with the fewest choices. It will deny these customers a share in the benefits of competition. CALLS will also establish a benchmark price that will guide the new oligopoly to its optimal profit position. Finally, CALLS will provide the incumbents with a reserve fund to purchase entrants or to finance price squeezes to eliminate entrants.

The second neoclassical solution to the common cost problem is to use the max/min rule. The maximum price is the stand-alone cost of service and minimum price is the incremental cost of service. These conditions insure that no service is paying or receiving a subsidy.[35] For any service, the firm can establish a price anywhere between these extremes. The firm will then be able to devise a pricing strategy that recovers all of its common and service-specific costs.[36]

The first problem with the max/min rule is that the firm's incentives are to reduce prices in competitive markets and raise prices in monopoly markets. The max/min rule allows the firm to implement such a strategy but constrains price increases in monopoly markets and price decreases in the competitive markets. The resulting prices will resemble Ramsey pricing, with the inelastic markets priced well above incremental cost and the elastic market prices set close to incremental cost. This pricing strategy will transfer most, if not all, of the benefits of joint production away from monopoly customers and to customers of competitive services.

The second problem is that in practice the stand-alone cost of monopoly services is seldom estimated. Instead, the incremental cost for each competitive service is estimated and prices are set equal to or above their incremental cost. Next, it is shown that if the rates for all services are above their incremental cost, it is impossible for the rate of any service to be above its stand-alone cost. Therefore, it is not necessary to estimate the stand-alone cost of service.[37] This assertion regarding stand-alone cost is true if, and only if, the total cost recovered through rates is equal to the total economic cost of providing the services. However, the total cost recovered is usually greater than the economic cost of service, because either innovation has lowered the economic cost or the total cost contains inefficiencies excluded from the economic cost. When total cost is above economic cost and the competitive services are priced at incremental cost, then monopoly services must be priced above stand-alone cost for the firm to break even. This leads to a situation where the monopoly services are responsible not only for common costs but also for inefficiencies due to the gold plating of investment, the pass through of excessive expense and management error, and the higher costs associated with old technologies.[38]

The third problem is that incremental costs are not uniquely defined by an objective set of input prices and output. Additional assumptions must be specified prior to determining incremental cost. These assumptions include but are not limited to the size of the increment, the starting position of the decision making, and the quality of the output. Changing any of these assumptions changes the incremental cost estimate.[39] Thus, a competitive market will not result in setting price equal to unique incremental cost. Multiple prices could be established. Moreover, it is not clear which price is optimal. In practice, these assumptions are always made to justify a particular political or economic power position or market strategy. Thus, given the existence of economic power, setting prices equal to incremental cost merely reinforces the firm's economic power-retaining strategies.

The prices established for Centrex service exemplify this problem. Centrex service allows a business customer to call internally using four digits. It provides many features, such as three-way calling and call transfer. It also provides each telephone station with a dedicated line to the central office. Thus, the number of copper pairs between the wire center and the customer equals the number of telephones used by the customer. All of the intelligence to provide these services to the customer is located in the telephone company's switch. If the customer had chosen to buy a private branch exchange (PBX), the customer's equipment would have provided the advanced features and four-digit internal dialing. Because the internal calls never leave the customer's place of business, the number of loops required to connect the customer to the central office is significantly reduced. The customer's choice between purchasing a PBX and Centrex service should reflect the difference between the cost of using part of the central switch and a large number of lines and the cost of purchasing and maintaining a PBX and using a small number of lines. The telephone company, however, does not allow the customer to make that comparison. Instead, it claims that the loop costs are sunk and should not enter the decision process. Thus, the customer compares the cost of the PBX to a portion of the central office switching cost. This exclusion of costs associated with Centrex skews the comparison, thereby encouraging the purchase of Centrex services over PBXs. Thus, by strategically determining the starting position for calculating cost, the resultant incremental cost-based price directs the market toward the most optimal outcome for the company. Of course, the company must have economic power in at least one other market where it can recover the cost of the Centrex loops. However, the existence of such a market is rarely a problem for a major telephone company.[40]

Common Cost Recovery and Institutional Economics

In numerous articles, Trebing asserts that the alternative justifiable expenditure method is the best way to allocate common costs. As noted previously, this method will assign a portion of the common cost to all services and will prevent the strategic shifting of the benefits of joint production away from monopoly services. Previous studies have shown that the alternative justifiable expenditure method can accomplish these tasks.[41] This section discusses how to calculate the stand-alone costs of network services by varying the assumptions used to model telephone networks. In so doing, it demonstrates that the alternative justifiable expenditure model can be used in the current environment to determine a reasonable allocation of common costs. Several problems with this method are also discussed.

To implement the alternative justifiable expenditure method, it is first necessary to determine the number of services that the multipurpose network will provide. In the case of telephone networks, these services include local voice-grade, advanced switched data services, private line, and interexchange services. While the definition of local voice-grade service remains subject to debate, it is used here to mean voice conversations, and data sent over modems that operate within 300 to 3,000 hertz bandwidth.[42] Generally, voice-grade service limits modem speeds to less than 28 kilobits per second (kbps).[43] However, depending on the customer's location relative to a central office and the type of wire connecting the customer to the location, it is possible to send information at 56 kbps. Advanced switched data services include services such as asymmetric digital subscriber lines, (ADSL). ADSL operates at much higher frequencies than voice-grade service and is capable of sending information at 1,544 kbps in one direction and at slower levels of transmission in the other direction. Private line services connect to locations directly without using a switch.. Private line services vary from a simple voice connection to extremely high-speed connections capable of transmitting multiple television signals. Interexchange or toll service connects local exchange areas and can transmit information at various speeds.

The next step in the alternative justifiable expenditure method is to estimate the stand-alone cost of service for each service that benefits from network and thus will have common costs assigned to it. The most important common cost shared by all of the services described previously is the loop plant. In addition, circuit switches are shared by local voice-grade and interexchange services, and interoffice facilities are shared by all of the services. The loop plant connects customers to central offices. The design criteria changes with the type of services offered. Each different design criteria can be incorporated into a total cost model such as the synthesis model used by the FCC to estimate universal service support requirements. Depending on the design criteria used, the synthesis model would provide stand-alone loop cost for each service.

Currently, the loop design for interexchange and local voice-grade services is the same. The major design standard is that the maximum copper loop length is constrained to be eighteen thousand feet (kft).[44] Fiber systems are used to serve longer loops, and fiber is substituted for copper in extremely dense areas where very large copper cables exceed the cost of the fiber systems. For advanced services, the typical design standard is that the maximum copper loop length is twelve kft. In addition, fiber rings are installed to service dense business districts. The design standard for the private line loop system would be similar to the advanced services system. The private system, however, would not cover the entire service territory, due to the fact that private line services are generally purchased by business customers.

Next, for the switching and interoffice functions, the process of establishing design standards and running the model on a stand-alone basis for each service are be performed. Once the stand-alone cost estimates have been determined, service-specific costs, such as the digital subscriber line access multiplexer used to provide advance services, are subtracted from the stand-alone cost to determine the service-specific benefits. These service-specific benefits are entered into the alternative justifiable expenditure method to determine the portion of the common costs allocated to each service, and the service price ceiling is estimated as the sum of the allocated common costs and service-specific costs.

The two most important problems associated with the alternative justifiable expenditure method are the choice of services that the multipurpose network will provide and the inability to determine the stand-alone cost of basic service due to technological evolution. Strategic choice of services is a standard device used to force a particular outcome. For example, dividing local voice-grade service into residential and business services swings cost toward local service and away from interexchange and advanced services. If video services are added to the mix, the total cost increases significantly due to the requirements video places on the loop facilities, and a significant share of the common costs will be assigned to video services. Thus, the choice of services included in the study can determine the results.

The inability to estimate the stand-alone cost of basic service results from the fact that innovations required for advanced services are folded into facilities used to provide basic services. This results either in the shutting down of production of facilities designed just for the production of basic service or in the reducing of production levels so that average cost of these facilities increases. There are many examples of this phenomenon. First, copper cables augmented by loading coils were used to provide service loops greater than eighteen kft. Loading coils interfere not only with digital signals but also the ability to use modems. Thus, the industry has stopped using loading coils as a basic design. Second, analog stored program switches are no longer produced, even though sales of ISDN, the service that required digital switches, never matched the demand forecasts used to justify the replacement of analog switches with digital switches. Finally, digital loop carrier devices are being upgraded so that they can provide advanced digital services. In each case, the technological change allows the system to provide the entire set of services more efficiently, while increasing the stand-alone cost of basic service.

What Is Universal Service?

The debate over universal service centers on its meaning, how it is currently supported, and who should support it in the future. The traditional definition of universal service is that telephone service should be provided to all households, independent of income, race, and other demographic factors. In the context of this definition, universal service is measured by the telephone penetration rate, which measures the percentage of households with telephone service. In the United States, telephone penetration grew slowly during the monopoly era. The period immediately following the patent expiration saw a dramatic increase in penetration, led by the entrance of independent telephone companies and followed by the Bell response.[45] The growth rate slowed during the 1920s, and the percent of households with phones actually declined during the Great Depression. Following World War II, the penetration started its upward climb to the current level of 94 percent. While the increase in income in the post— World War II economy probably accounts for increases in penetration in urban areas, the growth in telephone service in rural areas was the result of direct government intervention through Rural Electrification Administration loans to small telephone companies.[46]

The overall high penetration rate hides pockets of low penetration among the poor. The penetration for households with incomes greater than $40,000 varies from 98.1 percent to 99.0 percent. For households with incomes less than $15,000 penetration rate varies from 77.2 percent to 91.0 percent.[47] Recent extensions of U.S. low-income programs are aimed at addressing this problem. Federal support for low-income rates was increased from $3.50 to $5.25 without state matching funds, and if states match a federal subsidy, a qualifying customer can receive up to $7.00 in federal aid and $3.50 in state aid for payment of the monthly local telephone bill and subscriber line charges. In addition, all companies wishing to participate in federal universal service programs must offer a low-income program.[48] Even so, there has not been any appreciable increase in penetration rates among the nation's poor during the first year of the new programs.[49]

Recently, a controversy has developed about what Theodore Vail meant when he first coined the term "universal service." It had been thought that Vail use the term to describe the traditional goal of providing telephone service to all households.[50] However, a second interpretation contends that Vail meant that one and only one telephone company should serve each geographic area.[51] This alternative interpretation traces its genesis to the problems the Bell telephone system was encountering during the early part of the century. Following the expiration of the basic patents in 1894, independent companies began developing franchises. While many of these franchises were in small towns that the Bell system had ignored, the independents also established systems competing directly with Bell franchises. Because the value of telephone service is directly related to the number of other persons with whom you can communicate, the existence of noninterconnected competing firms led to increases in the telephone penetration rate as each firm attempted to add value to its system. If one firm achieved a significant advantage in the competition for customers, this achievement would eventually translate into a monopoly.[52] Winning that advantage, however, required reducing prices and forgoing profits. To avoid such competition and to provide a stable foundation for the long-term growth of ATT, Vail favored the adoption of one universal system in each service territory. To legitimize the one-system approach, Vail endorsed state regulation of telephone companies.

The 1996 act, because it requires local service interconnection as part of its attempt to reestablish competition for the provision of local service, changes the nature of competition. Each firm no longer tries to increase the total number of customers with service. Instead, a firm tries to capture only highly profitable customers, leaving the low-profit customers— low income and those in rural areas—to rivals. This pattern of incentives is another source of tension between incumbent firms, who are required to serve low-profit customers, and entrants, who focus only on high-profit customers. This transforms universal service from a competitive prize to be captured by the firm with the most customers to a common cost that each competitor attempts to transfer to other competitors.

Service to households, however, is not the only dimension used to measure universal service. The other dimensions of universal service include the types of service, availability rather than usage, and service to other entitled clients, such as schools, libraries, and rural health care providers. The types of service generally included in a universal package are: single party access line, access to toll calling, local usage, tone dialing, access to emergency services, access to assistance services, statewide relay service, directory listing, and privacy protections.[53] It is important to note that for local and relay service, usage is included in the definition of universal service. For all other services, only access is required to be made available. The cost of access can be recovered through a separate charge or can be folded into basic service fees. Customer usage of these services will not be subsidized. The FCC adopted a similar approach in defining its universal service package. The 1996 act extended universal service to the provision of services to schools, libraries, and rural health providers. For schools, the FCC has ruled that the type of services available should include internal connections (inside wiring from the classroom to the telephone company's point of presence or the wireless equivalent) and internet access.[54]

Finally, the 1996 act requires the FCC to periodically review the definition of universal service. The availability of digital services to low-income and minority families is an issue that could be addressed in this review. This lack of availability, known as "the digital divide," is measured by the difference in computer ownership, E-mail, and Internet web availability between upper-income and low-income families, and between white and minority families. In 1998, 60 percent of households earning more than $75,000 used the Internet, compared to less than 10 percent of households with incomes below $20,000, while the white household Internet usage rate was more than two and half times that among black and Hispanic households.[55]

Universal Service and Efficiency

Neoclassical economists generally perceive universal service as an equity concern that is beyond the scope of economic inquiry. Their concerns are translated into insuring that universal service is provided efficiently. That is, if the concern is that low-income users obtain telephone service, then whatever subsidy is provided should go to low-income users rather than to companies. This leads to a desire to give out phone stamps or to support subsidized rates available only to low-income individuals. Second, there is an emphasis on recovering the cost of universal service efficiently. This concern leads to a desire to remove universal service recovery from usage rates and to transfer this recovery to flat rates.[56]

Institutional economists, however, view universal service as a means to increase the higher efficiency and progressive efficiency of an economy. Higher efficiency requires that economic institutions be designed to achieve social values with regard to equal opportunity and compassion. Extension of universal service to schools and libraries is a part of that proposition. A further extension of universal service to provide digital service to the student's home will improve the economy's ability to fulfill the promise of equal opportunity.

Progressive efficiency measures how well an economy is enhancing the well-being of its citizens through technology change. Institutional economists place heavy emphasis on technological change and how an economy creates resources, in addition to how an economy allocates existing resources.[57] Economic growth in an information-based society is dependent on an educated labor force and on an advanced communications network reaching all homes.[58] Extension of universal service to include the provision of digital services to the student is a way in which the economy creates the resources needed for a growing information economy. Therefore, this extension enhances the progressive efficiency of an economy.

Implementing policies that reduce the divide can be difficult. Telephone companies have promised to extend advanced services to residential and rural areas in return for regulatory favors. However, the most common outcome of these regulatory compacts has been that the regulatory favors are granted up front and the extension of advanced services does not occur.[59] To prevent a reoccurence of this history, the design of new universal services programs must require benefits to customers prior to or at the same time as companies receive funding.

Conclusion

The public interest vision of Harry Trebing defines the scope of regulation to include protecting the powerless from those with power, expanding choice through the development of new institutions, and creating a more efficient society. Trebing, like other public interest-oriented economists, does not limit the definition of efficiency to Pareto-superior allocations of resources.[60] Instead, he applies the broader notion of higher efficiency to measure economic well-being. In practice, Trebing continually demonstrates the shortfalls of neoclassical economic analysis. He shows that firms' desire to increase market power and their ability to use market power subverts the alleged regulatory reform proposals sponsored by neoclassical economists. Trebing guides us to the understanding that those proposals will not lead to efficient outcomes but instead will reinforce existing market power positions. Trebing contends that regulators must continue to employ measures to control market power. This chapter demonstrates that the alternative justifiable expenditure method can be used to reasonably allocate common costs in order to protect consumers and competitors from the power-enhancing strategies of incumbent firms. Finally, public interest regulation suggests that universal service funding is efficient because universal service supports the growing information economy and fulfills the mandate of higher efficiency to match economic outcomes to emerging social values and to build a more humane society.

Notes

1. Grant Lenahan, "Next Generation Networks: A Practical View of Network Evolution," (Washington, D.C.: Telcordia Technologies, Inc., 1999, photocopied), 1–2.

2. Martin Weiss and Junseok Hwang. "Internet Telephony or Circuit Switched Telephony: Which Is Cheaper?" in *The Twenty-Sixth Annual Telecommunications Policy Research Conference* Held in Alexandria, Virginia, 3–5 October 1998, 1.

3. Lucent Technologies announced that its 7R/E Packet Server evolves standard circuit switches to provide both voice and data services over IP networks. http://www.lucent-sas.com/news/7re_press.shtml.

4. Matthew Lucas and John Yin. "IP QoS," *Billing World* (September 1999): 28.

5. Harry M. Trebing, "Regulation of Industry: An Institutionalist Approach," *Journal of Economic Issues* 21, no. 4 (1987): 1733.

6. See generally, Bridger M. Mitchell and Ingo Vogelsang, *Telecommunications Pricing: Theory and Practice* (Cambridge: Cambridge University Press, 1991).

7. In his review of several books on Stephen Sondheim, Brad Leithauser compared Sondheim to "Lonesome George" because Leithauser believes that Sondheim is the last great composer of American musical theater. Brad Leithauser, "A Funny Thing Happened on the Way to Broadway," *New York Review of Books*, 10 February 2000, 35.

8. Harry M. Trebing, "Public Utility Regulation: A Case Study in the Debate over Effectiveness of Economic Regulation," *Journal of Economic Issues* 18, no. 1 (1984): 236.

9. Harry M. Trebing, "Telecommunications Regulation—The Continuing Dilemma," in *Public Utility Regulation: The Economic and Social Control of Industry*, ed. Kenneth Nowotny, David B. Smith, and Harry M. Trebing (Boston: Kluwer Academic Publishers, 1989), 102–6.

10. Harry M. Trebing, "Regulation of Industry: An Institutionalist Approach," *Journal of Economic Issues* 21, no. 4 (1987): 1731–33.

11. Philip A. Klein, "Institutionalist Reflections on the Role of the Public Sector," *Journal of Economic Issues* 18, no. 1 (1984): 45–68.

12. Alfred E. Kahn, "How to Treat the Costs of Shared Voice and Video Networks in a Post-Regulatory Age," *Cato Policy Analysis No. 264* (Washington, D.C.: Cato Institute, 1996), 12.

13. Harry M. Trebing, "Emerging Market Structures and Options for Regulatory Reform in Public Utility Industries," in *Telecommunications Reform: Principles, Policies and Regulatory Practices,* ed. William H. Melody (Lyngby: Den Private Ingeniorfond, Technical University of Denmark, 1997), 31–34.

14. Trebing, "Regulation of Industry," 1732.

15. This investment equals the total plant in service of all reporting local exchange companies as of 31 December 1998. Federal Communications Commission, *Statistics of Common Carriers 1998* (Washington, D.C.: Government Printing Office, 1999), table 2.9: Statistics of Reporting Local Exchange Carriers As of December 31, 1998 and for the Year then ended.

16. This estimate is only for nonrural companies local exchange plant. It excludes general support facilities. See Results.Zip file http://www.fcc.gov/ccb/apd/hcpm.

17. Robert Loube, "Price Cap Regulation: Problems and Solutions," *Land Economics* 71 (August 1995) : 292–96.

18. Trebing, "Emerging Market Structures," 35–36

19. Martin G. Glaeser, "Those TVA Joint Costs," *Public Utility Fortnightly,* 31 August 1939, 259.

20. Trebing, "Telecommunications Regulation," 121–22.

21. GTE Telephone Operating Cos. GTOC Transmittal No. 1148, CC Docket No. 98–79, FCC No. 99–41, Memorandum and Order, released 26 February 1999, para. 9.

22. U.S.C. Section 153(29).

23. See, for example, *Interconnection contract Between AT&T Communications of the Mountain States, Inc. and GTE Southwest Inc. Pursuant to 47 U.S.C. Section 252,* Docket No. 97–35-TC Before the New Mexico Corporation Commission.

24. *Implementation of the Local Competition Provisions of the Telecommunications Act of 1996,* CC Docket No. 96–98, First Report and Order, 11 FCC Rcd 15499 (1996), 677.

25. Ibid., 677.

26. Ibid., 683.

27. Ibid., 678.

28. AT&T Corp. Opening Brief of AT&T Corp. in Support of Complaint. *AT&T Corp., Complainant, v. Bell Atlantic Corp., Defendant.* FCC File No. E-98–05, 13 March 1998, 26–30.

29. Covad Oct 5 *Ex Parte.* Deployment of Wireline Services Offering Advanced Telecommunications Capability, CC Docket No. 98–147.

30. *Deployment of Wireline Services Offering Advanced Telecommunications Capability*, CC Docket No. 98–147, Third Report and Order, FCC 99–355, 132.

31. William J. Baumol and David Bradford, "Optimal Departures from Marginal Cost Pricing," *American Economic Review* 60 (1970): 265.

32. *Implementation of the Local Competition Provisions of the Telecommunications Act of 1996*, CC Docket No. 96–98, First Report and Order, 11 FCC Rcd 15499 (1996), 696.

33. Coalition for Affordable Local and Long Distance Service, *Memorandum in Support of the Coalition for Affordable Local and Long Distance Service Plan*, Price Cap Performance Review for Local Exchange Carriers, CC Docket No. 94–1, 2–8.

34. G. Kent Webb, *The Economics of Cable Television* (Lexington, Mass.: Lexington Books, 1983), 110–12.

35. Gerald R. Faulhaber, "Cross-Subsidization: Pricing in Public Enterprise," *American Economic Review* 65 (1975): 966.

36. William J. Baumol and J. Gregory Sidak. *Toward Competition in Local Telephony* (Cambridge: MIT Press, 1994).

37. Ibid., 84–85.

38. Robert Loube, "The Proper Use of Stand Alone Cost Studies," paper presented at the Ninth NARUC Biennial Regulatory Information Conference, September 1994.

39. William H. Melody, "Interservice Subsidy: Regulatory Standards and Applied Economics," in *Essays on Public Utility Pricing and Regulation*, ed. Harry M. Trebing (East Lansing: Michigan State University, 1971), 181–86.

40. Robert Loube, *Testimony*. Formal Case No. 814 Phase III, Investigation into the Impact of AT&T Divestiture and Decisions of the Federal Communications Commission on the Chesapeake and Potomac Telephone Company's Jurisdictional Rates.

41. See generally, Richard Gabel, "Allocation of Telephone Plant Investments," in *Adjusting to Regulatory, Pricing, and Marketing Realities*, ed. Harry M. Trebing (East Lansing: Michigan State University Press, 1983), 452–82.

42. Federal Communications Commission, Common Carrier Bureau Seeks Comment on Requests to Redefine "Voice Grade Service" for Purposes of Federal Universal Service Support, Public Notice, CC Docket No. 96–45, 22 December 1999.

43. Letter from Richard Clarke, AT&T, to William F. Caton, FCC, dated 8 April 1997, Ex Parte Presentation, CC Docket No. 96–262.

44. While it is possible to provide local and long-distance service on copper loops that are greater than eighteen thousand feet, this limitation is used in most forward-looking models to ensure that the outside plant will not have to be reengineered to accommodate the near-term provision of digital services. Bellcore, *Notes on the Network*, SR-2275, Issue 3, December 1997, Section 7; and *Federal-State Joint Board on Universal Service*, CC Docket No. 96–45, Fifth Report and Order, FCC 98–279, 68–70.

45. Richard Gabel, "The Early Competitive Era in Telephone Communications, 1893–1920," *Law and Contemporary Problems* 34 (1969): 340–59.

46. William H. Melody, "Efficiency and Social Policy in Telecommunications: Lessons from the U.S. Experience," *Journal of Economic Issues* 23, no. 3 (1989): 657–88.

47. Federal Communications Commission, Monitoring Report, CC Docket No. 98–202, June 1999, table 6–5: Percentage of Households with a Telephone by Income.

48. *Federal-State Joint Board on Universal Service,* Report and Order, CC Docket No. 96–45, 12 FCC Rcd (1997), 341–63.

49. Federal Communications Commission, *Trends in Telephone Service,* March 2000, table 8.2: Lifeline Assistance—Subscribers by State or Jurisdiction.

50. H. S. Dorick, "The Origins of Universal Service." *Telecommunications Policy* 14, no. 3 (1990): 223–38.

51. Milton L. Mueller Jr., *Universal Service: Competition, Interconnection, and Monopoly in the Making of the American Telephone System* (Cambridge: MIT Press, 1997), 4–10.

52. The last directly competing carrier prior to the Telecommunications Act of 1996 was the Keystone Telephone Company, serving Philadelphia until 17 September 1945. Alan Stone, *Public Service Liberalism: Telecommunications and Transitions in Public Policy* (Princeton, N.J.: Princeton University Press, 1991), 124–26.

53. New York State Department of Public Service, *Universal Service Issues,* A Staff Draft Report in Module 1, Case 94-C-0095, The Telecommunications Competition II Proceeding, 16 May 1995, 7.

54. *Federal-State Joint Board on Universal Service,* Report and Order, CC Docket No. 96–45, 12 FCC Rcd (1997), 56–87 and 424–25.

55. National Telecommunications and Information Administration, "Falling Through the Net: Defining the Digital Divide," *http://ntia.doc.gov/ntiahome/fttn99/part1.html#c,* 8 July 1999.

56. David L. Kaserman and John W. Mayo, "Cross-Subsidies in Telecommunications: Roadblocks on the Road to More Intelligent Telephone Pricing," *Yale Journal of Regulation* 11 (1994): 137–40.

57. Philip A. Klein and Edythe S. Miller, "Concepts of Value, Efficiency and Democracy in Institutional Economics," *Journal of Economic Issues* 30, no. 1 (1966): 267–77; and Thomas DeGregori, *A Theory of Technology: Continuity and Change in Human Development* (Ames: Iowa State University Press, 1985).

58. Francois Bar and Munk Riis, "From Welfare to Innovation: Toward a New Rationale for Universal Service," in *The Twenty-Sixth Annual Telecommunications Policy Research Conference* Held in Alexandria, Virginia, 3–5 October 1998, 2–3.

59. Lee L. Selwyn, Sonia N. Jorge, and Patricia D. Kravtin, "Broken Promises: A Review of Bell Atlantic-Pennsylvania's Performance Under Chapter 30," Economics and Technology, Inc., Boston, Massachusetts, June 1998, iii.

60. Edythe S. Miller, "Economic Efficiency: The Economics Discipline and

the 'Affected-With-A-Public-Interest' Concept," *Journal of Economic Issues* 24, no. 3 (1990): 719–32.

References

AT&T Corp. Opening Brief of AT&T Corp. in Support of Complaint. *AT&T Corp., Complainant, v. Bell Atlantic Corp., Defendant.* FCC File No. E-98–05, 13 March 1998.

Bar, Francois, and Munk Riis. "From Welfare to Innovation: Toward a New Rationale for Universal Service," in *The Twenty-Sixth Annual Telecommunications Policy Research Conference* Held in Alexandria, Virginia, 3–5 October 1998.

Baumol, William J., and David Bradford, "Optimal Departures from Marginal Cost Pricing," *American Economic Review* 60 (1970): 265.

Baumol, William J., and J. Gregory Sidak. *Toward Competition in Local Telephony.* Cambridge: MIT Press, 1994.

DeGregori, Thomas. *A Theory of Technology: Continuity and Change in Human Development.* Ames: Iowa State University Press, 1985.

Dorick, H. S. "The Origins of Universal Service." *Telecommunications Policy* 14, no. 3 (1990): 223–38.

Faulhaber, Gerald R. "Cross-Subsidization: Pricing in Public Enterprise." *American Economic Review* 65 (1975): 966.

Gabel, Richard. "The Early Competitive Era in Telephone Communications, 1893–1920." *Law and Contemporary Problems* 34 (1969): 340–59.

———. "Allocation of Telephone Plant Investments." In *Adjusting to Regulatory, Pricing, and Marketing Realities,* edited by Harry M. Trebing, 452–82. East Lansing: Michigan State University Press, 1983.

Glaeser, Martin G. "Those TVA Joint Costs." *Public Utility Fortnightly,* 31 August 1939, 259.

Kahn, Alfred E. "How to Treat the Costs of Shared Voice and Video Networks in a Post-Regulatory Age," *Cato Policy Analysis No. 264.* Washington, D.C.: Cato Institute, 1996.

Kaserman, David L., and John W. Mayo. "Cross-Subsidies in Telecommunications: Roadblocks on the Road to More Intelligent Telephone Pricing." *Yale Journal of Regulation* 11 (1994): 119–47.

Klein, Philip A. "Institutionalist Reflections on the Role of the Public Sector." *Journal of Economic Issues* 18, no. 1 (1984): 45–68.

Klein, Philip A., and Edythe S. Miller. "Concepts of Value, Efficiency and Democracy in Institutional Economics." *Journal of Economic Issues* 30, no. 1 (1996): 267–77.

Leithauser, Brad. "A Funny Thing Happened on the Way to Broadway." *New York Review of Books,* 10 February 2000, 35–38.

Lenahan, Grant. "Next Generation Networks: A Practical View of Network Evolution." Washington, D.C.: Telcordia Technologies, Inc., 1999. Photocopied.

Lewis, Arthur W. *Overhead Costs: Some Essays in Economic Analysis.* New York: Augustus Kelly, 1970.

Loube, Robert. "The Proper Use of Stand Alone Cost Studies." Paper presented at Ninth NARUC Biennial Regulatory Information Conference, September 1994.

———. "Price Cap Regulation: Problems and Solutions." *Land Economics* 71 (August 1995): 268–98.

———. *Testimony.* Formal Case No. 814 Phase III, Investigation into the Impact of AT&T Divestiture and Decisions of the Federal Communications Commission on the Chesapeake and Potomac Telephone Company's Jurisdictional Rates.

Lucas, Matthew, and John Yin. "IP QoS." *Billing World* (September 1999): 28–35.

Melody, William H. "Interservice Subsidy: Regulatory Standards and Applied Economics." In *Essays on Public Utility Pricing and Regulation,* edited by Harry M. Trebing, 167–210. East Lansing: Michigan State University Press, 1971.

———. "Efficiency and Social Policy in Telecommunications: Lessons from the U.S. Experience." *Journal of Economic Issues* 23, no. 3 (1989): 657–88.

Miller, Edythe S. "Economic Efficiency: The Economics Discipline and the 'Affected-With-A-Public-Interest' Concept." *Journal of Economic Issues* 24, no. 3 (1990): 719–32.

Mitchell, Bridger M., and Ingo Vogelsang. *Telecommunications Pricing: Theory and Practice.* Cambridge: Cambridge University Press, 1991.

Mueller, Milton L., Jr. *Universal Service: Competition, Interconnection, and Monopoly in the Making of the American Telephone System.* Cambridge: MIT Press, 1997.

Scotchmer, Suzanne. "Two-Tier Pricing of Shared Facilities in a Free-Entry Equilibrium." *Rand Journal of Economics* 16, no. 4 (1985): 456–72.

Selwyn, Lee L., Sonia N. Jorge, and Patricia D. Kravtin. Broken Promises: A Review of Bell Atlantic-Pennsylvania's Performance Under Chapter 30, Economics and Technology, Inc., Boston, Massachusetts, June 1998.

Stone, Alan. *Public Service Liberalism: Telecommunications and Transitions in Public Policy.* Princeton, N.J.: Princeton University Press, 1991.

Trebing, Harry M. "Market Structure and Regulatory Reform in the Electric and Gas Utility Industries." In *Salvaging Public Utility Regulation,* edited by Werner Sichel, 79–116. Lexington: Lexington Books, 1976.

———. "Public Utility Regulation: A Case Study in the Debate over Effectiveness of Economic Regulation." *Journal of Economic Issues* 18, no. 1 (1984): 223–50.

———."Public Control of Enterprise: Neoclassical Assault and Neoinstitutional Reform." Remarks upon Receipt of the Veblen-Commons Award. *Journal of Economic Issues* 18, no. 2 (1984): 353–68.

———. "Public Utility Regulation: A Case Study in the Debate over Effectiveness of Economic Regulation." *Journal of Economic Issues* 20, no. 1 (1986): 223–50.

———. "Apologetics of Deregulation in Energy and Telecommunciations: An Institutionalist Assessment." *Journal of Economic Issues* 20, no. 3 (1986): 613–32.

———. "Regulation of Industry: An Institutionalist Approach." *Journal of Economic Issues* 21, no. 4 (1987): 1707–37.

———. "Telecommunications Regulation—The Continuing Dilemma." In *Public Utility Regulation: The Economic and Social Control of Industry,* edited by Kenneth Nowotny, David B. Smith, and Harry M. Trebing, 93–130. Boston: Kluwer Academic Publishers, 1989.

———. "Emerging Market Structures and Options for Regulatory Reform in Public Utility Industries." In *Telecommunications Reform: Principles, Policies and Regulatory Practices,* edited by William H. Melody, 29–40. Lyngby: Den Private Ingeniorfond, Technical University of Denmark, 1997.

Webb, G. Kent. *The Economics of Cable Television.* Lexington: Lexington Books, 1983.

Weiss, Martin, and Junseok Hwang. "Internet Telephony or Circuit Switched Telephony: Which is Cheaper?" in The Twenty-Sixth Annual Telecommunications Policy Research Conference Held in Alexandria, Virginia, 3–5 October 1998.

The Role of Costing
as a Rate-Making Tool
in an Environment
of Dynamic Change

MARK A. JAMISON

Introduction

The future of rate making will determine the future of costing as a rate-making tool. If rate making is to play only a minor, brief role in telecommunications regulation, then costing does not matter. This was Stephen Littlechild's (1983) view of telecommunications rate making in the United Kingdom in the early 1980s. It led to his recommendation that the U.K. government deregulate most of British Telecom's prices immediately and use pure price cap regulation, based upon inflation and productivity indices, as a transitional mechanism toward complete deregulation of all prices.[1] His policy view was correct, but his industry assumptions were incorrect. Rate making is playing a long-term role in the United Kingdom's regulation of telecommunications. The government has adopted techniques that resemble rate-of-return regulation and has used costing as a basis for evaluating prices (Jamison 1998; Office of Telecommunications 1997; Berg and Foreman 1995). Indeed, in most developed and developing countries, with the notable exceptions of New Zealand, Switzerland, and Guatemala, regulatory rate making and costing are playing long-term roles as regulators address issues of price discrimination, control of market power, adequacy of revenues, and universal service.

Despite regulators' widespread use of costing in rate making, its use is controversial because of the inherent trade-offs regulators make between their pricing objectives, their credibility to investors, their legitimacy to the public, and their concerns over information rents. Pricing objectives

250

play a role because stakeholders and regulators sometimes seek to achieve desired pricing outcomes by choosing costing methods that support their preconceived results. Credibility refers to the concern that regulators might confiscate shareholder property by requiring prices that are so low that shareholders are denied the opportunity to receive a return on and a return of their investments. Legitimacy is the concern that the regulator is unable to achieve policy goals because the regulator is either captured by the industry interests or unable to overcome the utilities' information superiority. Information rents are excess benefits that shareholders and managers can extract from the regulatory process because of information asymmetries; that is to say, because they know more about their business than do regulators, the public, and other stakeholders.

In this chapter I describe how regulators have addressed these trade-offs and what they mean for the future of costing, assuming that rate making has a long-term role in telecommunications regulation. I explain the role of information rents and credibility concerns in leading regulators to adopt rate-of-return regulation in the early part of the twentieth century. Further concerns over legitimacy and information rents caused regulators to develop increasingly detailed techniques for rate-of-return regulation and eventually for jurisdictional and service costing. Jurisdictional costing is the process known as *Separations.* Separations' purpose is to determine how much of a telephone company's costs will be recovered through prices for interstate services, the services that the Federal Communications Commission (FCC) regulates. State regulators, called Public Utility Commissions or PUCs, regulate intrastate prices and are responsible for whatever costs are left over (Bolter et al. 1984). Service costing is the process of measuring costs for particular services or categories of services. Regulators first became interested in service costing in the 1960s, when certain telecommunications markets became competitive and regulators were called upon to protect against cross-subsidization.

Beginning in the 1980s, two factors—concerns over information rents and analytical research on the benefits of incentive regulation—led regulators to decrease their reliance on companies' own costs and to start using exogenous data for pricing purposes. The exogenous data included inflation and productivity factors in the case of price cap regulation, and computer models in the case of proxy costs. Regulators use price caps to limit overall price levels for regulated services, and use proxy costs to control rate design. Proxy costs are simply cost estimates from computer models that simulate the operations of a representative or virtual company, as opposed to an actual company. Rate design refers to the relative price levels of services and general structure of service prices; for example, whether residential prices are 25 percent or 75 percent of the level of business prices, or whether customers pay a flat rate or a measured rate for local service.

A revolution in the nature of telecommunications and its industry structure is prompting increasing concern among regulators over rate design and information rents that the incumbent industry could extract. Telecommunications was once a stand-alone system for carrying voice traffic between persons in fixed locations. It is now becoming a component of a larger, "always on" system that processes, stores, retrieves, and reformats all kinds of information with limited regard to location, means of input, and means of receiving output (Gibson 1999; Adler 1999). This means that telecommunications is a piece of a larger, rapidly changing, and rapidly growing information market. Because telecommunications was a stand-alone system, the government and industry were able to impose a monopoly structure, and they divided the market according to geographic boundaries. As technology changed, this monopoly structure was unable to withstand customer demands for lower prices, choices, and innovation, and nearby industries' economic interests in cracking the monopoly markets (Jamison 1999a), leading the government to remove most legal barriers to entry in telecommunications. Furthermore, the Telecommunications Act of 1996 requires incumbent local exchange companies (ILECs) to offer cost-based prices for exchange traffic with competing companies, cost-based prices for leasing unbundled elements of their networks to competitors, and cost-based discounts for competitors reselling ILEC retail services. As I explain in more detail later in the chapter, concerns that ILECs would estimate costs in ways that would promote ILEC business interests led regulators and competitors to begin using proxy cost models to develop cost-based prices.

I organize this chapter as follows. In the second section, I describe the emerging telecommunications industry and situations where regulators may choose to control prices. In the third section, I describe how utility rate making in the United States in the late 1800s and early 1900s was largely a matter of legislation or negotiations between utilities and municipalities. In some instances, the utilities' superior expertise gave them information rents. Yet at other times, prices were held so low that the utilities could not continue to operate. As a result of these problems, legislative and municipal regulation gave way to commission-style regulation, and the regulators adopted service-at-cost regulation, which became known as rate-of-return regulation.

In the fourth and fifth sections, I describe how, over time, it became clear to regulators that information asymmetries continued to exist and were giving rents to utilities and their management. Section four focuses on Separations and Section five covers service costing. Information rents created concerns for the public, new competitors, and the courts, who believed that regulators were unable to overcome utilities' information superiority. Their concerns, which challenged the legitimacy of the regulator, led regulators to develop increasingly detailed techniques for measuring costs. They also led regulators and the antitrust authorities to attempt structural control of the industry by means of forced divestitures and structural separations. This effort quickly lost favor because of fears that structural controls created production inefficiencies. As a result, regulators ended the structural controls and have renewed their efforts at service costing to deal with cross-subsidies, anticompetitive behavior, and price discrimination.

Section six provides recommendations. I recommend that regulators adopt benchmarking techniques for long-term control of telecommunications prices. The final section is the conclusion.

Rate Making in the Emerging Telecommunications Industry

Telecommunications was once a stand-alone, voice transmission service, provided over specialized wire-based networks. It is now transitioning to a mere component of an integrated communications system in which voice and other means of communications are simply software applications provided over interconnected networks that use both wire and wireless technologies. The basic components of this system are: (1) customer appliances, such as personal digital assistants and televisions; (2) network appliances, such as Internet servers; (3) networks; and (4) content/software, such as movies, personal planners, and e-commerce sites. The telecommunications industry primarily provides the networks.

This new type of telecommunications changes dramatically the role of networks. Instead of being based on geography and hardwired for voice service, as historically they have been, networks now operate in the space of connectivity and features. As a result, network providers compete on the basis of footprints and functionality. There are two types of footprints. One type represents the customers that directly connect to the network. Verizon's local exchange networks, Cox's cable television networks, and Vodafone's wireless networks are examples of this type of footprint. The second type of footprint represents content/software providers that are directly connected to the network and can be accessed through it. AOL Time Warner and NTL (a U.K. provider of integrated cable television and

Internet) are examples of network providers that have differentiated them-selves in terms of this second type of footprint. Functionality includes throughput (or network capacity) and the features that networks make available to customers and content/software providers.

Network providers compete based on footprints and functionality, which are interrelated. Network providers expand footprints and develop functionality to make their networks attractive to payers, which include customers, content/software providers, and packagers who pay fees to the network. MCI WorldCom's local-to-global-to-local strategy provides an example of a network provider competing in the development of footprints (Jamison 1999a). AOL Time Warner is an example of a pack-ager, who combines network, end-use customers, and content/software into an integrated service. Network providers make themselves attrac-tive to payers by simultaneously developing a critical mass of connected customers and providers who value communicating with each other, and providing functionality that makes it more valuable for these customers and providers to be connected to the same network than to be connected to separate networks. This functionality for communications on a single network is called internal functionality. Functionality for communications that pass between networks is called external functionality. Network providers supply different levels of internal and external functionality by providing different throughput rates (for example, by limiting net-work interconnection capacity relative to capacity for communications within the network) and by creating features that do not transverse to other networks, such as security features and service customization features.

Research to date is mixed on how this form of rivalry between networks affects the competitiveness of markets. In an earlier paper (Jamison 1999a) I argue that the drive to establish footprints creates more "local" compe-tition than is commonly recognized. Crémer, Rey, and Tirole (2000) argue that the opportunity to differentiate functionality allows large Inter-net backbone providers to discriminate against smaller Internet providers. In another paper (Jamison 2000) I show that large Internet backbone providers treat small Internet providers no worse than they treat them-selves and each other. Likewise, there remains considerable debate on whether regulation of network interconnection improves social welfare, with some arguing that regulation is critical (for example, Economides and White 1995) and others arguing that regulation can be counterproduc-tive (for example, Buehler 1999).

Furthermore, it is unclear whether network providers will be able to compete in functionality. It may be more profitable for businesses to provide functionality separate from network, similar to Microsoft's developing virtual networks of servers and end-use customers using Windows. If this business model dominates, networks may become commodities and network providers may revert to their traditional geography-based business model. In this case, local monopolies could re-emerge.

Without further evidence, it is difficult to tell where regulation of prices will play a long-term role. There are likely candidates, including customer connections in local areas (that is, footprints), backbone interconnection where demand is insufficient to attract multiple network providers, and software functionality, where high fixed costs result in monopoly or dominant firm market structures. Other likely candidates are rural areas, where policy makers are often concerned that relatively high service costs will result in prices that place an unacceptable burden on customers, even if the market attracts multiple network providers. In these cases, the regulator's role may be to use costing to quantify a subsidy amount rather than to provide guidance on limiting prices.

The rate-making framework that appears most appropriate for this environment is a modification of one recommended by Trebing (1984b). The Trebing model: (1) limits economic regulation to markets with residual monopoly power where competition does not appear to be sustainable; (2) incorporates clear welfare guidelines for social policies pursued through regulation, such as pricing for universal service; and (3) uses regulation of market structure to stimulate competition where feasible. Trebing's model could be viewed as assuming more stable technologies and markets than we have today. Also, its third element should be adapted to reflect the revolution in market structure that liberalization of telecommunications markets has unleashed. Given these points, an appropriately modified Trebing model would appear to have the following elements:

1. *Limited economic regulation.* Rate regulation should be limited to networks in areas where there is residual market power, where market power has actually emerged and companies have abused their market power, and to network services that are well established in the minds and lives of ordinary citizens as essential for living and engaging in normal economic activity. The scope of regulation should be significantly less than what the United States has today. There are two reasons for this. First, markets should be given the opportunity to work (Kahn 1998). Second, as I explain in later sec-

tions, extensive regulation in a dualistic environment of competition and monopoly strains regulators' legitimacy and credibility and causes stakeholders to seek to use regulated prices to gain advantage in the marketplace.

2. *Explicit and transparent welfare mechanisms that do not distort the competitive market process.* Regulators are making progress toward the formulation of explicit welfare objectives and transparent welfare mechanisms. However, the system emerging in the United States appears too expansive and complex to mesh well with competition. The United States would do well to examine the policies of countries such as the United Kingdom, Chile, and Peru, where universal service is limited to rural areas and to customers whose incomes are too low to allow them to afford service.

3. *Remove regulatory barriers that hinder efficient industry restructuring.* Despite the passage of the Telecommunications Act of 1996, there remain many barriers to an efficient industry structure. The Act itself singles out local exchange companies for special rights and obligations, even though one of the forces that drove the passage of the act was the meaninglessness of the distinction between local and long distance. The Act also establishes provisions that protect some rural ILECs from competition. Further, the Act treats cable television, wireless telecommunications, wireline voice telecommunications, and data telecommunications as separate, even though their convergence was also a driver of the passage of the Act. Lastly, regulators and antitrust authorities continue to rely upon traditional definitions of telecommunications markets when considering proposed mergers and divestitures.

The primary modifications to the Trebing model are: (1) regulation is limited to established network services; (2) social programs are modular so that they do not interfere with competition or deregulation; and (3) regulation of market structure is limited to removing entry barriers. Limiting market structure regulation to removing entry barriers is essential because the traditional industry structure is badly outdated and there is significant uncertainty regarding the most appropriate future market structure. It may even be that change will continue and that no single market structure will emerge as the most efficient.

For the remainder of this chapter, I will assume that regulators play a long-term role in telecommunications rate making. In the next section, I begin my description of the role that costing should play in rate making by describing the early history of regulation of utility prices.

Early Developments in Regulation

State legislatures and municipalities were the primary utility regulators in the United States during the late 1800s and early 1900s. In this section I explain how this form of regulation gave way to cost-of-service regulation because of concerns over information rents, legitimacy, and credibility (King 1912).

Regulation by legislatures resembled today's price cap regulation (Jamison 1988c). Legislatures would set maximum prices for extended periods and allow utilities to charge whatever prices they liked, as long as they were below the maximums. However, legislative bodies lacked expertise and data, so rate making was largely guesswork. Unforeseen demand changes, inflation or deflation, new technology, and competition often disrupted the arrangement. In some instances, company profits became so large that companies lowered prices to avoid public relations problems (Glaeser 1927).

Municipal regulation was somewhat different from legislative regulation, in that it relied heavily upon negotiations. Yet, as before, government officials lacked detailed data and expertise and so were at a disadvantage relative to the industry. Martin Glaeser remarked on the information asymmetries in the bargaining process: "The hope of reaping an exceptional reward or the fear of probably heavy loss were the imponderables that made bargaining a matching of wits between company and city representatives" (Glaeser 1927, 225).

Glaeser (1927) also observed that municipalities would sometimes attempt to renegotiate contracts when profits rose. Yet if profits turned against the utilities, municipalities generally held the companies to their contracts. As a result of such asymmetric (and opportunistic) treatment, rapidly increasing costs in the early 1900s jeopardized the financial viability of utilities under municipal regulation (Jamison 1988c).

The problems of legislative and municipal regulation led to the development of utility commissions (King 1912). During the development of utility commissions, several court cases limited regulators' discretion in overseeing utilities' prices. These cases ultimately forced regulators to allow prices that permit companies to operate successfully, maintain financial integrity, attract capital, and compensate investors (Kahn 1988). Rate-of-return regulation became the dominant mode of ensuring that this requirement was not violated.

The Influence of Separations

Overview of U.S. History in Telecommunications Costing

The development of costing techniques in U.S. telecommunications follows two tracks. One track is Separations. Separations plays a central role in telecommunications costing, for two reasons. First, until the 1960s, all telecommunications costing activity was in the development of Separations. As a result, many costing methods currently in use have their roots in the Separations process. The second reason is that Separations greatly affects price levels for local telephone service and the relative levels of interstate and intrastate long-distance prices. Costs allocated to the federal level are recovered through prices for interstate service. The remaining costs are left to the states to recover through state prices, largely intrastate long-distance and local services. The Separations process looks like a zero sum game and so has resulted in lengthy struggles between state and federal regulators as each has sought to limit the costs that are to be recovered in its jurisdiction (R. Gabel 1967).

The second track, service costing, determines how telephone companies can change prices in response to competition. As I explain in the following section, this track began in the 1960s when the FCC began using cost information to protect against cross-subsidization and the abuse of market power. This form of rate making generally determines minimum prices that regulated companies can charge in competitive markets, maximum price levels that they can charge in noncompetitive markets, or both (Bolter et al. 1984). In this track state and federal regulators have largely been allies, assisting each other in audits and information gathering. Exceptions to the cooperative relationship generally occur when federal rate-making decisions affect Separations or limit state jurisdiction.

Both tracks provide important lessons for regulators as they are attempting to decide how to control cross-subsidy and market power in the dynamic telecommunications environment. The history of Separations illustrates how regulators have tried to overcome companies' information advantage by adopting increasingly detailed costing rules, obtaining more data, and sharing data with other regulators. It also illustrates how companies and regulators have attempted to effect desired price changes by changing the cost allocation rules. Lastly, it shows that regulators are sometimes uneasy with extracting the full value of the cost information they obtain. For example, it is only recently that state and federal regulators began sharing financial data in a common format.

The history of service costing also illustrates regulators' desire to overcome information asymmetries and stakeholders' tendencies to obtain favorable pricing outcomes by affecting the costing process. In addition, it illustrates how regulators increase the possibility of confiscation of shareholder value when they increase their control of the costing formulas.

Lessons from Separations

Federal inaction marks the early history of the Separations process. Federal laws gave the FCC (and before it the Interstate Commerce Commission) jurisdiction over Separations. The Interstate Commerce Commission never used its authority and, for many years, neither did the FCC (R. Gabel 1967). Prior to World War II, AT&T developed its own policies for Separations and Settlements (the process by which AT&T shared long-distance revenues with local exchange companies) and used these policies to justify interstate price decreases and intrastate price increases. AT&T was satisfied with this arrangement because it gave the company considerable latitude in setting intrastate and interstate prices. The FCC was content because its policy goal, keeping interstate prices low, was consistent with AT&T's interests. Also, the FCC was able to follow a policy called *continuing oversight,* in which AT&T agreed to lower interstate prices from time to time as technology advances decreased AT&T's costs of providing long distance (Bolter et al. 1984).

Even though the FCC was satisfied with this arrangement, the states were dissatisfied, for two reasons. First, a growing disparity existed between interstate and intrastate prices. Second, AT&T's control of Separations allowed the company to use the process to its own benefit. Some states took unilateral action, making Separations decisions in the context of state rate cases. More generally, states used their national association, the National Association of Regulatory Utility Commissioners (NARUC), to press the FCC into action. The FCC responded in 1941 by opening docket no. 6328 and conducting hearings with state regulators. Despite extensive activity in this docket over a period of twenty-five years, the FCC did not reach a decision on Separations during this time (R. Gabel 1967).

Because of the FCC's indecision, Separations policy evolved through a negotiation process between the states, the FCC, and AT&T. Dissatisfied with AT&T's control of the process, NARUC proposed the first regulatory

Separations Manual in 1947. AT&T incorporated the manual into its Separations and Settlements processes later that year, and the FCC, rather than adopting the manual, notified AT&T that it would not object. Three years later, when the FCC was threatening to force AT&T to reduce interstate prices, AT&T sought to hold off the price decrease by working with NARUC on a modification of the 1947 *Separations Manual.* The modification would transfer costs from the state jurisdiction to the interstate jurisdiction (R. Gabel 1967). Under rate-of-return regulation, this cost shift had the effect of decreasing intrastate prices relative to interstate prices.

Even though the 1947 *Separations Manual* improved regulators' control of the Separations process, the states still perceived that AT&T was able to work the process to its favor. The states responded by conducting investigations into the allocation of costs of long distance lines in 1951–55, and expanded their investigations into almost all aspects of AT&T's operations and services in later years (R. Gabel 1967). By the late 1960s, the FCC finally adopted Separations rules and, in accordance with federal law, formed a Federal/State Joint Board to advise the FCC on changes in these rules.

The FCC's Separations rules and the Joint Board improved regulators' control of the Separations process, but they also formalized the use of cost allocations to achieve pricing goals. This has been particularly troubling to most economists, who have viewed cost allocations as arbitrary and counter to economic efficiency (Baumol 1979; Baumol, Koehn, and Willig 1987). Over the years, regulators have developed several Separations mechanisms to keep prices low for small local exchange companies, for local exchange companies with above average costs, and for state services in general (Federal Communications Commission, Common Carrier Bureau Staff 1996; Mueller 1993). A recurring theme in NARUC policy statements is that changes in Separations rules should not affect the amount of cost left to the state jurisdiction.

Through the Joint Board and through NARUC, the states have continued to press for greater regulatory control of Separations. Concerned that ILECs were reporting inconsistent information to federal and state regulators (ILECs were the primary companies subject to Separations after the breakup of AT&T in 1984), the states worked with the FCC on the development of a single system of financial reporting called *Automated Reporting Management Information System,* or *ARMIS.* This reporting system includes reporting of Separations and other ILEC data in an electronic format that is accessible to all regulators. The FCC now makes ARMIS data available on its Web site. Concerned that ILECs might not be following cost allocation rules as the regulators intended them, the states also began pressing for state and federal regulators to share resources in auditing the companies. To date, the states and the FCC have collaborated in several joint audits of ILECs.

Costing to Protect against Cross-Subsidy

Early Work by the FCC

The primary purpose of the second track of regulatory costing—service costing—is to prevent cross-subsidy and the abuse of market power (Trebing 1984a). The FCC laid the groundwork for regulators' use of costing in this area (Bolter 1978). The issue came to the FCC's attention around 1959, when the FCC allowed private users to build their own microwave systems. AT&T responded to the competition with deep price discounts for customers that might build their own systems (Brock 1981). The FCC's investigations of these discounts prompted the agency to launch an extensive inquiry into how to measure service costs. This inquiry spanned three dockets and fifteen years. The first docket, docket no. 14650, was opened in 1962, and the last docket, docket no. 18128, was decided in 1976.

Fully distributed cost and incremental cost emerged as the major costing philosophies for the commission to consider. Fully distributed cost is a general name for an almost infinite number of techniques for spreading a company's accounting costs across its services. Incremental cost is an estimate of how much a company's total economic cost would change if the company's output were to change by a certain amount. The FCC staff supported fully distributed cost, proposing that prices in competitive markets should cover their services' full allocation of costs. AT&T argued that prices should be acceptable as long as prices in competitive markets cover long-run incremental cost and prices in monopoly markets are no greater than stand-alone cost. Within these bounds, AT&T argued that it should be allowed to use Ramsey pricing, which raises service prices above marginal cost in inverse proportion to each service's price elasticity of demand. Similar in theory to marginal cost, long-run incremental cost is the extra investment and expense a company incurs to produce additional quantities of a service (Baumol 1979). Stand-alone cost is the total cost that would be incurred by a company if it served only the monopoly markets in question (Faulhaber 1975). The commission adopted the staff recommendation (Bolter 1978).

The differences between the FCC staff's fully distributed cost proposal and AT&T's long-run incremental cost proposal were substantial. Fully distributed cost uses data from companies' accounting records, so the costs are historical. Fully distributed cost allocates all accounting costs across all services with minimal regard to cost causation, so at best only a loose linkage exists between a service's fully distributed cost and the costs the service actually causes (Bolter 1978; Jamison 1988a). This is contrary to the conventional wisdom that fully distributed cost assigns direct costs and allocates only joint and common costs (Baumol and Walton 1973). Finally, because fully distributed cost allocates all costs, it also allocates all unused capacity and, in theory, forces a sharing of joint and common costs between competitive and noncompetitive services.[2]

In contrast to fully distributed cost, long-run incremental cost and stand-alone cost approaches are forward-looking. To make the cost measurement forward-looking, long-run incremental cost models typically measure costs for the technology that the ILEC plans to have in place in the near future and value the physical assets at current prices.[3] In theory, but not always in practice, long-run incremental cost also measures costs only for assets or activities, such as maintenance, whose costs are affected by the service whose costs are being measured. Lastly, the long-run incremental cost and stand-alone cost approaches force captive ratepayers to be responsible for paying all of the residual revenue requirements of the ILEC, and Ramsey pricing forces captive ratepayers to pay the bulk of joint and common costs (Trebing 1984a). Forcing joint and common costs onto captive ratepayers conflicts with regulators' generally accepted mission of protecting customers against monopoly pricing.

The FCC's preference for fully distributed cost and AT&T's preference for long-run incremental cost, stand-alone cost, and Ramsey pricing were predictable. Fully distributed cost supported the FCC's legitimacy by allowing the agency to show that all customers were sharing somewhat equally in covering AT&T's costs. Also, the fully distributed cost process is mechanical, making it simpler to satisfy legal requirements that regulatory policies not be arbitrary and capricious. On the other hand, AT&T's proposal, if implemented, would give AT&T the latitude to do exactly what it wanted to do: raise prices in noncompetitive markets and lower prices in competitive ones.

The U.S. Department of Justice viewed the FCC's efforts to control AT&T's anticompetitive actions, including cross-subsidy, as largely unsuccessful, so the Department of Justice reopened an antitrust case against AT&T in 1974. A settlement of this case in 1982 resulted in the breakup of AT&T in 1984. This breakup was, in effect, an attempt to use structural control to prevent cross-subsidy, by separating monopoly segments of the industry from potentially competitive segments. The Department of Justice and AT&T believed that the local exchange was a natural monopoly and that the remaining segments were potentially competitive. As it turns out, the distinction between local exchange and other industry segments was arbitrary. The conflicting business interests of local and long-distance companies brought the distinction to an end as each side sought regulatory policies that would allow companies to integrate local and long distance. This culminated in the passage of the Telecommunications Act of 1996.

Also in the early 1980s, regulators imposed structural separation requirements on the divested Bell Operating Companies, in part because of regulators' dissatisfaction with cost allocations. However, this experiment with structural control quickly gave way to concerns that it caused efficiency losses by surrendering economies of scale and scope, surrendering opportunities for technology and pricing innovations, and increasing transaction costs. Even though information asymmetries kept regulators from verifying the validity of these concerns, they largely abandoned structural control and went back to service costing. (Looking ahead in the story, the return to service costing meant a return to information rents and concerns for regulatory legitimacy. Regulators responded with price caps and proxy costs, but these tools have reopened the issue of regulatory credibility because they give regulators the ability to limit prices without reference to effects on shareholder property rights.)

After its decision to drop structural separation requirements for the Bell Operating Companies, the FCC had to develop a process for accounting separations to prevent the Bell Operating Companies from cross-subsidizing their non-telephone products and services. The FCC opened CC docket no. 86–111 to develop the cost allocation rules, which it would apply to all large ILECs. In this proceeding, the Bell Operating Companies and other ILECs generally supported incremental cost. State regulators and competitors to the Bell Operating Companies generally supported fully distributed cost. The agency adopted fully distributed cost guidelines and, to address information asymmetry concerns, stepped up its control of the costing process. The FCC required the large ILECs to file cost allocation manuals, subject to the agency's approval, and to have their compliance with the manuals and the FCC's rules audited on an annual basis. Over time, the FCC required large ILECs to develop uniform costing procedures and to electronically report the cost allocation results. These requirements had the effect of giving ILECs less discretion in how to allocate costs and of simplifying the FCC's enforcement of its cost allocation rules.

State PUC Efforts

State regulators began developing intrastate costing policies when they faced the same competitive pricing issues that the FCC faced. Their early decisions mirrored the FCC response. A 1988 survey sponsored by NARUC showed that 65 percent of the PUCs required cost support for pricing decisions. Fifty-five percent of these PUCs required fully distributed cost and 19 percent required incremental cost. Thirty-seven percent had or were developing policies on segregating costs between regulated and nonregulated services (Jamison 1988b).

After 1988, increasing numbers of PUCs began using incremental cost for rate making and began setting standards for how incremental costs would be calculated. The form of incremental cost that emerged is called *total service, long run incremental cost* (TSLRIC) (Larson and Parsons 1995). In theory, the differences between TSLRIC and long-run incremental cost, the cost measure that AT&T advocated in the 1960s, are that: (1) TSLRIC includes the investment and expense associated with producing the entire quantity of a service, whereas long-run incremental cost covers only a change in quantity; and (2) TSLRIC includes fixed costs caused by a service. These fixed costs—also called volume-insensitive costs—are caused by providing the service and remain constant regardless of the quantity of output produced. In practice, the difference between TSLRIC and long-run incremental cost is that TSLRIC includes fixed costs. As a result, TSLRIC can miss inframarginal costs, and generally understates the costs a service actually causes.[4]

In the late 1980s, MCI observed that ILEC estimates of TSLRIC for an item would vary depending on whether the price the costs supported was a wholesale price that MCI paid or a retail price against which MCI competed. The costs for retail services tended to be lower. Concerned that this meant that ILECs had too much discretion in calculating TSLRIC, MCI began advocating an approach called *Building Blocks.* Building Blocks would break services into components, estimate TSLRIC-like costs for each component, and then estimate service costs by aggregating the component costs that related to the service. In this way, component costs could not vary between competitive and noncompetitive services. Several PUCs shared MCI's concern and adopted the Building Blocks approach, writing detailed rules on how it should be implemented (Larson and Parsons 1995).

The Development of Proxy Costs

In recent years, regulators and competitors to ILECs have begun to develop their own cost models, taking the role of cost measurement away from the ILECs. These efforts decrease the information asymmetries between regulators and companies with respect to the inner workings of cost studies, but also risk decreasing regulators' credibility by increasing regulatory discretion in pricing.

The first effort by regulators to develop their own cost models occurred in the early 1980s, when the Kansas Corporation Commission led a group of PUCs in sponsoring a stand-alone cost study of selected Southwestern Bell exchanges in Kansas. They conducted this study to demonstrate the costs that long-distance service had imposed on the local exchange network. Their goal was to counter the industry position that long distance was subsidizing local exchange service and that competition in long distance meant that the subsidy could not be sustained. The PUCs conducted the study themselves because the industry was unwilling to conduct the study for them (Gabel et al. 1983).

Prompted by further reluctance by the regulated telephone companies to provide cost information that the regulators wanted, regulators continued to sponsor cost models. In 1985, David Gabel conducted a service cost study of Wisconsin Bell for the Wisconsin Public Service Commission (D. Gabel 1985). In 1987, the Michigan Public Service Commission, through the Michigan Divestiture Research Fund, funded Richard Gabel and David Gabel to investigate the incremental and stand-alone costs of Michigan Bell (R. Gabel and D. Gabel n.d.). Also in the late 1980s, the California PUC prompted a RAND study of the incremental costs of selected GTE local exchanges in California (Mitchell 1990). In the regulators' first break from estimating costs for specific ILECs, the National Regulatory Research Institute in 1991 funded David Gabel and Mark Kennet to develop a computer model that would estimate costs for hypothetical local exchange companies (D. Gabel and Kennet 1991). In 1992 the Maine Public Service Commission funded David Gabel to estimate costs for New England Telephone Company's services (D. Gabel 1992).

The introduction of local exchange competition caused other non-ILECs to become interested in conducting cost studies. In 1994, MCI sponsored a cost study to counter a United States Telephone Association study that suggested the cost of universal service was in the neighborhood of 25 percent of all ILEC revenues. The United States Telephone Association argued that local exchange competition would put at risk the money that subsidized universal service (Monson and Rohlfs 1993). Concerned that this argument for large universal service subsidies would cost MCI and delay local competition, MCI developed its cost study to argue that the cost of universal service was about one-third the amount claimed by the United States Telephone Association.

About this same time, two large ILECs, US West and Sprint, became concerned that local competition would hurt their ability to fund rural universal service from urban revenues. Their problem was that the FCC Separations rules severely limited the amount of universal service subsidy that large ILECs could receive. This meant that US West and Sprint had to generate subsidies internally to support what they felt were their unprofitable rural exchanges. Local exchange competition threatened their ability to do this. US West and Sprint saw MCI's cost model, called the *Hatfield Model,* as an opportunity to change the subsidy system so that subsidies would be based upon the cost of serving a rural area rather than upon the size and total cost of the ILEC. They teamed with MCI to develop what was called the *Benchmark Cost Model.* The Benchmark Cost Model used very little proprietary data, and regulators could run the model on their own computers. Eventually MCI dropped out of the alliance and returned to the development of the Hatfield Model, which gave lower cost results than the Benchmark Cost Model but could still be run by regulators on their own computers. Pacific Telesis, which had developed a competing model, joined with US West and Sprint, and the Benchmark Cost Model became known as the *BCPM.*[5]

As PUCs began allowing local competition, some PUCs adopted policies that allowed competitors such as AT&T and MCI the opportunity to lease unbundled network elements from ILECs. Unbundled network elements are simply pieces of telecommunications networks, such as local loops or parts of local switches. The Telecommunications Act of 1996 made this a national policy. At this time, AT&T and MCI were again concerned that the ILECs' cost support for unbundled network elements prices would produce results that favored ILECs. Wanting cost estimates that favored their own economic interests, AT&T and MCI joined together to refine the Hatfield Model so that it could estimate unbundled network element costs. The Washington Transportation and Utilities Commission, long frustrated with US West's reluctance to provide cost data that the commission could approve, was the first state to adopt the Hatfield Model for this purpose. This prompted other PUCs to seriously consider the Hatfield Model in their own jurisdictions.

With the passage of the Telecommunications Act of 1996, the focus of the costing debate returned to the FCC. The FCC began two proceedings that eventually led the FCC into proxy costs. In the first proceeding the FCC developed rules for pricing unbundled network elements and pricing reciprocal compensation. Reciprocal compensation is the arrangement by which ILECs and their competitors (the competitive local exchange companies, or CLECs) pay each other for terminating local telephone traffic. In this proceeding, the FCC adopted a near-TSLRIC, which the agency named *Total Element Long Run Incremental Cost* or TELRIC. The second FCC proceeding addressed universal service. In this proceeding, the FCC decided to develop its own TELRIC cost model to estimate the cost of universal service.

The main differences between TELRIC and TSLRIC are that (1) TELRIC assumes that the ILEC always uses the most current, least-cost technology, whereas TSLRIC is based on the technology that the ILEC actually uses; and (2) TELRIC assumes that the ILEC can always change cable routes to follow the most efficient routes that would satisfy current demand, whereas TSLRIC estimates costs for the ILEC's actual cable routes. The effect of these and other differences is that TELRIC gives lower cost estimates than TSLRIC, which means TELRIC further understates the costs ILECs actually incur (Jamison 1999b).

ILECs and PUCs objected to the FCC's pricing policies. The ILECs objected to TELRIC because the ILECs wanted to charge prices based on fully distributed cost, which they called *actual cost*. The PUCs objected to the FCC even having a pricing policy because they believed the 1996 Act gave them jurisdiction over reciprocal compensation and unbundled network element prices. The ILECs and PUCs collaborated in an appeal of the FCC's costing decisions and won an early court decision. However, the U.S. Supreme Court overturned the lower court decision and upheld many of the FCC's costing and pricing policies.

Conclusions Regarding Proxy Costs

While regulators' use of proxy costs has provided a remedy for their concerns regarding the credibility of ILEC-sponsored cost studies, proxy costs resurrect concerns about regulators' credibility and legitimacy that rate-of-return regulation was created to solve. Proxy costs revive these concerns because the flexibility that was once in the ILECs' hands is now in regulators' hands. Several experiences illustrate the discretion available in conducting economic cost studies from computer models, whether they be ILEC models, competitors' models, or regulators' models.

One event is the switch in industry perspectives on cost studies. Under the Telecommunications Act of 1996, regulators have begun using incremental cost as a standard for setting maximum prices in noncompetitive markets rather than minimum prices in competitive markets. This has caused ILECs and competitors to change their views on how to calculate incremental costs. ILEC economists once argued that long-run incremental cost models provided accurate estimates of incremental costs. Now that regulators have adopted these techniques for TELRIC and TSLRIC, ILEC economists argue that the techniques underestimate incremental costs by 50 to 70 percent. ILEC competitors, who once advocated fully distributed cost and were skeptical of low estimates of incremental costs, now endorse TELRIC and favor assumptions that cause TELRIC to understate incremental cost (Jamison 1999b).

The application of proxy costs in Chile provides an interesting example of the discretion built into these techniques. Prices for electricity distribution in Chile are regulated according to proxy cost models. The price for electricity distribution is calculated every four years. The procedure involves calculating the proxy costs of an efficient firm and then setting prices to cover these costs. Both the industry and the regulator (CNE) calculate proxy costs. The industry's estimate is given a weight of 33 percent, and CNE's estimate is given a weight of 67 percent, creating incentives for strategic behavior on the parts of the industry and CNE. As a result, discrepancies between the industry and CNE's estimates have exceeded 50 percent in some cases (Bitran and Serra 1994; Smith and Klein 1994).

A simplified cost model that the Public Utility Research Center has used in regulatory training workshops illustrates how small changes in cost model assumptions can have large effects on model results. Four critical assumptions in cost models are technology, depreciation, cost of capital, and capacity utilization. The technology assumption determines the value of the investment included in the cost study. The depreciation assumption determines the recovery period for the investment. The cost of capital assumption determines the profit allowed on the investment. The utilization assumption determines the number of units of service over which costs are spread. Changing these assumptions by as little as 5 percent causes a 13 percent change in the cost estimate. To put this in perspective, a 13 percent decrease in ILEC revenues in 1997 would have wiped out their entire net income.

A recent debate in telecommunications costing is the use of real options.[6] Real options are the value of resolving uncertainty before making a sunk investment. ILECs argue that estimates of incremental cost should be augmented with real option values because ILECs forgo the value of delaying investment by providing facilities today for unbundled network elements and reciprocal compensation. Without this addition to incremental cost, ILECs argue, they do not have an adequate incentive to invest and innovate. Opponents argue that the real option value is quite low, or even negative, so there is little to be gained by adding real option values to incremental cost estimates.

There is little question that regulated prices must be adequate to reward investment if regulators want investors to provide capital to regulated utilities. However, because estimating real option values is subjective and the values can be both negative and positive, it is unclear whether using real option values in rate making improves outcomes. Jerry Hausman (1999) illustrates the uncertainty involved in valuing telecommunications real options. Although he is an advocate for the use of real options, he is able to offer only a range of possible values that they could take. Lenos Trigeorgis (1996), who is one of the developers of the real options concept, explains that real options values can be positive or negative and shows that real options values depend upon the options considered (Trigeorgis 1999). These options vary among projects and place regulators in the position of assessing risk on a project-by-project basis. In an earlier paper (Jamison 1999b), I show that incremental cost studies can compensate for the uncertainty that real options values are supposed to resolve by incorporating realistic demand estimates.

Recommendations for Costing in the New Environment

The experiences that I described in the previous sections demonstrate that regulators and other stakeholders will often make strategic use of costing processes, if given the opportunity. If costing is to play a long-term role in telecommunications, policy makers should control this opportunistic behavior by adopting objective standards for costs and prices. I believe that price cap regulation and benchmarking are the best alternatives available.[7]

A price cap index would be used to limit overall price changes for the limited regulated services. In the near term, the index would reflect changes in the overall price level in the economy and how telecommunications differs from the rest of the economy in terms of input price inflation and productivity (Bernstein and Sappington 1999). As competition progresses in unregulated telecommunications markets, prices in regulated markets could be indexed to the unregulated prices, since the unregulated prices are presumably acceptable to consumers and profitable for companies, at least ex ante.

Price cap regulation can control overall price levels, but regulating the price structure is more difficult. Regulators will need to abandon current cost models as being too subjective and open to abuse by incumbents, competitors, and regulators. However, regulators cannot simply return to fully distributed cost. Fully distributed cost implies rate-of-return regulation, which creates opportunities for cross-subsidization and can be used to insulate shareholders from mistakes managers could make in competitive markets. Also, fully distributed cost is even more subjective than incremental cost models, because fully distributed cost has no underlying theory to indicate when a technique is good or bad.

Regulators should rely upon benchmarking to regulate prices, initially against observable industry costs and later against competitive prices. Because we know little about what competitive prices will look like for future services and noncompetitive network facilities, regulators will continue to rely upon economic cost models, but regulators should reconcile the results with observable industry costs. For example, the results of an economic model for loop costs should be compared and reconciled to the industry's accounting costs. This eliminates the opportunity to raise and lower regulated prices by simply changing cost model assumptions. Also, the reconciliation would be to industry costs rather than the costs of individual companies. This provides benchmark or yardstick competition among companies so that they have incentives to operate efficiently and report accounting costs that reflect the true underlying economics of their operations.

As competition develops, regulators should also rely upon rate structures in competitive markets as appropriate benchmarks for rate structures in noncompetitive markets. Two caveats are in order. First, the mix of services sold in competitive markets may be different than the mix sold in noncompetitive markets, making the competitive rate structures inappropriate for noncompetitive markets. For example, because competitive markets have attracted multiple service providers, one could expect competitive markets to have more profit potential than noncompetitive markets. One source of this profit potential could be the demand for advanced information services. If this is the case, companies in competitive markets might price basic services as *loss leaders*[8] in order to establish customer relationships and receive profits from the advanced services. Adopting the loss-leading prices for noncompetitive markets could be inappropriate because the demand for advanced services might be insufficient to make up for the losses on basic services. Cellular markets provide an example of such a situation. It is common in cellular markets for service providers to sell cellular telephones for as little as $1 in order to entice customers to sign up for service. In effect, the cellular provider is offering a two-part tariff in which the sign-up fee is below cost to attract risk-averse customers, who then make a sufficient number of calls to make the total package profitable.

The reverse could also be true. Competitive markets may have large numbers of customers whose incomes are high enough to make them more risk tolerant than customers in noncompetitive markets. This may make the prices for basic services in competitive markets too high for use in noncompetitive markets. The new PCS markets provide examples of this scenario. Some PCS providers have high monthly fees in excess of customer access costs. Customers pay these high fees to obtain low usage prices. This is optimal for these customers, but may not be for lower-income customers who could not afford the high monthly fees.

The second caveat regarding using rate structures in competitive markets to benchmark noncompetitive markets is that the underlying costs in the competitive markets may be different than costs in the noncompetitive markets. For example, high sunk costs discourage entry, so one would expect to see sunk costs more often in noncompetitive markets than in competitive markets.

Because of these caveats, it is likely that cost benchmarking across companies in noncompetitive markets will be necessary for regulating rate design. This benchmarking would serve two purposes. First, it would be a check to ensure that profits in noncompetitive markets are sufficient to encourage willing participation by service providers. Second, it would protect captive customers from providing profit windfalls to the monopolies.

Conclusion

The difficulties of cost-based rate making have increased exponentially in recent years. This fact makes regulators' lives difficult enough by itself, but it is particularly troubling when one realizes that we were unable to resolve cost measurement issues even in the simpler world. It is unlikely that we will solve these problems by going back to allowing companies to report their costs, either through fully distributed cost or incremental cost studies. It is equally unlikely that we will solve these problems by giving regulators the discretion provided by proxy cost models, since regulators once had to give up such discretion and adopt a more objective standard—rate-of-return regulation—because of concerns with regulatory legitimacy and credibility.

What seems more promising is to adopt a modified Trebing regulatory framework and benchmark regulated prices against competitive prices and against observable industry costs. Regulators would still have discretion in selecting industry benchmarks and benchmarking formulas, but this level of discretion has proven to be manageable in countries such as the United Kingdom and Norway, where benchmarking has proven to be an effective means of regulating utilities.

Notes

I would like to thank Harry Trebing, Sanford Berg, Warren Samuels, and Edythe Miller for their helpful comments on earlier drafts of this paper. I would also like to thank Harry, David Brevitz, and Richard Gabel for their guidance on this topic over the years. All errors and omissions are my own.

1. For an excellent overview of price cap regulation in telecommunications, see Sappington and Weisman (1996). Bernstein and Sappington (1999) describe how to develop price cap indices based on inflation and productivity.

2. Joint costs are costs that, once incurred, produce two or more products in fixed proportions. Common costs are costs that, once incurred, are freely available to produce two or more products. The distinction has not been very important in telecommunications.

3. The telephone industry rarely, if ever, performed a stand-alone cost study.

4. Inframarginal costs are all of the volume-sensitive costs caused by the service. If marginal costs are decreasing with output, measuring volume-sensitive costs at the margin understates the total amount of volume-sensitive costs.

5. BCPM is not an acronym. It is derived from the acronym *BCM*, which stood for Benchmark Cost Model, and Pacific Telesis's name.

6. A recent book (Alleman and Noam 1999) captures most of this debate.

7. In informal discussions, people sometimes object to my referring to price cap indices as cost estimates. My rationale is that the price cap indices are simply estimates of how much telecommunications companies costs change (Bernstein and Sappington 1999). This makes a price cap index a proxy cost, although not to be confused with the proxy cost models.

8. A *loss leader* is a product that is deliberately sold at a price near or below its incremental cost in order to sell more of a product that is priced farther above its incremental cost.

Bibliography

Adler, Robert. 1999. Projecting the telecommunications industry in 2009. In *The new global telecommunications industry and consumers,* edited by Jorge Schement, 12–18. University Park: Pennsylvania State University's Institute for Information Policy

Alleman, James, and Eli Noam, eds. 1999. *The new investment theory of real options and its implications for telecommunications economics.* Boston: Kluwer Academic Publishers.

Baumol, William J. 1979. Minimum and maximum pricing principles for residual tegulation. *Eastern Economic Journal* 5 (1–2): 235–48.

Baumol, William J., Michael F. Koehn, and Robert D. Willig. 1987. How arbitrary is 'arbitrary?'—or, Toward the deserved demise of full cost allocation. *Public Utilities Fortnightly* 120 (5): 16–21.

Baumol, William J., and Alfred G. Walton. 1973. Full costing, competition and regulatory practice, *Yale Law Journal* 82 (4): 639–55.

Berg, Sanford V., and Dean R. Foreman. 1995. Price cap policies in the transition from monopoly to competitive markets, *Industrial and Corporate Change* 4:671–81.

Bernstein, Jeffrey I., and David E. M. Sappington. 1999. Setting the X factor in price-cap regulation plans, *Journal of Regulatory Economics* 16 (1): 5–25.

Bitran, E., and Pablo Serra. 1994. Regulatory issues in the privatization of public utilities: The Chilean experience, *Quarterly Review of Economics and Finance* 34:179–97.

Bolter, Walter G. 1978. The FCC's selection of a "proper" costing standard after fifteen years—What can we learn from docket 18128?" in *Accessing new pricing concepts in public utilities,* edited by Harry Trebing, 333–72. East Lansing: Michigan State University Press.

Bolter, Walter G., Jerry B. Duvall, Fred J. Kelsey, and James W. McConnaughey. 1984. *Telecommunications policy for the 1980s: The transition to competition.* Englewood Cliffs, N.J: Prentice-Hall.

Brock, Gerald W. 1981. *The telecommunications industry: The dynamics of market structure.* Cambridge, Mass.: Harvard University Press.

Buehler, Stefan. 1999. A further look at two-way network competition in telecommunication. Unpublished working paper.

Crémer, Jacques, Patrick Rey, and Jean Tirole. 2000. Connectivity in the commercial Internet. *Journal of Industrial Economics* 48(4): 433–72.

Economides, Nicholas, and Lawrence J. White. 1995. Access and interconnection pricing: How efficient is the "efficient component pricing rule"? *Antitrust Bulletin* 40 (3): 557–79.

Faulhaber, Gerald R. 1975. Cross-subsidization: Pricing in public enterprises." *American Economic Review* 65 (5): 966–77.

Federal Communications Commission. 1985. Guidelines for dominant carriers' MTS rates and rate structure plans: Memorandum opinion and order," 50 Fed. Reg. 42, 946.

———. 1986. Amendment of sections 64.702 of the commission's rules and regulations (third computer inquiry), 104 FCC 2d 958.

Federal Communications Commission, Common Carrier Bureau Staff. 1996. Preparing for addressing universal service issues: A review of current interstate support mechanisms." Unpublished paper.

Gabel, David. 1985. A study of the stand-alone and marginal telephone category cost of service. Unpublished paper.

———. 1992. *Testimony of David Gabel on behalf of the Commission Advocacy Staff,* Before the Maine Public Utilities Commission, Docket No. 92–130.

Gabel, David., and Mark Kennet. 1991. *Estimating the cost structure of local telephone exchange network.* Columbus, Ohio: National Regulatory Research Institute.

Gabel, Richard. 1967. *Development of Separations principles in the telephone industry.* East Lansing: Michigan State University Institute of Public Utilities.

Gabel, Richard, and David Gabel. n.d. Cost characteristics of Michigan Bell: A study of the stand-alone and incremental costs for Michigan Bell's major categories of service. Unpublished paper.

Gabel, Richard, William Melody, Bob Warnek, and Bill Mihuc. 1983. The allocation of local exchange plant investment to the common exchange and toll services on the basis of equalized relative cost benefits. Unpublished paper.

Gibson, Robert. 1999. Technology and change. In *The new global telecommunication industry and consumers,* edited by Jorge Schement, 37–43. University Park: Pennsylvania State University's Institute for Information Policy.

Glaeser, Martin G. 1927. *Outlines of public utility economics.* New York: Macmillan.

Hausman, Jerry. 1999. The effect of sunk costs in telecommunications regulation." In *Real options: The new investment theory and its implications for telecommunications economics,* edited by James Alleman and Eli Noam, 191–204. Boston: Kluwer Academic Publishers.

Jamison, Mark A. 1988a. Applying part X allocations to intrastate costs. Paper presented at the Fourteenth Annual Missouri Rate Symposium.

———. 1988b. Report on intrastate cost allocations for the NARUC Communications Committee and Staff Subcommittee on Communications. Unpublished paper.

———. 1988c. Social contract regulation: Have we been this way before? *NRRI Quarterly Bulletin* 9 (July): 299–310.

———. 1998. Regulatory techniques for addressing interconnection, access, and cross-subsidy in telecommunications. In *Infrastructure regulation and market reform: Principles and practice,* edited by Margaret Arblaster and Mark Jamison, 113–29. Canberra, Australia: Commonwealth of Australia.

———. 1999a. Business imperatives. In *The new global telecommunications industry & consumers,* edited by Jorge Schement. University Park: Pennsylvania State University.

———. 1999b. Does practice follow principle? Applying real options principles to proxy costs in U.S. telecommunications. In *Real options: The new investment theory and its implications for telecommunications economics,* edited by James Alleman and Eli Noam, 50–75. Boston: Kluwer Academic Publishers.

———. 2000. An oligopoly model of market concentration and competition in network industries. Unpublished working paper.

Kahn, Alfred E. 1988. *The economics of regulation: Principles and institutions.* Cambridge, Mass.: MIT Press.

———. 1998. *Letting go: Deregulating the process of deregulation, or: Temptation of the kleptocrats and the political economy of regulatory disingenuousness.* MSU Public Utilities Papers. East Lansing: Michigan State University, Eli Broad

Graduate School of Management, Institute of Public Utilities and Network Industries.

King, Clyde Lyndon. 1912. The need for utility commissions. In *The regulation of municipal utilities,* edited by Clyde Lyndon King. New York: D. Appleton and Company.

Larson, Alexander C., and Steve G. Parsons. 1995. "Building block" cost methods for pricing and unbundling telecommunications services: Implications for the law and regulatory policy. *Jurimetrics Journal* 36 (1): 59–97.

Littlechild, S. C. 1983. *Regulation of British telecommunications profitability: A report to the secretary of state for trade and industry.* ?????

Melody, William H. 1971. Interservice dubsidy: Regulatory standards and applied economics. In *Essays on Public Utility Pricing and Regulation,* edited by Harry M. Trebing, 167–210. East Lansing: [Institute of Public Utilities], Division of Research, Graduate School of Business Administration, Michigan State University.

Mitchell, Bridger M. 1990. *Incremental costs of telephone access and local use,* Technical Report R-3909-ICTF. Santa Monica, Calif.: RAND.

Monson, Calvin, and Jeffrey H. Rohlfs. 1993. The $20 billion impact of local competition in telecommunications. Unpublished paper.

Mueller, Milton. 1993. Universal service in telephone history: A reconstruction. *Telecommunications Policy* 17:352–69.

Office of Telecommunications. 1997. *Network charges from 1997,* May 1997, http://www.oftel.gov.uk/pricing/ncc1.htm#CHAPTER 1, downloaded 25 March 2000.

Sappington, David E. M., and Dennis L. Weisman. 1996. *Designing incentive regulation for the telecommunications industry.* Cambridge, Mass.: MIT Press and Washington, D.C.: AEI Press.

Smith, Warrick, and Michael Klein. 1994. *Infrastructure regulation: Issues & options for East Asia.* Washington, D.C.: World Bank.

Trebing, Harry M. 1984a. Public control of enterprise: Neoclassical assault and neoinstitutionalist reform. *Journal of Economic Issues* 18 (2): 353–68.

———. 1984b. Public utility regulation: A case study in the debate over effectiveness of economic regulation. *Journal of Economic Issues* 18 (1): 223–50.

———. 1987. Regulation of industry: An institutionalist approach. *Journal of Economic Issues* 21 (4): 1707–37.

Trigeorgis, Lenos. 1996. *Real options: Managerial flexibility and strategy in resource allocation.* Cambridge, Mass.: MIT Press.

———. 1999. Real options: A primer. In *Real options: The new investment theory and its implications for telecommunications economics,* edited by James Alleman and Eli Noam, 3–33. Boston: Kluwer Academic Publishers.

Meeting Low-Income Energy Needs through Public Benefits: Selecting Energy Assistance and Weatherization Funding Levels

DENNIS J. RAY AND JACK R. HUDDLESTON

Introduction

Low-income energy policy issues are getting increasing attention at the state and federal levels as the electric industry restructures. These issues are being raised because of concerns that the changes the restructuring is bringing may not be in the best interest of low-income households, particularly if they result in lower funding for programs that target assistance to those households.[1] This is of particular concern, given the trend in declining federal funding of low-income energy programs. One of the ways state legislators have been addressing low-income funding concerns is through the provision of low-income public benefits funds.

The scarcity of funds for helping low-income households manage their utility bills suggests that close attention should be paid to the use of the available funds. There is an ongoing policy and program management debate regarding allocation of the funds between energy assistance and weatherization programs. To what extent should funds be used for long-term support through improved efficiency of energy use by low-income households rather than for short-term support through bill payment assistance? This chapter examines this allocation question quantitatively using simulation and optimization analysis of the low-income energy program in Wisconsin.

Low-Income Energy Assistance and Weatherization Programs

Energy affordability is a serious concern for low-income households in the United States. Finding ways to help households manage their energy bills has been a challenge for industry and government agencies. Various forms of energy assistance and weatherization (or energy efficiency) programs are being used. Energy assistance is a form of direct financial assistance, principally to assist low-income households in making payments for utility bills or for covering arrearages that may have been incurred. Weatherization programs target the use of energy, often by improving the efficiency of the building structure or envelope in order to produce lower energy use for heating and cooling.

Government Assistance

Energy assistance programs are principally designed to help eligible low-income households pay their bills. The Low-Income Home Energy Assistance Program provides funds for proactive assistance, crisis assistance, or furnace repair or replacement.[2] With proactive assistance, households receive assistance if heating costs are beyond their ability to pay, as defined by program eligibility criteria. The payments must be used to pay for energy. The actual payment levels depend upon available funds and the number of applicants, as well as various household demographics. In Wisconsin, a cold-weather state, the amount of the assistance averages around $280 per year, whereas average residential energy bills are about $1,000 annually.[3]

Some of the Low-Income Home Energy Assistance Program funds are also used for crisis assistance. Crisis assistance is essentially emergency assistance needed to deal with an existing or imminent threat to a low-income household getting energy for heat. Another use of the funds is for furnace repair or replacement when there is a threat to health or life. This use of funds is for health and safety reasons only, although energy efficiency is typically enhanced by the installation of new, energy-efficient furnaces.

Another federal program is the Weatherization Assistance Program, which provides funds for improving the energy efficiency and comfort of low-income dwellings. Around $2,750 is spent in Wisconsin on each eligible low-income household's home.[4] Evaluations of the Weatherization Assistance Program have shown that weatherization savings increased demonstrably in the 1990s, as compared to the 1980s, reaching up to a 33.5 percent reduction in the energy required for home heating.[5] Savings estimates to date in Wisconsin have been more modest, with about a 26 percent savings reported.[6] Weatherization Assistance Program funds can be used for work on rental units when a sufficiently high percentage of the tenants are eligible for the program.

Funding for the federal programs has dropped considerably over the last ten years. These programs are currently funded at about 50 percent of what they were in mid-1980s.[7] Nationwide, funding is about $1.1 billion for the Low-Income Home Energy Assistance Program and $138 million for the Weatherization Assistance Program.

Utility Programs

The second important source of support for low-income energy affordability is utility programs. These programs vary from state to state. Included in the utility programs are rate discount programs, affordable payment plans, arrears forgiveness programs, energy efficiency programs, and a range of other types of special assistance programs. Utility rate assistance programs (including affordable payment plans) for low-income households total almost $500 million. Under restructuring legislation passed but not yet implemented, that amount could increase by another $145 million nationwide.[8]

The rate assistance programs take various forms. For example, California utilities provide a 15 percent discount for eligible households. Under restructuring legislation, Texas utilities will be offering a 10 percent discount to up to one million eligible households. The discount could rise as high as 20 percent. All of Massachusetts' utilities offer discounts ranging from 25 to 35 percent.

Another form of rate assistance is a percent of income payment plan. In Ohio, all utilities offer a percent of income payment plan that typically caps total energy payments by participating low-income households at 13 to 15 percent of their gross monthly income, irrespective of what their bill is. The revenue shortfalls are funded through utility rates.

Another version of the percent of income payment plans, also called affordable payment plans, incorporates arrears forgiveness. For instance, Wisconsin Gas Company has an affordable payment plan in which the utility works with the consumer to set up a level payment schedule that represents about 5 to 7 percent of household income. In these affordable payment plans, some form of arrears forgiveness is common, since the affordable payment levels may not generate enough revenue to cover current bills plus the entire amount owed.

Participation rates among eligible low-income households are a concern. It has been estimated that paticipation rates average less than 40 percent of the eligible population.[9] Discussions have occurred in California about the utilities funding a statewide low-income energy needs assessment that would include a study of how to increase participation rates.

Public Benefits

Generally speaking, the 1990s trend toward lower utility funding for low-income programs in the United States appears to have been reversed as the electric power industry is being restructured. Many states have either passed comprehensive restructuring legislation (about twenty-two to date) or have regulatory commissions that have found they have the authority to restructure their state's electric power industry (two states to date). In many of these states, a public benefits funding mechanism has been instituted to support low-income programs, energy efficiency programs, and renewable energy programs.

- In Massachusetts, a 0.025 cent/kWh charge on every electric customer raises about $10 million for low-income energy conservation.
- California provides almost $190 million in public benefits funding to support the rate discount (of about $130 million) and energy efficiency (of about $60 million) programs. The funding of the electric rate discount and energy efficiency programs is accomplished through a systems benefit surcharge paid by residential and business consumers. That charge is approximately 0.1 cent/kWh for the low-income programs.
- In Pennsylvania, electric utility restructuring legislation mandated that existing programs be continued. Through individual utility restructuring settlements, 1999 funding more than doubled prerestructuring funding (from $23 million to $57.7 million), and funding will increase each year through 2002.
- Wisconsin passed legislation in 1999 that authorized approximately $50 million in public benefit support over and above federal funding levels. In the future, the level of public benefit support from utilities will vary depending upon the federal support level and an estimate of need developed by the state.[10]

The amount of public benefit support varies widely across the states, with many states still not having reached a decision about public benefits.

Choice of Energy Assistance and Weatherization Levels

There is a degree of tension in the funding of energy assistance and weatherization programs. This tension arises because the two services compete for what has become a progressively smaller pot of funds. There is also a philosophical dimension to the tension. Making utility bills more affordable through weatherization is often viewed as being a superior approach to energy assistance, because the benefits of weatherization last well into the future. Weatherization can help a low-income household for the life of installed energy efficiency measures. Energy assistance, on the other hand, provides a direct transfer of cash to cover current bills, thus easing today's financial hardship. However, it does little to address the potential for a repetition of that same hardship for the household. Thus, the philosophical debate concerns whether public funds should be used for short-term or long-term solutions to affordability issues for low-income households.

The tension lies on the presumption that there is inherent substitutability between weatherization and energy assistance as means for reaching affordability. In other words, whether through direct financial assistance for bill payment or through a weatherization "investment" that improves energy efficiency, the result is the same: a more affordable bill for the household. What we will illustrate later is that substitutability does not necessarily mean that only one approach should be used.

The current public benefits debate raises many issues about the overall funding required to make utility bills affordable. Little is heard in that debate about the public policy objective that drives the determination of the level of public benefits support. A fundamental question that is frequently not publicly debated is what the measure of affordability should be that would determine the structure and funding of such a public benefits program. There is also little heard about the effects of the choice of funding levels for energy assistance and weatherization on the overall public benefits funding need.

In this section, the interaction between energy assistance and weatherization expenditures will be analyzed in the context of an explicit policy objective of reaching an average level of affordability for the low-income segment as a whole.

Choice Framework

As discussed earlier, many public and utility programs are using energy burden, or the percent of income spent on energy, as a measure of affordability and as a criteria for determining the level of support for a particular household. In Wisconsin, the funding for low-income programs will be based on a formula that is designed to ensure that the total level of funding for low-income programs, from all sources, is the same proportion of a given year's low-income need as is provided by the base funding for the program. The need is the difference between estimated energy expenditures by low-income households and what the expenditures would have been had their average energy burden been 2.2 percent.[11]

Energy burdens can be quite high for low-income households across the United States. In 1993, the average energy burden for households at or below the poverty level was estimated to be 22 percent.[12] The burden for households at between 100 and 150 percent of the poverty level was estimated to be 9 percent, while that for higher income households was 3 percent.

We are going to assume that average energy burden is the measure of affordability needed to set the overall level of funding for energy assistance and weatherization. In addition, we are going to assume that policy makers are seeking to minimize the funding of low-income programs over time by choosing energy assistance and weatherization funding levels to achieve the selected measure of affordability.

The fundamental problem that must be solved is how to insure that the utility bills remain affordable from the start of the program while rolling out a weatherization program that may take a number of years to reach a market penetration objective. The trade-off between the two kinds of programs, from a present value perspective, is that the payoff from the weatherization investment of public funds occurs in the form of less energy assistance due to greater end-use efficiency. For instance, a weatherization investment of $200 million dollars over a five-year period will reduce the present value of future energy assistance funds beyond that five-year period. If the relevant discount rate were zero, then it would be wise to invest the $200 million only if more than $200 million in energy assistance savings could be realized.

Therefore, for this analysis, the formal objective will be to minimize the present value of future energy assistance and weatherization funds subject to the constraint that in every time period, the target average energy burden is attained for the eligible low-income household segment. This analysis will be done in the context of low-income energy assistance and weatherization programs in Wisconsin. There are three empirical questions of interest.

1. Should funding be provided for one or the other, or both energy programs (energy assistance and weatherization)?

2. When should the weatherization investment occur in the planning horizon?
3. How does any trade-off between the two programs affect the overall level of public benefit support of low-income programs?

In the short run, whether or not there should be energy assistance funding will depend upon the difference between the actual average energy burden and the target energy burden. If the actual energy burden is greater than the target, then there will need to be energy assistance, at least for some period of time. In the long run, the need for energy assistance funding will depend upon the effectiveness of the weatherization. Weatherization effectiveness will depend upon such factors as which measures are installed, given conditions of the low-income housing stock and energy-using devices, and energy-use patterns and levels. If the weatherization investment is highly effective, then it could be the case that the realized average energy burden would be less than the target energy burden. However, this possibility is identified more for theoretical completeness than as an expected outcome.

Whether or not there should be funding of weatherization will depend upon the discount rate. We posit that there is a weatherization boundary discount rate below which any selected discount rate will produce a positive amount of weatherization funding in the funding minimization problem. The higher this boundary discount rate, the greater the likelihood that weatherization funding should be used, for any given range of discount rates. The boundary discount rate is illustrated in figure 1. This illustration suggests that the boundary rate depends upon the relative "marginal" effectiveness of weatherization versus energy assistance funding in reaching the target energy burden. The more effective an additional dollar of weatherization funding is, relative to energy assistance funding, the higher the boundary discount rate would have to be to cause the policy maker to be indifferent between funding only energy assistance or a mix of energy assistance and weatherization.

Model Description

The analysis requires two steps. The first step is to estimate the technical relationship between the energy assistance and weatherization funding levels and the average energy burden. This is done with the Low-Income Policy Response Simulation Model (LIPRSM) based on empirical data from Wisconsin.[13] The relationship is essentially a linear expansion around a selected operating point (that is, the base case) for the low-income energy programs.

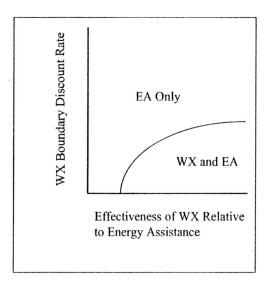

Figure 1 Weatherization Boundary Discount Rate vs. the Mix of Funding for Energy Assistance and Weatherization.

The second step is to optimize the choice of incremental changes in energy assistance and weatherization funding over a future time period. With a linear programming model, the optimal incremental changes were computed over an eight-year period (2000 to 2007) with an extension period to 2030 over which the energy assistance savings from the weatherization investments continue to accumulate. The extension period is needed since energy efficiency measures have lives that could be as long as twenty-five to thirty years. The optimization problem was structured as follows:

Objective: Minimize the present value of future changes in the real dollar levels of energy assistance and weatherization funding over base funding levels

Subject to the constraints:
1. Each year's changes in energy assistance and weatherization funding must cause that year's average energy burden to reach or to be lower than the target energy burden for the eligible low-income population;
2. Each year's change in weatherization funding must not exceed a given level ($40 million used here); and
3. Total change in weatherization funding over the optimization period (2000 to 2007) must not exceed a given level ($275 million used here).

The objective function minimizes the present value of future public benefits funding for energy assistance and weatherization at a chosen discount rate. This discount rate is referred to as the "policy discount rate" because it reflects policy-maker perspectives on the relative value of providing for assistance to low-income households in the future versus assistance to low-income households today. In addition, program benefits may occur in various forms, some quantifiable, such as bill savings, and others more difficult to quantify, such as increased comfort and reduced financial hardship or vulnerability. The policy makers involved in setting the actual public benefit levels vary. Implemented public benefit levels can be affected by legislative, regulatory, and state agency decisions.

The first constraint, the requirement that incremental changes in energy assistance and weatherization funding result in the attainment of the target energy burden, involves both technical and policy considerations. The technical parameters of the constraint equation were based on the simulation model results. Using the simulation model, how much higher funding levels lowered each year's average energy burden was estimated, normalized, and then incorporated into each year's technical relationship between funding level changes and changes in energy burden.

The target energy burden was chosen as the average measure of affordability that would serve as the basis for setting overall funding levels. For this analysis, energy burden is defined as the percentage of income spent on energy net of any energy assistance payments. Energy burden is frequently used as an affordability measure.[14] The difference between some reference energy burden and the actual energy burden is taken as a measure of how much "burden" energy payments are for a low-income household.

Energy burden is also frequently used as a policy objective. Many low-income programs use target energy burdens such as the affordable payment plans and percent of income payment plans mentioned previously. Public benefits legislation in Wisconsin defined overall funding need relative to an average residential energy burden. The target burdens in this analysis range from 7 to 9 percent, within the general range of burdens used in low-income program designs around the United States.[15]

The second constraint keeps the incremental increases in weatherization funding from exceeding a specified value. Rather than a capital constraint, this constraint was imposed to recognize that there may be effective constraints on production capability in delivering weatherization services. These constraints could be physical or economic. For instance, to increase productive capability in Wisconsin in response to the recent increase in weatherization funding authorized under the public benefits legislation, local nonprofit program agents will likely have to use more subcontracts with for-profit companies. Therefore, increased funding will require expanded internal productive capability along with new managerial responsibilities for cost-effective contract management.

Finally, the third constraint was used to limit the overall amount of incremental weatherization funding to a portion of the total number of low-income homes. At about $2,750 per home, on average, a $275 million overall expenditure will limit the weatherization to about one-third of the low-income households during the planning period.

Base Case Assumptions

The base case assumptions are summarized in table 1. The optimization occurs for funding of two low-income programs: heating assistance provided by the Low-Income Household Energy Assistance Program and energy efficiency improvements provided by the Weatherization Assistance Program. The base case funding levels for the heating assistance and weatherization are indicative of the support provided in Wisconsin. Administrative and outreach funds are included in the overall level of public benefit funding that these two programs provide.[16] These two programs are the largest low-income energy programs in Wisconsin and most other states.

The base case energy burdens based on the LIPRSM simulation are given in table 2. The burdens are reported for four different household types

Table 1   Base Case Assumptions.

Item	Assumption
Currency Reference Year	1999
Rate of inflation	3%
Energy assistance delivered to households	$24.7 million in 2000 declining in real dollars at 3% per year
Administration and outreach for energy assistance	10% and 1.8% of total energy assistance funding respectively
Weatherization funding delivered to program contractors	$10.9 million in 2000 declining in real dollars at 3% per year
Contract weatherization costs (including administration and outreach)	$2,750 per home in real dollars
State administration of weatherization program	3.8% of total funding
Heating energy savings due to weatherization	26%
Energy prices	Constant in real dollars
Growth in the number of low-income households	1% per year

Table 2   Base Case Energy Burdens (in percent) by Energy Assistance (EA) or Weatherization (WX) Program Participation.

Year	No EA or WX	EA Only	WX Only	EA and WX	Average
2000	10.68	8.54	9.52	7.87	9.92
2007	10.69	8.55	9.52	7.88	10.01

based on participation in the energy assistance (EA) or weatherization (WX) programs. The average burden across all households in the target group is also reported. The target group is defined as those households at or below 150 percent of the poverty guidelines, the same eligibility criteria used in the Low-Income Household Energy Assistance Program in Wisconsin.

Effects of Discount Rates on the Funding of Energy Assistance and Weatherization Programs

Table 3 gives the simulation and optimization results for a base case. For a policy discount rate equal to 2.81 percent (that is, the boundary rate), no increase in weatherization is chosen. From $79 to $88 million are needed in additional energy assistance funding annually over the eight-year period to reach a target energy burden of 8 percent. In part, the incremental

Table 3   Incremental Energy Assistance and Weatherization Expenditures (in Million Dollars) vs. Discount Rate to Achieve an 8 Percent Average Energy Burden*

	Policy Discount Rate					
	2.81%		2.50%		1.46%	
Year	ΔEA	ΔWX	ΔEA	ΔWX	ΔEA	ΔWX
2000	78.76	0	78.76	40	78.76	40
2001	80.17	0	78.18	40	78.18	40
2002	81.52	0	77.54	0	77.54	40
2003	82.87	0	78.89	0	78.89	40
2004	84.23	0	80.25	0	80.25	40
2005	85.60	0	81.62	0	81.62	40
2006	86.98	0	83.00	0	83.00	35
2007	88.36	0	84.37	0	84.37	0

energy assistance funding is needed to make up for the decline in real base level energy assistance funds.

As shown in table 3, at a policy discount rate of 2.5 percent, the optimal level of additional weatherization funding is $40 million for the first two years in the planning period. When added to the base level funding, total weatherization support comes to almost $51 million in those two years, an amount that is a little higher than the amount originally expected to be set aside for low-income weatherization support under Wisconsin's public benefits program. When the discount rate falls further to 1.46 percent, then the optimal weatherization funding calls for $40 million in years 2000 to 2005 and $35 million in 2006.

The results answer the question of how much weatherization funding should be used under the base case assumptions. If the policy maker's discount rate exceeds the boundary rate of 2.81 percent, then only energy assistance should be provided. If the discount rate falls between 2.81 and 1.46 percent, then weatherization should occur, but not all of the targeted number of homes should be weatherized. Finally, if the discount rate is 1.46 percent or lower, then all of the targeted homes should be weatherized.

The results also answer the question of when the weatherization should occur—as soon as possible up to the productive capability of the program. The sooner the weatherization occurs, the sooner the benefits of reduced energy assistance funding will be realized.

Effect of Effectiveness of Weatherization and Energy Assistance on the Boundary Rate

As indicated in the previous sections, the weatherization boundary discount rate determines the extent to which weatherization funding should be used for any given policy discount rate. The boundary rate is affected by the effectiveness of incremental changes in weatherization and energy assistance expenditures in reducing the actual energy burden.

One way to examine how the relative effectiveness of program funding affects the boundary rate is to change the technical coefficients in the energy burden constraints in the optimization model. The technical coefficients give the rate of change of the energy burden with respect to weatherization and energy assistance funding. Table 4 shows how the boundary rate is affected by improvements in the weatherization technical coefficients. With a 10 percent increase in each year's technical coefficient over the planning horizon, the boundary rate increases from 2.81 to 3.55 percent. If the improvement is 20 percent each year, then the boundary rate increases further to 4.27 percent.

Table 4   Boundary Rate vs. Percent Improvement
in Weatherization Effectiveness in Decreasing
the Energy Burden.

Improvement	Boundary Rate
0	2.81%
10%	3.55%
20%	4.27%

Numerous factors affect program effectiveness. Three are illustrated in table 5. If real energy prices rise 2 percent per year faster than the base case, then the boundary rate increases from the 2.81 percent base case value to 3.56 percent. In this case, weatherization is made more effective in reducing energy burden, because energy expenditures have risen, thus giving weatherization's assumed 26 percent savings a relatively larger effect than before on energy burden. On the other hand, energy assistance is slightly less effective, because the constant dollar reduction in utility bill has fallen in size relative to the large energy expenditure.

The increased effectiveness of weatherization when energy prices are rising is an important result. In periods of rising energy prices or of rising uncertainty about future energy prices, weatherization can be viewed as an important policy approach to mitigate affordability risk for low-income households.

A 1 percent decline in the income growth rate from the base case of zero real growth produces very little change in the boundary rate. In this case, energy expenditures have not changed, so weatherization and energy assistance effectiveness have both improved.

Finally, when the energy bill savings from lower heating costs increases from the base case of 26 percent to 28 percent, the effectiveness of weatherization commensurately increases by about the same 8 percent. This results in the boundary rate increasing to 3.39 percent, as shown in table 5.

Table 5   Sensitivity of the Boundary Rate to Selected Variables.

Case	Boundary Rate
Base Case	2.81%
+2% per Year Increase in Energy Price Growth Rates	3.56%
−1% per Year Decrease in Income Growth Rate	2.73%
Increased Weatherization Savings Rate from 26% to 28%	3.39%

Although energy prices and income growth rates are largely out of low-income energy policy makers' hands, the weatherization savings rate might not be. The savings rate can be improved by more efficient delivery of weatherization and by technical advances in materials and installation techniques. Those technical advances, in turn, can be driven by investments in research and development that could be publicly funded, such as through a public benefits fund.

Effect of Target Energy Burden on Public Benefits Expenditures with and without Incremental Weatherization Expenditures

Is there an interaction between the funding levels of weatherization and energy assistance, and the total amount of public benefit funding needed to reach the target average affordability level? The answer is, not surprisingly, yes, given the results of the optimization given above. Tables 6 and 7 show how weatherization and energy assistance funding interact to produce lower public benefit funding requirements when it is optimal to use both types of programs (that is, when the policy discount rate is lower than the boundary rate). Table 6 shows that the annual levels of required energy assistance decline as more weatherization is used. This does not occur in 2000, however, because there is assumed to be a one-year lag in achieving the 26 percent heating savings per weatherized home served by the increased weatherization funding.

Table 7 shows that the even though the public benefits support level would be higher in the initial years of the planning period, due to the mix of weatherization and energy assistance, in the long run, the public benefits levels are lower when weatherization is used. Without discounting future public benefit levels, total future public benefit funds are $95 million lower for both target energy burdens.

Conclusions

This analysis has provided estimates of the public benefit funding required to reach a target energy burden for eligible low-income households. In so doing, it has shown that there are policy trade-offs in choosing how to allocate public benefit funding between energy assistance and weatherization. Some of the principal results are given below.

Table 6 Energy Assistance Funding (in million $) with and without Incremental Weatherization for Seven and Nine Percent Target Energy Burdens.

Year	Target Energy Burden of 9%		Target Energy Burden of 7%	
	EA w/ΔWX	EA (no ΔWX)	EA w/ΔWX	EA (no ΔWX)
2000	62.55	62.55	144.43	144.43
2001	60.81	62.80	143.55	145.55
2002	59.06	63.04	142.62	146.60
2003	57.33	63.30	141.72	147.69
2004	55.62	63.59	140.84	148.81
2005	53.94	63.89	140.50	149.96
2006	52.29	64.22	139.20	151.14
2007	50.90	64.57	138.68	152.35

Table 7 Total Low-Income Public Benefit Support (in million $) with and without Incremental Weatherization for Seven and Nine Percent Target Energy Burdens.

Year	Target Energy Burden of 9%		Target Energy Burden of 7%	
	ΔWX > 0	ΔWX = 0	ΔWX > 0	ΔWX = 0
2000	113.46	73.46	195.34	155.34
2001	111.41	73.40	194.15	156.15
2002	109.35	73.33	192.91	156.89
2003	107.32	73.29	191.71	157.68
2004	105.32	73.29	190.54	158.51
2005	103.36	73.31	189.42	159.38
2006	96.43	73.37	183.34	160.28
2007	59.78	73.45	147.55	161.23

- Energy assistance and weatherization funding may be needed to cost-effectively reach a target level of average affordability for low-income households.
- Whether energy assistance and weatherization are needed depends upon how much policy makers value assisting low-income households in the future versus assisting them today. The more policy makers consider the welfare of future low-income households, the greater the attractiveness of a mix of energy assistance and weatherization funding.

- When weatherization is used, it should occur as quickly as productive capability allows and as production economics dictate.
- The mix of energy assistance and weatherization also depends upon the relative effectiveness of energy assistance and weatherization in reducing average energy burden. The more effective weatherization is, relative to energy assistance, the greater the likelihood that it should be funded. The effectiveness of weatherization can be improved through program design (such as targeting the most inefficient housing), implementation, and technological advances.
- Weatherization can be an important hedge against affordability risk in periods of rising energy prices or of growing price uncertainty, since the relative effectiveness of weatherization rises as base level energy expenditures increase.

The results show that the level of public benefits needed to reach a target level of affordability for the low-income household segment can be lowered through a mix energy assistance and weatherization programs.

Notes

The authors express their appreciation to Bobbi Tannenbaum of the Energy Center of Wisconsin and Tony Link of the Wisconsin Division of Energy and Public Benefits for their assistance in providing data used in the analysis.

1. Roger Colton has identified policy concerns about the possible impacts of restructuring. Roger Colton, *Assessing Impacts on Small-Business, Residential and Low-Income Customers* (The National Council on Competition and the Electric Utility Industry, 1996). Location: http://www.ncsl.org/programs/esnr/colton.htm#retcompetition.

2. The U.S. Department of Housing and Urban Development provides public housing to over twenty-three million low-income households who are expected to pay about 30 percent of their income on rent, including utilities. Studies have shown that the rental assistance provided to these households is often not sufficient to cover utility bills. As a consequence, many states allow Low-Income Home Energy Assistance Program payments to be made to public housing tenants. For more information, see LIHEAP Clearinghouse, "Subsidized Housing and LIHEAP," August 1998, at http://www.ncat.org/liheap/pubs/440.htm.

3. State heating and crisis assistance levels are summarized at the LIHEAP Clearinghouse's Web site, http://www.ncat.org/liheap/tables/fy99bene.htm. Additional information was obtained from the Division of Energy and Public Benefits, Wisconsin Department of Administration.

4. Those eligible for the Low-Income Home Energy Assistance Program and the Weatherization Assistance Program typically include households with incomes up to 150 percent of the federal poverty level. Currently the poverty level for a household size of four is an annual income of $16,700.

5. Linda Berry, *State-Level Evaluations of the Weatherization Assistance Program in 1990–1996: A MetaEvaluation that Estimates National Savings*, ORNL/CON-435, Oak Ridge National Laboratory, Oak Ridge, Tennessee, January 1997.

6. Evaluations in the early 1990s in Wisconsin showed about a 26 percent savings. The Energy Center of Wisconsin is about to undertake a study to update that impact evaluation result.

7. A historical summary of LIHEAP and Weatherization Assistance Program funding can be found at http://www.ncat.org/liheap/tables/lhhist.htm.

8. LIHEAP Clearinghouse, "Low-Income Assistance Tally Growing as State Restructures," *LIHEAP Networker* 33 (October 1999), available at http://www.ncat.org/ liheap.

9. LIHEAP Clearinghouse, "Low-Income Programs Under-Enrolled, Advocates Ponder How to Increase." *LIHEAP Networker.* 33 (October 1999), available at http://www.ncat.org/liheap/newslett/33net.htm.

10. Wisconsin passed public benefits legislation before restructuring the state's electric power industry. In October 1999, Wisconsin's governor signed the biennial state budget bill that incorporated "Reliability 2000" legislation with a comprehensive public benefits package. This legislation provided approximately $64.8 million for low-income energy programs. When added to the $43.7 million in federal support (in 1998), the total funding appeared to amount to about $108 million. However, the final utility contribution is still being debated before the Public Service Commission of Wisconsin. Eventually, 47 percent of the total funding (or about $50 million) is to be used for weatherization and conservation services. Wisconsin Legislative Council Staff Memorandum, "Overview of New Law on Electric Utility Regulation—The "Reliability 2000" Legislation (Part of 1999 Wisconsin Act 9)," 2 December 1999.

11. During the 1990s several states estimated low-income energy funding needs. These included Colorado (*A Report from Governor Romer's Energy Assistance Reform Task Force*, February 1998) and Maine (*Report of the Blue Ribbon Commission on Energy Policy for Maine's Low-Income Citizens*, 30 November 1990). The analysis used in this chapter is the first attempt to estimate funding needs by optimizing across energy assistance and weatherization programs.

12. Meg Power, *A Profile of the Energy Usage and Energy Needs of Low-Income Households* (Association for Energy Affordability, 1999).

13. Jack Huddleston, Dennis Ray, and Rodney Stevenson, *Low-Income Policy Response Simulation Model: Technical Documentation* (Energy Center of Wisconsin, October 1997).

14. Affordability measures, including energy burden, are described in Roger

Colton, *Funding Fuel Assistance: State and Local Strategies to Help Pay Low-Income Home Energy Bills* (Belmont, Mass.: Fisher, Shehan and Colton, May 1996).

15. The optimization targets an average energy burden rather than a program that assures that each participating households' energy burden equals the target. The modeled program designs in the simulation are based on program parameters used in Wisconsin in the mid to late 1990s.

16. The administration and outreach expenses are not used in determining the effects of energy assistance on energy burden, but are used in determining the best allocation of funds between energy assistance and weatherization.

Part 4

Market, Regulatory, and Deregulation Failure

Social Control of Rail Transport in the United States

JOHN C. SPYCHALSKI

The exercise of political power to promote and restrain has been a critical determinant of the performance and condition of rail transport ever since its emergence circa 1830. In some instances during its evolution, the rail mode has been the direct object of the exercise of such power. In others, it has been an indirect target (intended or unintended) thereof. The basic instruments for the social control (construed broadly) of rail and all other forms of transport are depicted in summary form in figure 1. It must be acknowledged that the array of elements presented in figure 1 represents a broad construct of social control. From a traditional perspective, it is possible to view economic regulation, antitrust, and government ownership as the core, if not the sum, of social control. However, in the view taken here, all public sector instruments that do or can affect efficiency and equity in transport merit attention.

This essay seeks to provide a historical review and critique of the exercise of various of these instruments, primarily within the rail mode, from the nineteenth century through the present. The evolution of direct and indirect social control of rail transport falls within the following five distinct phases, partially overlaid in time.

- Major Support of Rail Industry Expansion–Circa 1830–1871.
- Regulation of Rail Market Behavior—Circa 1870–Present.
- Regulation of Safety, Environmental Impacts, and Labor and Personnel Relations—Circa 1893–Present.
- Major Support of Expansion of Nonrail Modes—Circa 1916–Present.
- Minor Support of Rail Rehabilitation and Development—1976–Present.

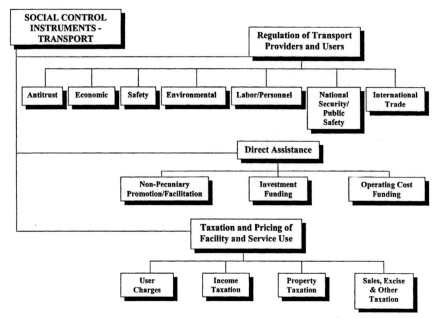

Figure 1

Significant events and conditions that have occurred and prevailed in each of these phases will serve as focal points in the following sections of the essay.

Support of Expansion—Public- and Private-Sector Roles

Soon after its entry onto the socioeconomic stage of the nineteenth century, rail technology burst to front and center with dramatic image and impact. The overwhelmingly superior service quality and cost characteristics of rail carriage vis-à-vis other then-extant modes fueled feverish enthusiasm for its rapid and wide expansion among both government officials and a majority of the public. Communities and business interests quickly came to see access to rail service as indispensable for economic survival and growth (Locklin 1972, chap.6; Meyer 1948, chaps. 11–15; Ripley 1912, chap. I). Opposition to railway construction by vested interests in sectors such as canal and wagon freight transport, although often vigorous and initially somewhat obstructive, ultimately disintegrated.

The single most significant hurdle for rail development was aggregation of financial capital in magnitudes sufficient to fund the construction of fixed plant; the purchase of motive power, rolling stock, and other equipment and supplies; and the initiation of operations under conditions in which operating revenues did not immediately (or within a relatively short-to-intermediate time frame) cover operating costs. Three alternatives for surmounting this hurdle emerged: (1) public sector financing, ownership, and management; (2) private enterprise financing, ownership, and management under the corporate form of organization; and (3) public sector assistance of private sector financing, ownership, and management under the corporate form of organization.

Pursuit of the first alternative was scant. Unlike the governments of some European countries, the American federal government exhibited no vision or will for the planning, construction, and operation of either a single comprehensive national rail system or a group of regional systems. Several states did launch rail ventures during the early period of rail development between 1830 and 1850. However, most withdrew from them prior to 1850, when the industry still consisted mainly of relatively short-distanced and largely unconnected lines. In some instances, state withdrawal from ownership and management was the result of spectacular financial failure involving repudiation of state indebtedness and allegations of administrative incompetence, malfeasance, and poor services (Harlow 1947, 214–19; Hargrave, 1932, 15–71; Larson 1984, chap. 2). These failures inspired constitutional proscriptions against any further direct state involvement in transport enterprises.[1]

The task of building long-distance rail links and joining them with existing localized segments to create an interconnected multifirm national network thus was left to the private corporate enterprise and private corporate enterprise-cum government assistance alternatives (Goodrich 1960, chaps. 2, 3; MacGill [1917] 1948, chap. 16; Ripley 1912, chap. 2).[2] These alternatives presented institutional features that, in tandem with inherent technological and economic characteristics of rail firms, were destined to inspire public policy choices that would cast influence on rail transport and collateral parties long into the future.

Detailed coverage of the role of public sector assistance in nineteenth-century railway development exceeds the ambit of this essay. However, linkages between such assistance and other early social control instruments discussed later require a capsule view of its principal features. Aid at all governmental levels was provided in both pecuniary and nonpecuniary forms. State, county, and local governments subscribed to railway stock issues, made loans via the purchase of railway bonds and other devices, served as guarantors of railway bonds, and made donations to railways in the form of cash, land, equipment, materials, labor, and government securities (for example, state bonds, which railway companies or their "inside construction companies" could sell for cash). Two nonpecuniary state-level aids of enduring significance were the power of eminent domain and the enactment of general railway incorporation laws. Possession of eminent domain power by private railway companies was deemed necessary and justifiable to enable the acquisition of property needed for providing railway service (such service being considered public in nature) from non-consenting owners, in exchange for "just compensation." General incorporation laws, which first appeared in New York and several other states about 1850, greatly simplified and speeded up the process of railway corporate formation. Before the advent of such laws, founders of businesses using the corporate form were required to obtain charters directly from state legislatures by special enactment (Locklin 1972, 119–31).

Land grants dominated federal rail aid. Their earliest use occurred in 1830 and 1833, when existing legislation providing grants of federal land to Ohio and Michigan, respectively, for canal building were amended to also include rail construction. The premier federal rail land grant program ran between 1850 and about 1871. Of the eighty-nine separate grants made under the program, recipients of seventy-two met the terms of the grants by building over 18,738 miles of line in ten Midwestern and four-teen western states and obtained a total of 131,350,534 acres. The remaining seventeen grants were forfeited for failure to carry out rail construction. Grant recipients obtained land for right-of-way use in widths of either two hundred or four hundred feet, together with varying numbers of alternating strips lying along each side of the right-of-way. These sections could be used for stations, shops, and other rail facilities, or sold for cash to assist with financing of construction or other corporate activities (Locklin 1972, 133–35; Holbrook 1947, 157).[3]

Threat of loss of the West to the Confederacy made construction of a rail link between the Midwest and California urgent for the Union. This urgency forced the only significant departure from the federal government's policy of confining railway aid to land grants. Legislation enacted in 1862 and 1864 cast the government in the role of incorporator, route planner, and specifier of technical standards, and provider of debt capital and land for a privately owned rail carrier, the Union Pacific Railroad Company. The 1864 legislation also authorized federal credit for the Union Pacific's western connector, the Central Pacific Railroad. Under the terms of this legislation, the two companies and their subsidiaries received U.S. government bonds totaling over $64,600,000. The railroad companies sold these bonds for cash. They then paid the proceeds over to inside construction companies, which acted as agents for the letting of contracts to firms that actually carried out railroad construction. Officers and directors of the railroad companies, among them public office holders, were also principals in the inside construction companies. Hence, they could and did reward themselves for their services, both handsomely and relatively quickly, with government bond-sourced cash. Whether their gains were justified in whole or in part by their rail development achievements and whatever risks of personal capital they bore is for debate elsewhere. The point of critical importance here is that the insiders' actions inflated the stated capitalization of the railroad companies above the total amounts paid out for railroad construction. Most notorious was the saga of the Union Pacific's inside construction company, the Credit Mobilier. Its actions saddled the Union Pacific with a capitalization almost twice the cost of construction, and tarnished members of Congress and other participants (Locklin 1972, 132–33, 138–39; Sabin 1919, chaps. 1–5; Ripley 1913, chap. 4).

Seeds of Economic Regulation

Significant federal assistance of rail development ended with completion of the Union Pacific—Central Pacific line to California in 1869 and termination of land grants in the early 1870s. Most state assistance programs had ended even earlier. It thus is with some irony that 1870 became the threshold of the greatest growth phase in the railway network. Between 1870 and 1910, line mileage rose from 52,922 to 240,293. However, 1870 also marked the beginning of a distinct turn in public attitude. Strong, widespread desire for expansion and improvement of railway service continued, but hostility toward railway companies began to build. Conditions sparking this hostility included the following:

- Violations of public trust by government officials in actions involving railway companies, as in the aforementioned Credit Mobilier affair.
- Violations of fiduciary trust and bribery of government officials, including members of the judiciary, by railway officers and directors. Ranking high in egregiousness and notoriety among episodes in such misbehavior was the manipulation of the Erie Railway by Daniel Drew, James Fisk, and Jay Gould in the late 1860s (Ripley 1913, chap. 1).
- The existence of "insufficient facilities, unfair discriminations, and extortionate charges," as reported in 1874 by the Windom

Committee, a special Senate committee appointed in 1872 to seek possible ways for obtaining lower-cost transport service for movements between interior points and the eastern seaboard (U.S. Senate 1874, 71).

- Agrarian discontent manifested in the Granger movement, stemming from declining market prices for agricultural products and rail price discrimination. Farmers and allied interests believed that rail freight rates on inbound supplies and outbound products could and should be reduced to alleviate their economic suffering. This belief was based at least in part on the sharp differences between freight rates at points where intramodal and intermodal (water transport) competition existed, and those at points captive to a single rail carrier.

- Discontent among industrial and mercantile freight shippers about what they perceived as excessively high freight rates. This reaction was sparked by the shrinkage in freight shippers' income during the five-year economic depression that followed the stock market panic of 1873.

- Losses to investors and burdens on taxpayers from rail financial failures. Subscribers to stock of failed railway companies experienced evaporation of share value and expectations of dividend income. They often also faced the burden of mortgage loans taken to fund their stock purchases. Taxpayers' obligations increased in instances where railway companies defaulted on loans made by state and local governments to assist rail construction.

Underlying these sources of public hostility against rail firms were three more fundamental interrelated conditions. First was the scale and scope of a typical rail firm relative to most other types of business entities in existence up to the 1870s. Second was vertical integration of rail infrastructure and rail service operation. Third was the set of distinctive inherent economic characteristics of the rail firm, and their effects on rail pricing and service behavior, market structure, and market entry and exit.

To expand on the first of these conditions, the threshold costs of a public service railway exceeded the funding capacity of the proprietorship and partnership, which stood as the common forms of business organization at the dawn of the railway age. Accumulation of requisite financial capital thus demanded use of the corporate form when private rather than government ownership was the chosen policy alternative for railway development. The result was entry into the national economy of a group of firms and an industry possessing economic power, spatial reach, stakeholders (employees, suppliers, customers, creditors, shareholders), capability for exerting political influence, and social impact far above that of virtually any other then-extant business sector.

Turning to the second condition, operating experience with the earliest railways quickly demonstrated that rail carriers should either own or hold rights for exclusive use of the track and other infrastructure components on which they run trains and provide service. This integration of the function of providing the transport way with the function of supplying transport service meant that an individual railway possessed a technically driven monopoly of the service offered on its line or network. Thus, intramodal competition in rail transport could occur only through competition between different lines or networks, rather than between different carriers on the same line, as in road and water (and later, air) transport (Bonavia 1958, 37).[4]

Expanding on the third condition, the inherent economic characteristics of rail firms that distinguish them from firms in settings of pure or highly workable competition include the following:

- High threshold costs and high sunk costs resulting from large investments in long-lived, highly specialized site-fixed and semimobile infrastructure components such as track, drainage systems, bridges, tunnels, and communication and signal systems.
- Economies of density in line operation.
- Network economies and revenue-generating advantages of network size.
- Relatively high ratio of fixed costs to total costs within short- and intermediate-run time periods.
- Causally identifiable marginal costs below average cost over large ranges of output. The term "causally identifiable marginal cost" as used here refers to specific elements of cost that can be traced or assigned on the basis of observable cause-and-effect evidence to particular units of rail transport service. Non-causally identifiable costs, or indivisible costs, stem from the common use of rail infrastructure by large numbers of individual rail transport output and sales units and by gaps in size between such output and sales units. The rail transport output unit is a train or train movement between origin and destination points. Rail transport sales units range from individual less-than-carload shipments through carload and small multiple-carload shipments to unit train or full trainload shipments. There is no gap between the rail output and sales units in instances where service is sold in full trainload quantities (Milne 1960, chaps. 4, 5).

Before going farther, it should be acknowledged that the just-concluded elaboration on indivisible costs appears in full here rather than in an endnote despite its pedantic tone because of the critical influence which cost indivisibility has exerted on pricing and other management and regulatory decision-making areas throughout the railway industry's existence.

Network Growth and the Emergence of Regulation

As noted in the previous section, 1870 marked a major turning point on two fronts for the railway industry. On one front was the period of headiest growth in the railway network. On the other was fruition of the seeds of regulation.

Railway line mileage leaped from 52,922 to 193,346 between 1870 and 1900 (Locklin 1972, chap. 3). Motives for the myriad projects within this great expansion varied. Some lines were built purely for the generation of income from their long-term operation. Profits were not necessarily expected to materialize immediately. More often than not, new extensions were constructed in advance of the development of sources of traffic along them. Strategic and tactical considerations focused more on the revenue and profitability of a carrier's total system than on the earnings of a particular line segment also played a role in numerous instances. Here a typical objective was capture of a key route or source of expected future traffic to foreclose or delay entry by a rival (Overton 1965, chaps. 8–11; Waters 1950, chap. 3). The post-1870 period also witnessed acceleration of a trend that had begun to emerge even before 1860—the geographic expansion of individual carriers through a blend of merger of existing shorter lines and construction of new, often relatively long-distanced line extensions. This genre of railway expansion stemmed from three sources. First was the steady growth in demand for longer-distance movements of freight and passengers, which accelerated after the Civil War. Second was recognition of the fact that rail systems, aided by continuing improvements in technology, could achieve economies of scope through a wider traffic base and longer, broader service territory. Third was the ability to attract more traffic and revenues vis-à-vis competitors by providing single-line service, or interline service involving a lesser number of connecting railways (Ripley 1912, chap. 1).

Other line-building projects were carried out in part for the earnings that they might yield from operation, and in part for the capture of short-term gains by their promoters à la the aforementioned Credit Mobilier of the Union Pacific's construction saga. Still others materialized exclusively for the garnering of profits from their promotion and construction. Yet another phenomenon involved the building of new lines by new companies that closely paralleled existing mileage owned by older, established carriers. The objective was "to dragoon the older lines into purchasing the new ones at extortionate prices" (Ripley 1912, 29). Such behavior reached its pinnacle during the crest of the great railway expansion wave in the 1880s. It drove the building of much of the 70,335 miles of new line that appeared during that decade, in what Ripley (1912, 27) characterized as "veritable crazes of promotion and speculative activity, unequalled before or since in our railroad history."

Henry Carter Adams decried this torrid run of corporate individualism as having "led to the creation of twice as much railroad property in the United States as the needs of the country require." Hence, in Adams's view, it represented a monumental case of market failure, embodying "misapplication of capital, a misdirection of industrial energy . . . [that could] . . . have no other result than to obstruct healthful growth" (Adams 1887, 71).

Market failure in nineteenth-century rail transport was not, however, restricted to capital allocation for line expansion. Its proclivity in intramodal price competition had been revealed as early as the 1840s and 1850s (Harlow 1947, 228–29). The principal drivers were the presence of some degree of unused capacity and the previously noted inherent economic characteristics of the rail firm, which made it both possible and necessary for rail officials confronted by intense competitive pressure to cut freight rates and passenger fares to levels well below average cost (and sometimes even below causally identifiable marginal costs when competitive frenzy reached peak levels). There was but one unacceptable alternative to such severe rate and fare reductions (assuming they fell short of causally identifiable marginal costs)—loss of all revenue on the involved traffic.

Opportunities for such ruinous price competition proliferated during the great post-1870 boom in line construction. The last three decades of the nineteenth century saw a series of spectacular rate wars, particularly in the East and Midwest, where the duplication of lines criticized by Adams had reached its highest levels. Each war ended with quasi-cartelistic efforts to stabilize carriers' revenues and fares at more remunerative levels by means of either rate or pooling agreements. The latter were of two types, traffic pools and money pools. A traffic pool involved the division of traffic movements between competing carriers, while a money pool involved division of receipts on competitive traffic among carriers party to the pooling agreement. The early (pre-1880) rate agreements quickly broke down, but some of the pooling agreements succeeded in maintaining rates at profitable levels for varying periods of time (Locklin 1972, 314; Hadley 1888, 91–95).

Intramodal competition in rail transport was not (and is not) spatially pervasive within the networks of individual carriers. Some locations enjoyed service from two or more rail firms, while numerous others were captive to a single carrier. Similarly, intermodal competition from water carriage could occur only at selected points on a rail carrier's system. These conditions, coupled with the distinctive cost characteristics of the rail firm, set the stage for the practice of long-and-short-haul discrimination in railway pricing. This practice—bolstering income by subjecting shippers at captive intermediate points to rates higher than (or even identical to) those paid by shippers at more distant origins for movements of the same commodity to a common destination—received additional impetus from revenue-draining rate wars.

Imperfections in rail freight transport markets were not confined to the seller's side. Some shippers commanded greater bargaining power against railway companies than did their competitors. This induced the practice of personal discrimination, under which carriers gave preferential treatment in pricing (in the form of either lower rates or rebates) and service to such shippers. Other forms of discrimination—by type of commodity carried, direction of movement, time of movement, shipment size, and geographic location (in ways other than long-and-short-haul differentiation)—were (and are) also important members of the railways' pricing repertoire. Technically, there are no inherent differences between any of these forms of transport price discrimination insofar as their execution is concerned. All require the possession of some degree of monopoly power for their successful practice; they entail the sale of service to different shippers and groups of shippers at different price-to-marginal cost ratios, based on differences in price elasticity of demand between each shipper or shipper group. Within the setting of nineteenth-century transport markets, however, all were objects of criticism on equity grounds (except, presumably, by parties whom they favored), but two ranked highest in opprobrium—personal discrimination and long-and-short-haul discrimination. They were perceived as the forms most threatening and harmful (and therefore unfair) to the economic welfare of the businesses and locations disfavored by their practice. The validity of this perception was self-evident, given the railway industry's then all-but-complete dominance of inland transport markets. Indeed, the once popular saying in freight traffic circles that "the power to make freight rates is the power to build and destroy" was not a hollow aphorism. Even modest changes in rates on some items could dramatically alter the cost and range of access to raw materials, and the scope and profitability of access to markets, for transport users.

Elimination of the most objectionable forms of price discrimination, control of excesses in the practice of others, and restraint of rates and fares to "reasonable" levels were among the leading objectives of early political actions taken to regulate economic behavior in the railway industry. Legislative fruition of significant[5] economic regulation of the industry began at the state level in the 1870s and culminated at the federal level when President Grover Cleveland signed the Act to Regulate Commerce, later and better known as the Interstate Commerce Act (ICA), on 4 February 1887. [6]

Federal Economic Regulation—Entry of the ICC

The effective date of the ICA, 5 April 1887, marked the first use of commission regulation as a distinctive tool for federal control of market behavior in any sector of business. Its application to the railway industry, with periodic changes in scope, was destined to endure down to the present day. Key provisions of the ICA prohibited pooling agreements, personal discrimination, and "undue preference and prejudice"; imposed stringent limitations on long-and-short-haul discrimination; and required that all rates and fares be (1) "just and reasonable," and (2) published and given strict adherence as published. To administer these provisions, the act established a five-member agency, the Interstate Commerce Commission (ICC). The ICC, like various state railroad commissions that had been created in the 1870s and earlier 1880s, was to be a quasi-independent regulatory body, functionally separate and distinct from the executive, legislative, and judicial branches of government. As such, *in concept*, it was to enjoy insulation from capricious political interference and possess technical expertise and other resources required for fulfillment of its mission (Locklin 1972, 224–27, 288–89).

President Cleveland appointed Thomas M. Cooley as the ICC's first chairman. Cooley, who possessed impressive professional credentials well suited to the role of the new agency, worked strenuously to provide it with leadership and to preserve and enhance its power.[7] He harbored a deep sense of fairness and equity. While intrinsically good and eminently desirable for a commissioner to possess, this trait may explain at least in part why some scholars judged Cooley to be "largely responsible" for the passive, reactive, quasi-judicial case-by-case approach that the ICC followed from its inception. However, it is difficult, if not impossible, for an entity of any type with a capacity-straining workload to take a sustained proactive administrative stance; within a short time after the ICA's 5 April 1887 effective date, the short-staffed ICC found itself inundated with more than "a thousand complaints, grievances, and questions . . ." (Hoogenboom and Hoogenboom 1976, 21–26).

Cooley did believe that the commission should act on its own initiative when a need for intervention arose. In February 1888, a strike by locomotive engineers began on the Chicago, Burlington & Quincy Railroad (CB&Q). It soon grew bitter and prolonged and caused serious disruptions in interstate commerce. Cooley sought to have the ICC launch an investigation in an effort to facilitate a settlement, but none of the other four commissioners would support his proposed initiative (Hoogenboom and Hoogenboom 1976, 26–27; Overton 1965, 206–14). Cooley also manifested proaction in 1889, 1890, and 1891 by attempting to persuade Congress to bring intrastate rail traffic under the ICC's jurisdiction and make commission rulings less susceptible to delay and negation by the courts. Congress, however, rejected his pleas. Beset by deteriorating health, Cooley resigned from the commission in September 1891 (Hoogenboom and Hoogenboom 1976, 30–31).

Cooley did score a masterstroke of success in 1887 by appointing a distinguished economist, Henry Carter Adams, as the ICC's first statistician. Adams firmly believed that effective regulation required robust data for firms under the ICC's jurisdiction. His work in developing a mandatory uniform system of accounts for railways became his legacy as a public servant. Adams held a broad perspective. In addition to his work as chief statistician, he became a leading defender of commission regulation and a beacon of hope within the ICC through the post-Cooley years of the 1890s. During that time, the commission suffered from emasculation of its decisions by the courts, disregard for its actions by the railways, lack of support from the McKinley administration, and mediocre leadership among the commissioners (Dorfman 1954, 43–44; Hoogenboom and Hoogenboom 1976, 37–38).

Antitrust Law Applications

After 1887, the railroads (with minor exceptions) bowed to the ICA and terminated their pooling agreements. The traffic associations, which had administered pooling agreements, were recast to administer collective rate agreements. The ICC, under Thomas Cooley's leadership, did not bar such agreements. Cooley and his colleagues abhorred monopoly pricing but apparently recognized the inherent limitations on the workability of intense intramodal railway price competition and disliked the debilitating consequences of rate wars (Hoogenboom and Hoogenboom 1976, 28–29). Collective rate making produced relatively stable rates and earnings, until the stock market panic of 1893 triggered a severe depression. The ensuing decline in freight traffic ignited rate warfare as individual carriers, desperate for revenue, ignored the agreements and acted unilaterally to cut rates and offer rebates. Defaults on debt befell numerous railways, including companies as prominent as the Santa Fe (Waters 1950, 204–17). Efforts to end the conflict with new collective agreements succeeded in 1896. The ICC opposed at least one of these agreements (that of the Joint Traffic Association involving lines in eastern territory) because its terms violated the antipooling section of the ICA. However, ICC opposition did not stop its operation; antitrust enforcement did. U.S. Supreme Court decisions handed down in 1897 and 1898 found the rate-fixing actions of two organizations, the Trans-Missouri Freight Association and the Joint Traffic Association, to be in violation of the 1890 Sherman Antitrust Act.[8]

These rulings did not totally stop collective rate making. Yet the threat that they posed, together with the railways' quest for a device that would diminish, if not end, rebates to powerful monopsonistic shippers such as the Rockerfeller-ruled Standard Oil Company, gave impetus to initiation in the late 1890s of a nationwide movement toward railway consolidation and combination. Before the end of the next decade, extensive and somewhat intricate intercorporate stock acquisitions had created close communities of interest, which concentrated decisions on critical issues such as pricing in the hands of one or two dominant group-leading companies in each region of the country. Most of these groups escaped direct antitrust attack, but action by the Department of Justice forced several dissolutions, including separation of the Northern Pacific from the Great Northern in the famous Northern Securities Case decision, divestment of the Union Pacific's holding of 46 percent of the Southern Pacific's common stock, and separation of the Boston & Maine from the New York, New Haven & Hartford (Overton 1965, 262–63; Hofsommer 1986, 52–54; Locklin 1972, 322–23).

As figure 2 reveals, the community of interest combinations together with collective rate making stopped the long post–Civil War decline in average freight revenue per ton-mile and contributed toward a modest increase between 1900 and 1904. Passage of the Elkins Act amendment to the ICA in 1903 also helped bolster railway income by strengthening the ICC's power to stop personal discrimination, particularly in the form of rebating (Locklin 1972, 228–29). Additional benefit came from sharp increases in freight traffic, as the national economy recovered from its post-1893 depression. These increases, along with growth in passenger traffic, resulted in a series of heavy capital investment programs and projects focused on the upgrading and expansion of fixed plant and the acquisition of larger capacity motive power and rolling stock. Notable examples included the virtual complete rebuilding of track, bridges, and other infrastructure components on the Union Pacific, the quadrupling of mainline track on lengthy sections of the Pennsylvania Railroad, and the construction of massive New York City terminal facilities by both the Pennsylvania and the New York Central. Net new industry-wide investment rose from $232 million in 1898 to $859 million in 1906 and $1.5 billion in 1907 (Hofsommer 1986, 10–12; Burgess and Kennedy 1949, 463–503; Martin 1971, 130).

Progressivism, ICC Resuscitation, and Constraint

The community of interest combination movement produced a side effect unintended (presumably) by its architects—reinforcement of the railway industry's public visage as a rapacious monopoly. This, together with continuing widespread antirail sentiment stemming from the nineteenth-century-vintage root causes reviewed previously, incited political action

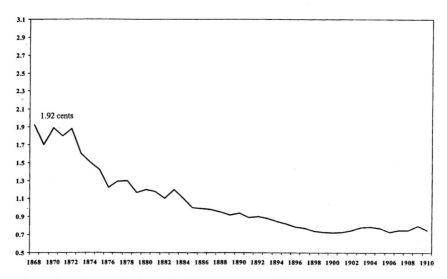

Figure 2   Average Railway Freight Revenue per Ton-Mile—1867–1910
Source: William Z. Ripley, *Railroads: Rates and Regulation* (New York: Longmans, Green and Co., 1912), 413.

that transformed the becalmed ICC into a potent instrument of constraint. A detailed review of the transformation belongs elsewhere. Suffice it to note here that its key drivers included Progressive Movement leaders such as Presidents Theodore Roosevelt and William H. Taft, Wisconsin governor (and later, U.S. senator, 1906–25) Robert M. La Follette Sr., and Iowa governor (and, beginning in 1909, U.S. senator) Albert B. Cummins (Hoogenboom and Hoogenboom 1976, chap. 2). The legislative results of their efforts were the Hepburn Act (1906) and Mann-Elkins Act (1910) amendments to the ICA. Of greatest significance among the numerous provisions of these amendments were those empowering the ICC to (1) prescribe maximum rates in instances where it found existing rates to be unlawful, and (2) suspend proposed changes in rates pending investigation to ascertain their reasonableness and lawfulness (Locklin 1972, 229–37). The ICC itself was reinforced by Roosevelt's and Taft's appointments of commissioners favoring strong control of private monopoly. [9]

Although rejuvenated in power and personnel, the commission did not attempt to step beyond its previously established quasi-judicial case-by-case approach and develop a comprehensive set of balanced principles for guiding the performance of the railway industry. Instead, it hewed to the narrow-framed policy focus set by its enabling statute—to negate railway behavior when and where required to protect shippers and passengers against extortionate and unjustly discriminatory rates and fares. Price thus stood at the center of this focus. Service adequacy received attention only insofar as it related to discrimination in treatment of individual customers and customer groups by carriers. The impact of carriers' financial condition on service adequacy was not of primary concern; the commission, within the bounds of its statute, "had no particular responsibilities toward the carriers" (Locklin 1972, 242).

This narrow focus was manifested in a series of landmark rate case decisions between 1911 and 1917. Before 1910, railroads sought to implement rate increases on an individual rather than a collective basis. However, in April of that year, rising labor and other costs moved the Western Traffic Association, representing twenty-four carriers operating west of the Mississippi River, to file an application with the ICC for a general rate increase. A short time later, the large eastern railways operating north of the Ohio River and east of the Mississippi filed a similar application. Evidence presented by rail carrier witnesses during the commission's hearings paled in impact in comparison with testimony given by shippers' representatives, one of whom was Louis D. Brandeis. Brandeis's tactics included testimony from expert witnesses who specialized in the development and application of scientific management practices in an effort to demonstrate that (1) railroads were experiencing significant inefficiencies, and (2) remediation of such inefficiencies would obviate the carriers' need for increases in rates. Such testimony proved persuasive to the commission; its thrust drew positive acknowledgment in the text of the final decision on the case. In addition to this challenge, lack of unit cost data undermined rail witnesses' attempts to prove the reasonableness of rates on particular commodities that were within the scope of the proposed general increase.[10] Early in 1911, the commission resoundingly denied both the eastern and western carriers' applications.[11]

Continuing increases in railway operating expenses, resulting in part from general inflation and in part from state and federal government-mandated and influenced increases in rail labor costs,[12] brought four additional general rate adjustment decisions—in mid- and late 1914, mid-1915, and mid-1917. The commission granted increases in each of these cases, but they fell far below the carriers' claimed levels of need. Simultaneously, state commissions contributed to the constraint of railway revenue by exerting steady downward pressure on rates and fares for intrastate traffic (Hines 1928, 4–5; Martin 1971, chaps. 7–11).

Operating conditions on the railway network lent credence to its owners' pleas that the commission's (and the ICA's) exclusive focus on rate minimization for maximizing shippers' and passengers' economic welfare was seriously flawed. Investment in fixed facilities and rolling stock lagged, and "traffic congestion became at times exceedingly serious" (Hines 1928, 5). Growth in traffic from post-1914 British and French purchases of American-made war matériel aggravated these conditions.

Concern over rail service inadequacy caught the attention of President Woodrow Wilson even before the start of World War I. In his annual message to Congress in January 1914, Wilson viewed the prosperity of the railway industry and the nation as inseparable, stated that railway executives had "spoken very plainly and very earnestly" of these needs, and that "we ought to be quick to accept" actions for meeting those needs (Hoogenboom and Hoogenboom 1976, 72). Perhaps not without coincidence, Winthrop M. Daniels was at this time one of the two newest members of the ICC. Prior to becoming a commissioner, Daniels had been the ICC's economist. Earlier, he was a colleague and friend of Wilson at Princeton University, and had served on the New Jersey public utility commission. (Establishment of that agency was an initiative of Wilson during his tenure as governor of New Jersey.) Daniels joined the ICC in time to participate in all but the first of the landmark rate level case decisions. He consistently voted in favor of granting at least some increase in each case. In instances where he provided comments (usually dissenting) on his vote, Daniels cited economic evidence of the need for rate increases, criticized (in one case)[13] colleagues for including muckracking-type sentiments in their rationale for denial of an increase, and exhibited "broader administrative concern for the welfare of the carriers and the health of the economy" (Hoogenboom and Hoogenboom 1976, 74).[14]

President Wilson grew increasingly concerned about the performance of the railway industry and the ICC. In addition to service problems, line mileage operated by railways in receivership had grown to 42,000—more than at any time since the depression of the 1890s. On 7 December 1915, in a special message to Congress, he sought the appointment of a "commission of inquiry" to investigate the "transportation problem" and identify ways in which the statutory powers and processes of regulation could be altered to better "the conditions under which the railroads are operated" and make them "more useful servants of the country as a whole" (Hines 1928, 5–6). After additional prodding, the Senate and House established a joint subcommittee in July 1916 to conduct a broad-based inquiry. The subcommittee, chaired by California senator Francis G. Newlands, initiated hearings in November 1916 and continued to gather evidence sporadically through November 1917. Its work ended abruptly, unfinished, on 26 December 1917, when epic-level rail traffic congestion so threatened the war effort that the federal government took administrative possession and control of the railroads by presidential proclamation.[15] However, evidence gathered by the subcommittee helped set the foundation for a wider understanding of "[t]he need for comprehensive and constructive railroad legislation . . ." that would be fulfilled by passage of the Transportation Act of 1920 (Hines 1928, 5–6, 224; Martin 1971, 340–45).

Comprehensive Planning and Control

Wilson's proclamation nationalized managerial control of the railroads taken over (but not their ownership) under the auspices of the United States Railroad Administration (USRA).[16] The proclamation overrode the antipooling provisions of the ICA and the anticollusion intent of the Sherman Act and enabled the USRA to manage the carriers under its control as a single unified national network. Maximum effectiveness in the movement of traffic was Wilson's primary objective.

Railway labor scored dramatic gains under federal management. Collective bargaining was extended to all USRA-controlled railroads. A series of wage increases upped hourly rates by a total of 100 percent and added

$965 million to railway operating expenses. Pay bases were altered and standardized. Changes in work rules were promulgated, notably by classification of employees' tasks "in great detail so that one class of employees would not be permitted to do the work of another class, and so that it might be necessary for several employees to work on a single job which prior thereto could have been done by one employee" (Hines 1928, 177, 180–81; Hoogenboom and Hoogenboom 1976, 87). These inefficiencies proved conspicuously burdensome and difficult to eliminate later; some still exist.

Unlike the ICC, the USRA moved quickly to boost income in the face of rising operating expenses. In 1918, it ordered increases of approximately 25 percent in freight rates and 18 percent in passenger fares on both interstate and intrastate traffic. These increases "were made without giving the shipping or traveling public any opportunity to be heard . . . ," without formal consultation with the ICC, and without any consultation with the state commissions (Hines 1928, 193–95). However, neither the increases nor record wartime traffic volume produced revenues sufficient to offset jumps in operating costs. When federal control ended on 1 March 1920, the USRA had accumulated a deficit of $1.2 billion, but had succeeded in breaking the wartime rail traffic jam and demonstrating the achievability of economies from coordinated operation of competing carriers' facilities and equipment (Hines 1928, chaps. 4, 15; Hoogenboom and Hoogenboom 1976, 88).

At the close of World War I, most public policy analysts and decision makers perceived the dominance that rail transport had possessed since the 1870s as impregnable. Thus, policy choices surrounding the transition from wartime federal control were centered on how best to shape the future performance and condition of an industry that was seen as (1) possessing a virtual monopoly as a mode of transport, but that simultaneously was (2) beset by duplicate capacity in excess of peacetime transport demand, and (3) populated by a mixture of financially strong and weak carriers.

Continued federal control of management and nationalization of ownership were advocated by Joseph B. Eastman and Glenn E. Plumb. Eastman, a protégé of Louis D. Brandeis who had joined the ICC in early 1919 after service on the Massachusetts Public Service Commission, believed that federal ownership would (1) give access to low-cost financial capital for funding improvements, while simultaneously providing the best means for (2) maintaining rates and fares at reasonable levels, (3) rationalizing duplicate facilities, equipment, and operations, (4) solving the weak-strong road problem, and (5) fostering sound labor relations. Plumb, general counsel for the railway unions and acting on their behalf, developed a proposal for railway nationalization that envisioned federal purchase of rail assets through the sale of $18 billion in bonds and vestment of rail network ownership in a government corporation governed by fifteen presidentially appointed directors. However, Eastman's view met with opposition from most of his fellow ICC commissioners, and Plumb's plan drew strong hostility from shippers, farmers, railway investors and management, and the general public. By the fall of 1919, the political climate favored only one policy track—retention of private ownership and return of managerial control to the railway companies, coupled with an improved framework for commission regulation (Hoogenboom and Hoogenboom 1976, 90–92).

The result was passage of the Esch-Cummins Transportation Act of 1920. It vastly expanded the ICA,[17] with provisions intended to shift the ICC from its pre-1918 emphasis on rate and fare minimization to "effective but constructive . . . regulation . . ." (Hines 1928, 226) attuned to "the needs of both the shipping public and the carriers" (Hoogenboom and Hoogenboom 1976, 97).[18] Provisions of the act of immediate interest here include the following (Locklin 1972, chap. 11; Hines 1928, 224–25):

- A revised rule of rate making, by which carriers taken as a whole on either a nationwide or regional basis were to be permitted (but not guaranteed) aggregate net railway operating income equal to a fair rate of return on the aggregate value assets used by them in providing transport service.[19] Congress prescribed 5.5 percent as the fair rate of return for the first two years beyond the act's effective date (after which determination of fair rate of return was to be left to the ICC), but authorized the ICC to add an amount no greater than 0.5 percent to fund improvements and betterments.
- Power to recapture excessive earnings; because administration of the rule of rate making on an industry-wide or regional basis rather than an individual company basis could give some companies earnings in excess of the prescribed rate of return and leave others with inadequate earnings, Congress mandated that one-half of the net operating income of an individual railway company in any year that exceeded 6 percent was to be paid to the ICC and placed in a railroad contingency fund. From this fund, interest-bearing (6 percent) loans were to be made to needy carriers for funding capital expenditures or refunding maturing debt obligations. Alternatively, the ICC was authorized to purchase railway equipment with recaptured earnings and lease it to carriers in need at charges sufficient to cover depreciation and yield a rate of return of at least 6 percent.[20]

- Empowerment of the ICC to set minimum and exact rates for the purpose of protecting weak railroads from destructive competition.
- Imposition of ICC control over a rail carrier's (1) abandonment of an existing line, and (2) extension of service to new territory through either use of an existing line (obtained via trackage rights or purchase) or construction of a new line.
- Elimination of the absolute prohibition of pooling in the 1887 ICA and empowerment of the ICC to approve pooling agreements between competing railroads when the commission judged that they would improve service and/or reduce costs without unduly restraining competition.
- A mandate that the ICC prepare and adopt a plan for consolidation of all U.S. railway companies into a limited number of competing systems.
- Empowerment of the ICC to approve consolidation of two or more railway companies into one entity in instances where it found consolidation to be in the public interest and in conformance with the plan for industry-wide consolidation that the commission was directed to prepare. Under this provision, antitrust law was subordinated to ICC judgment in rail merger cases.
- Empowerment of the ICC to compel the joint use of terminal facilities if justified by the public interest and capable of being implemented without impairing the facility owner's ability to handle its own traffic.

Taken at face, these provisions gave the ICC the authority and inspiration to transcend its thirty-three-year fixation on the quasi-judicial case-by-case method of regulation and proactively plan and implement initiatives for improving railroad industry structure and performance. However, such a reformation was not to be.

The premier proactive provision was the directive for preparation and adoption of a plan for railway consolidation. Substantive effort toward fulfillment of the directive began with the commission's engagement of Professor William Z. Ripley of Harvard University. Ripley presented a preliminary plan to the commission on 31 January 1921. The commission modified Ripley's twenty-one-system plan into a nineteen-system tentative plan released on 26 September 1921. During the next two years, the commission held extensive hearings on its tentative plan. They drew strong hostility toward both details of the plan and consolidation per se from railway management and labor, and from communities and other stakeholders. These outpourings of negativism intimidated and divided the commission and destroyed its resolve to block consolidation proposals in conflict with its plan. In a 1923 case decision, the ICC narrowly interpreted the 1920 act to permit consummation of consolidations approved by state commissions without ICC consideration of the impact of such consolidations on the commission's consolidation plan. Dissenting with anguish, Commissioner Joseph B. Eastman decried the decision as gravely impairing if not totally destroying the commission's power to successfully fulfill the intended purpose of the consolidation plan directive in the 1920 act. Within a year after this decision, the commission found itself unable to agree on a final plan for consolidation. Annually from 1925 through 1928, it pleaded unsuccessfully with Congress to be relieved of its obligation to plan consolidations. Finally, in 1929, the commission reluctantly adopted a nineteen-system consolidation plan similar to its tentative plan of 1921. The 1929 plan languished on paper through the 1930s. In 1940, Congress relieved the commission of its failed responsibility to provide leadership through comprehensive consolidation planning (Dearing and Owen 1949, 318–21; Locklin 1972, 266; Hoogenboom and Hoogenboom 1976, 105–7).

This failure might have been avoided *if* Congress in 1920 had (1) empowered the ICC to compel consolidations in conformance with its comprehensive plan, and (2) required that railway intercorporate combinations accomplished through either lease or stock ownership as distinguished from merger be in conformance with the commission's plan.[21] The loophole created by these voids in ICC power enabled various large railroads opposed to the corporate groupings in the ICC's proposed consolidation plan to subvert it. During the 1920s, they paid substantial sums, inflated by the stock market boom of that decade, to obtain working control of smaller competing and complementary carriers. Holding companies and voting trusts served as vehicles for such transactions.[22] The commission itself became an accomplice in this subversion by approving requests for interlocking railway board appointments in instances where they crossed boundaries between the corporate groups in the commission's proposed consolidation plan. Had the ICC's final plan of 1929 been implemented, it would have required substantial divestment of intercorporate securities holdings and key changes in railway directorates (Burgess and Kennedy 1949, 574–81; Hoogenboom and Hoogenboom 1976, 105–9; Rehor 1965, 171–79).

Less-than-stellar administration also befell other key provisions of the 1920 act bulleted above. Of immediate noteworthiness here, however, is the fact that failures in the process of their application would prove in retrospect to be of less significance than rapid diminution of their conceptual relevance and basic workability.

The core provisions of the 1920 act, as envisaged by Congress, had as their basic objective the maintenance of adequate railway service on all or most of the lines within the national railway network of 1920. Maximum spatial coverage of service and access thereto were seen as essential to public well-being in a setting in which the railway held center stage; it was the exclusive or almost exclusive supplier of universal inland intercity common carrier transport service, with both the technical ability and legal obligation to accommodate virtually every conceivable type of freight in consignments of all sizes, as well as mail, express, and all classes of passenger service.

The principal challenge to maintenance of this geographically comprehensive universal service network was seen as the aforementioned weak-strong road problem—disparities in earning power and financial capital structure that left some railways well able to fund asset renewal and improvement and bear the relatively high-cost labor agreement conditions instituted during wartime government control, and others less able or unable to do so. External subsidization of weak roads was not seen as an option for meeting this challenge. The sought-after solution in the 1920 act was internal cross-subsidization within the framework of a privately owned self-financing industry, and the pivotal tool for achieving this solution was development and implementation of the plan for consolidation mandated by the act. Hence, in the act, Congress specifically instructed the ICC to group the companies so that:

> the cost of transportation as between competitive systems and as related to the values of the properties through which the service is rendered shall be the same, so far as practicable, so that these systems can employ uniform rates in the movement of competitive traffic and under efficient management earn substantially the same rate of return upon the value of their respective railway properties. (Dearing and Owen 1949, 318).

With this scheme, Congress sought to restructure the industry as a set of homogeneous firms comprising a regulated quasi cartel, justified by the expected benefit to the public of an assured supply of adequate, universal, and vital common carrier freight and passenger service. Congress obviously did not seek maximization of economies of density and minimization of rail service supply costs through rigorous rationalization of duplicate lines, facilities, and equipment. It subordinated, if not supplanted, price competition with service rivalry.

To function as envisaged, Congress's scheme required continued existence of the rail mode's long-standing near monopoly of intercity transport. However, even as the 1920 act was being drafted, technological and institutional changes were emerging that would soon breach and ultimately decimate rail market dominance through (1) reincarnation of inter-city road transport, (2) revival of inland water transport, and (3) development of commercial air transport. Government initiatives played indispensable roles in the success of these thrusts. Detailed coverage of each is not possible here. However, it must be noted that post-1916 engineering-based planning and construction of road, water, and air transport infrastructure, conducted by executive branch agencies and sustained by public funding, cast a sharp contrast in effectiveness with efforts toward planning by the ICC (Seely 1987, chaps. 3–9; U.S. Department of Transportation 1976, 90–319).

Motor freight carriers' penetration of the railway traffic base grew steadily during the 1920s, aided by continuing advances in the technology of trucking equipment and government-funded construction of hard-surfaced road mileage. Revival of inland water freight service, stimulated by federally funded navigation improvements and establishment and operation of a federally owned barge line, also siphoned off rail traffic, albeit in a lesser number of freight transport markets. Nevertheless, growth in business activity enabled rail freight revenue to remain relatively steady despite selective rate reductions to meet the new competition; it stood at $4.42 billion in 1920, reached a high of $4.90 billion in 1926, and was at $4.89 billion in 1929. In the passenger sector, however, the competitive impact of increased private automobile and motor bus usage was severe. After rising steadily to a peak of over 47 billion passenger-miles in 1920, rail volume fell to just over 31 billion in 1929. Much of this loss was in short- and intermediate-distance day-coach traffic; commuter and Pullman (first class) patronage remained stable. Passenger revenue declined from $1.3 billion to $876 million between 1920 and 1929, but this drop did not impair financial performance of rail operations. The industry's operating ratio (operating expenses divided by operating revenue) declined from an unsatisfactory 94.4 in 1920 to 71.8 in 1929. This improvement in performance stemmed primarily from increased productivity made possible by greater carrying capacity of freight equipment, higher horsepower per locomotive unit, and other technological improvements (Moulton and Associates 1933, 28, 87–96).

The Great Depression and Eastman's Grand Design

Continuing increases in intermodal competition after 1929, coupled with the devastating effects of the Great Depression on traffic and revenues, quickly ended the ten-year run of relatively favorable financial performance that the railway industry had enjoyed and set the stage for extension of federal economic regulation to motor, air, and water transport. The rationale and model legislative language for such extension was articulated in reports prepared under the direction of ICC commissioner Joseph B. Eastman during his tenure as federal coordinator of transportation, charged with administering the Emergency Railroad Transportation Act of 1933. Among the act's provisions was a directive that the federal coordinator survey conditions in the various modes of transport and suggest means for improvement to the ICC, which in turn was to submit them with its own comments to Congress and the president (Locklin 1972, 261; U.S. House 1935).[23] Eastman found most carriers to be financially malnourished and exhibiting service deficiencies, including (in the case of motor transport) inability to maintain equipment in safe condition, and judged inter- and intramodal price competition to be excessively intense. He recommended that the comprehensive regulatory framework already applicable to rail transport be extended to the other three modes for the purpose of moderating competitive pressure on carrier earnings and restoring financial stamina to each of the modes in measures sufficient to enable them to provide common carrier service of adequate quantity and quality. He viewed competition as desirable, but contended that "it must be held within reasonable limits and kept from assuming destructive and wasteful forms" (Eastman 1940, 124–25; U.S. Senate 1934, 14, 22–23). In addition, Eastman saw comprehensive regulation of all modes by one agency as a means for achieving intermodal coordination. He envisaged regulation of competing carriers in such ways that each would be fitted more closely to the particular types of service for which it was economically best suited (U.S. Senate 1934, 24). Eastman's model bills formed the foundations for (1) the Motor Carrier Act of 1935, which subjected intercity for-hire motor freight and passenger service to economic regulation; (2) the Transportation Act of 1940, which imposed economic regulation on domestic for-hire water freight and passenger carriers; and (3) the Civil Aeronautics Act of 1938. The acts did, however, differ in various of their provisions from those proposed in Eastman's model bills. In the Motor Carrier Act, Congress granted exemptions from regulation for commodities defined as agricultural. In the Transportation Act of 1940, exemptions from regulation were provided for the water transport of various types of dry and liquid bulk commodities. Eastman had recommended that air transport regulation be administered by the ICC, but Congress placed it under the jurisdiction of a new agency, the Civil Aeronautics Authority (later the Civil Aeronautics Board). The new legislation thus fell short in its comprehensiveness from the all-encompassing grand design for regulation envisioned by Eastman. Also outside the framework of commission regulation were private carriage by truck, water, and air, and infrastructure provision (vested in federal, state, and municipal administrative agencies and departments).

1940–1976—Grand Design Unrealized

Congress prefaced the Transportation Act of 1940 with a statement of national transportation policy intended to serve as an overarching guide for the ICC's administration of the ICA. Echoing the tenets of Eastman's grand design, Congress defined the national transportation policy as

> fair and impartial regulation of all modes of transportation subject to the provisions of the Act, so administered as to recognize and preserve the inherent advantages of each, to promote safe, adequate, economical, and efficient service and foster sound economic conditions in transportation and among the several carriers; to encourage the establishment and maintenance of reasonable charges for transportation services, without unjust discriminations, undue preferences or advantages, or unfair of destructive competitive practices; to cooperate with the several States and the duly authorized officials thereof; and to encourage fair wages and equitable working conditions;—all to the end of developing, coordinating, and preserving a national transportation system by water, highway, and rail, as well as other means. . . . [24]

Principles enunciated in this policy statement were destined to provoke controversy in the ICC's adjudication of intermodal rate competition and, by doing so, contribute to future legislative curtailments in the commission's authority to control such competition. As noted above, regulation of intermodal price rivalry ranked high in Eastman's grand design, and cases involving it began to demand ICC attention soon after passage of the Motor Carrier Act of 1935 gave truckers the ability to invoke exercise of the commission's minimum rate power in defense against truck-competitive rate reductions by railways. These early cases moved Commissioner Eastman to acknowledge in a December 1939 presentation before the Transportation and Public Utilities Group of the American Economic Association that they posed difficult challenges for the ICC (Eastman 1940, 124–29). The causes of these challenges were rooted in the following interrelated conditions:

- Wide gaps between causally identifiable marginal costs and average costs of providing rail service, as explicated earlier in this essay.

- Heterogeneity between the cost structures of rail firms on the one hand, and those of motor and water carrier firms on the other, that is, differences in (1) ratios of fixed to variable costs, (2) gaps between marginal and average costs, and (3) postponable versus nonpostponable costs, stemming from disparities in the physical lives and degrees of sunkenness of carriers' asset bases.
- Lack of refined costing systems for providing relatively accurate unit cost data, coupled with inherent difficulties in providing such data in the rail mode due to the presence of significant indivisible costs, as noted earlier.

The World War II freight traffic boom strained the capacity of all three modes to their utmost limits, thus bringing a temporary respite from intercarrier pricing disputes. They reappeared and proliferated after the war, and came to dominate the commission's caseload as rail carriers fought growing inroads from motor and water transport with selective rate reductions. The result was a thirty-year (approximate) quagmire of ambiguous decision making by the ICC, and a rising tide of criticism from railroads and transport economists contending that the commission was engaging in so-called umbrella rate making—that is, prescribing minimum rates that were in excess of the costs of the lowest-cost mode of transport party to the rate dispute. The commission, together with motor and water carriers, argued that the practice was justified by Congress's directive in the above-quoted national transportation policy statement that regulation be conducted in such a way as to preserve a national transportation system by all modes, and to prevent destructive competitive practices. A 1958 amendment to the ICA was intended to curtail the practice, but the ICC continued to manifest an umbrella or "share the traffic" policy in the 1960s (Coyle 1969; Harbeson 1962; Williams 1958; Nelson 1959, 138–47).

Two case decisions in that decade became widely cited in arguments supportive of regulatory reform. The first was the ICC's denial (later reversed after being fought to the U.S. Supreme Court) of the Southern Railway's proposal to use incentive pricing (involving rate reductions of up to 60 percent) for the movement of grain in innovative one-hundred-ton-capacity covered hopper cars constructed of aluminum (ICC 1963, 1965). The second was the disallowance of rail rates based on incremental costs for the transport of heavy ingot molds. The commission judged that (1) such reduced rates would not preserve the inherent advantages of competing barge lines whose rates were based on average costs, and thus (2) that the reduced rates were in violation of the 1940 Statement of National Transportation Policy (ICC 1965).

Other dimensions of rail regulation also came under significant criticism as early as the 1950s. Attempts to partially deregulate were made by the Eisenhower administration in the mid-1950s and the Kennedy administration in the early 1960s, but both failed in the face of strong opposition from trucking and water carrier interests (Nelson 1975, 18).

Rail Financial Malnutrition and Diminished Economic Regulation

By the late 1960s, the intercity rail passenger service sector was rapidly approaching extinction in the wake of post–World War II market share capture by air carriers and the private automobile, aided by massive public sector investments in infrastructure. Rail commuter passenger service traffic remained strong, but operating conditions made it unprofitable to provide. Almost simultaneously, on 21 June 1970, the Penn Central Transportation Company entered bankruptcy. Penn Central had been formed on 1 February 1968 by merger of the Pennsylvania and New York Central Railroad companies. As a condition for approval of that merger, the ICC had ordered Penn Central to absorb (in 1969) the already bankrupt New York, New Haven and Hartford Railroad. Penn Central was the nation's largest remaining operator of intercity rail passenger service, and the largest commuter rail passenger operator. This cast Penn Central as bearer of the largest share of the railway industry's annual passenger service deficit (more than $100 million in 1970), a burden that the company's financial plight rendered unbearable. Profits from freight operations had fallen below the level where they could be used to cross-subsidize passenger services.

Confronted by the specter of total cessation of rail passenger service in territory containing about 40 percent of the nation's population and locus of many of the most prominent centers of influence in business and politics, Congress enacted the Rail Passenger Service Act of 1970 in October of that year. The act created the government-sponsored National Railroad Passenger Corporation (Amtrak) to take over operation of intercity passenger service from the railway companies. Similarly, responsibility for most commuter passenger services passed from the railway companies to local, regional, and statewide public authorities between the 1960s and 1980s. One result of this transition from private- to public-sector ownership was the virtual elimination of economic regulation within the rail passenger sphere. Amtrak and the commuter authorities came to possess degrees of freedom in pricing and other business decision areas that had not existed since 1887 (U.S. Senate 1973).

Economic regulation of rail transport thus became a "freight service only" activity. However, changes would soon occur in that sphere as well. By the early 1970s, the Penn Central had been joined in bankruptcy by five of its competitors—Erie-Lackawanna Railway, Reading Company, Lehigh Valley Railroad, Central Railroad of New Jersey, and Lehigh & Hudson River Railway. It soon became apparent that none of these companies could regain solvency through adjustments in the claims of security holders. Their cash flows had become insufficient to support capitalization of any magnitude. Loss of most rail freight service in the populous Northeast—which then contained more than 50 percent of all manufacturing plants in the nation—thus became an imminent threat. Congress met this threat by establishing the government-funded Consolidated Rail Corporation (Conrail), which took over equipment, infrastructure, and service operations from the insolvent carriers on 1 April 1976.[25] Conrail became the sole provider of rail freight service within much of its service territory (Perritt 1983).

To fund the start-up of Conrail, and to give the entire freight railway industry greater freedom for improving its financial performance and condition, Congress enacted the Railroad Revitalization and Regulatory Reform Act of 1976 (4R Act).[26] The 4R Act provided for the first significant contractions in federal rail economic regulation since its inception in 1887. Key provisions included (1) curtailment of the ICC's power to limit reductions in railway rates for the purpose of protecting competing modes (by specifying variable cost as the floor for rail pricing); (2) limitation of the ICC's power over maximum rate levels to situations in which a carrier was judged to possess market dominance; (3) empowerment of the ICC to exempt specific categories of railway traffic from regulation in situations where competitive conditions had rendered regulation unnecessary; and (4) placement of time limits on the ICC's issuance of decisions in cases involving railway mergers and consolidations (U.S. House 1976).

Congress intended that Conrail be self-sustaining. However, the company suffered losses totaling $1.5 billion between 1976 and 1980. In the same period, two historically weak but extensive western carriers, the Chicago, Rock Island & Pacific, and the Chicago, Milwaukee, St. Paul & Pacific, entered bankruptcy. These events persuaded Congress that avoidance of continued government funding of Conrail's losses and improvement of the entire railway industry's financial condition required further reductions in economic regulation, particularly those providing greater freedom in pricing and in the disposal of unprofitable lines. Passage of the

Staggers Rail Act of 1980 and the Northeast Rail Service Act of 1981 (NERSA) reduced the ICC's powers over freight railways' managerial discretion far below what they had been even after passage of the 4R Act four years earlier. Among the most important features of the Staggers Act was a provision allowing rail services to be marketed on a contract basis. This led to a shift from traditional published tariff rates to confidential contract charges for the movement of much rail traffic. Until 1980, the ICC had viewed contract rail services as being in violation of the statutory prohibition of personal discrimination dating from 1887.

The Staggers Act applied to the entire railway industry, while NERSA focused on changes needed to assist Conrail's efforts to become self-sufficient, including (1) expedited line abandonment procedures (for a limited period of time); (2) termination of Conrail's obligation to operate commuter passenger services on a contract basis for public-sector agencies (some of which allegedly underpaid or were slow to pay Conrail); (3) preemption of full-crew laws within various states, which required larger-than-necessary numbers of on-train operating employees; (4) relief from obligations for employee protective and severance payments; and (5) a mandate that Conrail either meet two profitability tests by 1983 or be dismembered and sold (U.S. House 1980; U.S. House 1981).[27]

Exit ICC; Enter STB

The fourth and latest statutory change in rail economic regulation occurred on 29 December 1995, when President Clinton signed the ICC Termination Act of 1995 (ICCTA) into law.[28] The act abolished the then-108-year-old ICC on 31 December 1995 and created a new agency, the Surface Transportation Board (STB), to administer the vestiges of economic regulation that survive under the ICCTA. The basic policy thrusts of these vestiges insofar as they involve rail freight transport are as follows (Spychalski 1997, 135):

- Rely on market forces to determine price and service quality levels wherever competition is judged sufficiently workable.
- Regulate price and service quality in markets where economic injury from abuse of monopoly power could occur. The statute specifies an average revenue to variable cost ratio of 180 percent as the threshold above which a rate can be challenged as indicative of the possible existence of excessive market power.

- Maintain connectivity between railway companies to facilitate inter-line services.
- Facilitate transfers of railway infrastructure ownership in ways that hold promise for maintaining service and improving economic performance (for example, sale of lines by larger carriers to short line or regional railways, which can operate them at lower cost and higher levels of customer service).

Results under Diminished Economic Regulation

Performance of the freight railroad industry under diminished economic regulation has been neither disastrous nor stellar. There are variations in progress between different performance factors. The 87 percent rise in rail ton-miles (table 1) between 1975 and 1997 is, by itself, an excellent improvement, and has been accompanied by a modest increase in market share. However, changes in market share for tons carried and revenue (tables 2 and 3) have been, respectively, moderately unfavorable and very unfavorable. An extensive examination of total factor productivity belongs elsewhere. However, it can be noted (table 4) that freight revenue ton-miles per employee and employee-hour have leaped dramatically. It is arguable that several key drivers of this improvement, including large-scale rationalization of track and other physical assets, and trucking competition-induced pressures for reformation of contracts with labor unions, became fully feasible only with deregulation. Indeed, plant rationalization and labor cost reductions were critical to the ultimate success of Conrail. Actions taken by its management that were facilitated by the Staggers Act and NERSA (which temporarily exempted Conrail from ICC line abandonment criteria and procedures) enabled the company to

Table 1   United States Freight Transport Market Share—Ton-Miles (Billions)

	Rail		Road		Oil Pipeline		Water		Air		Total
	Amount	%	Amount	%	Amount	%	Amount	%	Amount	%	(rounded)
1975	759	36.74	454	21.97	507	24.54	342	16.55	3.73	0.18	2,066
1997	1,421	39.23	1,051	29.01	628	17.34	508	14.03	13.87	0.38	3,622

Source: Rosalyn A. Wilson, *Transportation in America 1998* (Washington, D.C.: Eno Transportation Foundation, Inc , Sixteenth Edition, 1998), 44

Table 2 United States Freight Transport Market Share—Tonnage (Millions)

	Rail		Road		Oil Pipeline		Water		Air		Total
	Amount	%	Amount	%	Amount	%	Amount	%	Amount	%	(rounded)
1975	1,471	29.65	1,744	35.15	879	17.71	865	17.43	3.2	0.06	4,962
1997	1,972	25.00	3,745	47.47	1,142	14.47	1,015	12.86	16.3	0.20	7,890

Source: Rosalyn A. Wilson, *Transportation in America 1998* (Washington, D.C.: Eno Transportation Foundation, Inc., Sixteenth Edition, 1998), 46.

Table 3 United States Freight Transport Market Share— Revenue (Millions)

	Rail		Road		Oil Pipeline		Water		Air		Total
	Amount	%	Amount	%	Amount	%	Amount	%	Amount	%	(rounded)
1976	16,509	14.48	84,843	74.39	2,220	1.94	8,221	7.20	2,256	1.97	114,049
1997	35,349	7.08	401,684	80.43	8,735	1.74	25,346	5.08	28,294	5.67	499,408

Sources: Rosalyn A. Wilson, *Transportation in America 1998* (Washington, D.C.: Eno Transportation Foundation, Inc., Sixteenth Edition, 1998), 40; and *Railroad Facts* (Washington, D.C.: Association of American Railroads, 1998), 3.

Table 4 Revenue Ton-Miles Per Employee and Employee-Hour

	Freight Revenue Ton-Miles Per:	
Year	Employee (millions)	Employee-Hour
1975	1.6	690
1980	2.1	863
1985	2.9	1,196
1990	4.8	1,901
1991	5.1	2,020
1992	5.4	2,176
1993	5.8	2,280
1994	6.3	2,509
1995	7.0	2,746
1996	7.5	2,965
1997	7.6	2,973
1998	7.8	2,955

Source: Railroad Facts (Washington, D.C.: Association of American Railroads, 1999), 41.

meet its congressionally mandated profitability tests and avert dismemberment and sale.

Other performance factors reveal more modest results. The combination of (1) a plateauing of Class I carriers' constant-dollar operating revenue and net railway operating income (table 5); (2) an almost unbroken decline in revenue per ton-mile since 1982 (figure 3), coupled with the previously noted significant increases in ton-miles of traffic, and (3) the persistence of shortfalls between rate of return on assets and cost of capital (table 6), indicates that the railways have been "hauling more for less" through most of the 1980s and all of the 1990s. Consequently, the significant gains achieved through dramatic increases in productivity have been captured more fully by rail shippers than by rail carriers.[29]

End-of-Century Discontent

Paradoxically, shippers' capture of much of the gain from sharply improved rail productivity has been accompanied by rising shipper dis-

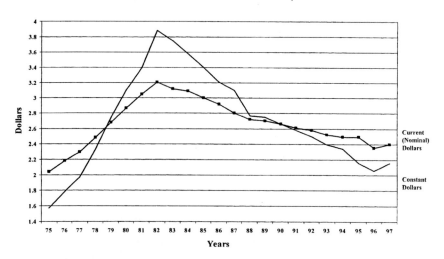

Figure 3   United States Railway Freight Revenue Per Ton-Mile in Current (Nominal) and Constant 1990 Dollars (1990–100).
Source: Computed from data presented in Rosalyn A. Wilson, *Transportation in America 1998* (Washington, D.C.: Eno Transportation Foundation, Inc., Sixteenth Edition, 1998), p. 49. Constant dollar values are based on the Producer Price Index, published in *Economic Indicators* by the President's Council of Economic Advisors.

Table 5 Financial Performance of United States Class I Freight Railroads—Operating Revenue and Net Railway Operating Income—Selected Years, 1975–1997

	Nominal Dollars		Constant Dollars (1990 = 100)[3]	
Year	Operating Revenue[1]	Net Railway Operating Income[2]	Operating Revenue	Net Railway Operating Income
1975	$ 16.4 billion	$ 351 million	$ 24.8 billion	$ 530 million
1980	28.2 billion	1.33 billion	35.5 billion	1.68 billion
1985	27.5 billion	1.74 billion	30.8 billion	1.95 billion
1990	28.3 billion	2.64 billion	28.3 billion	2.64 billion
1992	28.3 billion	1.95 billion	27.3 billion	1.88 billion
1994	30.8 billion	3.39 billion	29.2 billion	3.21 billion
1995	32.2 billion	2.85 billion	29.8 billion	2.64 billion
1996	32.6 billion	4.33 billion	29.3 billion	3.88 billion
1997	33.1 billion	3.98 billion	29.6 billion	3.55 billion
1998	33.1 billion	3.69 billion	29.8 billion	3.33 billion

[1] Includes revenue from freight movements plus income from switching (shunting), demurrage and incidental charges.

[2] Excludes non-operating income and expenses and fixed charges (interest expense).

[3] Calculations based on Producer Price Index data presented in Rosalyn A. Wilson, *Transportation in America 1998*, 17th ed. (Washington, D.C.: Eno Transportation Foundation, Inc, 1999), 49.

Source: Railroad Facts (Washington, D.C.: Association of American Railroads, 1999), pp.12, 17.

Table 6 Financial Performance of United States Class I Railroads —
Rate of Return on Net Investment vs. Regulatory Cost of Capital —
Selected Years, 1975–1997

Year	Rate of Return on Net Investment[1] %	Regulatory Cost of Capital (Debt plus Equity)[2] %	Difference Between Rate of Return on Net Investment and Cost of Capital— Favorable, (Unfavorable)
1975	1.20	N/A	N/A
1980	4.22	12.1	(7.88)
1985	4.58	13.6	(9.02)
1990	8.11	11.8	(3.69)
1991	1.30	11.6	(10.3)
1992	6.30	11.4	(5.10)
1993	7.06	11.4	(4.34)
1994	9.37	12.2	(2.83)
1995	7.04	11.7	(4.66)
1996	9.36	11.9	(2.54)
1997	7.57	11.8	(4.23)
1998	7.00	10.7	(3.70)

[1] Ratio of net railway operating income (NROI) to average net investment in property used for conducting rail transport service. NROI excludes non-operating income and expenses and fixed charges (interest expenses).

[2] Based on the Surface Transportation Board's annual determination which calculates pre-tax cost of debt and post-tax cost of equity.

Source: Railroad Facts (Washington, D.C.: Association of American Railroads, 1999), 18–19.

content toward the railway industry. Manifestations of this include the introduction of legislative proposals in recent sessions of Congress providing for partial restoration of economic regulation or competitive access requirements. None of these proposals, which differ in content, have moved close to enactment.[30] Frustrated by this inertia, interest groups supportive of the proposals orchestrated the drafting and transmittal of a letter, dated 26 September 2000, to the chairman and the ranking member of the Senate Commerce Committee. Signed by almost 270 chief executive officers of major corporations and trade associations, the letter asks "that shipper concerns with current national rail policy be given priority for Commerce Committee action next Congress. . . ." (Attachment 2000). Impetus for this lobbying effort stems from dissatisfaction of shippers and their political allies with the following real and/or perceived conditions (Attachment 2000; Buxbaum 2000; U.S. General Accounting Office 1999; Gallagher 1999; Gallagher 2000).

- Various dimensions of rail price discrimination, including access pricing in so-called bottleneck situations,[31] and pricing (and operational) access for captive shippers in terminal areas.[32]
- Increased concentration and decreased intramodal competition resulting from industry consolidation that reduced the number of independent Class I U.S. and Canadian railroads from thirty in 1976 to seven in 2000.
- Service degradation, in some instances massive, from which recovery was slow, following merger of the Union Pacific and Southern Pacific systems in 1996, and the split of Conrail's network between Norfolk Southern and CSX Transportation on 1 June 1999.
- Imposition of larger minimum-volume requirements for the tendering of rail shipments.
- Unresponsiveness of the STB to complaints against rail carriers.

A full assessment of these conditions exceeds present space. Suffice it to observe that the first bulleted point is indicative of a quest for further rate reductions. Shippers apparently are not satisfied with the long post-1982 decline in rail charges revealed by the average revenue per ton-mile trend in figure 3. This may stem in part from the fact that rates have not declined proportionately for all shippers. A study of changes in rates for all major rail freight commodity groups between 1982 and 1996 revealed greater average annual decreases for some groups than for others. Also contributing to differential distribution of decreases is discrimination in rates for movements within the same commodity group or subgroup, based on locational, directional, and time characteristics. Further, rates for some movements have not fallen (U.S. General Accounting Office 1999, chap. 3).

As noted previously (tables 5 and 6), the freight railway industry has not been generating monopoly profits (even though a study for the years 1990–96 found that about one-third of its total revenues came from shipments carried at rates that generated revenues exceeding 180 percent of variable costs) (U.S. General Accounting Office 1999, 61–63). Indeed, data presented in table 6 portray inadequate returns. This raises the question of how shippers' desire for lower rates through reductions in freight rate discrimination can be reconciled with the industry's need to generate funds sufficient to (1) cover the large blocks of indivisible costs that stand between total costs and causally identifiable costs in rail firms' cost structures; (2) fund renewal and improvement of capital intensive infrastructure as well as motive power, rolling stock, and other vital components of its asset base; and (3) improve customer service. Some legislators apparently believe that this question should not be a matter of concern for regulators. A bipartisan bill sponsored during the current session of Congress by Senators John D. Rockefeller IV and Conrad Burns would eliminate the STB's responsibility for providing analyses of railway revenue adequacy (Buxbaum 2000, 1A). If such a measure wins enactment, it will mark a step back toward the pre-1920 narrow-focused ICC philosophy that equated minimization of rates with maximization of shipper welfare.

Concluding Observations

Infrastructure—its financing, construction, ownership, degree of sunkenness, the pricing of its use, and its disinvestment—stands at the base of 170 years of issues and choices in the social control of rail transport. Integration of infrastructure control with vehicle (service) operation within privately owned firms set the combination of conditions that made invention and application of economic regulation necessary in the nineteenth century—large aggregations of financial capital and their attendant power, the presence of substantial economies of scope and density, large gaps between causally identifiable transport service (sales) unit costs and total costs, and significant externalities.

Throughout its existence, economic regulation of transport as a process has proven capable of acting, albeit not consistently, as a potent instrument of constraint and as a grantor of permission with its quasi-judicial case-by-case approach. However, it has never on its own initiative proven capable of developing and administering comprehensive long-range plans for the performance of the industry (or industries) under its jurisdiction. In the one instance where Congress gave it a mandate (but, arguably, insufficient power) to plan—railway consolidation, in the Transportation Act of 1920—regulation not only failed but aided the implementation of private plans for corporate combinations that conflicted with its own tentative plan.

Extension of federal economic regulation to all nonrail modes of transport between 1935 and 1940 was Joseph B. Eastman's grand design. It was a vision achieved with the power provided by his role as federal coordinator of transportation rather than as a member of the ICC, and a vision intended to prevent the self-destruction of a Depression-beleaguered transport system. Yet even Eastman lacked a clear perspective of how the comprehensive framework would function insofar as it applied to rate competition between rail transport and other modes following the post-1945 proliferation of motor and inland water carrier services. Umbrella rate making benefited motor and water carriers and localities dependent on their freight traffic flow patterns, but imposed opportunity costs on rail carriers and shippers who were in a position to benefit from competitive rate reductions.

Present-day challenges confronting the STB are strikingly similar to some of those faced by the ICC in earlier phases of its existence. In particular, further consolidation of the railway industry requires guidance in ways that hold promise for avoiding deterioration in service quality and preventing the loss of sustainable intramodal competition in markets large enough to support it. Equally important, aggregated bargaining and political power of shippers in industries and even individual firms far larger than the entire railway industry must be prevented from capturing gains in the form of reduced rates or enhanced services that leave railway companies unable to recapitalize themselves. Monopsony and oligopsony require surveillance and control no less than monopoly.

Notes

1. Writing in the mid-1880s, Henry Carter Adams (Dorfman 1954, 117) decried such constitutional provisions. In his view, they restricted the supply of inland transport service, a function of high public importance and responsibility, to private corporations that wielded power over legislation and the behavior of public officials in magnitudes such as to "menace the stability of society. . . ."

2. In a few instances, municipalities have engaged in railway ownership and operation, or ownership with operation leased to a private railway company. Most such ventures have been local connectors to nearby main lines of privately owned carriers. A notable exception is the Cincinnati Southern, extending from Cincinnati, Ohio, to Chattanooga, Tennessee. Built and owned by the city of Cincinnati and opened for traffic in 1877, it has been operated under lease since 1881 by the present-day Norfolk Southern Railway and predecessor companies.

3. Approximately 150 railway companies also obtained land for rail operational purposes only under legislation that granted rights-of-way through federally owned public lands (Locklin 1972, 132).

4. Partial exceptions to such vertical integration can be seen in trackage rights agreements under which one railway can operate trains over the line of another, but with restrictions (usually absolute) on access to customers of the "landlord" carrier, thus preserving the latter's monopoly position. Another exception arose in the 1990s in the United Kingdom, when infrastructure ownership was split from ownership of freight and passenger service operation as part of the privatization of that country's nationalized rail system.

5. Less significant was charter regulation, which involved the inclusion of public interest protection provisions in early railway charters of incorporation granted through state legislation. Such provisions proved largely ineffective. Also of lesser significance were the railroad commissions that were established in the 1830s and 1840s in some New England states. Their powers and accomplishments were limited.

6. 24 Stat. 379 (4 February 1887).

7. Before joining the ICC, Cooley served as a professor of law at the University of Michigan and as a justice of the Michigan Supreme Court. At the time of his appointment to the commission, he was a receiver of the bankrupt Wabash Railway's lines east of the Mississippi (Hoogenboom and Hoogenboom 1976, 19).

8. *United States v. Trans-Missouri Freight Association*, 166 US 290; and *United States v. Joint Traffic Association*, 171 US 505.

9. In particular, Franklin K. Lane, a Californian who had fought railroad monopoly in that state; Charles C. McChord, who had drafted Kentucky's rail regulatory statute and chaired the Kentucky Railroad Commission; and Balthasar H. Meyer, a distinguished scholar of transport history, economics, and policy who had moved from a faculty position at the University of Wisconsin to the Wisconsin Railroad Commission.

10. The Mann-Elkins Act of 1910 placed burden of proof of the reasonableness of individual rates on the carrier.

11. Joining in this vote was Commissioner Balthasar H. Meyer. Earlier, while a member of the faculty at the University of Wisconsin, Meyer had written a volume on railway legislation (as one in a series of works edited by Professor Richard T. Ely) in which he presented a reasoned critique of both railroad management practices and public policy toward rail transport. One writer has suggested that (1) Meyer's vote in the 1911 rate case decision and his actions in the two that followed were at variance with his earlier writings, and (2) that this variance could be explained by Meyer's desire to retain the favor of his political sponsor for membership on the ICC, Senator Robert M. La Follette Sr., of Wisconsin, who opposed rate increases and detested rail corporate behavior (Martin 1971, 180–81; 357–58].

12. The Erdman Act of 1898, and the more stringent Newlands Act that replaced it in 1913, gave the ICC's chairman and the U.S. commissioner of labor authority to mediate disputes between rail labor and management. Exercise of this power resulted in substantial wage increases for operating employees. State

governments imposed additional labor costs by passing so-called full crew laws, which required additional personnel for operation of trains beyond specified lengths. They also mandated railway capital outlays for safety-related projects such as grade crossing elimination and installation of warning devices. In 1916, to avert a strike by train and engine service personnel, Congress and President Wilson passed the Adamson Act, which established eight hours as the basic workday in freight train service. This entailed overtime payments for time on duty beyond eight hours and caused a substantial increase in railway wage expenses (Hines 1928, 5; Hoogenboom and Hoogenboom 1976, 59).

13. In partial support of their August 1915 denial of a request by railways in the West for a selective 2 percent increase on ten heavily trafficked commodities with very low rates, commissioners voting in the majority cited violations of fiduciary trust by officials of the Chicago, Rock Island & Pacific, the Chicago & Alton, and the St. Louis-San Francisco. Daniels decried this as having punished owners of railways managed "with integrity and honesty" as well as the "luckless shareholders" of the looted companies (Hoogenboom and Hoogenboom 1976, 76).

14. Daniels' policy perspective in the rate cases aroused anger among Progressive Republicans. When President Wilson submitted Daniels' name to the Senate for reappointment in January 1917, Senators Robert M. La Follette Sr. (Wisconsin), Albert B. Cummins (Iowa), and William E. Borah (Idaho) tried to block it. They failed. Daniels was confirmed by a vote of forty-two to thirteen (Martin 1971, 316–18).

15. Federal control officially took effect at noon on 28 December 1917 (Hines 1928, 247).

16. The federal government compensated carriers subjected to its control with payments "not exceeding their respective average annual net railway operating income from operation in the three years ending June 30, 1917" (Hines 1928, 28).

17. Technically, the title, Act to Regulate Commerce, was used until 1920; after that date it was referred to as the Interstate Commerce Act (Locklin 1972, 243).

18. Senator Robert M. La Follette Sr. voiced strong objection to this change in regulatory philosophy. In essence, he believed that it would result in an unjustifiable transfer of income from shippers and passengers to railway companies (Hoogenboom and Hoogenboom 1976, 95).

19. Valuation of railway property for use in rate making had been an issue of longstanding debate, as a result of rail capitalization practices mentioned earlier in this essay that caused so-called stock watering and the carrying of assets on balance sheets at values in excess of their actual acquisition costs. In an effort to obtain an accurate measure of the value of the industry's asset base for use in rate regulation, Congress passed the Valuation Act of 1913. To carry out this task, a Bureau of Valuation was established within the ICC. The bureau embarked an exhaustive engineering-based inventory and evaluation of the assets of each

individual railway company. This work consumed substantial resources and took twenty years to complete (Locklin 1972, 237–38; Moulton and Associates 1933, chap. 17). In rate cases handled prior to completion of the valuation project, the ICC was to devise alternative means for determining the value of rail assets.

20. "The other half of the excess was to be retained by the carrier, but was to be placed in a reserve fund for the payment of interest, dividends, and rentals to the extent that its income in any year fell short of 6 percent on the value of its property, and the fund might not be drawn upon for any other purpose. When the reserve fund amounted to more than 5 percent of the value of its property, the carrier was to be permitted to use its share of further excess earnings for any lawful purpose" (Locklin 1972, 245; Moulton and Associates 1933, chap. 18).

21. Compulsory power for railway consolidations was proposed by Senator Albert B. Cummins in 1919. However, Cummins envisaged that it would be administered by a new transportation board rather than the ICC. It thus is not surprising that the commission opposed Cummins's compulsory approach under a separate administrative body, and "favored permissive consolidation under its supervision" (Hoogenboom and Hoogenboom 1976, 93–94).

As in the United States, the close of World War I and the turn of the decade marked a watershed for transport policy in the United Kingdom. Like the United States, Britain considered and rejected government ownership (at that time). Unlike the United States, however, it compelled by legislation (the Railways Act of 1921) the amalgamation of 120 privately owned railway companies into four large privately owned systems (Simmons and Biddle 1999, 197).

22. Commissioner Joseph B. Eastman contended that some of these transactions violated the Clayton Antitrust Act (Hoogenboom and Hoogenboom 1976, 108).

23. The centerpiece of the Emergency Railroad Transportation Act of 1933 was a provision requiring that the Federal Coordinator provide assistance and leadership to the railway industry in achieving reductions in the cost of rail operation through coordination and consolidation of duplicate terminals, rolling stock, motive power, personnel, and other items. Eastman's attempts to fulfill this duty were frustrated by opposition from railroad management and organized labor and, in the judgment of Latham (1959, chap. 21), Eastman's own administrative style.

24. 54 Stat. 898 (18 September 1940).

25. The planning for a reorganized northeastern rail network based on the properties of the bankrupt carriers was conducted by the United States Railway Association (the second rail-focused government agency within the century to have the initials USRA). In addition to its planning function, this agency served as the conduit for the payment of government funds to Conrail, and as a monitor of Conrail's performance during the early years of its existence (Perrit 1983).

26. Public Law 94–210, 5 February 1976.

27. The Northeast Rail Services Act was included in the Omnibus Budget

Reconciliation Act of 1981. This was an adroit political maneuver. It prevented NERSA from being subjected to separate consideration on the floor of either the Senate or the House of Representatives, and thus defused the lobbying power of railway labor and other stakeholders in the measure.

28. ICC Termination Act of 1995, Public Law 104–88, 104th Congress, 109 Stat. 803 (29 December 1995), 49 USC 101.

29. Portions of this section and the preceding section are based on an unpublished paper by the author (Spychalski 1999).

30. Two of the bills introduced in the current session of Congress would (1) mandate that the STB insure reasonable rail rates where there is no competition; (2) eliminate volume requirements; (3) overturn STB bottleneck decisions; (4) change rules for captive shippers in terminal areas; (5) eliminate analyses of product and geographic competition in rate cases; and (6) eliminate railroad revenue adequacy analysis by the STB (Buxbaum 2000, 1A).

31. "Bottleneck" refers to a situation in which a single railway serves a facility that either originates or receives rail traffic, although another railway is able to carry that traffic for part of its through or overall movement.

32. A rail carrier that serves a particular locality cannot access shippers or receivers of freight with private sidings located on the line of another railway serving the same locality unless (1) a reciprocal switching or trackage rights agreement is in place between the two carriers; (2) the charges for reciprocal switching or trackage rights usage are affordable; and (3) the carrier owning the line does not hinder movement of the other carrier's traffic with artificial operating constraints.

References

Adams, Henry Carter. [1887]. 1954. *Relation of the state to industrial action and economics and jurisprudence*. New York: Columbia University Press.

Attachment. 2000. Hundreds of business lenders unite in message to Congress, *News Release*, American Chemical Council, et al., 27 September.

Bonavia, Michael R. 1958. *The economics of transport*. Digswell Place: James Nisbet and Company, Ltd. and Cambridge: Cambridge University Press.

Burgess, George H., and Miles C. Kennedy. 1949. *Centennial history of the Pennsylvania Railroad Company*. Philadelphia: ThePennsylvania Railroad Company.

Buxbuam, Peter A. 2000. Captive shippers lobby Congress for relief, *Journal of American Transport*, 13 March, 1A, 9A.

Coyle, John J. 1969. The ingot molds case and competitive ratemaking, *I.C.C. Practitioners' Journal* 36 (4): 1654–72.

Dearing, Charles L., and Wilfred Owen. 1949. *National transportation policy*. Washington, D.C.: Brookings Institution Press.

Derleth, August. 1948. *The Milwaukee road*. New York: Creative Age Press.

Dorfman, Joseph. 1954. Introductory essay. In *Relation of the state to industrial action and economics and jurisprudence,* by Henry Carter Adams. New York: Columbia University Press.

Eastman, Joseph B. 1940. The adjustment of rates between competing forms of transportation, *American Economic Review* 30 (1) Supp. Part 2: 124–29.

Gallagher, John. 1999. NS-CSX shipper requests emergency service order; STB wants more data, *Traffic World,* 15 November, 52–53.

———. 2000. CSX wants rates to reflect "seller's market" but shippers wonder "what about service?" *Traffic World,* 7 February, 10–11.

Goodrich, Carter. 1960. *Government promotion of American canals and railroads, 1800–1890.* New York: Columbia University Press.

Hadley, Arthur T. 1888. *Railroad transportation.* New York: G.P. Putnam's Sons.

Harbeson, Robert W. 1962. The regulation of interagency rate competition under the Transportation Act of 1958, *I.C.C. Practitioners' Journal* 30 (3): 287–308.

Hargrave, Frank F. 1932. *A Pioneer Indiana railroad.* Indianapolis: Wm. B. Burford Printing Co.

Harlow, Alvin F. 1947. *The road of the century.* New York: Creative Age Press.

Hines, Walker D. 1928. *War history of American railroads.* New Haven, Conn.: Yale University Press.

Hofsommer, Don L. 1986. *The Southern Pacific, 1901–1985.* College Station: Texas A&M University Press.

Holbrook, Stewart H. 1947. *The story of American railroads.* New York: Crown Publishers.

Hoogenboom, Ari, and Olive Hoogenboom. 1976. *A history of the ICC.* New York: W.W. Norton.

ICC. 1963. 1965. *Grain in Multiple-Car Shipments—River Crossings to South.* 318 ICC 641; 325 ICC 752.

———. 1965. *Ingot molds from Pennsylvania to Steelton, KY.* 323 ICC 758.

Larson, John L. 1984. *Bonds of enterprise—John Murray Forbes and western development in America's railway age.* Boston: Division of Research, Graduate School of Business, Harvard University.

Latham, Earl. 1959. *The politics of railroad coordination.* Cambridge, Mass.: Harvard University.

Locklin, D. Philip. 1972. *Economics of transportation.* Homewood, Ill.: Richard D. Irwin, Inc.

Martin, Albro. 1971. *Enterprise denied.* New York: Columbia University Press.

MacGill, Caroline E.. [1917]. 1948. *History of transportation in the United States before 1860.* Carnegie Institution of Washington Publication No. 215c. Forge Village: Murray Printing Company. Reprinted by Peter Smith.

Milne, A. M. 1960. *The economics of inland transport.* London: Sir Isaac Pitman & Sons.

Moulton, Harold G., and Associates. 1933. *The American transportation problem.* Washington, D.C.: Brookings Institution Press.

Nelson, James C. 1959. *Railroad transportation and public policy*. Washington, D.C.: Brookings Institution Press.

———. 1975. The changing economic case for surface transport regulation. In *Perspectives on federal transportation policy*, edited by James C. Miller III. Washington, D.C.: American Enterprise Institute for Public Policy Research.

Overton, Richard C. 1965. *Burlington route*. New York: Alfred A. Knopf.

Perritt, Henry H. 1983. Ask and ye shall receive: The legislative response to the northeast rail crisis *Villanova Law Review* 28 (2): 271–377.

Rehor, John A. 1965. *The nickel plate story*. Milwaukee, Wisc.: Kalmbach Publishing Co.

Ripley, William Z. 1912. *Railroads: Rates and regulation*. New York: Longmans, Green, and Co.

———. 1913. *Railway problems*. Boston: Ginn and Company.

Sabin, Edwin L. 1919. *Building the Pacific Railway*. Philadelphia: J.B. Lippincott Co.

Seely, Bruce E. 1987. *Building the American highway system*. Philadelphia: Temple University Press.

Simmons, Jack, and Gordon Biddle, eds. 1999. *The Oxford companion to British railway history*. Oxford: Oxford University Press.

Spychalski, John C. 1997. From ICC to STB: Continuing vestiges of U.S. surface transport regulation. *Journal of Transport Economics and Policy* 31 (1): 131–36.

———. 1999. Two decades of diminished economic regulation: results and challenges for the United States railway industry. Paper presented at International Conference on Regulatory Reforms in the Railway Sector, 14 June, at Stockholm School of Economics, Stockholm, Sweden.

U.S. Department of Transportation. 1976. *America's highways 1776/1976: A history of the federal-aid program*. Washington, D.C.: GPO.

U.S. General Accounting Office (USGAO). 1999. *Railroad regulation—Changes in railroad rates and service quality since 1990*, Report to Congressional Requesters, GAO/RCED—99–93.

U.S. House. 1935. *Report of the federal coordinator of transportation, 1934.* 74th Cong. H. Doc. 89.

———. 1936. *Fourth report of the federal coordinator of transportation on transportation legislation.* 74th Cong. 2d sess. H. Doc. 394.

———. 1976. *Railroad revitalization and reform act of 1976*. Report of the Committee Conference on 5.2718. 94th Cong., 2nd sess. H. Report, no. 94–781.

———. 1980. To reform the economic regulation of railroads and for other purposes. Report of the Committee on Conference on S. 1946. 96th Cong, 2d sess. House Rept., no. 96–1430. 307–52.

———. 1981. *Northeast Rail Services Act of 1981*. Omnibus Budget Reconciliation Act of 1981, Conference Report. 97th Cong. 1st sess. Rept. no. 97–208.

U.S. Senate. 1874. *Transportation routes to the seaboard*. 43d Cong., 1st sess. Senate Rep., no. 307.

————. 1934. *Regulation of transportation agencies.* 73d Cong., 2d sess. S. Doc. 152.

————. 1961. *National transportation policy.* 87th Cong., 1st sess. Preliminary Draft of a Report Prepared for the Committee on Interstate and Foreign Commerce, U.S. Senate, by the Special Study Group.

————. 1973. *The Penn Central and other railroads.* 92d Cong., 2d sess.

Waters, L. L. 1950. *Steel trails to Santa Fe.* Lawrence: University of Kansas Press.

Williams, Jr., Ernest W. 1958. *The regulation of rail-motor rate competition.* New York: Harper.

Trucking Deregulation Disproves Positive Political Theory

KENNETH D. BOYER

"Positive Political Theory" builds a model of regulatory behavior on the assumption that regulators, like other economic actors, are maximizing a private interest.[1] The private interest that is maximized is "political support," or the probability of getting reelected or reappointed. Transferring resources from an unorganized part of the population to a group that knows its own self-interest and is willing to spend to promote it can increase this probability. According to this theory, the essence of regulation is taxation of one group and subsidization of another with the goal of reelecting the regulator.

The appeal of Positive Political Theory is to treat regulators as individuals with the same assumed motivations as consumers and producers, not as selfless public servants maximizing an ill-defined "public interest." Americans have historically been distrustful of their governments. Positive Political Theory, with its scent of corruption and vote buying, finds a resonance within this anti-government tradition. The actors of Positive Political Theory seem much more human and believable than the fair, sober-minded, and disinterested social planners often assumed in economic models.

Yet simply because Positive Political Theory makes the plausible claim that regulators should be seen as self-interested maximizers rather than as public servants does not make the theory correct. This chapter uses what is probably the most important U.S. deregulatory event—trucking deregulation—to argue that Positive Political Theory simply misses the mark as a tool for understanding the motives of regulators and the impetus for regulatory change.

Trucking deregulation is more than a minor event—one that can be dismissed as an unimportant or aberrant instance in which Positive Political Theory failed to coherently provide an explanation for the action. Trucking is the major transportation industry, far larger than either railroads or airlines. To the academic economist, there was no industry more deserving of being deregulated. Trucking deregulation is also considered (at least by academic economists) to be the major unalloyed success of the deregulation movement.[2] It is the archetypal example of an industry where deregulation produced major benefits and no problems to the public. Motor carrier deregulation did not lead to rapid increases in rates for some shippers and a significant contraction in service for others, as railroad deregulation did. Unlike the airline industry, where deregulation continues to be plagued by problems of inadequate competition, trucking deregulation went smoothly and has generated no complaints from the using public. For Positive Political Theory to be taken seriously, it must give us insight into the timing and logic of trucking deregulation. It is the thesis of this chapter that Positive Political Theory fails this test.

This chapter first discusses how trucking regulation was practiced. As emphasized in the following, regulation covered many practices that do not fit well with Positive Political Theory. The two phases of trucking deregulation are then discussed. The chapter shows that Positive Political Theory can explain neither the form that trucking regulation took nor the timing of when trucking regulation disappeared. Positive Political Theory thus fails the test of consistency of prediction and observation.

The chapter concludes by showing that trucking deregulation can be understood if regulation is seen as motivated by the issues of equity and stability. This chapter does not claim that deregulation was made inevitable by the economic climate in 1980 and 1994–95. The institutional change was not forced by economic conditions. The 1980 bill was the direct result of some strategic blundering by the trucking industry. In the case of the 1994–95 bills, it was forced by outside interests. However, the public policy discussions in 1980 and in 1994–95 revealed that regulatory intervention in the trucking industry was not doing what it was supposed to—neither stabilizing an inherently unstable industry nor correcting equity failures that were the natural result of the economics of the industry. It became quite clear, in fact, that equity was being badly skewed in this case and that the institution was causing efficiency problems as well. This revelation of the true nature of trucking regulation made it difficult to make the affirmative case for continued regulation of the trucking industry.

How Trucking Was Regulated

Regulation is portrayed in economics classrooms by drawing a straight line across a set of cost curves, indicating that the regulator fixes prices rather than allowing prices to be set by market conditions. The interesting question, then, is the level at which those prices are set. If the horizontal line is drawn at average cost, shown as P_1 in figure 1, we can tentatively accept the hypothesis that regulators are motivated by the aim of maximizing the sum of consumer plus producers surplus subject to a break-even constraint. If a line is drawn above average cost, shown as P_2 in figure 1, the analysis supports Positive Political Theory—or at least the idea that there is a motive other than the maximization of economic efficiency at work in the determination of pricing in this industry.

Yet this analysis is a bad cartoon of what trucking regulation really did. It draws attention away from the goals and problems of regulation, both of which focused on the structure of prices and services, rather than on the average revenue level.[3]

Trucking regulation cannot be understood without recognizing the historical setting in which it developed. When Congress passed the Motor Carrier Act of 1935, the emerging trucking industry was seen as suffering from low rates brought about by excessive competition.[4] The same problem had been identified as afflicting railroads fifteen years earlier, a problem that was apparently solved through railroad regulation. It was then only natural that a successful agency like the Interstate Commerce Commission (ICC) would be asked to take on the responsibility of dealing with what appeared to be problems in the trucking industry that were similar to those in the railroad industry. This solution had the added benefit of curbing excess intermodal competition—a problem that was beginning to affect the ICC's ability to control prices and services in the railroad industry.

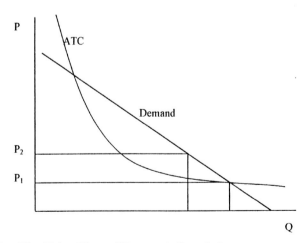

Figure 1   The Naive View of Economic Regulation.

The analysis of the trucking industry as suffering from ruinous competition was, however, incorrect from the beginning. Railroads theoretically may have a problem with excess competition, but the trucking industry does not. Trucking and railroad economics have little in common, other than that they are both network industries. The ICC also did not view trucking control as its primary function—it was the railroad industry whose behavior took up most of its regulatory attention. The trucking industry, far from being the focus of attention of its regulatory agency, was regulated by a distracted agency, following the railroad model—a model that was inappropriate for its economic conditions. It is generally not recognized how pervasive and how inappropriate trucking regulation was for the industry. The following discussion highlights some of the elements of trucking regulation.

The Route Structure

The first tasks of the new trucking regulators were to set up a route structure for each motor carrier and to draw up rules of traffic interchange that were borrowed directly from the railroad industry. There is no economic reason that trucking firms should have a fixed network. They have no fixed facilities other than the terminals that they use to collect, break, and distribute that part of their traffic that is less-than-truckload shipments. One of the advantages that trucking firms have over railroads is that they are not bound to a route. If they lose a customer in one traffic lane, they can easily switch their equipment to a different lane. By requiring all motor carriers to have a route certificate (granted by a simple showing that the company had carried goods on this route before 1935) for all connections that they might wish to serve, regulation forced trucking companies to take on some of the economic characteristics of railroads. It also prevented trucking companies from achieving the advantages of traffic density that an efficient hub and spoke system provides. The licensing procedure also effectively protected small local trucking companies from competition from larger firms with a broader national coverage. New route certificates were granted only upon showing that existing services on a route were inadequate. There were strict criteria used to evaluate the adequacy of service, with the burden of proof placed on the applicant. A showing that that the applicant could provide cheaper service between two endpoints was not sufficient to show that existing service was inadequate.[5]

The Rate Structure

In addition to forcing the trucking industry to adopt railroad-style route structures, the Interstate Commerce Commission also adopted techniques for rate regulation borrowed from railroads. Under this system, there were two different procedures, one for average rate levels and one for individual rates. Rate level regulation took the form of a request from the industry for a percentage increase in freight charges—for example, a 3 percent increase in all rates. This general rate increase was supported by data on fuel and labor costs or the decline in the average profitability of a typical firm in the industry. The logic of general rate increases required collective rate making; hence, regulation permitted and encouraged firms in each mode of transport to get together to prepare rate requests. The ICC then played a passive role in approving or denying requests prepared by the industry as a whole.

While general rate increases were the most visible part of rate regulation, they were not the most important part. The regulated rate structure consisted of a set of high list prices combined with a regulatory-approved set of rate reductions for each commodity and locality. The rate reductions were negotiated between shipper and carrier and were then passed on to the industry rate bureau. If a rate proposed for one shipper was sufficiently low that it threatened the profitability of traffic moved by another carrier, the rate could be disapproved by the rate bureau. If confirmed by the rate bureau, it was passed on to the Interstate Commerce Commission for approval or disapproval. If it was rejected by the rate bureau, a carrier who wanted to put the rate into effect had to bear the expense of publishing the rate itself and defending it before the regulatory commission. Few chose to do so.

The rate structure that developed was very complex. Since effective rates were applicable for specific commodities in specific sizes between very finely defined end points, published rates numbered in the billions (at a time before computer retrieval of information) and there was little indexing. Given the vast number of rate changes that required action, the commission had little choice but to approve most of them. The Interstate Commerce Commission, even if it were inclined to closely supervise rate setting, did not have the practical ability to do so.

Were regulation as simple as was shown in figure 1, it would have been possible to effectively control rates. Railroad regulation clearly was effective in altering the rate from what it would have been had the regulatory authorities not intervened. Yet railroads have only a handful of customers on each line. Regulation using a system of individualized rates is possible in this situation. By contrast, it was impossible to give more than nominal oversight to rate making in the trucking sector, with its millions of customers and billions of routes. Throughout the rise of the trucking industry in the 1950s and 1960s, the regulation of trucking prices should be seen as collusive price setting with little more than nominal control by a government agency.

The Control of Operations

Regulation gave each trucking company a fixed network with limited coverage. If shippers wished to move goods to a point off the route system of the originating carrier, a connection was necessary to a second carrier, and sometimes to additional carriers. One way of exercising market power was for a motor carrier to leverage a strong position when making a traffic interchange—perhaps by insisting on a high rate division or interchanging only a small quantity of traffic. In order to prevent this from occurring, and to insure that the transportation map would be operated as a unified system, the ICC created rules for the interchange of freight and equipment—regulations again borrowed from the railroad industry. An important part of these rules was the prices that carriers could charge for services that they provided to one another. In particular, the ICC had the power to control the division of rates between originating, terminating, and bridge carriers. All this was done to promote the ideal of common carriage in the trucking industry.

Regulatory commissions were also charged with insuring carrier safety. Under this charge the ICC controlled the number of hours that drivers were permitted to be behind the wheel and how hazardous materials were to be handled—regulations that are still enforced today by the ICC's successor agency, the Surface Transportation Board. Trucking regulatory rules also contained extensive labor protection paralleling that adopted for railroads, insuring that a motor carrier could not abrogate a labor agreement simply by selling the concern to another carrier. Labor protection rules were credited with facilitating the organization of trucking labor by the Teamsters Union.[6] The ICC enforced rules on the extent to which drivers could be asked to load and unload their own trucks as well as conditions under which owner-operators could lease their services to major carriers. All of these actions affected trucking industry costs as well as the ability to exercise market power.

Criteria for Regulatory Decisions

Regulation in the trucking sector entailed much more than deciding on the level at which the price line should be drawn across figure 1. Regulation gave great discretion to the regulatory agency on the structure of the industry, its pricing, and its operation. Knowing that the agency had discretion, however, does not tell us how decisions were formed. Under the Interstate Commerce Act and the laws that amended it, the regulatory authority was directed to, "promote safety, honesty, and efficiency; to avoid 'undue' concentration of economic power; to encourage energy conservation; to promote the national defense; to encourage fair wages and working conditions; and to encourage sound economic conditions in transportation and among carriers." The regulatory agency was also directed to further the "public interest" and the "public convenience and necessity."[7] When the agency made its rate decisions, prices were required to be "just, reasonable, and non-discriminatory."

The field of economics has a long history of ignoring professed explanations for behavior. The directive that rates be just, reasonable, and nondiscriminatory was thus widely ignored in the economic analysis of the trucking regulation. Yet the ICC did give meaning to the words through its interpretation. The criteria used, however, were not those of private optimization. For example, in evaluating rates, the regulatory agency tried to insure that large shippers could not use their bargaining power to get lower rates than small shippers and similarly that rural areas—with their necessarily sparser route network—were not disadvantaged relative to urban areas.

Transportation regulation cannot be understood without attempting to analyze concepts of fairness used by the regulatory commissions. Regulators tried to create a transportation system in which everyone—carriers, customers, and the wider community—was treated fairly. Regulation, in short, was supposed to serve the ideal of common carriage, where transport operators would be a silent, neutral, invisible service provider. Just as a water or sewage system is not supposed to maximize profits by discriminating against different landowners, similarly transportation was supposed to facilitate movement without giving preference or prejudice to different individuals.

Regulators also saw themselves as promoting transportation safety. It was part of their congressional charge. By providing financial stability to the trucking industry, it was hoped that motor carriers would have the resources and the financial incentive to maintain their fleets in good operating condition. Licensing requirements were seen as a way to eliminate the "fly-by-night" operator who was considered to be most likely to create safety problems. That licensing also provided a means to exclude new competition, and the benefits that such competition would give to customers were not initially appreciated. In fact, since the original concern that prompted trucking regulation was ruinously low prices, entry limitations were seen as part of the solution to the problem, not a source of concern.

Throughout the era of trucking regulation, cost considerations were given only minor attention. There was general skepticism that costs could be found that were a sufficiently accurate approximation to real costs to be useful in rate making. The insistence on fixed route structures and the implicit increase in bargaining power bestowed upon labor by regulation increased trucking costs significantly.[8] Yet carriers could pass cost increases on to customers without fear of entry. That they did so, and benefited greatly from the process, is not in doubt. In fact, if the simplified analysis in figure 1 is to be used to understand trucking regulation, the effects of regulation should have been twofold: first to raise the average total cost curve and then to set the price line somewhat above the intersection of the demand and the ATC curves. The first of these two effects was more important than the second.

The Circumstances of Interstate Deregulation

After the passage of the Motor Carrier Act of 1935, trucking companies quickly learned that the regulation to which they were subjected provided them with two great advantages: (1) the route certification process effectively protected the industry from new competition; and (2) the rate regulation process could be used to control competition among carriers on any route. Collective rate making, inevitable under the railroad-style regulation chosen by the Interstate Commerce Commission in 1935, was a collusive arrangement that would have been illegal in the rest of American Industry—a violation of Section 1 of the Sherman Act. Yet when it was permitted as part of economic regulation, the trucking industry had an advantage that illegal conspirators did not have. The regulator hired agents who could stop truckers on the highway and ask to inspect their papers, and one of the elements that could be checked for was whether or not a good was being carried at the tariffed rate.

The ability to set rates collectively and the protection that the route licensing requirements provided for the industry afforded an ideal environment for trucking companies to profit.[9] Operating margins throughout the period of regulation were so high and consistent that trucking companies were considered to be very low risk. Tom Donohue, president of the American Trucking Associations, speaking more than a decade after interstate trucking deregulation, described regulated trucking as such an easy business that you could "send a second son into it." [10] Motor carriers took this opportunity to invest by borrowing heavily, using as collateral their route certificates—which became extraordinarily valuable as demand for trucking services increased far faster than new certificates were awarded. This financial leverage, combined with lack of any capacity controls under regulation, left the industry vulnerable when deregulation appeared.

The first break in trucking deregulation occurred due to an accident of politics when President Carter appointed some "policy entrepreneurs"— people with a "public interest" perspective—to the Interstate Commerce Commission. The increased focus on efficiency and implicit reduction in the importance of the other goals of regulation was justified as a means of reducing the rate of price inflation in the economy as a whole. It should also be recognized that the new group of commissioners, those with the perspective assumed by the Public Interest Theory of regulation, was considered to be making decisions in a fundamentally different way than those who had sat on the commission for the previous forty years. When the deregulation-oriented commissioners appointed by the Carter administration chose to eliminate policing functions, it was an odd spectacle to have the regulated industry suing the regulators for not enforcing rules that were presumed to restrict regulated firms.

There were several pieces of evidence used by the new members of the Interstate Commerce Commission to come to the conclusion that trucking regulation was unnecessary. The existence of a parallel unregulated sector (carrying agricultural and other exempt commodities) showed that unregulated trucking could be a quite stable industry. A number of academic articles made a similar point.[11] The newly appointed commissioners were also not convinced that the equity goals of trucking regulation were being met. The obvious profitability of the industry, the high value of route certificates, and high wages of drivers made it appear that the main beneficiaries of trucking regulation were not small businesses or rural areas, but the trucking firms and their drivers.

Administrative deregulation followed quickly behind the appointment of the new commissioners. The Interstate Commerce Commission granted certificates at request to carry freight between any of the forty-eight contiguous states. By administrative decision, the ICC abandoned the practice of forcing interstate trucking companies into the fixed-route mold of railroads. Blanket approval was also given to trucking companies to raise or lower rates from the regulated levels within ever widening bands, thus effectively abandoning the regulation of rate structures that had been the focus of regulatory activity for forty years.

The Motor Carrier Act of 1980 simply ratified the new status quo established by the Carter-appointed members of the Interstate Commerce Commission. The fact that the Teamsters Union and the Regular Route Motor

Common Carrier Association stood alone in defending interstate trucking regulation, unsupported by any of the supposed beneficiaries of government oversight, was an obvious sign to members of Congress that the institution had outlived its usefulness. Still, it seems unlikely that Congress would have deregulated trucking, had not the regulatory agency moved first. Passage of the bill was assured only when it was revealed that the Teamsters Union had attempted to bribe senators to vote to retain regulation.

The Circumstances of Intrastate Trucking Deregulation

The 1980 law affected only interstate trucking. In the case of railroads, interstate deregulation was sufficient to effectively deregulate the whole industry, since intrastate railroad movements are of trivial importance. Such is not the case in trucking. Most of the activity of trucking companies is short-distance. The number of shipments that travel one thousand miles is a small fraction of those that travel less than one hundred miles.[12] Shipments traveling fewer miles are, of course, less likely to cross state lines. Geography, then, determines the importance of intrastate trucking regulation, which was unaffected by the 1980 law.

During the 1980s and early 1990s, a firm wishing to make a shipment out of state could decide which trucking firm to use among the unlimited number who had or could get authority to serve them. Shippers could then negotiate for the best deal. By contrast, if the shipment was intrastate, a firm with the appropriate route certificate needed to be found and the tariffed rate had to be charged. Since intrastate route structures were not optimized for large-scale hub-and-spoke operations, they tended to have higher costs. In addition, the dynamic of higher wages and higher profit margins allowed by collective rate making continued to affect costs and rates in the intrastate industries. Not surprisingly, intrastate rates throughout the 1980s and early 1990s tended to be higher than those charged on interstate routes. Moreover, there was a gross inefficiency of first having interstate freight collected by one carrier, and then having a second carrier calling at the loading dock for intrastate freight. For some shippers, the economical solution was to have all shipments picked up by the interstate carrier and taken out of state for sorting. Those shipments bound for addresses in the same state were then shipped back across state lines in a second unregulated movement.

Despite the fact that academic economists saw traditional forms of regulation as fundamentally inappropriate for the trucking industry, there was no general movement toward intrastate trucking deregulation between

1980 and 1994. One reason may be that the concern about possible economic instability in the deregulated industry was quite genuine. Interstate trucking deregulation was successfully portrayed to state regulators as having been a disaster, leading to widespread bankruptcies among trucking firms, layoffs among employees, rapid consolidation of traffic in a few firms, and unsafe operations. Deregulation at the state level threatened the same economic dislocation.

The characterization of interstate trucking deregulation as leading to financial instability was entirely justified.[13] With deregulation, the trucking industry began to develop an efficient hub-and-spoke system for collecting, transporting, and delivering freight for a large and diverse enough group of shippers to assure a consistently high load factor. It was also immediately apparent to industry members that the ability to develop a route structure freely would give overwhelming advantages to firms with the most extensive route structures. With mergers ruled out by problems of unfunded pension liabilities, the trucking industry embarked on a program of terminal building. This capacity expansion occurred in the early 1980s, at precisely the period when a severe recession reduced the amount of freight being moved. The logical consequence of the resulting overcapacity was financial pressure on the for-hire industry. Unfortunately, the financial leverage that the industry had taken on during the period of regulation—leverage allowed by the high value of route certificates—left it vulnerable when competition and overcapacity appeared. A majority of the top twenty trucking firms prior to deregulation slid into bankruptcy in the years following deregulation and stopped service.

Not all of the members of the trucking industry felt the financial pressures of overcapacity and competition equally. Nonunion regional carriers expanded rapidly at the expense of the high-cost unionized firms. In addition, a group of three carriers with national route structures (Roadway, Yellow, and CNF Transportation) took advantage of the network economies and expanded to carry traffic formerly moved by the failing companies, often by buying the facilities of bankrupt carriers. The Big Three of the trucking industry also developed their own regional nonunion carriers to compete for traffic.

Network economies are especially important for collection and distribution of traffic, and this is the main function of the Less-Than-Truckload (LTL) sector of the industry. In this sector, deregulation produced a rapid increase in concentration.[14] It is now clear that regulation maintained an artificially competitive structure in the LTL industry by protecting inefficiently small carriers; regulation, instead of working against competition in the trucking industry, in fact was the protector of the competitive structure.

Academic economists dismissed the instability argument against intrastate trucking deregulation as nonsensical, disproved by the fact that there were no disruptions of service following interstate deregulation and essentially no complaints among any customer groups. The bankruptcies of the 1980s were simply an adaptation to a new equilibrium for an industry that had overexpanded and taken on too much financial leverage in the period before 1980. Yet among the regulatory community, the fear that deregulation would return us to depression-era conditions was widely believed.[15]

During the 1980s and 1990s, a few states liberalized trucking rules, but at least one—Michigan—strengthened controls on intrastate trucking. The majority of states continued to regulate in the classic form. It seems unlikely that any major change would have occurred, were it not for the wish of the package express industry to integrate their air express and ground express businesses and to expand both businesses into heavier freight. In 1993, Federal Express, the big air express operation, successfully sued to exempt its small package business from state regulations in California. Several states then quickly followed, passing statutes to exempt from regulation the intrastate carriage of small packages by air express companies. The logic of the California court decision made it appear inevitable that all states would eventually have to deregulate the ground carriage of small packages by air express companies. The discussion then switched to how an air carrier was to be distinguished from a regular trucking firm.

As in the case of the Motor Carrier Act of 1980, intrastate trucking regulation did not fall due to an internal collapse of the institution—it appeared to be quite stable in the majority of states. In particular, it did not fall due to shrinking of regulatory rents. Rather, Congress was given the opportunity to confirm a change in the status quo that had occurred through no action of its own. When it became clear that intrastate trucking firms would be unprotected from competition with the ground operations of air freight carriers, the American Trucking Associations changed its stance on intrastate trucking deregulation from opposed to neutral on the subject. The Federal Aviation Administration Authorization Act of 1994 formally preempted the regulation of intrastate trucking by state regulatory authorities. In December 1995, the ICC Termination Act eliminated the structure that had been in place for regulating motor carrier operations, and deregulation was complete.

Making Sense of Trucking Deregulation

Trucking regulation should not be mourned by anyone outside of the owners of regulated companies and their employees. The structure of regulation did not allow for the social control of industry. Instead, the collective rate making that was an inevitable part of the attempt to force the trucking industry into the mold of railroad regulation allowed the trucking companies to control their customers. The Interstate Commerce Commission overzealously supervised the railroad rate structure to insure that no railroad exercised economic power over rail shippers. In the process, the agency pushed much of the railroad industry into bankruptcy. The trucking rate structure was effectively unsupervised, allowing the industry to use the institutions of economic regulation to establish a government-sponsored cartel.

The fact that the regulation developed in this way was primarily a historical accident. The industry was perceived in the mid-1930s to have the same problems that railroads were having and was given the treatment that appeared to be successful for railroads at that time. The fact that the industry was deregulated in two steps is also in large part historical accident. It was the appointment of deregulation-minded commissioners in response to inflation worries that created the effectively deregulated status quo for interstate trucking in 1980 that could be ratified by a legislature intensely interested in reducing the rate of inflation. In 1994, it was the challenge to the legal basis of intrastate trucking regulation by the air express industry that allowed Congress to confirm the status quo of preemption of intrastate trucking.

Under Positive Political Theory, deregulation is predicted to occur when the wealth to be transferred through the political process declines to a sufficiently low level to no longer justify the expenditures of the benefited group.[16] Yet prior to passage of the Motor Carrier Act of 1980, the trucking industry was financially very healthy. The only financial threat to the institution was the possibility of deregulation. Similarly, the only challenge to the profits of intrastate truckers in the 1990s was the threat of the loss of regulatory restrictions on the industry.

There were no economic forces that made it inevitable that the trucking industry would be given rules in 1935 that effectively precluded the public from establishing oversight that would have been necessary to insure an efficient and equitable outcome. There was nothing in 1980 that would suggest that the institution would collapse. There was nothing in the 1980s and early 1990s that can explain why state legislatures chose such a different path from that followed by Congress. Positive Political Theory could not have predicted the elimination of trucking regulation as part of a challenge from the air express industry in 1994.

Positive Political Theory fails as an explanation for regulatory motivation during the period when trucking was under the control of the Interstate Commerce Commission. It also fails in its attempt to explain trucking deregulation. There is no question that regulation was beneficial to trucking companies and their employees. There is no evidence, however, that this was intentional or part of a system to capture for regulators the support of stockholders of trucking companies or of their drivers.

Conclusion

Positive Political Theory can explain neither the form that trucking regulation took nor the timing of trucking deregulation. Unless the trucking industry is considered to be a statistical aberration, the inability of the theory to explain and predict behavior would normally cause us to reject the theory in favor of the alternative.

To call the trucking industry a statistical aberration, however, is to suggest that there are other stochastic factors that are influential in determining regulatory motivation and behavior. Yet the trucking industry cannot be considered to be a statistical fluke. It is *the* canonical example of the success of deregulation. It was often given as the classic example of regulators "captured" by the industry. In this key example, the data do not fit Positive Political Theory. Moreover, Positive Political Theory is set up as a deterministic theory of behavior. The theory is not set up as forecasting tendencies but as a complete framework for understanding regulatory motivation and behavior. In such a complete framework, any failure to predict invalidates the theory.

It must be conceded that there is no alternative theory with similar ambitions to Positive Political Theory that has better explanatory power. Indeed, there are no other theories with similar ambitions. Positive Political Theory is a break with past tradition in the field of regulatory economics—an attempt to build a deductive, predictive model of regulatory behavior and motivation. Deductive models are justified by hypothesis testing, typically in the form of nested hypotheses. The failure of the alternative hypothesis to explain behavior then calls for acceptance of the maintained hypothesis. Yet Positive Political Theory is not nested within a broader class of explanations. Thus the inability of the theory to explain and predict does not suggest an alternative on which to fall back.

The tradition from which Positive Political Theory was a distinct break is well represented by the writings of Harry Trebing, who argued that regulation was a response to problems of equity and industry stability.[17] Approaching regulatory motivation from this perspective provides a consistent framework for understanding the practice of trucking regulation and congressional acquiescence in its demise. This is not a claim that Positive Political Theory can make. Deregulation did not occur because the beneficiaries were no longer benefiting from it enough to justify organizing costs and payoffs to legislators. Shippers did not rise up and organize themselves to demand deregulation. Moreover, it is hard to square the idea that regulation is organized corruption to benefit well-organized groups at the expense of weaker groups when the targeted beneficiaries of regulation are often parts of the population (for example, the urban and rural poor) with very low voter participation rates. The intellectual support for trucking regulation disappeared when it was shown that regulation was neither necessary to prevent service disruptions nor required to advance equity. The inability of the industry to make a coherent argument based on stability and equity made it difficult to argue that outside events that had interrupted the regulatory equilibrium should be reversed.

The trucking industry is not the only one in which regulatory change can be understood as reflecting equity and stability. Railroad deregulation can also be explained by it. Railroad deregulation followed a long period of financial and physical decline in the industry. It is not often appreciated that by common consensus, for several decades railroads were not earning a normal rate of return on invested capital. Railroad regulation was maintained since it was seen as critical to maintaining an equitable rate structure. Had it not been the case that railroad financial problems led to service disruptions and a crumbling roadbed, in turn causing serious safety problems associated with frequent derailments, it is likely that equity concerns would have continued to provide a basis of support for railroad regulation. Since the institution in the 1970s failed to achieve stability for the shipping public, it was abandoned.

Similarly, airline deregulation is also consistent with the approach to regulatory motivation that stresses stability and equity. The spark for airline deregulation was the academic studies that demonstrated that unregulated intrastate airline service provided a stable and lower-cost alternative to the regulated carriers. The existence of the unregulated sector showed that regulation was unnecessary to insure stability in the industry. The fact that the unregulated competitors had much lower ticket prices seemed to argue that airline regulation was redistributing wealth from the traveling public to the regulated airlines, in contradiction to common concepts of equity.

It cannot be denied that political influences have helped to shape regulatory decisions. Trucking deregulation shows that the mechanism of institutional change identified by Positive Political Theory is at best incomplete, and at worst misleading. Regulators are motivated by, among other factors, considerations of equity and stability. The most compelling argument against undoing trucking deregulation was that these twin goals were not being met. Regulation in this industry was unnecessary for stability, and was working against the interests of equity. When this truth was revealed to legislators, historical accidents that shifted the status quo were allowed to remain by eliminating the old regulatory statutes.

Notes

1. This approach is summarized in Roger G. Noll, "Economic Perspectives on the Politics of Regulation," in *Handbook of Industrial Organization,* vol. 2, ed. Richard Schmalensee and Robert Willig (Amsterdam: North Holland, 1989.) The original contribution was Sam Peltzman, "Towards a More General Theory of Regulation," *Journal of Law and Economics* (August 1976): 211–40.

2. Clifford Winston, "Economic Deregulation: Days of Reckoning for Microeconomists," *Journal of Economic Literature* 31, no. 3 (1993): 1263–89.

3. An extensive description of the importance of relative prices and service levels to regulatory authorities is found is D. Philip Locklin, *The Economics of Transportation,* various editions from 1935–1972 (Homewood, Ill.: Richard D. Irwin). See also Kenneth D. Boyer, "Equalizing Discrimination and Cartel Pricing in Transport Rate Regulation," *Journal of Political Economy* (April 1981): 270–86.

4. James C. Nelson, "The Motor Act of 1935," *Journal of Political Economy* 44 (1936): 464–504.

5. This was established in the supreme court decision, ICC v. J-T Transport Co., 368 US 81 (1961).

6. See Peter N. Perry, Charles R. Waring, and Craig M. Glick, *Deregulation and the Decline of the Unionized Trucking Industry* (Philadelphia: Industrial Research Unit, The Wharton School, University of Pennsylvania, 1986.)

7. Interstate Commerce Commission, "Study of Interstate Commerce Commission Regulatory Responsibilities Pursuant to Section 210(a) of the Trucking Industry Regulatory Reform Act of 1994," 25 October 1994, 4–5.

8. Nancy L. Rose, "Labor Rent Sharing and Regulation: Evidence from the Trucking Industry," *Journal of Political Economy* 95, no. 6 (December 1987): 1146–78 and idem., "The Incidence of Regulatory Rents in the Motor Carrier Industry," *Rand Journal of Economics* 16, no. 3 (autumn 1985): 299–318

9. This perspective is articulated, among many others, in Thomas Gale Moore, "The Beneficiaries of Trucking Regulation," *Journal of Law and Economics* 21, no. 2 (1978): 327–43.

10. Quoted at meeting of the Surface Freight Transportation Committee of the Transportation Research Board, Washington D.C., 30 June 1993.

11. See, for example, Paul W. MacAvoy and John W. Snow, *Regulation of Entry and Pricing in Truck Transportation* (Washington, D.C.: American Enterprise Institute for Public Policy Research, 1977).

12. U.S. Department of Transportation, Bureau of Transportation Statistics, *1997 Census, 1997 Commodity Flow Survey* (Washington, D.C: U.S. Government Printing Office, 1999).

13. This section is based on Kenneth D. Boyer, "Deregulation of the Trucking Sector: Specialization, Concentration, Entry, and Financial Distress," *Southern Economic Journal* 59, no. 3 (1993): 481–95. See also, Clifford Winston et al., *The Economic Effects of Surface Freight Deregulation* (Washington, D.C.: Brookings Institution, 1990).

14. Robert W. Kling, "Deregulation and Structural Change in the LTL Motor Freight Industry," *Transportation Journal* (spring 1990): 47–53

15. As representative of this work, see Paul Dempsey, *The Social and Economic Consequences of Deregulation: The Transportation Industry in Transition* (Westport, Conn.: Greenwood Press and London: Quorum Books, 1989).

16. Sam Peltzman, "The Economic Theory of Regulation after a Decade of Deregulation," *Brookings Papers on Economic Activity*, Special Issue (1989): 1–59.

17. Trebing's approach is outlined in Harry M. Trebing, "Equity, Efficiency, and the Viability of Public Utility Regulation," in *Applications of Economic Principles in Public Utility Industries*, ed. Werner Sichel and Thomas G. Gies (Ann Arbor: Division of Research, Graduate School of Business Administration, University of Michigan, 1981.)

Public Control, through Ownership or Regulation, Is Necessary in Electric Power

EUGENE P. COYLE

> . . . there is no competitive equilibrium in an industry characterized
> by quite plausible cost and demand conditions. All we need for this
> conclusion is falling long-run average cost, stochastic demand, and
> some cost associated with having idle plants. An implication of these
> largely negative results concerning competition is that some non-
> competitive, cooperative solution to market allocation is necessary. By
> extension, the importance of this line of reasoning for antitrust is that
> *it becomes unrealistic to expect competitive behavior in certain markets*
> *because firms could not behave competitively even if they wanted to.*
>
> George Bittlingmayer

"Decreasing Average Cost and Competition: A New Look at the Addiston Pipe Case" (emphasis added)

Introduction

Electric power, in common with other network industries, has character-istics that make public control necessary, through either regulation or public ownership, to minimize the cost to society of providing the service and to deliver just, reasonable, and nondiscriminatory rates.

The goal of "just, reasonable, and nondiscriminatory electric rates" has been memorialized in the statutes and policies of many states and at the Federal Energy Regulatory Commission (FERC). The argument for dereg-ulation of electric power is that competition will deliver economic efficiency, and lower prices, which are just and reasonable, more effectively than can regulation. The discussion of competition, furthermore, is carried out in terms of a single product with a single price. Neoclassical microeconomics

358

is simply applied to the analysis of any and all industries, without regard to the cost conditions, or the characteristics of the product involved. We will see that this type of analysis cannot be fruitfully applied to electric power. At the same time, we will see that serious and respected economists from wildly different branches of thought have repeatedly shown that competition can deliver neither economic efficiency nor just, reasonable, and nondiscriminatory rates in industries such as electric power.

A very brief review of the standard and familiar economic argument for the benefits of competition follows, as set forth by prestigious proponents of deregulation.[1] A discussion of why product and cost conditions in electric power will not allow textbook competition, or any competition, as that term is conventionally used in economics, then follows.

The heart of the chapter is a review of the long recognition, by some of the most distinguished economists of successive generations, that for industries like electric power, public control over pricing, and thus ultimately over investment and other decisions, is required for economic efficiency and for just, reasonable, and nondiscriminatory prices. The first remarkable thing about this showing is that it has had little effect on the mainstream of the profession. This despite the second remarkable thing, which is that the recognition that competition cannot deliver in the case of electric power is developed by economists starting from widely different theoretical branches and political perspectives.

The Economic Theory behind the Drive for Deregulation

It is useful to begin with a brief review of how competition is supposed to deliver benefits to customers. A paper by three prominent economists, William Baumol, Paul Joskow, and Alfred Kahn, supporting electric deregulation lists as its first "central conclusion" that

> Properly structured, competition in the supply of generation services can be a better guarantor of efficient performance than is regulated monopoly. Efficiency improvements should be the primary goals [sic] of policy reform.[2]

In the paper, funded by the private power companies' national trade association, the Edison Electric Institute, Baumol, Joskow, and Kahn make an argument for moving from regulation to competition, based on economic theory. They assert that

> Regulators, legislators and providers have become increasingly receptive to the idea of relying on competition to improve the industry's performance. They have been influenced in important measure by mounting evidence

from other regulated industries that wherever effective competition is feasible, it can yield lower costs and a wider range of consumer choices than traditional cost-of-service regulation.[3]

Note that Baumol, Joskow, and Kahn assert that there might be lower costs, but they say nothing about lower prices. There is a difference, and the goal of a profit-oriented business is to keep prices as far above costs as possible. Profits are, after all, the difference between costs and prices.

Economic efficiency is the overriding objective of microeconomists. It is achieved, simply enough, through decisions by individuals as to what to buy and produce. These individual decisions supposedly result in three things: maximization of consumer benefits, maximization of profits, and best utilization of society's resources. This comes about, the theory says, through competition. The lowest-cost producers gain market share by selling profitably at low cost. Others must follow prices down in order to sell at all, and eventually prices are driven down to the marginal cost of the lowest-cost producer. This is the theoretical basis for deregulating electric generation.

Having prices equal to marginal cost is the sine qua non for economists, and price *will be* equal to marginal cost under competition, it is claimed, if we simply deregulate electric power. (We shall see that there is no basis for this claim.) The U.S. Department of Energy's Energy Information Administration, in advocating deregulation on behalf of the Clinton administration, asserted that prices would be set at marginal cost in a deregulated future:

> If fully competitive electricity markets develop, prices will *not* be set to *average* costs. . . . With prices set to marginal costs, the market will clear; all suppliers willing to provide power and all consumers willing to purchase power at the market price will be doing so" (emphasis added).[4]

Yet price will not and cannot equal marginal cost in electric power. Thus the economists' justification for deregulation, that price will equal marginal cost, cannot support deregulation. In addition, we should quickly recall that the argument that marginal cost pricing results in "economic efficiency" has been shown repeatedly to be an empty one.[5]

At this point we turn back to the paper by Baumol, Joskow, and Kahn to show that they themselves recognize that under the cost conditions of electric power, competition and pricing at marginal cost fails. A single page has the following text and footnote:

A. The Proper Goal Is Enhanced Efficiency

The case for competition, to which we subscribe as a general principle, is that it is a better guarantor of efficient performance than regulated monopoly—with efficiency defined in terms of the costs as well as the quality and variety of service options presented to consumers.

There are two ways in which the historic arrangement of franchised monopoly subject to traditional regulation tends to produce less efficient results. First, because of its inherent cost-plus character, it tends to provide inadequate incentives and inadequate pressures to minimize costs. Second, government price regulation has a strong inherent tendency to promote allocative inefficiency by setting prices—both prices overall and the structure of prices to different categories of users—at levels that do not reflect or come as close as possible to reflecting marginal costs as they would be reflected in competitive markets.* (We refer to the consequent inefficiency as "allocative" because the prices consumers pay, by failing to reflect the costs society incurs by producing somewhat more of the mispriced services or that it would save by producing somewhat less, induces . . .)

*Standard economic analysis demonstrates that efficiency requires the price of each service sold by a firm to equal its marginal cost, provided that the firm's services or other products are produced under conditions of diminishing or constant returns to scale. That is because the marginal cost of a unit of service is, by definition the cost caused by the process of supplying that unit of service. Consequently, if its price is set equal to marginal cost, consumers are said to be given "the right signal." That is, they pay an amount for the service that it costs the economy to supply it. Consequently, the consumer is not lured by a price below cost to use the product wastefully, and is not deterred from appropriate use of that service by an excessive price.

However, where the supply of some product entails a large fixed cost or entails substantial scale economies for some other reason, as may well be true of the cost of transmission, then a fundamental problem arises for the setting of prices at marginal cost. In these circumstances, such prices will bring the firm total revenues that are inadequate to cover its total costs. *The reason is most easily seen in the case where fixed costs are present.* There, a price set at marginal cost makes no contribution to coverage of fixed cost because, by definition, the supply of a unit of output causes no addition to fixed cost. In such a case, to prevent insolvency of the firm, prices must deviate from marginal costs. Economists have derived a formula for the (second-best) efficient prices in these circumstances; those are referred to as *Ramsey Prices* (after their discoverer).

Henceforth, whenever we refer to prices set at marginal costs in this paper, we will mean either what that term literally implies or, instead, we will be referring to Ramsey prices, whichever is appropriate under the circumstances in question at that point in the discussion (emphasis added).[6]

The point here is that Baumol, Joskow, and Kahn recommend competitive pricing for generation at the top of the page and then agree in the footnote that it cannot be used in an industry with generation's cost structure.[7] It should be noted, moreover, that Ramsey pricing is, per se, discriminatory pricing.

The Product and Cost Structure Precludes Competition in Electric Power

Competition is the hallmark of the U.S. economy, and the belief is widely held that its emphasis on efficiency drives forward prosperity and growth. There are certain industries, however, that have characteristics such that competition does not play its textbook role. Electric power is one such industry. This chapter addresses at some length two characteristics in particular: First, where the product sold is an undifferentiated commodity, like corn or soybeans, and, second, where production requires large fixed investment, or "overhead costs."

Electric power generation, remarkably, has both of these attributes—a product, the kilowatt hour, that is an undifferentiated commodity, and also high overhead or fixed costs. Either of these attributes leads us to the expectation of failure of competition. Finding both together assures us that textbook competition will not appear in this industry.

To be profitable, industries with either of these characteristics must find ways to discriminate among the customers to cooperate or illegally collude to set prices, or to do both. Kilowatt-hours per se are undifferentiated at the customer's meter, and power production requires large up-front investment. Tight oligopoly, which is the direction in which the industry is clearly headed, is characterized by the absence of price competition, the result of a recognition of a common interest in avoiding price cuts.

In 1999 a new record for fines in an antitrust case—$725 million—was set when the world's two biggest vitamin makers, Roche and Rhone-Poulenc, agreed to pay to settle charges in a massive price-fixing conspiracy. The chief executive at Roche, paying $500 million of the fine, said at a news conference:

> You will understand that this was not part of our responsibility. It is certainly not easy to understand the reasons for the actions of employees who in secrecy organized a conspiracy of this kind.[8]

In fact, however, it is easy to understand the behavior. The conspirators were not sociopaths or born criminals, nor did they have a predilection for crime. Rather, they simply tried to cope with the business they were in.

The economic theory section of this chapter provides the background for understanding why these actions occurred: Acceptable profits without collusion were hard to achieve. A gentleman convicted in the notorious electrical equipment case, in an industry struggling with excess capacity and large overhead costs, understood the point, "No one attending the gatherings was so stupid he didn't know the meetings were in violation of the law. But it is the only way a business can be run. It is free enterprise."[9]

The vitamin conspiracy is simply the new record holder in terms of the dollar amount of the fines. New records have been occurring frequently since Archer-Daniels-Midland (ADM), also in a commodity conspiracy, agreed to pay $100 million in 1996. Two officials of ADM were each sentenced in July 1999 to two years of incarceration.

Our first step will be to review some history, first of commodity pricing, and, second, of pricing of products produced under conditions of high overhead cost. A century of history shows that selling an undifferentiated commodity is not the path to profits.

Agricultural Commodities

Economic forces in undifferentiated commodity businesses require coordinated control of output. In agriculture, acreage and other controls on wheat, corn, and milk served a coordinating function for most of the twentieth century. Congress, attempting a form of deregulation of agriculture in 1996, passed the "Freedom to Farm Act," hoping that "the market" would work in agriculture. By the summer of 1999 a farm crisis had emerged, and in the year 2000 the federal government spent more than $25 billion to sustain farmers when marginal-cost pricing will not.[10]

Farmers understand better than most that when they produce a bumper crop, as happened in 2000 for corn, sugar, soybeans, and other farm output, prices crash. Farmers selling commodities, often held up as a good example of how the market works, have either been driven to the wall by excess production or are dependent on one or another of a series of agricultural laws for control of production and for price supports.

In contrast with farmers, manufacturers and corporate vendors of undifferentiated commodities have found ways within the law to cooperate to keep prices up, or failing that, have colluded outside the law to fix prices.

Cooperation and Collusion—A Long History in Commodities

Cooperation or collusion to fix prices occurs repeatedly in industries with undifferentiated commodity products. Examples of price cooperation or collusion from these industries abound. We report first from a commodity industry, where Professor Fritz Machlup cites an example where sealed bids identical to six decimal places were submitted: "On April 23, 1936, officers of the United States Engineering Office of Tucumcari, New Mexico, opened the sealed envelopes containing price bids for the delivery of 6,000 barrels of cement. Eleven firms had submitted their bids and every one of them named a price of $3.286854 per barrel."[11]

The cooperation on prices that led to identical bids was facilitated through the "basing-point system"—legal at the time of the cement bids just noted, but found illegal by the U. S. Supreme Court in 1948. The basing-point system was complicated, with many permutations, but in its simplest form it amounted to this: An industry selected a particular plant as the physical basing point and agreed on a selling price. Then suppliers added freight charges from the basing point to the customer, regardless of whether their own production was located closer to or further from the customer. Thus all suppliers charged the same price and added identical delivery charges. The price was identical even though the cost of production might vary, and the cost of shipping likely would vary, between suppliers.[12]

Machlup shows that, from the 1890s forward, industries like cement, steel, and corn products needed to cooperate on prices in order to be profitable, and found successive ways to do that as each innovation in price cooperation was put outside the pale. The vitamin pricing conspiracy mentioned earlier, together with Machlup's research, shows over a century of legal problems with the sale of undifferentiated commodities. These vitamins, of course, are industrial inputs, not the little bottles at the neighborhood drug store.[13]

No one wants to be in an undifferentiated commodity business—profits are small or nil in such a business unless you cooperate to set prices, as the basing-point system facilitated for cement. The corn products industry also used the basing-point system to set prices, and the industry had skirted antitrust for decades before.[14] Corn products' long history in that regard is described by Fritz Machlup, later president of the American Economic Association: "this industry deserves a place in an historical account of the basing-point system. Its chief claim to fame is the valor and determination with which it has kept up its brave fight against the law of the land. It fought one bout after another against the United States; no sooner had it lost one than it renewed its persistent efforts to beat the antitrust laws."[15]

Although corn products have changed over the years since Machlup wrote, the persistence of the industry's involvement with the antitrust laws has not. Machlup traced the history of the industry from competition in 1890 through a wave of mergers and then pricing via trade associations until the U. S. Supreme Court decided, in 1945, in favor of the Federal Trade Commission in condemning all discriminatory pricing practices, including those inherent in the basing-point system.[16]

The corn products anti-trust case of the 1990s set a record for the dollar amount of fines. The price fixing for lysine, citric acid, and corn syrup by a number of producers, including Archer-Daniels-Midland (ADM) and others resulted in ADM alone paying a then record fine of $100 million.

In an undifferentiated commodity business, price is driven down to where profits are unattractive. As a result, commodity vendors attempt to dress their product in various disguises, to establish brand names, to add logos or other distinguishing marks in order to avoid selling merely a commodity. The commodity environment has led to mergers and then, when concentration is high enough, to various schemes to share markets— schemes either illegal when embraced or declared illegal upon review by the Federal Trade Commission or other agency. Survival in an undifferentiated commodity business without merger or collusion requires product differentiation and market segmentation.

Large Overhead Costs—Another Blow to Competition

A second way in which the textbook version of competition does not apply for producers and fails to deliver benefits for all consumers is under a cost structure where fixed or overhead costs are a large part of the total.

The cost structure of electric power is heavily weighted toward overhead costs. Large up-front investment is required before sales can take place, and the annual charges related to the investment must be covered whether sales occur or not. Depreciation, capital cost, and even fuel bought under long-term contracts are costs that continue whether sales are made or not. Fixed cost puts pressure on the owners to operate the plants at high capacity factors so that the annual costs can be spread over a high volume. There is a virtuous circularity to this. With high volume, the per-unit share of the overhead costs is low, and the product can be priced low enough to attract sales that will result in a high capacity factor.

The problem is to attract the high sales volume without pricing below the average cost of production—that is, without pricing at a loss. The solution, widely practiced over the years by a variety of industries, is to discriminate among customers. The strategy was developed by the railroads over a century ago: charge some customers high prices, much higher than average cost, and achieve high volume by offering other customers lower prices.

Selling some output below cost (i.e., below average cost) adds to profit if the price makes even a small contribution beyond the out-of-pocket cost. This is the logic of selling in an industry with overhead cost. It is familiar in our everyday lives, with airline tickets perhaps the most obvious example. Discriminatory pricing is widespread in our economy. Hotels now practice "yield management," sometimes offering rooms at bargain rates, but only in restricted volume, with volume and price changing on a daily basis. In fact, only those selling an undifferentiated product sell at a single price. Farming is the familiar example.

Selling a part of output below average cost has been, furthermore, a common practice in the electric power industry. Some industrial tariff sales even today under regulation seem clearly lower than the full cost of service. Off-system sales under regulation were frequently made for just slightly more than the fuel cost.[17]

The U.S. Department of Energy's Energy Information Administration and others have forecasted large consumer benefits resting on marginal-cost pricing. The promise of benefits to consumers when prices are driven to marginal cost will not materialize, however, because that cannot be profitable. Selling at marginal cost when there are substantial overhead costs leads to bankruptcy. It is not possible to be profitable while pricing at marginal cost in such an industry.

Selling all output at a single profitable price—for example, at average cost or higher—is also not feasible. The full price might be so high as to discourage sales. If sales were not large enough to fully employ the capacity of the plant, or to come close to that, then total costs would not be covered. The solution, long understood and employed by electric utilities, is price discrimination and cross-subsidization. Utilities and other industries like them struggle mightily to avoid pricing at marginal cost.

Even if the vendors are few in number and reach an accommodation to charge more than marginal cost (that is, to charge enough so that total costs are covered), price discrimination will be required to avoid redundant capacity and low rates of return on investment. It can be argued that collusion in an industry with many firms is hard to achieve and even harder to perpetuate. Yet, over time, failure of prices to cover total costs leads to mergers and high concentration, and since there will be a *need* for concentration, there *will be* concentration.[18] Mergers will proceed until collusion and cooperation can be effected. The airlines provide an example of cooperation. They have reached pricing détente through posting prices through a common computer. Upstart carriers are now tolerated if taking only small bits of the market, or are targets of price wars if more of a threat.

The combination of large overhead costs and excess capacity requires mergers, cooperation, or collusion for profitability. Consider the electrical equipment (not electric power) industry. In February 1960, the U.S. Department of Justice named forty-four electrical manufacturers and twenty-eight individuals as conspiring to fix prices.[19] There were subsequent indictments and, in early 1961, twenty-nine companies were convicted and fined. Many individual executives were fined and given suspended sentences, and seven executives actually served time. The prosecution was triggered by the revelation of identical bids in a newsletter: "The TVA weekly newsletter, dated for release on Wednesday, May 13, 1959, reported that seven sealed bids for conductor cable had come in at an identical $198,438.24."[20]

Identical bids for conductor cable, down to the odd twenty-four cents, manufactured by different companies in factories at different locations, raised the question of collusion. Investigation and prosecution revealed that collusion on prices, not only for cable but for transformers, turbine generators, switchgear, steam condensers, meters, and many other products had gone on for a long time.

Two books, *The Gentlemen Conspirators* and *The Great Price Conspiracy*, relate the story of what was then the greatest antitrust conspiracy in American history. The price fixing and allocation of market share came to be known in the press as the "Phases of the Moon" case, after the formula used by the conspirators to determine which company would make the low bid on a particular job.

John Herling noted that

> The records of the Antitrust Division indicate that certain companies appeared to have a predilection for violating antitrust laws.*

*In December, 1961, the Justice Department sought a court order to make the General Electric Company subject to unlimited fines if it ever tried to fix prices or violated any other requirement of the antitrust laws. This order would cover everything GE manufactures, not only the heavy electrical equipment where they were already found guilty of price fixing and bid rigging. The department listed 39 antitrust actions against GE, 36 of them since 1941. These included 29 convictions, seven consent decrees, and three "adverse findings" of the Federal Trade Commission. To the Justice Department this indicated "General Electric's proclivity for persistent and frequent involvement in antitrust violations" in all branches of industrial production. Westinghouse could show almost as cluttered a record in antitrust violations.[21]

The conclusion that "certain companies" have a predilection for violating the antitrust laws, a conclusion that echoes the idea that certain nationalities or ethnic groups are predisposed to crime, isn't satisfactory.

We need to look for the conditions that *cause* this behavior. In the case of the electrical equipment manufacturers, the cost structure of the industry explains the urge to cooperate and collude.

Deregulated electric generation combines an undifferentiated commodity business with a cost structure heavily weighted to fixed costs. As a result, price fixing and discrimination must occur for the industry to be profitable.

The Economic Theorists

We turn now to a review of the various branches of economic theory that, stretching for over a century, have shown that in industries like electric power, competition cannot deliver economic efficiency.

The key diagram in a student's first college course in microeconomics is "the U-shaped cost curve of the representative firm." That diagram continues to be the basis of the analysis of business behavior through graduate school in economics. It is also the heart of the Energy Information Administration's analysis of electric power deregulation, and of the analyses of the economists advocating deregulation.

This chapter opened with a quote from an economist working in core theory. The core theorists show that under the cost conditions of electric power generation, competitive behavior won't emerge. It is useful to provide here more of that previously quoted statement:

> The most startling result to emerge from work in this area is that, barring only a few special cases, there is no competitive equilibrium in an industry composed of independently operated plants with identical, U-shaped average costs curves. The cost conditions are, of course, those from the textbook case of the Viner industry, but I think many if not most economists are surprised that this ineluctable result concerning equilibrium is contained in the most familiar of models. A broader and more practical result is that there is no competitive equilibrium in an industry characterized by quite plausible cost and demand conditions. All we need for this conclusion is falling long-run average cost, stochastic demand, and some cost associated with having idle plants. An implication of these largely negative results concerning competition is that some noncompetitive, cooperative solution to market allocation is necessary. By extension, the importance of this line of reasoning for antitrust is that *it becomes unrealistic to expect competitive behavior in certain markets because firms could not behave competitively even if they wanted to* (emphasis added).[22]

Interestingly, John Maynard Keynes listed a very similar set of "complications" in the 1920s in two lectures. He noted, like Bittlingmayer, the cost and demand conditions under which competition doesn't—can't—emerge. Keynes then went further, to explain how economists move from simplifying assumptions to abandonment of the actual facts, and to conclude that their model is what reality is.

> The beauty and the simplicity of such a theory are so great that it is easy to forget that it follows not from the actual facts, but from an incomplete hypothesis introduced for the sake of simplicity. Apart from other objections to be mentioned later, the conclusion that individuals acting independently for their own advantage will produce the greatest aggregate of wealth, depends on a variety of unreal assumptions to the effect that the processes of production and consumption are in no way organic, that there exists a sufficient foreknowledge of conditions and requirements, and that there are adequate opportunities of obtaining this foreknowledge. For economists generally reserve for a later stage of their arguments the complications which arise—(1) when the efficient units of production are large relatively to the units of consumption, (2) when overhead costs or joint costs are present, (3) when internal economies tend to the aggregation of production, (4) when the time required for adjustments is long, (5) when ignorance prevails over knowledge, and (6) when monopolies and combinations interfere with equality in bargaining—they reserve, that is to say, for a later stage their analysis of the actual facts. Moreover, many of those who recognise that the simplified hypothesis does not accurately correspond to fact conclude nevertheless that it does represent what is "natural" and therefore ideal. They regard the simplified hypothesis as health, and the further complications as disease.[23]

John Maurice Clark and Overhead Costs

John Maurice Clark, at about the same time as Keynes gave his lectures, or perhaps earlier, explicitly undertook the investigation of the implications of cost structure in courses given at the University of Chicago, and published his analysis in *Studies in the Economics of Overhead Costs*.[24] Clark was attempting to break from the static economics that erroneously tells us today that competition will result in economic efficiency. His book

> studies the discrepancies between supply and demand; indeed the whole subject of the book might be defined as a study of discrepancies between ever fluctuating demand and a relatively inelastic fund of productive capacity, resulting in wastes of partial idleness, and many other economic disturbances. *Unused capacity is its central theme* (emphasis added).[25]

Clark describes the gradual discovery of overhead costs, by businessmen and economists alike. Businessmen have remembered these costs, while most economists have either not considered or have forgotten them.

Clark wrote:

7. Overhead Costs on Railroads

However, this fact did not have its full effect until the largest mechanical unit of all—the railroad—had reached maturity and had had its transforming effect on industry, making possible the fullest development of mechanical production in other lines by enabling the output of mammoth plants to find a market. There resulted the struggle for world-markets, cut-throat competition, discrimination, the modern forms of the business cycle, and the growth of monopoly. But it was the railroad itself that first brought the notion of overhead costs into real prominence with economists. When railroads were new, their rates were commonly uniform, or nearly so, based on weight and distance, and were uniformly high. Soon it was discovered that additional traffic could be carried at little or no additional cost and that reduced rates, if confined to classes of traffic not already moving, would increase the net earnings of the company. Thus classification was born and the foundations were laid for cheaper railroad carriage than would ever have been possible without discrimination.

Along with it or after it, however, came many other less innocuous types of discrimination, often without rhyme or reason, and harmful even to the roads that used them. Rate wars and receiverships followed. Shippers at local points saw goods hauled past them to junctions beyond at lower rates than they paid for their shorter hauls, and with simple logic reason that if the lower through rate was adequate, the higher local rate was obviously extortionate. Under pressure of contending interests, with the need of justifying practices against attack, the theory underlying discrimination became vocal and explicit, and the world learned that railroads were different from other industries because such a large part of their costs were "constant" or independent of traffic.

Thus the world of economic thought was made aware of a fact, which is older than railroads, older than economic science and, far from being a peculiarity of one business or a group of highly capitalistic businesses, is universal. From the present point of view the thing that seems more in need of explanation is why economists should have thought that other industries were different from railroads or why they should have thought that they had explained the prices of single goods by showing that they tended, under competition, to cover the expenses of production.

So far as railroads were concerned, the chief use made of the notion of overhead costs was to justify discrimination as a general practice, on the ground that added traffic was not responsible for those costs which did not increase as traffic increased, and that in any case it was impossible to determine the proper share of costs traceable to one shipment or one unit of business. . . . The upshot was that the makers of rates were assumed to know their own interests, and while it was clear that no one in or out of the railroad business knew the "variable cost" of any given class of traffic, it was assumed that the facts of cost justified wide discriminations, and the practice of "charging what the traffic will bear" was given the benefit of the doubt so far as cost was concerned. The question of distinguishing fair from unfair discrimination was left to be argued on other grounds.

8. Overhead Costs in Other Industries

It soon became evident that railroads were not the only industry using large fixed capital and subject to the "peculiarities" of constant and variable costs. It also became evident that discrimination was not the only untoward result of such a condition. Rate wars on the railroads often abolished the regular classifications and brought all rates to a level far below cost. Large companies, railroad and industrial, failed, were re-organized, and continued in business, often more formidable competitors than before. It became evident that economic law did not insure prices that would yield "normal" returns on invested capital, because the capital could not get out if it wanted to, and so had to take whatever it could get. The business cycle had become a recognized part of the order of things, with its recurring periods of excess producing capacity, during which active competition tended to lower prices until even efficient concerns could make little or no return on their investment. "Cut-throat competition" was seen to be a natural thing, and it was seen to be equally natural that business should adopt protective measures, whether combinations, pools, gentlemen's agreements, or a mere sentiment against "spoiling the market."[26]

Clark makes a number of points that bear emphasis. The first of these is that price discrimination was common, leading to greater utilization of capacity, increased earnings, and more service for the public at cheaper rates than would have been possible without discrimination.

Clark goes on to note, however, that "rate wars and receiverships followed." "So far as railroads were concerned," Clark says, "the chief use made of the notion of overhead costs was to justify discrimination as a general practice."

Finally, Clark notes how natural it was "that business should adopt protective measures, whether combinations, pools, gentlemen's agreements, or a mere sentiment against 'spoiling the market.'"[27]

Clark quotes A. T. Hadley, another economist making actual observations of behavior. Hadley's language of 1896 is dated, but his analysis is as modern as the unregulated airline industry:

> Each producer can extend his output with a gain, rather than a loss in economy. If he can increase his sales, there will be only a slight increase— perhaps none at all—in the expense for wages and materials, and a decided

decrease in the share of the charges on fixed capital which each unit of product must pay. There is no fixed standard of cost which we can treat as the normal price; for the cost per unit of product depends on the quantity sold, falling as sales increase.

The price which will induce new competitors to enter the field is also much higher than that which will lead old ones to withdraw. No concern will quit competition as long as it can pay an appreciable part of its interest charges. It is better to lose part of your interest on every piece of goods you sell than to lose the whole of it on every piece you do not sell. As long as the price received more than covers the expense of wages and materials, each of the old factories will continue to compete. Even if it changes ownership by foreclosure it will remain in operation. But, on the other hand, no new competitor will be called into being unless the price is high enough to afford a liberal profit, after paying interest, maintenance, and other charges on fixed capital invested under modern methods. Thus prices, instead of constantly tending to gravitate toward an equitable figure, oscillate between two extremes. The rate of production, at figures which give a fair profit, is usually either much larger than the rate of consumption, or much smaller. In the former case, prices are unremunerative and unjust to the producer; in the latter case, they are oppressive to the consumer. The average price resulting from such fluctuations may perhaps be a fair one; but the wide changes of price are disastrous to all parties concerned.

In some cases the industrial units which are necessary for proper utilization of labor have become so large as to produce actual monopoly. . . . Even in cases where the necessity for concentrated management is not quite so marked, . . . the competition of different concerns always involves a loss, from the need of maintaining too many selling agencies, the expense of unnecessary advertising, and the lack of proper utilization of fixed capital.[28]

Recent Recognition of the Issue of Cost Conditions

Distinguished economists have long recognized the implications of the peculiar cost structure of an industry. In fact, the most prominent of all economists of each generation have seen that under conditions of large overhead costs, "competition" does *not* deliver economic efficiency. From Alfred Marshall, the father of today's "neoclassical" school of economics, on down to today, this insight is acknowledged by the mass of economists, who then go on to make contrary assumptions and to prescribe policy that cannot work.

Regulation Has Constrained Price Discrimination while Rationalizing Capacity

Regulation is commonly thought to be about controlling monopoly profits, but important functions of regulation are preventing "undue price discrimination" and rationalizing investment. Price discrimination exists under regulation, of course, with different customer classes charged different prices for a kilowatt-hour of electricity, but the discrimination is based, ostensibly at least, on cost differences. Without regulation, no test of a cost basis will exist.

Railroad regulation was actually spawned in the late 1800s by the demand by some customers for control of price discrimination, combined with the railroads' own need for outside control of "cutthroat competition." Gabriel Kolko makes a convincing case that federal railroad regulation came out of a demand by customers who were discriminated against, in alliance with the railroads themselves.[29] Rockefeller's Standard Oil was getting low rates, plus rebates, and rival oil companies joined with the railroads themselves to push legislation. The railroads embraced regulation because they were unable to self-enforce price agreements and wanted the government to police the cheating among them on what were then legal price pools.

Electric power companies under the leadership of Samuel Insull later embraced exclusive territories under the supervision of regulators, so that "cutthroat competition" would not break out to bankrupt them. The regulators' most important functions over the years became control over price discrimination within service areas and determining capacity levels deemed "used and useful." With a protected territory, a utility favors industrial customers as a way to raise growth in sales and earnings and, hence, its value on the stock market.[30] Sales and investment grew apace, to maintain the return on investment at a profitable level.

Exclusive territories did successfully preclude the cutthroat competition among electric utilities that had plagued the early railroads. Yet it is clear that even deregulated power production will be protected from ungentlemanly price wars by emergence of tight oligopoly or collusion. Deregulation of the airlines did at first lead to price wars, which bankrupted many carriers, some more than once. Very helpful in ending the price wars has been consolidation through mergers and alliances, leaving very few players to compete or cooperate, as the case may be. The airlines have found a way to "cooperate" on pricing, followed by steady price increases. Yet price discrimination remains severe.

Overhead Costs through the Lens of Game Theory: The Work of Lester Telser

A modern subset of game theory, called "the theory of the core," offers a rich explanation of pricing in an industry with the cost characteristics of electric generation. An economist from the University of Chicago, Lester

G. Telser, followed by other scholars, has explored, through the lens of game theory, the impact of cost conditions on behavior. He concludes that "cooperation" is necessary for economic efficiency under the cost conditions of electric power.

Telser addresses cost conditions that, when present, make equilibrium (and single) prices very unlikely. We focus on two of these, overhead cost and the need for inventory larger than expected demand—or, for electricity, capacity larger than expected peak, since the product is produced at the instant of demand.[31] We discuss each in turn.

Game theory is a mathematical exploration of mutual interdependence. A branch of game theory that Telser develops is core theory. Telser concludes that the players in the game—producers of electricity, for example—should "cooperate" to reach economic efficiency, that is, the best solution for society.[32] Telser shows that under the cost conditions of electric power, the neoclassical competitive outcome will not occur. Without cooperation, a stable equilibrium and efficiency cannot happen. Core theory is mathematical, but Telser's conclusions are fully consonant with the prose descriptions provided by John M. Clark and by Hadley's work of a century ago.

Telser notes that

> Competition is a means to an end, not an end it itself. In my view a proper end is an efficient equilibrium. In such an equilibrium changes are not possible that would make someone better off without making at least one other person worse off. Were this not true it would show that the original situation was inefficient. Therefore, the problem is to learn when competition can give an efficient equilibrium. A central thesis of my argument is that competition does not always result in an equilibrium. It can lead to chaos.[33]

Core theory, in exploring the conditions necessary for economic efficiency in an industry with large overhead costs, reaches the same conclusion as we find using common sense. In an industry with large overhead costs, economic efficiency cannot occur in the absence of collusion among producers. Telser situates his work in the mainstream of economics, showing that distinguished economists have reached this same conclusion.

> As we shall see, competition may require some *cooperation* in order to obtain efficiency. Some of my analysis stems from theories of very distinguished economists, including Edgeworth, Bohm-Bawerk, Marshall, J. M. Clark and F. H. Knight. I take the argument further than they did, partly because since their time the economy has moved strongly in the directions that support the relevance of my theoretical analysis. These ideas are not

fads or idiosyncrasies. They come from the mainstream of economic theory and help us understand the modern economy (emphasis added).[34]

In an earlier book, *Economic Theory and the Core*, Telser put it this way:

> The mathematical reason for an empty core is that the characteristic functions that represent the situation are unkind. ["unkind" here is a mathematical term describing a function.] In order to restore an equilibrium it is necessary to impose restrictions on which coalitions may form. If there are too many coalitions, then in the face of an unkind characteristic function an equilibrium cannot emerge. *One may say that there is too much competition,* which prevents having a stable outcome. This resembles the conclusions of J. M. Clark in his *Studies in the Economics of Overhead Costs* (1923) (emphasis added).[35]

Telser's highly mathematical work derives the necessary conditions for the existence of a stable equilibrium. He stresses that the nature of cost conditions is of central importance. When large fixed costs are present, he finds, an equilibrium cannot exist unless "restrictions" are imposed.

> One of the principal conclusions from these applications of core theory to economics is the central importance of the nature of the cost conditions. Unless the firms in the industry are small and numerous, a neoclassical perfectly competitive equilibrium cannot exist. Specialization, fixed costs, and indivisibilities give a stable equilibrium only with *restrictions* on which coalitions may form (emphasis added).[36]

Telser's restrictions, we shall see, include public ownership or public control if cooperation among producers is to be permitted.

Coalitions are subsets of producers who agree in some fashion on the total capacity that society needs and agree on prices to result in efficiency. In other words, cooperation or collusion is required to get the right amount of capacity—neither shortage nor excess—for society's need. In an industry with huge capital requirements relative to revenue, as electric generation is, "competition" in the simple textbook sense cannot work to produce economic efficiency.

Telser notes that when supply conditions enter the picture of competition, they bring complications.

> The bulk of these complications arise from the fact that costs are lower if producers make commitments in advance of the revenue they expect to receive. . . . By choosing production methods capable of making complicated articles at low cost, provided the means of production are ready before the appearance of the actual demand, producers become hostage to the vagaries of uncertain future demand.[37]

A strong believer in economic efficiency, Telser notes nevertheless that under certain conditions of supply, including those in electric power, "competition may require some *cooperation* in order to obtain efficiency (emphasis added)."[38]

In other words, it is more efficient to plan an electrical power system than to rely on the market to produce the optimal one. Telser's conclusion can be interpreted as support for regulation or for public power as a way of devising the appropriate terms between customers and suppliers. Absent such control, or unless producer cooperation (now illegal) were to be permitted, economic efficiency cannot occur in electric power, regardless of measures to curb market power.

A separate issue for electric power, the question of how to have the right amount of capacity in place for customers whose demand fluctuates seasonally and diurnally, is also explored by Telser.[39] To make his next point he works through a complicated example about the correct amount of inventory to satisfy customer demand and at the same time result in a profitable business The example is germane for electricity, which cannot be economically stored. Telser writes:

> Thus with marginal inventory cost a constant and equal to the price as required by the condition for optimality of the inventory level [for electricity substitute optimal capacity in mW], expected receipts would be less than the total cost of the inventory. The single price fails to generate enough revenue to cover the total cost. . . . Explicit agreement between the suppliers and their customers on the inventory level, the price per unit, and a provision for sharing the difference between expected receipts and total cost in the form of long-term contracts could give a mutually acceptable arrangement among all of the parties that would be efficient.[40]

In working through the mathematics of his example, Telser shows that

it is optimal to have more stocks on hand than are expected to be sold. Since the optimal level of inventories is where

$$(b + t)[1 - F(y_0)] = \partial C(y_0)/\partial y, \tag{7}$$

it follows that $(b + t) >$ the marginal cost at the optimal y. Although this formulation describes the necessary condition that must be satisfied in order to obtain the optimal level of stocks, it leaves open the question of the nature of the arrangements that are capable of achieving the optimum.

The point is this. There is no adversary relation between customers and their suppliers. There is a gain they can share. The expected value of this gain is the difference between the expected benefit and the cost. . . . It is as if the customers owned the stores and the managers of the stores were their agents. Even so, there would remain the problem of devising appropriate terms between customers and their agent-suppliers so that the latter would choose the optimal inventory level.[41]

The notion that "the customers owned the stores and the managers of the stores were their agents" is a description of public power.

A Lawyer's Reply to the Argument for Allowing Horizontal Agreements

Many of the economists following Telser advocate relaxing or repealing antitrust laws to make collusion legal in such industries. Letting producers agree on prices and total capacity is, of course, now illegal. They aim at getting the "efficient" amount of capacity through "cooperation," and would then expect innovation to be driven by rivalry between competitors. Some of these economists come from what is called the public choice theory school, libertarian in policy proposals. They are trying to reconcile the problem of the behavior of firms with large overhead costs with the repeal of antitrust laws. They recognize that with large overhead costs the capacity in place is going to fluctuate severely around the optimum. There will be either too much capacity, leading to price wars, or too little, leading to price spikes. That is not *efficient*. They would recommend that the competitors cooperate, that is, collude, legally, so as to build the "correct" amount of capacity.

John Shepard Wiley Jr., professor of law at the UCLA School of Law, writing in 1987, defended the enforcement of antitrust law against the core theorists. He begins:

> Economists have kicked antitrust law around a lot in the last couple of decades but one thing has seemed clear: at least they have agreed that antitrust should outlaw per se horizontal agreements that explicitly and exclusively fix prices or restrain output. Recently, however, some economists have challenged even this remnant of doctrinal tradition.
>
> Using a part of game theory known as core theory, these economists suggest that horizontal agreements among competitors to restrain output sometimes can be essential for productive efficiency. One commentator rightly remarks that this work "strike[s] at the root of orthodox antitrust doctrine, even of the economic kind." Professor Lester Telser of the University of Chicago Department of Economics is the most prominent advocate of core theory (footnotes omitted).[42]

Wiley does not dispute the rigor of the analysis offered by Telser and the others. He does defend the antitrust laws, and asserts that policy makers should ignore the "good idea" of core theory. He says:

II. The Core: A Good Idea for Policymakers to Ignore

A. Quotas That Work Will Be Pretty Scary

Telser's quotas aim to improve productive efficiency, but in practice they necessarily empower industry to inflict on consumers the cartel costs of overly restricted output, unnecessarily high prices, and, possibly, dampened innovation. To avoid these losses, Telser's proposal would require that judges do what they always have refused to do: use antitrust law to regulate industry as if it were a public utility. There is every reason to respect this traditional judicial reluctance.[43]

With respect to electricity, however, it is not evident that the economists supporting core theory ideas, and specifically Telser, would recommend allowing power producers to cooperate unsupervised. On the contrary, Telser himself asserts that constraints on the "cooperators"— amounting to public utility regulation—would be necessary to result in economic efficiency:

> These constraints assume a variety of shapes in the real world. The state may intervene either by outright ownership of the plants or by regulation of the activities of the single firm supplying the output from its plants. Sometimes the state intervenes by acting on behalf of the buyers, or the buyers may form their own coalition to act in concert. In contrast to the cases where the core is nonvoid for a wide range of firm-size distributions, in this case with decreasing average cost at the plant level, few alternatives are compatible with an equilibrium. Under these cost conditions we may say there is either a natural monopoly or a natural monopsony.[44]

We conclude this section on game theory (the theory of the core) with further remarks from George Bittlingmayer, the "core theory" economist whose bold statement began this section: "These observations suggest that explicit cartelization, tacit collusion, and horizontal merger can be viewed, in many instances, as the noncompetitive arrangements that the firms in an industry *must necessarily adopt*."[45]

An Industry Where Cooperation Is Legal

There is an industry with legal antitrust exemptions that permit "cooperation" among rivals. It is ocean shipping. William Sjostrom has investigated ocean shipping in light of core theory. Sjostrom tests whether the ocean shipping conferences are cartels or a means to cope with an empty core. He notes that economists have argued that the practices of shipping conferences are consistent with cartel behavior, but sees difficulties with that argument. He concludes that "The results, although certainly not definitive, offer further evidence for the proposition that market arrangements that appear to be cartels may be attempts to solve the problem of an empty core."[46]

The American Bar Association's Hypothetical and the "Rule of Reason"

A hypothetical case to test whether "cooperation" will stand up to antitrust law was argued at an American Bar Association meeting in Chicago in 1996. The hypothetical looks at a situation where a utility and an IPP agree to a joint venture, rather than each building a power plant, where a market exists for only one new plant. In other words, they "cooperate" to not build competing plants. The case was argued before an invited federal judge, with a surprising result:

> The deal raises serious questions about the legality of agreeing not to compete and dividing markets. "Believe it or not," said Bolze, "what we (bar seminar attenders) came out with was that the decision would rely on the rule of reason and not treat the question as a *per se* violation (illegal on the face of it) and there's a good chance you could win this thing," Bolze predicted.[47]

The Theory of Positive Feedbacks

Finally, and roughly chronologically, we call the reader's attention to the work of Paul David and Brian Arthur. Their work provides a possible path for future research with respect to electric power production and, separately, the market for electricity. It incorporates two strands of thought, each of which is important in understanding network industries: One strand is increasing returns and the second is path dependence.

The first of these, increasing returns, was discussed earlier in reviewing the work of Telser and Bittlingmayer in the "theory of the core." Arthur focuses his analysis on technology and the new information economies, but the analysis fits electric power production quite well. In some ways the argument is similar to Telser's work, but Arthur strongly stresses that he is talking of increasing returns, as distinct from increasing returns to scale. Arthur writes:

Conventional economic theory is built on the assumption of diminishing returns. Economic actions engender a negative feedback that leads to a predictable equilibrium for prices and market shares. . . . According to conventional theory, the equilibrium marks the "best" outcome possible under the circumstances: the most efficient use and allocation of resources.

Such an agreeable picture often does violence to reality. In many parts of the economy, stabilizing forces appear not to operate, instead positive feedback magnifies the effects of small economic shifts: the economic models that describe such effects differ vastly from the conventional ones. Diminishing returns imply a single equilibrium point for the economy, but positive feedback—increasing returns—makes for many possible equilibrium points.[48]

A world of multiple equilibrium points cannot expect a market to control investment and pricing. Hence, electricity, as Telser shows, requires public control to reach optimal levels of investment, capacity, and pricing.

The discovery, or, rather, the rediscovery, of increasing returns seems to have led to the trendy "new natural monopolies," for example. pharmaceuticals and software. Secretary of the Treasury Larry Summers noted in a recent speech:

An information-based world is one in which more of the goods that are produced will have the character of pharmaceuticals or books or records, in that they involve very large fixed costs and much smaller marginal costs. . . .

The greater salience of these characteristics has crucial implications for business and for the functioning of the economy as a whole. For one thing, it means that the only incentive to produce anything is the possession of temporary monopoly power—because without that power the price will be bid down to marginal cost and the high initial fixed costs cannot be recouped.[49]

Secretary Summers focused on information-based industries, but the same cost structure, very large fixed costs and much smaller marginal costs, predominates in electric power production, and with the same implication: Without monopoly power (or cooperation in a tight oligopoly) the high initial fixed costs cannot be recouped.

Summers's speech seems to follow Paul David's notion of "path dependence."[50] David's argument is quite sophisticated. Summers's speech goes on to simplify the idea:

The same characteristics also mean that what engineers call positive feedback, philosophers call self-fulfilling prophesies, and what others call rolling snowball effects are increasingly important.

> The old economy is a negative feedback economy. Consider the classic Smithian model of wheat: when prices rise, farmers produce more, consumers buy less, and equilibrium is restored at a lower level of demand. By contrast, the information economy will increasingly be a positive feedback economy: one in which rising demand drives higher efficiency and higher returns, drives lower prices and yet higher demand. In such a world, the avalanche, rather than the thermostat, becomes the more attractive metaphor for economic policy.
>
> Another way to capture the distinction would be that the traditional industrial economy was a Newtonian system checks and balances, in which disequilibria of demand and supply arose, only to be equilibrated by adjusting prices. While the right metaphors for the new economy are more Darwinian, with the fittest surviving, the winner frequently taking all, and, as modern Darwinians have come to understand, accidents of history casting long and consequential shadows.[51]

It is interesting that the secretary of the treasury supports monopoly power as the driving force behind profits, and thus investment, for industries with large overhead costs, while at the same time the secretary of energy, to reach the same goal, advocates the elimination of monopoly in electricity.

Conclusion

Electric power, in common with other network industries, has characteristics that make public control necessary, through either regulation or public ownership. Only in this way can the cost to society be minimized. Only through public control can we have "just, reasonable, and nondiscriminatory rates."

We have shown that pricing at marginal cost in an industry with large overhead costs is unprofitable. Agriculture and the new high-tech and information industries, as well as electricity, provide examples. Although the mainstream of economists cling to the idea that pricing at marginal cost will provide efficient allocation of society's resources and maximize the wellbeing of the population, it has long been well known that that argument has no foundation.

In a chapter headed "Marginal Cost and the Just Price," J. de V. Graaff writes, "The measure of acceptance the marginal cost pricing principle has won among professional economists would be astonishing were not its pedigree so long and respectable."[52]

He concludes his chapter by defining the just price:

I suggest that the only price a public enterprise or a nationalized industry can be expected to set is what we may as well call a *just price—a price which is set with some regard for its effect on the distribution of wealth* as well as for its effect on the allocation of resources. Definite value judgments are naturally required for its determination—and a good deal of positive knowledge (italics in original).[53]

Regulatory commissions at both the state and federal level are charged with providing "just, reasonable, and nondiscriminatory rates." The conclusion here is that the market cannot do that job.

Notes

1. Later we will show that some of the same proponents in fact recognize that their standard arguments fail for industries like electric power.

2. William J. Baumol, Paul L. Joskow, and Alfred E. Kahn, "The Challenge for Federal and State Regulators: Transition from Regulation to Efficient Competition in Electric Power," append. A, p. 3. Paper submitted to FERC, Docket No. RM 958000 et al., 4 December 1994.

3. The authors do not provide any "mounting evidence" or citations for the assertion. The experience with telecommunications and airlines now suggests to many regulators and legislators that the evidence runs the other way. Price spikes in California's deregulated electric market in 2000 have convinced many legislators and regulators that electricity must be regulated or otherwise publicly controlled.

4. *Electricity Prices in a Competitive Environment: Marginal Cost Pricing of Generation Services and Financial Status of Electric Utilities,* Energy Information Administration, DOE/EIA-0614, August 1997, p. 11.

5. Repeated showings have had almost no impact. Perhaps the most elegant source reaching the conclusion that marginal cost pricing does not provide "economic efficiency" is J. de V. Graaff's *Theoretical Welfare Economics* (Cambridge: Cambridge University Press, 1963).

6. Baumol Joskow, and Kahn, "The Challenge for Federal and State Regulators," 19. As a quick aside, Ramsey pricing enjoys amazing acceptance among economists as a so-called second-best approach to setting prices equal to marginal cost. Ramsey pricing is difficult to distinguish from simple textbook monopoly pricing, where the profit-maximizing rule is to squeeze each customer for the maximum revenue possible. Recent work by Ron Baiman of Roosevelt University, "Why 'Second Best' Ramsey Pricing Doesn't Maximize Static Social Welfare: A Simple Progressive Social Pricing Theory," forthcoming, shows that Ramsey pricing minimizes, rather than maximizes, social welfare.

7. They put their example in terms of transmission rather than generation, but the overhead cost problem is the same in both.

8. Quoted in the *New York Times,* 10 June 1999, C1.

9. F. F. Loock, president, general manager, and sales manager of the Allen-Bradley Company, quoted in John G. Fuller, *The Gentlemen Conspirators* (New York: Grove Press, 1962), 14. Loock pled guilty and was fined $7,500 in 1961.

10. *Wall Street Journal,* 15 August 2000, B6.

11. Fritz Machlup, *The Basing-Point System* (Philadelphia: Blakiston, 1949), 2. Machlup's cite is to *Federal Trade Commission v. The Cement Institute et al.,* 333 U. S. 683 (1948) 68 S. Ct. 793, 809.

12. Agreeing on meeting a price sounds vaguely illegal, but vendors meeting announced price increases often justify the action in the news media as "competition."

13. The U.S. Department of Justice said about the crime, "The conspiracy lasted from January 1990 into February 1999 and affected the vitamins most commonly used as nutritional supplements or to enrich human food and animal feed—vitamins A, B2, B5, C, E, and Beta Carotene. Vitamin premixes, which are used to enrich breakfast cereals and numerous other processed foods were also affected by the conspiracy." Department of Justice *Press Release,* 20 May 1999.

14. See Machlup, *The Basing-Point System,* for the history of corn products until midcentury.

15. Ibid., 83.

16. Although Machlup considered the corn products industry less important in the overall economy than others he discussed in his book, he devoted eight pages to reviewing its antitrust history. See ibid., 83–90.

17. Sales between utilities were priced at "split savings." The difference between the running costs (system lambda) of the two systems was calculated and the price set halfway between them. The selling system thus got its fuel cost plus half the difference between the two running costs as a contribution to overhead.

18. Arthur Burns, the Alan Greenspan of the 1960s, makes this point. See *The Decline of Competition* (New York: McGraw-Hill, 1936).

19. Herling, *The Great Price Conspiracy,* 68.

20. Fuller, *The Gentlemen Conspirators,* 10.

21. Herling, *The Great Price Conspiracy,* 320, 320n.

22. George Bittlingmayer, "Decreasing Average Cost and Competition: A New Look at the Addyston Pipe Case," *Journal of Law and Economics* 25 (October 1982): 202.

23. J. M. Keynes, "The End of Laissez-Faire," in *The Collected Writings of John Maynard Keynes,* vol. 9, *Essays in Persuasion* (London: Macmillan Press, 1972), 284. Cited in James Crotty, "Was Keynes a Corporatist? Keynes's Radical Views on Industrial Policy and Macro Policy in the 1920s," *Journal of Economic Issues* 33, no 3 (September 1999). The essay was published as a pamphlet in 1926 and based on lectures given in 1924 and 1926.

24. John Maurice Clark, *Studies in the Economics of Overhead Costs* (Chicago: University of Chicago Press, 1923).

25. Ibid., ix.

26. Ibid., 11. Clark's footnotes have been omitted.

27. Note, as well, that one of his examples of railroad price discrimination of perhaps a century ago—"Shippers at local points saw goods hauled past them to junctions beyond at lower rates than they paid for their shorter hauls, and with simple logic reason that if the lower through rate was adequate, the higher local rate was obviously extortionate"—is an airline pricing scheme today!

28. A. T. Hadley, *Economics* (New York: G. P. Putnam's Sons, 1896), 151–54, quoted in Clark, *Studies in the Economics of Overhead Costs,* 12.

29. Gabriel Kolko, *Railroads and Regulation* (Princeton, N.J.: Princeton University Press, 1965).

30. See the work of Myron Gordon, who shows how share prices depend on the rate of growth of earnings. Myron J. Gordon, *The Investment, Financing and Valuation of the Corporation* (Homewood, Ill: Richard D. Irwin, 1962). See also Robin Marris, "Recent Developments in Theory of the Growth of The Firm," Mimeo, 1967, and "Prepared Direct Testimony of Eugene P. Coyle," Investigation No. 9108002, California PUC, 7 May 1993.

31. Abigail McWilliams notes that Telser identifies six characteristics that result in the "pathology" of having no competitive equilibrium. Abigail McWilliams, "Rethinking Horizontal Market Restrictions: in Defense of Cooperation in Empty Core Markets," *Quarterly Review of Economics and Business* 30, no. 3 (autumn 1990): 4.

32. "Noncooperative" game theory has entered the discussion of electric deregulation. It is used to provide the basis for arguing that an equilibrium can be attained without cooperation or collusion. A stable equilibrium, in turn, is the support for the belief that "the market" can work. See, for example, Borenstein, Bushnell, and Knittel, "Market Power in Electricity Markets: Beyond Concentration Measures," PWP-059, April 1998, and cites provided there. Telser addresses "noncooperative" game theory as well.

33. Lester G. Telser, *A Theory of Efficient Cooperation and Competition* (New York: Cambridge University Press, 1987), 45.

34. Lester G. Telser, *Journal of Law and Economics* (1985): 272. Telser repeats this passage in his 1987 book.

35. Lester G. Telser, *Economic Theory and the Core* (Chicago: University of Chicago Press, 1978). Interestingly enough, in the 1923 J. M. Clark book cited by Telser is found the 1896 quote from A. T. Hadley, cited in our note 29 above.

36. Ibid., 90.

37. Lester G. Telser, "Cooperation, Competition, and Efficiency," *Journal of Law & Economics* 28 (May 1985): 276.

38. Ibid., 272.

39. This is distinct from the problem of having an equilibrium amount of capacity over time. Even with the "correct" amount of total capacity, the seasonal or diurnal swings create a conflict between buyers and sellers.

40. Telser, "Cooperation, Competition, and Efficiency," 284.

41. Ibid., 280

42. John Shepard Wiley Jr., "Antitrust and Core Theory" *University of Chicago Law Review* (spring 1987): 556.

43. Ibid., 569.

44. Telser, *Economic Theory and the Core*, 65.

45. Bittlingmayer, "Decreasing Average Cost and Competition," 203.

46. William Sjostrom, "Collusion in Ocean Shipping: A Test of Monopoly and Empty Core Models," *Journal of Political Economy* 97, no. 5 (1989): 1177. Professor Sjostrom very generously introduced me to much of the core theory literature.

47. Conclusion of a moot court at "Overview of Key Antitrust Issues: Predatory and Strategic Behavior," in *Power Struggle: Antitrust and the Changing Rules of Electric Utility Competition* (Chicago: American Bar Association, 1996). Reported in PMA OnLine Magazine, October 1998.

48. W. Brian Arthur, "Positive Feedbacks in the Economy," *Scientific American*, February 1990, 92. Arthur makes the distinction between increasing returns and increasing returns to scale and stresses that he addresses the former. He sees the latter as the old smokestack industries, while the former are information based. Yet his description is very similar to that in Bittlingmayer's work on why competition could not work in processing industries in the 1890s.

49. Lawrence H. Summers, "The New Wealth of Nations," remarks at the Hambrecht & Quist Technology Conference, San Francisco, California, 10 May 2000.

50. Paul David, "Path Dependence, Its Critics and the Quest for 'Historical Economics,'" in *Evolution and Path Dependence in Economic Ideas,* ed. Garrouste and Ioannides (Cheltenham, U.K.: Edward Elgar, 2001).

51. Summers, "The New Wealth of Nations." It is outside the scope of this chapter to explore this, but think of a company like Enron, which has gotten very large in the trading of energy futures—that is, electric and gas. The advantage of being early and large leads to further advantage. This is the premise under which investors have supplied huge amounts of capital to Amazon.com while it unprofitably "gets big fast." Exploring how a very few large trading companies may come to dominate the electric power market in the future is a topic still to be researched, and would fruitfully start with David and Arthur's work.

52. De V. Graaff, *Theoretical Welfare Economics,* 142.

53. Ibid., 155.

Taking the Road Less Traveled: Harry Trebing and the Mythology of Deregulation

THOMAS C. GORAK

Introduction

Over the past seventeen years, the regulation of public utilities has undergone a massive change, particularly in the telecommunications, natural gas, and electric industries. Traditional "hands-on" regulation by duly authorized public agencies and commissions has been abandoned—to various degrees—at the federal and state levels. Theoretically, the reason for this change is to inject competition into these formerly regulated utility industries, with the lofty goal of decreasing prices and increasing services for all consumers. However, as is often the case, the goal is not reflected in reality, and there is a danger that deregulation has created the exact antithesis of competition—that is, industries that will be controlled by either monopoly or oligopoly power.

In a body of work spanning many years, Professor Harry M. Trebing anticipated that the experiment in light-handed regulation would fail, predicted that the result of this failure would be the emergence of oligopoly power, and posited that there is a workable remedy for these failures that will satisfy both those who seek more competition in utility industries, and those who worry that deregulation is proceeding in a fashion that is decidedly harmful to so-called captive residential and small commercial customers.[1] This chapter explores the deregulation of the utility industry, primarily through a discussion of the deregulation of the interstate natural gas pipeline industry, and how the concerns raised by Professor Trebing have, unfortunately, come to fruition. The chapter concludes with an analysis of Professor Trebing's remedy for the problems plaguing the utility industry today: the structural separation of the network and basic utility services from competitive services.

Professor Trebing has never lost sight of the fact that the goal of both regulation and deregulation should be the same; that is, to protect the public interest. While the "public interest" standard is perhaps viewed as an outdated concept by those who tout deregulation, Professor Trebing has reminded the public utility industry again and again of its importance. Moreover, he has frequently observed that a public utility company is something more than a manufacturing firm or processing plant; instead, "public utility networks have come to be recognized as an integral part of the nation's infrastructure" (Trebing 1994, 379). Thus, deregulation also raises social concerns, which have been succinctly summarized by Professor Trebing:

> Can the establishment, utilization, and maintenance of an infrastructure that is of fundamental importance in a globalized economy be entrusted to the signals, motivations, and penalties associated with substantially deregulated electricity, natural gas, and telecommunication markets? (Trebing 1994, 379)

These issues are seldom addressed in any depth in the current debate over deregulation of the utility industry. Yet, as Professor Trebing has recognized, these issues should be addressed both in reviewing the success of deregulation to date and before deciding whether to continue current deregulation policies in the future.

It has become increasingly clear to Professor Trebing (and the author) that while decreased reliance upon regulation and increased reliance on competitive forces in the telecommunications, natural gas, and electric industries has led to lower prices for industrial and larger commercial customers, the same is not true for smaller commercial and residential customers. More importantly, if the present template for deregulation continues to be applied, there is the possibility that prices will actually increase while service decreases for residential and most commercial customers.

The problem is that, despite the many changes fostered upon the utility industry in the name of competition, competition has not been achieved. As Professor Trebing has observed:

> growing patterns of market concentration in the major transportation and utility industries clearly challenge the prospects for competition. High concentration gives the firm discretionary control over markets, prices, and investment. At the same time, since profits are linked to market share there is a strong incentive to capture market share, thereby further increasing

concentration. . . . Without [consumer] activism, the residential and small business player will be effectively removed and major decisions regarding price, investment, and service in network industries will be determined largely by newly redefined utilities, potential entrants, large-volume buyers, and a greatly diminished regulatory presence. Furthermore, when concentration radically changes industry structures, new problems will arise that are not immediately evident when individual consumers attempt to choose between supplier A and supplier B. (Trebing 1999, 427)

Those that champion deregulation would do well to review Professor Trebing's work, which demonstrates that deregulation as currently practiced is inferior to traditional regulation in terms of protecting captive customers against the abuse of market power, and may, in fact, foster that abuse.

Fundamental Regulatory Principles

As a prelude to a discussion of the current status of deregulation, it is helpful to understand the legal and economic forces that have shaped the regulation of the public utility industry in the United States. Public utility companies are companies that supply continuous or repeated services through permanent physical connections between the supplier and the consumer—generally, electricity, gas, communications, water, and sewer. Traditionally, such companies were said to share certain basic characteristics. *First,* public utilities tend to be monopolies, because the given industry operates more efficiently as a monopoly. *Second,* and related, it is less costly for a single firm to provide service in a given area than it is to have multiple firms competing to provide that service. *Third,* public utilities are generally privately owned, although there are a large number of publicly owned electric utilities, as well as some publicly owned gas utilities. *Fourth,* these companies are publicly regulated. For example, states grant "exclusive" service area franchises in return for agreement by a public utility company to serve all customers that seek service at tariffed rates. Those utilities that operate in interstate commerce make a similar regulatory compact, and are subject to regulation by federal agencies, such as the Federal Energy Regulatory Commission (FERC).

While a detailed review of the legal principles which have developed with respect to public utility companies is beyond the scope of this chapter, certain key principles must be addressed in any discussion of deregulation. The basic authority to regulate is derived from common law; simply stated, businesses essential to commerce have an obligation to serve the public fairly. The United States Constitution encompasses the basic authority to regulate in the Commerce Clause.[2] In a longstanding series of decisions, the Supreme Court has held that property becomes clothed with a public interest when used in a manner to make it of public consequence, which affects the community at large.[3] Therefore, when one devotes his property to a use in which the public has an interest, he, in effect, grants to the public an interest in that use, and must submit that use to be controlled by the public for the common good. States generally derive their power to regulate from their police powers as protected by the Tenth Amendment to the United States Constitution; in general, a state is free to adopt whatever economic policy may reasonably be deemed to promote the public welfare, and to enforce that policy by legislation adapted to its purpose.[4]

What is immediately noticeable, of course, is the great opportunity for engaging in all sorts of mischief under these principles. Virtually no one could disagree with the notion that companies endowed with the public interest should be regulated so as to protect that interest. However, the devil, as they say, is in the details, and perhaps more importantly, in who controls the details. The public interest standard is, at best, a vague one, and is subject to different interpretations at different points in time. These differing interpretations are what permitted the massive changes in regulation that are now occurring without any major changes in the underlying legal precedents or applicable statutes. Instead, these changes are based on "creative" new ways of interpreting and applying these precedents and statutes by a set of regulators and judges that have different economic and policy views than those of their predecessors. The issue is whether these new standards do, in fact, protect and promote the public interest.

To be sure, the public interest standard is not totally undefined. Loose interpretations of the public interest standard to be applied by regulatory authorities are generally set forth in enabling legislation. Hence, the interstate natural gas industry is primarily regulated under (appropriately enough) the Natural Gas Act of 1938 (NGA);[5] the interstate electric industry is primarily regulated under the Federal Power Act of 1935;[6] and intrastate electric and gas utilities are regulated under a variety of state statutes.[7] Generally, these statutes provide that public utility companies shall operate in the public interest. The following principles have emerged to guide regulators:

- Public utility companies must be regulated so as to protect the "public interest."
- The rates charged for public utility services must be "just and reasonable."

- Public utility companies may not "unduly discriminate" among customers.
- Public utility companies may not provide "undue preferences" to particular customers.

None of these principles is subject to precise definition, and each can be shaped to address different circumstances. Moreover, their interpretation in the first instance is left to the agency that is charged with their enforcement. This places tremendous power in the agency's hands to interpret these principles in the light of the "hot" economic or business theory of the day. Currently, the "hot" theory is that deregulation will do a better job at keeping prices and services competitive than will traditional regulation.

Regulation of the Interstate Natural Gas Industry

This chapter focuses on changes in the interstate natural gas industry to illustrate the problems with deregulation and the attempt to inject competitive forces into an industry that is, by its nature, noncompetitive. The principles discussed are, however, equally applicable to the electric power and telecommunications industries. The key issues to consider, from a legal perspective, are whether, and to what extent, the public interest is served by deregulating traditionally regulated industries, and what can be done to close Pandora's box in the event that the experiment with competitive forces fails.

As noted previously, the foundation for the regulation of interstate natural gas pipelines is the NGA. The NGA allows interstate pipelines to transport gas from producers to local distributors and direct end users in other states, as well as to purchase gas and resell it on their own account. Pipelines may transport gas purchased by end users and distributors directly from producers, but have no "common carrier" obligation to do so. The rates that these pipelines may charge are regulated by what is now called the Federal Energy Regulatory Commission, or FERC.[8]

Importantly, in accordance with the general principles discussed above, the NGA prohibits interstate natural gas pipelines from engaging in conduct that is unduly discriminatory, or that provides an unreasonable preference to any customer.[9] Stated differently, the NGA prevents pipelines from offering rates or services that discriminate among similarly situated customers. Moreover, on its own motion, FERC may adopt corrective measures to remedy any unjust, unreasonable, unduly preferential, or unduly discriminatory rates or services.[10] What is, perhaps, more interesting about the NGA are the conditions that led to its passage. The NGA was prompted by the emergence of huge, unregulated firms in the natural gas industry. These firms exerted considerable market power, and the NGA was Congress' response to the abuse of this monopoly power by pipelines and producers.[11]

For the next forty years or so, the industry followed a traditional regulatory model. Pipelines became vertically integrated; they or their subsidiaries or affiliates produced the gas at the wellhead, "bundled" that gas with the physical pipeline capacity necessary to transport it to the buyer, and charged a bundled rate for the entire service. These rates were established under traditional cost of service regulation methods, as approved by the courts. That is, federal and state regulators determined a just and reasonable rate by looking at a representative level of expenses and investment, and establishing a reasonable rate of return for the company. Professor Trebing describes this period as an age of traditional regulation (Trebing 1994, 380).

In addition, under a seminal 1954 United States Supreme Court case, known as the *Phillips* case, federal regulators were given the authority to regulate the price of the gas commodity at the wellhead—that is, to set the maximum prices that producers could charge.[12] There was not a great deal of differentiation in the transportation services offered by pipelines; a buyer could purchase firm service, which would guarantee that a certain amount of gas would be delivered on a given day, or interruptible service, whereby the buyer agreed to permit interruptions of its service on short notice in return for a much lower rate.

The Deregulation of the Natural Gas Industry

As frequently observed by Professor Trebing, the problems that led to the current deregulation movement began in the late 1960s (Trebing 1994, 380).[13] In the natural gas industry, the FPC (FERC's predecessor) used its *Phillips* authority to keep the price of gas below a market clearing price—that is, at an artificially low level. Because gas did *not* have to be sold into the interstate market, but could instead be sold within the borders of the state where it was produced or simply shut in hopes that prices would rise in the future, producers unwilling to accept these low market prices withheld their gas supplies from the interstate market. The result was the gas shortages and curtailments of the late 1970s.

In an effort to assuage these shortages, Congress, in 1978, passed the Natural Gas Policy Act of 1978, or NGPA.[14] The NGPA basically reversed the *Phillips* decision and terminated over time FERC's authority to set wellhead prices for natural gas. Congress attempted to substitute market forces for cost-based priced controls to establish the price of gas production at the "wellhead" market. However, rather than simply permitting the market to establish the price of gas at the wellhead, the NGPA instead instituted a complex pricing scheme that set the maximum price level for gas produced at different types of wells and adjusted these prices upward by way of an index.

The 1978 predictions of 1985 gas markets were in error, and a gas surplus resulted. Factors contributing to this surplus included the increased wellhead prices, impending total decontrol under the NGPA, greater energy conservation, and lower prices of competing fuels. At the same time, the maximum permissible price for gas under the NGPA rose above market prices, so that an anomaly occurred: consumers were faced with rising prices in the face of a gas surplus. Longstanding notions of supply and demand were violated.

Another problem was also developing. Given the curtailments of the late 1970s, pipelines had entered into long-term (twenty-year) contracts during the period from 1979 to 1981 that locked them into purchases of NGPA and regulated gas at volumes and prices based on 1978 expectations, that is, above market prices. This led to the so-called take-or-pay problem; simply stated, pipelines had to pay for this gas whether or not it was taken.

These conditions provided the genesis for deregulation. If all consumers had been price inelastic, that is, if they did not have any alternatives to the use of natural gas, rates most likely would have been structured so as to apportion the above-market prices between *all* pipeline customers and the pipelines' shareholders. However, certain customers, notably industrial dual-fuel end users, had the ability to substitute oil for natural gas. Faced with higher-than-market prices for natural gas as a result of the NGPA, they did precisely that. The result was that inelastic customers— residential and commercial consumers with no alternatives to natural gas—were not only left to pay the above-market NGPA prices, but an additional $6 billion that was the result of contracts signed by the pipelines that had so-called take-or-pay clauses stating that the pipeline either had to take the gas or pay for it (General Accounting Office 1993, 15–16). Pipelines took the gas, and those unlucky consumers that could not switch to some other fuel source—that is, captive residential and commercial customers—were left with both substantial take-or-pay costs as well as the high commodity prices for natural gas under the NGPA.

It was clear at this point that traditional regulation was butting up against heretofore unheard of market conditions. The just and reasonable rate that pipelines wanted enforced at this time was one that permitted them to recover the costs of operating the pipeline, the price paid for the gas commodity (the NGPA above-market price), and any take-or-pay costs. According to the pipelines, they were not responsible for the curtailments of the 1970s, and they were entitled to recover the costs associated with long-term contracts they had signed to avoid a recurrence of those conditions—even if they had locked into above-market prices for an inordinately long period of time. Consumers, on the other hand, argued that a just and reasonable rate could not include any take-or-pay costs because they, as the pipelines' remaining customers, were not responsible for causing those costs since they had remained natural gas customers and continued to purchase gas at or above historic levels. Something had to give.

Something did. As a basic proposition, if a monopolist wants to maximize its profits, it extracts the highest price possible from its inelastic customers (that is, those who have no ready alternatives to its product) and charges whatever price it can to its elastic customers, so as to collect at least some profit from them. It is this ability to segment markets to maximize profits that led to regulation of monopolies in the first place. Yet, in responding to the market conditions existing in the natural gas industry in the early 1980s, FERC—either unwittingly or wittingly—provided the monopolies under its control with the ability to maximize profits in precisely this fashion. FERC approved—in the name of just and reasonable, nondiscriminatory, and nonpreferential rates—a special marketing and blanket certificate program that permitted pipelines to segment their customers into two separate classes.[15] Those customers with access to alternative fuels, primarily oil, were permitted to avoid buying the pipeline's above-market priced NGPA gas and to purchase transportation-only service from the pipelines. Captive customers, including residential and small commercials, were prohibited from utilizing transportation-only services to purchase market-priced gas supplies, and, instead, were forced to buy the pipelines' overpriced gas supplies.

In a series of cases now known as the *Maryland People's Counsel* (*MPC*) cases, captive residential, commercial, and other customers of local distribution companies (LDCs) argued that they should have the same access to market-priced supplies of gas that their industrial counterparts had obtained through the SMPs.[16] Utilizing the same regulatory principles previously discussed, these customers argued that FERC's decision to bar them from programs that permitted access to market-priced gas were unduly discriminatory and preferential. On appeal, the United States Court of Appeals *agreed* with these captive customers that the discriminatory aspects of those programs had not been justified. The court stated, again using traditional regulatory notions of discrimination and undue preference, that the argument that the SMPs enabled pipelines to price discriminate, that is, to sell their own overpriced gas to captive consumers while still retaining fuel-switchable customers by serving them at market rates, was simply not answered by the FERC.

In 1985, in response to the *MPC* decisions and changes in the industry, FERC issued a series of orders, beginning with Order 436,[17] that completely restructured the industry—a process that is continuing today. In Order 436, FERC stated that nondiscriminatory access to pipeline transportation and storage services was the cornerstone of its new rule. Under Order 436, interstate pipelines were required to unbundle their sales and transportation services into two separate and distinct services instead of one bundled service, and to provide nondiscriminatory access to all customers to pipeline transportation (capacity) service. Thus, residential and commercial customers, through the LDCs that served them, now had access to lower-priced gas supplies. Unfortunately, there was still the thorny problem of take-or-pay liability; as noted previously, consumers wound up paying almost $6 billion to pipelines for the pipelines' contracting mistakes.

The courts upheld FERC's authority to promulgate Order 436, stating that FERC had properly exercised its NGA power to stamp out undue discrimination based upon its finding that pipelines continued to wield substantial market power by denying sales customers access to competitively priced gas.[18] Hence, traditional regulatory standards were once again applied in a non-traditional way to further the public interest, as it was perceived at the time.

Even given their substantial and unwarranted contribution to the pipelines' take-or-pay woes, captive customers might have come out ahead had FERC left well enough alone after Order 436. Coupled with the fact that Congress completely deregulated the price of gas at the wellhead in 1990, Order 436 attempted to ensure fair and equitable access for all customers to pipeline capacity at rates that remained regulated subject to the just and reasonable standard. This allowed all customers (industrial, commercial, and residential alike) to purchase competitively priced gas supplies from a large number of suppliers. At the time, FERC referred to this as the "level playing field."

Unfortunately, FERC did not choose to leave well enough alone. Having created a pipeline network that allowed buyers nondiscriminatory access to capacity, and sellers the opportunity to interact with all types of buyers, FERC decided—again in the name of nondiscriminatory and nonpreferential rates—to "untilt" the level playing field. In the process, FERC has created conditions that, if left unchecked, will lead to amalgamation of market power and an industry that is controlled by a few large entities. What is more, these entities will largely be beyond regulation, a result that is decidedly not in the public interest, no matter how one chooses to define it, and that may have particularly detrimental impacts on commercial and residential customers.

The first major step down this road was Order 636.[19] In that order, FERC essentially decided that pipelines should no longer be in the business of selling the gas commodity; they should instead, FERC said, sell only transportation and storage capacity. If a pipeline wanted to sell the gas commodity, it would have to do so through an affiliate, and the sales price would be unregulated. In addition, Order 636 shifted virtually all of a pipeline's fixed costs into the demand charge—a fixed charge that is paid by firm service customers every month whether or not gas is actually taken. This rate design—the so-called straight fixed-variable or SFV rate design— is harmful to residential and commercial customers that must contract for a substantial level of firm pipeline capacity in order to have service available on the coldest of days. In essence, it shifts a disproportionate amount of the costs associated with construction and operation of pipelines to inelastic residential and commercial firm service customers. In addition, Order 636 instituted a so-called capacity release program. The essence of the program is that unused capacity may be sold by the capacity holder to other buyers in the market. The program may promote full utilization of the pipeline system, but, as will be discussed later, also raises the specter that unregulated entities can gain control of the pipeline system.

Since the inception of Order 636, FERC has embarked on a number of other rate and service initiatives. For example, FERC has routinely permitted so-called negotiated rates and has considered permitting negotiated services.[20] In a nutshell, under FERC's negotiated rate program, as long as a pipeline agrees to provide a tariffed rate or service that was once established under traditional regulatory methods, it may negotiate *any* rate or service with *any* customer. It takes no particular expertise to conclude that those parties that will be able to negotiate lower rates and more flexible services are those parties that have significant market power, such as large industrial users. Pipelines will again segment their markets into two classes, shippers that have market power and access to alternatives, and shippers that have neither. Pipelines will negotiate rates and services with the former and refuse to do so with the latter. Those consumers that have little market power will be left to pay stale, nonmarket rates for services and may well see the quality of their service decline as the pipeline provides more and better negotiated services to its larger customers.

Moreover, pipelines may attempt to coerce shippers that lack market power into paying *higher* rates for less flexible services under this policy.

Obviously, such results would not be compatible with the traditional consumer protection mandate of the NGA. Stated simply, permitting pipelines that possess substantial market power to act as if they do not possess such power will lead directly to anticompetitive behavior and the maximization of monopoly profits. This result underscores the point that deregulation does not necessarily result in a competitive market nor serve the public interest. In addition, it should not go unnoticed that this type of market segmentation is exactly the type of segmentation that was found unlawful in the *Maryland People's Counsel* cases as unduly discriminatory. Yet, to date, courts have not struck down the negotiated rate program, although invited to do so.[21]

In the year 2000, FERC has issued a new industry-wide order, Order 637.[22] According to FERC, the purpose of the order is to "improve the efficiency of the gas market and to provide captive customers with the opportunity to reduce their cost of holding long-term pipeline capacity while continuing to protect against the exercise of market power."[23] To achieve these goals, FERC made a number of changes to its regulation of pipeline services. Chief among these changes is FERC's decision to permit LDCs and other captive customers to charge a price *above* the maximum lawful cost-based tariff rate for short-term sales of capacity that these customers hold but do not always need under firm contracts ("released capacity").[24] According to FERC, this change will enhance the efficiency of the market, while, at the same time, the continued regulation of pipeline rates and services—including interruptible service—will provide protection against the exercise of market power.[25] As discussed below, while Order 637 is a step in the right direction, pipelines are already taking steps to undermine the value of these changes to captive customers.

Order 637 also addressed so called term-differentiated rates, changes in scheduling procedures, revisions to penalty procedures, and changes in reporting requirements that are designed to provide more "transparent" pricing information and to permit more effective monitoring for the exercise of market power and undue discrimination. Again, the expressed goal for these changes is to enhance competition; the question is whether these changes, without more, can achieve that goal.

FERC also instituted a new process to undertake a continuing examination of the market and the relationship of its rules to the market.[26] This examination involves questions of rate design and risk allocation in light of changing long-term contracting policies, improving market centers, creating greater integration of capacity allocation, and scheduling processes with the growing trend toward e-commerce, and reexamining the methods for setting and reviewing pipeline rates.

With respect to the latter, FERC stated that it will, in the future, consider whether rate design policies need to be changed to establish incentives for pipelines to enhance quality and efficiency and reward pipelines appropriately. One example of such rates would undoubtedly be price caps; that is, FERC would set a price cap for pipeline transportation services, which would periodically be increased to account for inflation and decreased to account for increases in productivity. However, price caps do not protect captive, inelastic consumers. Instead, they encourage the pipeline to permit cross-subsidization of large customers by small customers by setting a high capped rate for captive customers and a low rate for noncaptive customers.

The Failure of Deregulation to Protect the Public Interest

As discussed, FERC has opined that policies such as open access, negotiated rates, and incentive or performance-based rates will maximize competition, mitigate the ability to exercise market power, and provide flexibility in rates and terms for pipeline services. However, as the experience in the natural gas industry shows, it is unlikely that FERC's policies will achieve these goals. In fact, it is more likely that FERC has established the basis for the reemergence of significant market power by pipelines and producers, and, at the same time, has reduced the ability of consumers to take action to remedy these abuses. Order 637, while somewhat helpful to captive customers, does not directly address these market power problems.

The reason for this gloomy outlook is that FERC has failed to account for the effects of existing and emerging market power on its open-access policies and proposals. New concerns with respect to the market power of unregulated entities—that is, marketers, brokers, producers, and entities other than pipelines—are rapidly emerging. For example, while the interstate natural gas supply—as opposed to the capacity—market is now generally considered to be competitive, this conclusion may be reversed in the not-too-distant future. Following Order 636, there were few barriers to entry into the supply market and many new large and small third-party suppliers emerged. However, if dominant third-party suppliers evolve (as current evidence suggests that they will), through either growth, acquisition, or merger, barriers to entry will develop.

If these patterns persist, gas supplies will be controlled by an oligopoly. Professor Trebing has summarized the problem this way:

> The current popularity of deregulation and marketization of public utility services rests on the belief that new, profit driven incentives and new systems of supply will enhance efficiency, accelerate innovation and eventually lower real prices to all classes of customers. Whether this is a realistic expectation depends on the emergence of effective competition across the board. If deregulation results in industries characterized by high market concentration and tight oligopoly, then an entirely different outcome can be anticipated. (Trebing 1998a, 61)

As Professor Trebing recognizes, the changing industry structures in electricity, telecommunications, and natural gas (as discussed previously) appear to be moving toward tight oligopoly, rather than high levels of competition:

> If this is correct, primary reliance on price caps, incentive allowances, and open access to the network (so-called light regulation) will not assure levels of industry performance that maximize their contribution to the national infrastructure. That is, light regulation will either be ineffectual or irrelevant in dealing with oligopoly. (Trebing 1996a, 71)

As Professor Trebing has often observed, the simplest definition of an oligopoly focuses on market structure. In his view, market dominance exists when one firm has 40 to 100 percent of a market and barriers to entry are high; tight oligopoly exists when the leading four firms, combined, have 60 to 100 percent of the market and barriers to entry persist; and competition exists when no firm has more than 40 percent of the market and there are five or six firms of comparable size which will serve to prevent collusion (Trebing 1996a, 71).

If oligopoly exists, prices will no longer necessarily track costs, and profits will be higher than those that would have prevailed under either traditional, stringent, rate-base regulation *or* competition (Trebing 1996b, 564). Equally important, there will be strong incentives for cross-subsidization, price discrimination, and risk shifting (ibid). In the gas industry, the large unregulated supplier will be able to structure its sales portfolio precisely as pipelines did under the special marketing programs that were struck down in the *Maryland People's Counsel* cases. Suppliers will segment their markets into captive and noncaptive segments, increasing prices to those with no alternatives, that is, residential and small commercial consumers, and decreasing prices to those with market power or access to alternatives, that is, industrial consumers.

Mergers may also have a direct effect on the future viability of existing market participants, leading to a decidedly less competitive supply market. New mergers and acquisitions in the energy sector are announced on a seemingly daily basis. This trend has been readily apparent in the natural gas industry since shortly after the promulgation of Order 636. For example, in 1996, the Energy Information Administration (EIA) reported that the top ten natural gas marketers in 1994 accounted for 31 Bcf in average national daily sales, or about 42 percent of U.S. consumption, but that following a series of proposed and completed mergers, this same percentage of sales would be provided by the four largest marketers (Energy Information Agency 1996, 22–23). In 1998, EIA reported that although the market share of the four major marketers had declined somewhat for the period from 1992 to 1997, sales had more than doubled (Energy Information Agency 1998, 152–53). EIA also observed that, for the energy sector, the 1990s marked a period of intense merger activity and sweeping corporate combinations (Energy Information Agency 1998, 148). EIA further reported that mergers and acquisitions among companies in the natural gas industry increased fourfold between 1990 and 1997, and that the value of mergers throughout the energy sector increased more than fourfold between 1992 and 1997 (Energy Information Agency 1998, 147).

As noted, this trend is not confined to the natural gas industry. EIA reported that from 1997 through April 2000, twenty-three convergence mergers involving gas electric companies with assets valued at $0.5 billion or above were completed or pending completion (Energy Information Agency 2000, 98). A convergence merger is defined by EIA as a merger in which one company's primary business activity is natural gas production, processing, transportation, or sales, and the other company's primary business activity is electricity generation, transmission, or sales (98). The potential benefits of such mergers to the companies involved include the transfer of a gas company's experience in marketing and trading to an electric company that is relatively new to these areas, diversification of products and services, potential for increasing market share through cross-selling, and expanding access to a fuel supply for electric power plants (103). As discussed herein, the benefits—if any—for retail customers are far from clear. As EIA observed, while the intent of convergence mergers is to strengthen the company's position in the competitive industry, it is not clear whether "electric customers will be better off as well" (108). The same conclusion holds true for gas customers.

FERC underscored these trends in Order 637:

> The pace of mergers and alliances raises questions about the future structure of the industry. Mergers between pipeline corporations can decrease competition in markets where the merged firms previously competed. Vertical mergers between pipeline companies and gas fired power generators

raise concerns about the ability of the integrated firm to injure competition by favoring its vertically integrated affiliate. The increasing use of asset managers by LDCs and other shippers to manage their pipeline capacity could result in the concentration of pipeline capacity in a few hands, reducing the competitiveness of the capacity resale market.[27]

These trends do not bode well for the development of a truly competitive market. Smaller marketers will find themselves under increasing economic pressure as margins they earn from buying and selling gas become squeezed by the entry of large firms into the market. If only a few dominant players control the price of supplies and the terms and conditions under which they will be sold, the competitive supply market will soon cease to exist. FERC will then be faced with the unenviable task of dealing with an oligopoly of unregulated suppliers.[28]

There is yet another significant danger posed by unregulated marketers. Marketers and other nonregulated third-party suppliers are now purchasing and holding substantial amounts of pipeline transportation and storage capacity, and may sell that capacity packaged with their own supplies as a bundled service.[29] EIA has observed:

> Marketing companies are playing a key role in the restructured gas market by offering the aggregation and bundling function previously provided by pipeline companies. Consumers contract separately for gas purchases and transportation, receiving transportation from the pipeline company and local distribution company. Customers can purchase supplies from any seller. Many customers use marketing companies to rebundle services. Marketing companies are not regulated.[30]

Serious problems will emerge if control of large portions of pipeline capacity falls into the hands of a small number of unregulated entities. For example, LDCs that serve residential and commercial needs may not be able to negotiate directly with a pipeline for additional firm capacity to serve growing needs because third-party suppliers hold all of the available excess capacity. The only option available to these shippers may be a take-it-or-leave-it bundled service that includes a premium over market prices for supplies. In other words, the suppliers would offer to sell the necessary interstate pipeline capacity to an LDC at the FERC-established rate, *provided* that the LDC agrees to purchase its gas supplies from the same supplier at an above-market price. Because the gas supplier is not regulated by FERC, there is no direct relief to the consumer. In order to seek redress for this market power abuse, the consumer would have to file an antitrust suit, which is both expensive and time consuming.

Solutions to the Problems

The obvious question is how to deal with these problems. With respect to interstate pipelines, the most direct way to address market power abuses is to ensure that all shippers continue to have nondiscriminatory access to the interstate pipeline network. Pipelines should be required to make available to all shippers an established, nonnegotiable menu of firm and interruptible transportation and storage services; this requirement is similar to that imposed on common carriers. If a pipeline desires to provide a new service, or a variant of an existing one, to a shipper, that service should be made available to all other shippers as well. In other words, the availability of a new or more flexible service should not be limited to a shipper or shippers that have significant market power.

As noted previously, FERC's Order 637 does acknowledge increasing concerns with market power.[31] However, FERC does not provide a long-term, structural solution to these problems. Instead, it addresses a number of discrete issues within the order (such as removal of the short-term capacity release price cap, penalties, scheduling, and the provision of additional data), and states that "whether more fundamental changes are needed will depend on future market developments and especially how the industry responds to the changes adopted in [Order 637]."[32] FERC intends to address other issues through a series of discussions on an industry-wide basis.

As to the discrete issues, while many of the changes in Order 637 are long past due, they are, at best, narrowly focused solutions to specific problems. For example, removing the maximum rate cap for capacity releases by LDCs and other captive customers may, in limited circumstances, permit those customers to recover a portion of their SFV demand charges. Other changes under Order 637, such as reducing penalties, streamlining scheduling, and encouraging new services to address imbalances, are welcome but do not address the fundamental structural problems discussed in this chapter.

Moreover, pipelines are already devising ways to undercut this change through a combination of negotiated rates and service restructuring. For example, pipelines have sought approval of a "limited firm transportation" (LFT) service.[33] In exchange for a customer's promise to permit interruption of service for a period as short as one day, the pipeline would provide the customer with LFT transportation service that is otherwise indistinguishable from firm service on all other days in terms of delivery and receipt point priority, scheduling, and curtailment.

When this proposal is coupled with the pipeline's existing authority to negotiate rates that can also exceed the maximum rate cap, the pipeline clearly has the means to undercut an LDC's price under the new capacity release rules. If that occurs, the stated goal of Order 637—to protect captive customers, fairly apportion the revenue responsibility between captive customers with limited alternatives and short-term shippers with greater options, and, at the same time, prevent pipelines from exercising market power—will have been effectively nullified.[34]

As noted, in Order 637, FERC has stated that it will address market power and other issues in the future. The problem is that this discussion will apparently include certain issues, such as performance-based or incentive rates and so-called two track rate making (which would permit cost-based rates for captive customers and market-oriented rates for noncaptive customers)[35] that, for the reasons addressed by Professor Trebing, will exacerbate, rather than remedy, market power problems.

To remedy the problems associated with market power abuse, a more fundamental change is required. Professor Trebing has long championed the use of structural separation as a means to negate oligopoly power, increase customer options, and strengthen the infrastructure:

> Many of the domestic issues of market power associated with tight oligopoly could be addressed directly by introducing a full, mandatory separation of the network from all services deemed to be competitive that utilize the network. With structural separation, the network would have common carrier status with an obligation to serve all comers. It would be subject to appropriate state and federal regulation, and it would not be protected from the threat of bypass. (Trebing, 1998b, 66)

According to Professor Trebing, structural separation would entail an independent network with its own financing and board of directors, and would be subject to regulatory control (Trebing 1998c, 14). In his view, such an entity would have a strong incentive to "expand usage on the system, minimize bottlenecks, and develop a rate structure that would promote overall efficiency" (ibid.). At the same time, any tendency to restrict capacity would be nullified by a requirement to provide adequate service, which is similar to the traditional utility obligation to serve (ibid.). The network would not be permitted to enter into joint ventures of any type with deregulated marketing affiliates, or any other group or entity using its service (ibid.).

Professor Trebing has discussed the numerous benefits associated with structural separation. Most importantly, market concentration among buyers and sellers would decline as steps were taken to expand network access and coverage, which would lead to a decline in oligopoly power (ibid.). Other benefits include, but are by no means limited to, the following: (1) the incremental cost of adding new services would fall as the size of the network increased; (2) capital markets would be better able to appraise the risk inherent with the operations of an independent network; (3) there would be an incentive to achieve all inherent network and coordination economies; (4) there would be no incentive to denigrate service or disinvest in the network, since the network would have no financial ties to any other group or entity; (5) the network would have an incentive to innovate and modernize because it would be subject to bypass; (6) an independent network would be free from the need to consider the ramifications of its actions on other parts of the corporate organization; (7) price volatility in secondary markets could potentially be minimized because an expanded network could provide greater opportunities for arbitrage; (8) as the size of the network increased, the ability of oligopsony buyers to extract price concessions would diminish because sellers would have other options; (9) as the size of the network increased, the market power of individual sellers would decrease because more buyers would have access to more sources of supply; (10) as the number of buyer options increased, the number of captive customers should decrease; and (11) structural separations would minimize the opportunity to cross-subsidize between regulated and unregulated activities or combine them through tie-in sales via supposedly separate marketing affiliates (Trebing 1998c, 14; Trebing 1998b, 66–68).

The obvious question, of course, is whether such a structure—which would require a FERC order or legislation requiring that interstate pipelines be totally divorced from their parent corporations and their affiliates—could be imposed on the interstate pipeline system. Both legal and FERC precedent indicate that FERC has the necessary power to achieve this goal. As noted in the *AGD* case, FERC's remedial powers are at their zenith when FERC is addressing issues of market power, discrimination, and anticompetitive behavior.[36] Furthermore, FERC has already forced pipelines out of the merchant business through Order 636, finding that traditional bundled service was hindering the development of a truly competitive market. It is, of course, virtually certain that any attempt by FERC to impose structural separation of pipeline (or electric transmission or telecommunication) facilities would be challenged in the courts; if a court struck down such a program, the only recourse would be through legislation.

Implementation of structural separation would not be a panacea, nor would it be without problems. As Professor Trebing has recognized, there are three main issues that would be raised by structural separation. *First,* the boundaries of the network would have to be established (Trebing

1998a, 61). This is more easily accomplished in the natural gas industry than in the electric industry, because there is more of a "bright line" distinction between transmission (the interstate pipeline) and distribution (the local distribution company) than there is in the electric industry.

Second, if an independent network is established, it will be necessary to establish, cost, and price the network's services (Trebing 1998c, 15). With respect to structurally separate interstate pipelines, FERC would need to consider a new cost allocation methodology for the establishment of just and reasonable rates. The current method (the straight fixed-variable or SFV method), which assigns all fixed costs to peak-sensitive customers, penalizes firm shippers, like LDCs, that have public service obligations, and fails to recognize that *all* shippers—firm and interruptible, captive and noncaptive alike—benefit from network economies.

FERC should, instead, investigate a cost allocation methodology that assigns the costs of the interstate pipeline network to customers in direct proportion to the benefits that they derive from the use of the network. To accomplish this task, Professor Trebing has long advocated the use of the *Glaeser* model, which assigns common and joint costs on the basis of the relative benefit derived from the use of the network (Trebing 1998b, 68). Applying this cost-based methodology to the interstate pipeline industry would result in each service paying its direct costs, plus a share of a pipeline's joint or common costs. To determine the share of common costs to be allocated to each service, the cost of the "next best alternative" would be compared to the cost of using the network, and ratios for allocating these costs would be developed. This approach has several advantages in addition to assigning costs on a fair and equitable basis. For example, it eliminates uneconomic bypass of the pipeline. It assigns revenue requirements on the basis of cost causation and minimizes the potential for cross-subsidization. Finally, such initiatives as individually negotiated rates and services would be abandoned as inconsistent with the goal of providing all shippers with nondiscriminatory access to standardized services. The services provided by the network would be standardized, subject to rate regulation, and available to all comers.

Third, as Professor Trebing recognizes, even with structural separation, there will remain numerous opportunities for the employment of oligopolistic strategies that cannot be handled by way of structural separations (Trebing 1996a, 79). For example, within the interstate gas industry, the regulatory response to problems associated with the market power exercised by unregulated entities involves extremely complicated issues. The only recourse against abuse of market power by an unregulated entity is through the antitrust laws, a remedy that is difficult, expensive, and time-consuming.

Obviously, it may be difficult to address market power abuses by third-party suppliers without a revision to the NGA that provides the FERC with direct regulatory control over these parties. However, consistent with Professor Trebing's view, the Commission should, at a minimum, take the following steps to begin to address these problems. FERC should collect and monitor data concerning the market concentration of pipeline-affiliated and nonaffiliated unregulated entities by major market areas. By monitoring this data, FERC should be able to discern trends and potential problems. The revised data reporting requirements set forth in Order 637 are a step in this direction.

Next, FERC must address issues associated with the hoarding of pipeline capacity by unregulated entities. As previously discussed, the most direct way to address this problem is through structural separation and continued regulation of basic service. In addition, FERC could impose reasonable terms and conditions on the provision of essential capacity services through pipeline tariffs. Thus, for example, the commission could limit the amount of time that a party may buy and hold firm pipeline capacity for speculative purposes. Parties that are not direct end users or that do not have a direct public service obligation would not be permitted to automatically extend or roll over contracts for excess capacity. Moreover, a pipeline tariff could be used to prohibit tying a purchase of supply to the purchase of capacity.

Conclusions

As can be seen, deregulation is not the answer to the problems associated with regulated utilities; it merely poses an entirely new set of questions. The current trend in utility regulation is to substitute competitive market forces for traditional, hands-on regulation. Yet, there is no evidence that this trend will further the public interest, result in just and reasonable rates, or eliminate undue discrimination and preferences. In fact, as discussed here, not only does deregulation fail to provide comfort with respect to these issues, it also raises a whole host of issues concerning whether all consumers, and not just those with significant market power of their own, can be protected from the abuse of monopoly or oligopoly power. Moreover, there is the question of how abuses by unregulated entities can be kept in check.

Professor Trebing's work has provided not only a detailed analysis of why deregulation as currently practiced cannot result in competitive markets, it has also provided concrete proposals for protecting the network—and captive customers—while permitting the development of competitive supply alternatives. Professor Trebing's work has been—and remains—a source of encouragement for those whose primary mandate is to protect captive residential and small commercial customers. Thank god for Harry Trebing.

References

Energy Information Agency (EIA). 1996. *Natural gas 1996, issues and trends.* U.S. Department of Energy. December.

———. 1998. *Natural gas 1998, issues and trends.* U.S. Department of Energy. April.

———. 2000. The changing structure of the electric power industry 2000: An update. U.S. Department of Energy. October

———. 2001. Natural gas transportation—infrastructure issues and operational trends. U.S. Department of Energy. October.

General Accounting Office (GAO). 1993. *Natural gas—Cost, benefits and concerns related to FERC's Order 636.* U.S. General Accounting Office Report to Congressional Requesters. November.

Gorak, Thomas C., and Dennis J. Ray. 1995. Efficiency and equity in the transition to a new natural gas market. *Land Economics* 71 (3).

Phillips, Charles F. 1993. *The regulation of public utilities.* Arlington, Va.: Public Utilities Reports.

Trebing, Harry M. 1994. The networks as infrastructure—The reestablishment of market power. *Journal of Economic Issues* 28 (2).

———. 1996a. Adapting regulation to tight oligopoly. *NRRI Quarterly Bulletin* 17 (1): 71.

———. 1996b. Achieving coordination in public utility industries: A critique of troublesome options. *Journal of Economic Issues* 30 (2): 564.

———. 1998a. Concentration and the sustainability of market power in public utility industries. *Regulatory Assistance Project Issues Letter* (March): 61.

———. 1998b. Market concentration and the sustainability of market power in public utility industries. *NRRI Quarterly Bulletin* 19 (1): 66.

———. 1998c. Promoting consumer protection in a changing electric industry. Published by *The Consumer Research Foundation,* p. 14.

———. 1999. New challenges for the consumer movement in an era of utility deregulation. *NRRI Quarterly Bulletin* 19 (4).

Notes

1. For the purposes of this paper, captive customers are defined as those customers who lack either alternatives to the particular public utility service at issue or market power of their own.

2. Article I, Section 8, Clause 3, of the United States Constitution provides: "The Congress shall have power . . . to regulate commerce with foreign nations, and among the several states, and with Indian tribes."

3. See, e.g., *Munn v. Illinois*, 94 U.S. 113 (1887); see also *American Power and Light Company v. SEC*, 329 U.S. 90 (1946); *Railroad Commission Cases*, 116 U.S. 307 (1886).

4. See, e.g., *Nebbia v. New York*, 291 U.S. 502 (1934); see also *United States v. Carolene Products*, 304 U.S. 144 (1938).

5. U.S.C. 717, et seq.

6. U.S.C. 791a, et seq.

7. See, e.g., *Maryland Public Utility Companies Article*, Annotated Code of Maryland, PUC 1–101, et seq.

8. FERC is the successor to the Federal Power Commission (FPC).

9. U.S.C. 717c.

10. U.S.C. 717d.

11. "The Natural Gas Act has the fundamental purpose of protecting interstate gas consumers from pipelines' monopoly power. See Sen. Doc. No. 92, part 64A, 70th Cong., 1st Sess., 588–91 (FTC Utility Corporations Rep. 1935)." *Associated Gas Distributors v. FERC*, 824 F.2d 981, 995 (D.C. Cir. 1987).

12. *Phillips Petroleum Company v. Wisconsin*, 347 U.S. 672 (1954).

13. Phillips (1993, 691–743) and Gorak and Ray (1995, 368–86), among others, provide a more detailed discussion of the events summarized here.

14. U.S.C. 3301, et seq.

15. See *Columbia Gas Transmission Corporation*, 25 F.E.R.C. (CCH) ¶ 61,220 (1983); *Interstate Pipeline Blanket Certificates for Routine Transactions*, Final Rule, Order No. 234-B, 24 F.E.R.C. (CCH) ¶ 61,099, FERC Statutes and Regulations (CCH) ¶ 30,476 (1983); and *Sales and Transportation by Interstate Pipelines and Distributors*, Final Rule, Order No. 319, 24 F.E.R.C. (CCH) ¶ 61,100, FERC Statutes and Regulations (CCH) ¶30,477 (1983).

16. *Maryland People's Counsel v. FERC*, 761 F.2d 768 (D.C. Cir. 1985); *Maryland People's Counsel v. FERC*, 761 F.2d 780 (D.C. Cir. 1985).

17. *Regulation of Natural Gas Pipelines After Partial Wellhead Decontrol*, Order No. 436, FERC Statutes and Regulations (CCH), Regulations Preambles 1982–1985, ¶ 30,665 (1985), et seq.

18. See note 11

19. *Pipeline Service Obligations and Revisions to Regulations Governing Self-Implementing Transportation; and Regulation of Natural Gas Pipelines After Partial Wellhead Decontrol*, Order No. 636, III F.E.R.C. Statutes and Regulations (CCH), Regulations Preambles ¶ 30,939 (1992); *on reh'g*, Order No. 636-A, III F.E.R.C. Statutes and Regulations (CCH), Regulations Preambles ¶ 30,950 (1992); *on reh'g*, Order No. 636-B, 61 F.E.R.C. (CCH) ¶ 61,272. These orders are referred to collectively as "Order 636" throughout this chapter.

20. The term "negotiated services" implies that a customer could negotiate the physical aspects of its service, such as curtailment priority, delivery and receipt

point flexibility, interruptions, etc. Negotiated services were addressed in FERC Order 637. *Regulation of Short-Term Natural Gas Transportation Services and Regulation of Interstate Natural Gas Transportation Services,* Order No. 637, III FERC Statutes and Regulations (CCH), Regulations Preambles, ¶ 30,091 (9 February 2000); *on reh'g,* Order No. 637-A, III FERC Statutes and Regulations (CCH), Regulations Preambles, ¶ 31,099 (19 May 2000);Order No. 637-B, 92 FERC ¶ 61,062 (26 July 2000). These orders are referred to collectively as "Order 637" throughout this chapter.

In Order 637, FERC determined not to provide pipelines, at this time, with authority to file for preapproval of the right to negotiate terms and conditions of service for individual customers. Given the changes in the market, FERC said that it was not yet clear that this authority was necessary. FERC will continue to explore the need for and effects of negotiated terms and conditions of service and their relation to long-term regulatory issues. Order 637, ¶ 30,091 at 31,342–44.

21. See *Northern Municipal Distributors Group, et al. v. FERC,* Nos. 96–1455, et al. (consolidated) (D.C. Cir. 1998) (court rejected request to overturn negotiated rate program on grounds the appeal was not ripe because no direct injury had yet occurred).

22. *See* footnote 20, infra.

23. Order 637, ¶ 30,091 at 31,270–87.

24. Ibid., at 31,263.

25. Ibid.

26. Ibid. at 31,264–69.

27. Order 637, ¶ 30,091 at 31,260–61.

28. The Enron Corporation (Enron) bankruptcy occurred late in 2001 and after this chapter was written. A discussion of the various reasons behind Enron's failure and the effects of that failure on the industry are beyond the scope of the chapter. However, it should be observed that Enron's marketing arm was the largest gas trader in the United States. In 2001, EIA reported that "the volume of gas traded by [Enron] in 2000 was almost double the volume in 1999 and twice that of second-ranked Duke Energy Marketing" (Energy Information Agency 2001, 18). The fact that the market for gas supply continued to function following the Enron debacle does not prove that the market is—or will remain—truly competitive. Instead, it underscores the fact that the market is becoming controlled by a few very dominant firms, which, in turn, raises the concern that a competitive supply market will not exist in the future. For example, in 2001, EIA reported that the largest instance of consolidation was carried out by El Paso Energy Corporation (17). EIA observed that while El Paso Energy Corporation once owned only one interstate pipeline, since 1997, it had acquired eight others, providing it with access to markets across all of the lower forty-eight states. At the same time, El Paso Merchant Energy Company, the original marketing arm of El Paso Natural Gas Pipeline, became one of the top ten natural gas and energy marketing companies. To the extent that Enron's customers are absorbed by one of the dominant players, the problems presented by a market consisting of

an unregulated oligopoly of firms are exacerbated. Moreover, as discussed herein, these marketers may also pose a threat to consumers through their control of substantial amounts of interstate pipeline capacity.

29. EIA reported that, in 1997, approximately 23.5 percent of all firm pipeline capacity was held by marketers (Energy Information Agency 1998, 134).

30. Energy Information Agency 2001, 17n. 28.

31. See note 27 and accompanying text.

32. Order 637, ¶ 30,091 at 31,264.

33. See for example, *Northern Natural Gas Company*, FERC Docket No. RP00–223, filed 27 March 2000.

34. *Northern Natural Gas Company*, 91 FERC ¶ 61,075 (2000); *on reh'g*, 95 FERC ¶ 61,088 (2001). In the Northern case, FERC ultimately approved the LFT service in the market area, but *only* during the summer period when excess capacity is available.

35. Order 637, ¶ 30,091 at 31,265–68.

36. *Associated Gas Distributors v. FERC*, 824 F.2d at 1001.

Harry M. Trebing and Three Classic Errors of Deregulation

WILLIAM G. SHEPHERD

This chapter summarizes some of the lessons that have flown from Harry M. Trebing's contributions to the understanding of regulation and deregulation.

There is a four-stage process that often leads deregulation into failure. I explain that process and then discuss the main reasons why deregulation may fail. Then I cover the three cardinal errors that often occur during deregulation: excessive haste, permitting strategic price discrimination by the former monopolist, and allowing anticompetitive mergers. Finally, I discuss the possible cures for deregulatory failure.

The chapter draws on Harry M. Trebing's skepticism, technical skills, and intellectual leadership, as displayed over many decades of research and action since the 1950s.

Harry M. Trebing has helped to identify the classic errors that have marred deregulation in the United States. Three of the errors have been foremost:

1. dropping regulations too hastily,
2. allowing dominant firms to use strategic price discrimination against smaller competitors, and
3. permitting anticompetitive mergers that obstruct the rise of competition or actually reverse it.

The errors have scarred deregulation's peak period in the United States, during the years from 1975 to 2000. Furthermore, the errors are continuing, repeatedly and sometimes with remarkable ineptitude. As a result, the 1975–2000 period may come to be reproached as the Deregulation-to-Dominance Era.

Harry M. Trebing has been a leading scholarly critic of these errors, applying his unsparing skepticism and high technical skill in hundreds of settings, including hearings, conferences, publications, private briefings, and many others. Since the 1960s he has become a powerful force in the thinking about regulatory policy, on two levels: one level is about the proper design for good regulation and deregulation, and the other level is about understanding the effects of badly done regulation and deregulation.

In particular, Trebing has been a pervasive presence in advising and guiding regulatory authorities in the United States and leading foreign countries. In addition to his academic career at Michigan State University (1966–92), Indiana University (1962–66), and the University of Nebraska (1957–62), he served as chief economist for both the Federal Communications Commission (1965–66) and the U.S. Postal Rate Commission (1971–72).

Trebing's leading role and influence have been greatly magnified by his twenty-five years as the director of the Institute of Public Utilities at Michigan State University, during its Golden Era of 1966–91. There he promoted research, managed publications, and created the annual Williamsburg conference as a major regulation forum.[1]

Also, from 1973 to 1991 Trebing was the administrator of the education programs of the National Association of Regulatory Utility Commissioners (NARUC). This involved a prodigious array of conferences for the United States's leading regulatory authorities and staff members, eventually including well over nine thousand people.[2] It can fairly be said that he has known—and has had beneficial influence on—everyone that has mattered in utitlities regulation.

He set extremely high standards of fairness and breadth in the many conferences and publications that he prepared and led. His leadership neatly fit the 1950–1990s period when regulation became fully mature and deregulation then became the vogue and developed its special benefits and dangers.

Trebing is perhaps the most distinguished recent scholar and participant in a long line of leading intellectuals, activists, and officials. They guided America's experiments in regulating monopolies, and then some of them have watched the deregulation of many of the major regulated sectors. Among these leaders have been Henry Carter Adams, Richard T. Ely, Martin Glaeser, James M. Landis, James C. Bonbright, and Alfred E. Kahn.

Trebing has applied fundamental economic analysis to increasingly sophisticated and intricate problems. With intellectual power, he has avoided the theoretical fads and policy deceptions that have infected the field and marred much of the actual deregulation.

Many of the deregulation experiments since 1970 have had some success, but there have been some serious errors and failures.[3] The removal of regulation has often allowed the monopolist quickly to entrench itself in a dominant position. That blocks the chances for effective competition, and thus it defeats the rosy hope of the deregulation.

Deregulation has had its best luck in the transport, banking, and finance industries, where the underlying technology often favored "natural competition" rather than "natural monopoly." In many of those cases, deregulation was overdue even before 1950.[4] Pure monopoly wasn't entrenched in those industries, and competition was ready to burst out.

In telecommunications and electricity, however, natural monopoly conditions have existed and have persisted in some markets. Therefore, regulation was more suitable for these situations. Regulation was often reasonably effective after all. It was never deeply questionable, despite some heated ideological attacks by free-market advocates and some mild research hints of inefficiencies.[5]

Accordingly, as Trebing and others have pointed out, much of the deregulation of telecommunications and electricity has had less to offer, and some of it may leave things worse off, not better. Virtually all cases of deregulation have been hurt by errors and by a careless tolerance of anti-competitive mergers and strategic price discrimination.

At this point, some extremists are urging that deregulation be stretched to reach dubious, intractable cases (such as water and city transit). In this overhyped situation, it is suitable to appraise what has worked and what hasn't, in dealing with pure monopolies.

There have been several main patterns and errors in the failures. *First, deregulatory failure often follows a four-stage process:*

1. *overoptimism* at the start,
2. a *too-hasty removal* of regulation,
3. casual permission for *anticompetitive mergers and strategic pricing* by dominant firms, so that
4. the industry becomes *trapped under powerful dominant firms,* which are now free of any protections for consumers.

I'll present these stages in the first section. They have varied somewhat from case to case. Yet moving a former franchised pure monopoly down to fully effective competition—electricity and telecommunications are prime cases—can be quite difficult.[6]

The next section covers—again drawing on Trebing's own extensive discussions—some of the main *underlying problems that make deregulation fail.* They include especially: strong corporate pressures; large imperfections in the regulated firms and markets; the very slow pace at which dominant market shares usually recede, if at all; adverse surrounding conditions, such as the 1990s merger boom; and the weakness of antitrust policies.

These troubles have repeatedly destabilized and distorted the efforts at deregulation, leaving scores of powerful dominant firms. The difficulties have caused competition to be weak and spotty in many deregulated markets, ranging from airlines and railroads to telecommunications. The prospects for many telecommunications and electricity markets are, in fact, not favorable.

The actual failures came from the three cardinal errors, already noted:

1. dropping regulations too hastily,
2. allowing dominant firms to use strategic price discrimination against smaller competitors, and
3. permitting anticompetitive mergers that obstruct the rise of competition or actually reverse it.

I'll discuss them in a third section.

Finally, are there cures for the errors and failures? I will explore some possibilities in a concluding section. The main lesson is that antitrust criteria and policies need to be tightened sharply, both against horizontal mergers and against strategic price discrimination. Avoiding the errors (that is, prevention) is much superior to trying to reverse them or cure their impacts afterward.

Yet, a new strictness now seems quite unlikely to happen. On the contrary, deregulation is besieged, under severe difficulties. Furthermore, U.S. merger policies seem likely to remain weak and vague, and this literally multiplied the underlying merger incentives and generated an entirely unprecedented cascade of mergers in the 1990s. The Antitrust Division's Section 2 case against Microsoft can be seen as a belated effort by the Antitrust Division to seem strict, despite the laxity of its merger policies.

Hence there is this sobering practical lesson: the efforts to deregulate and create competition will frequently be overwhelmed by pressures and distortions. The old monopolists will often manage the deregulatory process for their own benefit, rather than acquiesce in situations of effective competition. Deregulation will often continue to fail.

The crucial role of market shares. In this whole complex topic, *market shares* are squarely at the intellectual center. The former monopolist's market share usually indicates (approximately) the degree of monopoly it still holds. That market share—plus the numbers and market shares of smaller rivals—show best whether and when it may be prudent to deregulate.

Market shares also determine whether a firm's mergers and pricing actions will be pro-competitive or anticompetitive. Against this, there have been vociferous efforts by some pure theorists, and by the dominant firms themselves, to claim that market shares are now "irrelevant," proven by "new" theory to be obsolete.[7] Despite these claims, good economics and virtually universal business thinking continue to regard market shares as the main anchor of market power.

A Four-Stage Process of Deregulatory Failure

Initial Overoptimism

Academic theorists and some politicians routinely promise that deregulation will be easy and quick, once the legal bars to new entry are removed. They assume that the markets are essentially perfect: everyone possesses complete and accurate information, all changes are frictionless and instantaneous, and all consumers have total rationality and information, with no fears or loyalties. The theorists and politicians also say that, in any event, the onrush of radical new technology will soon sweep away all monopoly advantages.

This optimistic rhetoric is not always wrong, but it is often naive and hazardous. The imperfections in the market are often large, as Harry Trebing has often noted and as I note in the next section. An important negative example is railroads, where imperfections, natural monopoly conditions, and unchanging technology tend to frustrate the chances for effective competition. In the airlines industry, the persistence of powerful "fortress hubs" also illustrates the power of established monopoly positions.

Premature Deregulation

The foremost danger is *premature deregulation*. Regulators often commit this error by dropping the protective constraints while the formerly franchised monopoly still holds high dominance over the market. Instead, deregulation should occur only *after* the dominance has faded, so that fully effective competition has been established.

Effective competition exists only *when there is reasonable parity among numerous competitors, who are able to apply strong mutual pressure.*[8] There must also be a large enough number of competitors that the incentives to compete overcome the temptations to collude in fixing prices and other conditions.

In concise form, there are three main conditions of effective competition:

1. At least five comparable competitors, as a bare-bones minimum number.
2. No dominance by one or several firms.[9]
3. Reasonably easy entry by new competitors.

Permitting Anticompetitive Mergers and Strategic Pricing

The old monopolist will use mergers as much as it is permitted, so as to increase its dominance and capture the firms that might be competitors. If mergers are constrained, then the monopolist may resort to alliances or other forms of quasi merger in order to obtain the same advantages.[10]

The dominant firm will also use price discrimination in strategic ways to defeat small rivals. As the literature and antitrust policies have long recognized, such systematic dominant-firm discrimination tends to be anticompetitive.[11] It stifles smaller competitors and prevents the emergence of full competition.

Stable Dominance, Which Lasts

The market needs to move from monopoly down through dominance and tight oligopoly, in order to reach loose oligopoly and the goal of fully effective competition.[12] Instead, however, the market may become trapped in single-firm dominance, where the entrenched firm holds over half of the market. In this case the former monopolist actually welcomes the presence of a fringe of mild competitors, and it claims that these little rivals are powerful.

Yet, in actuality, the dominant firm—deeply entrenched by its many decades as monopolist—is usually able to control the market outcomes in substantial degree and deter new competition. If so, then deregulation has removed the reasonably effective regulations while leaving consumers with no protection against the dominant firm.

The Main Reasons for Deregulatory Failure

Deregulation can yield good results, of course: competition may arise from independent forces, especially if the old monopolists invade each others' adjacent areas.[13] Yet the old monopolists have powerful incentives to retain their supremacy and prevent strong new competition, and that can make deregulation fail. There are five main causes for adverse outcomes.

Unrealistic Optimism and Strong Corporate Pressures

Deregulation is always started amid expectations that competition will prevail immediately or within a year or two, at most. The monopolists claim that competition will quickly triumph, and the publicists for aspiring new-entrant firms spread bright hopes that they will succeed. Journalists bandy about large numbers of potential competitors and future competitive possibilities. Some economic theorists declare that market shares are irrelevant and that entry and "contestability" have eliminated any danger of monopoly. The merger-promoting industry creates blue-sky claims that the opportunities for profits and mergers are unlimited.

All of these loose ideas create false illusions that the established regulations, which have protected consumers for decades, are now merely "in the way of progress." Moreover, the commercial pressures and investor expectations push the pace, forcing regulators to scrap rules lest they be accused of shaking the stock markets.

The monopolists are rationally maximizing their market positions, using classic methods: competition-reducing mergers, strategic price discrimination, allowing fringe competition, and political maneuvering including the use of economists as advocates. Some of the tactics appear to be devious (for example, the strategic price-discounting deals that are made secretly and then kept hidden, often by the regulatory commissions' own rulings).[14] Still other tactics attempt to manipulate and subvert the policy process (for example, using attacks in the public media to apply political pressures on supposedly impartial regulatory hearings).

Such corporate tactics are hard for academic economists to deal with. The tactics employ simple, seemingly logical free-market theories in ways that deliberately misrepresent and distort policy situations that are quite complicated. These tactics are particularly baffling because they arise at the awkward overlap between

1. *standardized regulatory processes* (which apply pricing and profit formulas to the static-efficiency conditions of an existing franchised monopolist) and
2. *sophisticated antitrust situations* (which require entirely different concepts for evolving, dynamic competitive processes). For example, the possible static-efficiency *virtues* of "Ramsey pricing" (a variant

of price discrimination) instantly become *threats* to effective competition, once deregulation begins.

The issues usually mingle economic and political actions in ways that simply do not fit game theory, the mathematical formulations of criteria, or pure theories. Yet, theoreticians are often brought in to hearings in order to declare precisely the opposite. In this context, oddly enough, being merely a pure theorist is often claimed to be a strength, rather than a limitation. These theorists habitually make flat declarations, rather than encourage balanced and careful discussions.[15]

Therefore, the current fashions in economics have not been very useful or appropriate. On the contrary, the monopoly firms have taken advantage of these current economic styles in order to conceal and justify the real monopoly-enhancing actions.

The general bias toward naive optimism at the start of deregulation can be intense. Regulators and politicians, who lack training in the sophisticated and complicated antitrust issues, often yield to the heavy pressures to adopt this hasty optimism.

Market Imperfections

Imperfections

Decades of franchised-monopoly operation create large market imperfections, which entrench the monopolists and help them block the rise of competition. The monopolists seek to obstruct the emergence of rivals, rather than accept the move to a "level playing field." Their incentives are to prevent competition with all possible force and all possible stratagems. They also try to capture and control the changes in technology, which might otherwise undermine their positions.

Among the twenty main kinds of imperfections that have been discussed extensively in the literature, several important ones are especially relevant to telecommunications and electricity. Figure 1 presents them in more detail.

For the old franchised monopolists, the monopoly came from *artificial origins,* rather than from fair competitive struggles in open markets. In every market, dominant firms can gain from imperfections because they control over half of the entire market, often for several decades or more. The firms also take actions to enlarge the imperfections further.

In formerly regulated markets, however, the imperfections are usually even larger than they are in never-regulated markets. Many decades of monopoly have given the firms huge advantages of reputation and

Figure 1 Nineteen Categories of Market Imperfections

1. *Pecuniary Gains May Be Obtained by Some Firms.* They occur when a firm is able to gain access to cheaper inputs than its competitors have. That may reflect the firm's use of monopsony power or the exploiting of advantages of large scale at the supplier level. The pecuniary gains let the firm obtain supra-normal profits that are not based on superior performance.

2. *Consumers May Exhibit Irrational Behavior.* Some or many of them may have preferences that are poorly formed, unstable or inconsistent. They may pursue goals other than maximizing utility in the ideal manner assumed in neo-classical microeconomic theory. They may let elements other than self-interest (e.g., values of other people, other institutions, or anti-rational groups) interfere with their decisions. The consumers may be unwilling to consider new suppliers; that puts them in the role of "captive customers." The loyalties may be created or intensified by advertising, de signed to change the choices made by consumers.

3. *Producers May Exhibit Irrational Behavior.* Some or many of them may have limited or inconsistent decision-making abilities. They may pursue goals other than pure profit maximizing. They may include external effects and other interests in their choices.

4. *There May Be Large Uncertainties, Which Interfere with Rational and Consistent Decisions by Consumers and/or Producers.* Main elements of decision situations may be unknown, or may be known to change unpredictably, so that consumers or producers cannot make complete or consistent decisions.

5. *Lags May Occur in the Decisions and/or Actions of Consumers or Producers.* Actions may not be timely, permitting firms to take strategic actions which prevent competition and/or beneficial outcomes. The firms may gain advantages not arising from economic efficiency.

6. *Consumer Loyalties May Exist.* They may be instilled or intensified by advertising and other marketing activities, which prevent objective choices by consumers. The loyalties may permit the charging of supra-normal prices, not based on efficiency. The loyalties may also make the consumers behave as captive customers, not changing to other goods when they are overcharged.

7. *Some Firm Managers may also Hold Non-rational Loyalties.* They may remain with the firm throughout their careers, rather than moving freely to other employers when the other jobs are superior. The loyalties may permit the firms to pay sub-normal salaries and rewards without losing their services.

8. *The Segmenting of Markets May Be Accentuated and Exploited.* If producers can segregate customers on the basis of their demand attributes, then the producers may be able to use price discrimination strategically so as to extend and sustain monopoly power. The segmenting also permits a maximizing of the monopoly profits, and they can be used in later strategic efforts. The segmenting violates the single-good, single-price assumptions of the simple pure-market case. It can prevent effective competition by rivals and entrants throughout the whole of the market. Dominant firms may develop extreme price discrimination so as to repel new competition.

9. *Differences in Access to Information, including Secrecy.* If some firms have superior knowledge compared to their rivals and/or consumers, then these firms may gain supra-normal profits without having superior efficiency. The patterns of innovation may also be distorted. Dominant firms may be particularly able to accentuate such asymmetries of access to information, to the point of complete secrecy about crucial information. That will work to their advantage even if the dominant firm is not superior in true efficiency.

10. *Controls Over Key Inputs and Technology.* Firms may obtain specific controls over crucial inputs, such as superior ores, specific talents of expert personnel, favorable geographic or urban locations, and patents or other access to critical technology. These

controls may permit a direct exclusion of competitors and an exploiting of consumers.

11. *Barriers Against New Competition.* New entry may be blocked or hampered by a variety of conditions which raises entry barriers. Some economic causes of barriers may be exogenous and basic to the market. Other barriers may be endogenous and created deliberately by actions of the incumbent firms. At least 18 sources of barriers are known to be significant in real markets. The barriers may occur both at the outside edges of the market and among segments of the market ("barriers to mobility" within the market).

12. *Risk Aversion.* Some consumers and/or producers may be strongly risk averse. That may make them unwilling to take the normal range of competitive actions. It makes the risk-averse managers vulnerable to threats by firms seeking to control market outcomes.

13. *Transactions Costs and Excess Capacity May Be Significant.* They may occur naturally or be increased by firms' deliberate actions. These costs and rigidities may cause the market to deviate from instant and complete adjustments in line with true costs.

14. *Firms May Have Sunk Costs, including Excess Capacity and Switching Costs That Arise from Past Commitments.* These sunk costs may prevent the firms from making free and rapid adjustments. They may also curtail or prevent new entry.

15. *Because of Principal-Agent Problems, Firms May Deviate from Profit-maximizing.* Managers may seek their own gains, in conflict with shareholders' interests.

16. *Internal Distortions in Information, Decision-making and Incentives may Cause X-Inefficiency and Distorted Decisions.* There may be misperceptions and conflicts of interest between shareowners and managers, and between upper and lower management groups. These problems often arise in large, complex organizations, in the form of bureaucracy, excess layers of management, and distorted information and incentives.

17. *Shareholder and Other Financial Owners of the Firm's Securities May Be Unable to Coordinate Their Interests and Actions Perfectly.* In addition to principal-agent problems between shareholders and managers, the owners may be unable to organize among themselves with perfect information and efficiency. That reduces their ability to enforce efficient behavior by managers.

18. *In International Markets, There May Be Artificial Exclusionary Conditions, Including Barriers at Borders.* Attempts by firms to operate freely across borders may be impeded by customs levies, taxes, required permissions, formalities, and other artificial burdens. Also, cultural and social differences may prevent free exchange of standardized goods among global markets.

19. *In International Markets, Firms May Often Have Differences in Information About Languages and Cross-Cultural Variations.* That may give advantages to some firms and prevent the perfect-market outcomes that could occur in cross-national firms and markets. Some firms may ignore real opportunities or problems, make inefficient mergers, or incur added costs and inefficiencies.

---

consumer loyalty, knowledge of the market and technology, irrational and fearful consumers, lags in adjustments, costs for entrants, and many others.

Accordingly, many of the monopolists can retain control despite being equal or even decidedly inferior to their rivals in terms of their performance.[16] Furthermore, monopoly-retaining activities do not use up the monopoly rents, despite new Chicago School claims that they usually will.[17] Thus, the dominant firms have even more resources for resisting and controlling competition.

Technology

As for rapid changes in technology, they might eventually have strong impacts. Yet the effects may currently still be weak. Although the changes might be *exogenous*—outside the industry's control—often they are *endogenous*. This means that they may be controlled by the dominant firms in ways that block competition rather than permit it..

In telecommunications, for example, the entrenched firms such as AT&T and the local Baby Bells have tried to capture cell-phone operations as a way of heading off new technological choices. Another case in telecommunications is the rise of consumers' satellite-dish access to broadcasts, as an alternative to local monopoly cable TV systems. Leading cable TV systems tried to buy satellite dish companies in 1998 but were successfully resisted by antitrust enforcers.

As for the electricity industry, so far it seems almost immune to any strong new technology changes that could undermine the dominant firms.[18] The only possible exception may be the emergence of cheaper generating technology using natural gas, often in small-scale units.

Slow Declines of Dominance

Schumpeter's process of creative destruction requires that dominant firms will decline rapidly and be completely replaced.[19] Without such a rapid and complete displacement, the Schumpeterian theory of "creative destruction" has little validity or relevance. Other writers have also developed the rapid-decline theme, and the "declining dominant firm" became a popular idea in the literature by the 1960s.[20] Yet this was merely a casual theory, not a research fact. By the time that Darius Gaskins first applied complex analysis to it in 1970, there had never been systematic research done on the actual rate of decline.[21]

My research since the 1960s has suggested that the average rate of decline has been quite slow, usually less that 1 percent per year.[22] Other studies have reached similar conclusions. The leading examples in business history during the twentieth century fit this pattern of slow decline. Figure 2 gives some prominent examples of dominant firms that have averted declines for more than four decades. In many cases, these firms exhibited inferior efficiency even while retaining their dominant positions.

Despite this observed glacial pace of dominant firm decline, it might conceivably be true that the rate of decline has speeded up in recent

Figure 2   Long-Lasting Dominance in Selected U.S. Industries (other than in franchised utility sectors).

Name of Dominant Firm	Years of Dominance (approximate)	Length of Dominance (approximate)
Eastman Kodak	1900—continuing	95+ years
IBM	1950s—1990 (continuing?)	40 years
General Motors	1930–1985	55 years
Alcoa	1900–1950	50 years
Campbell Soup	1920s—continuing	70+ years
Procter & Gamble	1920s—continuing	70+ years
Kellogg	1920s—1980s	60+ years
Gillette	1910—continuing	85+ years

decades, perhaps in some industries at least. Yet I doubt it, and there is no research basis for believing it.

Possibly, too, the franchised-monopoly positions under deregulation might somehow be more fragile than average, under the crushing impact of new competition. Yet that also is not plausible, given the degree to which franchised monopolists' advantages naturally tend to deepen and harden over the decades. The formerly regulated monopolies are thus likely to secure an even slower decline than average, not a more rapid decline.

Hostile Surroundings; Especially the New Wave of Mergers that Enhance Market Dominance.

The Merger Wave

Deregulation has been unavoidably affected by the powerful, still-rising merger wave of the 1990s, which has spread across all major sectors of the U.S. economy.[23] This merger mania not only encourages mergers by the deregulated firms. The merger craze is also spawning a startling, widespread rise in mergers that substantially increase market dominance in hundreds of important markets. This has created a setting that tolerates competition-reducing mergers by telecommunications and electricity firms. Without this general stampede, most of the telecommunications and electricity mergers would not have been acceptable.

The 1990s merger wave exploded to a scale far beyond any and all previous waves, at least three times the volume of the 1980s wave that broke all previous records. Electricity mergers are just one small part of that massive flood, and they are expected to increase as the current wave grows.[24]

Alliances are also increasingly important, as a way of uniting firms' conditions without the formal step of actual mergers. These alliances are weakening deregulation particularly in the airline and telecommunications industries, but their role in electricity may also become important.

The 1990s mergers-and-alliances boom—with scores of combinations that created or increased market dominance—is remarkably parallel to the first great U.S. merger wave, a century ago. Back then, antitrust regulation was embryonic and it did nothing at all as a flood of mergers formed many scores of dominant firms (as John Moody's *The Truth About the Trusts* showed).[25] History gives consistent lessons that warn against the market-power impacts of many current mergers. Many if not most of the 1897–1901 dominance-creating mergers quickly failed and faded away.[26][7] Yet many of them did have sharp monopoly effects, and some of those firms (such as General Electric) are still dominant a century later.

Many dominance-creating mergers also flowered in the 1980s and 1990s, across a wide range of U.S. industries. Amid the extremely rapid flow and very large volume of mergers, there have been an increasing number that create or restore dominance. They go far beyond any previous merger waves, except for the true mania of monopoly-creating mergers during the great 1897–1901 first wave. Figure 3 presents some of the most prominent recent instances.

The resulting increases in market dominance may be fewer than in 1897–1901, but some of the dominance cases are surprisingly large and important. By December 1998, mergers were being announced almost daily that would create leading or actually dominant positions in their markets. Those in figure 3 are a partial listing, but they are remarkably numerous and important. They include aircraft, telecommunications, computer-related and software-related activities, railroads, electricity, broadcasting (especially radio chains), military manufacturers of many kinds, dominant health care firms, banking, securities firms, and real estate, even snack foods and legal publishing! Repeatedly, high market shares (and HHI levels) are being accepted by the antitrust and regulatory agencies.

Rhetoric Claiming to Justify Dominance-Enhancing Mergers

The justifications now given are surprisingly similar to the rhetoric used a century ago.[27] The supposed "New Global Age" talk includes the following:

"There is a mandate for bigness. Bigness is necessary for survival in today's markets." Yet this has little research basis; small-scale technology and operations are better in many, if not most, markets.

Figure 3   Some Examples of Recent Dominance-Enhancing or Dominance-Creating Mergers

Industries	Firms
Aircraft	Boeing and McDonnell-Douglas 1997
Petroleum	Exxon and Mobil 1998
	BP and AMOCO 1998
Telecommunications	AT&T and McCaw Cellular 1995
	Bell Atlantic and NYNEX 1997
	SBC and Pacific Telesis 1997
	MCI and WorldCom 1998
	SBC and Ameritech 1998
	Bell Atlantic and GTE
	WorldCom-MCI and Sprint 1999
Computer-related	Intel and Chips & Technologies
	America On Line and Netscape and Sun Microsystems
Railroads	Union Pacific and Southern Pacific
	Burlington Northern and Santa Fe
	Conrail, Chesapeake and Ohio, and Norfolk and Western
Electricity	Numerous mergers since 1992, including Union Electric and Central Illinois 1997
	American Electric Power and South West Power 1998
Broadcasting	Various radio chains
	Westinghouse CBS and American Radio Systems
Military weapons	A large number of mergers including Raytheon and Hughes Electronics
Health care	Numerous hospital chains and other health-related firms
Banking	Extensive mergers among banking and related firms:
	Bankers Trust and Deutsche Bank 1998
	Fleet Bank and Bank of Boston 1996
	Citigroup and Travelers Insurance
Major accounting firms	Numerous large firms, including
	Price Waterhouse and Coopers & Lybrand and others
Grain trading	Cargill and Continental
Automobiles	Daimler Benz and Chrysler 1998
Paper	International Paper and Union Camp 1998

Sources: recent issues of the *Wall Street Journal* and *Business Week* magazine.

"Global markets are now the rule. They dominate all important sectors and apply overwhelming pressures." Yet many markets are actually narrow and/or local, and many have large national barriers.

"Markets are virtually perfect. That is enforced by the new age of the Internet, which is making all previous conditions irrelevant." Yet imperfections are actually still many and large, in many or most of the important sectors, as I have noted.

"Free entry prevails everywhere. This is the age of deregulation, and new commercial sources are ubiquitous." Yet much of this is just loose talk. There are about twenty major causes of barriers to entry and the endogenous causes alone can be overwhelming in many markets.28

"Mergers are good, generating synergies and new creativity." They can do that in selected real cases, but economic and business research forcefully rebuts this optimism as a general matter. Since the 1960s, as many economic and business experts have shown and all intelligent business officials are now aware, mergers have generally tended to worsen efficiency and innovation, not improve them.29

"Deregulation naturally calls for consolidating. It is important for markets to shake out excess fragmentation and organize more efficiently." This idea has little economic basis and is often merely a self-serving rationale for increasing market power.

"In any event, all free-market actions are, by definition, justified and superior." This claim is mere rhetoric, and it is refuted by recent business experience: over half of the substantial mergers actually hurt the companies and shareholders.

The 1990s merger boom (like the 1980s boom and, in fact, all great merger waves) was also been stimulated by the looseness of antitrust constraints on mergers.

The resort to alliances—and various other forms of quasi merger—reinforces this pattern. Alliances are largely free of antitrust constraints, partly because they are not concrete and are not subject to formal legal provisions.

Each of the cases can be debated, but many of the mergers and alliances pose disturbing questions about antitrust's economic basis. Technology has been moving strongly toward smaller economies of scale, especially in the formerly regulated industries, including electricity. Yet the merger promoters offer only ancient rhetorical cliches, as just noted. These claims were common a century ago, during the first 1897–1901 merger wave. They were also offered in the Roaring Twenties, in the 1950s, and of course in the 1980s.

The claims deny the emerging reality since the 1970s favoring smaller scale in many sectors. Rising small-firm innovation and flexibility have reflected fundamental conditions as well as the spread of computer and telecommunications-related progress. There has been a strong case for tighter horizontal-merger limits, not looser ones.

Weak Antitrust Constraints on Mergers. Unfortunately, U.S. antitrust policies toward horizontal mergers and alliances—which are crucial to electricity's chances for effective competition—are currently both lax and random. Since helping draft the original antitrust "Merger Guidelines" in

1968, I've watched the Reagan-era guidelines with limited hope, and increasingly with dismay.

From 1958 to 1980, antitrust policies restrained mergers from reinforcing dominance. The 1968 Merger Guidelines articulated that strictness, holding horizontal mergers usually to no more than a 10–15 percent combined market share, or 20 percent in exceptional cases.[30]

After 1980, merger policies became quite lax and vague. New guidelines were issued in 1982, 1984, and then 1992. The agencies have claimed that these guidelines were more scientific. Yet instead they have become an obscure mix of many "screens" and possibly relevant conditions. The borders of policy have become lax and vague to the point of confusion. In the 1990s, the borders may be somewhere between 20 and 50 percent, but actual case outcomes are virtually impossible to predict. Officials will merely "consider" various conditions, or "take unfavorable views." Prosecutorial discretion is extremely wide.

The laxity often permits dominance-creating or dominance-enhancing mergers, even beyond what was permitted in the minimal-antitrust 1980s. The randomness is large; the agencies' actions often veer sharply between moderate constraints and complete passivity. The antitrust treatment of alliances is even weaker. Only in the passenger-airlines industry has there been significant effort to assess and resist leading-firm alliances.

Two Main Additional Weaknesses of Antitrust

Not only are antitrust merger policies now defective. Antitrust is also inherently weak against precisely the two core problems of monopoly deregulation:

1. reducing dominant-firm market power, and
2. dealing with dynamic strategic price discrimination.

The general weakness of Section 2 of the Sherman Act in trying to deal with monopolizing is widely recognized. When the monopolist has become entrenched by decades of monopoly-franchised privileges, the weakness of Section 2 is even more evident.

The failures of deregulation are a subset of the wider rise after 1980 of new market dominance. Competition did spread and increase in the U.S. economy between 1960 and 1980.[31] Yet antitrust enforcement was drastically cut back by Reagan-administration officials after 1980, under the sway of New Chicago School thinking. The stunting of antitrust led to a rise of market dominance in numerous industries, partly via horizontal

426 · WILLIAM G. SHEPHERD

mergers. The deregulated-monopolists' two main retaliatory actions—horizontal mergers and strategic price discrimination—are simply the long-familiar responses to competition by all dominant firms. They have been quite common in human history, and surely for well over a century in the United States, since the abuses of the Standard Oil monopoly created by the Rockefellers.

Moreover, the responsibilities created by deregulation have placed antitrust enforcement under even more strain, even though it is already overburdened and it holds only limited powers. Merely removing regulation is not a sufficient step to obtain effective competition. There must be powerful policies to reduce the dominance and prevent its entrenchment or restoration. The actual weaknesses of antitrust can therefore frustrate deregulation.

Three Cardinal Errors of Deregulation

Finally, we come to the cardinal errors of deregulation, as they emerge from the discussions above.

Premature Deregulation

The removal of regulation is a fateful step, which has been extremely difficult or impossible to reverse. Deregulation should occur only after the old monopolist's market share is below 40 percent, there are at least five comparable strong competitors, and entry by new rivals is clearly easy. Yet the monopolist demands immediate deregulation, claiming that the fringe competitors are actually powerful and sure to push the monopolist aside. Much of this is posturing, as when AT&T and the Baby Bells have demanded deregulation even when their market shares are above 80 percent. Yet it sets the stage for negotiating a "compromise," and the regulators may accept it.

A leading example is the FCC's official decision in 1989 that AT&T no longer held market dominance, even though AT&T actually did (with a market share of at least 65 percent). Other examples include scores of states: during 1985–87 they totally deregulated dozens of telecommunications-related markets—including even the Yellow Pages monopolies!—even though virtual monopolies still existed.

These naive actions have usually been caused by a trust in "contestability" theory and very easy entry conditions. Contestability ideas also played a large role in the enthusiasm for airline deregulation, even though the theory was soon admitted to be irrelevant even by its main advocates.[32]

Mergers and Alliances

I have discussed previously the errors of lax policies toward mergers and alliances. Economic research and long-standing antitrust traditions have focused on the 20–25 percent market-share range as the appropriate limit for most horizontal mergers. Virtually all mergers by electricity firms, and most horizontal-related mergers by telecommunications firms, would easily violate this standard.

Yet antitrust and regulatory officials have permitted scores of such mergers, and there are few signs of any significant shift against them. Railroad mergers have involved even higher degrees of monopoly enhancement.[33]

Strategic Pricing by the Dominant Firm

Strategic price discrimination is often the most important device that the dominant firm uses to prevent new and effective competition.[34] It is usually the monopolist's first weapon. Yet the monopolist usually tries to stop new competitors from following its own actions: it attacks discrimination by the new competitors, calling it "cream-skimming."

Price discrimination may have some value for encouraging static-efficient allocation under the regulation of pure-monopoly declining-cost utilities. The notion of "Ramsey pricing" grew from the ancient literature of the 1930s, but Ramsey pricing has major defects in any practical use.[35]

Yet in any event, Ramsey pricing becomes a deadly threat to competition in the instant that deregulation and competition begin. Discrimination is the crucial dynamic process of price discounting, used relentlessly by dominant firms since time immemorial in order to block and stifle competition.

Perhaps the strongest uses of strategic price discrimination have been by airlines (related to the dominance of airlines' fortress hubs) and by railroads. AT&T has also made extensive use of discrimination, with its Tariff 12 and Tariff 15 pricing starting in the 1980s. The local Bells have been using it to block small rivals and prevent entry by potential rivals.

In the 1990s, electricity firms have developed extensive special-discount pricing, much of which is clearly anticompetitive.[36] I have observed little restraint in state-level acquiescence to such pricing. Yet it seems clearly to be frustrating the ability of new entrants to compete in electricity markets.

An interesting parallel case involves Telmex, the deregulated telephone monopoly in Mexico. Telmex's use of complex, extensive pricing devices nicely illustrates the general phenomenon.[37] Telmex has also resorted to unusually rough tactics in stifling rivals, even powerful ones from the United States and elsewhere.[38]

Possible Cures for Deregulatory Failure

Harry Trebing has long clarified the main lessons for managing the onset of competition. This chapter has fit his main criteria, and so do the cures for deregulatory failure. Market shares continue to be crucial to the design of all successful efforts at deregulation. Market shares are not "obsolete," and the very vehemence with which theorists and dominant firms try to belittle market shares is a good sign that they continue to be centrally important. The cardinal errors of deregulation mainly occur from ignoring market shares, and the safeguards and cures rely on market shares.

Slowing Down Deregulation, Based on Market Shares

Virtually all firms with market shares over 40–50 percent hold substantial market power, and such dominance blocks effective competition. Constraints should be retained or applied anew to such situations. When hasty removal has stripped the constraints too soon, the jibe of supposedly "restoring old, discredited regulation" should be rejected. Mild and specific constraints may be enough to fully cure harms caused by the hasty deregulation.

For example, price caps or other hybrid constraints are available. They could be applied to sections of markets and firms (for example, to the "captive customers," or to submarkets where new entry is being blocked), even if not to the entire firms. Still other creative methods—prohibitions on specific actions, prevention of certain kinds of price discrimination— might be fit to the situation.

The task is difficult, and it has bedeviled antitrust policy's century-long efforts to reduce monopoly under Section 2 of the Sherman Act. Yet the difficulties do not justify pretending that there is no problem or that nothing can be done.

The dominant firms will resist fiercely: the better the policy is, the angrier the denunciations will be. The firms will try to smear the constraints as merely crude "re-regulation," which, they will sneer, is politically absurd. If public officials are firm, however, well-designed constraints can have beneficial effects on the market situations and results.

Preventing Anticompetitive Mergers

Stopping harmful mergers is a clearer and easier task. Mergers are a well-worn and highly developed antitrust topic that does not pose deep mysteries. Deregulation should generally bar any horizontal mergers by dominant firms, adjacent monopolies, or other potential competitors. Enforcement can be undertaken by regulators, with antitrust participation, or vice versa, by antitrust cases, with participation by the regulators.

All combinations should usually be kept under a 20 percent market share. The current antitrust agencies' Merger Guidelines should *not* be relied on for clarity; they are a mass of obscure, vague, and unpredictable notions. Instead, a critically minded focus on market shares and entry barriers can usually provide reasonably clear guidance about anticompetitive mergers.

Preventing New Sharp Price Discounts by Dominant Firms, and Voiding Past Ones

Especially where there is a clear scarcity of new and strong rivals, sharp price discounting should be recognized to be likely to block effective competition. Where strategic discrimination has already gone far—especially in electricity—the special discounts should simply be voided by regulators. Voiding is currently not a realistic political possibility. Yet it is both economically correct and crucial. Regulators, consumer advocates, and economists should hammer this point relentlessly, seeking to get legislative action to permit the voiding.

The bar should be removed only after the dominant firm's market share has receded below 40 percent and there are at least five comparably strong competitors in the market.

Where voiding is not possible, regulators should try to keep the dominant-firm's strategic price discounts to a brief period, a year or less. Furthermore, the discounts should always be made fully public—repeat: fully public—rather than being hidden in regulation-approved secrecy. That secrecy is now common, and it is quite pernicious to the chances for effective competition.

All of these points and lessons have been made abundantly clear in the writings and discussions of Harry Trebing. That his lessons have often been ignored is a sign of the powerful forces that are distorting deregulation. Yet, to be powerfully correct and responsible—though denied and disparaged by privileged interests—is in an ancient and exceedingly honorable tradition.

Notes

Professor of economics, University of Massachusetts, Amherst, MA 01003; and general editor, the *Review of Industrial Organization.*

1. He edited nineteen volumes of papers from those conferences (five of them coedited with Patrick C. Mann). He also published over sixty papers, book chapters, and edited (or coedited) volumes, on all of the important regulatory topics.
2. They included these NARUC programs:

1. *1973–91,* the Annual Regulatory Studies Program, a two-week course for commissioners and staff from all state and federal regulatory agencies and state consumer counsels. Over seven thousand people attended this program.
2. *1979–91,* the Technical Education Conference for Commissioners, a semiannual one-day program confined to state and federal commissioners and focused on policy issues.
3. *1984–91,* the Advanced Regulatory Studies Program, a semiannual one-week advanced course for commissioners and senior staff only. It was a sequel to the annual program noted above.
4. *1985–91,* the Regional Introductory Training Program, a three-day program for new commission employees, on a regional basis.

3. "Early critiques were by Horace Gray, "The Passing of the Public Utility Concept," *Journal of Land & Public Utility Economics* (February 1940): 16–35; Walter Adams and Horace Gray, *Monopoly in America* (New York: Macmillan, 1955); John R. Meyer, Merton J. Peck, John Stenason, and Charles J. Zwick, *The Economics of Competition in the Transportatiion Industries* (Cambridge, Mass.: Harvard University Press, 1959); Richard E. Caves, *Air Transport and Its Regulators* (Cambridge, Mass.: Harvard University Press, 1962); and William G. Shepherd and Thomas G. Geis, eds., *Utility Regulation: New Directions in Theory and Policy* (New York: Random House, 1965).

Some of the best analysis has been by TPUG members, including especially Harry M. Trebing, James R. Nelson, William Melody, Edythe Miller, Kenneth D. Boyer, Paul M. Joskow, and Douglas N. Jones, to mention just a few. A substantial portion of it has appeared in the *Journal of Economic Issues.*

4. Meyer, Peck, Stenason, and Zwick, *The Economics of Competition,* provided fine guidance. See also Almarin Phillips, ed., *Promoting Competition in Regulated Industries* (Washington, D.C.: Brookings Institution, 1975).

5. William G. Shepherd, *Regulation and Efficiency: A Reappraisal of Research and Policies* (Columbus, Ohio: National Regulatory Research Institute, Ohio State University, 1992).

Attacks included George J. Stigler and Claire Friedland, "The Economic Effects of Regulation," *Journal of Law & Economics* (1963); Stephen Breyer and Paul W. MacAvoy, *Regulation by the Federal Power Commission* (Washington, D.C.: Brookings Institution, 1974).

Research hints included Leon Courville, "Regulation and Efficiency in the Electric Utility Industry," *Bell Journal of Economics* (spring 1974): 53–74; H. Craig Peterson, "An Empirical Test of Regulatory Effects," *Bell Journal of Economics* (spring 1975): 111–26, and Robert M. Spann, "Rate of Return Regulation and Efficiency in Production: An Empirical Test of the Averch-Johnson Thesis," *Bell Journal of Economics* (spring 1974): 38–52.

6. I noted twenty-five years ago, before the deregulation crusade got under way, that deregulation is much more difficult, time-consuming and unstable than its advocates admit; see William G. Shepherd, "Entry as a Substitute for Regulation," *American Economic Review* (May 1973): 98–105.

7. This is especially true of the Baumol group, with its claims about "perfectly contestable" markets; see William J. Baumol, John Panzar, and Robert D. Willig, *Contestable Markets and the Theory of Industry Structure* (San Diego: Harcourt Brace Jovanovich, 1982). Also, many game theorists who focus on abstract duopoly situations have claimed that market shares are merely an effect of behavior, not a strong influence on performance. See Jean Tirole, *The Theory of Industrial Organization* (Cambridge, Mass.: MIT Press, 1988).

8. This definition has emerged from many decades of the research literature. See William G. Shepherd, *The Economics of Industrial Organization*, 4th ed. (Englewood Cliffs, N.J.: Prentice-Hall, 1997), esp. chapters 1 and 3; and F. M. Scherer and David Ross, *Industrial Market Structure and Economic Performance*, 3d ed. (Boston: Houghton Mifflin, 1991).

9. The economics literature has agreed on the definition of single-firm market dominance: a market share of at least 40 to 50 percent, with no close rival, and with difficult entry conditions. That allows effective control over the main outcomes in the market.

There is a similar definition of market power held by "tight oligopoly" with just three or four firms: a combined market share of about 60 to 70 percent. Some analysts put it in terms of Hirschman-Herfindahl indexes. A threshold HHI value of 1,800 to 2,000 is the usual range.

10. Airlines recently have exemplified this development. Major alliances involving all leading U.S. airlines have been recognized on all sides as attempting to gain the effects of mergers while avoiding formal merger constraints. The alliances are so important that the normally lenient antitrust agencies have offered some resistance.

11. See Scherer and Ross, *Industrial Market Structure and Economic Performance*; Shepherd, *The Economics of Industrial Organization*, chapter 10; and Shepherd, "Assessing 'Predatory' Actions by Market Shares and Selectivity," *Antitrust Bulletin* 31 (spring 1986): 1–28. The leading antitrust cases include the first IBM case and the United Shoe Machinery decision of 1956.

12. On oligopoly, see especially the classic discussion in Carl Kaysen and Donald F. Turner, *Antitrust Policy: An Economic and Legal Analysis* (Cambridge, Mass.: Harvard University Press, 1959).

13. The airline industry has seemed to exemplify regulatory success, because many of its markets quickly became highly competitive after 1978. Yet that case differs radically from franchised-monopoly regulation, such as in telephone and electric service. Airlines already had a history of some competition, plus numerous and diverse airlines that were already fully in business. Merely removing the

legal barriers to entry was enough to unleash powerful competition. In regulated-monopoly cases, in contrast, competition must start from scratch, against entrenched monopolies.

It is also notable that airline deregulation underwent a sharp partial failure during 1985–88. A number of markedly anti-competitive mergers were permitted, and flexible price discounting was chanelled into a rather tight structure of rules and limits.

14. This has happened in electricity, in many or most states. See W. G. Shepherd, "Anti-Competitive Impacts of Secret Strategic Pricing in the Electricity Industry," *Public Utilities Fortnightly,* 14 February 1997.

15. Among the leading examples of this certainty have been William J. Baumol and Robert D. Willig, especially when discussing their concepts of "perfectly contestable markets" and "sustainability of prices." The overstatements have been especially striking when these theorists have been testifying for dominant firms in regulatory hearings about mergers and pricing.

16. For a critique of the new Chicago School optimistic "efficient-structure" doctrines, which hold that dominant firms never actually involve market power, see William G. Shepherd, "Three 'Efficiency School' Hypotheses about Market Power," *Antitrust Bulletin* (summer 1988): 395–415.

17. Richard A. Posner, "The Social Costs of Monopoly and Regulation," *Journal of Political Economy* (August 1976): 807–27; and Fred S. McChesney and William F. Shughart, eds., *The Causes and Consequences of Antitrust* (Chicago: University of Chicago Press, 1995).

18. The rise of smaller-scale generating technology since the 1980s has seemed to allow small-firm entry. Yet instead, so far, it seems to be mainly under the control of the established firms.

19. Joseph A. Schumpeter, *Capitalism, Socialism, and Democracy* (New York: Knopf, 1943). See also my analysis of it in *The Economics of Industrial Organization,* chapter 2.

20. Perhaps the earliest and most one-sided version of it was Dean W. Worcester Jr., "Why 'Dominant Firms' Decline," *Journal of Political Economy* 65 (August 1957): 338–47.

21. See the review in Shepherd, *The Economics of Industrial Organization,* 206–8, including Dean A. Worcester's paper, "Why 'Dominant Firms' Decline," and Darius W. Gaskins Jr., "Dynamic Limit Pricing: Optimal Pricing Under Threat of Entry," *Journal of Economic Theory* (3 September 1971): 306–22.

22. William G. Shepherd, *The Treatment of Market Power* (New York: Columbia University Press, 1976); Shepherd, *The Economics of Industrial Organization,* 204. See also Paul Geroski's summary chapter in Donald Hay and John Vickers, eds., *The Economics of Market Dominance* (Oxford: Basil Blackwell, 1987).

23. There is a clear parallel with the 1920s, when the utility merger craze went far to block the early efforts to apply effective *regulation* to electricity firms. Now the merger craze is likely to undermine *deregulation,* by creating monopoly power that prevents effective competition.

The causation may run the opposite way, too. Deregulation has helped to stimulate the utility-firm merger craze by removing restraints. This has spurred the whole rush to merge now-deregulated firms. Though antitrust officials should have blocked this onrush, they have been both weak and overwhelmed.

24. The past merger waves were:

First wave (1897–1901): mergers mainly created dominance. Yet many positions were weak or quickly faded.

Second wave (1920s): mergers mainly created tight oligopoly.

Third wave (1950s): mergers mainly created conglomerate firms. Most of those firms then came apart in the next decade or two.

Fourth wave (1980s): mergers mainly involved leveraged buyouts, the creation of market dominance, and the formation of very large conglomerates. Many of them became fiascos.

Fifth wave (1990s): many mergers created or enlarged dominant firm positions.

25. John Moody, *The Truth About the Trusts* (Chicago: Moody Publishing, 1904).

26. See A. D. H. Kaplan, *Big Business in a Competitive System* (Washington, D.C.: Brookings Institution, 1958), among others, on this pattern.

27. Charles J. Bullock, "Trust Literature: A Survey and Criticism," *Quarterly Journal of Economics* 15 (February 1901): 167–217.

28. Shepherd, *The Economics of Industrial Organization,* chapter 9.

29. David Ravenscraft and F. M. Scherer, *Mergers, Sell-Offs and Economic Efficiency* (Washington, D.C.: Brookings Institution, 1987); Dennis Mueller, *The Determinants and Effects of Mergers* (Cambridge, Mass.: Oelgeschlager, Gunn & Hain, 1981).

For recent findings, see Jeffrey L. Hiday, "Most Mergers Fail to Add Value, Consultants Find," *Wall Street Journal,* 12 October 1998, B9C, covering two financial-market studies. One, by A. T. Kearney, covered 115 mergers made between 1993 and 1996; 58 percent of them "didn't add value. A similar study by Mercer Management Consulting came up with a 57 percent failure rate."

See also Mark L. Sirower, *The Synergy Trap: How Companies Lose the Acquisition Game* (New York, Simon & Schuster, 1998), which finds that of 268 mergers during the 1980s and 1990s, about two-thirds lost money for shareholders. See also Gretchen Morgenson, "Mergers May Not Be Music to Investor Ears," *New York Times,* 6 December 1998, page 1, section 3.

Further, see the extensive coverage by Gretchen Morgenson, "A Cautionary Note on Mergers: Bigger Does Not Mean Better," *New York Times,* 8 December 2000, C1, C12.

30. I helped draft those guidelines in 1968, while I was special economic assistant to Donald F. Turner, then the head of the Antitrust Division. They were direct, concise, and clear.

31. William G. Shepherd, "Causes of Increased Competition in the U.S. Economy, 1939–1980," *Review of Economics and Statistics* (November 1982): 613–26.

32. See William G. Shepherd, "Contestability versus Competition," *American Economic Review* 74 (September 1984): 572–87. The main sources of the contestability notion are William J. Baumol, "Contestable Markets: An Uprising in the Theory of Industry Structure," *American Economic Review* 72 (March 1982): 1–15; and Baumol, Panzar, and Willig, *Contestable Markets.*

For further praise of the idea, see William J. Baumol and Robert D. Willig, "Contestability: Developments since the Book," *Oxford Economic Papers,* November 1986, Special Supplement. In contrast, Marius Schwartz, "The Nature of Contestability Theory," ibid., shows that contestability is not a robust concept.

33. The most notorious recent example of such regulatory failure is the Union Pacific-Southern Pacific merger, with its calamitous aftermath. The merged firms endured over two years of chaotic inefficiency. Of course, this merely recapitulated some of the most disastrous errors and failures of the merger between the Pennsylvania Railroad and the New York Central Railroad in 1969.

34. It has various nicknames, including sharp-shooting and pin-point pricing.

35. One important recent discussion can be found in William J. Baumol and J. Gregory Sidak, *Toward Competition in Local Telephony* (Cambridge, Mass.: MIT Press, 1994). A critique is found in William G. Shepherd, "Contestability vs. Competition—Once More," *Land Economics* 71 (August 1995): 299–309. See also William G. Shepherd, "Ramsey Pricing: Its Uses and Limits," *Utilities Policy* 1 (October 1993): 295–98.

The idea is popular among pure theorists. For example, another favorable discussion of Ramsey prices can be found in Tirole, *The Theory of Industrial Organization.*

36. William G. Shepherd, "Anti-Competitive Price Discrimination. . . .," *Public Utilities Fortnightly,* 14 February 1997.

37. Elliot Spagat, "Mexican Telecom Regulators Take Steps to Curb Telmex, Boost Fledgling Rivals," *Wall Street Journal,* 7 December 1998, B7C.

38. Jonathan Friedland, "U.S. Phone Giants Find Telmex Can Be a Bruising Competitor," *Wall Street Journal,* 23 October 1998, A1, A8. "AT&T's Alestra SA and MCI's Avantel SA now have a 25% share of the $3.5 billion long-distance market, down from a peak of 28%. And unless conditions change, executives acknowledge, neither will make money anytime soon.

The reason: Telmex has outfoxed them at every turn in defending its stake in the busy U.S.—Mexico long-distance corridor. In an ironic reprise of the defense AT&T once used against interlopers in the 1970s, Telmex has priced its services aggressively, made shrewd use of Mexico's feeble regulatory and legal systems. . . .

Part 5

Regulation and the Clash
of Economic Philosophies

Implications for the Social Control of Business of Competing Economic Visions

EDYTHE S. MILLER

From the beginning, public utilities were recognized as requiring special treatment because of operating conditions perceived as rendering them unsuited to market control. Accordingly, public utilities were granted special status, in the United States as regulated monopolies, and in much of the rest of the world as publicly owned enterprises. Of late, perceptions have changed. Market forces now are viewed by many as sufficient for control of economic power, resulting in significant movement toward deregulation and privatization. It is at least arguable that the most important and far-reaching current international trends are those of deregulation, consolidation, and globalization. In this chapter, I propose to examine these trends in regard to public utilities and transportation in the United States, and to explore the role played by the economics discipline in these developments.

Neoclassical economics has been the dominant orthodoxy in the Western world for more than a century. Institutional economics, from its inception in the late nineteenth and early twentieth centuries, challenged the theoretical and analytical framework and policy implications of this system. The new institutional economics (NIE),[1] a.k.a. transaction cost economics, and game theory (GT) are recent entrants into the domain of neoclassical economics. Each has received comparatively rapid acceptance in terms of adoption into college curricula, publication in "leading" economic journals, and professional esteem. Although it sometimes is suggested that mainstream economics is challenged on two fronts, internally by NIE and GT and externally by institutionalism, I contend that the perceived internal challenge is not a challenge at all. Not only are NIE and GT positioned snugly within the neoclassical paradigm but their core theoretical and policy stances are virtually identical to those of the mainstream. I apprehend them therefore as support rather than challenge to the mainstream, and view them as shaping a stronger, tighter orthodoxy. There also is dispute about whether these are two fields or one; GT often is viewed not as a separate field but as an application of NIE (see, e.g., Langlois 1986, 17–18; Shen 1991, 306–7).

Yet however they are viewed, there is no question that the new approaches offer a distinctive perspective, and that they have achieved extensive prominence.[2] Moreover, in addition to academic, curricula, and publication predominance, both schools have received worldly tribute. For example, economists within each have been named Nobel Laureates.[3] It is evident that the ideas and methods of these branches of neoclassicism have influenced popular and professional views of the nature of economics and the economy, and have had important effects on the formulation of public policy.

This chapter consists, first, of a review of how the trends toward deregulation and consolidation are playing out in the United States. I will examine briefly some recent developments in public utilities and transportation. I then will explore the theory, method, and prescripts of each of these schools for perspective on the explanatory value, relevance, and implications for policy on questions of industrial organization and economic power.

Industries are said to have market power when they possess characteristics that impair market forces and hinder the development of competition. These industries are sometimes identified as natural monopolies or oligopolies. In this regard, mainstream economic attention for the most part has focused on the economies of scale that mark industries as natural monopolies. Yet, additional characteristics also signal the presence of market power. For example: (1) interdependence that necessitates joint planning and interconnection; (2) requirements for high, up-front, sunk costs; (3) wide use of nonfungible assets; (4) control of monopoly focal points; (5) high proportions of joint in total costs; (6) important externalities; and (7) a significant embodiment of necessity in demand. The presence of such attributes indicates ability to discipline market forces, to control entry and exit, and to influence consumer choice; that is, the possession of market power. The views of NIE, GT, and institutional economics on questions of the existence and extent of, and the desirability of control of, private market power are of particular interest and will constitute the gist of this chapter.

This task requires analysis of differences in the conceptual frameworks and policy conclusions of each of these schools. Areas to be examined include: (1) The relationship between deregulation and competition and between (2) consolidation and competition. (3) The role of government in the economy. (4) Market control and efficiency and (5) equity. (6) Views on the "natural" or "normal" in the economy. (7) Assumptions of rationality, and of (8) methodological individualism. (9) The concept of a public interest. Many of these topics center to a large extent on the issue of (10) the factual base of contending theories, that is, the question of whether the models reflect reality, and whether a link to reality matters. Consideration of these differences will help to establish the ability of the schools to address real-world problems. The first order of business, however, is to identify some of those real-world problems.

Deregulation and Consolidation in Public Utilities

The terms "deregulation" and "competition" often are used as synonyms. They are not. Deregulation does not lead inexorably to a competitive utopia. Neither is deregulation invariably the win-win scenario portrayed. Recent experience demonstrates that deregulation will have both winners and losers. An inquiry into the course of recent deregulation in the United States sheds light upon both the process and the identities of its victors and victims.

The implementation of deregulation in recent years primarily is attributable to the political strength of special interests with high stakes in the result. At the same time, much of the academic support was supplied by the U.S. neoclassical mainstream. The branch of neoclassicism known as the Chicago School, in particular, is identified with policies of limited government. From about the late 1960s, and accelerating thereafter, deregulation also received increasing public favor, surviving even the damping of the inflation that initially had sparked it. Decontrol was proposed in the name of efficiency and decreases in costs and prices, and was implemented for a broad range of industries. Regulation was terminated for federal transportation. Natural gas pricing was partially and then fully deregulated, entry liberalized, and policies of open access adopted for transmission pipelines. There was increased reliance on negotiation and private contract.

In electricity, the 1978 Public Utility Regulatory Policies Act (PURPA) was not strongly deregulatory. Its rate structure reform, enacted in the name of efficient usage, largely reflected neoclassical principles. PURPA also included provisions to encourage development of alternative energy sources, such as cogeneration. In contrast, the 1992 Energy Policy Act (EPA) was deregulatory. It created a new class of producer, an "exempt wholesale generator" (EWG), to include both utility-affiliated and nonaffiliated wholesale producers, amending the Public Utility Holding Company Act (PUHCA) of 1935. If found to qualify by the Federal Energy Regulatory Commission (FERC), EWGs now could build and operate facilities in one or more states, absent state regulation. The act also opened transmission networks to all (for greater detail, see Miller 1993a, 325–28).

At the state level, the deregulation of electricity started in 1996 in California. Deregulation in this context refers to a division of electricity functions, with transmission and distribution remaining under regulation and generation and marketing transferred to the market. Generators are permitted to set the price of power sold into the wholesale market, with EWGs of traditional utilities expected to be among the principal players in this arena. The incentive to producers to cut costs is seen as the ability of buyers to shop for the cheapest power. Power marketers then would sell to retail distributors. It is anticipated that the attention of electricity marketers[4] primarily would be directed at high-volume customers, which have been the focus of sellers for every sector under deregulation. Changing industrial circumstances augur the potential for price volatility. For example, heat spells in the summers of 1998 and 1999 brought severe power shortages, soaring prices, interruptions of power, and the cessation of power sales to some customers, forcing plant closings (Kranhold 1998, R4; McKay 1999, C21). As it turned out, this was to be but a pale harbinger of even higher price spikes and longer power interruptions in subsequent years. Utilities also are breaching traditional boundaries to obtain distant power plants (Kranhold 1998, R4), and actively acquiring international companies (Gumbel 1999, A9). To date, final consumers are protected from the most direct price impacts of the market activity because prices to end users are frozen during the transition to deregulation.

In telecommunications, the AT&T settlement and divestiture of 1984 was more deintegrating than competitive or even deregulatory. The local loop—the so-called last mile—remained under control of the seven divested regional Bell holding companies (RBHCs); that is, local service remained a monopoly. Furthermore, although long-distance service often is described as competitive, this is a mischaracterization. AT&T retains a high percentage of market share. Moreover, the pattern of alternating price wars and lock step price change among the major interexchange carriers (IXCs) suggests not competition but oligopoly and price leadership or collusion. The settlement ushered in a wave of "alternative regulation" at the federal and state levels (see Trebing 1989, 117–20; Miller 1994, 803–7). Yet, the removal of restraints on profits and earnings thus sanctioned, together with the relaxation of previous prohibitions contained in the settlement agreement, seemed to provide a warrant not for competition but for unconstrained diversification. In the years after the settlement, AT&T and the Bells ventured ever farther afield (both geographically and functionally) into related and unrelated fields.

The aim of the 1996 Telecommunications Act was achievement of the local competition that had eluded reach. The act denies RBHCs entry into the long-distance market until local competition is attained. It specifies that the RBHCs must permit access through connection to their networks or resale. The FCC rules call for the RBHCs to make available unbundled components of the local network, including the local loop, at a discount, the amount of which has been a matter of dispute. The FCC has a four-teen-point test that incumbent carriers must pass to be allowed into inter-state long-distance markets (Mehta 1998b, R8; Cauley 1998, R14-R15). RBHCs have been successful in winning FCC approval to provide long-distance service in some of the states they serve. The competition expected in these markets as a result of this entry has not yet materialized.

The major effect of the 1996 Telecommunications Act appears to have been not encouragement of competition but facilitation of a merger and acquisition (M&A) movement of vast proportions, a movement also man-ifest in airlines, railroads, and electricity during this period. Nor is the M&A movement confined to the public utility sector. It is part of an econ-omy-wide trend and of worldwide dimensions. Consolidation and con-centration also is evident in banking, finance, oil and gas, pharmaceuticals, health care, broadcasting, and many other industries, in addition to telecommunications and other public utilities. The movement has been expedited by prevailing market-oriented, deregulatory convictions. It is further encouraged by a run-up in stock market values, which permits cash-free or almost cash-free purchase financed by highly appreciated stock and debt, and facilitates the purchase of large firms by much smaller companies. It is animated by a legal environment that rejects antitrust in the same spirit that it embraces deregulation, and is galvanized by an eco-nomic environment that surrenders skepticism in regard to size of opera-tion. In today's environment, large size is accepted almost as a survival requirement.

The merger movement has resulted in the number of major railroads dropping, according to a recent calculation, from forty in 1980 to "just a handful" at present (Machalaba and Mathews 1999, A2). With the takeover of Southern Pacific (SP) by Union Pacific (UP), the merger of Burlington Northern (BN) and Santa Fe Pacific (SF), and the Norfolk Southern and CSX acquisition of Conrail, only two western (BN/SF and UP/SP) and two eastern (Burlington Northern and CSX) rail systems remain. In the energy industries, a similar pattern of conglomeration emerges, including the melding of potentially rivalrous gas and electric companies. Yet no industry has seen activity on this front comparable to that of telecommunications, which has been the scene of multi-billion-dollar acquisitions, bidding wars, hostile takeovers, settlements, and trial marriages/breakups, and new unions.[5] Along the way, amidst cross-industry conglomeration and expansion, cable, Internet, telecommunications, information, and entertainment industry lines are becoming blurred, and companies interact now as combatants and then as allies. Power companies also are edging into telecommunications through their fiber networks. The following examples of completed and pending[6] M&As convey only a hint of the convoluted nature of recent deals and near misses. They are also an indication of the sophisticated strategies and vast consequences—that is, the kind of gaming and the nature of the escalating stakes—involved in current real-world jousting.

AT&T has acquired Teleport, a long-distance business provider, the cable company TCI (formerly pledged to Bell Atlantic), and the USWest spin-off MediaOne (besting Comcast). AT&T also has formed an alliance with Time Warner's cable unit. With the acquisition of MediaOne, AT&T will have the ability to reach about 60 percent of all U.S. cable households (Cauley and Blumenstein 1999, A3). Speculation is rife that the cable acquisitions will permit AT&T to offer local telephone service through cable, although conversion of broadband cable one-way video into an interactive, two-way transmission system requires costly upgrades and equipment. In the nearer term, the acquisition of cable will permit AT&T to offer speedy internet hookup, with a major controversy brewing over the question of whether "open access" (or, in AT&T's terminology, "forced access"[7]) to these facilities should be required.

The RBHCs now are down to four from seven, with the acquisition by SBC of Pacific Telesis and Ameritech, and the merger of Bell Atlantic and Nynex. In addition, SBC has purchased SNET, Bell Atlantic and GTE have merged, and the little-known WorldCom has acquired the much larger MCI, previously courted by both British Telecom and GTE. Bell South, to date neither an acquirer nor an acquiree, owns a 10 percent interest in Qwest, the maximum—in one of the few legal restrictions that remains—allowed by law for an RBHC of an IXC. A prolonged bidding war to acquire USWest and Frontier (the former Rochester Telephone Company) by Qwest and Global Crossing was avoided by settlement, with the two suitors dividing the prize. A Bell Atlantic/Vodafone alliance has been announced. The turmoil makes it easy to overlook the fact that potential rivals are joining forces. Cable and telephone, seen as possible functional rivals, and the RBHCs, seen as potential geographic rivals, are instead combining. At this juncture, some see the phone industry eventually evolving into a few worldwide supercarriers offering global service including local and long-distance voice, data, and video carriage and Internet access (see, for example, Mehta 1999, B1).[8]

A consideration of winners and losers under deregulation indicates that the winners include new entrants into the fields; senior executives of acquired companies, enriched by stock options and exit payments; stockholders, enriched by run-ups in stock prices; and large-volume customers, courted with discounts and special treatment. Low-volume customers, however, are not much advantaged. The ordinary customer in many of these markets does not receive much in the way of decreased rates, better service, or increased choice of carrier or product. Indeed, in current telephone markets, as stock prices increase, "local telephone rates are rising . . . [and] service is slipping" (Mehta 1998a, B1). On-the-spot reports in the business press have portrayed deregulation in the electric and telephone industries, respectively, as resulting in decreased bills for large-volume and increased bills for low-volume users, and as encouraging concentration rather than competition (e.g., Kranhold 1998, R4). Moreover, these reports express the concern that "[a]s the industry titans battle for the choicest customers, some people—and some communities—may find themselves left on the sidelines" (Mehta 1999, B1). That is, informed observers raise the specter that institutional economists have articulated from the start, and against which Trebing in particular in recent years has raised an often-lonely voice (for example, 1987, 1724). In other words, they point to the strong probability that the unique operating conditions of these industries will engender consolidation and concentration, encourage cross-subsidization and price discrimination for joint products in segmented markets, and result in isolation and polarization of vulnerable persons and communities. The economic schools that we will be scrutinizing view these matters from distinctly incompatible perspectives.

The New Institutional Economics

It generally is recognized that Ronald Coase established the basis for NIE in his 1937 "The Nature of the Firm." The article was well received, although its ideas were not extensively applied. In the words of the author, the essay was "much cited and little used" (Coase 1991, 51). It was not until the appearance in 1960 of his "The Problem of Social Cost" and the subsequent work of Oliver Williamson in the 1970s that the analytic treatment took hold. Williamson credits Coase with having planted the seeds for an approach that was to set the tone and determine the direction of many sub-specialties, including public utility economics, and spawn the new subfield of law and economics.

Both Coase and Williamson emphasize that NIE is not a substitute but a complement and supplement to neoclassicism. The point is well taken. The analysis relies heavily on microtheory. Coase notes that a criterion employed in his formulation of the emergence of the firm is that it be compatible with competition (Coase 1991, 54), a hallmark of neoclassicism. The framework of the analysis is forthrightly individualistic; social costs and values play no part. Moreover, and as discussed in the following, the theoretical core of NIE is basically neoclassicist.

Williamson distinguishes NIE from neoclassicism in that the key unit of analysis in the former is the transaction; hence, transaction cost economics. That is, he distinguishes the approach in terms of its focus upon exchange rather than production. Transaction cost economics purports to explain the choice between the firm and the market, between "make or buy" decisions. Williamson famously comments: "In the beginning, there were markets" (1975, 20). That is, he seeks the basis for firm formation from an initial state of market-based activity. He finds it in the minimization of transaction costs, identified as the costs of search, negotiation, and enforcement. Firms are formed as alternatives to the market to maximize efficiency by internalizing and economizing on transaction costs. This is in accord with the overall tendency of the NIE to explain the emergence of institutions as a result of rational individual action from an initial institution-free condition (Hodgson 1998, 176). Williamson emphasizes that a key difference between transaction cost and standard theory is that the former views the firm as a contracting body rather than a "production function," with efficiency parameters determined by technology. That is, transaction cost minimization is added to production cost minimization, and posited as determining market structure.

Bounded rationality, opportunism, and asset specificity are explicitly identified as central concepts, and cited as differentiating features. Although not identified as core ideas, concepts of equilibrium and certainty also are implicitly central, underscoring the continuity of NIE with neoclassicism. NIE also adopts the neoclassical emphasis on economic rationality and individual self-interest, although they are qualified. Thus, rationality, in a concept borrowed from Herbert Simon, becomes bounded rationality, restricted by human computational and coordinating limitations. The neoclassical self-interest is modified and presented as opportunism, defined as self-interest plus guile, indicating the potential for untrustworthy action. Asset specificity (nonfungibility) occurs when redeployment of resources (including human resources) would negate or reduce productivity. It affects optimal firm size and bargaining options. The economic norm is that of private individual negotiation to achieve highest benefit at lowest cost. Social cost and benefit are excluded from consideration.

The subfields influenced by this approach uniformly accept and apply what has come to be known as the "Coase Theorem," which counsels that absent legal liability and with zero transaction costs (ZTC), parties will negotiate until they achieve maximum allocative efficiency, whatever the initial distribution of property rights. This occurs because through bargaining and exchange the property right appropriately will vest with the person who assigns to it the highest value (Langlois 1986, 16). This distribution will also ensure that the agent who will use the property most productively (that is, will be most likely to pursue efficiency and return maximization) will have ownership rights (Lorenz 1999, 302–3).

Notwithstanding the attempt at differentiation, both the vision and message of the Coase Theorem are neoclassical: That individual negotiation, contract, and exchange are "natural " ordering principles of society, that efficiency is the goal of economic activity, that private processes are preferable to public ones. The Coase Theorem contains an additional implicit message. By extending the concepts of commodity and transaction to include the purchase and sale of rights to inflict harm (Reder 1982, 22), it informs that with ZTC, parties will bargain to achieve the most efficient solution, irrespective of legal liability. Freedom of contract is established as the norm; equity considerations are depreciated. Only in the event of high transaction costs is intervention considered appropriate. Moreover, such departures from the norm are aberrational and require justification (Horwitz 1980, 908–9); the burden of proof thus is assigned to advocates for intervention. Moreover, if high transaction costs mandate government intervention, the intervention should be fashioned so as to mimic the market.

Hence, efficiency takes precedence over equity; contract takes precedence over tort. Parties will negotiate until they reach the efficient solution. Only private individual costs and benefits are included in the calculation. Efficiency is conceived in a strictly individualistic sense, and equated with maximum individual pecuniary return. Social costs and benefits play no role. The ability of the powerful, or the deep-pocketed, to finesse the powerless, manipulate events, and turn things to account is ignored. The mutually acceptable result of the individual bargaining process is the equilibrium position, the point at which no party can be made better off without making some other party worse off. Not to be overlooked is the spirit of Pareto that hovers, like Banquo's ghost, at this table. We will meet it again in our discussion of GT.

Continuity, perhaps even unity, with the "mother theory" also is shown by the conclusion: Reliance upon individual negotiation and transacting ensures efficiency; achievement of efficiency secures the maximization of social welfare. It ensures that consumers who (again, following neoclassicism) direct production will be able to purchase desired goods at the lowest possible price. It achieves superior resource allocation and maximizes output. It effects firm profitability that, in turn, assures firm survivability. Consumer and social welfare thus are maximized. This utopian cornucopia is achieved by following the "natural" ordering process of individual negotiation, contracting, and exchange in a free private market.

NIE retains the core of neoclassicism, although trimmed around the edges. The themes explored are the same, the core assumptions only slightly varied, the conclusions indistinguishable. Each is methodologically individualistic. In each, the individual transaction is interpreted as consensual. It is equated with freedom. In each, government action is viewed as coercive. Williamson makes the point that abuses of private power are exaggerated, and the potential for "government failure" is large. Moreover, he contends that the use of sophisticated contracting will provide for most market contingencies (Williamson 1985, 327; idem 1975, 220; see also Miller 1993b, 1051–54). Individuals are affirmed as the appropriate moving parties, and viewed as unaffected by social norm and convention, to say nothing of circumstance. Individual preferences are given and innate. Humans are rational optimizers. Power imbalances are ignored. The concept of a public interest is absent, except as the sum of private individual interests.

Strong statements on survival, that is, the judgment that efficient firms survive because efficiency translates into profitability that, in turn, translates into survivability, are found in both NIE and neoclassicism (see, for example, Williamson 1985, 236; Friedman 1953, 21–22). In NIE, as in its wellspring, the survivability contention is justification for the status quo. That is, the efficiency criterion that informs bargains ensures superior economic performance. It is also justification for almost any degree of private vertical integration. NIE contains a strong, implicit condemnation of regulation, antitrust, or any form of social control. If firms are formed and structured to economize on transaction costs so as to achieve efficiency, and efficiency is the overriding goal, how is vertical integration to be challenged? As with so much of neoclassicism, the thinking is profoundly tautological. That is, firms survive because they are efficient. The proof of their efficiency is their survival. Pareto optimality is tautological in much the same sense. Rational individual choice results in a Pareto-optimal equilibrium. The evidence that it is Pareto-optimal is that it is the result of individual rational choice.

Model tractability plays a significant role in standard neoclassicism. It is one of the reasons that certainty and complete knowledge are so central. It is also important to NIE and, as we shall see, to game theory. Yet, the later formulations maintain that in their systems of thought certainty is rejected and uncertainty affirmed, in large measure because they view individuals as boundedly rational. In the absence of certainty, however, the optimization goal is problematic. The resolution is a substitution of the ability to assign probability distributions, and therefore calculable risk, to all possible outcomes. The capacity to model choice on the basis of relative returns thus is retained. Models assume either certainty or, alternatively, that it is possible unambiguously to assign probability distributions to all potential outcomes. The situation is then determinate. One may calculate returns on which to base decisions (Lorenz 1999, 304).

The solution, of course, is no solution at all. As Frank Knight indicated years ago in distinguishing uncertainty and risk, probability distributions may be assigned to risk, but not to uncertainty. It is possible to insure against risk, but not uncertainty. In fact, under conditions of uncertainty, a probability distribution cannot conceivably incorporate all possible contingencies. Some possible outcomes cannot be anticipated. Uncertainty is a void, a black hole, a mysterious space about which there not only are no precise answers, but for which it may not even be possible to formulate meaningful questions. What is called uncertainty in NIE is not uncertainty, but simply a variation on neoclassical certainty. Neoclassicism unquestionably errs in assuming perfect knowledge; NIE just as assuredly errs in its variation on the principle. As we shall see in the following, GT bears a striking resemblance to NIE in its approach to this question, and to many others.

Game Theory

Game theory is described as "rampant in economics" (Gibbons 1997, 127). The depiction is well deserved. Over the past several decades GT has all but taken possession of pure theory and has greatly expanded its role in an increasing number of subspecialties. Above all else, GT values "precision and generality of the underlying ideas and emphasizes the usefulness of abstraction and formalism" (Gul 1997, 163). Logical consistency is highly prized (Mailath 1998, 1351). As game theorists increasingly fill the professional ranks of the discipline, "more and more, the language of game theory has become the language of economics" (Gul 1997, 163).

The ascent of GT within the discipline can be traced to John von Neumann and Oskar Morgenstern's *Theory of Games and Economic Behavior* (1944). By most accounts, it was intended as a break with neoclassicism and with use of the method of the differential calculus. Von Neumann and Morgenstern hoped to substitute for the neoclassical "metaphor of the machine," which they viewed as inapplicable to social experience, an analysis of structure based upon the axiomization of psychological phenomena to allow for indeterminacy, probability, and discontinuous change (Leonard 1995, 755–56). The axiomatic method was held to be applicable to all science, social as well as physical. It was postulated that through the application of reason and logic and the expression of hypotheses in formal, mathematical terms, truth would be revealed (Ingrao and Israel 1990, 176, 185, 193). The formalism of GT implicitly is based on the concept that because economic behavior is lawlike in its regularity, it can be explored rigorously and quantified through the use of mathematics. Logically consistent hypethetico-deductive mathematical methods are utilized to derive the laws governing human behavior. GT, as is its neoclassical parent, is by its nature a prioristic.

Game theorists draw a distinction between "rationalistic" and "evolutionary," also designated noncooperative and cooperative, GT (for example, Mailath 1998, 1347). Evolutionary GT seeks a rationale for the emergence of cooperation, and is characterized by repetitive play of games (also called supergames) by boundedly rational players (Weibull 1988, 1). Noncooperative GT instead concentrates on the playing of one-shot games by perfectly rational players. A key factor identified for the emergence of cooperation is the requirement that play be infinite because of a perceived tendency, in a one-shot (or finite) game, to try to achieve an immediate personal advantage. Cooperation is more likely to develop as an equilibrium strategy if the probability of future interaction between players is high (Axelrod and Hodgson 1994, 82–83; Field 1994, 273). In addition, in cooperative games, it is assumed that players are able to make binding agreements, although it is not clear how these are to be enforced (Field 1994, 272).

The model most frequently utilized clearly shows the affinity of GT and NIE. It is that of the rational agent choosing one action from a set of possibilities, with outcomes depending upon which of a set of mutually exclusive "states of nature" is believed to exist. The agent is assumed to allot values in terms of utility to all possible outcomes and, because certainty is not achievable (rationality is bounded), to assign probabilities to each (with probabilities and acts assumed independent). The value of outcomes is the probability-weighted sum of its utility; the rule is that acts must be chosen that offer at least as high a utility as any other (Runde and Anand 1997, 4–5). That is, a "belief profile" specifies a probability distribution for each set of outcomes; the probability attached to these beliefs determines the plays that will be made (Binmore 1987, 191). GT is a representation of interactive decision theory, with individual choice defined as a choice of strategies. Opposing players rationally choose from among possible strategies with the aim of achieving the maximum payoff. A major difference between rationalistic and evolutionary game theory is that in the latter, the attempt is to maximize the payoff to the individual by maximizing the payoff to the group, rather than seeking immediate advantage. The rationalistic theory relies on rationality and certainty; the evolutionary on bounded rationality and probability distribution. It is much the same difference as between neoclassicism and NIE.

The games employed in game theoretic analysis are intended as analogies to real-world conditions. For example, Edward Lorenz describes a well-known game theoretic treatment of incomplete contracts involving a moral hazard problem. The moral hazard is alleviated and efficiency improved by vertical integration (Lorenz 1999, 302–3). The familiar Prisoners' Dilemma (PD) game is a metaphor for the difficulty of achieving satisfactory results (that is, highest payoffs) when self-interested individuals play one-shot games and there are no mechanisms for binding agreements and enforcement. A shift of play to a supergame demonstrates that cooperation, resulting in higher payoffs, is achievable (Axelrod and Hodgson 1994, 82). Repetitive play may result in cooperative equilibria with efficient payoffs (Fudenberg and Maskin 1990, 274–75) because the knowledge that there will be continued interaction will lead to a desire to preserve future relationships (Gul 1997, 170).[9] A frequently referenced (for example, Field 1994, 273) experiment organized by Robert Axelrod as a PD supergame yielded the result that the most successful strategy adopted was not joint defection, rational for individuals in one-shot PD games, but a tit-for-tat strategy, in which players repeat opponent's prior moves.

The experiment raises interesting questions about the nature of learning in game theory. For example, reinforcement and imitation are viewed as among the most, if not, indeed, *the* most important categories of learning (Weibull 1988, 7–9). Individuals learn by reinforcement when they repeat their own past successful (that is, high-payoff) behavior; they learn by imitation when they model the successful (high-payoff) behavior of others, as in the tit-for-tat strategy. The population will increase its use of successful behavior, decrease that of unsuccessful behavior (Mailath 1998,

1355). Game theory holds that rational players will never use a strictly dominated strategy (Binmore 1987, 193). A strategy is termed "strictly dominated" if it consistently yields lower payoffs than other strategies. Over time, the dominated strategy will therefore disappear. In a variation on the survivability thesis, successful behavior becomes more prevalent both because the market selects against the unsuccessful and because agents replicate their own past successful behavior and imitate the behavior of those who succeed (Mailath 1998, 1348). The related issue of how progress is to occur in this system is also of interest. If learning occurs primarily through repetition or imitation of successful "moves," there seems to be little room for transformation and development.

The emphasis given by game theory to model tractability also lends credence to the view of it as an application of NIE. Mailath notes that in an ideal world, analysis would be extended to a study of more complicated games than are presently studied. Yet complicated models are not tractable. He contends that if understanding is to be enhanced, it is necessary to pose problems that are soluble. It therefore is necessary to use simple and tractable models. He notes: "the role of models is to improve our intuition and to deepen our understanding of how particular economic or strategic forces interact. . . . [T]o progress, we must analyze . . . simple and tractable games. . . . In order to better understand these issues, we need to study models that can be solved . . ." (1998, 1356). Accordingly, models are restricted in the interest of manageability. Porter points out that although multiperiod games are most analogous to industrial interaction, oligopoly game theory relies primarily on static models because of their greater tractability (1991, 557). Mailath indicates that in examining the robustness of an evolutionarily stable strategy (ESS) to perturbations (a key concept in evolutionary game theory), the simplest of models are used.[10] For example, ESS is examined for its robustness to any single episode of perturbation, but not to a series of shocks (Mailath 1998, 1369).

Beyond this, however, it is to the concepts and processes that unite mainstream NIE and GT that we must look for the factors that most influence their ability to construct these simple, elegant, and logically consistent models. Each abstracts from reality to make underlying assumptions about human nature, behavior, and incentives. Core ideas of rationality and maximization are accepted or modified in ways that preserve their essential meaning. Tastes, preferences, rules of the game—all are accepted as constants or given. Despite lip service to interactivity, the methodological individualism of neoclassicism survives. Recognition of the influence of the social on the individual is lacking. The flow is solely from the individual to the collective. Rational choice is the motive force behind all action, and therefore responsible for all final states. The concept of a final state is important to the model. Equilibrium continues as a focus and a goal, and Pareto-optimum play is a common strategy.[11] For example, a Nash equilibrium is defined as a situation in which a set of strategies exists such that no player benefits from change when other players' strategies are unchanged.[12] Efficiency is defined in terms of allocation of resources to their highest (pecuniary) use or as maximization of returns, sometimes conflated. Moreover, recognition of the effects of disparities of power commensurate with their importance in real-world arrangements uniformly is absent. When recognized, it is commonly for purposes of justification.[13] The very procedure adopted accentuates a weakness of the method. While certain real-world conditions can more or less be simulated in games, others present obstacles. For example, while it is not too difficult to switch play from a one-shot to a supergame, it is problematic to represent and model through game-theoretic experiment disparities in power.

GT claims as a major advantage its ability to provide determinate answers to unmanageable problems (Gul 1997, 162). The answers may indeed be determinate, but also irrelevant to solution of real-world problems. In light of the resistance of the world to the resolute efforts of economists and others to purge it of complexity, application to it of simple tractable models would seem to be of questionable value. The real world is notably intractable. That GT performs little empirical work (Porter 1991, 554) serves only to compound the problem.

Institutional Economics

Unlike NIE and GT, institutional economics is cognizant of the existence and effects of power, perceives human behavior as multifaceted, understands the interaction of economic and other sciences, and is firmly rooted in the real world. This equips it to deal with questions of market maneuvering and economic might.

Williamson notes that NIE takes its name in large part from the fact that both he and Commons advance the transaction as the major analytic unit and rely upon analysis of institutions (see, for example, Williamson 1975, xi; idem 1985, 3). Yet the most cursory reading of their work reveals the deep divide that separates their treatment of these concepts. NIE finds the derivation of the firm in economic rationality, transaction costs, and free individual exchange between relative equals. Institutions develop in response to economizing by rational agents in a free market. Commons, in contrast, is interested in varieties and characteristics of rational and irrational human interaction. He distinguishes three types of transactions. Two are typified by inequality of power. Furthermore, he is at pains to point out that even when it comes to the bargaining transaction, most closely approximating one of equality, there exists legal but not economic equality. That is, Commons's analysis is cognizant of power imbalances; NIE all but ignores them.

The institution also is differently construed within the two approaches. NIE views institutions as developing from institutionless beginnings through freedom and rationality. For institutionalists, the concept of institution-free "beginnings" lacks meaning. Veblen defines institutions as "settled habits of thought common to the generality of men." Commons sees it similarly, as "collective action in control of individual action." Humans are born into existing cultures. The institution is social and behavioral rather than individualistic and structural. Custom and convention, authority and law direct and control behavior.

Institutional economics differs from the mainstream in assumption, methodology, and conclusion. It rejects concepts of individuality, rationality, and maximization accepted as axiomatic by standard theory. It sees human action as grounded in an amalgam of incentives. It perceives individuals as active seekers of explanation and wielders of and adapters to influence rather than solely as passive reactors to monetary stimuli. The Veblenian dichotomy distinguishes instrumental propensities such as workmanship and the parental bent from ceremonial ones such as status striving and the urge for dominance. Veblen and Commons draw distinctions between the "going plant" and the "going business," with goals, respectively, of "making goods" and "making money," and engaged, respectively, in workmanship and salesmanship. Institutional economists see creative and exploitative, technological and institutional tendencies operating conjointly.

Institutional economics discerns individuals who are shaped by even as they shape their environments. It thus apprehends concepts of innate preference and "consumer sovereignty" as incorrect and misleading. Institutionalists maintain that characteristics posited by neoclassical economics as given and constant are variable, and importantly so. Human tastes and preferences are not given. Social standards and mores color individual preference, and people are subject to manipulation and coercion by many factors, not least of all the persuasive and coercive will of others and the lifestyles of those above them on the social ladder. Thus Veblen opines that "invention is the mother of necessity," rather than the converse. John Kenneth Galbraith describes a "revised sequence" in which supply determines demand. Mainstream theories ignore the fact that choice is socially shaped and determined, that cultural norms and standards are internalized, that convention and law do not simply codify but confer legitimacy. They overlook the ability of market power to manipulate and coerce the powerless to its ends. Institutional economists do not accept as "normal" or "natural" specific individual attributes, market structures, or social conditions. In keeping with the pragmatic and experimental character of their thought, they advocate that solutions be shaped to the nature of problems, rather than to such prespecified goals as competition and market determination, and be varied as situations change.

Institutional economics focuses on process. It supplants equilibrium with evolution, seeing neither beginning nor end point to development. It substitutes process irreversibility for equilibration between states of rest. It is indeterminate and nondeterministic, envisioning neither prescribed path nor final term for the economic continuum. As such, it posits an implacable uncertainty. It is interdisciplinary, seeing the economy and economics itself as forged and conditioned by all the sciences, physical and social. The penetrating influence of the polity and technology, for example, on the economic is recognized. Institutionalism does not confine itself to the use of "economic" tools, or to the observation of "economic" phenomena. Mathematical and statistical analysis is not dismissed, but viewed as the tool rather than the core of economic theory.

The universe of inquiry for institutional economists is the economy as it is, rather than as specified by an ideal type or as required to be neatly encompassed in "tractable" models. Institutionalism is experiential, fact based. It apprehends an economy characterized by flaws and departures from the competitive model, including the possession of power that confers discretionary ability to determine outcomes. Veblen, for example, defines industrial sabotage as the "conscientious withdrawal of efficiency." As an instance of this, he and Commons identify the ability to restrict output to increase scarcity, and thereby price, made possible by the existence of private market power. Thus, in a significant departure from the competitive vision of the neoclassical schools, producers are depicted as "price makers" and not "price takers," a result of the operation of the "going business" driven by salesmanship. Institutionalists do not accept the rules of the game as given, any more than are tastes and preferences, but recognize that market power permits its possessors to make and change the rules. Institutionalism sees economics as a problem-solving discipline, with the aim of providing causal explanation for economic condition, and experimenting with arrangements that improve it.

Institutionalists see efficiency as a social rather than an individual, and as a real rather than a pecuniary phenomenon. Efficiency is viewed as the expression of the full productive potential of the economy, including most particularly the productive human potential. Thus, efficiency is perceived in a communal, rather than an individualistic, sense, and includes the concept of social responsibility. For example, public utilities and network infrastructure are viewed as part of the social capital of the economy—that is, part of the commons—requiring oversight to ensure wide accessibility and to guard against use as a hostage to fortune.

Efficiency is not viewed as allocation of scarce resources to a "highest" (pecuniary) use to achieve given ends, or as return maximization. The maximization of returns serves a private pecuniary purpose; the maximization of productive potential satisfies a public interest. Resources are not scarce, ends are not given. Periods of high unemployment and overcapacity are commonplace facts of human history. Time and again the problem faced is not scarcity but glut of resources, often a result of the "conscientious withdrawal of efficiency." Goals are not anterior to the economic process, nor are they established exogenously, but through human interaction. Inefficiency is viewed as commensurate with waste, especially the waste of human life. This may be the result of abuses of private market power. Institutionalists do not uncouple efficiency and equity, as do all versions of mainstream economics. For institutionalists, efficiency has a sizable equity component, and the public interest is a meaningful concept.

Institutional and mainstream economists take different views also of learning and progress. The neoclassical schools view learning as a response to pecuniary incentives, and progress as the conjuncture of economic rationality and freedom, as they define these terms. Institutionalists see the unregulated market, most often equated with freedom by traditional schools, as frequently controlled by private power. They see learning as occurring through workmanship, curiosity, and experimentation that (when not impeded by Veblen's "imbecile institutions") yield technological and intellectual advance and improved standards of life. Institutionalists recognize learning as transformative, developmental, building upon itself and carrying growth of new ideas, understandings, capabilities, habits of thought, tastes and preferences, methods of procedure, and technique.

Institutional economists observe industries in the public utility sector in which, in the absence of public restraint, strong centralizing tendencies will permit the amassing of private power. This is not dependent upon the existence of natural monopoly conditions. That is, institutionalists do not perceive an economic world that is sharply segmented into naturally monopolistic and competitive markets. They see, rather, a world in which oligopoly is a pervasive market form. Market power enhances the ability, for example, to favor large-volume at the expense of small-volume consumers, power respecting power; that is, oligopoly favoring oligopsony. It also encourages the cycle of vertical and horizontal integration that we see today, which only a short time ago was prevented by law. Institutionalism does not call for social control if workable competition exists. However, it does not view workable competition as an inevitable result of laissez-faire. It follows that marketization or deregulation is not an end in itself. When workable competition does not exist, institutionalists see the need for public regulation to control private economic power. Neoclassical economics envisions market forces as almost invariably free and neutral, even benign, and sufficient for control of market power. Institutionalism recognizes that market forces may be ill matched to the task of controlling market power. It maintains that when workable competition is absent, the existence of centralizing tendencies, together with the existence of goods or services with high elements of necessity in demand, establishes a strong prima facie case for social control.

It follows that the institutional approach to markets and regulation differs from the prevalent popular version, or that embedded in GT or NIE. In the institutionalist view, the models of markets and market value found in GT and NIE do not address current real-world problems of market failure and market concentration. Institutionalists see situations such as these as calling for vigorous regulation, a position distant from the market views of GT or NIE. Moreover, institutionalists view regulation itself as evolutionary, requiring change in form and method to meet changing circumstances and needs. Evaluation of regulatory results then needs be in terms of its ability to meet the problem at hand, rather than in terms of its approximation to a market solution, or conformity to any other ideal.

Thus, institutional economists reject the contention that the current industrial combination and consolidation is a means of economizing on transaction costs, and see it instead as often an exercise in private power. They dismiss the idea that it is an expression of rationality, however qualified, seeing it rather as a predatory drive toward dominance and advantage. Furthermore, they deny the laissez-faire content of the mainstream message, which they see either as an endorsement of the status quo or as an "anything goes" statement. They call, when market control is inoperative, for application of a deliberative and evolving means of social control in a public interest.

Conclusion

It is clear that institutional economics stands in sharp contrast to NIE and game theory in virtually all respects, from basic assumption to policy

conclusion. It is equally clear that NIE and game theory are in fundamental accord. Their foundational precepts are virtually indistinguishable.
Their policy conclusions are allied, if not equivalent. In fact, the contention that game theory is an application of NIE is compelling.

Game theory commonly is depicted as uniquely equipped to deal with
problems of oligopoly because it offers a model of interactive decision theory. Thus, action is viewed as in some measure a response to anticipated
actions and reactions of opponents. However, a system based upon
methodological individualism, economic rationality, and maximization is
at odds with real-world circumstances of interactivity. It does not come to
grips with worldly conditions of interdependence and dominance. A
model of bargaining between relative equals in an environment of certainty, or in which complex contracts and probability distributions compensate for their absence, is ineffectual for analysis of arbitrary and
capricious power in unregulated markets. Nor will a system that views firm
formation, organization, and expansion as an expression of its efficiency
goal be useful in examining the problems that may arise as a result. It also
is unlikely that a model that attributes survival to and equates revenue
maximization with that same efficiency is equipped objectively to assess
the relative contributions and just desserts of real-world winners and
losers. Finally, a system that minimizes "market failure" and points instead
to "government failure" (Williamson 1985, 327) is impeded in neutrally
evaluating issues of market position and in controlling for its effects.

Despite the record of academic and publication achievement, one is
somewhat hard pressed to find practical applications of NIE and game theory. NIE is lauded for its advancement of the utilization of complex contracts, and for the boost it has given negotiation in decision making. Game
theory is praised for its part in popularizing auctions and designing Federal Communication Commission (FCC) auctions of spectrum (Leonard
1995, 730–31; Gul 1997, 172). However, the practical success of these
techniques is questionable. For example, recent FCC auctions have been
plagued by missed deadlines, default, and pleas for restructuring of debt
(Pearl 1994, B3; Mills 1995, 20; Gruley and Hardy 1997, A3). Auctions
and bidding are promoted as market-oriented alternatives to regulation.[14]
The difficulties that have been encountered confirm the major benefit of
auctions as a tool, rather than a substitute, for regulation.

Yet at bottom what most recommends game theory to many is the
effect it has had upon the manner in which economists reason. That is, its
major accomplishment is viewed as encouragement of the utilization of
formal, abstract, rigorous methods (Gul 1997, 172) and the mandate for
a logically consistent approach. However, what is accepted as its greatest

strength may be its major weakness. The centrality to the model of mechanical procedure results in a depreciation of substance. Not only are central issues not properly addressed; they are not addressed at all. Close to four decades ago the philosopher of science Thomas Kuhn, in distinguishing normal and revolutionary science, noted that normal science, or science in thrall to a prevalent system of thought, contents itself with the working out of puzzles that extend or flesh out the prevailing theory. He made the point that the working out of puzzles is primarily useful for displaying the ingenuity or skill of the analyst, rather than for producing a socially useful result (Kuhn 1962, 36–37; for additional detail, see Miller 1991, 994–95). Game theory is the ultimate propounder of puzzles. Bruna Ingrao and Georgio Israel have stated that the "axiomization" of economics had the result for the discipline of "emptying [it] of content" (1990, 183). Economists have long displayed an affinity for analysis of "empty economic boxes." We seem to be at it once again.

References

Axelrod, Robert M., and Geoffrey M. Hodgson. 1994. The evolution of cooperation. In *The Elgar companion to institutional and evolutionary economics I*, edited by Geoffrey M. Hodgson, Warren J. Samuels, and Marc R. Tool, 80–85. Aldershot: Edward Elgar.

Ball, Deborah. 1999. Olivetti's win may reshape telecom industry. *Wall Street Journal*, 25 May, A22.

Binmore, Ken. 1987. Modeling rational players. *Economics and Philosophy* (October): 179–214.

Cauley, Leslie. 1998. Changing picture. *Wall Street Journal*, 21 September, R14–15.

Cauley, Leslie, and Rebecca Blumenstein. 1999. Comcast, in AT&T accord, abandons MediaOne. *Wall Street Journal*, 5 May, A3.

Coase, Ronald H. 1991. The nature of the firm: Meaning. In *The nature of the firm: Origins, evolution and development*, edited by Oliver E. Williamson and Sidney G. Winter, 48–60. New York and Oxford: Oxford University Press.

Farhi, Paul. 1999. From Ma Bell to Ma Cable? *Washington Post Weekly Edition*, 3 May, 18.

Field, Alexander J. 1994. Game theory and institutions. In *The Elgar companion to institutional and evolutionary economics*, edited by Geoffrey M. Hodgson, Warren J. Samuels, and Marc R. Tool, 271–276. Aldershot: Edward Elgar.

Friedman, Milton.1953. The methodology of positive economics. In *Essays in positive economics*, 3–43. Chicago: University of Chicago Press.

Fudenberg, Drew, and Eric Maskin. 1990. Evolution and cooperation in noisy repeated games. *AER Papers and Proceedings* (May): 274–79.

Gibbons, Robert. 1997. An introduction to applicable game theory. *Journal of Economic Perspectives* (winter): 127–49.

Gruley, Bryan, and Quentin Hardy. 1997. Wireless bidders act to restructure debt. *Wall Street Journal*, 26 June, A3.

Gul, Faruk. 1997. A Nobel Prize for game theorists: The contributions of Harsanyi, Nash and Selten. *Journal of Economic Perspectives* (summer): 159–74.

Gumbel, Peter. 1999. Steep rate cuts proposed in U.K. jolt U.S. *Wall Street Journal*, 13 August, A9.

Hodgson, Geoffrey M. 1998. The approach of institutional economics. *Journal of Economic Literature* (March): 166–92.

Horwitz, Morton J. 1980. Law and economics: Science or politics? *Hofstra Law Review* (summer): 905–12.

Ingrao, Bruna, and Giorgio Israel. 1990. *The invisible hand*, translated by Ian McGilvray. Cambridge, Mass.: MIT Press.

Kranhold, Kathryn. 1998. Current event. *Wall Street Journal*, 14 September, R4.

Knight, Frank H. [1921]. 1971. *Risk, uncertainty, and profit*. Chicago: University of Chicago Press.

Kuhn, Thomas S. 1962. *The structure of scientific revolutions*. Chicago: University of Chicago Press.

LaBorde, Allyson. 1998. Learning the hard way. *Wall Street Journal*, 4 September, R8.

Langlois, Richard N. 1986. The new insitutional economics: An introductory essay. In *Economics as a process*, edited by Richard N. Langlois, 1–25. Cambridge: Cambridge University Press.

Leonard, Robert J. 1995. From parlor games to social science: von Neumann, Morgenstern and the creation of game theory. *Journal of Economic Literature* (June): 730–61.

Lorenz, Edward. 1999. Trust, contract and economic cooperation. *Cambridge Journal of Economics* (May): 301–15.

Machalaba, Daniel, and Anna Wilde Mathews. 1999. Shippers criticize railroads, charging lack of competition is hurting service. *Wall Street Journal*, 5 April, A2.

Mailath, George J. 1998. Do people play Nash equilibrium? Lessons from evolutionary game theory. *Journal of Economic Literature* (September): 1347–74.

McKay, Peter A. 1999. Soaring prices in the electricity market may prompt state, federal regulation. *Wall Street Journal*, 2 August, C21.

Mehta, Stephanie. 1998a. Consumers get put on hold in phone deals. *Wall Street Journal*, 11 May, B1.

———. 1998b. Locked out. *Wall Street Journal*, 21 September, R8.

———. 1999. In phones, the new number is four. *Wall Street Journal*, 8 March, B1.

Miller, Edythe S. 1991. Of economic paradigms, puzzles, problems, and policies;

Or, Is the economy too important to be left to the economists? *Journal of Economic Issues* (December): 993–1004.

———. 1993a. A consideration of contracting and competitive bidding as alternatives to direct economic regulation in imperfect markets. *Utilities Policy* (October): 323–32.

———. 1993b. The economic imagination and public policy: Orthodoxy discovers the corporation. *Journal of Economic Issues* (December): 1041–58.

———. 1994. Economic regulation and the social contract. *Journal of Economic Issues* (September): 799–818.

———. 2001. The impact of technological change on market power and market failure in telecommunications. Journal of Economic Issues (June): 385–93.

Mills, Mike. 1995. An interactive dream unfulfilled. *Washington Post Weekly Edition,* 10–16 July, 20.

Myerson, Roger B. 1999. Nash equilibrium and the history of economic theory. *Journal of Economic Literature* (September): 1067–82.

Pearl, Daniel. 1994. FCC says some license bidders have defaulted. *Wall Street Journal,* 17 August, B3.

Porter, Robert H. 1991. A review essay on handbook of industrial organization. *Journal of Economic Literature* (June): 553–72.

Reder, Melvin W. 1982. Chicago economics: Permanence and change. *Journal of Economic Literature* (March): 1–38.

Runde, Jochen, and Paul Anand. 1997. Special issue on rationality and methodology: Introduction. *Journal of Economic Methodology* (June): 1–21.

Shen, T.Y. 1991. Handbook of industrial organization: A review. *Review of Industrial Organization* (June): 301–11.

Trebing, Harry M. 1987. Regulation of industry: An institutionalist approach. *Journal of Economic Issues* (December): 1707–37.

———. 1989. Telecommunications regulation—The continuing dilemma. In *Public utility regulation,* edited by Kenneth Nowotny, David B. Smith, and Harry M. Trebing, 93–130. Norwell, Mass.: Kluwer Academic Publishers.

Weibull, Jorgen W. 1988. What have we learned from evolutionary game theory so far? Mimeo, 7 May, 1–29.

Williamson, Oliver E. 1975. *Markets and hierarchies: Analysis and antitrust implications.* New York: Free Press.

———. 1985. *The economic institutions of capitalism.* New York: Free Press.

Notes

1. The term "new institutional economics" is used to denote the school that has become prominent in the last several decades, and includes as predominant members Ronald Coase and Oliver Williamson. Institutional economics is utilized in its usual sense to refer to the school that originated with Thorstein Ve-

blen and John R. Commons at about the turn of the twentieth century, and has as a leading contemporary member Harry M. Trebing.

2. For example, Robert Porter notes the strong influence of NIE on the theory of the firm and the "dramatic change" in research that has occurred within the field of industrial organization over the past several decades, from general equilibrium to noncooperative game theory. He maintains that this has resulted in the "revolutionizing" of the subspecialty (Porter 1991, 556, 553, 567). Roger Myerson describes Nash equilibrium game theory as "one of the outstanding intellectual advances of the twentieth century," and a "watershed breakthrough" in economic thought (1999, 1067).

3. Ronald Coase, who generally is acknowledged to have laid the initial basis for NIE, was awarded the Nobel Prize in 1991. In 1994, the Nobel Prize was awarded to John C. Harsanyi, John F. Nash, and Reinhard Selten for their contributions to game theory.

4. In California, many of the companies that initially entered this market subsequently withdrew, with the number of companies registered declining in a short span of time from two hundred to twenty-five (LaBorde 1998, R8, 18).

5. Although the United States is a front-runner when it comes to M&A in these industries, other regions of the world seem to be learning by example. For example, Olivetti recently was a protagonist in a hard-fought hostile takeover of the much larger Telecom Italia, winning out over the friendly merger proposal of Deutsche Telecom (Ball 1999, A22). The British company Vodafone was successful in the acquisition of AirTouch, besting Bell Atlantic. Of late, multinational joint ventures seem to have become part of the ordinary course of business.

6. Most of those pending are awaiting regulatory approval. To date, all requests for approval that have been acted upon have been granted, albeit some with conditions.

7. Needless to say, AT&T does not object to "forced access" for itself to facilities of the RBHCs.

8. Since this was written, dramatic changes have occurred in the telecommunications industry. These include an announced restructuring of a debt-laden AT&T, by now experiencing rapidly plunging stock prices. Among the changes that the restructuring would entail was the spin-off of the Liberty Media Group by AT&T and the sale of the AT&T Broadband unit, the successor company to Telecommunications Inc. (TCI). The restructuring seemed effectively to bring to an end AT&T's dream of becoming a full-service company, capable of delivering voice, data, and video through one pipe (for greater detail, see Miller 2001, 388).

9. An example of a real-world failure of evolutionary game theory is the inability of the RBHCs and IXCs, despite the certainty of future interaction, and despite the fact that agreement would be in the interest of the group, to negotiate interconnection agreements.

10. An evolutionary stable strategy is a strategy that is not invadable by any other strategy. Perturbations refer to the introduction of extraneous elements. Perturbation may occur because of experimentation or entry, or for other reasons.

11. Although equilibrium is the focus of game theory, the equilibrium is not necessarily unique. Some game-theoretic models (for example, supergames) allow for multiple equilibria. Porter (1991, 558) notes that this, in fact, is a source of internal criticism. In some games, internal critics remonstrate, any result is possible. George Mailath advises (1998, 1348–49) that equilibrium is best understood as a community "steady state," where individuals are "groping toward maximizing behavior," thus evoking memories not only of Pareto-optima, but also of Walrasian tatonnement.

12. Nash equilibrium game theory, widely cited in the new oligopoly literature, is an example of noncooperative game theory. It adopts the rationality assumption, viewing individuals as consistently acting so as to maximize payoff, in light of the predicted behavior of other players. Nash equilibrium is a set of strategies in which each player's strategy maximizes his or her expected welfare. If behavior of all players in a game can be predicted, the prediction is a Nash equilibrium (Myerson 1999, 1069–70).

13. For example, the claim is made that the existence of market power is not of consequence if its possessors are more innovative as a result. A variation on this is that the antitrust laws should be relaxed for firms facing global competition because consortia of firms are a source of innovation (Porter 1991, 565–66).

14. See Miller 1993a, 323–32, for an examination of some of the shortcomings of the auction mechanism examined within the context of an analysis of a range of proposed market-oriented substitutes for direct economic regulation.

I would like to thank Warren J. Samuels, William G. Shepherd, and Harry M. Trebing for thoughtful and insightful comments and suggestions for this article. I would also like to express my gratitude to Harry M. Trebing for his generous counsel and encouragement extending over many years.

What Was the "Public Utility Category Problem" All About? An Essay in Interpretation

WARREN J. SAMUELS

The objective of this chapter is to interpret and critique the legal-economic institution of public utility regulation that has been the principal subject of Harry Trebing's work as an economist.

Background and Basic Problem

All business is subject to general legal controls. In a period in which the dominant mindset is against "government intervention" and in favor of market solutions, deregulation, and privatization, it is easy to forget that

> the economic system operates within a legal (and nonlegal) framework, for example, John R. Commons's *legal foundations of capitalism;*
> the basic economic institutions are in part a function of the law;
> actual markets, as distinct from the pure abstract a-institutional conceptual market of neoclassical economic theory, are in part a function of and give effect to the body of laws that forms, structures, and operates through them;
> the legal system, the substance of law, and the details of legal rights, for example, property, the corporation, contract, have undergone continuous and cumulative transformation;
> "regulation" is one mode through which the rights of property, corporation, and contract have been created and changed;
> government deals willy-nilly with fundamentals of the economic system, and is both inevitably activist and important;

economy and polity are not given, self-subsistent, independent, mutually exclusive categories but are each formed and reformed in the legal-economic nexus; and so on.

All that being the case, it is also true that

property is not protected because it is property, but is property because it is protected;

the issue in matters of regulation of property is not property as an independently given category versus government control, but what is to constitute property;

property consists of protected interests, with regulation changing the interests protected as property by government;

what is the interest to be protected as property or otherwise is the precisely the point at issue;

government helps determine the structure of freedom and of control that willy-nilly marks all economies;

the economic significance, for example, value of property, is a function of markets, which are themselves in part a function of government;

government is engaged, in part, in the exercise of coercion in protecting certain private parties from the coercive actions of other private parties; this being an aspect of government in the larger context of government helping to determine the distributions of power both between nominally private power holders and government and between nominally private power holders—all within the legal-economic nexus;

the law has changed from protection of value in use, use-value, to value in exchange, exchange-value, and regulation changes the exchange-value of property, in part by changing the use-value of property, typically differently for different parties; and so on.[1]

Some business (and its property) has been singled out, by commission and omission, as it were, for more intensive regulation, especially with regard to entry, prices charged consumers, and conditions of service. For present purposes, this intensive regulation commenced in the last third of the nineteenth century and was coupled with the eventual advent of the regulatory or administrative commission. The genesis of this intensive regulation was a set of beliefs, including: that the outputs of certain businesses were so important to the public welfare that they could not be left to the vagaries of the market and business practice; that the businesses producing these outputs were particularly strategically situated; that these businesses were typically able to charge prices that were both monopolistic and discriminatory; and that these businesses had certain attributes of being "natural" monopolies, in part because of economies of scale and the wastes of duplication. The original name given these business—that is, the category under which they were grouped for purposes of intensive treatment—was "businesses affected with the public interest." Eventually they came to be called public utilities, or public service companies, and the regulatory agencies came to be known as public utility or public service commissions.

The "public utility category problem" has therefore been the determination of which businesses were to be singled out for intensive regulation as to entry, rate, and service, while still remaining controlled by both market forces and the common legal framework.[2]

The Legal Complications

The social control of business, all business but especially perhaps public utilities, takes place within a particular legal system. That legal system evolves over time but always constitutes the framework within which regulation of any kind arises, is debated and legislated, and is subject to judicial review. The principal complications that arise in this context are the following.

1. The division of the power of governing between state and federal governments and between the executive, judicial, and legislative branches of government on each level. These dual divisions of power enable, if not generate, conflicts between the branches on each level and between levels. Apropos of public utility regulation, the principal conflicts have been between federal and state jurisdictions, between state legislatures and state and federal supreme courts, and between the U.S. Congress and the U.S. Supreme Court.

2. The juxtaposition of the police power to the requirement of due process of law. The police power involves, in one definition, the power to exercise control in the interest of the public health, safety, welfare, and morals; and, in another, the power to modify the rights of property and contract for a public purpose without paying compensation.

   The requirement of due process centers on the idea that legal action must accord with regular procedures. Procedures can change over time—for example, to utilize new technology of communication and to give effect to new ideas of just treatment—but must not vary from case to case in a capricious manner that evades procedural safeguards. This is procedural due process. Substantive due process involves the courts in passing judgment on the substance of legislation, that is, the conflict between legislative discretion and judicial review and judicial discretion. Apropos of public utility regulation, the substantive issues have been over, first, conceptions of free markets, the rights of property, and the nature and role of competition, on the one hand, and legislative protection of interests deemed to be exposed to concentrated and actually or potentially abusive and discriminatory power, on the other; second, the existence and scope of a category of businesses affected with a public interest; third, regulation of price versus lack of non-price regulation; and so on.

Apropos of the Fifth Amendment's clause requiring compensation in the event of a taking, which initially applied to physical takings, the juxtaposition is between the logic of the police power and that of eminent domain newly applied to the limitation of earning capacity of an otherwise protected interest. The broadest application of eminent domain reasoning would require government to compensate owners whenever legal change wrought a reduction in the value of their property, which would severely limit the police power as defined previously. In the case of public utility regulation that restricted the monopoly earnings of a utility company, eminent domain reasoning would have required payment of compensation the logical effect of which would have guaranteed the monopoly earnings.

3. The juxtaposition of different notions of property, as shown previously, and different definitions of the efficacy of markets. Further complicating beliefs about the absolute versus relative nature of property was the widespread affirmation of competition, even though competition might erode the value of losers' property, and of markets as a system of social control of property. In the case of public utility property and markets, the key issue was the relevance of the power of competition as a check on the power of the utility companies.

4. Conflicting private interests and a comparable set of conflicting public interests. On the one hand were the interests in maintaining the integrity and viability of both the institution of private property and the utility companies' provision of service; on the other, the interests in having private power restricted and in the ability of government to do so. Pervading these conflicts were the aforementioned disagreements over the relative responsiveness of private enterprise and government, and over the extent and efficacy of competition as a regulatory system. From one point of view, therefore, the issue was

one of the integrity and viability of private property as an institution; from the other, the issue was one of the relative efficacy of competition and government as regulatory systems.

5. Power. Insofar as the adoption of intensive regulation of firms deemed to be affected with a public interest involved government changing the interests to which it gave its support, one issue was the power of present-day government in comparison with past governments.

The Legal Arguments

The contest over intensive regulation of firms deemed to be affected with a public interest turned in part on whether there was either no such category or a closed category of such firms.

Arguments affirming either that no such category existed or, if it existed, that it was a closed category included the following:

1. The power to regulate is to be distinguished from, and does not include, the power to regulate price.
2. Price regulation is applicable only to businesses or property already in the category.
3. Unless a company is in the category, the right to determine price is an inherent property right as part of the common right to engage in any lawful business.
4. The inclusion of a business or property in the category is dependent upon (*a*) a public grant, (*b*) regulation from time immemorial, and (*c*) the business having become clothed or affected with a public interest due to (*i*) the indispensable nature of its service and (*ii*) its charging of exorbitant prices and its discriminatory treatment of customers.[3]
5. The regulation of entry, price, and service of a business not in the category takes property without due process of law per se. (It will be noticed, first, that this involves a narrow notion of the police power, but, second, does accept legal determination of the existence and content of the category, that is, an affirmation of the police power.)
6. Price regulation is inappropriate and inexpedient in relation to the evil to be remedied.
7. A denial of ultimate legislative discretion and an affirmation of broad judicial review of legislation.
8. Mandatory adherence to precedent, upon consideration of and adherence to doctrines of constitutionalism, a government of stable laws and not caprice, and the limited economic role of government.

Arguments affirming that the idea of a category is no absolute restriction upon the police power of the states included the following:

1. The category question, while perhaps a useful fiction capable of serving to frame arguments and as a medium of conflict resolution, can be—and, indeed, has been—carried too far:
   a. The present use of the category question begs the fundamental issue: whether to regulate intensively or not.
   b. No closed category exists.
   c. There is no common law definition of the category that is final or dispositive as to the composition of the category.
   d. Present government is no less capable than past government to govern, that is, to determine which businesses should be intensively regulated (be within the category).
2. There is no valid distinction between price and nonprice regulation, as, all regulation affects price. The power to regulate, that is, a broad definition of the police power, includes the power to regulate price.
3. Legislative discretion should bind the courts unless clearly restrained by express constitutional provision, that is, narrow judicial review.
   a. Determination that a business is affected with a public interest is a matter of legislative discretion, and no distinct and closed category thereof exists.
   b. The wisdom of legislative discretion is no matter for judicial review.
   c. Judicial invocation of due process should be narrow, and extend to procedural and not substantive due process.
   d. The viability of the police power (of the power of the legislature to govern) should be upheld over the erection of prejudice or ideology into legal principle.
4. Regulation should be dependent upon a broadly defined affectation with the public interest, in terms of
   a. degree of market control, including the character and strategic position of the business and the efficacy of competition as a regulatory system.
   b. the essentiality of the good.
5. Regulation of price is an appropriate regulatory instrument.

A Sample of Legal Holdings

Munn v. Illinois.[4]   This was the first modern U.S. case raising the public utility category problem. At issue was a state statute declaring grain elevators subject to the prescribing of maximum charges. The court held that although grain elevators had not hitherto been included in the common law list of businesses affected with a public interest, grain elevators were of such economic importance and in such a strategic position that their intensive regulation to avoid monopolistic and discriminatory pricing was warranted under the police power. Accordingly, the statute was found not to be taking property, since the right to price in a monopolistic and discriminatory manner was not included in the rights constituting private property.

The business of grain elevators was thus newly to be included in the group hitherto encompassing millers, ferrymen, innkeepers, wharfingers, bakers, cartmen, and hackney-coachmen, because, like them, the owners of grain elevators "stand . . . in the 'very gateway of commerce,' and take toll from all who pass" (131). The police power could be used, in all such cases, to regulate both the use and the price of the use of private property used therein.

The court did not further elaborate rules or tests by which such intensive control by state law would be permissible. Indeed, it is likely impossible to state fully and in advance the dividing lines involved in adjudicating the police power from eminent domain reasoning. Yet the court did state an affirmative position:

> This brings us to inquire as to the principles upon which this power of regulation rests, in order that we may determine what is within and what without its operative effect. Looking, then, to the common law, from whence came the right which the Constitution protects, we find that when private property is "affected with a public interests, it ceases to be *juris privati* only." This was said by Lord Chief Justice Hale more than two hundred years ago, in his treatise *De Portibus Maris,* I Harg. Law Tracts, 78, and has been accepted without objection as an essential element in the law of property ever since. Property does become clothed with a public interest when used in a manner to make it of public consequence, and affect the community at large. When, therefore, one devotes his property to a use in which the public has an interest, he, in effect, grants to the public an interest in that use, and must submit to be controlled by the public for the common good, to the extent of the interest he has thus created. He may withdraw his grant by discontinuing the use; but, so long as he maintains the use, he must submit to the control. (125–26)

The focus on property is to be noted, as is the preeminent (but not exclusive) position given to *common* law as against statute law.

Two further points are worth noting.

First, the logic of the decision focuses on the decision by the owner so to use his property, such that "He may withdraw his grant by discontinuing the use; but, so long as he maintains the use, he must submit to the control." This raises the problem at the heart of much public utility regulation, that of electric power, water, gas, and telephony: modern conditions do not permit the businesses to cease operation. Regulation here must maintain the operating and financial integrity of these companies. Such an issue did not arise, however, in regard to grain elevators within the ambit of the law of the public utility category problem; it did in practice later on, whenever a local elevator went bankrupt, for whatever reason, and in the context of local grain cooperatives.

Second, the phrases "used in a manner to make it of public consequence, and affect the community at large," "a use in which the public has an interest," and "controlled by the public for the common good" are inconclusive. One does not know, and one does not have specific criteria by which to determine, when these conditions hold and when they do not.

One implication of the immediate foregoing is that not all "businesses affected with the public interest" came to be regulated as "public utilities." In time, all business came to be subject to new types of regulation by federal, state, and local levels of government, for example, protective labor legislation, health and safety legislation, environmental legislation, and so on. The domain of "businesses affected with the public interest" became transformed into that of public utility regulation, with its focus on entry, rate, and service, which goes beyond most, if not all, other types of regulation.

At any rate, in *Munn,* the dissenting arguments did not carry the day. These arguments centered on such propositions as

If the legislature of a State, under pretence of providing for the public good, or for any other reason, can determine, against the consent of the owner, the uses to which private property shall be devoted, or the prices which the owner shall receive for its uses, it can deprive him of the property as completely as by a special act for its confiscation or destruction. (142)

The legislation in question is nothing less than a bold assertion of absolute power by the State to control at its discretion the property and business of the citizen, and fix the compensation he shall receive. (148)

The problem, of course, is that private property is not independent of the law of the police power; it is a function of the law of the police power. Property is a function of the evolving doctrines of property law, the police power, and eminent domain. The operative issue is one of a change of the interests to which government, in continuously molding the details of the institution of private property, will give its protection as property.

German Alliance Insurance Company v. Kansas.[5] This case involved a statute that regulated fire insurance rates, and an order by the superintendent of insurance, under the statute, to lower insurance premiums by 12 percent. The company claimed that the fire insurance business was private and not subject to the regulatory power of the state. The Court held that fire insurance was a virtual necessity, not immune from state regulation. As for the argument centering on the novelty of the regulation of fire insurance, the Court criticized "that conservatism of the mind, which puts to question every new act of regulating legislation and regards the legislation invalid or dangerous until it has become familiar" (410) and the view "that government possessed at one time a greater power to recognize the public interest in a business and its regulation to promote the general welfare than government possesses to-day" (411). In a dissenting opinion, Justice Lamar argued, inter alia, that "For great and pervasive as is the power to regulate it cannot override the constitutional principle that private property cannot be taken for private purposes" (424), neglecting the fact that the law in this and in many other cases must choose between conflicting claims of property right—here the claim of the company to charge whatever it wants versus the claims of insurance buyers to be protected against monopoly pricing—quite aside from the question of whether such a principle is "in" the Constitution.

Wolff Packing Co. v. Industrial Court.[6] The decision in this case represented a limitation on, or a contraction of, the police power. At issue was a Kansas statute creating a Court of Industrial Relations with power over wages in all businesses affected with a public interest. The Supreme Court declared both that meat packing was not within the class of businesses "affected with a public interest," and that even if it were, wages might not be regulated.

The Court distinguished three classes of business "clothed with a public interest justifying some public regulation" (535). These were

(1) Those which are carried on under the authority of a public grant of privileges which either expressly or impliedly imposes the affirmative duty of rendering a public service demanded by any member of the public. Such are the railroads, other common carriers and public utilities.

(2) Certain occupations, regarded as exceptional, the public interest attaching to which, recognized from earliest times, has survived the period of arbitrary laws by Parliament or Colonial legislatures for regulating all trades and callings. Such are those of the keepers of inns, cabs, and gristmills.

(3) Businesses which, though not public at their inception, may be fairly said to have risen to be such, and have become subject in consequence to some government regulation. They have come to hold such a peculiar relation to the public that this is superimposed upon them. In the language of the cases, the owner, by devoting his business to the public use, in effect grants the public an interest in that use, and subjects himself to public regulation to the extent of that interest, although the property continues to belong to its private owner, and to be entitled to protection accordingly. (535)

Extension of the class required a determination of "the indispensable nature of the service and the exorbitant charges and arbitrary control to which the public might be subjected without regulation" (537), deemed to be the basis on which inclusion of "nearly all of the businesses included in the third group rested" (537). The Court found, after elaborate consideration, that this was not the case in the food industry in general and meat packing in particular. As for the fixing of wages, this was held to be "in conflict with the Fourteenth Amendment and deprives [the packing company] of its property and liberty of contract without due process of law" (543).

Tyson & Brother v. Banton.[7]   This case involved New York state legislation limiting the increase in price charged by theater-ticket brokers. In declaring that the statute contravened the Fourteenth Amendment, the Court, considering the ticket broker an appendage of the theater, relied on Wolff Packing to strike down the ideas that the business was in the category and that therefore its power to fix prices could be regulated. Of particular interest, however, in view of later developments, are positions made in dissenting opinions. Justice Oliver Wendell Holmes wrote that "the notion that a business is clothed with a public interest and has been devoted to the public use is little more than a fiction intended to beautify what is disagreeable to the sufferers. The truth seems to me to be that, subject to compensation when compensation is due, the legislature may forbid or restrict any business when it has a sufficient force of public opinion behind it" (446). In his dissenting opinion, Justice Harlan Fiske Stone argued that reliance on so vague and illusory a phrase as "business affected with a public interest" begged the very question to be decided. He also could find no distinction between price and other regulation. (It might usefully be noted that during the same period, the 1920s, the issue of minimum-wage laws was also before the Court, the laws being disallowed.)

Ribnik v. McBride.[8]   This decision refused to include private employment agencies within the category of business affected with a public interest and to permit regulation of price, though allowing regulation in such matters as fraud and extortion. The Court continued both to distinguish between private and public and to limit entry into the category.

New State Ice Company v. Liebmann.[9] The Court similarly declined to hold constitutional legislation that required a license to engage in the ice business, the purpose of which was to prevent competition deemed excessive from depriving some communities of all ice service. The Court found the statute to deny or unreasonably curtail "the common right to engage in a lawful private business" to a business that bore "no such relation to the public as to warrant its inclusion in the category of businesses charged with a public use" (277).

That it was becoming increasingly clear both that the category did not define itself and that, were the majority's approach to persevere, judgments in individual cases would continue to have to be made, was implied in Justice Brandeis's statement in dissent that "The notion of a distinct category of business 'affected with a public interest,' employing property 'devoted to a public use,' rests upon historical error. The consequences which it is sought to draw from those phrases are belied by the meaning in which they were first used centuries ago, and by the decision of this Court, in *Munn v. Illinois,* 94 U.S. 113, which first introduced them into the law of the Constitution. In my opinion, the true principle is that the State's power extends to every regulation of any business reasonably required and appropriate for the public protection" (302–3).

Two ironies ensue, however: First, Brandeis thus shifts the question of inclusion in the category to another phrase that does not decide itself, "reasonably required and appropriate." Second, in discussing "the State's power," Brandeis undoubtedly was referring to the legislature; but if one understands or interprets the phrase to include the Court, the matter is more subtle: To the business whose intensive regulation the Court upholds, it is perhaps doubly the state which has the power. The state, in the combination of legislature and court, has the power. Insofar as the Supreme Court, or a majority thereof, wants to act, it is the Supreme Court that determines, for example, what is and what is not to be protected by law as property, the Supreme Court thereby being "the State."

Brandeis makes one other relevant point. He acknowledges that the Court has the power to evaluate whether state statutes, in matters of substantive law and procedure, are "arbitrary, capricious or unreasonable." "But," he wrote, "in the exercise of this high power, we must be ever on our guard, lest we erect our prejudices into legal principles. If we would guide by the light of reason, we must let our minds be bold" (311). One person's principle is, however, another's legal principle; if distinctions are to be made on the basis of what is and what is not "arbitrary, capricious or unreasonable," some normative premise, some ideology, some "prejudice" is inexorable.

Actually, however, the effective gravamen of these cases is different: It is whether the category is to be narrowly or broadly interpreted, which is the functional equivalent to whether the state legislature is to be either allowed its discretion or given a presumption, albeit rebuttable, of constitutionality. This is still ideology, still "prejudice," after a fashion.

Nebbia v. New York.[10] In a case establishing a Milk Control Board with the authority to fix minimum wholesale and retail fluid milk prices, the Court upheld the legislation at issue. The Court reaffirmed the power of the state to regulate property and correlative interpersonal business relations. Also, the distinction between price and other regulation was rejected, it was decided that competitive nonpublic utility businesses could be intensively regulated, and the category concept was so expanded as to no longer serve as a check on intensive regulation. The memorable statement was made that

> It is clear that there is no closed class or category of businesses affected with a public interest. . . . The phrase "affected with a public interest" can, in the nature of things, mean no more than that an industry, for adequate reason, is subject to control for the public good. . . . there can be no doubt that upon proper occasion and by appropriate measures the state may regulate a business in any of its aspects, including the prices to be charged for the products or commodities it sells. (536, 537)

One authority has written, "The final consequence of the Nebbia opinion must logically be either the broadening of the affected-with-a-public interest category to include all conceivable industries that may require regulation in the interest of the public welfare, or the interpretation of the concept out of existence" (Barnes 1942, 12–13). Yet there remains the task of adjudicating "proper occasion and by appropriate measures," and this permits the reintroduction of "prejudice" (here used as a nonpejorative synonym for "ideology").

Further Legal or Legal-Economic Complications

The history of the problem of the public utility category, from *Munn* to *Nebbia,* and beyond, manifests some combination of a change in the political power of adversely affected groups, a change in ideology with regard to the economic role of government, and, inter alia, a new chapter in the historic pragmatism that the people of the United States brought to their use of their government. This history was but part of the larger legal-economic scheme of things in which government structured markets, in part, by determining whose interests would be protected and whose would be exposed to the power of others, power based on the legal protection of their interests as property or otherwise; and in which the legal foundations of the economic system underwent gradual or incremental change.

Yet this history was not simple; it was laden with complications and with consequences that were unforeseen and unintended, at least by some people. Some of these complications and consequences are as follows:

1. Early in the history of the category question, consideration of the exposure of the value of utility property (the value of the companies as going concerns) to "confiscation" led to the adoption of a formula derived, as it were, from a phrase in the decision in *Smyth vs. Ames*.[11] The Court held that regulation could regulate and restrain monopoly profits, but that nonetheless the company was entitled to a fair return on the fair value of its property.

   Three matters directly derived from such a formula: First, the formula contains a fallacy. The value of property (as a going concern) is the capitalized valuation of the income from that property. To determine rate of return is ipso facto to determine value. Value is not independent of rate of return, and to regulate rate of return is to regulate value.

   Second, although the notion of "confiscation" was typically anathema to jurists (and others), the very nature of regulation was to limit, ergo to confiscate, the monopoly return that the company, absent regulation, would receive. Regulation, therefore, even under the fair return on fair value formula, would not eliminate confiscation (in the form of prevention rather than taking, of course); it would determine its magnitude, judged against unregulated return.

   Third, because the formula of fair return on fair value seemed reasonable and appeared to have judicial, that is, constitutional, mandate, commission regulation became centered on rate cases in which commission decisions would identify the stated fair value on which the stated fair return would be earned, and the rates (structure and level) that would lead thereto.

2. Resolution, as it were, of the public utility category problem thus led to several other problems at the heart of public utility regulation. These were

   (*a*) the problem of the valuation of the company, which involved such further issues as (*i*) reproduction versus original cost of assets, that is, the treatment of inflation and deflation; (*ii*) the value of physical assets as such versus valuation of their use in a going concern, (*iii*) depreciation, and so on;

(*b*) the problem of necessary and proper expenditures constituting the operating cost of production and doing business;

(*c*) the problem of fair rate of return, which involved such further issues as (*i*) determination of the embedded cost of debt, which entered into the rate of return; (*ii*) the appropriate structure of debt versus equity, which affected the cost of debt; (*iii*) the appropriate and necessary rate of return on equity, which in turn depended upon risk, perceptions of risk, the rate required or deemed to be required by investors relative to other utilities and to unregulated companies, and so on; and

(*d*) the problem of rate structure (to yield the level of revenue called for by commission decisions regarding the foregoing), which involved such further issues as (*i*) classifying types of customers and (*ii*) pricing on the basis of either marginal cost (which involved determination of the operative margins) or elasticity of demand, either of which (but especially the latter) reintroduced an element of price discrimination, though with a cap on earnings.

3. In addition to the perceived if not mandatory requirement to approach regulation in terms of the fair return on fair value formula, the regulatory commissions found themselves in a peculiarly complex, at least binary, position. On the one hand, regulation was to constrain the monopoly and discriminatory power of the public utility companies under their jurisdiction. This was the raison d'etre or genesis of regulation. On the other hand, regulation had to assure both the producing companies and the consuming public of continuity of provision of service. The companies were not criminal enterprises; they produced services needed and desired by the consuming public, services indeed vital to the welfare, if not also the existence, of society and economy. At the one extreme, regulation has to deny the realization of the practices and fruits of monopoly; at the other, regulation has to assure the operational and financial integrity of the regulated companies. This conflict of interests (in the nonpejorative sense) entered into the resolution of the four further problems listed previously, especially the first three but also the fourth, inasmuch as rate structure did need to yield the requisite revenue: valuation, expenditure recovery, rate of return, and rate structure. This situation was inevitably aggravated by the conflict between those who

wanted to keep rates low, and thereby to hold the companies to strict budgets, and those who wanted to err on the side of not endangering operational and financial viability. The problem was exacerbated by the absence of any formula or metric by which one could reach clear and conclusive numerical results; accordingly, rate cases, not least in matters pertaining to rate of return on equity but actually in all quantitative matters, tended to have an aura of numerology.

4. In time, specific company interests came to be articulated, either seriously or disingenuously, that is, pragmatically, in terms of the conduct of regulation. The same was true of most if not all other parties. Companies sought rates of return on equity more or less comparable with those of unregulated companies, and consumer interests sought lower rates of return on equity due to perceived lower risk, due, arguably, to the nature of the product, the market, and regulation's protection itself. During periods of inflation, companies sought asset valuation on the basis of reproduction cost, and customers sought original cost-based rates; the opposite was true for each during periods of deflation.

5. Commissions were widely understood to be exercising discretionary power delegated to them by the legislature (and confirmed eventually by the courts) so as to enable regulation to be based on technical expertise and to be independent of politics. This meant that the commissions had rights given to them by statute. It also meant that the commissions, in exercising the rights given them to protect certain interests, were the source of rights. In every aspect of their case decisions, commissions protected certain interests and not others. A conspicuous example is decisions that enabled poor customers to acquire utility services at more or less nominal cost. More subtle examples are decisions as to rate of return on equity and as to principles of rate making (marginal cost or elasticity of demand).

6. Commissions did not exist in a legal-economic vacuum. No more and no less than the other branches of government, including the judiciary, those either elected or appointed to positions of commissioners inevitably had biases arising from politics, economic ideology, personal experience, and their conceptions of the ideal economy and of ideal regulation. All of the conflicts noted previously could, and typically did, arise within commission regulation. In time, new commissioners fell into the established routines of administering their staffs and of hearing and deciding cases. Those elected or appointed to commission positions were concerned, moreover, with

their own lives and careers, that is, their political or job prospects after leaving office.

7. The problem of the public utility concept or category, of a class of businesses clothed with the public interest, has passed. It passed because after Nebbia it could be said that there was no closed category, hence, with a more permissive Court, no problem. Not all businesses that might have been were regulated as to entry, rate, and price. Intensive regulation along such lines was principally limited to the now-traditional public utilities. After the New Deal, the day of the modern regulatory state was in more or less full swing. After the mid-1970s, the modern regulatory state became increasingly "deregulated." The public utility category problem was for some a means of extending and legitimizing intensive regulation; for others, it was a means of limiting such intensive regulation. It was, thereby, a linguistic jurisprudential means of redetermining what constituted "private property" and "business."

The public utility category problem passed for another reason. The institution of commission regulation continued to provide for the redress of consumer grievances and for introducing some economic humanism and considerateness in the face of enormous inequality of economic power. However, commission regulation soon became institutionalized, routinized, and bureaucratized, and thereafter lacked the antimonopoly zeal that somewhat marked its early days. This was also due, in part, to the need to promote as well as restrict the regulated companies; after all, their products and services were, in fact, too important to endanger. It was also due, in part, to the fact that, as contemplated by at least some early corporate executives, regulation came to be dominated by the premier, hegemonic position of the regulated companies, their allies in the legislatures and the courts, and their mindset; the capture hypothesis is indeed widely accepted.

8. It is not easy to reach a firm, unequivocal position on the historic performance of commission regulation. Such data as one may draw upon is limited for purposes of evaluation, and evaluation is largely driven by selective perception, wishful thinking, and ideology.

At the very least, to reiterate, commissions have tended, it would seem, to protect against some of the excesses of unchecked power, by offering aggrieved customers some recourse, protection, and satisfaction.

The story of the operation and regulation of public utilities lies in the details, including alternatives both chosen and not chosen, and policies arguably more akin to financial gains versus those seen as sensible from more or less objective operating criteria. It is to the pursuit of more sensible, consumer- and system-oriented, rather than corporate empire-building, policies that Harry Trebing devoted his professional activities.

Conclusion

1. The foregoing picture requires that we contemplate the public utility institution within the complex and recondite legal-economic nexus. In this nexus what transpires in the nominally private sector is profoundly influenced by the nominally public sector, and what transpires in the nominally public sector is profoundly influenced by the nominally private sector. The public utility institution is a microcosm of the larger legal-economic nexus. It reflects the aforementioned pragmatism and principle of the use of government no more and no less than any other segment of the nexus.

2. It is not too much to conclude, however, that public utility administrative regulation had been captured—to use the common word (though some prefer "co-opted")—by the interests that such regulation was intended to control. This is not especially unique: government in general is an instrument available for the use of those in a position to control and use it, for example, to put their own private view of the constitution, law, and the good society to work. The capture view was manifest early on by some far-seeing, if cynical, Machiavellian corporate executives who looked forward to putting regulation to their own use. It was articulated by scholars on the left and on the right, and by those arguably in the center—sometimes emphasizing the duplicity of government, sometimes the cupidity of business, sometimes both, but almost always implicitly calling into play the answer given by labor leaders when asked what workers wanted: More. It was at least the condition felt by those who sensed a system of symbiotic if not fraternal relations between regulators and regulatees in a system that is at bottom largely plutocratic and kleptocratic.

   The question arises, however: if capture was successful, why have the public utility industries been so enthusiastic about deregulation? The answer has several parts.

   First, deregulation is the analytical equivalent of regulation, the difference being that whereas Alpha had been regulated in favor of

Beta, now Alpha is freed of regulation such that Beta is now exposed to the actions of Alpha. If regulation had been captured by Alpha, its freedom relative to Alpha had not been so limited. Deregulation, so-called, comprises only a change in Alpha's mode of hegemony.

Second, a new generation of utility management bought into the deregulation ideology.

Third, deregulation, so-called, is a misnomer. We have not had "deregulation," by its popular definition. Not everything has been "deregulated" or could have been. Deregulation has been selective. Regulation continues in certain aspects of public utility company business, although not in others. The companies retain the protection that captured regulation provides while now having the freedom that regulation, even captured regulation, did not provide. A great deal of regulation frames the wide range of newly permissible financial, operational, and organizational activities, such as mergers, consolidations, and joint ventures. Abetted and encouraged by the deregulation ideology, the growth of Internet communications, and the rising stock markets, utility companies have newly become vehicles for financial manipulation.

Deregulation is both the consequence and the cause of new opportunities, especially in the expanding world of communications. What is particularly uncertain now is the regulators' ability to pursue their former identification of the public interest with the financial, hence operating, viability of the regulated firm. What will happen if and when the world of high corporate finance stumbles, in the public utilities area and in the commercial banking-investment banking field, now that Glass-Steagall has been repealed, is uncertain.

In sum, deregulation does not indicate the falsity of the capture theory. It points to a new mix of ways in which, still under the umbrella of regulation, the firms' managements are able to advance their interests. Capture is not what it once was; it has been transformed, following the logic of politics as economics by other means.

3. Public utility regulation—and the entire public utility institution inclusive, of companies, commissions, other agencies of government, consumers, and other interested parties (the interveners in rate and other cases)—was never going to be a once-and-for-all-time solution to the relations between companies, consumers, and governments. It was only going to be the arena in which tentative, workable, problematic, experimental solutions had to be worked out.

4. The "special" position of the public utility companies relative to

other parties, notably consumers, is largely due to the fact of their concentrated, intensive interest relative to the dispersed and less intensive interests of, say, consumers, and to the fact that government in a pluralist society must be responsive to all interests, though it tends to be more responsive to the persistent claims of those with concentrated, intensive interests, especially of a pecuniary, plutocratic kind. It is these interests that have come to dominate, that is, to be given effective protection by government. That the comparative general operating success of the electric, telephonic, and other utilities in the United States in providing their services has been largely a by-product of other concerns and interests has not meant that consumers have not benefited. Regulation may indeed work in mysterious ways to advance the public's diverse interests.

5. The interpretation and evaluation of public utility regulation, indeed, the entire public utility institution, can be undertaken in two contexts, each involving two bases, the two contexts together comprising a widely applicable model of policy analysis.

The first context is that of ideal versus actual. One basis is an idealized notion or model of how regulation in particular and governmental decision making in general should be conducted—of which several different versions exist. By this approach, any actual system will appear deficient. Another basis is a realistic picture of how all systems of regulation and of governance actually work in the real world—of which, too, several different versions exist.

The second context is that of structure versus results. The interpretation and evaluation of public utility regulation, indeed the entire public utility institution, also can be undertaken on two other bases. One involves criteria of structure, such that given an agreed-upon structure, any policy result is considered a priori acceptable. The other involves criteria of results, such that any structure is evaluated on the basis of how well it achieves the desired policy result(s).

6. One's attitude toward public utility regulation will be profoundly influenced by one's faith—faith is indeed the apposite word—in markets. If one accepts that any market result under the conventional law of private property is a priori desirable, then intensive regulation is unnecessary and undesirable. If, however, one accepts that markets are in part structured by and give effect to the laws that enable them, that no market solution is uniquely optimal in the sense of Pareto optimality, that markets are not necessarily competitive, that private property need not include the right to charge monopolistic or discriminatory prices, and so on, then regulation may be, in

principle, necessary, inevitable, and desirable. Yet one must not compare idealized models of markets and of regulation. One must consider how markets and regulation actually work. Thus, one must consider the nature of "competitive" behavior, the definitional scope of "market," the workings of administrative commissions, and so on. These do not involve simple, self-answering questions, and, as in so many other human affairs, there is no simple answer. Yet there is a difference between proceeding in blind faith in either markets or regulation and with the nitty gritty of how things actually work in practice, like it or not. There is also a difference between defining and interpreting phenomena, including institutions, in terms of certain ideals, and comparing and evaluating them with the ideals. No institution is ideal, but they can be compared with an ideal. The problem then becomes this: just as there is no singular definition of an actual institution, there is no singular ideal by which it can be evaluated.

7. The concepts of "business affected with a public interest" and "public utility category" constitute a linguistic exercise within which certain normative decisions are framed and expressed. The decisions have to do with the organization and control of the economic system, the structure of power, the determination of who can do what to whom, and, especially, the change of legal rights through law. These are exquisitely delicate problems, especially that of when to change the law governing relative rights, exposures to the rights of others, and immunities therefrom.

These concepts are linguistic and ultimately subjective and normative. The categories and clauses of Constitutional (and Common) Law are not uniquely and unequivocally dispositive of the issues on which they are brought to bear. These categories and clauses are artifacts; they have no independent, given, transcendent existence or meaning. They do not dispose of issues by themselves; a key role is played by ideology understood as a theory of a good society, of how society should be organized and controlled. Just as the meanings of words are a function of their definitions (and of the definitions of the words used in the definitions), the meaning of a category or clause is a function of the legal or jurisprudential theory brought to bear on and made to operate through it.

Yet the use to which these concepts and clauses are put have material consequences with regard to the organization and control of the economic system. Their use, as has been noted, begs the question at issue. Is or is not manufacturing a matter of interstate commerce, and thus a matter for congressional legislation? Is a business within the category? Is regulation of price different from other regulation? The questions are stated in "is" rather than "ought" terms, but fundamentally they are "ought" questions.

Consider the question that arises in these cases: What is property? Property is subject to two modes of definition. On the basis of police power reasoning, property is subject to law that seeks to promote the public health, safety, welfare, and morals through the modification of rights of property and contract; in which case property is defined by and a function of law. On the basis of eminent domain reasoning, any regulation is a compensable "taking;" in which property exists independent of law.

All business is subject to general law. Some businesses are, through the exercise of discretion, made subject to more intensive control. Whether this should be the case and when it is to occur are matters of choice, that is, of policy. Judges who do not want to intensively regulate have an array of constitutional and jurisprudential lines of reasoning, such as categories and clauses, through which to project and in which to express their decisions and to state their policy.

The Court held in *Wolff Packing* that the extension of the class required a determination of "the indispensable nature of the service and the exorbitant charges and arbitrary control to which the public might be subjected without regulation" (537). It should be perfectly obvious both that the formulation is not itself explicitly found in the Constitution and that the key terms in that formulation—indispensable, exorbitant, arbitrary—are matters of selective perception. The meaning and evidence of such relevant terms as competition, concentrated power, relevant market, monopoly pricing, discriminatory pricing, and so on vary from economic theory to economic theory. Both the meaning attributed to them and the uses to which they are put are matters of selective perception; and their uses are modes of expression of decisions somehow reached, but not reached unaided through reference to constitutional clauses. In terms of the category of a business affected with the public interest, the justices individually and en banc had to make normative decisions; they then had to determine how to express the reasons for their choice in terms of constitutional language, selectively chosen, selectively conceptualized, and selectively applied.

This is possible because of the institution of judicial review. Judicial review of legislation is an institution that enables a frankly elite-positioned group to disallow legislative (and executive) decision-making.

This situation reflects the division of governmental power between the levels of government and among the branches on each level. It enables, for example, the federal Supreme Court to pass judgment on state legislative policy. It reflects a seemingly almost universal acceptance of judicial determination of "constitutionality." The situation is no different in principle than that articulated by Holmes in *Tyson and Brother v. Banton:*

> the notion that a business is clothed with a public interest and has been devoted to the public use is little more than a fiction intended to beautify what is disagreeable to the sufferers. The truth seems to me to be that, subject to compensation when compensation is due, the legislature may forbid or restrict any business when it has a sufficient force of public opinion behind it. (446)

So, too, the judiciary, ultimately the Supreme Court, may forbid or restrict any legislature when it has a sufficient force of public opinion behind it—a force that may comprise only an influential minority.

Thus does judicial review contribute to the performance by government of the division of power within the public sector and between the public and private sectors, so-called.

Argument in terms of the public utility category did not solve the issues of when and who to regulate intensively. The terms of the category were, however, the language in which the decisional results were stated, however reached.

Given the category frame of reference, the exegetical problem arises as to when and how to change relative rights and the correlative exposures and immunities of the respective parties. No rule as to when and how is self-executing and conclusively and unequivocally dispositive of particular cases. Rules need to be interpreted and applied, and ideology, or worldview, and wishful thinking inexorably enter the decision-making process.

What is true of the takings clause is also true of the public utility category problem. Legal policy is confronted with the need for the social reconstruction of society under conditions of radical indeterminacy and selective perception, and the matrix of legal principles combined with the matrix of legal rights serving as the framework of legal policy making and articulation and as a check on arbitrary and tyrannical power (whatever that may be). Reliance on constitutional and other principle serves as psychic balm and legitimation, including the inducement to losers to accept their losses, subsumed under the feeling that they had their day in court (see the articles by

Samuels and Mercuro on the compensation principle in Samuels 1992a, especially 267–92).

I have used the words "arbitrary and tyrannical power (whatever that may be)." These are matters of selective perception. The observer is always able to feel that some decisions are laudable and others depressing. My present point is more than a bit different, however. Intensive regulation under the rubric of the public utility category was an attempt to juxtapose the coercive (nonpejoratively used) power of government with the coercive (nonpejoratively used) power of certain businesses. Wherein resides the "arbitrary and tyrannical power" used pejoratively is the point at issue: by the private wielder of power or by the governmental wielder of power—*including the Supreme Court.*

8. The interpretation given here has been intended to be neither a jeremiad nor a Panglossian whitewash of the history of public utility regulation. Elements of both are necessarily present, though, however much the putative reality of regulation differs from various Platonic idealizations of it.

References

Barnes, Irston R. 1942. The economics of public utility regulation. New York: Appleton-Century-Crofts.

———. 1997. The concept of "coercion" in economics. In *The economy as a process of valuation*. Edited by Warren J. Samuels, Steven G. Medema, and A. Allan Schmid, 129–207. Lyme, N.H.: Edward Elgar.

Samuels, Warren J. 1992a. *Essays on the economic role of government*. Vol. 1, *Fundamentals*. London: Macmillan and New York: New York University Press.

———. 1992b. *Essays on the economic role of government*. Vol. 2, *Applications*. London: Macmillan and New York: New York University Press.

———. 1993. The growth of government. *Critical Review* 7:445–60.

———. 1995. Society is a process of mutual coercion and governance selectively perceived. *Critical Review* 9, no. 3 (summer): 437–43.

———, ed. 1989. *Fundamentals of the economic role of government*. Westport, Conn.: Greenwood Press.

Samuels, Warren J., and Nicholas Mercuro, eds. 1999. *The fundamental interrelationship between government and property*. Stamford, Conn.: JAI Press.

Samuels, Warren J., and A. Allan Schmid. 1997. The concept of cost in economics. In *The economy as a process of valuation,* edited by Warren J. Samuels, Steven G. Medema and A. Allan Schmid, 208–29. Lyme, N.H.: Edward Elgar.

———. 1987. The idea of the corporation as a person: On the normative significance of judicial language." In *Corporations and society: Power and responsibility*, edited by Warrnen J. Samuels and Athur S. Miller, 113–29. Westport, Conn.: Greenwood Press.

———, eds. 1981. *Law and economics: An institutional perspective*. Boston: Martinus Nijhoff.

Notes

The author is Professor Emeritus of Economics at Michigan State University. He is indebted to Nicholas Mercuro, Edythe Miller, and Harry Trebing for comments on an earlier draft.

1. The analyses grounding the foregoing are elaborated in Samuels 1987, 1992a, 1992b, 1993, 1995, 1997; Samuels and Mercuro 1999; and Samuels and Schmid 1981, 1997.

2. This problem must be distinguished from those posed by the antitrust laws: which businesses are to be controlled by virtue of their being a monopoly or attempting to become a monopoly, or by virtue of their acting in a monopolistic manner? Public utilities were often given monopoly franchises by or in combination with their administrative regulation, as an alternative to both nonregulation and government ownership and operation.

3. Barnes (1942, 13–19) lists the following legal and economic theories of the public interest. Legal: holding out, implied contract, constructive grant, and all-inclusive police power. Economic: monopoly and social disadvantage.

4. US 113–134, 1877.

5. US 389–434, 1914.

6. US 522–544, 1923.

7. US 418–456, 1927.

8. US 350–375, 1928.

9. US 262–311, 1932.

10. US 502–559, 1934.

11. US 466–550, 1898.

About the Contributors

Robert E. Babe is the first holder of the Jean Monty/BCE Chair in Media Studies at The University of Western Ontario, London, Canada. He is author or co-author of six books, including *Telecommunications in Canada: Technology, Industry and Government; Communication and the Transformation of Economics;* and *Canadian Communication Thought: Ten Foundational Writers.* He took Harry Trebing's course on the Regulation of Public Utilities at Michigan State University in the late 1960s.

Johannes M. Bauer is an associate professor in the Department of Telecommunication at Michigan State University where he is also the associate director of the James H. and Mary B. Quello Center for Telecommunications Management and Law. He received his Ph.D. in Economics from the Vienna University of Economics and Business Administration.

Kenneth Boyer is Professor of Economics at Michigan State University. He received his Ph.D. in Economics from the University of Michigan. His primary research interests are in the economics of transportation and the economics of regulation. Professor Boyer is the author of *Principles of Transportation Economics.* He has done research in transportation economics in Germany and has taught at the Sino-American Training Center in Shanghai, China. He has recently served on numerous advisory committees of the National Academy of Sciences' Transportation Research Board.

Eugene Coyle earned his Ph.D. from Boston College in 1969. He has participated in the national and international debate on electric deregulation, testifying in several U.S. states and lecturing and testifying in Australia and France. The House of Representatives in Brazil invited him to address it in 2001. His consulting practice has focused on natural resource economics since 1974.

Maurice Estabrooks is an economist and research consultant living in Ottawa, Canada. His personal research interest is the dynamics of science and technology, public policy and the institutions of economic society. Trained in the physical, social, and management sciences, he is the author of several books, including *Programmed Capitalism: A Computer-Mediated Global Society* and *Electronic Technology, Corporate Strategy and World Transformation.*

David Gabel is a Professor of Economics at the City University of New York and a visiting scholar at MIT. His work has appeared in various journals, including *The Journal of Economic History, Harvard Journal of Law and Technology, Journal of Regulatory Economics, Law and Policy, Federal Communications Law Journal,* and *Telecommunications Policy.* He has also coauthored monographs on the cost structure of the telecommunications industry and the regulatory policies of the United Kingdom and New Zealand. He is the co-editor of *Opening Networks to Competition: The Regulation and Pricing of Access.*

Thomas C. Gorak, Partner, Gorak & Bay, L.L.C. Mr. Gorak provides legal advice, consultation, and others services to a variety of clients, including privately and municipally owned gas and electric utilities, cooperatives, marketers, state public utility commissions and other state agencies, and several trade associations. He has lectured extensively on the problems that restructuring and deregulation pose for the natural gas and electric industries, and has authored several papers on those subjects. Mr. Gorak was co-counsel in the *MPC v. FERC* cases; the successful appeal of those cases led to the promulgation of FERC Order 436. For the past 18 years he has been a faculty member at the Institute of Public Utilities' NAEUC Annual and Advanced Regulatory Studies Program.

Jack R. Huddleston is Professor of Urban and Regional Planning and a member of the Energy Analysis and policy Program at the University of Wisconsin-Madison.

Mark A. Jamison is Executive Director of the Public Utility Research Center at the University of Florida. He is also Associate Director for Business and Economic Studies of the university's Center for International Business Education and Research. He specializes in communications policy and business strategy.

Michele Javary is currently researching developments in the United Kingdom Internet Service Providers' market for a project funded by the Economic and Social Research Council (ESRC).

Robin Mansell holds the Dixons Chair in New Media and Internet, London School of Economics and Political Science.

William Melody is Professor, Economics of Infrastructures, Delft University of Technology, and Guest Professor, Center for Tele-Information, Technical University of Denmark. He is Managing Director of LIRNE.NET, www.lirne.net, and Director of the World Dialogue on Regulation for Network Economies, www.regulateonline.org. His edited book, *Telecom Reform: Principles, Policies and Regulatory Practices,* has been used in more than 100 countries.

Edythe S. Miller is a former commissioner and chairwoman of the Colorado Public Utilities Commission. She is an adjunct professor of economics at Denver University, University College, Denver, Colorado.

Dennis J. Ray, Ph.D., is the Executive Director of the Power Systems Engineering Research Center, a multidisciplinary center involving twelve universities across the U.S. focusing on challenges associated with electric power industry restructuring. His research covers policies associated with that restructuring activity.

David Schwartz received his Ph.D. from the University of Wisconsin in public utility economics in 1950. He has worked in the field of public utility economics for more than 50 years as a teacher, practitioner with regulatory agencies, and as an expert witness before many state regulatory commissions, including West Virginia.

William G. Shepherd has been Professor of Economics at the University of Michigan and the University of Massachusetts, and also general editor of the *Review of Industrial Organization,* 1990–2002. He has published and testified widely on competition and deregulation and was president of the Transportation and Public Utilities Group of the American Economic Association in 1976 and of the Industrial Organization Society in 1989.

John C. Spychalski is professor of business logistics at The Pennsylvania State University. His research and teaching focuses on the economic performance and management of transport systems. He is also editor of the *Transportation Journal.*

Printed in the United States
945500003B